KU-489-275

li. 1952.

FRANZ VON PAPEN

MEMOIRS

FRANZ VON PAPEN

FRANZ VON PAPEN

MEMOIRS

TRANSLATED BY
BRIAN CONNELL

ANDRE DEUTSCH
LONDON

First published 1952 by
ANDRE DEUTSCH LIMITED
12 Thayer Street, Manchester Square
London W1

Printed in Great Britain by Tonbridge Printers Limited,
Tonbridge Kent, on paper supplied by Spicers Ltd, and
bound by James Burn & Co. Ltd, London and Esher

PUBLISHER'S NOTE

The Publishers would like to express their thanks to Mr Brian Connell, whose task has involved not merely translation, but, in collaboration with the author and his son, responsibility for sifting and presenting the large amount of material assembled by Herr von Papen as a basis for his Memoirs.

CONTENTS

PART ONE

FROM MONARCHY TO REPUBLIC

1	EARLY YEARS	1
2	INTERLUDE IN MEXICO	15
3	AMERICA AND THE WAR	29
4	RETURN TO GERMANY	53
5	ON ACTIVE SERVICE	66
6	AFTERMATH	90
7	GERMANY IN DECAY	111

PART TWO

THE DECLINE OF WEIMAR

8	BRÜNING'S ERROR	131
9	THE CHANCELLORSHIP	146
10	LAUSANNE	171
11	HITLER DEMANDS THE CHANCELLORSHIP	188
12	CONSTITUTIONAL CRISIS	207
13	FROM SCHLEICHER TO HITLER	225

PART THREE

HITLER IN POWER

14	HITLER	250
15	THE ENABLING LAW	264
16	THE CONCORDAT	278
17	THE NIGHT OF THE LONG KNIVES	303
18	THE HINDENBURG TESTAMENT	328

PART FOUR
MISSION TO AUSTRIA

19	A NEW TASK	337
20	RELATIONS IMPROVE	352
21	AGREEMENT AND AFTERMATH	368
22	THE SITUATION DETERIORATES	386
23	ANSCHLUSS	406

PART FIVE
FROM ANKARA TO NUREMBERG

24	WAR BREAKS OUT	440
25	HITLER'S FATEFUL DECISION	454
26	DUEL FOR TURKEY	470
27	AN APPROACH TO ROOSEVELT	485
28	'OPERATION CICERO'	506
29	ARREST	529
30	PRISON	545
31	THE TRIAL	556
32	ENVOI	575

Appendix I	589
Appendix II	599
Index	600

LIST OF ILLUSTRATIONS

Franz von Papen — Frontispiece

Court Page, 1897 — *Facing page* 20

In England, 1903 — 20

Von Papen with his Defence Minister, von Schleicher — 21

The Lausanne Conference — 182

Dissolution of the Reichstag: the defeat of the Papen Cabinet — 183

Nazi election slogans — 214

The author and Hitler, with Generals von Fritsch and von Rundstedt — 214

Riding in Berlin — 215

Signing the Concordat — 278

The old style and the new — 279

Von Hindenburg: '*Ich hatt' einen Kameraden!*' — 279

Conversation piece at Berchtesgaden — 310

At Hitler's headquarters with Ribbentrop — 311

A last talk with King Boris — 502

A discussion with M. Saracoglu — 502

Nuremberg: a cell — 503

Nuremberg: the trial — 534

The denazification trial — 535

Acknowledgments are due to Copress; Helmut Laux; Verlag Ullstein; Münchner Illustrierte Presse; Heinrich Hoffmann; G. Felici and to Liselotte Strelow for the use of many of these photographs.

IF FORTUNE has removed you from the foremost position in the State, you should nevertheless stand your ground and help with words, and if someone stops your mouth you should nevertheless stand your ground and help in silence. The service of a good citizen is never useless: by being heard and seen, by his expression, by his gesture, by his stubbornness and by his very walk, he helps.

SENECA: *Tranquillity of Mind*

PART ONE

FROM MONARCHY TO REPUBLIC

CHAPTER I

EARLY YEARS

Difficulties of autobiography – The salters of Werl – Cadet, court page and officer – Steeplechasing – A visit to the Shires – Marriage – The General Staff – A surprise appointment – Interview with the Kaiser

MEMOIRS are something of a drug on the market these days. The apocalyptic period through which we have just passed has led to a spate of attempts by all kinds of people to trace some of its causes and effects, and to place their own activities against the background of recent history. I do not wish to be ranged with those who have sought only to defend their mistakes and failures.

Historical developments are the product of the most diverse forces, both good and evil, within the various nations. I have written this story of a life between two eras because Germany's rôle in the events of these fifty years can only be understood in the context of historical continuity, a factor of which many of my compatriots are ignorant, and which a large number of contemporaries abroad do not recognize. I think I am entitled to ask that my own activities should be judged against this background.

My own life seems to a very large extent to have been written for me, and it may well take greater efforts than mine to put matters in a clear perspective. A number of biographies, and innumerable stories put out in the heat of the propaganda battles of two world wars, have pictured me in every conceivable guise. I have been represented as a master spy and mystery man, a political intriguer and plotter, and a two-faced diplomat. I have been called a stupid muddler and a naïve gentleman rider, incapable of grasping the true implications of a political situation. I am written off as a black-hearted reactionary who deliberately plotted Hitler's rise to power and supported the Nazi régime with all the influence

I

at his command. I have been arraigned as the architect of the rape of Austria, and the exponent of Hitler's aggressive policy when I was German Ambassador in Turkey during the second world war.

My personal vicissitudes have, indeed, been widely varied, and when I think of some of the paradoxes that have beset my life, I realize what a splendid subject I must have been for the propaganda machines. I have run the whole gamut, from being Chancellor of my country to appearing as a war criminal in the Nuremberg dock on a capital charge. I served my country for almost fifty years and have spent half the time since the second world war in gaol. I stand accused as a supporter of Hitler, yet his Gestapo always had me on their liquidation list and assassinated several of my closest collaborators. I spent the better half of my life as a soldier, protected on many battlefields by some benevolent angel, only to escape death by a hair's breadth at the hands of a hired assassin with a Russian bomb.

Paradox could be carried even further. As a convinced monarchist I was called upon to serve a republic. By tradition a man of conservative inclinations, I was branded as a lackey of Hitler and a sympathizer with his totalitarian ideas. By upbringing and experience a supporter of true social reform, I acquired the reputation of being an enemy of the working classes. By family connection and conviction an outspoken protagonist of Franco-German *rapprochement*, I have seen both countries beat each other to a standstill in two world wars. Seeking only a peaceful solution of the German-Austrian problem – and thereby incurring the bitter hatred of the Austrian Nazis – I stand accused of organizing Hitler's Anschluss. After fighting all my life for a strong position for Germany in Central Europe, I have had to watch half my country engulfed by the despotism of the East. Although an ardent Catholic, I came to be regarded as the servant of one of the most godless governments in modern times. I am under no illusion as to the reputation I enjoy abroad.

Now that I have, for the first time in my life, enough leisure to give my own account of all these events, I find myself almost the sole survivor of my past associates. It would be hard to devise conditions more difficult and more discouraging for such work. The personal files and public archives to which a person in my position would normally have had access, have been denied to me. Most of my own papers have been seized by one or other of the Allied powers, or destroyed in the final stages of the war. The result is that I have often had to rely on memory, on newspaper cuttings or the kindness of friends to refresh my recollections and bring them into focus.

Let me emphasize that this book is not written in self-justification. I made many mistakes and errors of judgment. But I owe it to my family to see some of the more outrageous misrepresentations corrected. The facts, considered dispassionately, provide an entirely different picture. This, however, is not my main concern. In the twilight of a life that has spanned three generations, I am much more concerned with obtaining greater understanding of Germany's rôle in the events of that period.

Not many people seem to realize the extent to which Hitler was a corollary of the punitive clauses of the Treaty of Versailles. It took decades even for historians to appreciate that the thesis of Germany's exclusive guilt for the first world war simply did not bear objective scrutiny. Yet for years we laboured in a condition of moral repression amid the economic morass imposed on us by reparations. Better pens than mine have described the physical misery of mass unemployment, the proletarianization of our middle classes after the inflation and the collapse of moral and Christian values in the 'twenties. Hitler and his movement were in essence a reaction against hopelessness, and for that sense of hopelessness the victorious powers must bear their full share of responsibility.

Hitler became Chancellor with the support of almost 40 per cent of the German electorate. It is not enough to pretend that his rise to power was the result of the intrigues of a few 'industrialists, militarists and reactionaries', as the Nuremberg indictment chose to put it. The German political parties of the Weimar period, from right to left, must, without exception, accept their share of responsibility. Instead of blaming others we should rather recognize our own mistakes in order to avoid a repetition of them.

We are all of us products of our environment. If I am to set my own activities against the background of the historical events in which I became increasingly involved, perhaps I may be allowed to give a short account of my early years. They probably differ little from the reminiscences of any other young man of my upbringing, but as I can at least claim to have been consistent in my conservative opinions throughout life, no harm can be done in tracing their beginnings in a world that has since vanished.

My family came from Werl, near Soest, in the western German province of Westphalia. We belonged for centuries to a small group of hereditary salters, with a right to work the local brine wells. Salt was an important commodity in medieval times and these families of free salters appear in chronicles of the eighth century. We were first mentioned by name in a decree of Count Gottfried III of Arnsberg in 1262, and in 1298 a certain Albert Pape was confirmed in what must have been long-standing rights in the brine wells by the city of Werl. They were certainly being worked at the time of Charlemagne, and the field on our property in which we used to play as children formed part of what is called the *Regedem* – the *regum domus*, over which King Henry the Falconer used to hunt in the tenth century.

Although earlier records are fragmentary, we can trace our descent in a direct line from Wilhelm von Papen, who died in 1494 as mayor of Werl and owner of the nearby Koeningen estate. The manor house remained in our unbroken possession, and my elder brother was the last owner of the entail. The local parish church, built in 1163, at the time of Henry the Lion, gives eloquent testimony to the services of my family to the community through the ages. Our rights and duties were as jealously guarded as they were faithfully carried out, and in 1900 I myself, in a chapel of the little church, took a formal oath to uphold our statutes. They had become largely a matter of tradition by then, the brine wells having ceased to flow after the industrial revolution, when the underground mine shafts diverted their course.

These old tales and traditions formed the background of my upbringing. Members of my family had served the Holy Roman Empire and the Archbishopric of Cologne throughout the centuries. When the old empire broke up under the attacks of Napoleon, the family maintained its allegiance to the Emperor in Vienna, and when I was called, in my turn, to make some contribution to the history of the German race as Ambassador to Austria in 1934, I felt that I was maintaining an old tradition. Our connection with Prussia was of a much later date. My father, who was born in 1839, took part in the wars of 1864, 1866 and 1870, which led to the unification of the German States as part of Bismarck's policy.

He was an officer in the Düsseldorf Uhlan regiment, but by the time I was born he had retired to the management of his modest estate. I was sent to the local village school, and spent several years in close contact with the countryside and its simple but splendid people. There was no hint of class consciousness. My first school friend was the son of a basket weaver. When I was asked at an early age what I wanted to do in life, I seem to have had no other thought than that of becoming a soldier; not, as I suppose many of my readers will hastily conclude, because I was brought up as a stiff-necked Prussian, but because I was passionately fond of horses and have remained so all my life. There was in fact little Prussian tradition in our family. My mother was a Rhinelander and many of our relations lived in Southern Germany. The estate, moreover, was entailed to my elder brother, and this meant I would have to become a civil servant, a soldier, or follow one of the professions in order to earn my living. My mother thought little of my choice, but I was insistent, and in April 1891 was accepted as a cadet.

I had little idea what a spartan profession I had chosen. We slept on camp beds, the great, vaulted rooms of the old castle of Bensberg were unheated even in the depths of winter, and the food consisted mostly of soup and bread. It was a harsh introduction to life for a boy of eleven, but it seemed to do me little harm. I grew up healthy and happy, and learned habits of hard work and personal discipline which I have kept all my life.

An elaborate misconception has grown up in the outside world of the imperialist and aggressive tendencies fostered in the German Army. I can only say I have no recollection of any such thing. Our training and education must have been much the same as that of similar establishments in other countries; our only concern was to protect the newly found unity of Germany from foreign attack. Aggressive militarism is one of those convenient generalizations that bear little relation to the true facts. When I was moved to Berlin for the last two years of my training, the cadet corps took part twice a year in the parade of the guard regiments before the Emperor. It was a thrilling experience to see the tattered standards of these famous regiments paraded before their Commander-in-Chief, but I do not believe these sentiments were any different from those of any other country with strong regimental traditions.

In the spring of 1897 I was among the ninety out of six hundred new ensigns to pass with sufficiently high marks to remain in the *Selekta* class. This involved submitting to the rigid discipline for a further year as an under-officer in the cadet corps, but it also provided an opportunity of entering the Imperial corps of pages, and meant that we would get our commissions six months earlier than our less successful colleagues. The pages were selected by court officials from photographs and my inclusion amongst the fortunate few brought me into intimate contact with the royal household. In our eighteenth-century uniforms we attended the Emperor on state occasions – the opening of the Reichstag or the Prussian Landtag,[1] royal levées and investitures. Here and at the court balls I obtained a lasting impression of the pomp and circumstance of monarchy. We came face to face with the great figures of the *Kaiserreich* – soldiers, politicians, such as Heydebrandt, the leader of the Conservatives and 'uncrowned king of Prussia', Bennigsen, the head of the Liberals, and Windthorst, the chief of the powerful Zentrum party. Little did I think that one day I would be following in their footsteps.

When I look back on these youthful impressions I am thankful to have seen the German Empire in all its power and majesty. The House of Hohenzollern was forced to give way to a republic which at best had only uncertain roots, and whose processes were never fully understood. The German nation, brought up in monarchist traditions of authority, obedience and a sense of duty, was to learn how scandalously these characteristics could be misused by unscrupulous leaders. If we had been allowed to retain the institution of the crown there would never have been a Hitler. If President Wilson and his advisers had known Europe better and had had a greater appreciation of the historical processes that had formed it, we might have been given an opportunity to develop our own form of modern democracy, instead of having forced on us a parliamentary system which, by 1932, had reduced itself to absurdity.

In Berlin's eastern sector the old royal palace has now been demolished, the site marked only by the red flag of Asiatic slavery. I cannot believe that this is an irrevocable decision of history. Central Europe will have to rise again as a bulwark of Western

---

[1] Prussia, like other German states, had her own parliament, the Landtag, generally called the Prussian Diet.

thought against the advance of totalitarian ideas. But this can only occur if Germany's political rebirth is based on the principle of authority under God. That was the principle I saw put into practice in the grand days of the monarchy at the turn of the century.

When I had completed my officers' course, I reported as a second lieutenant in my father's old Westphalian 5th Uhlan regiment. Düsseldorf was in those days a considerable cultural metropolis. The regiment's reserve of officers included not only such names as Haniel, Poensgen, Carp, Heye and Trinkhaus – sons of the rich industrial families – but also representatives of the arts, such as Oeder, Eckenbrecher, Roeber and Matthes. The famous *Malkasten*, which the artists used as a sort of club, had seen the work of Peter Cornelius, Wilhelm von Schadow, Arnold Boecklin, and many others. Goethe had been there as a guest. It was one of the most important centres of the romantic tradition and I remember years later, when I was in Washington, I used to tease some of my American friends about an artist named Emanuel Leutze, one of the founders of the *Malkasten*. When they said they had never heard of him, it was easy to win a small bet by offering to prove that they knew one of his pictures well. He was, in fact, the man who painted the famous scene of *Washington Crossing the Delaware*, that hangs in the foyer of the White House and reproductions of which hang in countless American homes.

The easy, cultured existence of such people was something of a revelation to an unsophisticated eighteen-year-old lieutenant. One of my friends, Count Erich Hopffgarten, kept a small stable of hunters and racehorses, and it was not long before I was able to bring home my first steeplechase cup. I suppose our carefree existence would be frowned upon in these more austere days. Parties often went on all night and many times I found myself exercising horses at dawn, having had no sleep at all. Nevertheless, our regimental duties still had to be carried out, and the personal discipline involved in such endless activity was by no means a bad training for the more onerous duties of life.

I became a not unsuccessful gentleman rider, although my normal weight in those days was near eleven stone and I often had to bant to make the weight. I had very little money, and although I was able to buy and sell an occasional selling plater, I was dependent on friends for my good mounts. When I became Chancellor thirty years later, my critics were quick to pounce on my years as a gentleman rider as proof that I was totally unsuited to occupy such a post of state. I can only say that there are few better ways of developing character. Steeplechasing requires considerable self-discipline, endurance and powers of decision, as well as a fine contempt for broken bones – by no means a bad training for a politician.

I spent the years 1902–4 in the cavalry school at Hanover. It was there that I first came across Whyte-Melville's wonderful books on riding in England, particularly his *Market Harborough*, and I made up my mind to see something of hunting in the Shires. One of my Düsseldorf friends was August Neven du Mont, a reserve officer of the regiment, who had gone to live in Bexhill-on-Sea. He was a great friend of Whistler's and was himself quite well known as an English landscape painter. Another friend, named Campbell, who lived at Windsor, was an enthusiastic horseman, and had taken part, as a volunteer officer in the 7th Regiment of Cuirassiers, in the cavalry charge at Mars-la-Tour in the campaign of 1870. I obtained leave from the regiment and set off for England with a fellow officer named Klenze. In those days no passports were necessary: one simply bought one's ticket and went wherever one wanted to go.

The British Empire at the turn of the century was then at the height of its glory, and I shall never forget the first impact of London. Armed with a letter of introduction from Campbell, we both went to see Mr Hames, a gentleman horse-dealer in Leicester. I remember him as a man of few words. Giving us a searching look, he asked: 'Are you good horsemen?' We replied somewhat diffidently, 'We hope so', and he agreed to send us two horses for the Belvoir meet the next day. We expected to be palmed off with a couple of hacks in order to see how we shaped, and our surprise can be imagined when our mounts turned out to be two superb thoroughbreds. We must have performed well enough to gain his confidence, because never in my life have I ridden better horses than during these weeks with the Shire packs – the Queen's, Quorn, Belvoir, Pytchley and Mr Fernie's. And all for four guineas a day!

After some weeks in Market Harborough we went to stay with Neven du Mont, who had taken over Lord De La Warr's manor house and was Master of the East Sussex Foxhounds. Things were indeed different in those days, when such a position could be held by a German. The riding bore no comparison with that in the

Shires, but the social life was much more pleasant, and I had many dinners in London at the Junior United Services Club and the Cavalry Club.

I paid another short visit to England in November, 1913, just before I left Germany for Washington. This time I had been asked by the Kaiser's Master of the Horse, Count Westphalen, to accompany him in search of some stud horses. We were invited to ride with Lord Annaly's pack and I remember being impressed by a wonderful grey. When we asked its owner whether the horse could be bought for the Kaiser, his answer was: 'Not even for the King of England, sir!'

I have not seen England since and have no great wish to experience its present-day austerity. Even so, I still envy the British their constitutional monarchy, although I have never really been able to understand how such a country, basically conservative – in spite of its Liberals and Socialists – could have supported so readily the abolition of the monarchy in Germany. If only heads had been clearer and emotions less violent at the end of the totally unnecessary first world war, a more forgiving peace would never have robbed Central Europe of its rôle as the bulwark of the West.

When I got back to Germany in 1905 it was time to settle down. One of my cousins had married the second son of Privy Councillor von Boch-Galhau, at whose lovely house at Mettlach, in the Saar, I was a frequent visitor. In May 1905 I married the youngest daughter, a happy union that has stood the test of time through all these difficult years. The Boch-Galhaus were a completely cosmopolitan family, and my constant preoccupation with Franco-German affairs can trace many of its origins to my wife's family. They came partly from Lorraine and partly from Luxembourg. Of my father-in-law's three sisters, one had married a French officer, another the Marquis d'Oncieu de Chaffardon, and the third the Luxembourg Count Lamoral Villers. My wife's eldest sister had married a grandson of Baron Nothomb, one of the founders of Belgian independence. From her uncle, Adolphe von Galhau, my wife inherited the estate of Wallerfangen in the Saar, which was to become our family home. All these border families had suffered in the endless wars from the time of Louis XIV and it is no surprise that they had predominantly internationalist sentiments, which were in due course transmitted to me.

At our engagement party my father-in-law spoke in French, the language normally in use in the house. To my annoyance I could understand barely half of it. He had told my wife that the officers he chiefly respected were those on the General Staff, whom he considered men of culture and intellect with interests far outside the military sphere. I was left in little doubt as to what was required of me, but it meant accepting a formidable challenge. The General Staff was made up of the cream of the Army's brains and involved a career of constant study and hard work. Competition was fierce. Nearly one thousand officers applied each year, and of these only about one hundred and fifty were accepted for the preliminary course. It had no small attraction for an officer in one of the provincial garrisons because it involved three years' service at the Staff College in the capital. I am a person far more industrious than inspired, and I still regard my inclusion amongst the lucky 15 per cent in the year 1907 as something of a minor miracle. However, in October of that year I said goodbye to Düsseldorf to begin what was virtually a new career.

I had enjoyed my life in the regiment. The contact between officers and other ranks was very close, and although discipline was strict, a human relationship was built up that lasted all our lives. The families of the Rhenish and Westphalian peasants, who made up most of our strength, were glad to let their sons serve in the Army. They were taught habits of punctuality, good behaviour, cleanliness and a sense of duty, which made them better members of the community. To this day I frequently receive letters from old members of the 5th Uhlans who served in my squadron half a century ago.

Every General Staff aspirant had to spend three years in the War Academy. Only those who survived the rigid discipline of endless work, application and constant examinations, were finally chosen as members of the General Staff. The old War Academy building in the Dorotheenstrasse may have looked like a university, but its régime was very different. There was no question of attending occasional lectures and supplementing them by outside study. Every lecture began with military punctuality, and the day's curriculum lasted exactly five hours. The gifts and industry of each individual were stretched to breaking point and only the fittest survived. My fellow officers came from every part of the country and I made a number of friendships that were to last a lifetime. Many of them, like Freiherr von Hammerstein, Freiherr von

Fritsch and the later Field-Marshal von Bock, were in due course to reach the top of their profession.

Part of the training consisted of detached service with different branches of the Army. I spent a period in Strasbourg with a Saxon infantry regiment, and in Trier with the field artillery. This brought me once again in contact with the problem of Franco-German relations in the Saar, and during my third year at the War Academy I was able to take a long leave in France to improve my knowledge of the language and the people. Of the one hundred and fifty officers who survived this three year's course, only thirty or forty were chosen for a trial period of one year's service in the General Staff, and there was a wait of nearly six months before the decision was known. The normal procedure was to return in the meantime to one's regiment. My colonel in Düsseldorf, von Pelet-Narbonne, had meanwhile taken over command of the 1st Regiment of Uhlans of the Guard in Potsdam. He requested my transfer to his new command, for which I was grateful, since it meant that if I received a General Staff appointment my family would be near Berlin.

On April 1, 1911, I was told that I had been accepted for General Staff duties. The next two years were probably the happiest in my life. We had a delightful house in Potsdam, opposite the Marble Palace – the residence of the Crown Prince and his wife – and I was able to combine work in the capital with the pleasant existence in this neighbouring garrison town. Field-Marshal Count Schlieffen, who had commanded the 1st Uhlan Guard before becoming Chief of the General Staff, gave me a particularly warm welcome, delighted that a young officer from his old regiment had joined the *Rote Bude*, as the General Staff building in the Königsplatz was known.

By the time I took up my appointment, Schlieffen had already been replaced by the younger Moltke, a nephew of the great Field-Marshal. My first duties were with Section 10, the Austrian Department. There were, in fact, few secrets as far as the Danube Monarchy was concerned, for there was a constant exchange of staff officers, and the Austrian Commander-in-Chief, General Conrad von Hötzendorf, enjoyed the confidence of the whole German General Staff. However, his views on the inevitability of war with Russia as a result of aggressive pan-Slavic policies were not shared in Berlin.

We worked incessantly. Further training was constantly added to the routine work of the office. The demands on our industry, intelligence and powers of concentration were tremendous, and the senior officers were soon able to sort the wheat from the chaff. Above all, we were required to develop independent judgment and full responsibility for our decisions. Many years later these were the principles that Hitler set out to destroy, thereby robbing the members of the General Staff of one of their principal qualities. In later years I was myself to be criticized for the suddenness of my decisions and the directness of my methods. In a politician these may well have been failings, but I do not seek for one moment to deny their origins.

Coming events were already casting their shadows. Agadir, trouble in Tripoli between Turkey and Italy, and conflict in the Balkans, were all portents of coming catastrophe. I was only a small cog in a great machine, but from my level of observation I saw nothing in the work of the General Staff that in any way hastened the coming of war. On the contrary, our intimate knowledge of the effects of modern weapons and the scale of European armaments made us much more anxious to maintain peace than most of the politicians.

For all that, it was our duty to maintain the German war machine in a constant state of readiness. Mobilization and campaign plans had to be prepared by April 1 each year. I remember that in January 1913 we received an order from the Emperor that no plans for a campaign against Russia were to be worked out for the coming year. The normal procedure had always been to prepare one plan for offensive operations against France with defensive measures in the east, and another for offensive operations against Russia accompanied by defensive measures in the west. The second half of this work was cancelled, presumably on the assumption that the Russian secret service would obtain some knowledge of such an unusual measure and that this would serve to relieve the tension. A few months later, as relations with Russia deteriorated over the Balkan crisis, we received a counter-order to prepare the plan after all. I remember well our disgust at having to accomplish months of work in a few weeks.

My other outstanding memory is of the efforts of General Conrad von Hötzendorf, the Austrian Chief of Staff, to persuade Germany to join Austria in offensive operations in the Balkans.

He contended that time was on the side of the Russians, and that as a conflict between Austria and Russia was inevitable, the sooner it started the better. The military weakness of our ally was, however, well known to us, and Moltke, the German Chief of Staff, being strongly against any preventive measures, did everything in his power to restrain his Austrian colleague. Hötzendorf used to insist that the Russians were bound to attack sooner or later, and that it would be far better to take the initiative. The situation bore a close parallel to that of today. Now many people are convinced that the aims of world Communism can be achieved only by war, and that a conflict is therefore inevitable. Moltke had much the same views as General Eisenhower. The Western Powers must never engage themselves in a preventive war. Moltke's constant theme was: 'We will never engage in a European war merely because of what may happen in the Balkans.'

I was finally accepted as a permanent member of the General Staff on March 9, 1913. At the time it seemed as if I had achieved my life's ambition, but my pleasure was nothing compared with my surprise in the autumn when I was offered the post of military attaché in Washington. The normal practice had been to appoint much older staff officers to this post. Professionally, the post was not particularly attractive. There were few developments of military interest on which to report, and the United States seemed completely divorced from the European system of alliances. There were probably two reasons for this sudden promotion. I have already mentioned how impressed I was during my visit to England by the vitality and strength of the British Empire. In fact, I had acquired the reputation of being an almost exaggerated Anglophile. Indeed, my fellow officers used to chaff me by saying, 'You already have got British breeches, boots and saddles: next time you will come back in a British uniform.' My senior officers were well aware of my opinions, but probably thought that if I was to be trained as a possible military attaché for the important London post, a few years in the United States would provide an excellent preparation. Moreover, I had shown a keen interest in European politico-military problems, and had been called upon to deliver a number of lectures on the subject. Perhaps, for once, industry earned its reward.

I was in two minds whether to decline the appointment, but the idea of seeing an unknown continent, of whose potentialities we

had all heard so much, appealed to me greatly. I therefore accepted
and was granted an audience with the Kaiser before I left in December. He was most gracious, retained me for lunch, enumerated all
his friends and acquaintances in the United States, and told me
how fortunate I was to be taking up such a post. 'Learn to speak
English well, study the mentality of the people, and I will send you
to London in due course,' he told me. As I took my leave he gave
me a special message of good wishes for Theodore Roosevelt, to
whom he had taken a great liking. A few days later I was on my
way, leaving my wife and children behind. We were expecting an
addition to the family, and my wife planned to join me in the
summer. Little did I imagine that it would be more than two
years before I should see her again.

CHAPTER II

INTERLUDE IN MEXICO

A warning from Bernstorff – Civil war in Mexico – State of siege in the capital – United States intervention – Clouds gather in Europe – Lunch with Admiral Cradock – War is declared – Notes on its causes

WASHINGTON in those days had an almost rural charm. The German Embassy occupied a modest building on Massachusetts Avenue, with the Chancery on the ground floor and the Ambassador's residence occupying the upper part. Count Bernstorff greeted me in a friendly fashion, with a mild warning that it was no part of the military attaché's duty to make political reports. He had been obliged to recommend the recall of my predecessor, von Herwarth, for his failure to adhere to this rule. However, Herr von Haniel, a member of the Düsseldorf family, was the Counsellor, and Freiherr von Lersner, another acquaintance of my Uhlan days, when his own regiment had been stationed at Bonn, was the First Secretary, so I was among friends. The naval attaché was Captain Boy-Ed, with whom I was to share many vicissitudes after the outbreak of war. He was an excellent fellow, very quiet and reserved.

From the military point of view there was practically nothing with which to occupy myself in Washington. Life seemed to consist of a continual social whirl, and as I had always had a taste for work, I felt somewhat out of place. Endless invitations came from people I had never met, and the whole rhythm of life was in complete contrast to the more formal habits of the old world. Among the many acquaintances I formed at this time, I still remember meeting at the Chevy Chase Country Club a young American named Franklin D. Roosevelt, without suspecting for one moment what a tremendous rôle he was to play in the history of his country. I also met a young American captain named McCoy, adjutant to General Leonard Wood, who, with General Pershing, was the outstanding military figure of those days. I often exchanged compliments with General Wood during my early-morning canters

15

in Rock Creek Park. He later took up residence on Governor's Island, off New York, and never denied me his friendship even in the most difficult days of the war.

President Wilson gave his first official reception at the White House in February 1914. He was kind enough to give me a few moments of his time and asked me what my plans were. I told him I had made up my mind to pay a short visit to Mexico, where I was also accredited, and he exclaimed: 'How I envy you! I have always wanted to go there myself.'

My plans, in fact, were vague enough. The Kaiser had told me to travel as much as possible and see all I could. Mexico was embroiled in a civil war and would certainly be more interesting than the social life of Washington. I therefore set off with Lersner and Berckheim, the Second Secretary, via Cuba and Vera Cruz, and presented myself to Admiral von Hintze, our Minister in Mexico City.

My first contact with the officials of this new country was bizarre enough. When I went to pay my respects to the Mexican Minister of War I was halted by the guard at the entrance to the Presidential palace. I was in full uniform and sought to explain my presence by declaring in my best Spanish: '*El agregado militar alemán.*' He pointed to a flag hanging up behind him and demanded that I should salute it before proceeding. I saw no point in causing a scene, and duly did so, only learning later that it was the banner of the 29th Infantry Regiment, which had so far been responsible for carrying out all the successful revolutions in the city. General Blanquet, the War Minister, a worthy old gentleman, greeted me kindly and, presumably in order to impress his personality upon me at the earliest possible stage, told me that he had been the sergeant in charge of the firing squad which had executed the Emperor Maximilian at Querétaro.

I was hardly prepared for such frank admissions, but felt on somewhat safer ground when Blanquet made some approving remarks about the German Army, whose training methods he claimed to have adopted. I told him that I was delighted and would be glad to let him have any additional information that he might need. He was much less helpful when I asked for his assistance in enabling me to make a tour of inspection. I particularly wanted to visit the northern provinces, where the Government was in constant conflict with the revolutionary bands of Pancho Villa. He told me he could take no responsibility for my safety, and it was clear that if I was to get about at all I would need the support of the Mexican authorities.

The capital itself was more or less in a state of siege. For months another rebel leader, named Zapata, had been conducting nightly raids from the surrounding hills, and neither the army nor the police seemed to be able to deal with him. The whole European colony therefore decided to form a volunteer brigade to protect their property and lives, and as the only soldier in the Diplomatic Corps, I was asked to take command. The German cruiser *Dresden*, lying at Vera Cruz, sent a few sailors to our assistance with a couple of machine-guns, and a Japanese cruiser off the west coast also sent us a few weapons. We acquitted ourselves quite well, and the bandits sheered off whenever they were greeted with a few shots from the Embassy compounds. The excitement was in fact greater than the danger. We had a few alarms and excursions but nothing of any consequence.

Some of the gentlemen who have taken an interest in the various episodes of my life have been pleased to create a whole legend out of my activities in Mexico. In fact, my one official visit in search of information outside the capital degenerated into broad farce. General Blanquet finally authorized me to visit the Villa country, and I got as far as Saltillo, which was still in the hands of the Government. The local 'General' was probably twenty-five years old and his troops looked more like a musical comedy chorus than a military detachment. I managed to have a long conversation with one soldier, who was guarding a medieval cannon in the local citadel; but he must have had second thoughts about my identity, for on my way down the hill he chased me with a fusillade of shots, which fortunately missed. Tension between Mexico and the United States was already high and I expect he took me for a *gringo*. There seemed no point in risking my life to such little purpose, so I returned to the capital.

I arrived back to find the two countries to which I was accredited on the brink of war. An American flag had been hauled down by a Mexican mob in the oil port of Tampico, and the American press was clamouring for reprisals. The Atlantic fleet, under the command of Admiral Badger, appeared before Vera Cruz, and an expeditionary force was being organized. Among Government circles in Mexico City the atmosphere was one of extraordinary tension and confusion. I shall never forget an official reception that was held one evening in Chapultepec Castle. At one point in the proceedings the lights suddenly fused. When they came on again a few seconds later, all the ministers, and most of their guests, had formed themselves into a wary circle, each holding a pistol hurriedly pulled from his tail-coat pocket. In all the turmoil of my later life I have never seen a more astonishing spectacle.

In spite of all our efforts there was not much von Hintze or I could do to halt the impending conflict. The American ultimatum expired on April 19, 1914, and our chief preoccupation was to ensure the safety of the German and other European colonies. Huerta, the Mexican President, was in a difficult position, and although I had formed a higher opinion of him than had von Hintze, I gave what support I could to the moves by the different diplomatic representatives to get him to resign, as a means of preventing the conflict with the United States from spreading. The situation seemed grave enough at the time, but it has paled into insignificance compared with the world conflict that followed. The interesting point to remember is that the British were highly dissatisfied and suspicious of what they regarded as reawakened American imperialism. Relations between the representatives of the two powers were by no means cordial, and this should be remembered when considering the events that followed only a few months later.

In the end, I accompanied a train convoy of foreign nationals to Vera Cruz, where I found lying in the roads no less than seventeen battleships belonging to the interested nations. The new acquaintances I made included Rear-Admiral Sir Christopher Cradock, who was to command the British fleet at the Battle of Coronel, and young Lieutenant Canaris, later to become famous as head of the German Intelligence Service.

I was in the curious position of being officially accredited to both sides in the conflict. From the military point of view there was little of interest to be learned on the Mexican side; but my first view of an American expeditionary force led me to certain positive conclusions. I was made very welcome and given every opportunity to appreciate their organization. General Funston was in command, and one of his aides was called Captain MacArthur, with whom I had to deal on several occasions. I recall him as a virile and handsome man, always in an immaculate uniform, who appeared to enjoy considerable influence on General Funston's staff. When, the other day, I read H. H. Kiruna's biography[1] of this now most distinguished general, I learned of one incident in which Captain MacArthur crossed the Mexican lines from Vera Cruz, disguised as a cowboy, and brought back three Mexican locomotives. It was suggested that I had been of some assistance to him in this exploit. My pleasure at having made his acquaintance does not, I am afraid, entitle me to any share of the glory in this feat, of which I knew nothing until now. It is also a pure invention to suggest that General MacArthur intervened on my behalf at the Nuremberg trial and that this contributed to my acquittal.

Although small, the American Army had excellent officers and first-class troops. In my reports to Berlin I insisted, even at this early stage, that with American industrial capacity in the background, the United States would be able to expand their Army almost without limit within a very short time. I emphasized that if the already troubled European situation deteriorated into war, America was a major factor that must be taken into account.

Shortly after the fatal shots had been fired at Sarajevo I had lunch on board H.M.S. *Good Hope* with Admiral Cradock. He was a great admirer of the Kaiser, several of whose photographs decorated his cabin. Sir Christopher was a most charming person, and we had a long talk about the threatening situation in Europe. As we discussed the possible consequences I remarked that I hoped that if Germany became involved in a war on two fronts, Britain would at least remain neutral. His answer was typical of the British attitude in those days. 'England will never go to war against Germany,' he said, adding after a slight pause, 'even if only for the sake of our week-ends.'

Although the problems on the spot seemed vital enough, it was clear that the European powers had little further interest in the Mexican affair. It was a curious situation for us, as the friendly contact every day between officers of every nation contrasted vividly with the furious diplomatic and military activity in Europe. However, very little of this sense of urgency was transmitted to any of us, and my first indication that the situation in Europe was really to be taken seriously came from, of all people, the Russian

[1] Horst Heinz Kiruna: *General Douglas MacArthur*. Verlag Dr Paul Herzog, Tübingen, 1951.

Minister, Baron Stalevski. Even he was without direct information, but he told me that his military attaché, Colonel Goleyevsky, had been ordered back to Washington. When I asked the Baron whether he could guess the reason for this, he replied: 'All I know is that he has to go back and organize an intelligence service, although I am not clear as to its exact purpose.' It sounded ominous to me, and I immediately informed our General Staff of this development. I had taken similar steps myself before leaving the United States, although most of the groundwork had been done by my predecessor. An office had already been earmarked in New York for the purpose of obtaining and transmitting military information. In due course I shall give an account of our work.

I learnt about the actual outbreak of war in a curious fashion. On August 1 I was invited to dinner by General Funston. In the lounge of his hotel I met my Russian colleague, who was also a guest. The General came down the stairs waving a piece of paper, and remarked as he shook hands with us: 'Gentleman, I have an interesting piece of news for you. Germany has declared war on Russia.' Goleyevsky, the Russian, gave me a stiff bow and told the General that in the circumstances it would be impossible for him to remain to dinner. The General tried to persuade him that we had not personally declared war on each other, but Goleyevsky insisted, and in the end we both took our leave. Our chief concern was to get back to Washington as quickly as possible, and our departure next day, both in the same American destroyer, was not without a certain piquancy. Our many mutual friends stood on the dockside and gave three cheers for Germany and then three cheers for Russia, while every ship in the harbour blew its siren.

It was not a pleasant passage. The sea was rough, the ship was small, the heat oppressive, and it was very difficult for Goleyevsky and myself to avoid each other's company. I tried to establish some sort of formal contact with a few conventional phrases: '*C'est vraiment au détriment de l'Europe que la diplomatie n'a pas réussi à maintenir l'amitié traditionelle entre nos deux grands pays,*' I remarked. '*Nous deux, nous allons faire notre devoir maintenant – espérons néanmoins que cette épreuve ne durera pas trop longtemps.*'

The Colonel, who had been military attaché in London under Benkendorf, and was doubtless better informed about the political background of the Entente powers than I was, replied somewhat sharply, '*Ce n'est pas du tout étonnant que nous ne puissions plus*

Court Page, 1897 In England, 1903

Von Papen with his Defence Minister, von Schleicher

supporter cette maîtrise de l'Allemagne et tant de brusqueries de votre part. Et vous vous trompez profondément si vous croyez que cette affaire sera vite terminée. Cela va durer deux ans, trois ans, dix ans, si vous voulez!' And then he added with considerable emphasis, *'Jusqu'à un résultat définitif.'*

Many years later, when I became German Chancellor in 1932, I was surprised to receive a telegram of good wishes from my former colleague. He had fled from Russia at the time of the revolution and was then living in Paris. Perhaps he had had occasion to reflect on what the *résultat définitif* sought by his imperial master had led to – the bolshevization of his own country.

Two days later, on August 4, we landed at Galveston. I ran to the nearest newspaper kiosk, to be greeted by the headlines: 'German Army of 40,000 men captured at Liège' and 'German Crown Prince commits suicide'. I did not believe either of them, but I was appalled at the thought of this great clash of mass armies and the misery it must bring. That evening I caught a train to New York. The war had begun for me as well.

* * *

Perhaps I may be allowed to sketch briefly the development of the European situation and its deterioration to the point where this clash of the great powers, with its terrible consequences, could no longer be prevented. In the General Staff we had watched closely the growing tension and had seen at first hand how the moves of the major powers might affect the maintenance of European peace.

The General Staff reacted like a barometer to international political developments. Our geographical position between East and West meant that we were extremely sensitive to any shifts in the balance of power. During my service there I witnessed the increasing gravity of the political situation which finally led to the outbreak of war in 1914. A General Staff does not exist to make or influence political decisions. Its business is to make military preparations for any conflict likely to arise out of political developments.

The history of diplomacy in the period preceding the first world war has been minutely studied by historians in every country. There is no need for me to duplicate their conclusions, but I would like to give a short account of certain stages in the development of the situation as I saw it, because two aspects of it played a part in

my subsequent political career. The first was the situation caused
in South-East Europe and Turkey as a result of the Balkan Wars
of 1911–13; I was later called upon to hold both military and
diplomatic posts in this area. The second, and more important
aspect, was the gathering crisis, which included the world war and
ended in 1919 with the Versailles Treaty, based on the charge of
Germany's exclusive war guilt. This latter conception largely
determined the political developments of the nineteen-twenties,
and coloured every thought and action in German internal affairs.
As parliamentarian, Chancellor and Vice-Chancellor, it was the
main psychological problem with which I had to deal, and it cast
its shadow over the whole of my political activity.

This thesis has already been rejected by most historians in every
country. Nevertheless, it lives on as a popular myth. After the
second world war, for which Hitler was without any question
responsible, it has become customary to refer to Germany as a
congenital aggressor, entirely responsible for the war of 1870, and
for both the first and second world wars. It is only necessary to
study the ordinances of the occupying powers in Germany, or the
Nuremberg indictment, to see how this idea has taken root in
spite of all historical evidence to the contrary. On it are based
many of the measures that the occupying powers have instituted
in both the economic and political spheres.

When, as a member of the General Staff, I first became intimately concerned with major political trends, the decisive shift in
the balance of European political power was already well marked.
The turning point had come with the signature of the Anglo-
Russian Convention of August 31, 1907. In the days of Salisbury
and Bismarck, Russia was regarded as an Asiatic power whose
influence in European affairs should be neutralized, but with this
Convention the interests of the British Empire were given precedence over those of Europe. It divided Persia into Russian and
British spheres of interest and recognized British oil rights in the
Persian Gulf. Russia was granted greater security on her Asiatic
side by being given greater influence in Afghanistan and Tibet.
Two months earlier, France, Russia and Japan had agreed to maintain the *status quo* in China.

It had always been Bismarck's policy to lay down acknowledged spheres of interest within a framework of practical political
guarantees. This had checked Russian designs in the West, while

removing her fear of being attacked. This new constellation showed the extent to which German influence in Europe had lost ground. It must also be noted that neither the Kaiser nor the German Government made any attempt to take advantage of Russia's weakened condition after losing the war with Japan. If ever Germany had entertained the idea of a preventive war, this would have been the time for it, rather than later.

Sir Charles Petrie, the British historian, has advanced the thesis that the Anglo-Russian Convention saved Europe seven years later, because Germany was obliged to fight on two fronts. But this is a reversal of the true situation. The Convention not only completely shifted the European balance of power, but the threat of a war on two fronts was one of the main causes of the ensuing arms race and of the developments which finally led to the war.

The deterioration in our relations with Russia should have led to improved relations with the western nations, but other developments prevented this. French expansionist policies in North Africa excited the rivalry of the Italians, who sought in their turn to obtain some share of the tottering Turkish Empire. One of the first situations with which I had to familiarize myself on the General Staff was the increasing danger of an Italo-Turkish conflict over Libya. Turkey was in no position to resist Italian attack, but Enver Bey, at that time the Turkish military attaché in Berlin, where he was a close acquaintance of mine, set off for Libya to organize the resistance of the local tribes. This conflict placed Germany in an extremely difficult situation. On the one side we were allied with Italy, and on the other on terms of close friendship with Turkey. It had always been a major canon of our foreign policy to prevent the division of her Empire amongst the great powers. The General Staff therefore decided to make the gesture of sending only one young observer to the scene. Our sympathies were entirely on the Turkish side, but, as in the Boer War, we were activated more by sentiment than real political considerations. For their part, the Triple Entente powers made no formal protest against Italy's aggression, and Britain prevented the passage of Turkish troops through Egypt.

The Italians seemed to think that a modern army would have little difficulty in dealing with native tribes (they made the same mistake later in the Abyssinian war), but they had to contend with long and bitter resistance. The attack had its repercussions in

B

history: the Turks never forgot this invasion of a peaceful part of their territories. When Mussolini raised the cry of *Mare Nostrum* in 1939, with his attack on Albania, the Turks immediately entered into a military alliance with France and Great Britain.

This Libyan conflict was only a symptom of the rising tension in Europe, which was chiefly caused by Russia's designs in the south and west, and Austria's policy of extending her influence in the Balkans. The Entente Cordiale between Britain and France had shifted the European balance of power in Russia's favour and deprived Germany of the security she had once enjoyed through British support. Our relations with France had never recovered from the war of 1870.

When France arranged in July 1911 for Sultan Mulay Hafid to call her to his aid, and occupied Fez, Germany regarded this as a breach of the Treaty of Algeciras. The 'panther spring' to Agadir[1] – it is beside the point whether it served any purpose or not – had more serious effects in London than in Paris. Sir Edward Grey called it an 'unprovoked attack' and Lloyd George made a highly critical speech. It was clear that Britain regarded Germany's presence on the Moroccan coast as a threat to her interests in the Mediterranean.

Even British historians now take a more objective view of Germany's intervention in the Moroccan question. But there is little recognition for the fact that the Kaiser's action in August played an important rôle in achieving a peaceful solution. The French obtained everything they were after, and in 1912 formed their protectorate in Morocco. The most unfortunate result was the increasing divergence of opinion between Great Britain and Germany. Our sympathy for Turkey in the Libyan conflict had already led to a *rapprochement* between the Italians and the Triple Entente, and Italy gradually became more closely associated with

[1] After the Algeciras Conference of 1906 had internationalized Morocco's economy (with France's special position recognized by Germany), much friction continued between the two countries. It came to a head when, after a tribal revolt at Fez in October 1910 and the release of the besieged town by a French expeditionary force in March 1911, the German gunboat *Panther* appeared on July 1 'to protect German interests'. Since Britain stood firmly by the Entente Cordiale, war seemed imminent; yet, after complicated negotiations, agreement was reached on November 4, 1911 by conceding to Germany a slice of the French Congo.

Great Britain. This still further weakened the position of the Central Powers.

Increasingly friendly relations between Germany and Turkey, and the negotiations for the construction of the Baghdad railway, were viewed by the British as a threat to their Empire life-line. German foreign policy was at fault in not making our intentions perfectly clear. We had no wish to threaten the British position in the Near and Middle East, and only sought export markets for our growing industries. We were in no position to indulge in colonial expansion because we had entered the field a century too late. Surely our attempt to gain commercial markets by peaceful means should have been judged with a less critical eye, even if they seemed to conflict with established interests?

In October 1912 a peace treaty was signed in Ouchy which deprived Turkey of Libya and the Dodecanese. In the meantime Turkey was threatened from another direction. Under Russian patronage, Serbia, Bulgaria, Greece and Montenegro had formed a secret anti-Turkish alliance. In October Montenegro launched an attack, and by the beginning of 1913 the situation threatened war between Austria and Russia. The Kaiser declined to promise his country's assistance, and in this he was true to the Bismarckian tradition of never committing Germany in the Balkans unless the existence of our ally, Austria, was threatened. In close co-operation with the British Government, European peace was maintained. However, in spite of the London Treaty of December 1912, the Balkan conflict dragged on. Enver Pasha, the defender of Libya, brought down the Turkish Government with the *Progrès et Union* Committee. Peace was not finally signed until May 1913. Greece received Salonika and Crete, Serbia got North Macedonia, and Bulgaria obtained Thrace and the Aegean coast.

Shortly after this, Bulgaria attacked Serbia and the Greeks, but was defeated, while the Turks won back Adrianople. This conflict was settled by the Treaty of Bucharest in August 1913, by which Bulgaria lost Macedonia and the Aegean coast again and had to cede the Dobrudja to Rumania. To prevent Serbia from dominating the Adriatic coast, Albania was made into an independent state. A colleague of mine on the General Staff, Prince zu Wied, was suggested at the end of 1913 by Germany as monarch of Albania, but his short reign was something of a farce. I have never understood why some experienced servant of the Hapsburgs was not sent to this troubled corner of Europe in view of their intimate knowledge of its affairs.

That the complications of this Balkan situation did not lead to a general war was almost entirely due to close co-operation between the British and German Governments. Our hopes that this co-operation with Britain would lead to some lessening of the general tension were, unfortunately, not fulfilled. Our difficulties with France over the Moroccan affair increased and the link between Paris and St Petersburg continued to be strengthened. The British Government did little to allay the tension, even when the Czar announced that Russia would support Serbia in every way – a direct intervention in the Austrian sphere of interest, with which the French Government seemed fully in agreement.

Our efforts to come to an understanding with Great Britain were only partially successful. In June 1914 the conflict of interests caused by the Baghdad railway project was settled by German recognition of British rights in the Persian Gulf, in return for recognition of Germany's interests in Mesopotamia. However, this had no effect on major causes of disagreement in the European sphere or on the naval question. Lord Haldane's attempt to reach a compromise on the problem of the relative strengths of the two fleets had no success. Tension was still high when, on June 28, 1914, the fatal shots were fired in Sarajevo.

Again the question arose of whether to follow Bismarck's maxim that Germany's strength should never be committed in Balkan affairs. As soon as it became clear that there was no hope of localizing the conflict between Serbia and Austria, and that Russia intended to come to Serbia's assistance, the Danube Monarchy was in direct danger and Germany herself was threatened. The recognition of Russian aspirations towards Constantinople and in the Balkans would have meant abandoning the European balance of power to the policies of St Petersburg. Peace and Europe's equilibrium could only have been maintained if both Britain and Germany had brought pressure to bear on the same side. But the British Government chose to take another decision. For a short time the situation remained in doubt. The Austrian Government sought active German assistance, while we concentrated in the first place on preventing the outbreak of a general conflict. But German policy was weak and tentative. The Czar ordered a partial mobilization against Austria, but his War Minister, behind his back, also ordered total mobilization against Germany. Russia intended to make war.

I have mentioned the continuity that runs through German history. Since the days of Charlemagne, the conversion to Christianity of the territories between Elbe, Oder and Vistula, and the incorporation of Prussia and the Baltic by the German knightly orders, the Holy Roman Empire of German nations had always had the duty of defending in Central Europe not only the classical tradition of culture but the whole conception of Christianity. Whether it was Ghengis Khan at Liegnitz, the Turks at the walls of Vienna, or Russia's drive for the ice-free ports of the west, we had always taken the first shock in the defence of Europe against attacks from Asia.

The sense of this historical mission was deeply embedded in the consciousness of every German. The conflict presented by the first world war could only be viewed in this light. The objection may be made that there had been breaks in this continuity. From time to time Prussia had attempted to join with Russia for some limited purpose, and several attempts have been made in history to incorporate Russia into the European family. The alliances of Austria, Great Britain and Prussia with Russia against Napoleon were one example of this, but the statesmen of the time made the same mistake that Roosevelt committed at Yalta: Russia is an Asiatic power and cannot be Europeanized.

In the present world situation, the West is faced by the problem that confronted Germany for centuries. Perhaps it makes it a little easier to understand why I, and many of my countrymen, found the exclusion of Germany from her historical rôle under the terms of the Treaty of Versailles so unjust and so unreasonable, particularly as we found ourselves obliged to combat the doctrines of totalitarian Bolshevism. The fact that many of us saw in the anti-Communist attitude of the growing Nazi party the possibility of finding a new and useful ally may cause our errors to be viewed by historians in a slightly less critical light.

I do not seek to deny the many mistakes of the Wilhelmian era. After Bismarck disappeared from the scene, our foreign policy was confused and often high-handed, and our attitude to some of our neighbours psychologically ill-judged. Schemes for economic and colonial expansion, the result of our sudden industrialization, our naval policy, and our political intervention in areas which Bismarck had always recognized as belonging to other powers, had earned us the reputation of being a thoroughly awkward neighbour. For all that, the objective observer is obliged to admit today that the Kaiser did not seek war. The German people entered the conflict in 1914 in the honest conviction that they were engaging in a defensive war. French policy since 1871 had always been conducted with a view to regaining Alsace and Lorraine (*Pensons-y toujours, n'en parlons jamais*), and Russia sought to regain some of the prestige she had lost as the result of her defeat in the Far East by obtaining some of her European objectives. Germany and Great Britain entered the war without any territorial demands which required a war to satisfy them.

We are accused of having begun by violating the territory of a neutral country. There is no doubt that this act turned world public opinion against us from the very start, but, contrary as it was to international law, at least it was not based on territorial demands. It was chiefly due to the lack of correlation between the military authorities who had devised the campaign plan and the country's political leaders. From the purely technical viewpoint of the General Staff, a war on two fronts could only be fought if an immediate result was obtained on one of them. The immense distances to the east made any result in this direction out of the question, and this obliged us to concentrate on the French front. The Schlieffen plan envisaged an encircling movement round the northern part of the French defences, which could only be conducted through Belgium. The moment Russia entered the war, France was obliged under her treaty obligations to follow suit, and our own plan of campaign came automatically into action.

The fault of the country's political leaders lay in not instructing the General Staff to prepare alternative plans for a campaign against France which could be adapted to the prevailing political situation. I heard from friends in the General Staff that when the German Chancellor, Bethmann-Hollweg, expressed a desire to respect Belgium's neutrality, Moltke was obliged to reply that the plan of campaign led through Belgium, and could not be altered without running the risk of losing the war on the first day. I shared the conviction with millions of my countrymen that we were engaging in a purely defensive war for the purpose of protecting our historical position in the centre of Europe.

CHAPTER III

AMERICA AND THE WAR

Legends and facts – Bernstorff isolated – Organizing an intelligence service – The Welland Canal and Vanceboro Bridge affairs – Sir Roger Casement – We corner the munitions market – The U-boat controversy – The Lusitania *– The Albert papers – Von Rintelen – The Dumba letter – Persona non grata*

IF I had not been so intensely occupied all my life I would have taken some earlier occasion to correct the crop of rumours which has come to surround my name. Various more or less fictional biographies have appeared from time to time, tracing in lurid detail the various episodes of my career. Their common denominator has been to begin these accounts by inventing a highly coloured legend of my activities in the United States during the first eighteen months of the war.

I am supposed to have organized a widespread net of saboteurs, to have instigated strikes in the docks and munitions factories, to have employed squads of dynamiters, and to have been the master spy at the head of a veritable army corps of secret agents. A relation of the true facts will, I fear, prove very disappointing to those of my readers who would like to have the old sensational stories confirmed. It should be realized that the reputation I acquired in those days was deliberately fostered by the well-organized Allied propaganda services as part of their campaign to arouse emotions in the United States to the point of active intervention in the war. It was all part of a process which has now acquired the grandiloquent title of psychological warfare. In this the Allies enjoyed all the technical advantages of communications and, I might add, invention. Combined with the ceaseless flow of atrocity stories from the war fronts and the representation of Imperial Germany as the most undemocratic, militaristic and criminal régime in history, the alleged activities of the German military attaché provided another useful stick with which to prod the United States Government.

There was little opportunity at the end of the war to refute any of these stories, at least in a manner that would have attracted the attention of the general public. I was called as a witness before the commission set up by the German Government to enquire into the causes of the war, and was able to show how completely false all the propaganda about my activities had been. I do not imagine that this testimony has been much read in the outside world; in any case, it had acquired only academic interest by then. The official histories of the war mercifully gave me little mention, and it was therefore all the more embarrassing to see the old pack of nonsense rehashed in the more popular organs of the press when I became German Chancellor in 1932. Even then pressure of events prevented me from making any reply, and so much has happened since that it seems a little late to try. However, if this account of my life is to be complete, it is a period that cannot be ignored.

On my return from Mexico, I found myself in the unenviable position of being the only military representative of the Central Powers in the United States. Austria-Hungary, Bulgaria and Turkey had no service attachés in the United States, and the whole responsibility for keeping Germany and her allies informed of politico-military developments in the North American continent devolved on me. Moreover, the number of our officials was so limited and physical contact with Germany so impeded that I was called upon to engage in an ever-widening circle of activity.

The German Embassy in Washington became completely ineffective. The Foreign Office in Berlin was so unprepared for war that they had not even reckoned with the possibility of cable communications being cut by the British. The Royal Navy's command of the sea cut off Germany both politically and economically from the rest of the world and it was some months before Bernstorff was again able to send reports to Berlin, via Sweden.

At least in this respect, the General Staff had been somewhat more provident. Deposited in my safe at the Embassy was a long, thick envelope, which I knew to contain explicit instructions regarding my course of action in the event of war. A military attaché's normal duties consist of a form of officially recognized 'espionage'. However, when his country is at war, his duties become much more onerous and complex. I was a young officer, completely inexperienced in this type of work, and my emotions, as I broke the seals and took out the contents of the envelope, can well be imagined. I was called upon to furnish all possible information concerning enemy and neutral countries which might assist in the conduct of the war. The envelope also contained a list of addresses of commercial firms in neutral countries, together with a code which made it possible to send military information in the guise of commercial messages. I had also been given the name of a German firm with offices in Hanover Street, in New York, which I used henceforth as my permanent headquarters.

Our enemies had instituted rigid control of their press at a very early date, but it was still possible to derive a considerable amount of information by reading between the lines. The American newspaper correspondents in Great Britain still retained a great measure of freedom in the early stages of the war, and their dispatches contained many useful clues. For instance, I was able to advise the German General Staff that part of a British expeditionary corps of about 60,000 men had landed at Abbeville. The actual message I sent read, as far as my memory goes: '60,000 bales of cotton f.o.b. Alexandria bought for so many dollars for delivery in Genoa,' to which were added further details about a partial shipment already having arrived, with the possibility of more being made available in other Italian ports.

This message was sent to a number of cotton firms in Italy, Holland and Sweden. Other messages concerning sugar, oil and similar contracts in fact contained information concerning military operations in Belgium and France culled from the American press, or reports on United States reaction. My suggestions at a later stage for monopolizing the purchase of American-made arms and munitions were sent by the same route.

Unfortunately, this was for many months a one-way traffic. What was particularly galling for Germans in the United States were the completely false accounts given in the press of the operations in France. These spoke exclusively of German defeats, although a careful reader was able to appreciate that the place-names mentioned indicated fairly constant German advances on the right wing of their Army groups. I asked Berlin on a number of occasions to make the daily operational reports available to us, but nothing effective was done, and wireless communication with the still weak Nauen station was constantly interrupted by atmospherics.

The worst aspect of this isolation was the fantastic atrocity propaganda with which our enemies filled the vacuum. There is no question that our justification for marching into Belgium was extremely naïve. The Schlieffen plan, calling for a strong right hook at Paris, through Belgium and the Pas de Calais, with the purpose of taking the main French defence line of Belfort-Toul-Verdun in the rear, was based on the assumption that France would begin operations by marching through Belgium to attack the Ruhr. As no such French move materialized, the Western Powers were in a position to stigmatize our infringement of Belgian neutrality as a major crime against international law. These allegations found a willing ear in the United States, and the invasion of Belgium ruined our cause in American eyes from the start. Perhaps, even at this late date, it is only fair to point out that official studies of the period prove that the Belgian, French and British general staffs had in fact conducted binding talks covering just such an eventual French attack through Belgian territory.

We were at a further disadvantage, as Bernstorff had practically no contact with President Wilson. This was largely due to the atmosphere in which the American presidential election had been fought. Wilson had been elected as a protégé of William Jennings Bryan, whose principal electoral battle-cry was a philippic against the 'privilege-hunting and favour-seeking classes' as exemplified by J. Pierpont Morgan, August Belmont, and other financiers of the period. As these gentlemen belonged to the social strata in which moved most of the elderly aristocrats who made up the diplomatic corps, the Democrats were regarded more or less as social outcasts. Bryan, who became Secretary of State, was shunned as a wild man whom diplomatists would do well to avoid. Their contacts over the years had been almost exclusively with Republicans, to whom most German-Americans gave their instinctive support. It is interesting to speculate whether the United States would ever have entered the war if Theodore Roosevelt had been re-elected as President. It is far more likely that he would have exercised a mediatory rôle, similar to his efforts after the Russo-Japanese War. The Balkanization of Europe could only have been avoided by the influence of a neutral and objective Great Power, which the United States, after Wilson's advent, ceased to be.

We did what we could to organize an information service to present the German point of view to the American public, but communication difficulties meant that our messages and communiqués usually arrived too late for publication. A propaganda committee was formed with the support of a number of German organizations and of the German language press. German immigrants had long since formed various societies for the purpose of maintaining contact with the traditions of their mother country, and their sympathies naturally lay with Germany. Without in any way being disloyal to the country of their adoption, they sought to express their feelings by demanding rigid neutrality on the part of the United States. They soon came under violent attack in that section of the press which really controlled public opinion, and which called from the start for American intervention in Europe. The Germans in America had always exerted their political influence through the Republican Party, and had very few points of contact with the triumphant Democrats. It was therefore easy to counter their activities by simple methods of abuse, in which they were accused of having no conception of American ideals, and were charged, usually with the epithet of 'hyphenated Americans', with engaging in treasonable activities.

This was the atmosphere in which I was called to defend Germany's interests in the country which was to prove the decisive factor in the conflict. I wish to make no secret of the fact that I engaged in two forms of enterprise which were in conflict with the letter of United States law. On two occasions attempts were made to delay the transport in Canada of troop reinforcements for the European theatre by blowing up key points on the Canadian Pacific Railway line. The first occurred during the first winter of the war, and the second, under pressure from the German General Staff, in the subsequent summer. I also arranged for the manufacture of false passports for some of the key German personnel clamouring to return and serve in their country's armed forces. At the same time I wish to emphasize that neither activity endangered either American lives or security, although, in the strictly legal sense, it was improper to use neutral territory as the base of such operations.

During the first few weeks of the conflict I was plagued by all sorts of people with plans for the conduct of the war, new inventions, and all manner of unlikely projects. One of them was a young man who had the idea of hindering the transport of troops and war material from Canada in order to delay as far as possible the arrival of British aid in France. The idea seemed attractive to me, and the attempt to delay the arrival of British and Canadian divisions in France a worthwhile project. The young man in question suggested that the railway bridge over the Welland Canal in Canada should be blown up. Canada was a belligerent, and this sort of activity seemed perfectly justified. I gave him $500, and friends in New York provided him with explosives. The attempt misfired and two of the participants were arrested. The young man had presented himself to me under the name of Horst von der Goltz and in Canada went by the name of Bridgeman-Taylor. I found out later that his account of his past life and membership of the German Army were completely false. Another man was mixed up in this Canadian affair, a reserve officer named Werner Horn. He had been prevented by the Allied blockade from returning to military service in Germany and had placed himself at my disposal. He was sent to blow up the railway bridge over the St Croix river at Vanceboro, but was arrested while planning the attack.

I admit that this was not a particularly intelligent piece of work on my part, and it must be put down to the confusion of those early days and my lack of experience in this particular field. Even success in the attempt would never have been worth the political risk involved. I soon learned my lesson, as Goltz turned into a petty blackmailer, who was always threatening to make some disclosure if I did not keep him sufficiently sweetened. I decided to look twice at all such plans in the future and to keep on the right side of the United States law.

But in the summer of 1915 the German General Staff apparently decided to risk offending American public opinion to the extent of making another similar attempt and I received renewed instructions to interrupt the transport of troops on the Canadian Pacific Railway. A major offensive against Russia was planned, leaving only a screening force on the Western Front. The Allies had somehow to be prevented from receiving reinforcements, and if Japanese or Canadian troops were to be sent to the Western Front, then I was to arrange for the railway line to be blown up at suitable points. The legal justification for this step was based on the assertion that as the Monroe Doctrine prevented any European power intervening on the North American continent, the North American powers should not intervene in Europe.

Herr von Reisswitz, the German Consul in Chicago, introduced to me a man named Albert Kaltschmidt as a person who could be trusted, and I instructed him to make plans for attacks on the railway. He had, however, much bigger ideas and wanted to blow up munition factories. This I strictly forbade him to do. Two of his assistants were arrested while searching for a suitable point at which to attack the Canadian Pacific line, and made long and detailed confessions. This was as far as the matter got because no troops were being transported over the railway at the time, so no attempt was made to sever the line.

The passport forgeries were more or less forced upon us by the necessity of getting through the Allied blockade some of the thousands of German reservists who were storming the consulates and Embassy in their anxiety to return home and join their units. The British Navy was in complete control of the seas, and all Germans travelling in neutral ships were being taken prisoner. We therefore had to ask most of our young men to remain in America, but where they possessed particular technical or professional qualifications we did our best to supply them with some document that would get them home. I put a reserve officer named von Wedell in charge of this work and a number of our people got through.

I also endeavoured to harass our enemies as much as possible by giving what assistance I could to the Indian and Irish independence movements. I shall have a word to say about the Indians in due course, but the Irish were more important to us, especially in view of the large number of people of Irish extraction in America. Their leader was Mr John Devoy, publisher of the *Gaelic American*. He introduced me to Sir Roger Casement, whom I saw frequently in New York during the first weeks of the war. He was fanatically opposed to everything English and was prepared to consider every means to obtain Ireland's independence. He considered that the most direct method would be through a German victory and I recommended him to go to Berlin and discuss there the measures best calculated to ensure a British defeat. He had been greatly disturbed in the United States by the rising wave of pro-Allied feeling and the start of material support for the Entente Powers. When he got to Berlin he seems to have recommended above all that some effort should be made to interrupt this flow of war material by means of acts of sabotage.

On January 26, 1915, I received a message from the General Staff naming a number of Irish Nationalists who could be counted on for such work. However, after the uproar of the Vanceboro

Bridge affair I was strongly opposed to any further activities of this sort. The atmosphere in the United States by this time made it impossible to risk exacerbating public opinion by any acts of sabotage and I made no attempt to follow up Casement's suggestions. His later activities were all outside my sphere and I had no further connection with him. It will be recalled that he landed with a small group of men on the southern Irish coast from a German U-boat at Easter 1916. He was arrested and later hanged in Pentonville. I remember him only as an honest and fearless patriot prepared to risk his life in the service of his cause.

I soon found that I needed some professional assistance in gathering useful information. We also had to organize some system of security to guard our secrets from the prying eyes of the enemy intelligence services. The Hamburg-Amerika Line had employed a private detective named Paul Koenig in their New York harbour offices, and as their liners were no longer running, he was recommended to me. He was a completely reliable and most intelligent fellow to whom I assigned the task of obtaining all possible information concerning shipments of war material to Europe. In this he was most successful, and I was able to keep the General Staff constantly posted as to their quantity and nature.

Koenig was also responsible for keeping an eye on Allied stool pigeons and agents who tried to pry into our activities, and was in charge of the security arrangements. He had a number of agents working for him, most of whom were unknown to me, but neither he nor they at any time received orders to carry out acts of sabotage. On the contrary, when strangers used to approach us with claims of having carried out this or that act on behalf of the Fatherland, Koenig was instructed to check up on them. As I was a complete novice in this sort of cloak and dagger existence, he used to give me lessons in how to avoid being shadowed. We used to go to one of the big department stores, get in one of the lifts, change at different floors, and go up and down until none of the original passengers were left with us. Then we went down again and left the building by another door. This was considered a sovereign routine for shaking off shadowers, but I must admit that it was a form of activity little to my taste.

★ ★ ★

After the battle of the Marne, it became clear that the war was going to last a long time, and that victory would go in the last resort to the side which possessed the greater material reserves. The decisive factor was therefore the productive capacity of the United States. Even if the United States had remained neutral, there was little possibility of the Central Powers running supplies through the British naval blockade. However, there was no reason why as much of this productive capacity as possible should not be denied to the Allied Powers.

When I had paid my respects to the Kaiser and Moltke in December 1913, before leaving for the United States, they had both referred to the possibility of a European war. However, I had received no specific orders as to what line of action I should take in the event of war breaking out. It did not occur to either of them that America might be able to play any sort of decisive part. I had quickly got a very different picture of the potentialities of American industrial production, and in a report to the German War Ministry, dated September 12, 1914, I had suggested that the relatively few American war factories should be given enough German orders to occupy their full capacity. At such an early stage of the war this idea must have seemed peculiar, and I did not even receive a reply, in spite of sending a telegraphic hastener about a month later. In the meantime, Allied purchasing agents started to arrive in America in droves for the purpose of concluding arms contracts. There were considerable obstacles at first. As far as I knew, there was only one factory manufacturing gun barrels, and only two major concerns manufacturing explosive powder, the Dupont Powder Company and the Aetna Powder Company. The flood of new contracts could only be met by building additional plants.

Without any clear indication of how long the war might last, the Americans were not inclined to take undue commercial risks. They did not want to be left with a lot of surplus plant on their hands if the war came to a sudden end. The prices for these immense orders were raised to a level which offered some possibility of amortizing the cost of the additional plant, and the whole problem was the subject of protracted and difficult negotiations. I was kept well informed of all this, because most of the big American banks employed a large number of German-Americans, who provided us with very full information about all these transactions without our even having to ask for it. As soon as the pattern became clear, I made up my mind to take what steps I could to delay the building of these new armament plants. I submitted plans to the War Ministry which would allow us to do this within a perfectly legal commercial framework, and finally obtained permission to go ahead on March 24, 1915.

The plan was relatively simple. An American friend, Mr George Hoadley, was given a contract to build a large factory for the production of guns and ammunition, to be called the Bridgeport Projectile Company. It was to work, to all outward appearances, as an American company, and accept contracts from the Allied Powers. Every firm in the United States making machine tools, hydraulic presses and rolling mills for the manufacture of war material was given enough orders by our company to keep them occupied at full capacity for a couple of years at a maximum rate of delivery. When the Allies finally settled their price difficulties in the spring of 1915 and started to place their orders, they found that all the contractors with the equipment to build the necessary factories were fully booked with orders. Our secret had been well kept, and the general belief was that other American firms had bought up the machinery in order to produce for Allied accounts. I suppose in these days Mr Hoadley might very well be called before the Committee for Un-American Activities, but he was a perfectly good American patriot who did not see why his country's neutrality should benefit only one side in the conflict. A neutral could still do business with whomsoever he pleased, and in 1914 British propaganda had not yet been successful in convicting Germany of a desire to conquer the world.

The Bridgeport Company also succeeded in tying up the Aetna Powder Company's whole capacity for the production of gunpowder until the end of 1915, with an order for five million lbs. By chance a copy of my report to Berlin concerning the signing of this contract is still among the few documents I have been able to preserve. I see that my main preoccupation was where to store these enormous quantities of explosives, as we had contracted to pay one cent per lb. per month for storage, if delivery was not taken within thirty days. In the end we managed to erect suitable storage space on the Bridgeport Company's estate. We were able to put another spoke in the wheel by placing orders for a couple of years' production with all the firms making the special containers used in the manufacture of explosives.

The manufacture of explosives depends to a very large extent on the coking of coal, and the sudden expansion of orders called for a considerable increase in the number of coke ovens. The erection of this type of plant had been for many years the speciality of certain German firms which maintained branches with their own staffs of engineers working in close collaboration with American heavy industry. I prevailed upon them to slow down production as part of our overall plan.

The financing of all these measures came under Herr Albert, who was the financial adviser to the Embassy. The supply of funds presented no particular difficulty. Immense sums had been collected for the German Red Cross, and as this money could not be transferred in the normal way, Berlin was advised from time to time of the amount collected, and the Reichsmark equivalent was placed at the disposal of the Red Cross in Germany. We were then able to use the dollars in the United States. What did involve us in much public criticism was a further measure that we took concerning the large number of German artisans and employees in American firms working on orders for the Allies. All these people would have been required to serve in the forces if they had been at home, and in fact would have been repatriated for the purpose if it had been practicable. Many of them were trained engineers and foremen, holding down key jobs, and we felt that, providing they were not American citizens, the least obligation we could demand of them was not actively to assist the Allied war effort. We therefore asked them to give up their jobs in the armament industries, and opened a labour exchange which found them alternative work in firms still engaged in peacetime production. All this was completely legal.

As I have said, we found ourselves with increasing quantities of explosives on our hands, and sought some means of disposing of them which would still deny their use to the Allies. We were able to sell a certain amount of this material to Mexico as a normal commercial transaction. I know it has been suggested that this was all part of a long-term plot that reached its culmination with the famous Zimmermann telegram in 1917, proposing a Mexican declaration of war on the United States, but I am afraid that this is too convenient an assumption. We were also engaged in trying to get rid of this mass of useless war material by shipments to other neutral powers, such as Norway, Sweden and Spain, and it cannot be claimed that there was any intention of getting them to declare war on the Entente Powers.

My chief collaborator in the Mexican deals was Carlos Heynen, whom I had met in Vera Cruz, where he had been for many years the chief representative of the North German Lloyd shipping company. He also assisted me in another plan we developed for helping the Indian nationalists. We did not go so far as to suppose that there was any hope of India achieving her independence through our assistance, but if there was any chance of fomenting local disorders we felt it might limit the number of Indian troops who could be sent to France and other theatres of war. I obtained a credit of $200,000 from Albert, and Tauscher, the Krupp representative in the United States, saw to the purchase of the additional material.

The Indians had set up an office at 364 West 120th Street in New York, and our liaison officer with them was called Ernst Sekuna. We agreed that a shipment of arms and munitions should be sent from California to Mexico. At least that was to be the destination of the bills of lading. But when the s.s. *Annie Larsen*, in which the arms were loaded, left San Diego, she was to make straight for Socorro Island in the Pacific, where she would be joined by an oil tanker called the s.s. *Maveric*, which we had chartered specially for the purpose. The *Maveric* was to tranship the cargo of arms, hide them in the oil tanks, and make for Karachi.

The scheme went wrong, as the *Maveric* did not appear at Socorro Island at the appointed time. There was no fresh water on the island, and as the *Annie Larsen* had no condenser on board she was forced to return and put in to Hoaquim. In the meantime, the British Secret Service had got wind of the affair – how, I shall never know – and caught up with the *Maveric* when she finally arrived off Socorro. The ship was searched from top to bottom, but naturally nothing was found. However, the assistance of the U.S. Coast Guard was invoked, and the *Annie Larsen* was detained and her cargo seized.

★   ★   ★

In the meantime, the German cause had suffered irreparable damage in the United States through the U-boat controversy. Germany had declared the British and French naval blockade to be contrary to international law, as it was not 'effective'; that is to say, no attempt was being made to blockade German harbours or the North Sea coast. The German Navy rendered this impossible. The blockade was therefore carried out on the high seas with the object of cutting off the Central Powers from all overseas trade. The Government in Berlin considered it its duty to combat by every means in its power this attempt to starve a hundred and twenty million people. The only effective weapon left for the purpose was that of submarine warfare.

This brought Germany into direct conflict with the United States Government. Washington adopted the London attitude, that the U-boats must conform to the rules of cruiser warfare. That is to say, if the U-boat intended to sink a transport vessel it had to surface, halt the ship, examine its papers, personnel and cargo, and send it to the bottom only after the safety of the crew had been assured. It was impossible to apply these rules to submarine warfare. Most of the transports were armed and any surfaced U-boat would have been sunk before it could have started to comply with such regulations. In any case, it was quite impossible to take the crew of an ocean-going steamer on board a small submarine. At most, time could be given for the crew to take to the ship's boats. There is abundant proof that the German Navy discharged its duties in the most humane fashion possible, often at considerable risk to the submarine's own crew. Nevertheless, the British Government declared the U-boat campaign to be a breach of international law and the United States Government immediately concurred.

When the German Government prohibited the use of certain areas of the ocean to enemy ships and neutral ships operating on their account, under the threat of sinking without warning, Washington reacted violently. Proclaiming the principle of the freedom of the seas, they declared that Americans had the right to use the oceans as they saw fit, and that any restriction of this right would have serious consequences. It required nearly thirty years for international law to recognize the requirements of submarine warfare. In 1945 the German Navy was again accused at Nuremberg of having violated international law in its U-boat campaign. Admiral Nimitz, the American Fleet Commander, admitted that the United States Navy, in its turn, had received orders to sink enemy ships at sight from the first day of the war. While declaring that international law had been violated, the Tribunal took the view that as the Allies had adopted the same tactics no punishment was possible.

In 1915 the whole matter was brought to a head by the sinking of the *Lusitania*. In April Germany had announced the new phase of submarine warfare and had warned American citizens against travelling through the forbidden zones. On May 3 the news reached New York that the *Lusitania*, then one of the largest British passenger liners, had been sunk with fearful loss of life. She had sailed from New York with a number of American passengers and a small cargo of munitions. I still have a copy of the secret report I sent to Berlin on May 3, 1915, giving a list of arms shipments, which was provided by Koenig, the detective, in the course of his normal activities. It contained a list of twenty-eight ships sailing from American ports for various European destinations, and included the *Lusitania*. According to the report she was carrying 12 crates of detonators, 6,026 crates of bullets, 492 crates of sundry military equipment, and 223 of motor car wheels. The value of the shipment was given as exceeding half a million dollars. I would emphasize that this report was sent by mail on the day of the sinking and could have had no direct connection with it.

Press and public opinion in the United States exploded with rage at the news, and the country was flooded with protests against the 'satanic and inhuman' methods of warfare adopted by the Central Powers. By chance the German colony in New York had arranged for that very evening a gala performance of *Lohengrin*, to be given in aid of the German Red Cross at the Metropolitan Opera House. Count Bernstorff had agreed to appear as patron, but because of the outcry against everything German in the press, the management sought to cancel the performance. We told them we would be prepared to do so as a sign of respect for the victims of the disaster, but could not agree to a cancellation for political reasons. The performance duly took place amid scenes of near hysteria both inside and outside the theatre. The Ambassador decided at the last moment not to appear, and requested Boy-Ed and myself to act as official representatives. While the performance aroused scenes of great enthusiasm in the auditorium, Boy-Ed and I were publicly insulted during the interval by a group of British and American journalists, and the violence of the street demonstrations outside left us in no doubt about the rift that had been caused between the two countries. I realized how disastrous it would be for Germany if this atmosphere should develop to the point of American intervention.

The more pacifist-minded Bryan had been succeeded as Secretary of State by Lansing, and under his ægis the United States Government now adopted a much stiffer attitude towards Germany. The situation seemed sufficiently serious for Boy-Ed and myself to go to Washington and persuade our Ambassador to renew his broken contacts with the White House, so that he could discuss the whole problem of United States-German relations with the President. Bernstorff already had some acquaintance with Colonel House, but this was no substitute for direct contact. I was sometimes present at Bernstorff's meetings with House and although he maintained outwardly an attitude of complete objectivity, there was little doubt that House was an Allied sympathizer. I had good reason to suppose that he was constantly persuading the President to act as *arbiter mundi* in the world conflict. Like most Americans, he was unaware of the principle that Europe could only be a stable factor in world politics if the Central Powers remained strong enough to contain Slav aspirations. In the critical problem of submarine warfare he seemed unwilling to appreciate that Germany was not a real rival to Allied naval power and that our use of U-boats was only designed as a means of defeating the Allied blockade in order to reach a decision on land. The present-day concentration of the Soviet Union on submarine weapons is only another example of the same strategic conception. There is again no question of their wresting naval supremacy from Great Britain and the United States. House appreciated none of this, yet his influence on Wilson during these critical years was probably decisive.

The exchange of notes on the *Lusitania* affair coloured the whole relationship between Germany and the United States up to 1917, reinforced as it was by other incidents of the same order. Our earnest attempts to improve the atmosphere foundered on the rock of the U-boat controversy. In addition, America gradually became, both financially and materially, an inexhaustible arsenal for our enemies, until her alleged neutrality was no more than a fiction.

* * *

The Bridgeport Projectile Company scheme was working splendidly, and all the contracts it had placed were being fulfilled. The accounts were sent once a month from my office to Albert, the financial adviser, for settlement. One evening, as he was travelling home from his office, tired after the day's work, he fell asleep in the underground train. His brief-case, full of my reports and invoices, was stolen from under his arm, and ended up with the British or American Secret Service. I was having dinner in the German Club with two or three friends that evening, when Albert, in a state of terrible agitation, suddenly appeared and told us what had happened. We did everything in our power to locate the brief-case, but without success. Three days later the *New York World* brought out on its front page facsimiles of some of my reports, and continued to do so for a week. The sensation was tremendous. After the first wave of indignation at such 'underhand methods' of interfering with the American armament industry, one or two bolder commentators found the courage to remark that the whole procedure seemed perfectly legal and could quite fairly be called clever. However, they were only an objective minority. Almost everyone else, particularly those with a financial interest in supplying the Allies – the banks, the factories, and the British and French purchasing agents themselves – were outraged at having their business thus interfered with. Our contracts were challenged, cancelled or replaced by other 'priority' orders, and our scheme came to an end.

When General Falkenhayn sent me the order to prevent, at all costs, American war material reaching the Western Front, while he tried to smash the Russians in the east, his telegram said: 'If you can achieve this you will be able to claim a considerable share in our final victory.' But his hope of finishing the war by 1915 was not fulfilled. My plan would have been of no use in the long run, though until the end of the year only very small quantities of American war material were shipped to Europe. At least I had the satisfaction of knowing that, in spite of the business of the stolen documents, the plan had served its purpose during the period for which it was originally intended. The rumour got round, and has in fact been current all these years, that the papers had been stolen from me in a moment of fantastic negligence on my part. I am sure my friend Albert will not be annoyed if I put the affair in its correct perspective. The incorrect version was repeated in print only three years ago, in the American-sponsored newspaper *Neue Zeitung*, published in Munich. Although I obtained an affidavit from Albert giving the true version, the *Neue Zeitung* declined to publish it.

Perhaps I may also make some belated acknowledgment of Mr Hoadley's work. He put our plan through with the thoroughness and conscientiousness so typical of American businessmen. I have no idea whether he was a German sympathizer in his political affinities. I only remember that after the theft of the documents had made any further operations impossible, Hoadley visited me one day with a cheque for a very large sum. He explained that my position as principal in drawing up the contracts entitled me legally to a brokerage of one and a half per cent on the gross value of all the purchases. I was astounded and told him that it would be quite impossible for me to accept any remuneration for orders I had given on behalf of the German Government. It was now Hoadley's turn to be surprised. He could not understand my attitude and tried to persuade me to accept the cheque. In the end I got the Ambassador's permission to accept the amount for the German Red Cross, to whose account it was duly transferred. Mr Hoadley seemed somewhat perturbed at this rather unbusinesslike handling of his offer, and presented me instead with a handsome cigarette case, which I kept in grateful recollection of his help. It was taken from me by the G.I.'s in 1945 as a souvenir, with the rest of the contents of my house.

* * *

The possibility of using illegal methods to prevent arms shipments reaching the Allies was clearly viewed with greater favour in Germany than by Bernstorff and myself. A number of people in both Germany and America seemed to think that they would be justified in sabotaging what they considered to be a breach of neutrality in delivering this war material to one side only. I used to get dozens of letters a day, many of them from *agents provocateurs*, suggesting ways of interfering with these shipments. From the very beginning my attitude was that such methods could on no account be tolerated. The main problem after the battle of the Marne and the certainty of a long war was to counter the aims of British propaganda in its attempt to bring the United States into the conflict. Any activity by German sympathizers that could have been exploited in this direction had therefore to be strictly avoided. I was, of course, unable to prevent individual acts of sabotage by people who imagined they were serving the German cause; or, worse still, who boasted about it afterwards, as some of them did. There were numerous accidents in the new arms factories, though this was hardly to be wondered at with so many unskilled workers employed, and now and then someone would present himself to me, pretending that he had caused the explosion and therefore deserved to be awarded the Iron Cross. My files were full of such claims.

As I have mentioned already, I received a message on January 26 1915 authorizing acts of sabotage on American territory. This came from Section IIIB (Intelligence and Counter-Espionage) of the General Staff, not from the Ministry of War, to which I was responsible. At Casement's suggestion they had even named certain persons who might be used for this purpose. But as the telegram was an authorization, not an order, I ignored the proposal, which conflicted not only with Bernstorff's policy but with my own convictions.

The case that aroused most public interest was that of Captain von Rintelen. He was a naval reserve officer and a banker by profession. He spoke perfect English, for which reason, presumably, and because of his connections in the United States, the Naval High Command had sent him to America as an agent. One morning, at the beginning of April 1915, the door of my office in New York opened and Rintelen walked in. I had never met him. He told me quite openly that he had come to carry out acts of sabotage. He intended to organize strikes amongst the longshoremen, to hold up the loading of arms ships, or place bombs on board to damage them at sea. The whole story is told in his book *The Dark Invader*,[1] in which I am described as a 'foolish and stupid intriguer', and made the object of much of his resentment. One episode does not appear in the book; as soon as Rintelen stopped talking at our first interview, I said: 'And with these plans in your head you pay your first visit in the United States to the German military attaché! Don't you realize that everyone who comes to this office is photographed and shadowed by the British or American Secret Service?'

'That does not matter in the least,' Rintelen replied. 'I have no intention of hiding. As a matter of fact, what I would really like is

[1] Lovat Dickson, London, 1933.

an interview with President Wilson. I would like to have a really long talk with him, and I thought you might be able to arrange it.'

I was amazed. First of all I tried to convince him that there was no hope of carrying out his plans and – what was more important – any attempt to do so would have the worst possible political consequences for the rest of us. I tried to give him some idea of the general atmosphere in the United States, of which he was entirely ignorant, but without any success. I soon realized that he was a man of limited intelligence, completely ignorant of the situation that had developed in America, and obsessed with the personal ambition of pulling off some great *coup* for Germany. His idea of seeking an interview with Wilson was almost beyond the borders of sanity. Quite apart from the fact that an interview with President Wilson was extremely difficult for anyone to get, the least a man with Rintelen's intentions could do was to keep under cover.

I immediately consulted my colleague, Boy-Ed, who agreed with me that if Rintelen remained long enough to carry out any part of his plans, the consequences would be disastrous. With Boy-Ed's agreement I sent a telegram to the Supreme Command asking them to request the German Admiralty to recall Rintelen immediately. We chose this approach as we assumed that the naval authorities probably had an entirely false picture of the political situation in the United States and of the dangers involved in Rintelen's activities. The General Staff, on the other hand, had been kept fully informed of developments, and approved of my insistence that war material shipments should be restricted by legal methods only. Bernstorff also approved, and the telegram was sent off in code, communications with Germany having been by this time re-established. The rest of the story is told in Rintelen's book. After a few weeks, during which he went ahead with his plans for strikes and bombs, he was ordered home. In spite of travelling with a false passport, he was taken off a ship in the English Channel by the British in the middle of July 1915 and was later sent back to the United States. There he was put on trial and sentenced to a term of imprisonment in Atlanta. At the end of the war his sentence was remitted.

The fate of this man, imbued as he was with patriotic motives, was regrettable, but it was a risk that everyone in his position had to run. The extraordinary thing was that he himself was not prepared to accept the responsibility for the failure of his mission, and sought a scapegoat. This turned out to be me. He maintained that I had sent the telegram requesting his recall 'in clear' and thereby disclosed his identity to the British. In fact, the German diplomatic cipher had long since been broken by the British. It is also more than likely that he was as unguarded in his general conversation as he had been with me, and that the counter-espionage soon got wind of his activities.

The chief reason why Rintelen's name and mine have come to be coupled is probably because of a payment I made in the latter part of 1914 to a German chemist called Dr Scheele. He was engaged in research work on our account into a process for pulverizing oil, a scarce commodity in Germany. We hoped to be able to ship this product as artificial fertilizer through neutral countries, and for this purpose set up a plant called the New Jersey Agricultural Company. Rintelen sought him out, and in May 1915 Scheele started to make bombs and other contrivances to be placed in munition ships. He did this without my knowledge or permission, and as soon as I learnt of it I sent off a complaint to the War Ministry in Berlin. It only remains to add that at the end of the war, when a United States Senate Committee conducted an investigation into some two or three hundred alleged acts of sabotage, no question of the participation of any member of the German Embassy staff ever arose.

* * *

Our efforts to find other employment for nationals of the Central Powers employed in the American armaments industry led to a highly unfortunate occurrence. A large number of the people concerned were Austro-Hungarian citizens, and I had asked their ambassador in Washington, Constantin Dumba, for his support. He found the whole plan excellent and sent a report to Vienna in the summer of 1915 recommending support for the measures I had suggested. At the same time he commented very freely on the doubtful neutrality of the American Government and suggested that every possible step should be taken to combat this state of affairs. His report contained one sentence which, if taken out of its context, might have given the impression that we intended to disrupt the American economy by Illegal methods: 'we can disorganise and hold up for months, if not entirely prevent, the manufacture of munitions . . . which, in the opinion of the German military attaché, is of great importance, and amply outweighs the . . . small expenditure of money involved.'[1] This report, together with a number of others from the Austrian and German Embassies, was given to an American journalist called Archibald for delivery. He was a close friend of both Dumba and the Austrian Consul-General in New York, Herr von Nuber. Archibald, who was considered completely reliable, had been given facilities to report the war from the German side, and was on his way to Berlin. The whole packet of documents came into the possession of the British Secret Service and the contents were sent back to the United States, where their publication caused a furore.

We had always supposed that Archibald had been negligent in some way, and it was only quite recently that I learned what had really happened. A full account is given in the book *Spy and Counter-Spy*,[2] by Captain Voska, a Czech. During the first world war Voska, who had worked in close contact with Captain (later Admiral Sir) Guy Gaunt, the British naval attaché in Washington, had succeeded in planting Czech agents in the Austrian Consulate-General in New York. The Dumba report which caused all the trouble was written in Nuber's office by the Ambassador, who happened to be in New York at the time. The packet of documents for Archibald was made up in the Consulate-General, and it was not long before a full report of their contents and manner of transmission was in the hands of Gaunt, who immediately forwarded it to Naval Intelligence in London. The rest was easy. When the Dutch liner *Rotterdam* arrived at Falmouth it was duly searched, the packet was discovered and removed from the protesting Archibald.

As in all spy stories, Voska's book seeks to bolster some of his genuine successes with a certain amount of fantastic over-elaboration. In this instance he adds a number of details about a hollow walking-stick said to contain the most secret papers of all, which had been handed to Archibald by a certain Count Lynar, who was one of the German officers caught in America by the outbreak of war. He may well have made Archibald a present of a stick, a normal item of any gentleman's equipment in those days, as a gesture of appreciation for taking a letter to his wife. At any rate, the stick was never found, although it was mentioned in

[1] See footnote on p. 50.   [2] Harrap, London, 1941.

Gaunt's message and the ship was searched for it from top to bottom.

The British Government published a White Paper[1] on the contents of the Archibald documents. These included a report from me to the German War Ministry on the subject of the loss of the 'Albert papers', together with a copy of a memorandum I had written on the subject, which Count Bernstorff had handed to the State Department. This made it quite clear that we had not been attempting to buy up American munition factories, as the press was proclaiming. On the contrary, we laid down 'that the German Government would at any time be willing – and, indeed, glad – to sell and transfer to the United States Government any or all of the material it had purchased. . . . From the German point of view, purchases at this time by the German Government of war material manufactured in the United States, while it would involve the sacrifice of large sums of money, would be justified alone by the consideration of the humane effects such purchases might accomplish in the saving of the lives of the German soldiers whom, in the hands of the Allies, this war material would wound and slay. (signed) Papen.'

One of the most unfortunate documents was not an official report at all. I had asked Archibald to take a private letter to my wife. In it I made use of a slightly unparliamentary expression, referring to these 'idiotic Yankees', and the phrase was given great prominence in the press without indicating the context in which it had been written. However, the details of the Albert affair added little to what was already known on the subject. It was Ambassador Dumba's report that raised the major scandal. He was accused of intending to disorganize the production of war material by strikes and other illegal methods. Although this was completely untrue, he was declared to be *persona non grata* by the State Department, which demanded his immediate recall. His departure was a great loss to the Central Powers and a great blow to me personally. He was always most kind to me, and in 1934 when I went to Vienna we renewed our friendship and he assisted me in many ways.

I came heavily under fire as a result of the Dumba episode, and, with my colleague Boy-Ed, became the object of a violent campaign in the American press and elsewhere. This made great play

[1] Miscellaneous. No. 16 (1915) H.M.S.O. London.

with the 'criminal methods' employed by German agents to prevent the manufacture and shipment of war material for the Allies. Taken in conjunction with the revelations in Albert's brief-case this led to renewed efforts on the part of the Allied representatives to make my further presence in the United States impossible. The Welland Canal affair and the faking of passports had not yet been traced to me, but a minor episode in the autumn of 1915 showed what proportions the campaign against me had reached. In September I received an invitation from the military governor of New York, General Leonard Wood, to have tea with him. He was one of the most respected military figures in the United States and I have already mentioned how I had become closely acquainted with him as a result of our morning rides in Rock Creek Park in Washington. I visited him on Governor's Island and the first thing he did was to show me a plan for blowing up the New York subway and port installations, which the American Secret Service was said to have found in my office. We both had a good laugh about it, and I made use of the opportunity to have a frank discussion of the whole situation and, in particular, to complain about the campaign of which I was the victim. I told him that all the intentions attributed to me were ridiculous. We would have needed thousands of agents and a small army to have overcome the guards on the various installations we were accused of intending to attack. The underlying motive of the campaign was to prepare public opinion in America for a declaration of war. General Wood agreed with me, and I gave him an assurance that I would undertake and encourage nothing which might harm the interests of our two countries.

However, the furore caused by the publication of the Dumba report made any further activity in the United States extremely difficult. By December 1915 Boy-Ed and I finally fell victims to the Allied campaign against us. The American Government found it convenient to bow to the storm of criticism against the Central Powers and declared us both *persona non grata*. When the German Government asked for the reason for this step, they were told that we had engaged in 'unwarranted military and naval activity'. In fact, no specific charges were made against us.

Frankly, I was thoroughly pleased when the final break came. I was a regular soldier and had always felt ill at ease behind a desk, while my country was fighting for its existence. Moreover, my return would enable me to give a full account of the changed situation in the United States during the year and a half of war. I made up my mind to convince the highest personalities I could approach of the danger of some of their policies, particularly the effect of the U-boat campaign on American public opinion and its fateful consequences. During eighteen difficult months I had endeavoured to serve my country to the best of my ability. But I was a soldier, not a diplomat, and had therefore paid little attention to what the personal consequences of any of my activities might be. I could have made life much simpler for myself if I had taken no risks and spent the time far from the battle front under the protection of diplomatic immunity. At least I had got a very clear idea of the danger to Germany of a too close association between America and the Western Allies. The entry of the United States into the war could only mean our defeat. I now decided to present my convictions to my Government's policy makers.

CHAPTER IV

RETURN TO GERMANY

Incident at Falmouth – A White Paper – The Black Tom Case –
Interviews in Berlin – The Kaiser is displeased – I report to my regiment

I MADE a stormy winter crossing of the Atlantic on the S.S.
Nordam. We put in at Falmouth, and in spite of my travelling
under a safe conduct, a guard was put at the door of my cabin
and my baggage meticulously searched. Every document was
seized. A telegram of protest which I sent to the American Ambassador in London, Mr Page, complaining about this disregard of my
diplomatic immunity, remained unanswered. However, most of
the material was forwarded on to me about two months later. It
included my private bank statements and cheque stubs, which the
British apparently regarded as first-class material for their propaganda campaign. It should not be forgotten that the United States
had at this period still not decided to throw in their lot with the
Allied Powers. The British propaganda machine was therefore
concentrating all its efforts on convincing American public opinion
of Germany's 'criminal' intentions. Immense pains were taken to
present Germany as ignoring all laws and morals. Such methods,
it was made clear, could only be eradicated by a union of all the
freedom-loving peoples of the world to annihilate this enemy of
humanity.

At the time we found it convenient in Germany to describe the
payments shown by my cheques as personal outgoings, such as
laundry bills. In fact, some of them gave valuable clues to my
activities in the United States, although their importance was
grossly exaggerated. There were two payments to Bridgeman-
Taylor, alias von der Goltz, alias Wachendorf, in connection with
the Welland Canal affair. There was also a payment to Werner
Horn, who made the attempt on the Vanceboro bridge. Another
man involved was one Caserta, who was supposed to help
Bridgeman-Taylor and Horn out of Ottawa.

Most of the other payments were salary cheques to von Igel and ho were my assistants in the military attaché's office. lso payments to von Wedell, who had charge of the nd issue of false passports for those German nationals d to smuggle back to serve in our armed forces. ....her payments attracted great attention. One was for $68 to the Krupp representative, Tauscher, for a small supply of picric acid. As far as I remember, this was supplied to Horn as part of the Canadian affair. It was certainly not used for any illegal activities in the United States. Great play was also made with a payment for $19 to an explosives expert named Hoegen, with the annotation 'dum-dum enquiry'. This was used as evidence to prove that I had ordered the manufacture of these explosive bullets. In fact, the boot was on the other foot. We had reason to believe that the Russians had given an order for this type of ammunition and I obtained a specimen for analysis.

It may well be asked why I was carrying such incriminating material with me. There were two reasons. First of all, I had assumed that the safe conduct I had been given would cover my personal belongings. However, this apparently did not accord with the rules of war as interpreted by the British. I was also under an obligation to account for every pfennig that I had spent in the United States. The German authorities were very strict in such matters and demanded detailed accounts. They would have done much better in this case to waive their requirements, as the British filled a White Paper[1] with all the details and were able to make much propaganda capital out of the contents.

A curious episode during the final stages of my journey was my encounter with an English passenger who boarded the ship at Falmouth and sailed with me as far as Rotterdam. He gave me to understand that he was a senior representative of the British Government and asked me to let it be known in Berlin that Britain wished to make peace. Germany would have to evacuate France and Belgium, and Poland must in some way be reconstituted. I told him that I could see little hope of Russian agreement to an independent Poland, but undertook to explore the possibilities when I got to Berlin. I do not recall this gentleman's name, and have no reason to suppose that the one he gave me was correct. In any case, nothing came of the matter.

* * *

[1] Miscellaneous No. 6 (1916). H.M.S.O. London.

To round off this account of my experiences in the United States, I should like to deal with one of the most controversial events of the war. It will necessitate a jump ahead in time, but as the repercussions dragged on for years into the peace, it is perhaps not out of place to consider it here. I am referring to what became known as the Black Tom Case. In July 1916 and January 1917, German agents were alleged to have caused a series of explosions in marshalling yards belonging to the Lehigh Valley Railroad Company, and this firm, together with the Canadian Car and Foundry Company, presented a claim for damages amounting to $40 million against the German Government. I was accused of having organized the whole affair. This may have tied in very well with the reputation I had acquired, but it was quite another matter to prove my participation. The explosions in question, due allegedly to acts of sabotage, but more probably to the self-ignition of ammunition, took place seven and thirteen months respectively after I had left the United States. But the companies in question went to great pains to prove that I had received official instructions to carry out such acts of sabotage, and that 'my' agents were responsible.

Some years after the war, when I was living the life of a country gentleman in Westphalia, I received a large packet of documents from the German Foreign Office with a request that I should return them with my comments. The packet contained a collection of alleged affidavits concerning my private life in New York in 1915. Their contents gave me a good laugh. Here was apparent proof that I had lived an extremely loose sort of life, and had maintained an open liaison with a certain American girl who was in the habit of accompanying me on my early morning rides in Central Park. We were said to have organized an almost continuous series of parties attended by numerous friends – all of them agents, of course – accompanied by their girl friends. In 1915 I was reported to have held one such party in a certain down-town brothel: champagne was served and I had drunk to the health of the Kaiser and to our victory. Count Bernstorff also was described as having been present, and another guest was said to have been the man who had organized the Lehigh Valley explosions long after I had left the country.

I made a sworn statement that the whole collection of affidavits, and particularly one dated February 14, 1925, and made by some-

C

one named Mena Reiss, *née* Edwards, known as the 'Eastman Girl', were a complete invention from start to finish. I had never known a young woman of that name in the whole of my life; nor had Boy-Ed and I ever taken her to 123 West 15th Street, occupied by a Mrs Gordon or a Mrs Heldt. Both the address and the occupants were entirely unknown to me. The business about my rides in the Park was another piece of nonsense. The horse I hired from the Central Park Riding Academy loathed other horses and always had to be ridden alone.

When the plaintiffs saw that my complicity was not to be proved so easily, they produced an order I was supposed to have received from the German General Staff instructing me to undertake acts of sabotage. It was again relatively simple to dispose of this document. In a sworn statement I said: 'My alleged implication in these acts of sabotage is based on what is described as a "General Staff circular to the military attachés in the United States", dated January 15, 1915. This refers to a previous document, dated November 2, 1914, authorizing me to foment strikes and commit sabotage in factories and elsewhere. I never received either of these instructions and they are obvious forgeries. No officer named Fischer, whose signature appears on them, ever occupied a post in the General Staff or the War Ministry which would have placed him in a position to prepare such a document. Moreover, there has never been a function or rank described as *Generalrat des deutschen Heeres* [General Councillor of the German Army]. Further, the second circular is addressed to the military attachés in the plural, and can only have been concocted by a person who was ignorant of the fact that there was only one.' I went on to point out that the remaining contents of the circulars bore no relation to the facts. German banks were mentioned whose branches in the United States were said to have opened unlimited credits in my favour, with which to pay for acts of sabotage. If any German banks did, in fact, maintain branches in the United States, none of them had granted me any credits at all. All the funds used for our commercial operations had been placed at my disposal as required, by Albert, the commercial attaché.

I can only assume that the Lehigh Valley Company's investigators had in some way heard of the message I had received on January 26, 1915, from Section IIIB of the General Staff, which had contained some of the suggestions Sir Roger Casement had made in Berlin. As they did not have this document in their possession, I suppose they found it necessary to reconstruct something for their own purposes. In any case, the original message was only an authorization, and not an order, and, as I have already made clear, I did nothing about it.

All the documents seized from me by the British authorities at Falmouth on my way back to Germany were subsequently used as exhibits in this Black Tom litigation. They covered the whole range of my activities in the United States, but not one of them gave the slightest indication that I was in any way engaged in sabotage activities. Yet every legal loophole was explored in order to place responsibility for the explosions on my shoulders. Over the course of the years a variety of persons were found ready to swear that they were the agents who had caused the explosions on the orders of the German Government. At one period, Germany's Foreign Minister, Dr Stresemann, seemed prepared to pay a certain sum in damages. He had been told that the settlement of the affair would have a good effect on public opinion in the United States and that relations between the two countries would benefit. It must have seemed a tempting proposition at the time. Fortunately I got wind of his intentions. I went to see him and told him that in my opinion there was no reason for such a compromise: Germany had had no responsibility whatever in the matter. He insisted, however, that the political gain was worth the financial sacrifice. I therefore told him I would have a complaint brought in the Reichstag against such a wilful squandering of public funds. In the end he decided to make no payment, and in 1930 the Mixed Claim Commission, which had been set up to adjudicate in the matter, rejected the suit with costs.

That, however, was by no means the end of the matter. New material was produced on two occasions, but in March 1931, and November 1932, the Commission decided again in Germany's favour. An American friend of mine told me that the lawyer representing the Lehigh Valley Company had by that time collected about a million dollars' worth of fees. It is therefore hardly surprising that the matter was carried still further. Again new witnesses were found and the case reopened. In the meantime, the Nazis had come to power in Germany, and in negotiations with certain semi-official representatives it was indicated that a settlement for $40 million would influence American public opinion very much in their favour. The Nazis knew nothing about international affairs, and in their ignorance of the United States, fell for the suggestion even more heavily than had Dr Stresemann. One of the representatives on the American side was Mr John McCloy, now American High Commissioner in Germany, and at that time a member of the law firm of Cravath de Gersdorff, Swaine and Wood. I remained completely ignorant of the whole business, although I was at that time Vice-Chancellor in the Government, and, as one of the people most frequently mentioned in the case, could have expected to be consulted. One day, Neurath, the German Foreign Minister, asked me to call on him and showed me an agreement that had been drawn up between the Lehigh Valley Company and the German Government, on whose behalf it had been signed by a Herr von Pfeffer. This declared the German Government's willingness to close the proceedings by the payment of damages. Both Neurath and I were considerably nonplussed by this document. Pfeffer was one of Hitler's confidants and a constant member of his immediate circle, but he was in no position to sign such an agreement on behalf of the German Government. I told Neurath to look up the files on the proceedings and he subsequently had a number of talks with Hitler in an attempt to get the agreement annulled.

Rintelen also turned up in Berlin at about this time. I was told that the Americans had approached him with a view to obtaining affidavits from agents. By this time, I believe, he had become a British subject; otherwise I feel that his activities could well have been regarded as treasonable. He was also engaged in a claim against the German Government for compensation as a result of his imprisonment in Atlanta during the war. He had no success in either of these enterprises and returned to London, where he wrote a second book, *The Return of the Dark Invader*,[1] again consisting chiefly of a tirade against me. I really think that by this time his nervous energy was exhausted and that he was no longer fully responsible for what he said or did.

In the days before I became Chancellor I was visited at our country house in Westphalia by an American gentleman who claimed to be a representative of the Lehigh Valley Company. I will not give his name, because it was probably a false one. He

[1] Lovat Dickson, London, 1935.

indicated that the Black Tom Case would be easy to solve to the satisfaction of both sides(!) if I would be prepared to swear that I knew a certain agent had been employed by the German Government. This would not involve my personal responsibility at all, he said, making it quite clear that this assistance on my part would be suitably rewarded. Glancing over our modest property, he remarked: 'You could then settle down in a place three times as big as this, with all modern comforts.' I told him that I was very fond of my home and knew no agents who could thus be of service to him.

Later, when relations between the Nazi Government and the United States became increasingly difficult, the German representative of the Mixed Claim Commission, Dr Huecking, resigned. The Lehigh Valley Company then opened the case once more in May 1939, and it was decided in their favour, without determining any damages. The Black Tom Case might therefore be said to be still open, and the mysterious contacts I made as a 'master spy' probably still colour my reputation in the United States. No harm can therefore be done in reprinting the sworn statement I made before a notary in Dülmen on November 27, 1927, when the German Government first questioned me on the subject:

'Neither orally nor in writing, neither secretly, by suggestion, order, instruction nor authorization, did I at any time instigate the destruction of factories or stores of munitions; nor did I in any way support or further any such plans by others. Accusations that I organized violent or illegal measures to interfere with the American munitions industry are therefore completely without foundation. Most of the people mentioned by the American plaintiffs as members of an alleged sabotage organization are completely unknown to me. With certain others I was acquainted, but only in relation to activities in no way connected with the sabotage of American property. As far as the incidents at Black Tom Terminal and the Kingsland Plant are concerned, I can only say that I learnt the names of both these places for the first time from the American writ. The explosions took place seven and thirteen months respectively after I had been recalled from the United States and I had nothing either directly or indirectly to do with them.'

★ ★ ★

But to revert to my own story. I arrived in Germany on January 6, 1916, and saw my family again for the first time for over two years. In Berlin I found that I had acquired a reputation of having done everything in my power to defend Germany against the un-neutral attitude of the United States. I was the first official to return to Germany who had lived in the United States through the whole period since the outbreak of war, and my reports were much in demand. I was sent for almost immediately by the German Chief of Staff, General von Falkenhayn. I spent several hours with him, giving a detailed account of the atmosphere in the United States, the main bones of contention and the outlook for the future. Falkenhayn expressed his gratitude for everything I had done to delay the delivery of war material to the enemy and gave his approval to all the measures I had taken. His plans to end the war in 1915 had, however, come to nothing, and he saw little hope of limiting the effect of ever-increasing American aid to the Allies.

I laid particular stress on America's immense industrial capacity, which, I told him, would be able to deliver almost any desired quantity of material. It was simply a question of finance. The only matter still outstanding was the extent to which the United States was prepared to grant credits. The Allies were trying by every conceivable means to persuade the United States to enter the war. It was therefore my considered opinion that the greatest care must be taken to ensure that relations between the United States and Germany remained as friendly as possible. No attempt must be made by German agents to carry out acts of sabotage, and Germany should make an announcement that disputes over the proper use of U-boats would be settled, and no attempt made to intro-duce unrestricted submarine warfare. I tried to explain to the General how the *Lusitania* sinking had caused public opinion in the United States to become hostile to Germany. He shared the general disbelief of his compatriots at the growth of this sentiment, and could not understand why a nation in whose development people of German origin had played such a considerable rôle should devote all its sympathies to the opposite camp. I told him that although a referendum in the United States at that moment would probably show a clear majority for neutrality, 90 per cent of the press and the organs of public opinion sympathized with the Allies. One or two serious errors of policy on Germany's part must lead inevitably to a majority of the people in America favouring a declaration of war. Moreover, the United States was a sea power, even if its resources in this respect were only partially developed, and shared the British conception of the freedom of the seas. It was my absolute conviction that our manner of conducting the U-boat campaign would in the end lead to open conflict unless steps were taken to modify it.

The General then asked me what policy the Central Powers should adopt if the scope of U-boat warfare was limited. I said that we must make it quite clear to the world that we had not embarked on a war of conquest. There were no territorial problems on our frontiers which could be regarded as a *casus belli*. Our only interest was to protect our overseas markets and develop our colonial possessions in a peaceful fashion. Inept diplomacy had placed us in a bad position right from the start of the war. It was now our business to state these simple truths and demolish the accusation that we were waging a war of aggression. We had declared war to aid Austria-Hungary against the menace of the Slavs, and had no political ambitions which in any way conflicted with those of the United States. We must make it quite clear, particularly to the American public, what sort of Europe we wished to see at the end of the war. Such an appeal to reason was the only way of countering enemy propaganda.

Falkenhayn was an extremely intelligent man. He had travelled widely and had an intimate knowledge of foreign countries. There was little doubt that he realized the limitations of the resources at the disposal of the Central Powers. On the other hand, he was faced by a situation in which the German Navy, which occupied a highly independent position under the Kaiser, had a preponderant influence on the conduct of foreign policy. The Kaiser himself was a strong supporter of Tirpitz' naval policy, which before the war had led more than anything to the decline in our relations with Great Britain. It was therefore inevitable that the manner in which U-boat warfare was to be conducted would be a determining factor in our policy. Falkenhayn expressed full agreement with my opinions, but their practical implementation in the face of objections from the Kaiser and Tirpitz was quite another matter.

He closed our interview by saying: 'As a soldier and Chief of Staff, it is my duty to bring this war to a successful conclusion. As long as the naval blockade continues, military operations alone cannot bring about a decision. Admiral von Tirpitz maintains that unrestricted submarine warfare is the only way out of the *impasse*.' The Allied blockade, he said, did not conform to the rules of sea warfare, and condemned the Central Powers to slow death by hunger. Germany was therefore justified, both from the military and the moral point of view, in using every means to break it. 'I am under an obligation to use this weapon if the naval command guarantees its success. They have given me this guarantee.' I could only reply that I was still convinced that this decision, if put into practice, must lead inevitably to the participation of the United States. In that event, the war would be lost.

Falkenhayn rose and said: 'You now know my opinion as to how this war can be brought to a successful conclusion. I must ask you to consider whether, on reflection, it is not possible for you to modify your own views, after the considerations I have mentioned.'

'Your Excellency,' I replied, 'my convictions spring from an intimate knowledge of events in the United States during the last year and a half. I am afraid they remain unshaken.'

The next few days were full of interviews. I saw two leading naval officers, Admiral von Holtzendorff and Admiral von Müller. Their interest in my descriptions of life in the United States very soon gave way to astonishment when they found that I was an uncompromising opponent of their submarine policy. This was the one problem that exercised every mind in Germany at the time, and to have contrary views expressed to the country's leaders by someone with first-hand knowledge of the situation in the United States was very little to their taste.

Herr von Bethmann-Hollweg, the German Chancellor, also asked me to report to him personally. I repeated the arguments I had presented to Falkenhayn. Here was no soldier, concerned only with employing every technique at his disposal, but the responsible political head of the German Government. He saw the problem in its widest sense and sought some means of ending the war which would guarantee the continued influence of the Central Powers and not give the nation the impression that all its sacrifices had been in vain. The Chancellor also felt that the war could no longer be won with weapons alone, and shared my opinion that unrestricted submarine warfare would bring America into the war and lose it for Germany. He told me he would do everything in his power to prevent such a thing, but that I must realize that the partisans of the Navy's policy were not only very strong but controlled a large proportion of the press, and had the support of a considerable body of public opinion. The Supreme Command supported Tirpitz in his contention that the slow starvation of the Central Powers must, at all costs, be prevented. The alternative policy could only be carried out if public opinion was fully informed of the dangers inherent in continued U-boat warfare. The Chancellor suggested that the best method would be to assemble a group of journalists from all over Germany to hear my account of the situation in the United States. I said that nothing would please me more, but asked that I should be permitted first to have the audience with the Emperor which was being arranged. Moreover, I would need permission from the Chief of Staff, as I no longer came under the authority of the Foreign Office. The Chancellor did not seem to think that this would present any difficulty.

A few evenings later I received an order to report to General Falkenhayn the next morning and go with him to Potsdam to see the Kaiser. Before we set off I told him that I fully appreciated his opinions, but that I was firmly convinced that unrestricted submarine warfare would mean the certain loss of the war. He could reasonably expect a junior officer not to express opinions to the Emperor which might conflict with those of the Supreme Command. Therefore, I could only ask to be excused from the audience as I did not feel able to present any opinion to the Kaiser other than this one. General Falkenhayn answered: 'Come along, and tell the Emperor whatever you think fit.'

My reception turned out to be a grievous disappointment. I assumed that the Kaiser would ask for an explanation why relations with the United States had taken such a grave turn after all the messages of goodwill with which he had sped me on my way. I expected to give an account of the American attitude to the war at sea and of her potential aid to the Allies. Instead, after a brief greeting, the Kaiser launched into a long account of the situation in America as he saw it. I was hardly allowed to get a word in. He seemed to think that the Allies would never succeed in getting the United States to declare war. At this point I must have made some emphatic gesture to the contrary. He stopped talking and looked at me with astonishment. 'Your Majesty is perhaps not aware,' I said, 'of the extraordinary change that has taken place in America since the war. Everyone in our Embassy, from Count Bernstorff down to the most junior secretary, realizes that in the end Congress will do whatever the President demands. He has public opinion behind him, and is in a position to present Congress with a *fait accompli*. All your Majesty's representatives in America are convinced that war will come if no solution is found to the U-boat dispute.'

'No, no!' the Emperor answered, with an imperious gesture, 'my friend Ballin knows the Americans better. He tells me that Wilson is an obstinate fellow, but that he will never get Congress to agree to a declaration of war.' I could only reply that it was incomprehensible to me how Ballin could have arrived at such an opinion. Whereupon I was somewhat brusquely dismissed. It was clear I had fallen badly from grace. I was not invited to lunch, and was given no opportunity of presenting my arguments to the Emperor in a more informal fashion. Falkenhayn did not say a word during the whole audience, and I had the impression that the Kaiser had already been informed by the Navy of my opinions, and was not prepared to give me much scope. I met Ballin a few days later in the Hotel Esplanade and told this influential head of the Hamburg-Amerika Line how surprised I had been to learn the Kaiser's opinions. He seemed a little embarrassed that the Emperor had quoted him. I could only assume that he shared Tirpitz' conviction that this was the only way to end the war successfully and had therefore been at pains not to emphasize the inherent complications.

The Chancellor was considerably depressed at the result of my audience, but insisted, as did Herr von Jagow, the Foreign Secretary, that I should still hold my press conference. I had told Jagow, incidentally, of my meeting with the mysterious Englishman on board the *Nordam*, but he made it quite clear that the time was in no way propitious for such ideas to be discussed. Bethmann-Hollweg sent me a note one morning to say that the press conference had been arranged for 6 p.m. the next day in a private room at the Reichstag, and that Falkenhayn had been requested to give his approval. Two hours later I received one of the War Ministry's famous blue envelopes, with these urgent instructions: 'You will proceed to the Western Front within twenty-four hours and report to the 93rd Reserve Infantry Regiment of the 4th Guards Infantry Division as Battalion Commander.'

This probably seemed the best solution to the Naval High Command. There was certainly much to be gained by giving the German press a clear picture of the situation. But the High Command was doubtless delighted to be rid of such a self-opinionated junior officer, and considered me much better employed with my regiment. My field equipment had all been made ready and I left within the stated time.

There are two sequels to my connection with American affairs. While I was in Flanders, in 1917, I received a request from the General Staff to submit a memorandum on the possibility of the United States organizing an expeditionary force if the U-boat campaign led to a declaration of war. The general impression was that the peacetime strength of the American Army would permit no such development within a short space of time. I presented in the strongest possible terms the opposite opinion, but I doubt whether my report had much effect. My second intervention came after a request from the Foreign Office to comment on the plan to enter into an alliance with Mexico for the purpose of attacking the southern frontiers of the United States. I knew that the weakness and anarchy of Mexico would preclude any such possibility, and said so very forcibly. Again little attention can have been paid to my ideas, or the famous Zimmermann telegram would neither have been sent off nor intercepted. It will be recalled that this message, signed by the Under-Secretary of State, Zimmermann, was designed to launch this absurd project. It was decoded by the British in transit, and had its contents splashed across the front page of every Allied newspaper. Its interception was certainly a great intelligence *coup* and did us irreparable harm.

From a purely personal aspect, my stubborn advocacy in Berlin did not go unremarked or unrewarded. After Falkenhayn was replaced by Hindenburg and Ludendorff, and had been ordered to Turkey, he remembered the General Staff Captain who had predicted events in America so exactly, and sent for me to join his command as head of his operations division. But that is another story.

CHAPTER V

ON ACTIVE SERVICE

The Western Front – Transfer to Turkey – Plans to Recapture Baghdad – The Palestine Front – Command problems – Allenby's attack – Evacuation of Jerusalem – Liman von Sanders – Lawrence – East Jordan offensive – Visit to the Western Front – Ludendorff – Collapse in Palestine – Turkish Armistice – Representations to the Marshal – I escape to Germany – Interview with Hindenburg – I resign from the Army – Lessons of the peace

MY experiences as an officer on the Western Front differed in no way from those of millions of other service men on both sides. My regiment took part in the battles of Vimy Ridge and the Somme, and also fought in Flanders. The 4th Guards Infantry Division, of which my 93rd Reserve Infantry Regiment formed part, was used to plug the line at most of the places where the Allies threatened to break through. During the first difficult days of the Battle of the Somme I was called upon to replace the staff operations officer of my division. One memory which may be of interest is the Allied attack on September 1, 1916, between Ancre and Chaulnes, when for the first time the British and Canadian divisions were supported by tanks. The German communiqué of the day notes that deep penetrations were made in the German front, but that the 4th Guards Infantry Division succeeded in maintaining its position.

It was not as easy as this laconic report might indicate. As the day drew to a close, the battlefield seemed almost empty. I hurriedly collected batmen, cooks, orderlies and clerks from our own divisional headquarters and from a few neighbouring formations, and with them produced signs of activity as if fresh reserves had arrived. In fact, there was not a single reserve company for scores of miles behind us. A complete tactical break-through, the achievement of which the enemy dreamed, had taken place, although they did not seem to realize it. A few dozen administrative personnel was all that stood between the enemy and a major victory. By the time we had counted our losses the next morning, we found that our division alone had lost 72 officers and 4,200 men dead, but the stronger nerves had won the day. This curious failure of the British to exploit success was something I was to experience on several occasions.

In all, my division was thrown into the line three times during that terrible summer, and our final losses were 173 officers and 8,669 men. On Easter Monday, April 11, 1917, we were in action again at Vimy Ridge and Arras. In four weeks of fierce battles we managed to keep the Canadian divisions at bay, and it must have become clear to the enemy that their fantastic losses over the year had not in fact brought them any nearer victory.

The terrible losses caused in the Battle of the Somme, due to the manner in which relatively unimportant tactical positions were defended to the last, convinced every front-line officer that the German system of defence was out of date and far too rigid. The principal problem in any war has always been to use human lives as sparingly as possible. After the war of attrition on Vimy Ridge I had therefore, on my own initiative, introduced certain modifications in our defensive tactics along my divisional front in Artois. I manned my forward positions with relatively few men in a number of well camouflaged strongpoints arranged in echelon. This reduced the concentration of enemy fire, accustomed to a close network of thickly manned trenches. I do not claim to have been the inventor of this new system, the basic idea for which had been laid down by Ludendorff in a recent series of staff orders. However, my practical interpretation of his ideas proved unusually successful, and I was asked on one occasion to visit General Headquarters and made a personal report to both Hindenburg and Ludendorff.

It was not my first visit. My friend Lersner, whom I had known in my Düsseldorf days, and with whom I had worked in the United States and Mexico, was the Foreign Office liaison officer there, and from time to time I visited him. The Field-Marshal and Ludendorff were often kind enough to have a word with me, and on this occasion Hindenburg cross-examined me very closely on my experience with the new defensive methods, paying particular attention to the problem of whether the morale of the troops would not suffer if they were used in small independent units rather than in major formations under central control.

However, he agreed with me that this was largely a question of training and of the confidence felt by the other ranks in their officers. All my conversations with the Field-Marshal were purely military, but they laid the foundations of a personal relationship that was to develop in later years far beyond anything I could have imagined at the time.

* * *

One day in June 1917 I was called from the front line to the battalion field telephone and found Lersner on the line. 'You have been appointed operations officer in the Falkenhayn Army Group and you are to go to Mesopotamia with him,' he told me. I could not have been more astonished. 'Mesopotamia? Where on earth is that?' was my first question. But Lersner gave me no further details, and merely told me to report to Berlin immediately.

I would like to deal at some length with my experiences in the Middle East, for two reasons. Although they consist largely of the war reminiscences of a still relatively junior officer, I held an appointment which gave me a very clear picture of the campaigns in Mesopotamia and Palestine. These are given little attention in the official German war history and readers familiar with Allenby and Lawrence of Arabia may find something of interest in an account from the other side. Moreover, my experiences and the contacts I made with leading Turkish soldiers and officials were to be by no means unimportant when, more than twenty years later, I returned to Turkey as German Ambassador.

Falkenhayn had been replaced by Hindenburg and Ludendorff after the Battle of Verdun. For all his intelligence and clarity of conception, in the last resort he lacked the broad view. However, the campaign in Rumania had considerably raised his stock, and when Turkey sent her ally an urgent appeal for help, Falkenhayn seemed the right man to fill the gap. The German Field-Marshal, Colmar von der Goltz, had managed to beat off the British attack on Baghdad and a British army under General Townshend had surrendered to the Turks at Kut el Amara. Now Goltz was dead. The Turks had had immense confidence in him, and after his death suffered a number of reverses, including the loss of Baghdad. It was to be Falkenhayn's task to retake it. He paid a short visit to Turkey to reconnoitre the position and decided to accept the Supreme Command, providing operations in all four main theatres, the Dardanelles, the Caucasus, Mesopotamia and Palestine, were co-ordinated. This had been agreed after an interview with Enver Pasha, whom I have mentioned earlier and who by now was the leading personality in Turkey. In return, a small German expeditionary corps was being organized as a reinforcement for the Turkish Army. The Near East High Command therefore covered a tremendous area. I had little idea of the extraordinary difficulties and frictions that awaited us when I accepted my appointment. The immense area of territory involved, the extremely limited transport facilities, our ignorance of the country, its climate and people, and the totally different characters of the leading Turkish personalities, all played their part in our problems. Some of the difficulties could be overcome by military measures, others by a feeling for compromise which was to stand me in good stead when I returned to the country in later years.

When I arrived in Berlin I found preparations for the organization of the German Asia Corps well in hand. The main body of troops could not be expected to arrive in the Near East until the late autumn, and the immediate problem was for a small planning staff to proceed to Turkey and make all the necessary arrangements. We left for Constantinople, or Istanbul, as it is now called, in July. The plan for the recapture of Baghdad which we worked out in the fantastic heat of that Turkish summer was briefly this: the Turkish 7th Army was to be reorganized in and around Aleppo by the autumn and would receive the German Asia Corps as reinforcement. This force was then to proceed along the Euphrates, using the river as its line of communications, and march on Baghdad. A glance at the map will show the extraordinary difficulties with which we had to contend. The terrain was mainly desert. Barges and other vessels were not to be had, owing to lack of timber, and we had to fall back on the biblical coracle, made of inflated goat-skins.

The difficulties of keeping an army supplied by such measures can well be imagined. We did not even have enough coracles, and the problem of getting them up-river again was almost insoluble. We had to concentrate most of our efforts on making the roads practicable for the few lorries at our disposal. At that time two sections of the Baghdad railway, where it had been planned to cross the Taurus and Amanus mountains, were yet to be completed. Thousands of labourers were engaged in construction work, and the Amanus tunnel was ready by the end of the summer. The Taurus section, however, was not finished until the autumn of 1918. Its completion coincided exactly with the armistice that Turkey signed at Mudania. This railway was our main supply line, yet to get our supplies across the Taurus, everything had to be unloaded into a light field railway, taken over the passes and reloaded into railway trucks the other side. A chain is as strong as its weakest link. Every bullet, every stitch of uniform, every handful of coal and every pint of petrol had to pass along this tenuous link between Europe and the Turkish forces on the widely distributed fronts. The miracle is that the Turkish armies held out as long as they did.

Another yet more immediate problem occupied our attention. The southern Turkish front, on the edge of the Syrian desert between Gaza and Beersheba, was held by an army commanded by the German General Kress von Kressenstein, under the orders of the Governor-General of Syria, Cemal Pasha. After the failure of the Turkish offensive against the Suez Canal, Kress had built up his front in the most admirable fashion. He was well liked by his Turkish subordinates, and had already beaten off two British attacks on the oasis of Gaza, on the right flank of his line, with considerable success.

The Western Allies sent General Allenby from the Western Front to Egypt with the evident intention of mounting a major offensive in Palestine. Our intelligence services reported that the British, in their usual fashion, were building up their strength methodically. They had built a railway from Cairo to their forward areas in the direction of Gaza and had also installed a water pipeline, an absolute necessity in desert warfare. General Kress therefore had good reason to fear for his position. I had myself fought against Allenby's divisions at Vimy Ridge, and had little doubt that he would employ the methods he had used in France of preceding his attack by an overwhelming artillery barrage. If the Palestine front was threatened, then our operation against Baghdad was in danger. An enemy break-through would bring them into Syria and cut off our Baghdad Army from all its communications. Falkenhayn decided to pay a visit of inspection to the Palestine front and travelled down with his supply officer and myself.

For the first time in my life, I crossed the high Anatolian

plateau. This immense undeveloped region seemed practically un-inhabited. At Karapunar, high up in the Taurus, we had to leave the train and change into the improvised field railway which led over the mountains and down into the Adana plain. It followed the historic route of Alexander the Great and Cyrus. The further south we got, the hotter it became. Aleppo lay in a great cloud of dust from the armies and caravans. We went on through Damascus and Nazareth and finally arrived at Jaffa, where Kress was waiting for us. We inspected the whole front, a considerable strain in the pitiless brown desert after the unhealthy office life in Constantinople. Back in our railway car, Falkenhayn asked for my impressions.

The whole long front was very thinly held, but with the excep-tion of one or two modest reserve units, every available man was in the front line. There was no defence in depth. The field works might have been adequate in 1914, but they would never stand up to the sort of artillery bombardment to which we had become accustomed on the Western Front. Our own artillery and munition supplies were hopelessly insufficient, and although the troops had made a good impression, they had been in position for years with-out relief. Their rations were scanty and the supply system in-adequate. Half the mules, horses and camels had been eaten, and there seemed to be little likelihood of replacements. The front could only be held against Allenby's new methods if it was organized in depth. In its present condition the Palestine Army weakened the whole southern flank of the Aleppo Army Group.

Falkenhayn agreed with every word I said. We were convinced that Kress was still the best man on the spot, and sought only for some way in which to help him. But we were at a grave dis-advantage. The Allied supply lines, with their command of the sea and better overland communications, were superior to ours. As we worked out what units could possibly be spared from the Aleppo Army Group we received a fresh piece of bad news. A number of ammunition trains had been blown up at Haydarpasha, the Baghdad railway terminus on the Asia Minor coast opposite Constantinople, and valuable supplies for the Aleppo Army had been destroyed. Preparations for the Baghdad campaign had already fallen behind schedule and this new disaster set us back still further. The arrival of the German Asia Corps was also delayed.

Falkenhayn, who had been appointed a Turkish Marshal in the meantime, made up his mind to postpone the Baghdad enterprise and concentrate all his available strength to meet the coming attack in Palestine. The recapture of Baghdad was more a matter of prestige than of military necessity, while the collapse of the Palestine front would mean the loss of Iraq and Syria. While this decision was militarily correct, its consequences were regrettable. Falkenhayn demanded that if part of his army were to be placed at Kress's disposal, then he, Falkenhayn, must have the overall command, especially as he intended to make another drive on the Suez Canal after beating off the British attack. Cemal Pasha was not a man to surrender any part of his power, and fought with oriental tenacity against the idea of handing over the supreme command to Falkenhayn. We met Cemal in Damascus on our return journey and found that we had to deal with an extremely intelligent oriental despot, with a Chief of Staff, Colonel Ali Fuad, who was one of the most brilliant officers in the Turkish Army. Falkenhayn and Cemal came to no agreement, and the question of command was referred to the German and Turkish service chiefs.

I tried to convince Falkenhayn how unfortunate the consequences might be if Cemal were simply ordered to hand over his command. We would then have this powerful figure sitting resentfully in Damascus in control of all our lines of communication. But Falkenhayn was not to be moved. There was a stubborn, selfish streak in his character. He was a man who could not brook failure, and his pride had been wounded by his removal after Verdun from the post of Chief of Staff of the German Army. He now wished to carry out a campaign that would completely restore his fame and reputation. There could be no sharing of responsibility. In the end, Falkenhayn brought pressure to bear at Cabinet level and got his way. It was to be a Pyrrhic victory. From then on we met with passive resistance from the still powerful Cemal in everything that concerned our supplies and reinforcements.

Reports from Kress left us in no doubt that Allenby's attack was imminent. Falkenhayn therefore decided to send me down to Jerusalem to reorganize the defensive system and make arrangements for the quartering and deployment of the units of the 7th Turkish Army, which were to be sent from Aleppo under the command of one of the youngest and most energetic generals the Turks had, Mustafa Kemal Pasha, later to be known as Kemal Atatürk.

When I reported to General Kress in September, the situation had already become more threatening. A Turkish patrol had en-countered some English cavalry, one of whose horsemen had 'lost' his diary as they made off. This gave details of preparations for a major attack on Beersheba, on the extreme left of our line. There was no way of telling whether this was a trick or not, and as a matter of fact we learnt after the war that the British had hoped by this ruse to make us shift our strength to Beersheba while they attacked Gaza. An attack on the oasis of Abraham through the waterless desert seemed unlikely, but if it took place and was successful, the way to Hebron and Jerusalem would lie open to the enemy.

I took up the whole question of defence in depth with Kress. He agreed readily, but asked me to help him convince his Turkish officers. I therefore paid a visit to Gaza on the right flank, where General Refet Pasha commanded three divisions. He received me with great politeness and we had a long conversation in French, which he spoke perfectly. I told him of our experience with Allenby's methods on Vimy Ridge and explained that any attack was likely to be preceded by days of artillery bombardment. The thick cactus groves which surrounded the whole position appeared to offer an excellent defence, but once these were flattened, the desert offered no further cover. I asked him to keep two of his divisions in reserve and man the forward positions as lightly as possible. He gave me a charming smile and replied, '*J'ai bien compris, mon cher Commandant, mais j'y suis, j'y reste.*' All my efforts to convince him were useless, and I was more than a little perturbed at the apparent weakness of my powers of persuasion. We parted with mutual expressions of cordiality, and I begged him once again to reflect on his dispositions and the possibility of saving his troops the enormous losses that must result from the use of the enemy's superior artillery. The basic reason for his attitude, as I soon found out, was that the Turkish infantryman was accus-tomed to defending a given position to his last bullet and his last breath, but was not trained and had little taste for open warfare.

I was to meet Refet Pasha again in later years and he remem-bered our conversation well. He became War Minister under Atatürk and played a decisive rôle in modernizing the Turkish Army. My experience with him was repeated at other points along the front, and in spite of my feverish efforts things remained very much as they were. Kress saw little point in issuing operational orders that would probably neither be understood nor carried out, and so the position remained the same until, even earlier than we had feared, the storm broke.

Allenby's attack began at the end of October, and for me it was a repetition of the Easter battle at Arras. It began with a tremendous barrage from guns of every calibre. A detailed description of the fighting does not belong here. It is enough to say that although the Turkish troops fought like lions, their mass was cut up and destroyed by the enemy artillery before it came to hand-to-hand fighting. Gaza, the principal enemy objective, was captured after being practically razed to the ground. British and Australian cavalry units did in fact make the astonishing desert march to Beersheba, which fell in its turn. To block the road to Jerusalem, I asked Falkenhayn to divert to our threatened left flank two of the Turkish infantry divisions on their way from Aleppo. They were two of the best divisions in the Turkish Army, but when they finally reached our rendezvous they were in terrible shape through lack of water and supplies. At Abu Chuff, a water hole in the hills south of Hebron, I met Mustafa Kemal on his way south with the 7th Army. He was in a fearful temper and seemed to have had a misunderstanding with Falkenhayn over the measures to be adopted. It was a most regrettable situation, which led to his recall and replacement by General Fevzi Pasha, who continued in command of this army until the end of the war. In the post-war period Fevzi Pasha became famous under the name of Marshal Çakmak.

The position at the front went from bad to worse. Enemy aircraft attacked our supply lines and reinforcements, and the Turkish troops, completely unfamiliar with such methods, broke off to the north in disorder. At the first news of the attack Falkenhayn had hurried down to Jerusalem and issued a series of orders to restore the situation. With normal communications and unit commanders accustomed to independent operations, the day might still have been saved. But both these prerequisites were lacking. I tried to make this clear to Falkenhayn and in the end he came to the front himself. As soon as he saw that Kress's whole army had disintegrated, he acted with admirable determination. Every available Turkish and German staff officer was distributed on the roads in the rear areas with orders to stop every man and every unit and build up a new defence line. In the meantime he discussed with Kress and the German generals what the next step should be.

The enemy's right flank, in spite of its success at Beersheba, gave
no sign of following this up by marching on Jerusalem. This was a
tactical error which I have never understood to this day. As a
result, we were able to send the Turkish 7th Army units, which
were concentrating on Hebron, off to the west, where they were
able to attack the flank of the enemy advancing on that front. The
Turkish capacity for open manœuvre was insufficient to allow any
major success, but it was nevertheless possible to consolidate a new
position on Jaffa and behind the Audja, which brought the British
to a halt. Nobody could have been more astonished than we were
to deprive Allenby of the fruits of his break-through. It was the
story of the Western Front – Thiépval and Arras – all over again.
The enemy seemed to be content with his early success and now
paused for the regrouping of his own units. If Allenby had known
how near he was to a complete victory, he could have ended the
Palestine campaign in November 1917 and brought Turkey to her
knees a year earlier. Whatever criticisms may be directed at
Falkenhayn, his success in building a new front out of nothing
was a truly remarkable achievement; yet it would have been impossible without the fierce steadiness of the individual Turkish
soldier.

Our next problem was to make the enemy advance from the
coastal plain up to the heights of Jerusalem as difficult as possible.
We did not succeed in this for long. As soon as the British had re-
grouped, at the beginning of December, they advanced into the
hills on a broad front. We put up stiff resistance on the road from
Jaffa, but gradually had to give ground. One morning my radio
officer reported to me that the British transmitter at Caernarvon
had broadcast an announcement that the German troops defending Jerusalem had 'in the most impious fashion' blown up the
mausoleum of the Prophet Samuel to prevent it falling into British
hands. The broadcast then went on to bewail the horrors likely to
be perpetrated in the holy city of Jerusalem, which the 'Huns'
would probably raze to the ground.

On one of the hills outside Jerusalem there was in fact an old
Turkish burial place called Nebi Samvil, probably in memory of
the prophet. Two Turkish machine-guns had been stationed there
to enfilade the British advance, but they had been smoked out by
some well-placed artillery fire, which destroyed the building
before the capture of the hill by the British. This, I can only

suppose, provided the basis for the report of the 'shameful destruction of this biblical memorial by the Huns'. Nevertheless I found this broadcast rather perturbing. From my experience in the United States, I knew that even the most stupid and ill-founded propaganda could cause great damage, and the broadcast from Caernarvon was probably a sign of worse to come. I told Falkenhayn of my fears and begged him to evacuate Jerusalem before the town came under direct attack, causing damage for which we would certainly be blamed. The city had no strategic value and Palestine could be defended equally well three miles to the north. Its loss was therefore merely a matter of prestige. However, for Falkenhayn this was the decisive factor. 'I lost Verdun, I have just lost a new battle, and now you ask me to evacuate a city which is the cynosure of the world's attention. Impossible!'

But I did not give up. The prestige aspect seemed unimportant compared with the disastrous effect of the destruction of the Holy Places which must result if the city were invested. I sent a telegram to the German Ambassador in Constantinople, my old chief in America, Count Bernstorff, asking him to intercede with Enver Pasha for the evacuation of Jerusalem. I also cabled the German High Command explaining the necessity for the move. The order to evacuate the city was given on December 7 and carried out the next day, when we moved our headquarters first to Nablus and then to Nazareth. General Allenby's 'victorious' entry into the city achieved world fame, but it had no influence on the campaign. In spite of the collapse of the desert front we managed to hold down Allenby's armies in Palestine until September 1918, when the outcome of the war was being decided not in the Middle East but on the Western Front.

Rain, mud and the appalling state of the roads hindered operations on both sides during the winter of 1917–18. Our front had been stabilized. From the sea to the Nablus-Jerusalem road it was held by the Turkish 8th Army under Cevad Pasha. His Chief of Staff was Asim Bey, later to become the Vice-Chief of the Turkish General Staff. From there to the Jordan lay the 7th Army under Fevzi Pasha, whose Chief of Staff was my friend Falkenhausen, known later as Chiang Kai-Shek's advisor and Commanding General in Belgium. I was called upon to prepare a plan for an offensive campaign in the spring, but it was clear that without considerable reinforcements, nothing could be done. On the other hand, there was no doubt that Allenby would endeavour to follow up the result of his autumn offensive. The Turkish fronts in the Caucasus, in Mesopotamia and in Palestine were thinly held, there were no strategic reserves, and there was no hope of further help from the German High Command, which sought a final decision in the war on the Western Front. Falkenhayn saw no further employment for himself in Turkey and asked the Kaiser to relieve him.

His request was granted in February 1918, and he was given command of an army on the Russian front. He was succeeded by the chief of the German military mission in Turkey, Marshal Liman von Sanders, in his way an even more difficult character than Falkenhayn. Both had vain and obstinate personalities, but where Falkenhayn had undoubted operational genius, Liman had a better understanding of co-operation with our Turkish allies, and they responded quickly to the new appointment. In the early spring, the British launched an attack along the Jerusalem-Nablus road, where they came up against the Turkish 3rd Army Corps, under the command of General Ismet Pasha, later to become Turkey's second President. Two further attacks in the direction of Amman were also beaten off, and a new Turkish army, the 4th, was formed to hold this area. It was commanded by General Cemal Pasha, the 'Small One' as he was called, to distinguish him from the Governor-General of Syria. General Liman von Sanders ordered me to join this new formation as Cemal's Chief of Staff. He had his headquarters at Es Salt, a little Arab village on the way to Amman. I found him a corpulent and charming gentleman who maintained excellent relations with a great many Arab sheiks, including Emir Feisal, head of the Hashemite tribe, who was nevertheless allied to the British, and later became King of Iraq.

Es Salt lay about 5,000 feet above the Dead Sea, amid the peaks of the East Jordan mountains. The 4th Army held a sector from the left flank of the 7th Army on the Jordan as far as the Dead Sea. But we also had a 'front' in our rear. A Turkish division, commanded by Fahri Pasha, occupied Medina, the terminal of the famous railway to Mecca. This was the area in which Lawrence of Arabia was operating with his rebel Arabs in order to force the Turks out of the Holy Places. Their principal activity consisted in breaking this railway as it wound its way across miles of desert through Amman to Medina. The East Jordan mountains were almost devoid of communications. Apart from the single road that passed from Jericho through Es Salt to Amman, there were only mule tracks. Any British attack must therefore be directed against this road, which the surrounding mountains made relatively easy to defend. For this reason, the British forces had twice tried to reach Amman by an encircling movement, and open the road from the rear. I could expect them to try again.

The organization of the new 4th Army was only half completed when the British attacked again east of the Jordan. Before dawn several divisions made a frontal attack on our Jordan line, while at the same time three cavalry divisions crossed the Jordan north of Jericho and with the help of friendly Arabs made their way over mule tracks in the direction of Es Salt. It was perfectly clear to me that the fate of our whole position in Palestine was at stake. If the British cavalry divisions got as far as Dera and managed to cut the railway to Damascus, besides capturing the Jordan defile, then we should all be in a trap. We had good divisions on the Jordan front, but our only mobile reserve was an infantry battalion in Es Salt, which Cemal intended to retain for our own immediate defence. However, it was not going to be much use against three divisions, and I ordered it off to the front in answer to urgent requests for reinforcements.

By mid-morning the first British and Anzac cavalry appeared out of the hills in front of Es Salt. I mobilized the whole army staff and had them stationed in a ring round our headquarters. We intended to delay the advance as long as possible. I ordered our baggage to be sent off in the direction of Amman and despatched an urgent message to Liman to send reinforcements by railway to Amman in order to prepare for a counter-attack. By five o'clock in the afternoon we were almost completely surrounded, and decided to withdraw down the defile with as much dignity as we could muster. The situation by then was more than tense. An ammunition depot on the outskirts of the village blew up, presumably through an act of sabotage, and the defile was already under fire at one or two points. However, the British finally assisted us to break through. My Turkish friends had been loath to part with most of their belongings and our little cavalcade was followed by a fully laden camel caravan. As soon as the beasts came under fire, they panicked and tore down the narrow road at a gallop. We were hurled to the side of the road. I was unhorsed and lost a boot, and when I remounted I found that the camels had swept all before them. We followed them into safety as quickly as we could.

Our best course would have been to make for Amman, but there was no way of telling whether it had not fallen to a third encircling movement. I therefore decided to make for the nearest place where we could communicate with headquarters in Nazareth. This was another mountain village, called Jerash, the old Roman Gerasium, where there was a *gendarmerie* unit and a telegraph station. There, amidst the superbly preserved Roman ruins, I managed to learn that reinforcements and a howitzer battery were on their way. We rode off to meet them and attacked immediately, but were checked about a quarter of a mile from Es Salt. In the meantime, a Turkish cavalry division was attacking the British units on the flank. I went back to our telephone to ask Liman to support this attack as strongly as possible, but by this time his nerves were at breaking point and all I got was the shouted order over the telephone, 'If you have not retaken Es Salt by tomorrow I will have you court-martialled!'

The next morning I myself led an attack with machine-gun units and we managed to retake the village. I immediately informed the Commander-in-Chief, requesting at the same time my transfer to the Western Front. I did not feel that I could fight under his orders any longer. Allenby, incidentally, described the Es Salt attack as a mere demonstration on his part. For this, however, the forces involved were far too important, and a very real threat was only countered by the magnificent fight put up by the Turkish troops. Historians have seldom acknowledged the courage of these troops at this period, which is why I have devoted more space to the episode than would perhaps appear justified. For my own part, I received a number of Turkish decorations, one of which, my friends told me, bears the inscription 'Death to all Christian dogs'. Liman made no attempt to meet my request for a transfer and I let the matter drop. In due course he paid a visit to our headquarters and was able to appreciate the difficulties with which we were contending; as a result, our relations were somewhat restored.

* * *

We had considerably more success in our operations against the rebel Arab tribes under Lawrence. An expedition to El Tafile, in which the well-known German explorer Niedermayer took part, was highly successful and enabled us to renew railway communication with the Hedjaz. A truly remarkable performance on the part of our engineers enabled us to keep this railway running until the end of the war, in spite of the ever-repeated Bedouin attacks, and the Turkish division in Medina was maintained until the end. Nevertheless, there was a constant threat to our rear. Even if the military value of Lawrence's exploits was strictly limited, it was clear that his forces could menace our whole lines of communication if Allenby returned to the offensive.

The Arabian tribes who still adhered to Turkish suzerainty kept us continually informed about Lawrence's whereabouts. We had a small German air reconnaissance unit attached to our headquarters which had standing instructions to follow his movements closely. The oases were relatively easy to find and wherever the pilots saw a single white tent amongst a group of black, we were pretty sure of knowing he was in it. I often had an aerial photograph of his headquarters on my desk the day it was taken, but it was an unwritten law in the desert warfare, respected by the German pilots too, that a peaceful camp of this nature was not to be attacked. The conceptions of total warfare which developed in 1941 were fortunately unknown to both sides in the desert.

My army commander, General Cemal, maintained excellent relations not only with the nearby Arab tribes, whose sheiks often visited Es Salt to make their obeisances and bring gifts, but also with Emir Feisal and Ibn Saud. We were completely informed as to the internal differences and tensions in the Hashemite family and in King Hussein's household. Feisal's contacts went right back to Damascus with the great Cemal, and we had very much the impression that his basic intention was not to find himself on the losing side.

In the correspondence between Feisal and General Cemal, we did our best to discredit the promises which Great Britain made to the Arabs through Lawrence. It was an ingenious diplomatic game, carried out on what seemed to all intents and purposes a relatively unimportant front. The British can indeed count themselves fortunate to have had the services of a man with such understanding and affection for the Islamic world. From the military point of view his activities were probably not of great importance, but politically and economically they were of price-less value.

Cemal was never able to outbid the offers and promises of the British, nor was there any hope of persuading the Turks to give up their control of the Holy Places. What I did try to do was to have pressure brought on Enver Pasha to grant the Arab tribes and their leaders a wide measure of autonomy. To this end I had written, with Liman's permission, to my old chief Bernstorff in Con-stantinople, but he was unable to overcome the objections of the Turkish High Command. It seemed that this could only be effected by the strongest possible pressure from the German Supreme Command. I therefore decided to ask permission to visit German headquarters on the Western Front and enlist their assistance before Allenby renewed his offensive.

At the beginning of August 1918 I flew from Amman to Damascus and thence to France. On the Western Front I found a radical change in the situation. Russia was practically out of the war, and our defensive campaign in Flanders had been followed in the spring by the German offensive of 1918, on which all our hopes had been pinned. After starting off successfully, it had ground to a halt. The Americans, with their fresh divisions and endless material resources, had brought about the turning point at Château Thierry. By the time I arrived at General Headquarters it was clear that we would need a miracle to win the war. It was arranged for me to see General Ludendorff on the evening of my arrival at nine o'clock, but the interview did not finally take place until two in the morning, such was the pressure under which he was working. I gave him a short account of the general situation in Palestine, and particularly of the difficulties of my own army with its two fronts. I told him that a new enemy offensive was imminent and emphasized that unless the Turks made certain political concessions we would not be able to resist it. Ludendorff grasped the essentials immediately and told me to draft a telegram to Enver Pasha. This I did in a few minutes, calling for autonomy for the Arabs and making an urgent appeal for immediate political measures on the part of the Turkish Government. Ludendorff signed it. I had done everything humanly possible to meet the immediate threat.

While I was still in Germany on a short visit to my family, the British offensive broke on the whole Palestine front. A cavalry advance overran the German headquarters at Nazareth. Among the objects they captured was a trunkful of papers which I had left behind when I had first been ordered to Es Salt. In their raid on Nazareth the British cavalry just missed capturing Liman von Sanders, but they seemed to find my papers a compensation. They contained nothing but private letters that I had received from time to time, with comments on the general situation and the likely outcome of the war. They had no political importance, but the British propaganda machine was able to make a certain amount of use of them, especially as a sequel to the published version of my activities in the United States.

I packed my bags and caught the next Orient Express. Now that the blow had fallen, I was determined to be there. As far as I could gather, Allenby had attacked the 7th and 8th Turkish Armies, after his usual tremendous artillery barrage, but had left my 4th Army severely alone. Apparently he had learned to appreciate the difficulty of fighting in the East Jordan mountains. Unfortunately, my headquarters in Es Salt made the mistake of retaining the troops in their positions long after the 7th and 8th Armies had started to retreat. I was never able to find out what orders Liman von Sanders had issued to the 4th Army. Probably he had issued none. The only escape route for the disintegrating 7th and 8th Armies lay along the railway line and down the steep defile through Dera to Damascus. It should have been the duty of my army to keep this defile open at all costs. We should have broken contact and assured control in the Dera area before Lawrence's Arabs got there, but this was recognized too late.

Liman had not been able to repeat Falkenhayn's feat in the previous November of rallying a broken army in new defensive positions. This time defeat was final, even though isolated Turkish units offered stiff resistance near Damascus and further north. By the time I arrived in Istanbul General von Seeckt had taken over as senior German representative on the Turkish General Staff. As I could be of no further use in Palestine, I was given a new appointment.

The Bulgarian front had also broken, and it seemed probable that the Allies would advance on Constantinople across the Maritza. I was therefore instructed to take over a new defence line along the river. Some Turkish units were available, which were to be joined by a German territorial division transported from Odessa. It was a hopeless task from the beginning. The Turks were in no position to fight on. They had fulfilled their alliance with us to the last, and the fact that we could provide them with no further reinforcements was not our fault. Austria-Hungary had long been crying out for German divisions, and the German High Command was concentrating all its available reserves on the Western Front. Turkey was forced to begin armistice discussions, which were concluded at Mudania. In one clause the Turks insisted that all German troops should be honourably interned with their side arms and standards, and not treated as prisoners of war, but the Allies did not honour this engagement.

Amid the disintegration of defeat I was instructed to arrange for the homeward transport of the German survivors of the Liman von Sanders' Army Group, which was still concentrated in or to the south of the Taurus. I took the Baghdad railway for the last time and at Karapunar found the surviving units of the German Asia Corps. It had never been possible to commit them as a body. Their capacity for manœuvre and their fire power had made it necessary to send in individual units wherever the line was thin, and their losses had been high. One of the officers, Captain Guertner, was to become Minister of Justice in the cabinet I formed in later years. I do not need to go into details of their exploits, which have been described by better pens than mine. I cannot do better than quote the opinion of Lawrence of Arabia, who had this to say of their conduct during the final collapse:

'Exceptions were the German detachments; and here, for the first time, I grew proud of the enemy who had killed my brothers. They were two thousand miles from home, without hope and without guides, in conditions bad enough to break the bravest nerves. Yet their sections held together, in firm rank, sheering through the wrack of Turk and Arab like armoured ships, high-faced and silent. When attacked they halted, took position, fired to order. There was no haste, no crying, no hesitation. They were glorious.'[1]

With the Armistice Liman lost his post as Commander-in-Chief. The demobilization of the Turkish Army was being organized by Mustafa Kemal Pasha, and I paid him a last visit at Adana in order

[1] T. E. Lawrence: *Revolt in the Desert*. Jonathan Cape, London, 1927.

to arrange details for the transport of the German units. It was the beginning of his great rôle in rescuing Turkey from total collapse. He offered me what little assistance he could, but told me we would do better to look after ourselves. It had been agreed that the German troops were to be interned near Moda, a suburb of Constantinople, but the move was not completed until the end of November. It was high up in the grim Taurus, at Karapunar, that we had to endure the terrible news of our country's defeat. For most of us, it was the collapse of every value we had ever known, made even more painful by exile, and it was not easy to maintain discipline when we reached the camp at Moda.

The details only filtered through gradually, but for most of us the worst blow was the abdication forced on the Kaiser by the advice of Hindenburg and Groener, after President Wilson's refusal to deal with the existing German régime. Instead of the thousand-year-old monarchy, the Red Flag had been planted in the centre of Germany. It was the end of everything we had believed in for generations, the disappearance of all we had loved and fought for.

Liman von Sanders was allowed to take up residence on the Island of Prinkipo and had permission to visit the internment camp every morning. When the news trickled through that the revolutionaries in Germany were organizing soldiers' councils, this Imperial General suddenly made up his mind that similar institutions could properly be organized among the troops under his command. Had this happened, our authority would have quickly collapsed, and we would have been unable to withstand the Allies' demands that our arms be surrendered and the internment regulations stiffened. We discussed the situation among the officers and it was decided that I must represent to the Marshal on their behalf that it would be better, in view of his ill health, if he were to give up command of the German troops and return to Germany. We had a stormy interview, in which he refused to do anything of the sort, in spite of my contention that a further decline in discipline would result in the Allies treating us as prisoners of war. I then insisted, as senior General Staff Officer present, on getting in direct touch with Field-Marshal Hindenburg. As all the telegraph lines were now in the hands of the Allies, this would mean disclosing the whole affair to them. He became more thoughtful at this and ordered me to return to Moda, where he would let me have his decision within an hour. It came soon enough. I was to be arrested and brought before a court-martial on a charge of insubordination in face of the enemy.

This was too much. I would have been prepared to undergo a court-martial in Germany, but not in Moda, where it would only have made the situation worse. The only solution seemed to be to get back to Germany myself as quickly as possible. We were just at the turn of the years 1918–19. Among the many Allied ships lying off Constantinople was the hospital ship *Jerusalem*, still with its German crew. With one of my fellow officers, young Lieutenant Count Spee, a cousin of the Admiral, we made plans to smuggle ourselves on board. Disguised in civilian clothes that we had bought in one of the bazaars, we climbed a rope ladder in the dead of night and remained on board, undetected, until the ship arrived at Spezia. Italy appeared to be in a state of utter confusion, in spite of being one of the victorious powers, and we managed to make our way to the Swiss frontier. By January 6 we had arrived at the main station in Munich.

Here we were greeted by the revolution in full spate. The members of the soldiers' council on duty at the station tried to tear off my badges of rank, but I managed to get away and finally reached Kolberg, where Field-Marshal von Hindenburg had set up his last headquarters. His majestic figure looked the same as when I had last seen him in France, but his strong face was marked with care. I made my report on the final collapse of the Turkish Empire, the last battles, the internment of the German forces, and my dispute with Marshal Liman von Sanders. 'I am here to place myself at the disposal of a court-martial,' I said. 'Some steps had to be taken to maintain the honour of German arms in Turkey, and I accept full responsibility. When things became impossible, I made my way here, and now I request an investigation.'

A wry smile passed over Hindenburg's face. 'I know General Liman von Sanders' vanity pretty well. I don't need any further information about his attitude,' he said. 'There is no need for either investigation or court-martial. You may consider the matter closed.' It was a painful interview, and the last I was to have with him as an active soldier. From it I retained an ineffaceable impression of the strength of his character and of his modest, unassuming greatness in the hour of Germany's defeat. Here, I felt, was one personality to whom the nation could turn in time of stress.

Berlin, and every other German city, was torn by revolution. Liebknecht, Rosa Luxemburg, Eisner and their followers were fighting a bitter battle, setting up 'soviets' everywhere, against the more reasonable wing of the Social Democrat Party, led by Ebert and Noske. The Royal Palace was the scene of violent battles between Red sailors and more moderate elements. Nothing could have shown more clearly the decline of all authority that came with the collapse of the monarchy and the defiance of law, order and tradition. There seemed little place in this disruption for a soldier who had sworn an oath of loyalty to the Prussian King. The victors had decreed the demobilization of most of the Army, and the one hundred thousand men we were allowed to keep provided little chance of employment for regular officers. In March I received orders to report to military headquarters in Danzig as senior General Staff officer, but I had already made my own decision. With a heavy heart, I sent off my resignation from the Army, requesting permission, which was later granted, to wear the uniform of the General Staff on formal occasions, in memory of the work to which I had devoted most of my life. A new chapter was about to begin.

★ ★ ★

Before leaving this period I would like to make a few remarks on the development of the general world situation at the time of the peace treaty. Many decisions had been taken of which the full implications were not yet clear but which had a decisive effect on future events. Drawing up a peace which does not itself contain the germs of a new war requires a supreme effort of statesmanship. National passions, the thirst for revenge, demands for booty and compensation and the desire to underline military success by the annexation of territory or other political means, are all natural reactions which a true statesman is called upon to resist. The purpose of war can only be to arrive at a better peace, but in the case of the first world war the peace was already lost before the conflict ended. It may be said, perhaps, that the same is true of the second world war, but at least today it is encouraging to see how former errors are recognized and what efforts are being made to avoid their repetition.

In any war between coalitions, each seeks to strengthen its position by attracting fresh allies. But in doing so, it is most important to keep the ultimate goal of the conflict in mind. The problem by which the Great Powers were faced in 1914 was to seek a new, and if possible better, balance of Europe's conflicting forces. Neither the Central Powers nor the Entente remained true to this conception, and every attempt to consider possible peace terms during the course of the conflict failed completely. The offer by the Central Powers on December 12, 1916, to declare their war aims, in answer to President Wilson's invitation for all the belligerent powers to place their cards on the table, was dismissed by the Allies as a German propaganda manœuvre. It was a major error of German policy not to disregard this brusque response and to answer the pleas of both President Wilson and Pope Benedict XV by making a clear declaration of their aims, emphasizing that they had no territorial demands. The tragedy of Germany during this period was that there was no strong political leadership, with the result that the military leaders were obliged to determine policy. A high command always considers that to make an offer of peace when the military situation is unfavourable is a sign of weakness. When things are going well and success is in sight, their demands tend to become exaggerated. The Peace of Brest-Litovsk is a good example of what happens when military requirements predominate and political insight is lacking.

Those who know German history appreciate Bismarck's battle to impose his moderate demands on the country's military leaders. His overwhelming personality succeeded in placing political sagacity above military pride. When the German Reichstag conducted a post-war enquiry into the responsibility for the first world war, General Groener, later Minister of War in the Weimar Republic, testified: 'The German General Staff was fighting the British Parliament; not because militarism was paramount in Germany, but because there was no political power to match that of Great Britain in the conduct of our country's affairs.' Perhaps I may be allowed to ask whether the political sagacity of the Allies did in fact match the capacity of their military leaders.

When President Wilson made his famous speech to Congress on February 11, 1918, laying down the principles which should apply to any termination of the conflict, he did not know that their application had already been made impossible by the various secret pacts which the Allied Powers had signed. Wilson said that there should be no annexations, contributions, or punitive damages.

D

'. . . peoples and provinces are not to be bartered about from sovereignty to sovereignty as if they were chattels or pawns in a game.' National aspirations should be respected and peoples should be dominated and governed only by their own consent.

In November 1914, Great Britain had already advised the Russian Government that there was no objection to a Russian advance on Constantinople and the Dardanelles. An agreement between Great Britain and Japan had already deprived Germany of her position in the Pacific and on the continent of Asia. This may have freed Britain's rear, but in the end it weakened the European position in Asia. By 1915 it had been decided to partition the Turkish Empire. Russia was to receive the north-eastern territories, France was to get Syria, Adana and the south-eastern part of Asia Minor, while Britain was granted southern Mesopotamia, the Syrian ports of Haifa and Acre, and exclusive influence in the former neutral zone of Persia. In May 1916, France obtained a Protectorate over Syria under the terms of the Sykes-Picot Treaty.

Italy hesitated for some time before deciding at what price she would sell herself to the Entente Powers, after failing in her treaty obligations to Austria and Germany. A secret treaty, dated April 26, 1915, granted her the Trentino, the Adige Valley, Trieste, Istria and Dalmatia, Valona, Saseno, the Dodecanese and part of Asia Minor. This was later increased, by the Treaty of St Jean de Maurienne in April 1917, to include Smyrna. In November of that year the famous Balfour Declaration recognized Palestine as the national home of the Jews. This was drawn up, as Mr Lloyd George (as he then was) admitted to the Palestine Royal Commission in 1937, 'for propagandist reasons', the Allies wishing, at a time when the war situation was critical, to ensure support from the Jewish community throughout the world. The fulfilment of this promise could only offend the Arabs, while its failure must obviously antagonize the Jews. A wartime measure, designed to meet immediate tactical requirements, proved to have the most disastrous consequences. The resulting differences of opinion between Great Britain and the Arab world have led to a dangerous diminution in the influence of the Western Powers in one of the world's most important strategic areas.

Failure to sustain one of the fundamental principles of European policy – the maintenance of the Central Powers' position in Europe – led to a bad peace. Within a few years Europe had been brought near to collapse. In his ignorance of European conditions, President Wilson's insistence on the rights of self-determination led to the dissolution of the Danube Monarchy and lit the fuse of an endless series of disputes and conflicts. Germany was disarmed and the foundations of her economic life undermined by an irrational reparations policy. The thesis of her exclusive war guilt upset the moral equilibrium of the whole nation. The Allies even went so far as to regard it as a mistake not to have destroyed the unity of Germany which had been won by Bismarck.

There is a lesson to be learned in comparing the outcome of the world war peace conferences with the results achieved by Europe's statesmen a hundred years earlier at the Congress of Vienna. After the Napoleonic wars France was subjected to occupation and obliged to pay reparations; but three years after the war had finished, the Treaty of Aix la Chapelle ended the occupation and the reparations and proclaimed final peace. France was invited to join the councils of the four victorious powers – Russia, Austria, Great Britain and Prussia.

The economic and moral consequences of the Treaty of Versailles obliged the Weimar Republic to accept a burden which within a few years had caused its collapse. Fate provided me in 1932 with the opportunity to seek a new basis of European co-operation at the Lausanne Conference. My mission failed. The millstone which we had to bear became a stepping-stone on Hitler's route to power.

CHAPTER VI

AFTERMATH

A new life – Social problems – A dictated peace – Years of revolution – Parliamentary life – The Weimar Constitution – Drawbacks of independence – Hindenburg as President

THE world I had known and understood had disappeared. The whole system of values into which I had integrated myself and for which my generation had fought and died had become meaningless. The Kaiser's Empire and the Prussian monarchy, both of which we had regarded as permanent institutions, had been supplanted by a largely theoretical republic. Germany was defeated, ruined, her people and institutions a prey to chaos and disillusionment. The profession to which I had devoted my life had become one of the principal victims. I had to find some outlet for my energies. My whole training and upbringing had been in the service of my country, and now that disaster had intervened the obligation was still stronger. My chief problem was to decide the field of my future activity.

I considered several possibilities, in each of which a former officer could play a useful part, but my thoughts turned more and more to a political career. First of all I had to make up my mind exactly where I stood. The first object of my military training had been to instil discipline and obedience, and in this politics had played no part. The position of trust we had held under the Crown meant that we became conservative by nature. Now everything had changed. All these old traditions had been swept away by the Republic, and we were all free to adopt an independent attitude.

By background and upbringing I could hardly help being conservative, but even before the war I had found myself out of sympathy with the political development of the Conservative Party. It seemed to me a contradiction in terms to divide its members into progressives and diehards. A conservative must always be progressive. Tradition and principles are basic values, but conservatism implies their application to changing circumstances. Since the beginning of the Industrial Revolution, and at an ever increasing speed in the first half of our century, we have witnessed a gigantic and fundamental conflict. Advances in technique have tended to mechanize the human being, and individuality is in constant danger of becoming submerged in this vast levelling process. The threat to the body politic has increased with the conversion of individuals into 'the masses' – a Marxist weapon in the struggle to overturn the capitalist system. Collectivist philosophies, combined with the materialist conception of history, proclaim the overthrow of those Christian principles which have provided for two thousand years the basis of the Western world's growth. The Moscow brand of Communism has already triumphed in most of Eastern Europe, and the whole process of regarding the State as the tool of the 'repressed working classes' has made great inroads in other countries. The problem has been to find some means of combating these forces.

In the tumult of the post-war period, the duty of all conservative forces was to rally under the banner of Christianity, in order to sustain in the new Republic the basic conceptions of continuing tradition. The Constitution approved at Weimar in 1919 seemed to many a perfect synthesis of Western democratic ideas. Yet the second paragraph of its first article proclaimed the false philosophy of Jean-Jacques Rousseau – 'all power derives from the people'. This thesis is diametrically opposed to the teachings and traditions of the Roman Catholic Church. Over the centuries, the monarchy had represented the highest form of temporal authority in the State, but above it stood the still higher authority of spiritual teachings and Christianity.

Now we had to accept the proposition that the State was the ultimate factor in all our affairs, and its institutions, both administrative and parliamentary, the final repository of authority. This meant, as the Communist régimes based on these principles have proved, that the freedom of the individual and the framework of the law could be manipulated to suit the expediency of the State. But natural law should take precedence over State authority. It can only be maintained by making Christian principles the fundamental basis of all forms of government. And this is nowhere more necessary than in a democracy in which parliament arrogates to itself supreme powers.

Denis William Brogan, the Cambridge political economist, once said that tolerance and scepticism are the hallmarks of a free and democratic nation. Our Socialists in Germany exhibited neither. There was no scepticism concerning the omnipotence of the State and no tolerance for the cultural traditions of Roman Catholicism in a country of mixed religions. This provided us with yet another reason for closing our ranks in defence of these traditions.

Ever since the French Revolution and the *Contrat Social*, and its bastard offspring, the *Communist Manifesto*, the transfer from faith to reason has acquired increasing momentum. The philosophy of naked force has replaced the old relationship between power and authority, between reverence and piety on the one hand and force on the other. Worse than that, the masses have become a helpless tool in mechanized and total warfare in which the individual has become completely submerged. In some way we have to return from this conception of the mass to that of the individual as the most important component in our lives. In earlier times, those deprived of their rights and liberties found comfort in the teachings of the Church, which set the precepts of love against the doctrines of force. Marxism in all its forms has now set force against force, and the power of the masses against the authority of the rulers. In this process the relationship between a nation's citizens and its great personalities, based on conceptions of honour, true worth and true authority, has gradually deteriorated. Pandering to authority takes the place of reverence, and this inevitably entails a lessening in each individual's sense of responsibility. Power, and its exploitation, becomes an end in itself.

In the days when I first met my wife's family in Mettlach I realized the extent to which the solution of the social problem would be the dominating factor of our times. Mettlach was one of the principal industrial areas in the Saar. Here, and in other parts of Germany, as well as in France and Belgium, my wife's family had built during several generations a series of model factories for the production of ceramics. My father-in-law, Privy Councillor von Boch-Galhau, was one of a small group of enlightened industrialists who had recognized the inherent evils of the capitalist system. He tried to establish a relationship of mutual confidence between capital and labour, while yet retaining the traditions of a family enterprise. The shadow of class warfare was already on the horizon. The Socialists were propagating the principles of Marxism, and, in spite of the social reforms carried out under Kaiser Wilhelm II, were trying to organize the 'proletariat' on an international basis and detach the workers as a 'class' from the bourgeoisie.

Only a few industrialists had grasped the fact that the best way of countering these methods was to assume that, besides his wages, the worker should have a share in the prosperity of the enterprise and a dignified and satisfying existence. My father-in-law had been a leader in the provision of well-built modern houses, hostels and holiday estates for his workers, as well as medical care and pension and insurance rights. The results provided a striking example of what could be accomplished by applying the principles laid down by Pope Leo XIII in his Encyclical *Rerum Novarum* as a means of achieving social peace. In this family enterprise, the workers were treated as members of a vast family, and a strong bond of mutual interests held them together. Before he died, my father-in-law criticized bitterly the introduction of national insurance schemes. He considered this broke the bond between employers and employed, replacing the anonymity of State administration for the warm humanity of the old personal relationships. It was a solution designed to cover the new huge industries with their anonymous shareholders. To a very large extent the general manager was already replacing the old type of owner, with his sense of personal responsibility. Throughout my life my attitude to the social problem has been based largely on the successful experiments I saw carried out at Mettlach. I sought to the last some means of putting them into effect by parliamentary methods.

The background to these efforts was a disturbed one. It is difficult now to give a picture of the effect on the vast majority of Germans of the disappearance of their conceptions of order and authority. For over a thousand years the German nation had focused its loyalties on the monarchy, and under it had played a decisive part in building up Western civilization. At the time many of us regarded the sudden imposition of a republic as a fatal error, and we have seen our opinions reinforced over the course of the years. By destroying the historical framework to which most Germans had become accustomed, this drastic step made impossible the steady and peaceful development of Germany as part of an integrated Europe.

For the first time in recent history the victors applied the principle of totality to the terms of a peace: totality in the imposition of war guilt and its punishment, in the unilateral solution of territorial and ethnic problems, and all questions of reparations and finance: totality in the sequestration of all enemy private property, even in neutral countries, and totality in the formation of a League of Nations, from which only the vanquished were excluded. The question may well be asked whether this totality in the name of democracy did not plant the seed of later totalitarian political developments. Certainly it provided a poor example for the success of democracy in Germany.

The grave errors and injustices contained in the Versailles Treaty can only be explained by the state of hysteria engendered in the Allied Powers by years of hate-filled and untrue propaganda. Wilson's Fourteen Points were greeted with immense relief in Germany. Moreover, we were all convinced that the United States, having proved the decisive factor in the victory of the Allies, would play the principal part in the peace negotiations. I still remember how eagerly I discussed with the friends who were interned with me at Karapunar, in the Taurus mountains, what great opportunities Wilson's programme offered our defeated country. We wished for nothing better than to build a new world, as equal partners, conferring with other nations on our mutual difficulties. We still believed in Germany's historic mission as the stabilizing factor in Central Europe. The competition and rivalries which had caused a progressive deterioration in our relations with Great Britain seemed a thing of the past. We no longer represented a danger to anyone. Only our European mission remained the same as it was when we spread Christianity to the eastern provinces and the Baltic: to build a dyke against the threat of Slav aspirations and aggression.

Even if their fear of Germany had blinded the Allies to the threat of Russia, the least they could have done after our defeat was to restore Europe's equilibrium once the Revolution had placed Lenin in the Kremlin. They failed to understand that the era of nationalism had ended and could only be replaced by organizing a united Europe. Europe's wider needs were subjected to the Wilsonian principle of self-determination, which was, however, applied to the smaller nations only, and was ignored in the victors' irrational hatred of the defeated Central Powers. Thus nationalism was revived and exacerbated. We must be thankful today that President Truman and his advisers have shown more comprehension of the problem after the second world war. The Marshall Plan and France's Schuman Plan provide the means to overcome the dangers of nationalism. The League of Nations inherited the weakness of the misapplication of Wilson's principles. Now it is realized that a union of free nations must control its own executive.

After the first world war the Danube Monarchy was divided into its component parts. Czechs, Poles, Magyars, Croats and Serbs were released from the bonds of the former Empire, presumably in the hope that they would, between them, fulfil the rôle played by the Hapsburg monarchy in South-East Europe. In fact, as was to be expected, exaggerated nationalism took precedence over the interests of Europe as a whole. The destruction of the Hapsburg monarchy resulted only in the Balkanization of Europe, and this lack of statesmanlike vision fathered the treaties of Versailles and Saint Germain, designed to render the Germans as powerless as possible.

The effect of Germany's lost position in the world on the generation that had come through the war is understandable enough. It was reinforced by the fear that Germany was to be neutralized, even in Europe. Each day brought a new threat to our national existence. The Poles threatened our Silesian coal basin; East Prussia was placed at their mercy by a corridor that severed it from the main body of the country; the Saar was subjected to international control for fifteen years and its pits surrendered to France; the Ruhr was occupied by the French, who had their own plans for its ultimate disposal; and the union of Austria with Germany was formally forbidden, in complete defiance of the principles of self-determination. Within the country, the old conceptions of law and order and the devoted and excellent civil service were both threatened by internal chaos, although the permanent officials placed their services unreservedly at the disposal of the new form of government. Communists, who owed allegiance only to Moscow, combined with the Independent Socialists to impose by force a Soviet State on the Russian model. In Bavaria, the most conservative of all the states, Eisner succeeded in imposing the first local Soviet government, and civil war broke out in the Ruhr, Saxony and other industrial centres. Communist agents hoisted the Red Flag everywhere and the very existence of Ebert's Social Democrat Government was threatened.

But the more stable elements in the nation were not yet ready to surrender. The remnants of the disbanded German Army formed themselves, under determined officers and leaders, into Free Corps to harry the revolutionaries. The victorious powers called this a reawakening of German militarism. They refused to acknowledge that it was a matter of self-defence and that our only instinct was to save Germany from the Red flood, just as we are being called upon to do thirty-odd years later. I was not a member of any of the Free Corps myself, but on my arrival in Munich from Turkey I found it necessary to fight my way out of the station with their help. Their leader was an officer named Faupel, later to become the German Ambassador to the Franco Government in Spain.

Against this background of chaos I found myself denied access to my home in the Saar and saw little hope of continuing my Army career. The solution to my immediate problem was not easy, but in the end I decided to go back to the country life in which I had grown up. The people who worked the land had always been the well-spring of our nation's strength, and if sanity was to be restored to our affairs, these were the people with whom to work. For generations they had lived in an atmosphere of law and order and, in an industrial age, had kept their heads and their beliefs. If the precepts of Christianity were to play their due part in the life of the new Republic, then I would be in good company to combat the materialist spirit of the twentieth century and ward off the threat of decay, hopelessness and moral degeneration.

I acquired the lease of an estate in my native Westphalia, an old country house with stables and a little land, consisting largely of ponds and ancient oak trees. It was a primitive existence, without any of the modern amenities – no sewage or water mains, no electricity, and miles from the road and railway. But the neighbours of Haus Merfeld, as it was called, were splendid, simple people, with both feet planted firmly on the ground, strong in their religious beliefs and upright in their behaviour. They lived in a quietly ordered world of their own and it was not easy to gain their confidence, but once it had been won, it remained strong for life. We were not far from the borders of the Ruhr, and echoes of the Red revolt reached even our lonely lanes. I organized the local country people into a volunteer company to beat off the Red marauders, and we had to bury or hide our few valuables and reserves of food. Finally I had to ask the military commander in Münster to lend us a squad of soldiers to stiffen our defences. This intimate contact with the moral degeneration of civil war was infinitely more distasteful than anything I had experienced on the battlefields of Flanders.

It was during these troubled days that some of my neighbours, particularly the leader of the Westphalian Farmers' Association, Freiherr von Kerkerinck zur Borg, suggested that I should represent their interests in the Prussian State Parliament. It was some time before I could make up my mind to accept their request. The chief problem was to decide which party to join. I have already mentioned my distaste for formal conservatism, and its political representation in Prussia seemed compounded of too much prejudice and too many obsolete ideas. I thought I would do much better to join one of the centre parties, and the Zentrum Party in particular. This had been founded to represent Catholic interests at the time of Bismarck's struggle between the State and the Roman Catholic Church. Under Windthorst it had attracted many conservative-minded people from the Rhineland, Westphalia, Bavaria and Silesia. As a party of the centre it was essentially one devoted to compromise, and had always pledged itself to interpret the social precepts of Pope Leo XIII. Social problems were more than ever in the foreground, and I was convinced that I could put to good effect the experience of social relations I had gained in my father-in-law's factories. I felt that a party with a religious background would be best able to insist on those Christian principles which had been omitted from the Weimar Constitution. Moreover, my neighbours in Westphalia were all of the same faith and I felt that I could truly represent their interests.

* * *

Perhaps I may pause here to summarize some of the points in the new Constitution, and the electoral law that was part of it, which were to become matters of contention over the next twelve years or so. Both the Central and the State Governments suffered from the same constructional fault. Legislative powers were confined exclusively to a single chamber and there was no higher authority to provide for their correction and revision. The Reichsrat and the

Prussian Staatsrat were in no position to carry out these functions. There was also the problem, both in the Federal Government and the States, of a highly artificial electoral law and a serious lack of co-ordination between the Central Government and that of Prussia – the largest individual State. Amendments to the Constitution could only be made with the approval of a two-thirds majority, which, given the distribution of the parties, meant that no fundamental change was possible. The terms of the Constitution became a serious source of conflict between the left and the right wing parties.

I was particularly opposed to the list system of voting. It was praised as the most democratic in the world. Not a single vote was wasted or without effect. In point of fact, it corrupted the very basis of a healthy democracy. In Prussia, for instance, there was nominally one member for every 50,000 votes. However, this did not mean the formation of constituencies of this size. My electoral area consisted of half the province of Westphalia, with about two million voters. Of these, we could assume that about half a million were likely to vote for the Zentrum Party. Party headquarters therefore drew up a list with at least ten candidates, plus a few in reserve for the State list. After the votes had been counted, one member was elected for each complete 50,000 votes. Any votes that were over were added to the remainders in other areas, and these votes allotted to additional members. Under this system we finally had over thirty parties. No one had to win 50,000 votes in any one constituency, large as they were, and any eccentric or group of eccentrics was almost sure of getting at least one member into Parliament on the reserve list of additional votes. The consequent splintering of representation amounted to the suicide of democracy.

This system also did away with the need for by-elections. If a member died or resigned, his place would be taken by the next man on the list, and this meant that all contact with the fluctuations of public opinion became impossible during the four-year legislative period, except, of course, from the upheaval of a general election. Worst of all, the elected members had no sense of direct responsibility to the electorate. They had the central committee of their party to thank for their election, and could only maintain their position if they showed blind obedience to the party line. Moreover, although an attempt was made to give representation in party lists to the various professions, the result was usually that the individual preferred to become a spokesman for his particular group and lost sight of the broader issues. It became too much of a temptation to take things easily, vote for the party line as a guarantee of re-election, and exercise the minimum amount of original thinking or criticism. I know that party politics call for a certain degree of discipline on broad issues, but I contend that this method of election prevents the emergence of those political personalities who must ultimately form the *élite* on which even a democracy depends. The fact that a member was responsible to his party committee rather than to his constituents meant that he lost contact with them, and this made the individual voter lose interest in the manifestations of parliamentary life. Now, the Weimar Constitution has stood godfather to the Bonn Constitution. The Socialists clung to the list system, although the Christian Democrats made a half-hearted attempt to combine this with individual constituencies. It seems that some people never learn by events.

The relationship between the Federal and State Governments has been an issue ever since the days of Germany's minor principalities. It is not simply a matter of centralism or federalism, nor is it easy to determine the limits of State autonomy which still provide the Central Government with the powers necessary to render it a factor in European affairs. Bismarck, in his time, devised a solution which ensured wide autonomy for the individual States without endangering the authority of the Central Government. Prussia was far and away the largest and materially the best endowed State, including as it did the industrial centres of Rhine, Ruhr, Saar and Upper Silesia. Moreover, the Prussian King was at the same time the German Kaiser. Bismarck devised the idea of combining in one man the offices of Prussian Premier and Reich Chancellor. This greatly lessened the preponderance of Prussia, as the Chancellor, in the interests of unity, was compelled to make concessions to the other States to ensure their co-operation.

With the Crown gone, the Reich had lost its fulcrum. The minor dynasties in the smaller States had also abdicated. The new federal complex, deprived of its final authority, could not help being weak. The dualism between the Reich and its largest component, Prussia, became a very serious problem, which the Weimar Constitution made no attempts to solve and which escaped the

long-drawn-out deliberations of the Reichstag committee studying its reform. In due course I shall give an account of my efforts
as Chancellor to return to Bismarck's conceptions, although the
problem occupied my mind right from the start. The State
Governments went very much their own way, without paying
undue heed to the needs of the central administration, and the preponderance of Prussia could not be countered merely by reducing
its representation in the Reichsrat.

The Reich Government itself was in Berlin as the guest of
Prussia. It had no executive and no police force of its own. As long
as the Governments in both the Reich and Prussia had a similar
political complexion – in Prussia the Social Democrats were in unbroken power from 1918 to 1932 – the implementation of federal
law met with few difficulties in practice. However, if a right wing
coalition happened to be conducting the affairs of the Reich, it
was always possible for an individual Prussian minister to block
the implementation of measures decided upon by the Central
Government. Prussia became indeed a State within a State, and
this dualism provided a weak link in our whole political life. It
also meant that the political influence of a member of the Prussian
Landtag was often greater than that of a member of the Reichstag.

* * *

It seemed a bad time to embark on a political career. The country's
position was at its nadir. We had been beaten in war, we were embroiled in a civil war that threatened the very foundations of the
State, and laboured under a dictated peace which, in its reparations
demands, seemed to threaten the very basis of our economic
existence. Nevertheless, I threw myself into my new career with
the greatest enthusiasm. I was impatient of party dogma and the
narrow egocentric outlook which determined much of the current
thinking on internal and external problems. I refused to be tied
down to the party programme and even in my early speeches
insisted that a parliamentary representative should be responsible
for his own decisions. I was appalled at people's general ignorance
of foreign affairs and tried to awaken some interest in the activities
and opinions of the world beyond our frontiers. But at the same
time I appealed for some toleration and understanding among the
victorious powers for the situation in Germany. However, it was
too much to expect one man's voice to have much effect.

Our position became even more impossible when, at the height of the crisis, with the economy prostrate as a result of reparations and the inflationary devaluation of the currency, the French occupied the Ruhr, contrary to all their treaty undertakings. From Clemenceau's memoirs, *Les Grandeurs et Misères d'une Victoire*,[1] we know that Marshal Foch was insisting that the whole area be annexed. The value of the mark had dropped so low that it was no longer possible to support the miners' attitude of passive resistance by subsidies. Certain personalities in the Rhineland even advocated the establishment of a new independent Rhine Republic, with its capital at Cologne. One of these was Dr Adenauer, the Lord Mayor of Cologne. Although he held one of the highest offices in the state – that of President of the Prussian Staatsrat – he seemed to put the interests of his city above those of the country as a whole.

At an emergency meeting of the Zentrum Party organization I described the whole idea of a Rhine Republic as treasonable and had some hard things to say about these Rhineland defeatists. It was a moment Dr Adenauer did not forget, and in later years I received my own share of personal criticism in return. A few days after I had been acquitted at Nuremberg, Dr Adenauer issued a public denial that he intended to resign the chairmanship of the Christian Democratic Union in the British Zone in my favour. According to the version given in the *Westfalen Post*, published in Arnsberg on October 8, 1946, he is alleged to have added, 'von Papen is a traitor and was probably mixed up in the assassination of Dollfuss'. Many of my friends protested at this statement and called on Dr Adenauer to retract it, as I was under the surveillance of the Bavarian police and in no position to defend myself. But I can find no record of his having done so. However, in politics one must learn to forgive and forget. I am happy to do so now that it is clear that he has grown out of his somewhat narrow sphere of interests and is conducting the foreign affairs of the young Bonn Republic along the only possible lines of Franco-German *rapprochement* and European co-operation.

It seems to have long been forgotten that while France was hastening Germany's internal disruption and encouraging this sort of separatism, fourteen other nations, including Britain and the United States, had embarked on a course of armed intervention in

---

[1] *The Grandeur and Misery of Victory*. Harrap, London, 1930.

Communist Russia. German troops helped to free the Baltic States, and Pilsudski was supported in Poland as part of a *cordon sanitaire*, in which Mannerheim and the White Russian generals all played a rôle. Even Mr Churchill had called on other nations 'to help smash the Red nest before the hen lays any eggs'. Unfortunately it has laid only too many.

But Germany, bled white and internally disrupted, was denied any assistance against the attacks of the separatists, Spartacists and Soviet revolutionaries. Our own reaction was regarded as an attack on democracy and a manifestation of reawakened militarism. Germany owes a great debt to the Foreign Minister of the time, Dr Stresemann, who calmed the situation in the Ruhr while making it clear that the question of secession simply could not be entertained. In our fight to protect Germany and the West from the revolutionary hordes from the East we were thrown back entirely on our own resources. In spite of the economic quagmire into which we sank, under the load of reparations and the destruction of our currency, we succeeded. But our Government's blind insistence on meeting to the letter every outrageous demand on the part of our enemies resulted not only in financial and commercial disaster – the effect in terms of human relations was even more catastrophic.

People abroad have very little conception of the magnitude of this disaster. At the end of the inflation period I can remember how wages and salaries had to be paid daily, because the money received retained only a fraction of its worth at the end of another twenty-four hours. The Central Bank of Issue was unable to print money fast enough, and many cities issued their own currency, so that it became impossible to continue any ordered financial policy. It took a billion marks to purchase what one mark had bought before, and this meant that all savings, mortgages, pensions and investment incomes were completely worthless, and those without material belongings lost their entire capital. Those who had contributed to the many war loans suffered most. The middle classes, the artisans, pensioners and officials were proletarianized in the process. The industrious workman who had acquired a little property and substance had the basis of his economic existence destroyed and became a recruit to class warfare. This revolution in the social order provides the clue to the attraction of Marxist ideologies from the East and of Hitler's programme, born in these difficult days, and promising social justice to the worker and protection to the displaced bourgeoisie.

The nature of the threat to our social order can best be illustrated by a remark Lenin made to my old friend, General Ali Fuad Pasha, who went to Moscow as the first Turkish Ambassador to the new régime: 'The next country to become ripe for Communism will be Germany. If they accept Bolshevist doctrine I shall move immediately from Moscow to Berlin. The Germans are people of principle and remain faithful to ideas once they have accepted their truth. They would provide a much more reliable cadre for the propagation of world revolution than the Russians, whose conversion will take a long time.'

In November 1923, the introduction of the Rentenmark and the stabilization of the currency saved our economy from final collapse, but it remained a cardinal fault of our economic policy to seek to make up the lost ground by the uncontrolled floating of loans. An apparent degree of recovery was achieved, but the world economic crisis found Germany with such a load of reparations and indebtedness that collapse again threatened. Foreign creditors lost their money and Germany her record of financial honesty. Today, after an even greater disaster, many Germans seem unwilling to grasp the fact that a defeated country can only build up its administration and its economy by thrift and the avoidance of forms of expenditure which may cause offence to the outside world.

I became conscious at a very early stage of the hopeless inability of the National and State Parliaments to take decisive steps to deal with this social disaster, although none of us had any inkling at the time how it would fertilize the seed which Hitler was planting. But a great many people became increasingly dissatisfied with the inability of the established political parties to devise any real solution. Without a firm backbone of authority Germany was gradually sinking into the depths. As early as September 1923 I wrote a pamphlet with the title *Dictatorship or Parliament?* My thesis was that Germany was on the brink of complete collapse and that salvation would not be forthcoming through mechanical parliamentary methods or the sterile clash of rigid party doctrines. I called for a Government of independent, responsible people, without radical or dictatorial tendencies, who would use the last remnants of State authority to impose solutions designed to meet the emergency of the times. The words of a young member, practically unknown, carried little weight. Hitler was laying the foundation stone of his future much more securely with his march to the Feldherrnhalle[1] in Munich, in the reflected glory of one of our two great war commanders – General Ludendorff.

As in all times of revolutionary change, the radical parties were in the ascendant, and the various forms of Marxism attracted the largest measure of support. Fortunately for Germany, there were, amongst the Social Democrats, a number of civic-minded leaders like Ebert and Noske, who stood firm against the Bolshevist storm. In spite of their statesmanlike attitude, the basic programme of their party still exalted class warfare and the fight against religious influences. The cry for the 'dictatorship of the proletariat' was heard from all shades of Marxist opinion even though more moderate policies were actually put into practice. Germany's Social Democrats have always been regarded in the West as being much more democratic than they really are. This is largely due to the fact that Léon Blum's Socialists in France were much more tolerant in their attitude, while class warfare and anti-clericalism have not been official tenets of Labour Party policy in Great Britain, and American Trade Unionists still vote for one of the two established parties.

The opposite camp was made up of Conservatives and Liberals, neither of whom had been particularly constructive in their thinking, even before the war. During the Weimar period what they chiefly lacked was an outstanding leader with broad and progressive ideas. Hugenberg was a good administrator and a considerable financial expert, but he lacked the quality of a Conservative leader. The chief hope therefore lay in the parties of the centre – the newly formed Democratic Party, the Zentrum and the German People's Party.

The first of these three failed so lamentably that by 1931 it was reduced to four representatives, in spite of abandoning its democratic label and adopting the title of State Party. The German People's Party became the dominant member of this group, largely due to the leadership of Stresemann, who succeeded in giving Germany's foreign policy new form and content with the Locarno

---

[1] This refers to the abortive *Putsch* of 1923 which landed Hitler and Hess in Landsberg Gaol for a brief spell.

Treaty. He was the only major statesman produced during the Weimar era.

The only way of overcoming Germany's internal and external difficulties was to convince our former enemies of our genuine will for co-operation and to devise with them some peaceful way of lifting the discriminatory clauses of the Versailles Treaty. Hate, revenge and reprisals should not have been allowed to keep us from this goal. The Treaty of Versailles specifically permitted alterations in its terms by negotiation. If it had been possible to persuade France to allow this clause to be invoked, events might have developed differently. It was the great service of Stresemann and Briand that they recognized this possibility and paved the way with the Locarno Pact. Unfortunately neither of them obtained in their own countries the support necessary to complete the task, and Stresemann's early death was a tragic loss.

The chief responsibility of these centre parties should have been to give life to Germany's new democracy by ensuring that there was a healthy alternation of responsibility between the left and the right. Their failure to do so resulted in a numbing of the right-wing parties, who, instead of preparing themselves while in opposition to take over the responsibilities of government at any time, gradually adopted a policy of radical nationalism. The general condemnation in the outside world of Germany's conservative elements is both incorrect and historically false. The conservative opposition, which saw no possibility in the normal course of events of proving its capacity for government, lapsed into this attitude only too easily. I regard it as a particular fault of my own party, the Zentrum, that it failed to recognize this obligation. The proper functioning of democracy demands a healthy alternation between government and opposition.

When our institutions seemed likely to collapse at the end of the war, the Zentrum undoubtedly did right to combine with the Socialists, who were the strongest party. They were able to block measures of too radical a nature and prevented Germany from becoming a field for too many socialist experiments. This was a signal contribution to the conduct of our affairs. But the Weimar Coalition of Socialists, Democrats and Zentrum held obstinately to office once the first shock had been countered. In the Central Government, feeble attempts were made from time to time to incorporate representatives of the right wing parties. In Prussia, however, the Weimar Coalition remained in power without a break from 1918 until I became Chancellor. The Zentrum could never make up its mind to break with the Socialists in order to rescue the right wing parties from the torpidity of endless opposition. This was one of the major reasons for the collapse of the Weimar brand of democracy, and the growth of Hitler's party.

I shall always be grateful for the long contact I had with parliamentary institutions. They form an exacting school, which should oblige its members to accustom themselves to clear thinking and firm decisions. Unfortunately this does not always happen. It is very easy for a parliamentarian to live a comfortable life. He can accept his emoluments, travel free all over the place and attend all the debates assiduously, without ever concerning himself with fundamental problems. By always voting with the majority he can save himself anxiety and energy while still retaining a clear conscience about the services he is rendering his country. This, however, was an interpretation of our obligations that I was never prepared to accept. The German General Staff may have fallen into disrepute, but at least it taught its officers to form their own opinions and uphold them even when they were not popular.

I was soon to find out that such independence of mind could have unpleasant consequences. Elections in Prussia in 1924 left the Weimar Coalition with a majority of only two or three seats. I considered this a suitable occasion for an exchange of responsibilities, and endeavoured to persuade my Zentrum colleagues to form a coalition with the parties of the right. There was a heated debate in the party caucus, and in the end my proposal was voted down, with the demand that I should vote for the Prime Minister presented by the Weimar Coalition parties. Although twenty of my colleagues had supported me at first, only five remained with me by the time the vote was taken in the Chamber. The rest had submitted to party pressure. However, the six of us succeeded in rejecting the proposed ministry. There was a storm of angry protest and I was threatened with expulsion from the party. This soon died down, as it was not so easy to get rid of such an uncomfortable *frondeur*. I had acquired wide support amongst conservative groups in the country districts. The party limited my activities in another way, by excluding me from membership of all the committees. From that time on I became known as the 'black sheep' of the party.

A year later, President Ebert suddenly died. In the midst of extreme difficulties, he had succeed in maintaining the dignity and position of his office. But he had only occupied it by commission. The Socialists had never considered the occasion opportune to put his appointment to a free vote. With his death they lost one of their few leaders of any stature.

A deep longing had grown up among the people at large to see the post of President filled by an elected representative embodying the full weight of the State's authority. The old feeling for tradition which had become submerged in the immediate post-war years was now returning and sought for a man of undisputed character and international reputation to counter the appearance of disintegration at home and weakness abroad. None of the individual party leaders provided a personality of this sort. The left wing parties had little psychological appreciation of this need, nor indeed had the Zentrum, in spite of its more traditional background. In the end, the Weimar Coalition parties decided to nominate Dr Marx, one of the older Zentrum leaders, since the Socialists would not have been able to guarantee the success of a member of their own party. Dr Marx was a well-known judge, a man of sympathetic and very dignified personal characteristics, but devoid of the outstanding qualities of leadership demanded by such critical times.

The right wing parties adopted Field-Marshal von Hindenburg as their candidate. He had won the complete confidence of the nation during war, and at its end, when Ludendorff fled to Sweden, he brought back the shattered remnants of the Army to their homes. Both abroad and among left wing circles at home, his candidature was hotly criticized. France raised the cry: 'Hindenburg – c'est la guerre!' But no one could have been more devoted to the cause of peace than was this old soldier, who had witnessed the horrors of three wars. I admired his staunch, upright character and his overwhelming sense of duty, and I knew that he would never play the rôle of a political general if he was placed at the head of the country's affairs. Here, it seemed to me, was an opportunity to reawaken some of those traditions that had been lost with the collapse of the monarchy. I was never for one moment in doubt as to where my allegiance lay.

To ensure his election a certain body of support was needed among the centre parties, and this I set out to obtain, although it brought me into direct conflict with my colleagues of the Zentrum Party. I could not help feeling that the election of a head of the State should not be a party matter. With some friends I issued a declaration in the middle of April 1925, which regretted the action of the Zentrum Party in putting up a political candidate without any attempt to reach agreement with all the other parties. We pointed out that important sections of the population had lost faith in the type of society sought by the Weimar Coalition, based as it was, to too great an extent, on rationalistic and atheistic premises. We made no attack on Dr Marx, but insisted that it was not possible to elect a member of the Zentrum Party with the help of millions of socialist votes and then proceed with an anti-socialist policy. Calling for a return to the old Christian conception of government, we proclaimed once again Germany's historical duty to act as the watchman and bulwark of the western tradition in the heart of Europe. We felt that the election of such a God-fearing and devout personality as Hindenburg would provide the best guarantee for a return to this fundamental policy.

The effect of this document at Zentrum headquarters can be imagined. They published a counter-manifesto deploring this departure from the party line and insisting that their real task lay in providing a bridge between all professions and classes in order to bring about healthy co-operation in a spirit of tolerance. Not only was this no answer to the fundamental question we had raised, but both the Zentrum and left wing parties proceeded to tear Hindenburg's reputation to shreds in the course of the campaign. In 1925 he did not fit into their party political plans, although seven years later, when he became their champion for re-election, no praise was too great for him. The electoral campaign was bitter and protracted, but Hindenburg was duly elected and sent me a personal note of thanks for my intervention which, in the slender balance of forces, had probably been decisive.

This episode naturally made my position in the party extremely difficult. I had become an 'outsider', as the left referred to me in 1932, when I was proposed for the post of Chancellor. However, I was not entirely dependent on the party for my activity and had plenty of opportunity for expressing my convictions. When it became necessary in 1930 to elect a new leader for the party caucus in the Reichstag, I made a considerable effort to get Dr Brüning to accept this post. He had made a great reputation for himself as legal adviser to the Christian Trade Unions, and it seemed an admirable opportunity for placing such an intelligent and sympathetic person, with the best type of conservative leanings, in a position of decisive influence. However, he occupied the position for a relatively short time before exchanging it for that of Chancellor, a period of his career to which I shall have to devote a whole chapter in due course.

The year 1930 also saw Germany in the grip of the economic crisis. The collapse of the banks and the tariff walls erected abroad sent up the unemployment figure in Germany to dangerous heights. Millions of people, particularly the youth of the country, could find no work, and presented not only a unique economic problem but, with the rise of radicalism, an increasing political danger. As far as it was within my power, I endeavoured to support Brüning in his immense task. A speech I made in Dülmen on October 4, 1931, attracted considerable public attention:

Party politics, I said, lost much of their *raison d'être* when it became a question of calling on the nation as a whole to make a great combined effort. I could not understand why it was not possible to range the 'national opposition' behind Brüning in his historic task. His qualities of leadership and patriotism were not questioned by either side. The only reason I could see for the opposition's mistrust lay in the Chancellor's exaggerated political dependence on his Socialist colleagues in the Coalition. I suggested that in order to allay these suspicions, Brüning should appoint ministers without party affiliations. Under the threat of economic crisis, we needed to break away from the Socialists' collectivist theories and give individual entrepreneurs an opportunity to accept their share of the responsibilities within a framework of law and Christian endeavour. The Chancellor, I said, was in his person one of the greatest assets we had, both at home and abroad, and we relied upon him to choose his immediate colleagues from people who would ensure that he had the widest possible basis of support.

Right to the end of Brüning's Chancellorship I did all I could to ensure him a body of support amongst the parties of the right. My last act as a parliamentarian in 1932 had only this end in mind. Elections for the Prussian State Parliament were due to be held. Hindenburg had just been re-elected, but the right wing parties, particularly the Nazis, had shown a considerable increase in strength. Socialists and Zentrum feared to lose their majority, and in order to ensure the continuance in office of the Braun-Severing State Government, they resorted to a trick. The standing orders of the State Parliament were altered to require any new Prime Minister to be elected in the first and second rounds of voting by an absolute majority. Until then, in common with many other parliaments in the world, a relative majority had sufficed in the second round if no absolute majority was obtained in the first. They counted on the help of the Communists to prevent any bourgeois nominee from being elected to the post. In the event, the Weimar Coalition parties lacked a hundred seats for a majority, and by July 20 had failed to form a new cabinet, so that the previous one still remained in office.

The support by my party of such a completely undemocratic procedure seemed to me an affront both to the letter and spirit of parliamentary procedure. It could only serve to embitter the right even further, and increase the gulf between them and a Zentrum Chancellor. I tried in vain to dissuade my party colleagues from taking such a fateful step. However, I was unsuccessful, and in the end was the only one of their number to vote against the proposal.

I took no part in the subsequent election myself, as I had left my constituency in Westphalia and had been able to move back with my family into the Saar. My eleven years of activity in the Prussian Parliament therefore ended with a loud and public protest against a policy which I deplored and which I had already opposed back in 1923.

CHAPTER VII

GERMANY IN DECAY

Newspaper proprietor – The Herrenklub – The Reichswehr – Hinden-burg, Seeckt and Schleicher – Agricultural interests – Help from the Catholics – Franco-German relations – Moral degeneration

My controversial position in the Zentrum Party was further complicated by the predominant influence I obtained in its central organ, the *Germania*, a newspaper published in Berlin. During the wild inflation days of 1924 a considerable block of shares in this undertaking happened to come into the possession of a certain person. I learnt that it was his intention to get rid of them, and decided to purchase them myself. The war and inflation had seriously reduced our personal wealth and it was by no means easy to decide to invest a considerable proportion of the remainder in a way which might serve one's political interests but which would produce a very uncertain income.

The paper had been founded in 1870, and although it possessed its own printing plant it had only a limited circulation. It exerted considerable influence, however, through being the party's prin-cipal mouthpiece and because it appeared in the capital. The news that such an awkward *frondeur* had acquired about 47 per cent of the voting capital caused consternation at party headquarters. I immediately made it clear that I had no intention of altering the paper's character and would allow all shades of opinion to be expressed, on the grounds that discussion and constructive criticism form one of the cornerstones of democratic life. By agreement with Dr Florian Kloeckner, who possessed another block of shares, I took over the chairmanship of the board of directors. In addition to certain shareholders, I co-opted on to the board Count Galen, the Bishop of Berlin (who later became a Cardinal), and representatives of the Christian trade unions.

The eight years during which I held this post involved an im-mense amount of work, and I had to fight for every ounce of influence. I soon had difficulties with the management and the editor, who refused their co-operation and maintained that they alone were responsible for the paper's political line. In the end I was obliged to dispense with their services. This was not due to any attempt on my part to impose a political line on them, but because they refused to allow me any expression at all of my own political convictions. The other senior members of the editorial staff stayed on and continued to present the official policies of the party. On matters of major importance I often wrote leading articles myself, outlining the views of the conservative wing. I had no fundamental differences of opinion with party headquarters and co-operation on the board of directors was harmonious. In course of time the whole undertaking was modernized, and new and improved machines were installed.

The opposition press often accused me of playing the rôle of a dictator in our party organ, which I regard as quite unfounded. The moment I became Chancellor I resigned from the board and left the paper in complete freedom to criticize me as it wished. My work there certainly provided me with valuable instruction in the habits of the press. I made numerous friends amongst the German and foreign correspondents, and I have always been full of admiration for the devoted and conscientious manner in which they carry out their task of providing objective and unbiassed information. I learned a number of lessons which stood me in good stead both as Chancellor and diplomat.

The *Germania* remained an independent organ, with pronounced Catholic tendencies, well into the Hitler period. At the end of 1938 it finally fell a victim to Dr Goebbels' campaign for uniformity in the press. On December 31 of that year I wrote a final message for the last edition of a publication to which I had become most attached:

'Since the assumption of power by the National Socialist movement and the voluntary liquidation of the Zentrum Party, we have endeavoured to provide in the *Germania* a synthesis between the basic elements of practical Christianity and the demands of the new era. We considered it our duty, at a time when such momentous developments are determining the future of the Reich, to call on all those forces whose fundamental beliefs, active social conscience and patriotism could play a part in meeting the problems of our times. Today sees an end to this work . . .'

When Dr Goebbels read this, he had a fit of blind fury. He considered it outrageous at this late stage for us to maintain that our basic Christian conceptions had any further part to play in the Nazis' ideological struggle, and presumptuous of us to suggest that we were being forced to give up the fight. He insisted to Hitler that I should be disciplined, but the Führer declined to do anything. He probably already had his hands full with the situation caused by Goebbels' current anti-Semitic campaign.

If my dominating influence on the *Germania* roused the suspicions of the left wing parties as to my intentions as a young conservative politician, these suspicions were considerably strengthened by my membership of the Herrenklub. Perhaps I should say a word about this institution. In other countries political clubs have been for decades a perfectly normal manifestation of public life, and it would not occur to anyone to characterize them as nests of intrigue. The political immaturity of certain sections of the German population was never more clearly demonstrated than in the crop of rumours that came to surround our activities.

When the club was founded in 1923, our president, Count Alvensleben, defined the word *Herren* as implying a type of personality rather than the possession of worldly wealth. We granted every member the right to express his own political opinions, and only required that he should do so in a civilized fashion. Our aim was to bring together politicians of every shade of opinion to discuss their differences in the friendly atmosphere of a private gathering. Intellectuals of every type, scientists, artists, industrialists, farmers, employers and employees, ministers and members of every party were included in the membership. Our discussions were always on a high plane, whether the participants were socialists, liberals or conservatives, although the balance of membership probably tended to a conservative way of thinking.

I often spoke at its meetings, particularly on my favourite topic of Franco-German understanding. The annual dinner saw the leading personalities in every walk of German life assembled round the same table. In December 1932, I remember I used the occasion to offer our best wishes to the new Schleicher Government. Left wing accusations that the Herrenklub played a decisive rôle in the downfall of Brüning and my assumption of the Chancellorship were completely without foundation. Our 'intervention' took no other form than the discussion of the rapidly deteriorating situation, a subject on which I wrote a monograph in the club's publication, *Der Ring*. Rumours of unconstitutional pressure on Hindenburg were entirely false and betrayed only the lamentable German capacity to view changes in the occupancy of high office as some extraordinary event due to dark intrigue or occult influences. In other countries governments came and went in the normal course of events, but in Germany such a change always assumed the character of a *coup d'état*.

Even if our German leftists saw fit to accuse the members of the Herrenklub of all manner of reactionary intrigues, it is still astonishing that Great Britain, the country where club life was born, should have been so misguided as to accuse our members in a Military Government ordinance of May 30, 1946, as belonging to a criminal organization, thus forbidding them the right to stand for public office. Another contribution to our 're-education'! It only remains to add that the club premises in Berlin have been turned by the Communists into a club for their intellectuals – indeed a comment on the mutability of human fortunes.

*   *   *

I am often asked how it was that someone in my position, in a more or less continuous state of conflict with the other members of my party, and with no record of high public office, acquired sufficient influence to be offered the post of Chancellor.

There were two main currents of political thought in Germany during the 'twenties. The Weimar republicans, with the Socialists as the dominant partner, considered it their duty to eradicate all those manifestations of public life which belonged to the Kaiser's Germany. They attacked not only the stratum of society which had provided the country's leaders, but even abolished the national emblem under whose colours two million Germans, including Socialists, had died in war. They considered that the Reich was under an obligation to fulfil all the demands of the victorious countries and that resistance would only bring new sanctions. Whoever kept alive a sense of the old traditions was branded as a reactionary. The right wing, for its part, demanded the retention of what was good in the old way of life, insisted that the national honour should be upheld, and opposed the fulfilment of impossible demands. When, against the background of this fundamental conflict, a member of one of the Weimar Coalition parties protested loudly at what he considered opportunist party policies devoid of any feeling for principles and tradition, it is hardly surprising that wide interest was aroused. My efforts to persuade the Zentrum Party to adopt a position more independent of the Socialists and, if necessary, to join in a coalition with the bourgeois elements of the right, were naturally followed with sympathy in conservative circles. When I criticized the many weak points in our parliamentary system and opposed party decisions which I could not find it in my conscience to approve, I was made the object of severe criticisms by the Weimar Coalition stalwarts, but obtained a considerable degree of recognition in those circles which considered reform to be essential. I found particular appreciation for my political line of thought amongst my old colleagues in the Army.

Many officers with whom I had trained or served had come to hold high appointments in the Reichswehr. By tradition and instinct the armed forces were required to be a completely non-political instrument. Once the monarchy had disappeared as the culminating point in their hierarchy, and party politicians had taken over the representation of the Reich, it was not easy to keep this instrument of law and order divorced from the conflict of opinions. It should not be forgotten that in the civil disorders of the early 'twenties, when the very framework of the State seemed to be crumbling, the Army played a decisive rôle behind the political scene. The election of Field-Marshal von Hindenburg to the Presidency served to stabilize the situation. Between 1925 and 1930 it continued to become more normal, but under the threat of a new crisis, calculated to disrupt the foundations of our social life, the Army again became an important factor. We shall see that the Reichswehr did not intervene as a body in the affairs of State, but that the opinions of its outstanding personality, General von Schleicher, had a decisive influence on the decisions of the President. The growing tension between the right wing parties, particularly the Nazis, and the Government was viewed by the Army with increasing concern. Schleicher sought someone to head the Government who had close contacts with the centre parties while preserving the sympathies of the right. What was needed was a man of conservative tendencies, closely allied to the Zentrum Party, which was one of the pillars of the Weimar Coalition.

It may be something of an over-simplification, but it is probably true, to say that Schleicher's suggestion to offer the Chancellorship to me more or less represented the vote of the Army.

Its three outstanding officers in the post-war period were Hindenburg, General von Seeckt and Schleicher. I had not known Hindenburg before the war. As a member of the General Staff I came into contact with the leading personalities of Supreme Headquarters, including Ludendorff, who was head of the planning and operational section at the time. During the war, when I had to report from time to time to Supreme Headquarters or visited my friend Lersner, who was the Foreign Office liaison officer there, I not infrequently saw the senior officers. After the Easter battle of Arras I was called upon to make a personal report to Ludendorff, and also saw Hindenburg. In August 1918, after the critical failure of the spring offensive, when I hurried back from Palestine to report on my fears for the situation there, I saw Hindenburg again. I remember how impressed I was by his calm and determined attitude in the face of the rapidly deteriorating military situation.

As I have described, I saw him again on my return from Turkey after the unfortunate *contretemps* with Liman von Sanders. In his utter and selfless devotion to duty in the face of measureless disaster, he remained the one strong pillar of our honour and traditions. From then until 1932, apart from my intervention on his behalf in the 1925 Presidential election, I saw little of him, although he had not forgotten me, and always invited my wife and myself to the official receptions he held every winter in Berlin.

Hindenburg had an astonishing memory. He could recall every detail of a conversation and had a deep knowledge of Prussian political life. I could feel that he approved of my opposition in the Landtag and my expressed desire for more traditional policies liberated from party strife, although he would never have permitted himself an observation which conflicted with the duties of his office. When Schleicher suggested me for the post of Chancellor I was therefore no stranger, although our close personal relationship only dates from my period in that office. Walking through our adjacent gardens I then saw Hindenburg almost every day, presenting myself without previous announcement in his study. He always received me in the warm and sympathetic fashion which I found to be his normal approach to life's problems, and which even extended to his political opponents.

During one visit to his country estate at Neudeck he took me by the arm and led me into a small room containing a picture of Ludendorff. There was a revival of public controversy at the time as to whether the great military successes of the world war belonged to the genius of Ludendorff rather than Hindenburg. 'I am very sorry that our friendship came to an end,' the old Field-Marshal said. 'I still have the highest opinion of him.' And then, talking of Tannenberg, he added laconically, 'Ludendorff claims this was his victory. But if the encircling movement had gone wrong and success had lain on the other side, it is I who would have been blamed for losing the battle. After all, I know something about the business. I was the instructor on tactics at the War Academy for six years.' It was a typical remark. He cared little for the disputed glory. His only concern was to accept reponsibility and fulfil his duty. His great military authority and the aura of his personality compensated in a large measure for the disappearance of the monarchy, and thus prevented the Army from becoming a political tool.

Colonel-General von Seeckt, who built up the post-war Reichswehr, was its best representative and an outstanding personality in the early 'twenties. Abroad he was relatively unknown. He kept out of the limelight, and in this respect much resembled his predecessors, Moltke and Schlieffen. He shared, moreover, their strategic conceptions and powerful clarity of mind. He played a decisive rôle during the early years of the Republic and it is to be regretted that political reasons caused his removal from office, for he was in a category by himself.

Our paths had already crossed when I was serving with the Düsseldorf Uhlans and he was in command of a neighbouring company of the 39th Regiment. In 1918 he was in Turkey as Chief of Staff and there I disagreed with his views. For the first time he had to deal with Oriental problems; among them the ways and means of dominating large areas with limited forces. He showed little appreciation of the difficulties involved. In the summer of 1918 he devised a plan to occupy the Caucasus, capture Baku and advance on Baghdad over the Tiflis railway. This was pure fantasy. The fate of Turkey was already being decided on the Palestine front.

When I entered politics after the war we remained in contact. As the head of the one remaining stable element in the State, his position was extremely strong. In company with former General Staff officers such as Schleicher, Hammerstein, Busche and Harbou, we often discussed politics, particularly his relationship with Russia. He had no hand in the Treaty of Rapallo and only learned its details after it was signed. But he was a disciple of Bismarck in demanding an understanding with Russia, and saw in this the only means of obtaining the training of specialists in modern weapons for the ill-armed Reichswehr, and so preventing its decline into a completely outmoded force. This policy was carried out, as Seeckt himself told me, with the full agreement of Wirth, the Chancellor at the time.

Much has been made of the relationship between Seeckt and the Soviet Government. As Commander-in-Chief of an army forbidden to possess modern arms, he naturally wished to keep as many of his officers as possible informed of continuing technical developments. A means of doing this was first suggested in a letter written from Russia in August 1920 by Enver Pasha, who told Seeckt that Trotsky would welcome German instructors for the Soviet army. In September 1921, a preliminary conference took place at the flat of the then Colonel von Schleicher, where the possibility of German help to build up Russia's war industry was discussed. However, the Russians insisted on negotiating with Seeckt direct, and Radek had a number of meetings with him. Chancellor Wirth and his successor, Cuno, were kept fully informed. The main details were worked out by three of Seeckt's immediate subordinates, Hasse, Niedermayer and Thomsen. A small group of officers was sent to Russia to assist in the construction of aircraft, tanks and modern artillery, and to acquire training in their use.

The Rapallo Treaty established normal economic relations between the two countries and provided a framework for this military agreement, the scope of which was much more limited than the enemy powers chose to make out. Our Ambassador in Moscow, Count Brockdorff-Rantzau, opposed these military agreements at first, but the French policy of endeavouring to persuade Russia to underwrite the terms of the Versailles Treaty caused him to change his mind. Wirth, the Reich Chancellor, gave his approval to the formation of an Association for the

Encouragement of Industrial Co-operation, with branches in Berlin and Moscow. At first it received subsidies of about seven million Reichsmarks from the Army budget, but Wirth soon granted it a much larger amount. This was used to finance the construction of Army training camps in the interior of Russia, housing both German and Russian personnel. Some of our younger officers took part in Russian military manœuvres. The Junker aircraft company also built a factory near Moscow, where research work was carried out which benefited both countries.

The Treaty of Rapallo must be viewed against the background of Paragraph 116 of the Versailles Treaty, which Germany could only regard as a delayed-action threat. This clause reserved to Soviet Russia full rights to claim reparations and restitutions from Germany on the same terms as the other Allied powers. Radek told us in January 1922 that France had approached the Russian Government with a suggestion that it should invoke this clause. In return, France offered *de jure* recognition of the revolutionary régime, commercial credits and moderation of her intimate connection with Poland. It will be realized how important it was for us to prevent such a development by signing the Treaty of Rapallo. The circumstances today are so different that it is difficult to understand the West's constant fear that Germany might sign another Rapallo treaty. Fortunately Schuman comes from a different mould to that of his predecessor, Poincaré.

In September 1925, Chicherin visited Seeckt, a fact that was duly reported in the press. When Seeckt had to resign shortly after this, the Social Democrat, Scheidemann, complained violently in the Reichstag about the 'secret links' between the Reichswehr and Moscow. This was a purely political attack and gave the matter much greater importance than it really possessed.

Wirth, in his second capacity as Finance Minister, also provided the funds for what became known as the 'Black Reichswehr'. This was formed during the French occupation of the Ruhr, when it seemed that it might be necessary to prevent a French march on Berlin from the demilitarized Rhine zone. Members of the disbanded Free Corps, the Stahlhelm (the Old Comrades' Association) and the Socialist Reichsbanner groups provided the personnel for these Reichswehr reserve forces. This was a breach of the Versailles Treaty, but in view of the threatened incursion of Poles, the illegal occupation of the Ruhr (to which Great Britain took

E

exception), and Poincaré's threatened march on Berlin, the right of self-preservation was deemed to take precedence over the terms of the peace treaty. The Black Reichswehr formed an important item in the prosecution's case at the Nuremberg Tribunal. In fact it was only a modest attempt to strengthen the Reichswehr by a few thousand men and to provide some sort of frontier defence force against the Poles.

It is only too easy to forget the desperate German internal situation at the time. The currency had collapsed, a Communist government had been set up in the State of Saxony, the Socialists were engaged in violent political warfare against the hundred-thousand-man Reichswehr, and the Communists were making a renewed attempt to seize power by illegal means. I devoted my whole time to persuading my party to permit some strengthening of the military forces and kept Seeckt informed of my efforts. When, at the end of September 1923, passive resistance in the Ruhr collapsed, and the Palatinate sought to secede from the Reich as part of a new Rhine Republic, the Reichswehr was ordered by the Socialist President, Ebert, to restore law and order in two other troubled areas, Saxony and Thuringia. At the end of October the Bavarian State Government ordered the 7th Division, stationed on its territory, to transfer its allegiance to them from the Reich. Seeckt sent a message to the Commander, General von Lossow, saying 'such a step could only result in the disintegration of the Reich'.

I only learnt of this particular intervention many years later, although I had myself sent him an urgent communication begging him to do everything in his power to ensure the unity of the country. The simplest step, I suggested, would be to place himself at the head of a new Government as the only man capable of restoring the situation. But he was as opposed to military dictatorship as to the idea of becoming Chancellor, once Ebert had granted him full administrative powers. The Bavarian episode and the Hitler *Putsch* were suppressed without further intervention by the Army. But the question still remains whether the future course of events in the Weimar Republic would not have been very different if a man of Seeckt's integrity and capacity had taken over the reins of power. I remember reproaching him some time later with his failure to do so, and he repeated to me the phrase he had used to Ebert at the time. 'There is only one man in Germany in a position to organize a *Putsch*, and that is me. *Aber die Reichswehr putscht nicht!'*

I have always regretted that at this critical point in our history Seeckt did not make up his mind to bring order and authority into the chaotic state of our affairs. Even those circles in France who saw in him a representative of the old Germany – a general thirsting for revenge – and did everything possible to make things difficult for him, must now recognize how much better it would have been if the task of organizing a working democracy had been entrusted to a man whose whole nature was opposed to dictatorship and war. With a strong hand at the helm, the nerve centre of Europe would have been spared some of the developments which were to have such tragic consequences.

Seeckt's fall was due to a political trick. He had invited the eldest son of the former Crown Prince to take part in military manœuvres. This brought the left wing parties up in arms, crying 'monarchist reaction' and proclaiming that the Republic was in danger. The Socialists, and in their turn the National Socialists, were strongly apprehensive of the German people's continuing affection for the monarchy. In 1943 the Nazis considered it necessary to revoke the commissions of all the members of former royal and princely families serving in the Army. A man like Seeckt, who was a monarchist by conviction, would never have considered lending himself to a *coup d'état;* but Gessler, who was the Defence Minister when Seeckt was Commander-in-Chief, considered his position threatened by this 'affair of the prince', and Seeckt had to resign.

Seeckt's opinion of Schleicher is quoted in a biography by General von Rabenau,[1] which may not be known abroad. Seeckt regarded his fall from grace as Schleicher's work. At the beginning of 1926 Schleicher had persuaded Gessler to form a political section under the Minister's direct control, with himself at its head. His intention seems to have been to keep Seeckt out of political affairs and neutralize him at the first available opportunity. Rabenau quotes Seeckt as noting that the Black Reichswehr affair did not provide a suitable opportunity, as the Minister himself was too intimately involved. But Schleicher seems to have worked actively

---

[1] General Friedrich von Rabenau: *Seeckt. Aus seinem Leben.* Vol. II. Von Haase & Koehler Verlag, Leipzig, 1940.

for the removal of the man whose influence in the Army was second only to Hindenburg's, and who was a dangerous rival for the post of Chancellor. On June 5, 1932, Seeckt noted in his diary, with reference to the Reichstag elections then about to take place: 'To have to vote for Schleicher at the end of it all is really too much.'

In the Kaiser's Germany it would never have occurred to either officer or civilian to regard the Army as an instrument of internal politics. Even with the introduction of conscription the Army had never been used for political purposes. In the revolution of 1848 it merely undertook the personal protection of the sovereign. Until 1918 politics were regarded as a matter for the government and parliament, with the executive power depending in the last resort on the police. After the war the picture changed completely. The revolutionary Government of Ebert and Scheidemann possessed no authority among the mass of the nation. The Spartacist revolt was only mastered with the help of the Free Corps and the hastily organized units of the hundred-thousand-man army. When the situation had been stabilized in 1923 Seeckt was the first man to insist on the complete neutrality of the Army in political affairs. This was no easy task, as both the left and right wing parties sought to make the Reichswehr into a political instrument for their own purposes. An army's organization depends in the first instance on strong cadres of officers and N.C.O.s. The only trained personnel available in Germany after the war was steeped in the traditions of the Kaiser's time. Most of the officers had conservative leanings and their ideological affinities were naturally closer to the parties of the right. As a counter-measure, the left wing parties in power demanded 'democratic reforms' and a new form of personnel policy. These controversies became even more acute with the rise of the Nazi movement. A great many younger officers, disgusted with the sterility of party political warfare, were attracted to the dynamism of the Nazis.

As long as the President was a man with the military authority of Field-Marshal Hindenburg there was no danger of the Reichswehr being used for internal political purposes, although in the event of internal conflict the Central Government, deprived of an executive, would be at the mercy of the Prussian police. This was the situation in which I found myself on July 20, 1932, although we managed to maintain the state of emergency without calling on the Army. It should also not be forgotten that the Army, faced by the obligation of finding reserve forces for the defence of our eastern frontiers, found it necessary to call on the help of the organized party groups. In order to maintain its tradition of political neutrality, it was obliged to include those both of the right and the left, including the Nazis. This unpleasant obligation would never have arisen if the victorious powers had permitted us sufficient forces to provide for our own protection and defence.

Even this dependence on the internal situation would not necessarily have caused the Army to become a political instrument. The centuries-old tradition in the officers' corps was too strong, trained as they were to regard the defence of the country against outside attack as their only duty. The idea of a 'political general' was quite foreign in Imperial Germany, but the weak and uncertain governments of the Republic provided much more fruitful ground for this species. During the 'twenties Schleicher gradually became their prototype.

He belonged to the fourth generation of a military family and was just fifty in the fateful year of 1932. It was his good fortune to belong to the 3rd Regiment of the Guards, in which both Hindenburg and his son, Oscar, had served. There was therefore a bond between them from the start. On the General Staff before the war he had been in the railway section under General Groener, who later became Minister of War. He spent most of the war on Ludendorff's staff, right at the centre, where all the important decisions were taken. With the exception of one short period, he saw no active service, and was spoken of somewhat condescendingly in the Army as a 'desk general'.

The most important period of his life began in 1918. Hindenburg sent him from his headquarters at Spa to tell Ebert in Berlin that the Army would recognize the 'people's representative' and support the Social Democrats, if they would undertake drastic steps against the Communists and restore law and order. When a division of Red Marines revolted at the end of December and took Ebert and his colleagues into custody, it was Schleicher who succeeded in freeing them again. He also took part in the suppression of the Communist uprisings in Saxony and Thuringia. He was thus intimately concerned in the stormy events accompanying the birth of the young German Republic and the organization of the new Army.

He had a finger in every pie, and I have mentioned how the first negotiations with the Russians in 1921 took place in his flat. This taste for politico-military activity evidently gave rise to a desire for greater personal freedom of action, and led to the formation of the political department under his direction in the War Ministry. He soon came to exercise great influence on Hindenburg and managed to divorce his activities from the control of the ministers, Gessler and Groener, and his own military superior, Seeckt.

I had known Schleicher during our General Staff days and had often seen him during the war at Supreme Headquarters. He was a man of great clarity of vision, with a caustic wit and a cheerful extrovert manner which won him a number of friends. I cannot claim that I was one of them, though I liked him very well. During my parliamentary days I saw him whenever former members of the Headquarters or General Staff got together. He used to tell me that his ministerial department was designed to keep the Army out of politics. Any political questions affecting the Army were dealt with in this department for submission to the Minister. The Chief of Staff was restricted to purely military matters. But soon the suspicion grew that Schleicher was using his position to further his own ends.

I often used to discuss the situation with Schleicher, particularly after Hindenburg's re-election and the sudden increase in support for the Nazis in the spring of 1932, when internal affairs were reaching a crisis. At no time did I have the impression that he sought the limelight or wished to become Chancellor himself. His friendship with Oscar von Hindenburg and his intimate relationship with the Field-Marshal seemed sufficiently explained by their mutual tradition of public service. In due course I shall give an account of the subsequent development of his attitude during my own and his Chancellorship. I am often told that Schleicher was a manifestation unknown in the British or American Armies. That may well be so. Without the destruction of the monarchy in Germany, he would never have been able to play such a rôle.

★   ★   ★

In spite of my duties in the Prussian Diet, I found time for a number of outside activities. My close connection with country people and agricultural interests formed the basis of my political activity. My conceptions of the necessity for European co-operation led me to seek personal connections with France in an attempt to remove one of the chief obstacles to such policy. One of the best ways of doing this was to arrange for exchanges of opinion between leaders of Catholic thought in Germany and France. My connection with the land probably played a decisive rôle in my political career. I did what I could to improve the somewhat primitive conditions surrounding our estate at Merfeld in Westphalia. I assisted our local smallholders, had country roads built, together with a connection to the nearest railway, and arranged for a supply of electricity to the village. We also took steps to bring the surrounding heath country under cultivation. I formed a small riding school where the younger people could learn the care and management of horses. We balanced our local budget, paid off debts and managed to reduce our local taxes. It meant a lot of work for one's spare time, but the thanks and affection of my neighbours were sufficient reward. In the middle of the 'twenties I was elected honorary Mayor of the group of villages that surrounded us.

As I represented these agricultural interests in Parliament, it was not long before I was elected to the committee of the Westphalian Farmers' Union and the Agricultural Chamber of Commerce. This brought me into close association with agricultural organizations all over Germany, and the degree of influence I enjoyed was probably the principal reason why the Zentrum Party tolerated my independent attitude. Although we never succeeded in persuading the party to abandon its Socialist partner in the coalition, its leaders were always anxious to maintain the support of their more conservative elements.

A stable national economy can be maintained only if agricultural prices show a certain minimum return. During the 'twenties there were periods when they failed to keep pace with the rising price of industrial goods, and many farmers were threatened with bankruptcy. We often found that the best solution to our troubles was to conduct direct discussions with industrial leaders, and I got to know people like Springorum, Fritz Thyssen and Florian Kloeckner well. The latter was the chief representative of industry in the Zentrum Party. In any case, I had made the acquaintance of a number of these Ruhr families at a very early date, when many of their members were serving with me in Düsseldorf. Such were the Haniels and Poensgen, and I also knew Albert Voegler, head of the Vereinigte Stahlwerke, and the Krupp family, with whose daughters I had often danced in their house as a young lieutenant. But I must insist now, and will return to the matter later, that it is a complete fabrication of the left wing press to suggest that I used these friendships to obtain funds which were used for hoisting Hitler into the saddle. At no time was a single penny collected either by me or at my instigation for such a purpose.

The Zentrum Party's continual fight for religious freedom and denominational schools received strong support from the Papal Nuncio to Germany, Monsignor Eugenio Pacelli, who is now Pope Pius XII. It must be hundreds of years since a Pope knew Germany and the German people, with all their virtues and faults, as well as he does. It is a rare honour to have seen him at work and to have helped him in a modest way during this period of his career. When he moved to Berlin from Munich, the local foundation of the Knights of Malta, of which I was a member, undertook to refurnish his residence. His tastes ran to Spartan simplicity, but we were able to build a handsome private chapel. His task was not easy at first, because he was accused of wishing to convert the predominantly Protestant Prussia to Catholicism.

However, his personality was soon appreciated at its true value, and when he finally left Berlin, after signing a limited Concordat with Prussia, which at least gave the capital a Catholic bishop, he was seen off by immense crowds which had come to pay tribute to him rather than his religion. While he was living in Berlin I occasionally had the honour of inviting him to meet some of the country's leading conservative and Catholic personalities. One of these occasions, I remember, took place in a club, where he was probably the first Prince of the Church to be welcomed as a guest. I had no home of my own in Berlin at that time, so I invited some friends, including Count Galen, who later became a Cardinal, and several of my political colleagues, to the Guards Cavalry Club. The rooms were decorated with prints, paintings and mementoes of the old Prussian regiments, some of which had been presented by the Kings and Czars who had been their Colonels-in-Chief. Monsignor Pacelli was fascinated by this unusual atmosphere. As we were looking at a picture of the battlefield of Mars la Tour in the war of 1870, over which hung the famous bullet-riddled trumpet, he remarked, 'Too much blood has been spilt in the world. Let us hope that this trumpet will now sound a call for the peace which the world so sadly needs.'

I saw him again in Rome at Easter 1933, as Papal Secretary to Pope Pius XI, when I went to negotiate the terms of the Concordat with Germany. With his knowledge of the internal German situation and of the dangers inherent in Hitler's assumption of the Chancellorship, he gave me his fullest support in the efforts I was making to ensure the rights of the Church in my country. However bitterly I may have been attacked for my part in this agreement, however often my motives have been questioned and my efforts brought to naught, at least I have the satisfaction of knowing that one of the highest authorities in this troubled world took a much more objective view of my intentions.

One of the chief problems in restoring Germany's position in Central Europe was that of our relationship with France. I spent much time in encouraging every possible approach that might serve to wipe out the bitterness engendered by the war. The destruction in northern France had awakened on the one side a deep hatred of the *boches barbares*, while in Germany the moral stigma of the war guilt clause weighed more heavily than any material tribute we were called upon to pay. The chasm seemed impossible to bridge. The whole of France's post-war policy was based on the search for security. It manifested itself in the attitude of Tardieu, Massigli and Briand at Geneva, and in the plans for a Danube Federation and military alliances with Poland, Czechoslovakia and Russia. But these, in the end, could only result in an irrevocable division of Europe. It was essential to find some means of changing the mentality which lay behind this policy, and to seek some basis of co-operation in the interests of our common European heritage.

The universal bond of the Catholic faith seemed to provide one possible channel, and here I was able to do much good preliminary work through our family connections. In 1927 a German delegation attended the *Semaine Sociale* at the *Institut Catholique* in Paris, and this led to a frequent exchange of visits between leading personalities in both countries. We were happy to meet such people as François Marsal, Count Félix de Voguë, Louis Rolland, Champetier de Ribes, and many representatives of politics and the arts. One of my happiest recollections was of a visit to Berlin by a French delegation which included the famous Colonel Picot, President of the *Gueules Cassées*. At the end of a moving address he was kind enough to embrace me, as a sign of our fraternal devotion to mutual understanding between the two countries, and the whole meeting rose in a movement of spontaneous acclamation. In these days, the delegates to the Council of Europe at Strasbourg would do well to remember that the universal nature of our Catholic religion may still have a vital part to play in their deliberations.

These cultural contacts were reinforced by a similar, though more political organization called the Franco-German Study Group. This group was formed in May 1926 by Emile Mayrisch, the well-known Luxembourg industrialist, and included such personalities as the former French Ambassadors in Berlin, Charles Laurent and de Margerie, economists such as de Peyerimhoff and Pierre Lyautey, and well-known scientists and writers, among them the Duc de Broglie, Jean Schlumberger, André Siegfried and Vladimir d'Ormesson. The German members included the Catholic Bishop of Berlin, Dr Schreiber, the industrialists Poensgen and Frohwein, the bankers Warburg and Mendelsohn, and diplomats of the old school, such as Count Oberndorff and Prince Hatzfeldt. I have given these names in order to show the quality of this association and to contrast it with the committee which was later set up by Ribbentrop under the leadership of his friend, de Brinon.

Of these old friends, André Siegfried has since adopted a very different attitude. In his book *L'Ame des Peuples*,[1] he maintains that although the Germans occupy the key position in Europe geographically, there is some doubt as to whether we really belong to the West. He adopts the thesis of Madame de Staël, that there are two Germanies – the cultivated Westerners and the barbaric Prussians. This is unacceptable. Whatever may be thought about the Prussians, the territory east of the Elbe – and Siegfried even places the frontier at the Teutoburg forest – was converted to Christianity and defended by the Germans on behalf of the West for over a thousand years. It is we who have always taken the first shock from the East, not the French. The heritage we have to defend is a common one, although for years we waited in vain for some French statesman to accept the challenge of the real issues. Now M. Schuman has provided the lead we have all been seeking. We can only hope with all our hearts that it is not too late.

*   *   *

[1] Armand Colin, Paris, 1950.

I cannot close this brief sketch of the 'twenties without referring to another manifestation of German life which played a considerable part in the gradual decay of our social and political institutions. Great wars and great defeats often result in a moral vacuum. There was a particularly shameful reaction of this sort in Germany, which might have been countered if millions of our best citizens had not been killed in war and the country completely exhausted. Both literature and the visual arts sank to a level of depravity which was to a certain extent encouraged by the general denunciation of all the standards that Imperial Germany had stood for. The Governments in power were avowedly anti-clerical, and both parlour bolshevism and a denial of Christian ethics became fashionable attitudes. These factors were by no means the least on which the rising tide of nationalism in due course fed.

Although the Government made no attempt to counter this wave of decadence, some of us were sufficiently alive to its potentialities to take more positive steps. In 1929 I was instrumental in founding an Association for the Maintenance of Western Culture. It was a somewhat pompous title, but it signified an attempt to rescue something from the wreck while there was still time. I was convinced that a strengthening of the forces of religion was the real answer to these nihilistic ideas, which mere administrative measures could never hope to conquer. I had the support of Prince Löwenstein for the Catholics, Count Keyserling, representing the Protestants, and the Chief Rabbi of Berlin. Together, we set out to organize a programme of lectures, discussion groups and pamphlets, aimed at attracting to worship those to whom religion had become simply an empty word. I do not know whether our efforts had any great effect. The Socialists were merely sarcastic, and the Communists referred to our work as a reactionary attack on the rights of democracy.

The dreadful events in the years that followed were a direct result of the effect of this period of moral decay on the German body politic. The ideological battle which now threatens all Europe was fought out on our own soil. The political centre of Europe has become a victim of the most recent war, but although the Eastern powers control part of Germany, Asiatic totalitarianism has not yet captured the whole. The Western tradition is still strong, in spite of our political neutralization. The position in Europe is not dissimilar to that during the decline of Rome, when, despite the weakening of its political strength, its cultural traditions formed and fertilized the Renaissance. This process can still be repeated. In Germany the threat to individual freedom and Christian traditions, and the menace of State omnipotence, did not grow either unnoticed or unchallenged. There were still elements who did their utmost to defend our heritage.

PART TWO

THE DECLINE OF WEIMAR

CHAPTER VIII

BRÜNING'S ERROR

Reparation problems – Brüning as Chancellor – Government by decree – Reichstag election – The Nazis' success – Appeal to Hoover – Brüning in London, Paris and Geneva – Schleicher's intervention – Economic difficulties – Failure to combine with the Right – Plans for Hindenburg's re-election – Key to Brüning's policy

THE period I am now about to describe has been much misrepresented by historians. The Western Allies have preferred to regard National Socialism as a sudden manifestation, rather than as the result of years of development. My own Chancellorship has been described as a mere stepping-stone to the domination of Hitler, and the sequence of events has been so over-simplified that the current impression will be difficult to counter. I trust that in due course more able pens than mine will subject the German political scene between 1918 and 1932 to objective and critical scrutiny. For my own part, I must limit myself to a sketch of the situation in the years 1930–32, immediately preceding the formation of my Government, a period not without historical significance.

The substitution, on May 17, 1930, of the Young Plan for the 1924 Dawes Plan, caused many experts to have serious misgivings, even at that time. Later developments were to show that the plundering of German productive capacity for an indefinite period was a grave error. Any disturbance of Germany's economic equilibrium made the burden of reparations impossible. Moreover, it was clear that a country like Germany, whose economy was so dependent on the outside world, would be one of the principal victims of the general economic crisis. For this reason I had tried to persuade Dr Stresemann, who was then Foreign Minister, that the acceptance of the new financial burdens should be made conditional on a settlement of the Saar problem. The return of this industrial area to Germany would have placed our economy on a much firmer basis. But Stresemann saw little hope of achieving this, and in the end nothing was done. Nor were the right wing parties alone in their opposition to the Plan. Dr Brüning, who was shortly to become Chancellor, only supported the new arrangement on the understanding that wide measures of internal financial reform were introduced. 'The Young Plan,' he said, 'is not an agreement between equal partners. We have had to submit to dictation.'

It was a period when the very foundations of the Weimar Republic were being undermined. The Socialists were demanding measures to maintain the security of the State. Severing, the Minister of the Interior, aptly described the internal situation on March 13, 1930, when presenting the law for the defence of the Republic, by declaring: 'The right of assembly has become the wrongs of assembly, and press freedom has become press licence. We cannot permit demagogues to inflame the masses any further. Last year in Prussia alone three hundred policemen were wounded and fourteen killed in the course of their duties.' The disunity between the coalition parties concerning the financial reforms needed to meet the terms of the Young Plan led to the fall of the Cabinet headed by the Socialist Chancellor, Müller.

The President called on Dr Brüning, leader of the Zentrum Party in the Reichstag, to form a cabinet. The custom during the Republic had been to base each Government on a coalition majority in Parliament. Now that the Socialists had withdrawn their support from the coalition, the new Prime Minister should have sought his majority in combination with the right wing parties. This would have allowed the alternation in power of Government and Opposition which is normal in any democratic assembly. Dr Brüning was not prepared to adopt this approach because he feared having the Socialists in opposition at a period of economic crisis. He therefore chose to form a Government which did not enjoy a parliamentary majority, hoping to obtain the tacit approval of the Socialists for his measures by the mere fact of not having invited the collaboration of the right wing. The only way to put this solution into effect was to rule by Article 48 of the Constitution, which permitted a Government, in times of severe crisis, to enact legislation and seek the approval of Parliament at a later date. He gambled on the fact that though the Socialists would disapprove of many of the laws, they would vote for them in the end, if they were presented as emergency legislation. To risk a contrary vote would mean the dissolution of the Reichstag and new elections, in which the Socialists could only lose seats. This Ministry was known as a 'Presidential Cabinet', because it derived its authority not from Parliament and the political parties, but from the President. When I repeated the experiment two years later – seeking a majority with the right wing parties for my emergency legislation – the left wing christened me the 'gravedigger of democracy'. There was, of course, a considerable difference between Brüning's Cabinet and mine. As long as he enjoyed either Socialist support or toleration, his Government can be said to have had the backing of Parliament. In my case, the Zentrum Party refused this support and thus deprived me of parliamentary backing without making any attempt at co-operation.

The new Chancellor enjoyed the confidence of a high proportion of the population. He was known as a man of upright and impartial character, and had been the legal adviser to the Christian Trade Unions. He seemed ideally suited to the task of solving the social problems involved in the maintenance of the country's economy. I was completely in sympathy with Dr Brüning and his conservative way of thinking, and when it became clear that the Müller Cabinet was about to fall, I lobbied every group with whom I had influence in an effort to support him. If I have any criticisms to make of his Chancellorship, they are not based on personal grounds. I still have the highest regard for his personality and character, but his activities must be judged against the background of the needs of the time.

The Social Democrats were not represented in his Cabinet. It was the duty of such an important party not only to act in opposition, but also to accept the responsibilities of doing so. The Socialists, however, failed to observe this important tenet of democratic life. They supported Brüning and voted for his emergency measures, but declined to accept responsibility for them. If they had not supported him Brüning would have been obliged to seek his majority with the right wing. This would have involved the right wing parties in the obligations of active government and would have neutralized their radical elements. However, the Chancellor was not prepared to allow this free interplay of parliamentary forces, and relied exclusively on Article 48 of the Constitution.

Dr Schreiber, a Zentrum Party representative, was not far from the truth when he said, 'It is not a question of parliamentary institutions being threatened by dictatorship, but rather that dictatorship threatens because parliamentary institutions are so weak.'

The Chairman of the Zentrum Party, Dr Kaas, who belonged to the right wing of our party, defended the application of Article 48. He did not consider it a dictatorial weapon, but rather a means of educating the German people in rational political thought. Many party members were beginning to doubt the wisdom of continued coalition with the Socialists. On more than one occasion, because of their hostile attitude to Brüning, I had begged him to give notice of the ending of our agreements with them, at least in the Prussian State Parliament. At a Party Congress in July, Dr Kaas stated: 'It is up to the Cabinet rather than the party, to take the lead.' I may well ask why a statesman of the calibre of Dr Kaas did not accept the same proposition two years later when the President called on me to form a Presidential Cabinet which was to be independent of the parties.

Brüning wrote an article in the *Germania* newspaper in March, outlining the two courses that he considered practicable: one was to make use of his powers under Article 48; the other, to seek a stable majority through new elections. In spite of complaints by the Socialists that his emergency decrees were a breach of the Constitution, they continued to vote for them rather than risk an election, at which they would have to expect a loss of strength. They preferred to be guided by party doctrine rather than the requirements of the national welfare. But by the end of May the world economic crisis had caused a further worsening of the situation in Germany. The number of unemployed rose by over a million, and dole payments at the rate of 16.6 milliard marks a year failed completely to meet the growing distress. The Government made a new call for emergency legislation. At the second reading of financial measures to meet the crisis, the Chancellor threatened once again to apply his powers under Article 48. This time the Socialists demanded his resignation, and their leader declared: 'The Brüning Government is trying to wreck the foundations of democratic life.' The Communists described the Chancellor's speech as a preamble to a Fascist dictatorship. In the end, the Socialists refused to accept the measures, although they were unable to offer any better solution to the problem of raising enough money to pay the unemployment benefits. They were now prepared to risk a new election because Brüning's financial programme included a reduction in the relief payments. Being unwilling to subject their followers to such a sacrifice, the Socialists believed their opposition to it would provide electoral capital. Brüning had no alternative but to ask for the dissolution of the Reichstag.

Elections took place on September 14, 1930. It would be no exaggeration to describe the results as a turning point in German history. No less than fifteen parties took part, but this time the splinter groups were the losers and the extremists and radicals the winners. The Communists won twenty-three additional seats, and the Nazis increased theirs from twelve to one hundred and seven. The German Nationalists lost more than half their strength, largely because no one could any longer understand Hugenberg's brand of conservatism, which had refused to give Brüning the slightest chance. By far the most important fact was that the Nazis had become the second strongest party in the Chamber.

The fate of the Democratic Party was a startling indication of the way public opinion was moving. It had played an important rôle as one of the strongest parties in the framing of the Weimar Constitution, and its members and supporters included some of the most intelligent, freedom-loving and broad-minded representatives of the nation. Now that the very forms of democratic life were fast approaching bankruptcy, the party's representation had shrunk to a few insignificant members. Its very title seemed to have lost its attraction for the voters. Though it changed its name to the German State Party, even this failed to give it new life. Nothing could show more clearly the failure of Weimar democracy than this party's tragic end three years later, when its four remaining parliamentary representatives voted for Hitler's Enabling Law.[1]

Dr Brüning made his declaration of policy to the newly assembled Parliament on October 16, 1930. 'The world crisis has hit Germany particularly hard,' he said. 'It affects us at a time when our people are in a state of great moral perturbation, following the disasters and disappointments of the last few years. We are faced by a serious situation.' He announced that the Government

---

[1] This *Ermächtigungsgesetz* refers to the *carte blanche* Hitler demanded and obtained from the Reichstag after his assumption of power.

felt obliged to seek foreign loans to cover the budget deficit. In Germany's eastern territories agriculture faced a catastrophe. The main objective of both internal and external policy must be the achievement of national freedom, without which the younger generation was living in a state of complete uncertainty about its future. A number of countries, in defiance of international agreements, were continuing to build up their armaments and were threatening the peace and the security of the world. This was an intolerable situation and the German Government would insist on the right of the German people to bear arms in their own defence.

This is presumably the sort of statement that would be characterized abroad as showing the worst traits of German nationalism. Yet, in the circumstances, it is difficult to see what other attitude Brüning could have adopted.

The Social Democrats, in spite of their continuous complaints about the threat of a Fascist dictatorship, still continued to accept Brüning's emergency decrees. But nothing could halt the effects of the world economic crisis. Yet another plan for financial reform had to be presented in December, providing for increased appropriations for unemployment pay, cuts in the salaries of Civil servants, higher taxes, and further reductions in Government expenditure. This was again forced through as an emergency measure and again approved by the Reichstag, with the help of the Socialists. However, the year 1931 was to render Brüning's *Erfüllungspolitik* – the policy of meeting all the Allied reparation demands – no longer a practical possibility. Most foreign countries, above all the United States, met the economic crisis by increasing tariff barriers, thus making it impossible for Germany to maintain her foreign trade. One of the few measures that might have helped at this time would have been the organization of larger economic units. Brüning made plans to enter into a Customs Union with Austria, but was prevented from doing so by the victorious powers.

With the collapse of the *Kreditanstalt* in June 1931, Austria became the first victim of the world crisis and was brought to the verge of disintegration. She was only saved by political capitulation to the terms of the French Government. A similar fate awaited Germany. During the whole of this summer, the Chancellor, the Foreign Minister and the President of the Reichsbank made personal visits, cap in hand, to the capitals of the victorious powers.

They were received politely but came back empty handed. It was hardly surprising that each failure provided fuel for the propaganda of the nationalist-minded opposition. When Brüning and his Foreign Minister, Curtius, visited London, Mr Ramsay MacDonald showed understanding for their plight, but suggested that they should first seek salvation by internal measures. In the meantime the situation became worse. Germany's diplomatic representatives abroad were called home for discussion. The Reichsbank was faced by increased withdrawals of capital.

On June 20 the German President sent a personal message to President Hoover asking for help. Hoover responded with a suggestion that all the interested states should observe a year's moratorium on debts. To this the French Government objected, claiming that public opinion was not yet ready to accept the idea that reparation payments should cease. Brüning then suggested a Franco-German conference, but at first obtained no response. In the first fortnight of July Germany's financial crisis reached its peak. The President of the Reichsbank hurried by air from capital to capital in search of financial support, but found none. On the 13th of the month one of the chief German banks had to close its doors. Four days later Brüning and Curtius were invited to Paris.

This sudden invitation was probably due to French anxiety about the improved relations between Germany and Great Britain, which had followed Brüning's visit to London. But the atmosphere was hardly propitious. Brüning and Curtius had just had to swallow a serious defeat, resulting from the ban on their attempts to enter into a Customs Union with Austria. French public opinion had been alarmed by what it considered the spectre of a reawakening German hegemony in Central Europe. It took the disaster of the Hitler period to prove to Europe – and to France in particular – that national economic frameworks had become too narrow, and that the removal of arbitrary trade and tariff barriers was the only means then – as now – of putting Europe's economy on a healthy basis. Brüning's fight against the rising tide of nationalism was at a critical stage. His defeat on such a delicate issue as his efforts to reach agreement with Austria was disastrous.

How inadequately the situation was grasped in Paris can be judged from the suggestion with which Brüning was greeted in July 1931. The French Government proposed an Anglo-Franco-

American loan of $500 million against the pledge not only of certain material resources, but also of undertakings to respect the *status quo* for ten years, not to increase military expenditure, and not to undertake any alteration of the relationship between Germany and Austria. Seldom can a great nation's right to equality of treatment have been so disregarded by its neighbours. Brüning was quite correct in pointing out that an unlimited credit economy had already led to economic collapse and that its continuation would be fatal. What he failed to point out was that the mere publication of such conditions would cause a wave of nationalistic feeling in Germany and provide fuel for the right wing radical parties. His counter-proposals amounted to practically nothing, nor did he make it clear enough that it would be impossible to resume the payment of reparations after the Hoover moratorium had run its course. Not only did he fail to seek the co-operation of the victorious powers in granting such concessions as would subdue nationalist agitation; he even rejected the French idea of a consultative pact. Indeed, the result of his visit was meagre in the extreme. He would have rendered a much greater service if he had presented the dangers of the German internal situation in much more forcible terms.

When I appeared a year later as Brüning's successor at the Lausanne Conference I tried to make up in some measure for this lost opportunity. I told both Herriot and MacDonald that mine was the last 'bourgeois' Government they would see in Germany unless they were prepared to concede me some moral success, apart from the settlement of the reparations problem, which would enable me to counter the National Socialists' agitation. In my turn, I put up the idea of a consultative pact, without having any idea that Brüning had rejected such a suggestion. This episode I shall deal with in due course. European Union has now become the rallying cry of those engaged in organizing continental defence against the threat from the East. But in the period between the two wars the victorious nations were still thinking too much in terms of eighteenth-century balances of power and not one of them produced a statesman worthy of the name.

Brüning invited Briand and Laval to Berlin. Again little good was accomplished because Brüning failed to play his only trump card: the impossibility of controlling the nationalist wave unless certain imperative concessions were granted immediately. His minimum demands should have been: an end to reparations payments, the dropping of the thesis of Germany's war guilt, and her right to parity in defensive armaments with other nations. Instead, he tried to convince his visitors that he would eventually overcome the opposition forces with which he was surrounded.

The Hoover moratorium did little to help the economic situation. Brüning introduced rigid deflationary measures: salaries and pensions were reduced. But he incurred the violent antipathy of the agricultural community by fixing prices which were not sufficient for them to exist on, while industry also was driven out of business by low prices. The number of unemployed increased by millions. The Chancellor was compelled to adopt the only language calculated to take the wind out of the opposition's sails. In January 1932, the information leaked out that he had told the British Ambassador that Germany was determined not to resume reparation payments after the end of the Hoover moratorium. The effect on French public opinion can be imagined. The Paris newspapers overflowed with indignation and Laval had to resign. This, it was said, was the reason why Brüning had sought a *rapprochement* – as a means of avoiding his obligations. How much better it would have been if he had made the situation quite clear in Paris or in Berlin during the French Ministers' visit.

The new French cabinet, under Laval's leadership, adopted a much sharper tone. 'France will never forego her right to receive reparations,' it was announced. And in this atmosphere the reparations conference which had been called to meet in Lausanne, first on January 18 and then on February 4, was postponed until June. The delay could only complicate the crisis in Germany. Meanwhile the disarmament conference had met in Geneva and the French delegate, André Tardieu, produced his unexpected plan for the formation of an international army. Brüning saw in this a possibility of restoring German equality in defensive armaments and arranged a private meeting with Tardieu on April 21 to discuss the matter. Another meeting was arranged for the 29th at Bessinges, near Geneva, in the house occupied by the United States Secretary of State, Mr Stimson. Brüning got the impression that in the meantime the plan for equality of armaments suggested by him had been accepted by America, Great Britain and Italy at discussions under Mr Stimson's chairmanship. Only French agreement was lacking. But on the 29th Tardieu did not appear. Instead, he sent a message to say that he was indisposed. Brüning was convinced that it was only a diplomatic illness, and in fact had good reason for his suspicions.

During the whole of the preceding week, M. François-Poncet, the French Ambassador in Berlin, had been declaring to everybody that Brüning's position had become completely untenable and that I was about to become his successor. It seems clear that General von Schleicher, head of the Political Division of the Army High Command, had evolved a plan which he had communicated to François-Poncet before I had the least inkling of what was going on. I was at home with my family in the Saar at the time. Schleicher had clearly made up his mind to encompass Brüning's downfall and the last thing he wanted was for the Chancellor to return from Geneva with any sort of success to his credit. The best way of achieving this was to give the French Ambassador reason for telegraphing to his Government that there was no point in granting concessions to Brüning because he was about to be ousted.

It is difficult to imagine a more astonishing development. The head of the Political Division of the Army High Command had seen fit to divulge confidences to the French Ambassador which were kept secret even from the people concerned. Brüning claimed subsequently that he was advised of French agreement to his disarmament suggestion on May 31, the day before his dismissal. This piece of intrigue on Schleicher's part therefore cost six valuable months. I was never told that Brüning's formula had been accepted. I should still be interested to know what reasons he gives for not having passed on this important information. The success he claims to have achieved at Bessinges was not merely personal. It concerned the German Government, and he should not have allowed personal resentment towards his successor to have played any part in the matter. My own efforts to find a solution to the disarmament problem were only brought to fruition on December 8, but it was then too late, because within two months the effort to integrate the Nazis into a coalition Government with joint responsibility had finally collapsed. By then the political temperature had risen to such a degree that any success in the field of foreign policy could no longer be followed up. If only some agreement on the problem of disarmament had been reached in May 1932, before the Lausanne Conference, future developments might have been very different.

But I must return to the internal situation, and Brüning's attempts in the summer of 1931 to avert the impending catastrophe. Hoover's suggestion of a moratorium had been accepted at the London conference, but nothing had been done to fulfil the German Chancellor's hopes of a general settlement of the reparations problem. The Government's position in the Reichstag had become increasingly insecure. The boycott of the Reichstag by the one hundred and fifty-one members of the nationalist opposition – the German National Party and the Nazis – had turned the 'bourgeois' majority into a minority. Now, if ever, was the occasion for the Government to seek some sort of collaboration with the opposition. Instead of adopting one temporary measure after another, the Government should have won the confidence of its opponents by introducing a wide programme of the sort of reforms that had been discussed for years past. Dr Schacht, who had been the German representative at the Young Plan discussions, had pleaded with Brüning in the previous February to take the Nazis into coalition. Such coalitions existed in Thuringia, Brunswick and Oldenburg, where the Nazis had had to temper their programme to that of their coalition colleagues. There was no good reason why this could not be done in the Federal Government.

Brüning does not appear even to have considered this possibility. He preferred to make the fate of his Government dependent entirely on the attitude of the Social Democrats and resisted every suggestion of a coalition with the right. His Minister of the Interior, Dr Wirth, declared on March 5 that in view of the nationalist boycott of the Reichstag, and the impossibility of obtaining the required two-thirds majority, there was no hope of putting through any schemes for reform of the Constitution and the Electoral Law. Yet the Communist threat to German security had never been greater, and one of their Reichstag deputies, Ulbricht, now better known for his rôle in the East German Republic, declared in February, 'The working class will only come to power by an organized revolution to form a Soviet Germany.'

Great Britain and the United States have given us examples of successful coalition governments. In spite of their overwhelming majority, the British Conservatives took Labour representatives into the Government for the duration of the war, and Roosevelt appointed leading Republicans to his cabinet. Democracy in Germany never got further than attempts by each individual party to impose their programme on the others. The Nazis were by no means the first to make arbitrary use of the power of the press for their own purposes. In 1931 the Stahlhelm, the ex-servicemen's association, attempted to organize a referendum as a means of urging measures of reform in the State of Prussia. The Prussian Government, which had the same political complexion as the Federal Government, opposed by every means this perfectly legal activity. A violently worded communiqué was issued, warning people against taking part in the referendum, and every news-paper in the State was ordered by special decree to publish it. The Stahlhelm then complained to the Federal Chancellor of this attack on the right of every citizen to express his opinions freely, and asked him to prevent the Prussian police from confiscating the documents and papers prepared for the referendum. This high-handed act by the left wing Prussian Government provided in its way a foretaste of what we were to experience under Goebbels. What people were pleased to call my 'cabinet of barons' took no such steps to curb the freedom of expression.

* * *

Almost the only bond between the parties, with the exception of the Communists, lay in the personality of the German President. As late as September 1931, Hugenberg, leader of the German National Party, was calling on the President to respect the Con-stitution and claiming that the right wing parties formed the only workable majority in the State. The whole problem of the forth-coming Presidential election caused many of us great concern. In September I called on the Chancellor to draw his attention to the dangerous conflicts that must arise. The antagonism between the various parties made it most unlikely that they would ever agree on a new candidate. The only possible solution seemed to be the re-election of Hindenburg. The accusation has since been made that he was too old and no longer sufficiently in possession of his faculties to accept the responsibilities of office. However, at this period, his health and intelligence were in no way impaired. Moreover, any doubts that there might have been in 1925, that an elderly general possessed the necessary qualifications for a Presi-dent, had been stilled by the objective manner in which he had carried out his duties. The Socialists had never questioned his adherence to the terms of his oath of office and he had long enjoyed the confidence of the right wing parties. I suggested to the Chancellor that his re-election would provide the basis for some degree of agreement between the parties. I did not doubt that the Nazis would attempt to sell their co-operation, and would demand numerous concessions, and I begged the Chancellor to enter into negotiations with them while there was still time and work out an agreed programme. If this were done it would be possible for the Reichstag to confirm Hindenburg in office for a further period with the two-thirds majority necessary to effect this change in constitutional procedure. This, I told him, would avoid what I was convinced would be the disastrous consequences of a Presidential election in an atmosphere of political and party antagonism. Brüning replied that he saw no reason why the person of the President should be the cause of political strife, but undertook to study my proposition.

In the meantime the state of political anarchy increased. Towards the end of September the Federation of German Industry issued a warning that the economic situation was so serious that it could only be remedied by determined measures by the Cabinet, taken if necessary without reference to the political parties. They recommended that power be transferred from the Parliament to an authoritarian Cabinet. On October 6, 1931, Brüning made some ministerial changes to coincide with his third emergency decree covering further economic and financial measures. Curtius and Wirth, his Foreign Minister and Minister of the Interior respectively, both of whom had been heavily attacked, were forced to resign. But without coming to some agreement with the right wing parties, it was impossible for him to persuade any of their representatives to join the Cabinet. In the end he had to take over the post of Foreign Minister himself and appointed General Groener, the War Minister, to the Ministry of the Interior.

This failure to come to an agreement with the opposition, and the increased weakness of the Cabinet, helped to bring about a highly significant development. On September 11 representatives of the Nazi Party, the German National Party, the Stahlhelm and the Farmers' Association, together with Dr Schacht, and Colonel-General von Seeckt, and leading economists, held a conference at Bad Harzburg. An attempt was made to devise a common programme for the right wing opposition, and one of the most important speeches was made by Dr Schacht. He attacked the

Government for what he described as lack of backbone, and
declared that it was no longer possible to continue running Germany's economy on the basis of foreign loans. Such a policy
destroyed all confidence and respect abroad and the whole world
would welcome firm internal measures to meet the crisis.

Brüning had done what he could to weaken the 'Harzburger
Front' conference by persuading Hindenburg to receive Hitler the
day before it started. The only result was to encourage Hitler
in his arbitrary demands. He showed little willingness to co-
operate either with the Government or indeed with Hugenberg.
Nevertheless the opposition had made up its mind to get rid of
Brüning, and with renewed attacks from the left his position in
Parliament became practically untenable. The Communists referred
to General Groener as a military dictator, Brüning's association
with the Socialists became even more strained, and the much-
reduced party to which Stresemann had belonged left the coalition.
The threat from the extreme left grew more and more menacing.
On October 14 Severing, now Prussian Minister of the Interior,
announced that during the year Communist rowdies had caused
the death of thirty-four people and serious injury to one hundred
and eighty-six others. The moderates in the centre were being
threatened by the rising tide of radicalism from both wings and it
became increasingly difficult for them to provide Brüning with a
body of support.

In a speech at a conference of the Zentrum Party on November 5, Brüning declared: 'Our most important task during the
coming winter will be to prevent the antagonisms between the
political parties from becoming too explosive. . . . The Federal
and State Governments and the municipalities are faced by almost
insuperable financial problems next year. Tax receipts will be
based on 1931 incomes, reduced as they were by the economic
crisis, and even without the burden of reparations we shall have to
adopt still more stringent measures in every field of activity during
1932.' Brüning was certainly under no illusions concerning the
gravity of the situation, but this only makes it more difficult to
understand why he did not adopt the only possible solution and
take steps to include the opposition in the Government. Perhaps
his Minister of Labour, Stegerwald, gave the answer when he said
on the same day, 'There is no possibility of broadening the basis of
the coalition, either to the left or to the right. The left does not

provide us with a majority [Brüning already enjoyed the support of the Social Democrats], and co-operation with the right would cause difficulties in the field of foreign affairs and prejudice our position in reparation negotiations.'

This provides the key to Brüning's policies. The nationalist opposition was regarded as a hindrance when it came to negotiations with the victorious powers. Yet six months later, when my Cabinet had to rely on opposition support during the Lausanne Conference, we experienced no difficulties of any sort from the other powers.

Another emergency decree, containing the fourth set of financial and economic regulations, was promulgated on December 8, 1931. Brüning showed himself well aware of the increasing dangers of the situation when, in announcing the new regulations to the Reichstag, he declared, 'The Reich Government will tolerate no exercise of power not laid down in the Constitution. The President and the Government are the sole repositories of constitutional authority and we shall, if necessary, declare a state of emergency if this authority should be challenged by outside organizations.' It will be noted that in this declaration he makes no reference to Parliament or democracy. It is only fair to bring this again to the notice of historians who blame me for the collapse of the Weimar Constitution and my Government for the destruction of German democracy.

CHAPTER IX

THE CHANCELLORSHIP

The Presidency – Negotiations break down – Presidential elections – Rift with Brüning – Ban on the Storm Troopers – Brüning resigns – The decay of democracy – A call from Schleicher – An astonishing offer – I accept the Chancellorship – Zentrum opposition – I meet Hitler – First steps – The Osthilfe scandal

THE year 1932 opened with Brüning's attempts to ensure the re-election of Hindenburg by parliamentary methods. By January 7 he was negotiating with both Hitler and the Social Democrats. Hitler's first reaction was to make any agreement dependent on reaching an understanding with Hugenberg on the subject. His preliminary demands included recognition of the legality of the National Socialist Party in all its forms, and federal and state elections in the Reich and Prussia. The Social Democrats refused to acknowledge the need for any concessions to the right wing parties in return for their co-operation. If Brüning had been prepared to devise any sort of common programme with the right wing parties he could have countered their demand for elections. Even the price of new elections would have been worth paying in order to obtain Hindenburg's re-election. Brüning's position in the country would have been immensely strengthened if the President's term had been extended without party controversy. The Chancellor could have represented himself as enjoying the President's full confidence, and the opposition, especially the Nazis, would have been saddled with their share of the responsibilities of Government. However, he made no move and by January 12 negotiations had broken down.

Hugenberg, in a letter to the Chancellor, declined to co-operate in extending the President's term by a constitutional amendment. This, he declared, would not represent the true wish of the nation and instead of indicating a vote of confidence in the President would be taken rather as a sign of approval for those Government policies that the opposition was engaged in combating. Hitler in his turn submitted a memorandum in which he declared: 'The Reich Chancellor has expressed the opinion that elections at this time would prejudice the conduct of international negotiations, but he is not prepared to admit that any government that refuses to face up to the demands of the internal situation is not fully representative of the nation abroad.' This was surely a logical point of view.

Brüning made no further attempt to win the collaboration of the National Socialists and political tension in the country increased. The world saw the unedifying spectacle of a nation hopelessly divided on the question of choosing its Chief of State; the inevitable result being the tragedy of two bitterly fought Presidential elections. Brüning's failure to foresee that these elections must split the nation and further complicate the internal political situation, and his hesitation to take steps that would have made them unnecessary, were serious faults in his capacity as a statesman.

The nationalist opposition also showed little appreciation of the necessity for providing unanimous support for the person of the President. The Stahlhelm announced on February 14 that they would only support his re-election if there was a guarantee that the Government would change its course. Count von der Goltz, the leader of another right wing organization, turned against Hindenburg for having signed the Young Plan. Both Hitler and the Farmers' Association (Reichslandbund) declined to support his candidature. We were faced by the paradoxical situation of the right wing parties, which had elected Hindenburg in 1925 against the strenuous opposition of the centre and the left, now refusing their support. But disunity went even further. The parties united in the Harzburger Front could not even agree on a common candidate of their own. The nation was presented with a completely unknown Lieutenant-Colonel, named Duesterberg, put up by the German nationalists and the Stahlhelm as a challenger to the Great War's finest soldier – a soldier who had occupied the office of Chief of State, aloof from party political strife, for seven difficult years. As their candidate, the Nazis named Hitler.

In the circumstances Brüning did everything he could to support Hindenburg's re-election, but the first round of voting on March 13, 1932, failed to provide the absolute majority that was needed. Hindenburg won 49.7 per cent of the votes, Hitler 30.1

per cent, Thaelmann, the Communist, 13.3 per cent, and Duesterberg 6.9 per cent.

After another month of violent party propaganda a second
ballot was held. This gave Hindenburg a narrow majority with
53 per cent of the votes. Hitler increased his share to 36.8 per cent.
By refusing Hitler's demand for new parliamentary elections, in
return for his support in extending the President's term of office,
Brüning had subjected the country to two trials of strength, both
more bitter than anything yet experienced. The results showed not
only a striking increase in the strength of the Nazis, but also
astonishing evidence that more than a third of the population was
prepared to see Hitler appointed as Chief of State.

The psychological effect of this revelation was much more
serious than the outcome of a purely parliamentary election could
have been. It marks the real beginning of Hitler's rise to power. In
the elections held under the ægis of my Government a few months
later, the Nazis obtained almost the same figure. In spite of this,
the left wing parties have always maintained that the turning
point came in the July 31 elections. All the fears I had expressed to
the Chancellor in the previous autumn had unfortunately proved
well founded.

The course that the election took had further unpleasant consequences – relations between Hindenburg and the Chancellor
became increasingly strained. The President was upset by the
Chancellor's failure to organize the support of all parties for his re-
election. Though Brüning had not spared himself in the conduct
of the campaign, he had been unable to prevent unfair and unpleasant attacks on the President's good name by the right wing
parties. Hindenburg was particularly hurt at the course of events
which had led to his old wartime comrades campaigning against
him. His decision to act more independently of the political parties
was taken as a result of his experiences during and preceding the
elections, and the formation of my Presidential Cabinet was a
natural result of this development.

On April 13 the Government promulgated another emergency
decree banning the Nazi S.S. and S.A. organizations. Two days
later the President wrote to the Minister of the Interior, General
Groener, pointing out that this ban should apply to all the uniformed organizations that the different political parties had built
up. Groener at first declared that he had no reason to proceed

against the Communist Rotfront, the Socialist Reichsbanner, and similar organizations. A month later he resigned.

It may well be asked why it was found necessary in a civilized state for political parties to organize these 'protection forces'. The answer is simple. In Britain or the United States the police forces protect the activities of every political party. In the Weimar Republic things were different. Right wing meetings were continually broken up and interrupted by left wing radicals. The police, most of whom came under Socialist Ministers of the Interior in the States, did not or would not do anything about it. The right wing parties therefore found it necessary to organize their own police, and the Socialists in their turn found it necessary to organize the Reichsbanner as protection against the 'enemies of the Republic'. The Communists and the Nazis provided for the organization of these special corps in their party constitutions. Until January 30, 1933, they were all supposed to be unarmed, but after that date the S.A. and the S.S. began openly to carry weapons.

This ban on the Nazi Brownshirts was a vital factor in subsequent developments. It also throws an interesting light on the duplicity of General von Schleicher. Brüning has described in a letter published in the July 1947 issue of the *Deutsche Rundschau* how he held a meeting in the late autumn of 1931 with the German service chiefs – General von Hammerstein, Admiral Raeder and General von Schleicher – together with certain Social Democrat leaders, to discuss a plan for the suppression of the Nazi Party. The President declined to approve any steps which did not include the simultaneous suppression of the other revolutionary party, the Communists. Brüning now states that while he was stumping the country on the President's behalf, representatives of the Army and the Ministers of the Interior from the various German States came to an agreement on the Brownshirt ban. Although he now declares that he regarded the decree as premature, he overcame the President's objections by threatening that both he and Groener would resign. This he describes as the root cause of his rift with the President. According to Brüning, Schleicher not only insisted on the dissolution of the Brownshirts, but told Brüning that neither he himself nor Hammerstein could accept responsibility for the Army under any Government which included the Nazis in a coalition or which was unduly influenced by the Nazi Party. It is therefore clear that Brüning took this step only with Schleicher's approval and support, and at the risk of destroying his relationship with the President.

It was in April that the step was taken. If Schleicher had then changed his mind, and had come to believe that Nazi participation in the Government might yet solve the problem, it would have shown greater fairness if he and Hammerstein had told the Chancellor of this. The course of events can be explained only by the fact that Schleicher saw in the ban a means of forcing first Groener's resignation and then the Chancellor's. Hindenburg was right to insist on the dissolution of all the uniformed organizations. If the armed forces were to be called upon to maintain law and order in the country, they would need to act impartially against all disturbers of the peace. By his unilateral ban Brüning rendered this impossible.

The question may well be asked, who was in fact responsible for the overthrow of the Weimar Republic? A young Major-General, head of a Government department, without ministerial responsibility, apparently made up his mind that reasons of state demanded the resignation of the German Chancellor. From a purely personal point of view he may have been right, as the Army had become the one stable factor in the country after the Weimar conception of democracy had proved unworkable. The blame for the collapse of parliamentary government lies on many shoulders. Two months later, when I had become Chancellor and the ban on the Brownshirts was rescinded, so as to restore equal treatment to all parties, I was accused in the grossest terms of furthering the National Socialist cause. When I took over the post I had been assured by Schleicher that it was the wish of both Hindenburg and the Army that the decree should be annulled. He had promised Hitler that this would be done, against an undertaking that the Nazis would not act in opposition to my Government.

★ ★ ★

During the whole of this period I had pleaded in speeches and newspaper articles for a radical change in Brüning's policies. However, I was not informed about the increasing differences of opinion between Brüning and the President, and when the crisis came to a head I was at home in Wallerfangen.

On May 26 I received a telephone call from General von Schleicher, who asked me to come to Berlin on an urgent matter.

I arrived the next day without any idea of what was going on, and on the 28th I called on him at his office. He gave me a general survey of the political situation, described the crisis within the Cabinet, and told me that it was the President's wish to form a Cabinet of experts, independent of the political parties. It had become technically impossible to form a parliamentary Cabinet, because no combination could command a majority. The sole remaining constitutional solution was the formation of a Presidential Cabinet by the Chief of State. Schleicher gave me a colourful description of the impossibility of relying further on Brüning. His unilateral ban on the Brownshirts had placed the National Socialists even more sharply in opposition, and had at the same time put the President in an embarrassing situation constitutionally *vis-à-vis* the other parties. He no longer considered it possible to combat a party as strong as the Nazis by negative means, which had only resulted in the steady and threatening growth of their power. The Nazis claimed to be actuated by patriotic motives, for which a great many Germans found sympathy, and it was becoming increasingly difficult to prevent the younger Reichswehr officers from being attracted by their ideas.

Brüning had insisted, so Schleicher told me, that he would never sit at the same table with National Socialists. But there was no way of obtaining their co-operation in the affairs of Government if they were driven further and further into opposition and exposed to increasingly radical influences. Some solution had to be found. Hindenburg was also perturbed at the manner in which Brüning's emergency financial decrees were depressing the standard of living of those dependent on pensions and investment incomes. The economic crisis could only be solved by much more positive methods. The President was no longer convinced that the Chancellor's policies would protect the authority of the State and the country's economy from complete breakdown.

Schleicher left me in no doubt that he was acting as spokesman for the Army, the only stable organization remaining in the State, preserved intact and free of party political strife by von Seeckt and his successors. In the present parliamentary crisis, this instrument of law and order could only be spared from intervention in the civil war that threatened, if an authoritarian Cabinet were to replace the tottering party system. This was a theme we had often

F

discussed. From my public speeches Schleicher knew of my constant insistence that Brüning should form a national coalition Government and return to Bismarck's conception of uniting the post of Chancellor and Prussian Prime Minister, so that the Federal Cabinet might bring the Prussian services of public order under its authority and thus secure the stability of the Government.

I therefore found myself in complete agreement with Schleicher's train of thought. But I made it clear to him that the evil must be attacked at its roots and a supreme effort made to amend the Constitution. A system of individual constituencies would have to replace the present proportional representation system with its thirty parties, and an upper house reintroduced to give balance to the parliamentary system. Schleicher showed little enthusiasm for this. He lacked completely the practical experience of a parliamentarian and sought instead to reach a solution by lobbying and negotiations between the political parties, the trade unions, the Cabinet and the President. He then turned the conversation to the subject of who could lead the new Cabinet. We discussed various names and he asked for my opinion. There had been nothing out of the ordinary in our conversation so far, but to my amazement Schleicher now suggested that I should take over this task myself.

Looking at me with his humorous and somewhat sarcastic smile, he seemed to appreciate my astonishment. 'This offer takes me completely by surprise,' I said. 'I very much doubt if I am the right man. I know we seem to be agreed on the measures that have to be taken, and I shall be glad to help in any way that I can – but Reich Chancellor! That is a very different matter.'

'I have already suggested your name to the Old Gentleman,' Schleicher said, 'and he is most insistent that you should accept the post.'

I told him that he was taking things too much for granted. 'You cannot expect me to undertake such an immense responsibility on the spot,' I said.

Schleicher then took me by the arm and we walked up and down the room, talking like old friends. 'You have simply got to do Hindenburg and myself this service. Everything depends on it, and I cannot think of anyone who would do it better. You are a man of moderate convictions, whom no one will accuse of dictatorial tendencies, and there is no other right wing man of whom the same could be said. I have even drawn up a provisional Cabinet list which I am sure you will approve.'

I had to interrupt him. 'Give me time to think this over, Schleicher,' I said. 'Perhaps I can think of someone better. In any case, we have got to make up our minds what we can offer if we are to get the Nazis to collaborate in a Presidential Cabinet.'

'I have already had a word with Hitler about that,' Schleicher said. 'I told him we would lift the ban on the Brownshirts, providing they behaved themselves, and dissolve the Reichstag. He has assured me that in return the Nazis would give the Cabinet their tacit support, even though they are not represented in it.'

I must have made some gesture at the idea of dissolving the Reichstag, because Schleicher went on hurriedly, 'I have convinced Hindenburg that this is the correct thing to do if we are to rely on experts for a while rather than on the political parties. People are tired of endless political conflict in a crisis that goes from bad to worse. Hindenburg will earn everyone's thanks for any practical steps to put industry on its feet again and stop this incessant street fighting. New elections can only benefit the moderate elements of the right and centre.'

For the time being we left it at that. I said goodbye and told him I would think the whole matter over during the week-end (this was on a Saturday) and come to see him again on Monday. I left the War Ministry with my thoughts whirling. For ten years now I had contributed what I could to the rebirth of my country's affairs and had had to make a number of personal decisions which other people had preferred to avoid, either out of laziness or through a mistaken sense of party loyalty. I had never allowed party discipline to interfere with the dictates of my conscience, but here I was called upon to make a highly important decision which involved far more than personal responsibility.

Acceptance or refusal did not depend only on whether Schleicher or I were correct in our assessment of the situation. There was also the question of whether my personal capacity would suffice for a task of such importance. I was fully aware of my limitations, and my first reaction was to decline Schleicher's offer.

But I felt that I had to have a second opinion. It was not enough to put my own thoughts in order. So I set off for Neubabelsberg, on the western outskirts of Berlin, where my old friend Hans Humann lived. He was an enthusiastic yachtsman, and we spent most of the week-end on the Wannsee, discussing every possible aspect of the situation. We cruised up and down the beautiful lake without anyone to interrupt our thoughts.

Humann was the son of the famous archæologist who found the Pergamon Altar.[1] He had an almost Oriental detachment in his way of thinking, and a calm manner of judging people and events that had often helped me in making difficult decisions. He seemed far less astonished at Schleicher's offer than I was. 'It is quite clear they need someone from one of the centre parties,' he said: 'someone with enlightened conservative ideas to provide a contrast to the chaos in which the political parties have involved themselves.' (Of course, I cannot reconstruct his exact words, but this was roughly his line of thought.) 'The experiment could very well succeed, if there was any certainty that the political parties, deprived temporarily of their power, had enough good sense to tone down their opposition. I see that as the chief difficulty, and I cannot believe that they will. Your own party will be the worst problem. They idolize Brüning and will never forgive you for taking his place, even though the initiative was not yours. I see no reason why you should doubt your own capacity, but I still think you would be wise to decline the offer. I can understand very well why Schleicher and the President should have turned to you. They are looking for someone who understands people, knows the situation here and abroad, and has the courage of his convictions. From that point of view they chose very well. On the other hand, I don't think that the parties have yet realized that the whole apparatus of government under the present Constitution will break down completely if it is not reformed in some way. If only we had a competent right wing opposition, who could combine an enlightened outlook with their conservatism, I would recommend you to accept Schleicher's offer. The trouble is, there is not a statesman among them.'

My mind was made up. Early on Monday morning, the 30th – Brüning had not yet resigned – I set off for Schleicher's office again with the full intention of declining his offer. He received me with the smile of a man who sees deep-laid plans beginning to

---

[1] The Pergamon Altar, excavated and reassembled by Hans Humann, was one of the treasures of the Kaiser Friedrich Museum in Berlin, whence it found its way to Moscow in 1945.

succeed: 'Well, my dear Papen, what is the verdict?' he asked. 'I hope that someone as active as you are is not going to decline such an opportunity of serving his country.'

'I have been trying to answer your question all the week-end,' I said, 'but I am sorry to have to tell you that it can't be done. We can only resolve this situation by combining every constructive force in the country, both inside and outside the parties, and I am simply not the right man. If I were to take over from Brüning to-morrow, the whole Zentrum Party would turn against me. The Socialists already regard me as a Conservative, who would do any-thing to thwart their policies. The Trade Unions would oppose anyone to whom the Social Democrats objected, even if the new Government had enough freedom of action to reduce enemploy-ment and put the economy back on its feet. The one group we can't afford to offend is the centre. We must find some way of reforming the parties and getting parliamentary democracy to work, but we cannot ignore their existence and there would be no point in starting off with a constitutional crisis.'

'We have taken all this into consideration,' Schleicher answered with a smile, 'and I think you will find you are exaggerating the difficulties. Naturally, you and I will come in for a lot of criticism. But if we work out as quickly as possible a really comprehensive programme for reducing unemployment, we shall earn the grati-tude of the whole country; and I should like to see which party would oppose us then. Certainly not the Trade Unions; their funds are exhausted and their members are leaving because the unions can't offer them any solution to the problem of hunger. The only way to defeat radicalism is by providing work, and if we can do this the people who support the Nazis will soon quieten down. Brüning's purely negative methods are useless, and the Zentrum will soon appreciate this, if you can win over people of the intelligence of Dr Kaas. Hitler has already promised tacit co-operation with a Papen cabinet, and you will see what a difference it will make if we can get away from this civil war atmosphere.'

I must admit that Schleicher's arguments began to impress me. 'The only man who can do this is someone not too involved in party support,' he said. 'Let the nation as a whole decide. Hinden-burg is depending on you not to leave him in the lurch. He wants the quickest possible solution to the crisis and wants to see you later in the day.' There was little doubt that Schleicher's plans had been drawn up in great detail. He seemed to have presented Hindenburg with a firm proposal for the reorganization of the Brüning cabinet and had suggested no other name but my own. He had drawn up a complete list of ministers and had apparently discussed the matter with a number of them. The names he gave me were all of respectable non-political men of conservative tendencies.

But he had not talked me into it yet. I told him that I must first of all see Dr Kaas, the leader of the Zentrum Party. We also had to take some account of the reaction abroad. There would undoubtedly be plenty of people ready to warm up all the stories that had been told of my alleged activities in America during the war. 'I should not worry about that,' Schleicher said. 'People nowadays have a much more objective outlook on what went on during the war. The most important thing is that the French should give you a good press. They certainly ought to, after all your efforts to improve Franco-German relations, and you will probably be very glad to go even further in this direction.' To this I certainly agreed, and I mentioned how necessary it was to take some decisive step of this nature as prelude to the forthcoming reparations conference. We parted again on the understanding that I would give him a definite answer the next day and would also call on the President.

I finally managed to see Dr Kaas at three o'clock the next day, Tuesday the 31st. We had been on good terms ever since the party conference in Cologne had elected him as leader of the party in preference to Dr Stegerwald, and I had done all I could to support his policies. Stegerwald had been the Trade Union candidate for the leadership, while Dr Kaas belonged to the conservative wing of the party. He was a man of great intelligence and strength of character, but had been more than reluctant to accept the responsibilities of leadership and had only done so in order to bring enlightened conservative influences to bear on the affairs of the time. I found him in a very sombre mood.

I did not have to explain the reason for my visit. As I have already said, Schleicher had been dropping hints to the French Ambassador, François-Poncet, about Brüning's imminent replacement, and Berlin was full of rumours of political cabals and intrigues. There was no need to tell Dr Kaas that I had taken no initiative in the Schleicher development. He knew that I would not have been disloyal to Brüning. He went straight to the point and told me there could be no question of another member of the Zentrum Party taking Brüning's place because Brüning enjoyed their complete confidence. He begged me not to accept Hindenburg's offer.

This was just the attitude I had expected him to adopt. On the other hand, I told him plainly that Schleicher had convinced me not only of the wide breach between Hindenburg and the Chancellor, but also of the President's firm intention to seek other solutions. But Dr Kaas had confirmed my worst fears. I had already told Schleicher that not only would I not be able to count on the support of my own party, but that they would actively oppose my candidature. I therefore told Kaas that I would try to convince the President of the impossibility of confiding the Chancellorship to me and ask him to seek an alternative candidate. It seemed clear to me that this was the overriding argument against my accepting the post. Any man who did not enjoy the support of the centre parties would be to all intents and purposes powerless.

A quarter of an hour later I stood before the President. He received me with his usual paternal kindliness. 'Well, my dear Papen,' he said in his deep voice, 'I hope you are going to help me out of this difficult situation.'

'Herr Reich President, I am afraid I cannot,' I said.

I told him I agreed fully with the necessity for a change of course, and suggested that it might still be possible to get Brüning to take the necessary steps. Hindenburg thought there was little chance of this. It was his belief that Brüning had no other solution but that of his emergency decrees. Nor had he been able to convince Brüning that it would not be possible to ban the uniformed formations of the Nazis alone. But his chief complaint was the impossible situation in which he had been placed by his re-election by the left and centre parties alone, while the National Socialists had put up this 'corporal' against him. He had made up his mind to form a Cabinet out of people in whom he had personal confidence and who could govern without having arguments at every step.

I agreed with all this, but tried to convince him with all my powers of persuasion – and Kaas himself could not have been more articulate – that there was no point in calling on me in the hope that I would have the support of the Zentrum Party. If I accepted the post I would only incur the hate and enmity of my own party and he might just as well call upon the German Nationalists for the task.

I have often described the scene that followed. Rising heavily from his chair, the old Field-Marshal put both hands on my shoulders: 'You cannot possibly leave an old man like me in the lurch,' he said. 'In spite of my age I have had to accept the responsibilities of the nation for another period. I am asking you now to take over a task on which the future of our country depends, and I am relying on your sense of duty and patriotism to do what I ask you.' I can remember to this day the deep, heavy tone of his voice, so full of warmth, yet so demanding. 'It is immaterial to me if you earn the disapproval or even the enmity of your party. I intend to have people round me who are independent of political parties, men of good will and expert knowledge, who will surmount the crisis of our country.' The President's voice rose slightly. 'You have been a soldier and did your duty in the war. When the Fatherland calls, Prussia knows only one response – obedience.'

I struck my colours. Such a call, I felt, transcended party obligations. I clasped the Field-Marshal's hand. Schleicher, who had been waiting in the next room, came in to offer his congratulations. In view of the task I had undertaken, I felt rather that I needed his sympathy.

Someone – we never found out who it was – telephoned the information to the outside world. While Hindenburg, Schleicher and I sat down to a long discussion concerning the new ministers and the necessary new legislative measures, the news spread like wildfire. It soon reached the Reichstag, where Dr Kaas was giving the party caucus an account of my conversation with him and of my decision to decline Hindenburg's offer. The effect of the latest development can well be imagined, for Dr Kaas must have felt that I had deliberately misled him.

It was one of those situations where explanations were useless. If I had had any idea that the information would leak out so soon, I would have telephoned to Dr Kaas myself and told him why I had changed my mind. It would then have been possible for him to present the matter to the party meeting in a proper light. As it was, his colleagues, already furious at what they considered the shabby treatment of Brüning, became even more enraged. Without waiting to hear any further details, they made every sort of accusation against me and unanimously approved a resolution deploring what I had done. A few hours later I sent a long letter to Dr Kaas, explaining the sequence of events, but by that time the breach was irreparable, and was widened by Brüning's personal resentment. My letter expressed the hope that if the Zentrum Party and I were to go our own ways, we could at least co-operate on measures to resolve the country's plight. Above all, I said, our mutual wish to apply Christian principles to the conduct of the nation's affairs should bring us together again.

Subsequent developments were to show that there was no hope of reconciliation. The manner in which the news of my appointment was made public had severely reduced the chances of the new Government's success. It proved impossible to reform the party system or to persuade anyone to subordinate personality or party dogma to the urgent needs of the moment.

Our discussions concerning the Cabinet ended the next day. Schleicher had already sounded the obvious personalities and there was little left for me to do but to give my final approval and agree on our immediate objectives. Schleicher had certainly chosen well. Neurath, who had been approached by Brüning the previous November, took over the Foreign Office. Freiherr von Gayl, a reliable civil servant, who became the Minister of the Interior, was well suited to the problem of devising a reform of the Constitution. The Finance Ministry went to Count Schwerin-Krosigk, who had been for many years the head of its budget department. Dr Guertner, the Bavarian Minister of Justice and an old friend of mine from the Palestine campaign, became the Minister of Justice, and the other posts were occupied by people of similar qualities. Schleicher himself became the Minister of Defence, whose political liaison officer he had been for so long. This post assured him the strongest influence in the Cabinet he had brought into being.

We had some difficulty in filling the Economics and Labour posts. Schleicher had wanted to get the Lord Mayor of Leipzig, Dr Goerdeler, to take over one of the posts. In this connection it is interesting to note Brüning's post-war revelation that he had tried to persuade Hindenburg to accept Goerdeler as his successor. Whether the Lord Mayor felt that one ministry was less than his deserts I do not know, but he demanded both. However, as Schleicher and I considered it an impossible task for one man, we could not agree. In the end, Professor Warmbold took over the Economics Ministry and Dr Syrup, the permanent secretary, functioned as Minister of Labour. Within twenty-four hours I presented my Cabinet to the President to be sworn in. Not since the days of the Kaiser had any Government been formed so quickly. The bargaining between parties, which had often kept the nation in suspense for weeks, had been avoided entirely through Schleicher's efforts, and this caused a favourable first impression.

The problems facing us were extremely grave. In our first declaration of policy I stated that I had taken office not as a politician but as a German. The condition of the country required the collaboration and effort of every patriotic member of the community, whatever their political inclinations. The financial framework of Federal, State and local Government was broken. Plans for the basic reform of public life had never got beyond vague proposals. Unemployment was threatening the corporate life of the community and social security funds were exhausted. The post-war Governments had embarked on welfare schemes and a system of state socialism which were beyond the country's means and had turned it into a sort of charity institution. The moral strength of the nation had been weakened. Public life, if it was to combat Marxist and atheist teachings, would have to be rebuilt on the basis of Christian principles.

In foreign policy we declared that our desire was to achieve equality of rights and political freedom for Germany in consultation with other nations. Disarmament, reparations and the world economic crisis were all matters of vital concern to Germany. If her interests were to be properly represented abroad, the first task must be to clarify the internal political situation. For this reason the President had accepted the Government's proposal that the Reichstag should be dissolved and new elections held.

The Zentrum Party had already made its position clear in a communiqué which said:

'We condemn unanimously the events of the past few days, which have led to the resignation of Chancellor Brüning. Irresponsible intrigues by persons having no authority under the Constitution have halted the work of national reconstruction at a time when favourable developments could be expected from imminent international negotiations. The economic and social aspirations of every group in the country have had a grave obstacle placed in their path. . . . At a time of severe political unrest the Zentrum Party considers itself under an obligation to demand an overall policy leading to national freedom and equality, and a determined attempt to deal with the basic problem of unemployment. The Party therefore rejects the temporary solution provided by the present Cabinet, and demands that the situation should be clarified by placing the responsibility for forming a Government in the hands of the National Socialist Party.'

Historians who have accepted Brüning's later claim to have avoided all contact and collaboration with Hitler at this juncture, would be well advised to take note of this long-forgotten declaration. The relative blame might then be distributed more fairly. The Zentrum Party press, whose right wing came out in support of my Chancellorship, also suggested that National Socialists should be taken into the Cabinet. The right wing press in general gave me its support, while the chief accusation of the left was one of 'treason'.

Parliament was dissolved on June 4. I have already mentioned how Schleicher had promised Hitler that he would dissolve the Reichstag and have the ban on the Brownshirts lifted, providing the Nazis either supported my Government or entered it later on. When I told my Cabinet of this, they all agreed that even if no undertaking had been given to Hitler it would still have been essential to dissolve Parliament, so that the nation could express its opinion on the policy we intended to follow.

I have been accused ever since of ordering the dissolution only to do the Nazis a service. Brüning at least has had the grace to say in his *Deutsche Rundschau* article of July 1947, to which I have already referred: 'Papen was not responsible either for the Reichstag dissolution or for restoring the S.A. Schleicher had already made these concessions before Papen was appointed.' He also writes that Hindenburg had insisted on new elections in a conversation with him on May 30. It therefore seems clear that Schleicher had already told Hindenburg of the Nazis' demands before I was called in. Schleicher presented the matter to me as involving Nazi toleration for the time being and collaboration in the Government in due course. If this goal was to be achieved, then the dissolution would have served some purpose. Our most important task was to try, even at this late hour, to tame the Nazis by involving them in the responsibilities of Government, especially as the Reparations Conference with the Allies had been arranged to take place within a fortnight. Whoever represented Germany would have bungled the situation badly if he had not assured himself, before proceeding to the conference, that he had a solid basis of support in the country.

I met Hitler for the first time on June 9, 1932. The initiative had come from me. I wanted to hear his version of his arrangement with Schleicher and to try to gauge what attitude the Nazis would adopt to my Government. We met in a flat belonging to Herr von Alvensleben, a friend of Schleicher. I found him curiously unimpressive. Press pictures had conveyed no idea of a dominating personality and I could detect no inner quality which might explain his extraordinary hold on the masses. He was wearing a dark blue suit and seemed the complete *petit-bourgeois*. He had an unhealthy complexion, and with his little moustache and curious hair style had an indefinable bohemian quality. His demeanour was modest and polite, and although I had heard much about the magnetic quality of his eyes, I do not remember being impressed by them.

After a few polite formalities I asked him for his views on the possibility of supporting my Government. He brought up his usual list of complaints – previous governments had shown a lamentable lack of statesmanship in excluding a political party with such wide support from its due share in the affairs of the State at a time when an attempt should be made to correct the errors of the Versailles Treaty and restore full German sovereignty. This struck me as a most important point, and as he talked about his party's aims I was struck by the fanatical insistence with which he presented his arguments. I realized that the fate of my Government would depend to a large extent on the willingness of this man and his followers to back me up, and that this would be the most difficult problem with which I should have to deal. He made it clear that he would not be content for long with a subordinate rôle and intended in due course to demand plenary powers for himself. 'I regard your Cabinet only as a temporary solution, and will continue my efforts to make my party the strongest in the country. The Chancellorship will then devolve on me,' he said.

We were together for about an hour. As I left, I realized that it was up to me not only to show that a determined Government could achieve success at the forthcoming international conference at Lausanne, but also to initiate a comprehensive programme to combat unemployment and radicalism, so that the electorate might feel there was still an alternative to the assumption of power by the Nazis. We started under every handicap. The treasury was literally empty and the Government could barely meet the civil servants' June salaries. We therefore had to adopt at least part of Brüning's last emergency decree and reduce them. We started work on the problem of constitutional reform, encouraged the farmers and embarked on an economic programme to relieve the unemployed. By now they numbered some six or seven million, not including those on half-time, which would have brought their numbers nearer twelve or thirteen million, of which a million and a half were young people. In the fourteen days before the Lausanne Conference we covered an immense amount of ground. We were determined that people both at home and abroad should know exactly where they stood with the new Government.

We also honoured Schleicher's undertaking to lift the ban on the S.A. The President signed an order to this effect on June 16, and accompanied it by a letter to the Minister of the Interior, in which he said, 'I have met the Government's request for the present regulations to be relaxed in the expectation that political activity throughout the country will become more orderly, and that all acts of violence will cease. I am determined, if these expectations are not realized, to use every means in my power to halt abuses, and I authorize you to make known my intention in this respect.'

The parties of the left pretended then, and continue to do so now, that the lifting of the ban on the Brownshirts was the first step in my hoisting the Nazis into the saddle. I have no doubt they find it convenient to look for a scapegoat. All that had happened was that equal rights for all parties, including both the Nazis and the Communists, had been restored. At any rate, this lasted only for a month. Street clashes soon started again, and on July 18 the Minister of the Interior introduced a ban on political demonstrations throughout the country. This applied to the uniformed formations of every party. In certain States, such as Bavaria and Baden, the lifting of the original ban on the S.A. was never carried out. Both these State Governments had control over their own police, and if they did not agree with the measures of the Central

Government, they were free to ignore its regulations. Nor is it true to say that the relaxation influenced the result of the elections on July 31 in the Nazis' favour. The general ban on demonstrations was issued two weeks before the poll, and the street clashes were more likely to induce responsible voters to support the more moderate parties.

When I began my work as Chancellor I did not even have anywhere to live in Berlin. The Presidential palace was undergoing repair and Hindenburg had asked me if he could occupy the Chancellor's private residence for six months. I could hardly refuse. In the end I was given a flat at the back of 78 Wilhelmstrasse, which was usually at the disposal of the Permanent Secretary of the Ministry of the Interior. It was in a state of considerable disrepair, but we managed to give my study a new coat of paint. The cost, I remember, was 42.50 marks. I mention this figure because my successor in the flat, Frick, who later became the Nazi Minister of the Interior, spent 30,000 marks in having it done up; while our present Western German Chancellor, Dr Adenauer, was reported in the press to have had 230,000 marks spent on the Villa Schaumburg at Bonn, and another 160,000 marks on its garden. Yet one would have thought that there was even more reason for thrift in 1950 than in 1932.

In the days that followed the fall of Brüning the left wing press was filled with accusations that he had been brought low by the intrigues of the Junkers. It was alleged that they had acquired vast wealth as a result of the *Osthilfe*, the system of State subsidy designed to pay off some of the high mortgages on their East Prussian estates. Under the leadership of Herr von Oldenburg-Januschau they were said to have obstructed all plans for agricultural reform and to have exerted tremendous pressure on Hindenburg to dismiss Brüning, whom they called an agrarian bolshevist.

The former Prime Minister of Prussia, Otto Braun, even went so far in later years as to suggest that President Hindenburg had himself been compromised by the *Osthilfe* scandal, and had appointed Hitler as Chancellor to avoid the risk of public exposure. But when this was said Hindenburg was dead, and all my efforts to protect his name from an attack that exceeded even the bounds of defamation current in those days, came to nothing. Braun refused to publish a detraction, as did Dr Pechel, the owner of the *Deutsche Rundschau*, in which this accusation was first published. There is no space here to reprint all the material that proves these accusations to be false. But it is absolutely untrue to suggest that the *Osthilfe* affair played any part in bringing Hitler to power, or that it was used to bring pressure to bear on the President.

I must, however, make a few comments on the accusation that the big landowners east of the Elbe were responsible for the fall of Brüning, and whether there was, in fact, any scandal connected with the administration of the *Osthilfe*. All the fairy tales in the left wing press at the time have been reproduced in their entirety since the war. The most damaging accusation was made in the memoirs of Dr Meissner,[1] Presidential *chef de cabinet* under Ebert, Hindenburg and Hitler. According to Dr Meissner, three of these landowners, Oldenburg-Januschau and two of his friends, von Batotzki and von Rohr-Demin, visited Hindenburg at Neudeck in May 1932 to try to persuade him to veto the agricultural reforms planned by Brüning. Freiherr von Gayl, Minister of the Interior in my Cabinet, himself held an inquiry which proved that Oldenburg and Batotzki had no contact at this time with the President, either at Neudeck or anywhere else. Herr von Rohr, who is still alive, has declared under oath that he has never been to Neudeck in his life.

The series of post-war 'revelations' concerning this period rely largely on a book about Hindenburg written in 1935 by Rudolf Olden, a former member of the editorial staff of the *Berliner Tageblatt*. Olden accuses me of having led the Junker attack that resulted in the fall of Brüning, with a view to persuading the President to accept Hitler as Chancellor in order to prevent the details of the *Osthilfe* scandal from becoming public. 'The key to the capitulation to Hitler,' he writes, 'lies in the word Neudeck. This family estate was presented to Hindenburg on his eightieth birthday as a gift from German industry. It was then enlarged and subsidised by the *Osthilfe*, and when the scandal of the administration of these funds threatened to become public, Hindenburg preferred to betray the State to Hitler rather than risk exposure. Once again the nation was sacrificed for the benefit of the old ruling class.'

In fact, neither Hindenburg nor his son either claimed or

---

[1] Dr Otto Meissner: *Der Schicksalsweg des Deutschen Volkes 1918–45*. Hoffmann & Campe, Hamburg, 1951.

received a penny from the *Osthilfe*. The only 'accusation' that may hold water was that Neudeck had been assigned to Oscar von Hindenburg in order to avoid death duties. Such arrangements are common in many countries.

The *Osthilfe* affair and Brüning's agricultural settlement plan played no part in my own activities. Baron Braun, the Minister for Agriculture in my Cabinet, who now lives in the United States, has already published an affidavit confirming this.

The plain fact is that at the time of the world economic crisis agriculture was in a precarious condition in almost every country, and had to receive state subsidies of one sort or another. In the United States this was done under the New Deal, and in Germany through the *Osthilfe*. Dr Schlange-Schoeningen, now German diplomatic representative in London, and a member of Brüning's cabinet at the time, has revealed in his post-war book, *Am Tage Danach*[1] that a million and a half acres of land east of the Elbe were mortgaged at 150 per cent of their value, and that another three million acres were mortgaged up to 100 per cent. These debts, amounting to almost two milliard marks, were divided equally between large estates and small-holdings. If the mortgages had been called in, it would have been necessary to auction most of Germany's three frontier provinces. It can therefore be seen that in spite of the left wing opposition, state assistance was an absolute necessity.

It is almost inevitable that certain irregularities should have crept into the administration of such a large scheme of financial assistance. The Reichstag formed a commission to investigate the *Osthilfe*, and its report, published on May 25, 1933, was signed by, among others, representatives of the Zentrum Party, the Bavarian People's Party, and the German People's Party. Article IV of this report reads: 'Discussions in the Reichstag budget committee during January 1933 gave rise to violent attacks in the left wing press against officials administering the *Osthilfe*, in which reference was made to gigantic scandals, corruption, etc. This commission desires to state that none of the twenty-six cases of alleged corruption on the part of officials have been in any way proved, and the allegations must be considered to be without foundation.'

I have had access to the papers left by Gayl at his death, and

[1] Hans Schlange-Schoeningen: *The Morning After*. Gollancz, London, 1948.

among them is an important document so far unknown to most people, and for which no one will now accept responsibility. It is a draft law of the most radical nature for the resettlement of the East Prussian provinces, and was apparently drawn up in Adam Stegerwald's Ministry of Labour. It seems to have been worked out in agreement with Dr Schlange-Schoeningen, the Minister of Agriculture, although this he now denies.

Sir Horace Rumbold, the British Ambassador, reported to his Government on June 9, 1932,[1] that Brüning was preparing a plan 'providing for the settlement on bankrupt estates in East Prussia of a large number of unemployed. Dr Brüning has subsequently stated that it was intended to settle some 600,000 persons on these estates, i.e., 10 per cent of the peak figures of unemployment in Germany.'

With the poor quality of the soil in these territories, he would have needed to give each settler some sixty acres, involving an area of thirty-six million acres for the 600,000 settlers. The Ministry of Labour, which had a strong Trade Union bias, was in charge of the resettlement programme. It is not surprising that thousands of families whose homes had been in this area for centuries despaired of what might happen to them, if the issue should be decided by a bureaucracy so unfamiliar with their problems.

It is possible that Brüning knew nothing of this draft law, and although it must have got into the hands of the President, there is no means of telling who gave it to him. It is probably true that this question of the resettlement of the eastern territories played a part in Hindenburg's decision to make a change in the Chancellorship. But it certainly did not play an important part, and it was completely untrue for the Left to present the affair as a scandal involving a small clique of irresponsible landowners who sought, by conniving at the fall of Brüning, to hide the squandering of public funds voted for their assistance. The roots of the problem struck much deeper than this and it is high time that the truth was recognized.

★ ★ ★

Before leaving this account of the critical political events in Germany in 1932, I would like to emphasize once again what I

[1] *Documents on British Foreign Policy 1919–1939.* Second Series, Vol. III. No. 129. H.M.S.O. London, 1948.

consider to have been the main cause of the failure of the Weimar democracy. There is one fundamental reason why the Liberal Democratic ideas, proclaimed in 1848 at the Church of St Paul, in Frankfurt, never achieved success. When the Weimar Republic tried to embody these principles in the form of a Constitution, they forgot the one factor that makes democracy work in the Anglo-Saxon countries: that is the two-party system, which enables government and opposition to succeed one another, according to the needs and mood of the moment. There were eight parties represented at the Frankfurt Congress,[1] and their number had grown to thirty in the declining days of the Weimar Republic. Our parties were, and are in Western Germany to this day, founded on a basis of unalterable doctrine which has to be defended as if it were a religious dogma.

In America and Great Britain the two main parties are each formed on a basis of practical policies. Even the Labour Party which came to power in Great Britain in 1945 is not doctrinaire in the sense that the German Social Democrats have always been. The continent of Europe as a whole has only provided a very poor imitation of the Anglo-Saxon model. I would have thought that the disastrous consequences of splinter parties and the results of too narrow a defence of party doctrine would have taught us something; but post-war developments in Germany today show little sign of it. At least the parties based on the conception of religious denomination have had the sense to combine in one main middle-class party.

The politicians who held office during the Weimar Republic were faced with the problem not only of bringing Germany's economy to life again, but of giving her political existence a completely new content. None of the parties, either of the right or the left, can escape their joint responsibility. Their justified attempts to restore German sovereignty had given rise to conceptions of nationalism which took no account of Germany's obligations as a European state. International considerations played far too small a part and there was no statesman sufficiently able to give this aspect of the country's affairs its proper emphasis. The

[1] This refers to the Frankfurt Parliament of the late eighteen-forties (and early fifties) which was the first, if much frustrated expression of democracy in German political life.

narrow conception of nationalism which gradually grew up aroused passions in the whole nation, which fell an easy prey to the extreme and egocentric programme of National Socialism.

The German National Party's conception of conservatism lacked constructive and statesmanlike ideas as much as did the theories of the Social Democrats, who had become bogged down in doctrinaire Marxism. It was a tragedy that the Nationalist leader, Hugenberg, was never a true representative of enlightened conservatism. Formerly the financial head of Krupps, he was too steeped in commercial traditions to appreciate the spiritual values of true conservative policy.

The Social Democrats had emerged in 1919 as the principal pillars of the country, with 13.8 million votes. Even at the height of his legitimate support, shortly before he was made Chancellor, in the election of July 31, 1932, Hitler gained only 13.7 million votes. The Social Democrats were the dominant or Government party in the Reich and in Prussia almost without interruption for eleven years. Yet their constructive contribution to providing a European rôle for the Weimar Republic amounted to practically nothing. They were bound by ideological ties to the working-class parties in every other country, yet they failed miserably to instigate any common European policy to meet the disasters resulting from the fulfilment of reparations and the catastrophes due to the world economic crisis. The victorious powers may also like to reflect that they themselves were at their most difficult and intransigent during the period when the Socialists held this dominant position. When the situation got out of hand in 1930, the Socialists, at the very moment when their support was most necessary, deliberately retreated from their share of the responsibility.

My own party, the Zentrum, deserved even greater censure. For years I tried to convince my colleagues that one of the basic tenets of democracy was the regular interchange of government and opposition; but all to no purpose. I always contested their exaggerated collaboration with the Social Democrats, particularly in Prussia. It was this that held up a number of essential reforms, especially that of the Constitution, which would have been the only way of dealing with the abuses of democracy which had gradually developed. It was a tragedy that a man of Brüning's qualities should have made it impossible, when he became leader of the party again in June, for the new Cabinet to carry out those reforms which he himself recognized to be necessary. Everything in his power was done to restore the authority of the parties and combat that of my Cabinet. In view of his opinions concerning the Nazis, his failure to support the measures I proposed to check their rise and their totalitarian intentions was absolutely incomprehensible.

There were only two ways of meeting the situation by democratic means. One solution would have been to agree on a joint programme with the opposition and form a coalition Government. The right wing parties would then have had to abandon their propaganda of unrealizable promises and bear their share of responsibility for constructive co-operation. Their supporters would then have realized that there are practical limits to everything and would have lost much of their fanaticism. This step was an imperative necessity in 1930 and 1931, but it was not taken.

The other possibility required the removal of the conditions favouring the opposition's growth. The increasing radicalism of the Nazis was based on the constant increase in unemployment and the proletarianization of large masses of the population. It was essential to combat these two evils through policies of social security. Brüning chose exactly the opposite method. His policy of deflation only increased economic distress, led to the further impoverishment of the population, and to increasing radicalism. In fact, neither of these two possible solutions was put into practice, although the political parties of those days, and their descendants, now wash their hands of the responsibility. Brüning was an upright and straightforward man who attempted, according to his own lights, to do what he considered best for his country. But his personal unselfishness was matched by a political blindness that led him to continue the policy of fulfilling reparations when the internal situation in the country made the consequences of this policy disastrous.

CHAPTER X

LAUSANNE

High hopes – Conversation with Herriot – I present our demands – I suggest a consultative pact – Difficulties arise – MacDonald intervenes – Agreement on reparations – A final blow – Bad eggs and rotten apples

SETTLEMENT of the reparations problem had become one of the most urgent aspects of the world economic crisis. In his talks at Bessinges earlier in the year, to which I have already referred, Brüning had laid the foundation for German participation in an international conference to discuss all the implications, but the actual date had been postponed time and again. It is easy to understand his resentment at being deprived of the results of so much work. But when he claims that success was almost within his grasp – 'a hundred yards from the finishing line', as he himself expressed it – I can only say that he was over-optimistic. However, for many years his claim gave my political opponents yet another stick with which to belabour me. Brüning, they assert, would have had much more success at Lausanne.

In Volume III of the *Documents on British Foreign Policy*,[1] to which I shall frequently refer in this chapter, Mr Ramsay Mac-Donald is reported (document 103) as having stated on April 23, 1932, 'that Dr Brüning had said, privately . . . that, "he (Dr Brüning) would be accommodating towards any face-saving scheme such as that Germany should at some time pay some further capital charge. This would involve borrowing the money to pay it, and the sum would need to be small . . ." '

There is no reason to suppose that Brüning was not honestly convinced of his imminent success. He maintains that the victorious powers had promised him that they would reduce the outstanding reparations payments to five milliard marks and would accord Germany equality in the field of armaments. My answer to this is

[1]*Documents on British Foreign Policy 1919-1939.* Second Series, Vol. III. H.M.S.O. London, 1948.

that I obtained a reduction to three milliard marks under conditions which meant, in practice, that no further payment would be necessary. As far as re-armament was concerned, the Allies had no intention of making any such concessions. I went to Lausanne with far higher hopes and intentions than Brüning probably ever entertained. I was firmly convinced that the cessation of all reparations payments was not only an absolute necessity, but the goal of any responsible statesman. The economic idiocy and the disastrous consequences of this system of tribute had become painfully obvious. But I wished to go much further than this, and reach agreements with the outside world which would permit what could best be called the moral rearmament of Germany. If my country was to play its true part in the peaceful development of Europe, the causes of our inferiority complex would have to be removed. Germany had been reduced to a second-class nation at Versailles and deprived of many of the attributes of sovereignty. To the limitations placed on our purely defensive armaments were added the defencelessness of the Rhineland, the corridor that cut off East Prussia from the Reich, the international control of our Saar territory, and above all, paragraph 231 of the Versailles Treaty, the German war guilt clause. The development of the Nazi Party was based largely on its exploitation of these grievances. They accused every successive German Government of lacking patriotism, because of the failure to right these wrongs. The settlement of the reparations problem was largely incidental. Our greatest need was for moral support.

When the German delegation arrived in Lausanne on June 15, I made it my first business to contact the representatives of the world's press. Without waiting for the visits or requests for interviews of the assembled journalists, I got straight into my car and went down to press headquarters. This was something new from a German Chancellor and caused a minor sensation. I was surrounded by correspondents, to whom I expressed the hopes that Germany was pinning on the conference, and asked for the objective support of the world's organs of public opinion.

The next day, I paid a visit to the French Prime Minister, M. Herriot, in the Lausanne Palace Hotel. He was most cordial and I had no difficulty in establishing warm personal contact. We had a private talk lasting an hour and a half, in which I spoke frankly of the results I hoped to achieve at the conference. I gave him a full account of the background to the change of Government in Germany and emphasized that I was in a position to speak for the opposition as well. Our talk raised my hopes of advancing the French and German community of interest within the framework of the conference.

The first session took place in the banqueting hall of the Hotel Beau Rivage on June 17. The public was not admitted. It was my first experience of a gathering that included representatives of almost every European country. I had prepared my brief extremely carefully, and it was based to a very large extent on the memorandum which the Brüning Government had drawn up in the previous November. Moreover, I had agreed with my advisers that I should make my first speech in French. The usual thing was for each Prime Minister to speak in his own language, but as we knew that most of the Allied representatives did not speak German, we thought that my speech would have more effect if it was made in a language of which most people had a working knowledge. My experience has always been that even the best interpreter cannot reproduce the exact impression given by the original. I was criticized in the German press for doing this, so I made my final speech to the conference in German. The effect was as I expected. Everybody chattered throughout the speech, and when the interpreter gave his version, very little interest was aroused.

In my opening remarks I made it clear that we were not going to argue our case on purely legal grounds, or question the validity of earlier international agreements that Germany had signed. Our only interest was in dealing with the perils of the actual situation and how they might best be overcome. I gave a general survey of the world crisis in an attempt to show how the reparations payments had contributed to it. I compared the situation in 1929, when the Young Plan was signed, to the situation three years later, with mass unemployment everywhere, private and national bankruptcy, and the threatening social situation that had resulted.

At the same time I drew the delegates' attention to the little-appreciated consequences of our inflation. Foreign public opinion had come to assume that the liquidation of our internal indebtedness must be an advantage. But in social terms the inflation had been a disaster. Broad sections of the middle class had been ruined, and the country's financial reserves liquidated. The reparation demands therefore represented impracticable means to an un-attainable end. I appealed to the assembled powers to realize that a moratorium or similar temporary solution could never solve the problem. Immediate steps must be taken to rescue the world from total catastrophe, and the crisis could only be overcome by the co-operation of every European country. I told them my Government was prepared to take all the internal measures necessary to meet their share of responsibility. We wanted to serve as an equal partner in the reconstruction of a unified and peaceful Europe. I was frequently interrupted by applause and there seemed little doubt that my arguments had been received sympathetically.

I cannot ask for better evidence of what took place in the diffi-cult days that followed than the British Foreign Policy documents to which I have referred. They show with almost dramatic force how I tried day by day to abolish the root cause of European in-stability – the lack of mutual trust – by placing Franco-German relations on a new and more solid basis. Mr MacDonald at first played the rôle of honest broker with great skill and pertinacity. British policy envisaged the cancellation of our reparations obliga-tions in exchange for German participation in a 'political truce'. But towards the end he abandoned this rôle.

The new French Cabinet was three days younger than mine. But Herriot's fear of being ousted if he should return home with an unpopular agreement was infinitely greater than mine. This obsession with his internal position destroyed all hopes of statesman-ship on a European plane. He regarded closer ties with Britain and a large final payment of seven milliard Reichsmarks as being more important than any reconciliation with us. The result was that this last great opportunity of giving Europe a new start collapsed in a lamentable squabble about reparations payments.

As soon as it became clear that we were demanding the end of all these payments, there was a short recess while the delegations got in touch with their Governments. Herriot himself returned to Paris. His position was not an easy one, as his Cabinet was just preparing new schemes of taxation which still counted on the resumption of German payments. The financial experts in the French delegation were in almost constant session, and we learned that they were studying the possibility of demanding one final payment in the form of a mortgage on the German state railways. Schwerin-Krosigk, our Finance Minister, was instructed to prepare a brief to prove that this demand was impracticable and unacceptable. Count Grandi, the Italian Foreign Minister, paid me a visit in our headquarters at the Savoy Hotel, and we discussed with Neurath, how much support we could expect from the Italian delegation.

As soon as the leaders of the delegations were back in Lausanne, I tried to impress both on Herriot and MacDonald that they must realize mine was probably the last 'bourgeois' Government likely to hold power in Germany. If we returned home without achieving any success, we would be succeeded by the extremists, either of the left or of the right. Though Herriot has described this argument as blackmail, he continued to show considerable understanding for my Government's difficult position. I told him the conference would have achieved no lasting result if it did not lead to closer and more confident relations between our two countries.

The idea of Franco-German friendship has always been one of my chief obsessions, and now the time seemed ripe to take a practical step. In spite of the warnings of the highly intelligent and competent Permanent Secretary of the German Foreign Office, von Bülow, who sought to damp my enthusiasm, I tried to cut through the maze of diplomatic niceties by some drastic stroke. I suggested to Herriot that France and Germany should sign a consultative pact. We would undertake to subject our European policies to prior consultation with the French Government, and would expect them to do the same. It seemed the only way to restore relations of mutual confidence between the two countries. The important thing was to remove France's fear of Germany. The main question was how this was to be done. It was clear that if Germany was going to demand the revision of those clauses in the Versailles Treaty which effected her sovereignty and national honour, she must, in return, offer France some guarantee of security.

France and Britain had been enemies for centuries. Now there was complete understanding and confidence between the two countries. This alone was proof that ancient enmities could be surmounted if only the will was present. If France would be prepared to accord us the rights of a sovereign nation and allow us to possess the same armaments as other states, then Germany would be prepared to make some exceptional concession to convince the French of our peaceful intentions. The simplest way would be that of an outright alliance, but I realized that public opinion in both countries was not ready for this. The first step would therefore have to be the forming of something like a combined general staff. I suggested that on a basis of reciprocity, French General Staff officers should be allowed access to all the departments of our General Staff. France would then be informed on all German military matters. Some such step as this would do more to calm French fears than any number of political assurances. I then requested that this consultative pact should be crowned by a resolution of all the powers represented at Lausanne cancelling paragraph 231 of the Versailles Treaty, specifying Germany's war guilt.

On June 20 I told Mr MacDonald that: 'This Conference must give the French the idea that they have got greater security, and this should soften the political public opinion in France. . . . I want to get the whole Franco-German question settled once and for all. It is fundamental for Europe. Herriot ought to want it, too.'[1]

The next day I sent Mr MacDonald a letter, in which I explained that it would be impossible to accept any new obligations, such as a mortgage on the German railway system. However, I was prepared to make these constructive suggestions: German participation in all financial and economic measures for the reconstruction of Europe; we would be prepared, within the framework of a five-year disarmament convention, and in spite of the equality of rights that had been granted to us, to refrain from increasing our armaments to the permitted level; we were prepared to contribute to a lessening of the tension in Europe by entering into a consultative pact between France, Germany, Italy and Great Britain for the purpose of ensuring French security.

In spite of the difficulties he was having over the reparation problem, Herriot was apparently attracted by the suggestions I had made for improving Franco-German relations. He asked one of his secretaries of state, M. de Laboulay, to work out my proposals in the form of a draft agreement. De Laboulay had been Counsellor of the French Embassy in Berlin for many years, and I knew him as a fair-minded man and an able diplomat. Our detailed conversations soon resulted in a written draft. Herriot seemed to think that the next step must be to inform his British partner of our plans and obtain his agreement. To this I had no objection.

Matters now took an entirely unexpected turn. MacDonald

1 Op. cit. Vol. III, No. 141

appeared not only surprised, but appalled at what had been going on between Herriot and myself. I can only guess at the terms in which he expressed his astonishment to the French Prime Minister, but when, in response to an invitation, I called on him the next day, he informed me tersely that any such Franco-German pact was entirely unacceptable to the British Government. He begged me to abandon the whole idea, giving it as his opinion that a close *rapprochement* of this kind between Germany and France would upset the balance of European power.

On June 23 there came an unexpected intervention by President Hoover. A year earlier his suggestion of a reparations moratorium had come temporarily to Germany's assistance. Now he made concrete suggestions for general disarmament. Both Italy and Germany gave his proposals their fullest support, but in France they received little support, except from Léon Blum, and the proposed reduction in naval strength had little attraction for the British. The same day detailed talks between the French and British delegations in Lausanne came to an end. From what we could learn, it seemed that MacDonald's attempts to get the French to agree to a British plan for the settlement of the reparations problem had not succeeded. The conference was by now getting into severe difficulties.

The position of the Herriot Cabinet was becoming increasingly insecure. Their differences of opinion with the British considerably lessened the likelihood of their remaining in office, and my hopes of reaching an all-embracing agreement began to fade. The Belgian Foreign Minister, M. Hymans, and his financial adviser, M. Franqui, approached me with a view to acting as mediators, but there seemed little basis for us to work on. French proposals were taking the form of a further three-year moratorium, to be followed by a final payment of some seven milliard gold marks, the exact figure to be worked out by a committee of experts. This again I felt unable to accept, and Herriot left for Paris.

During this fresh lull I had occasion to attend a meeting on June 24 of the German colony in Lausanne. A number of German students from all over Switzerland took part, but its chief interest lay in the presence of many Austrians, including the Federal Chancellor, Dr Dollfuss. I knew him quite well, as he had always been a prominent member of the Austrian Peasant Movement, and we had met at a number of agricultural conferences. He had come to Lausanne to try to convince the heads of the various Governments of the necessity for a new international loan for Austria, and had already visited me that afternoon to tell me of his troubles.

His negotiations with Herriot had been disappointing. The French, as usual, were trying to attach political conditions to the granting of any new loan. He had been told that further support would only be forthcoming if the Austrian Government acknowledged, in the most formal terms, that they intended to adhere to the Treaty of St Germain and the Geneva Protocol, and would refrain from any *rapprochement* with Germany. This was the French reaction to Austria's attempt to place her economy on a sounder basis by entering into a customs union with Germany.

The German Foreign Office had usually taken the attitude that Austria's national pride could not be expected to accept discriminatory political demands as part of economic agreements. The Austrians had also been chary of permitting any such undertaking to affect their relationship with Germany. Faced with imminent financial disaster, Dollfuss was therefore in a cleft stick. Von Bülow had given me a background sketch of our policy towards Austria and had asked me to turn a deaf ear to Dollfuss' requests. Germany was not prepared to permit a widening of the artificial rift between the two countries by the imposition of new political obligations.

After Dollfuss had given me a description of his difficulties, I said to him, 'My dear friend, I am going to make a break with German policy in this respect. Our Foreign Office will not like it much, but I prefer to apply a little common sense. You have got to have this money. As far as I am concerned, the more the Western Powers let you have, the better. Sign all the political clauses concerning your relationship with Germany that they force upon you. I shall take no exception. One of these days our two countries will be united and then we shall see how the money is to be paid back.' Dollfuss' face broke into a smile and he thanked me heartily.

Herriot soon returned, and on June 27 had a conversation with MacDonald in which he explained that: '. . . if France abandoned reparation payments, she would be given economic and political compensations. . . . Herr von Papen had very definitely given him the impression in more than one conversation that these compensations would be given. . . . He added that Herr von Papen had spoken to him of a military alliance between France and Germany and of continuous contact between the General Staffs. . . . [Herriot had] put the alternative of reparation payments or compensations to the French Cabinet, and that he had urged very strongly that Franco-German reconciliation was better than a mere money payment. The Cabinet had accepted this view.'[1]

In giving these full details of what had been a highly confidential offer on my part, Herriot did not reveal that we had only spoken of the military alliance as a distant goal, and seems for some reason to have been under the impression that I had modified my opinions after a short visit I had paid to Berlin. This was completely unfounded and can only be due to some misrepresentation by M. Lauzanne, of the *Matin*, with whom I had had a confidential conversation, hoping it would help to rally French public opinion.

That same day I had a long talk with MacDonald: 'Herr von Papen continued that Germany had had to be negative on the reparation question. Elsewhere they had done their best to be constructive. . . . They had appealed to the French to put aside the troubled atmosphere of the last twelve years and to begin a new era. . . . he had done all he could to clear away the obstacles between France and Germany, even in the face of domestic criticism. He wanted to envelop reparations in some bigger scheme for Europe. . . .'[2]

MacDonald then intimated confidentially that France would in no circumstances abandon her demand for final payment, particularly as the United States were opposed to the cancellation of reparations, and then continued: 'He saw, however, in the Press suggestions of a military alliance. Any such idea would upset everything. It would completely destroy any chance of getting the U.S.A. to look favourably on such action as might be taken at Lausanne in regard to economic questions. . . . He felt himself in a state of bewilderment. . . . Herr von Papen asked permission to break in at this point. He had spoken of the French feeling that they lacked security. . . . France had the advantage of the Locarno Pact, which carried a British guarantee; they had the Kellogg Pact; they had the tremendous strength of their Eastern frontier, and they had their army. He had gone on to ask whether, if France had an alliance with Germany, it would give them any better security. . . . He had been misrepresented.' After this emphatic rejection of my

---

[1] Op. cit. Vol. III, No. 148   [2] Op. cit. Vol. III, No. 149

idea of a complete reconciliation with France, the British Premier concluded: 'He felt that things were going from bad to worse and emphasised the dangers to Germany which failure to reach agreement in Lausanne would have.'[1]

The next day Neurath and I had a fresh discussion with MacDonald and Herriot: 'Mr MacDonald said that he had been much disturbed by the communications made to him by M. Herriot and Herr von Papen on the previous evening. . . . He feared that what M. Herriot and Herr von Papen were doing at the moment was simply to increase what he might call their "military equipment" for the "battle" which they had fixed for the following day.' Both Herriot and I restated our positions. I emphasized that as far as I was concerned nothing had changed, and Herriot added that 'he wished to pay a tribute to the loyalty of the German Chancellor. . . . He had frequently said that he had only to congratulate himself on his relations with the German Delegates. . . . He understood that, if they could bring back from Lausanne a Franco-German reconciliation, that would be more important than any *solde*.' Moreover, Herr von Papen's suggestions were 'not essential measures or measures of reconciliation'.[2]

I repeated my offer again point by point: the general fund for the economic recovery of Europe, the voluntary restriction of our rearmament rights, and the consultative pact. To avoid embarrassing MacDonald I refrained from referring to my idea of a joint General Staff. However, it was quite clear that the atmosphere had changed completely over the last twenty-four hours. The British had obviously given the French to understand that any such *rapprochement* between France and Germany was most unwelcome, and that France should reject my offer. Herriot in fact replied that Germany's contribution to any such general fund would be of no positive advantage to France, that the rearmament question should not be coupled with that of reparations, and that he was prepared to study the suggestion of a consultative pact, but . . .

As the conversation continued, I insisted that the whole problem of equality in rearmament and all the discriminatory clauses of the Versailles Treaty should be dealt with. In a long discussion with Herriot I asked him to state what were his requirements for greater French security against Germany. He avoided the question by

[1] Op. cit. Vol. III, No. 149   [2] op. cit. Vol. III, No. 150

saying that he was not prepared to talk about political guarantees. He was only interested in the payment question. In the end I had to recognize that the French placed their friendship with Britain above any reconciliation with us. But the British had been most short-sighted in their policy.

It was the old policy of divide and rule all over again. It had served Britain's purposes for centuries, but her Prime Minister had apparently not recognized that it had become too narrow for modern European requirements. Nor did he seem to realize that the restoration to health and strength of a poverty-stricken Germany, threatened as it was by Russian totalitarianism, would guarantee Central European security in a form which could only be to Britain's advantage. When I saw MacDonald I did my best to argue with him, but the full force of my persuasive faculties made no impression on this stiff, unapproachable and unimaginative Scotsman. He simply would not see that the peace of Europe depended, in the first instance, on Franco-German amity.

My hopes had suffered a bitter blow. The purpose of the conference had now been reduced to the minor but difficult problem of settling the reparations question, which was to a very large extent a *cause jugée*. It was abundantly clear that the British attitude would prevent Herriot from giving any real support to my suggestions when he returned to Paris. I tried to recover what I could from the wreck by endeavouring to arrange some sort of resolution concerning the war guilt clause. This would have presented no great difficulty within the framework of a Franco-German agreement, but taken out of the context of the discriminatory terms of the Versailles Treaty, it represented a much more difficult concession. I can remember the indignation with which the Belgian delegate rejected the very idea. 'How can we be expected to reverse a historical judgment which is based to a very large extent on the German attack on Belgium?' he said.

As was only to be expected, Herriot told me that to his regret it would not be possible to continue our negotiations. France could not afford to risk a break with Great Britain. What he did not tell me was that he had adopted my idea of a consultative pact, and intended, more or less behind my back, to sign such a pact with Great Britain and the other nations represented at Lausanne. I learned of this development only after the conference had ended, and I must confess that this somewhat underhand manœuvre

caused me great offence. It is true that Germany was later invited
to take part, but after the breakdown of our personal negotiations
this was no longer possible.

The last week in Lausanne was taken up with a considerable
tussle to reach some agreement over reparations. The British
delegation was subjected to a time limit, and MacDonald, whose
presence was required at Ottawa, threatened to leave the conference. I was in no less of a hurry to get home, where a tremendous
amount of work had piled up. The German delegation was now
in a serious quandary. Should we maintain our firm attitude,
break off the conference, and return home empty-handed? The
measures that still had to be put into effect in Germany itself would
thereby have been seriously prejudiced. The left wing parties
would be given a wonderful opportunity of claiming that Brüning
in the circumstances, would have achieved a big success, and that
failure at Lausanne was due to the incapability of the new Government. All this would have had its effect on the elections due to
take place at the end of July. After a long discussion, we decided
that it would be better to return with some modest achievements
rather than with none at all. It was up to us to provide a bridge for
more hopeful developments in the future.

It is quite impossible to give here an account of the day-to-day
battle to settle the amount of the final payment, or of my efforts
to give the world the feeling that a complete and final solution of
our differences had been arrived at. Most people realized that any
further payment was impossible, and that if any such payment was
agreed in theory it would only represent a new and fateful deception. 'Herr von Papen asked why then the world should not be
told? Mr MacDonald said it would smash up the whole arrangement to do that.' But Mr MacDonald had already said a breach
must be avoided at all costs. He had heard that we were intent on
obtaining a cancellation of the Versailles war guilt clause. 'He
thought that might be managed in the event of an agreement.'[1]

But Herriot found even this impossible: '...the German Delegation was trying to settle the Reparation question . . . and the
question of the responsibility for the War all for a payment of
2.6 milliards of marks. He could not go home under those circumstances. . . . All this was humiliation for France.'[2] He made this

---

[1] Op. cit. Vol. III, No. 166   [2] Op. cit. Vol. III, No. 175

Lausanne. *Left to right*: M. Renkin (Belgium), Signor Grandi, Herr von Neurath, Herr von Papen, M. Herriot, Mr Duncan Sandys, M. Bonnet, Mr Ramsay MacDonald and, standing behind him, Sir Maurice Hankey (now Lord Hankey)

Dissolution of the Reichstag; the defeat of the Papen Cabinet

remark at a meeting between the British and French delegations on July 5, when he repeated again the details of my suggestions for co-operation between our two General Staffs – a confidential offer which he should not have passed on to MacDonald. But he wanted no political agreement. Mr Macdonald remarked that he was sure M. Herriot would never enter into a secret agreement.

That afternoon I saw MacDonald again. The protocol states: 'Mr MacDonald reported to Herr von Papen the reception by the French of his account of the offer which the Germans had made and described to him how greatly surprised he and Mr Chamberlain had been to hear the declaration of M. Herriot that he declined to accept any political condition whatever as part of the settlement.'[1] On July 6, Mr Chamberlain remarked to Count Schwerin-Krosigk: 'In fact we had been completely bewildered by what seemed to us an unaccountable *volte-face* on the part of the French.'[2]

What is one to say to such hypocrisy?

The remark is even more astonishing in view of what we now know to have occurred on the previous day, the 5th, when the British delegation handed the French the draft of a consultative pact, with this remark by the British Prime Minister: 'On all points raised by Germany and arising, now and in the future, in connection with the liberation of Germany from her obligations under the Treaty of Versailles, His Majesty's Government would return no definite answer to the German Government until they had first talked the matter over with the French Government. . . . The object of this understanding would be to protect both Governments against the dangers of piecemeal approaches by the German Government. . . . Candour is our policy.'[3]

This step was in direct negation of my earnest attempts to re-store mutual confidence in Europe. My plan for a consultative pact was turned into an instrument against Germany. The full account was presented on January 30, 1933, when Hitler came to power.

Tense negotiations had brought the French to the point where they were prepared to settle for a final payment of three milliard marks. This sum was only to be paid when Germany's balance of payments should be sufficiently strengthened by new international loans to make it possible. For our part, we had made up our minds

[1] Op. cit. Vol. III, No. 176   [2] Op. cit. Vol. III, No. 177
[3] Op. cit. Vol. III, No. 172

that the policy of my predecessors, of bolstering Germany's economy and finding the means to pay the reparations instalments on the basis of foreign loans, must finally be abandoned. If there were no further loans there could be no further payments, and our obligations would be purely theoretical. But the arrangements would make it possible for Herriot to appear before the French Chamber and declare: 'You see, Gentlemen, I have saved something from the wreck. France is to get another three milliards in future payments.' I remember well our final discussion on this point, when he said to me, '*Ne pouvez-vous pas comprendre l'impossibilité de me présenter à la Chambre et déclarer que la France ne reçevra plus un sou de votre part? C'est impossible! On me déblayerait à la même heure!*' This statesman felt himself entirely at the mercy of public opinion. Our concession of the three milliard figure seemed small enough, but it was to prove a millstone round my neck.

The evening the conference ended I addressed the German nation over the radio. I could give no hint of the defeat I had suffered in trying to create a new moral atmosphere for Germany's recovery, nor could I disclose that this was due to France's rejection of my wider proposals. All that remained was for me to present the result of the reparations negotiations in the most favourable light possible. In fact, the burden of our obligations had at long last been lifted. Under the terms of the agreement it was clear that in practice no further payment would be made, and I was able to explain that our undertaking was a psychological concession to our former enemies.

The whole problem of tariffs and trade restrictions had not even been touched, and had formed no part of the agenda of the Lausanne conference. On the contrary, America's New Deal and the decisions of the Ottawa conference served only to strengthen these barriers.

The Western Powers may well consider their share of responsibility for what followed. Their attitude at Lausanne, and their refusal to make the slightest concession which might have eased the Germans' sense of frustration and resentment, led three years later to Hitler's putting into force, unilaterally, by more violent methods, all the concessions for which I had begged. Germany's last bourgeois Government was simply not given a chance and there was no way of halting the rising tide of radicalism. I had been determined to reach international agreement by means of pacts and peaceful negotiation. Back in Germany, on July 12, I held a press conference, at which I attempted to prove that I had tried to put an end to a situation which had been gradually built up under previous Governments since the signing of the Versailles Treaty, and I added: 'The one thing we were not prepared to do was to resolve the situation by denying the validity of international agreements that Germany had been forced to sign, or by methods which do not belong in a modern state governed by the rule of law.' Hitler was not so scrupulous.

The Lausanne conference actually ended on July 9, and the payment of war debts, which had been postponed for all nations while the conference was in progress, was again postponed until such time as the agreement had been signed and ratified. In his closing speech MacDonald emphasized how difficult it had been to reach an agreement. Nations, like people, he said, are the slaves of their memories. The conference had been the end of an old chapter and the beginning of a new book. The whole system of reparation and war debt payments had weighed heavily on every country and had been the cause of all their difficulties. A simple and sensible solution had been found, and Germany had been drawn in to the work of European reconstruction. But he warned that there would be no security unless there was agreement on disarmament. In my own speech I declared myself satisfied with the result of the conference, but made it clear that Germany's contribution to European co-operation required much wider premises, and that financial arrangements were not enough. We signed our agreement under the golden seal of the city of Lausanne, first used in 1525 to cement the pact between the cantons of Berne, Freiburg and Lausanne.

The reception in the German press was, to say the least of it, cool. The left wing newspapers found the results of the conference shameful. Brüning, they declared, would never have agreed to a final payment. 'All our demands have been consigned to the waste-paper basket,' they wrote. Hugenberg had already announced at a meeting of the German Nationalist Party, in Bremen, that the results bore no relation to his demands that the payment of tribute should finally come to an end. The Zentrum Party press was even more disappointing. The Liberal-minded papers, published by Mosse and Ullstein, at least paid me the compliment of considering that I had carried Brüning's policies to a rational conclusion, but the *Germania*, over which I had renounced all influence on becoming Chancellor, considered that our success had been precisely nil and suggested that Brüning would have done very much better. The auguries for my Government could hardly have been worse.

When MacDonald made his report to the House of Commons he received an ovation. He expressed himself as particularly pleased that the proceedings at Lausanne had brought France and England even closer together. He did not say that this had been effected at the expense of Germany and the real interests of a general European settlement. Herriot in his turn received a great welcome from the French Chamber. His position had been strengthened. But when I returned to Germany our delegation was greeted at the railway station with a shower of bad eggs and rotten apples.

It was on July 13 that I suffered the sharpest blow. Sir John Simon, the British Foreign Secretary, announced in Parliament that contact between the French and the British delegation during the closing stages of the Lausanne conference had resulted in their agreement on a new step towards European understanding. The two Governments had undertaken to consult with each other in all matters arising out of the understanding reached at Lausanne, and hoped that other Governments would join them in the free and frank discussion on all problems of mutual interest. The British Government also intended to seek a solution of the disarmament problem and to work with other delegations at Geneva for an acceptable compromise. Sir John announced that invitations to adhere to this declaration had been sent to the German, Italian and Belgian Governments. The most astonishing and incomprehensible aspect of this manœuvre was that Herriot had rejected my suggestion for a consultative pact by saying, 'He thought this suggestion was in contradiction with Article 19 of the Covenant, which left every nation the right of defending its own interests.'[1] Perhaps M. Herriot can tell me today why the British draft was more in accordance with Article 19 of the Covenant of the League of Nations?

It should be added here that MacDonald had remarked to Herriot on July 8 that it would be inappropriate to inform the Germans for the time being of this new Franco–British pact, as 'the

[1] Op. cit. Vol. III, No. 179

Germans were receiving a good many blows at Lausanne . . . they must not make an announcement and give the impression that the French and British Governments had made in Lausanne a new alliance against Europe.'[1] And yet it was an alliance directed against European recovery.

German public opinion, as was only to be expected, assumed from this suggestion of a consultative pact that it ushered in a new era in the Franco–British Entente, and the press was quick to refer to the Franco–British initiative as another proof that the German delegation had blundered.

I was reminded of a speech Stresemann had made in 1929, shortly before his death:

> 'I have worked with all my heart for peace and reconciliation, and have subordinated everything to reaching an understanding between Great Britain, France and Germany. I have rallied 80 per cent of the German population to my support. I signed the Locarno Pact. I have given, given and given again, until my own countrymen started to turn against me. It is now five years since Locarno. If the Allies had made one single concession, I could have kept the support of my countrymen. I could still do so. But the Allies have given nothing in return. Their few small concessions always came too late. Now, the youth of Germany, which we had hoped to win for peace and a new Europe, is lost to both of us. That is my tragedy and their crime.'

[1] Op. cit. Vol. III, No. 184

CHAPTER XI

HITLER DEMANDS THE CHANCELLORSHIP

'Coup d'état' in Prussia – New elections – The Nazis obtain 230 seats –
Interview with Hitler – The Potempa case – Disarmament concessions

ONE of my first acts on returning to Germany from Lausanne
was to go to see Hindenburg at Neudeck. I found him in
excellent health, and full of understanding for the problems
that had faced us at the reparations conference and for the measures
my Government had felt it necessary to take. The internal situation
had deteriorated in my absence, the election campaign had led to a
fresh outbreak of street disorders, and it had become necessary to
limit again the freedom I had accorded to the Nazi Brownshirts. I
felt under little further obligation to Hitler after his newspaper,
the *Völkische Beobachter*, had greeted our work at Lausanne with
the comment: 'The spirit of Versailles has triumphed – Chancellor
von Papen has signed another promissory note in Lausanne.' The
President's warning that public order must at all costs be maintained had been disregarded by both the Communists and the
Nazis. I therefore suggested to Hindenburg that all the uniformed
party formations should be forbidden to hold demonstrations and
processions during the fortnight preceding the polling date, and to
this he agreed.

We were anxious about the situation in Prussia. It is probably
difficult for outside observers to understand to what extent the
Reich Government was limited in its executive powers. The protection of its administrative offices and personnel, and the guarding
of its ministries, was the responsibility of the Prussian police, over
which the Central Government had no authority. The Prussian
State Government suffered from the same party deadlock as the
Reich Government, and was equally threatened by the growth of
left and right wing radicalism. There was no point in taking firm
measures on a federal basis if we were to be threatened through the
back door, so to speak, by developments in Prussia. I had resisted
the idea of drastic measures as long as I could, but when I got back

from Lausanne, Schleicher told me of a report he had received from a senior official in the Prussian Ministry of the Interior. It seemed that negotiations had been going on between Abbegg, the Social Democrat State Secretary, and Caspar, a Communist member of the Prussian State Parliament. The two parties had always been at daggers drawn, but then so were the Nazis and the Communists, and they had been known to form local arrangements for the purpose of discomfiting the Socialists. An alliance between the two Marxist parties was by no means so unlikely, and if it came about, would present a most menacing situation. The world has seen more recently what happens to a Social Democrat party that allies itself with the Communists. Every Eastern European country has provided an example. The Communists' first action has always been to obtain control of the police. This was a possibility we could not ignore. Schleicher was also perturbed at the prospect of police power falling into the hands of the Nazis. Any increase in the party's power in the country as a whole would be reflected in Prussia, and it had always been parliamentary practice to confide the Ministry of the Interior to the strongest party. This would have placed them in control of the most important instrument of public order at the Government's disposal. We decided that this must be prevented.

I decided to recommend the necessary emergency decree to the President. This was promulgated on July 20, and took advantage again of the powers accorded to the President and the Chancellor in Article 48 of the Constitution. In my capacity as Chancellor, I was appointed Reich Commissioner for Prussia and authorized, if necessary, to dismiss the ministers of the State Government and appoint commissioners in their place. It was made clear in the preamble to the decree that Prussian independence under the Reich Constitution was not affected, and the hope was expressed that an improvement in the general situation would soon make the decree unnecessary.

I might mention that this was by no means the first time that such a measure had been introduced in Germany. President Ebert had made use of the same powers in 1923, when, to restore law and order, he appointed Reich Commissioners in Saxony and other States.

Severing, Hirtsiefer and Klepper, three of the Prussian ministers, were invited to a meeting in the Reich Chancellery on the 20th.

Otto Braun, the Prussian Prime Minister, was recovering from an illness and unable to attend. I told them that my Government had decided with regret to take emergency measures to combat the threatening situation in Prussia. I then read them the terms of the decree, emphasizing that it was only a question of taking over the offices of Prime Minister and Minister of the Interior for a short period. The other ministers would be asked to remain at their posts. I asked Severing, the Minister of the Interior, what attitude he intended to adopt. He replied that he considered the decree unconstitutional and would only yield to force. My assurances that there was nothing personal in our decision, and that it had only been taken in the best interests of the country, were of no avail. I told him that I was appointing as my vice-commissioner Dr Bracht, the Lord Mayor of Essen, a member of the Zentrum Party and a moderate and intelligent politician and administrator. I said that I hoped that the selection of such a man would convince the Prussian ministers that the Reich Government had no intention of conducting any unnecessary experiments in Prussia. Severing persisted in his attitude, and declared again that he would only yield to force. I got up and the meeting came to an end.

Schleicher and I had not really expected the affair to turn out otherwise, and we had already taken our precautions. Another decree of the same date had been signed by the President and counter-signed by Gayl (my Minister of the Interior), Schleicher and myself. This decree, declaring a state of emergency to exist in Greater Berlin and the Province of Brandenburg, was now promulgated, and Lieutenant-General von Rundstedt, the future Field-Marshal, was entrusted with the military measures necessary to put it into effect.

Klepper, who was the Prussian Finance Minister, gave his own account of this episode in the German magazine *Die Gegenwart*, in September 1947. He had been in Essen the day before he saw me, and had heard about the intended appointment of Dr Bracht. He hurried back to Berlin to warn his Prime Minister and colleagues. What I did not know at the time, and what would have served only to strengthen my resolve, was that a few days earlier, at Hirtsiefer's invitation, a meeting had been held of the South German State Prime Ministers, with Severing, Hirtsiefer himself, and Klepper. They had discussed the situation, and especially the possibility of meeting with force any attempt to appoint a Reich

Commissioner in Prussia. Rumours to this effect had already appeared in the press. The southern Germans had promised complete co-operation and it had been agreed that the Prussian Government, if its prerogatives were threatened, would declare a state of emergency and induct the uniformed Socialist Reichsbanner groups as auxiliary police. Hindenburg was to be discreetly neutralized, and the Reich Government, together with the leaders of the Nazi Party, arrested. The government of the country was to be taken over by a directorate consisting of the Prime Ministers of the five largest States. Klepper also claims that these plans were discussed with the President of the Prussian Council of State – the Upper House – Dr Adenauer, and State Secretary Dr Spiecker, both of whom had signified their agreement to this scheme.

As I say, all this was completely unknown to me at the time, but such highly treasonable intentions form an interesting background to what actually took place. The execution of the decree caused no incidents. Braun, the Prime Minister, was ill at his home, but as soon as he heard what had happened, he left for his office in the Wilhelmstrasse. There he was told that he would not be allowed to enter, so he returned home, where he immediately petitioned the State Supreme Court.

Severing had returned to the Ministry of the Interior and had instructed his police to pay no attention to the orders of the Reich Government. Von Rundstedt was then ordered to go to police headquarters with the new Police Commissioner, and ask the previous commissioner, the deputy commissioner and the head of the uniformed police, Colonel Heimannsberg, to resign. This they all refused to do, and they were then arrested by an officer and a squad of soldiers. They were released an hour later, after they had each signed a declaration stating: 'After being removed from office by force, I declare my willingness to refrain from undertaking any further duties.' The Minister himself, when informed that a lieutenant and twelve soldiers had arrived to demand that he surrender his seals of office, rose and declared 'I surrender to force', and left his Ministry.

That same evening, I addressed the nation on the radio. I explained that the alteration in the standing orders in the Prussian State Parliament by the Weimar Coalition parties had made it impossible to elect a Prime Minister. The two right wing parties, the National Socialists and the German Nationalists, had 47 per

of the seats. The refusal of the Zentrum Party to enter a
coalition with them meant that no majority could be achieved.
The Communists, with 16 per cent of the seats, were in a key
position and had acquired a dominant rôle in Prussian affairs. Their
purpose was to overthrow State and Constitution, their method
the destruction of the religious, moral and cultural values of our
people. Their terrorist groups had introduced violence and murder
as political weapons. I declared it to be the duty of every Government to draw a clear dividing line between enemies of the State
and those forces fighting for the future of the nation. The threat of
an alliance between the Socialists and the Communists made it
essential to take drastic steps.

Our new Berlin Police Commissioner, Melcher, a trustworthy
and thoroughly efficient civil servant of the old type, soon
succeeded in restoring normal conditions. The President's demand
that street warfare should cease was put into effect without the
slightest disturbance or loss of life.

In a broadcast to America, carried by the National Broadcasting
Company, I made it clear that my Government had been forced to
intervene by the danger of civil war, resulting from the conflict
between the left and right wing radical parties. My strictures on
the revolutionary nature and intentions of the Communists probably make more sense today than they did to the outside world
twenty years ago.

Germany's Socialists, and indeed the Nuremberg Tribunal,
refer to the events of July 20, 1932, as a *coup d'état* against the
Prussian State, designed to destroy the Social Democratic Party.
This act of violence, they declare, broke the back of the Weimar
Republic and cleared the way for Hitler. My emergency decree
was, however, neither a *coup d'état* nor an act of violence. On
October 25 the State Supreme Court, which had been considering
Braun's petition, declared the President's measures and mine to
have been completely constitutional. The decree was directed at
no party except the Communists, and its provisions affected only
the offices of Prime Minister and Minister of the Interior. The
other ministers refused to attend a second meeting on July 21 and
declined to work with my appointee. I therefore had no option
but to appoint commissioners in their place.

No historian can assert that this was the blow that disposed of
the Weimar Coalition. The State elections on April 24, 1932, had

already done that. The Weimar Coalition parties found themselves in a minority of more than a hundred seats. Perhaps they considered that democracy was only that state of affairs that provided them with a majority. A freely elected majority of other parties was presumably 'an attempt to overthrow the Republic'. Yet some Socialists even then were honest enough to recognize the signs of the times. One of their leaders, Karl Mierendorff, wrote in the *Sozialistische Monatshefte*, No. 8, 1932: 'The strength of the republican parties in Prussia had been broken by the results of the April election. A change in the balance of power, by purely constitutional methods, was only a matter of time.'

The national elections on July 31 brought yet another proof that the nation as a whole wished to break with the long series of Governments formed by the Weimar Coalition parties. Out of a total of 36.8 million votes, they only obtained 12.9 million between them. The Nazi vote, on the other hand, increased from 6.4 million to 13.7 million, and they gained 230 seats as against 110. Their share of 36.8 per cent of the total votes was almost exactly the same as they had gained in the second round of the Presidential election. They were now the key party and no parliamentary majority could be assured without them. This development, but perhaps more particularly the Prussian State election results of April, in which the Nazis had obtained 38.5 per cent of the votes, makes nonsense of the accusation that their increase in strength was due to my lifting the ban on the Brownshirts. By the end of July my Government had been in power for eight weeks. The real reason for the Nazis growth was Germany's desperate economic situation, combined with the general disappointment at the result of the Lausanne conference.

The day after the election I gave an interview to the Associated Press, in which I said:

'The result of the election shows that the time has come for the National Socialist movement to take an active part in the reconstruction work of the country. The present Reichstag, which now consists, to all intents and purposes, of one Chamber only, does not enjoy the system of checks and balances which the American Congress has in its Senate. We badly need an Upper House here in Germany, and it is essential that our electoral system be modified to establish the personal responsibility of each member. We are not concerned here with altering the character of the State, but rather with restoring some sort of order within our present framework.'

In this, I still contend, I exposed the weak point of the Weimar Constitution. A new voting system with individual constituencies was absolutely essential.

Press reactions to the election results varied widely. The Zentrum and the Bavarian People's Party were pleased that the country had been spared a Nazi majority Government, and believed that Hitler would now have to compromise. The right wing was discomfited by so many of their votes having gone to the Nazis, and noted with regret that Stresemann's former party had been practically wiped out. Foreign comment was by no means unfavourable. The Paris *Matin* considered that a Cabinet of independent experts had become even more necessary; while the London *Daily Telegraph* was pleased to note that the hypnotic appeal of the Nazis had received a relative check. The *Daily Mail* hoped that I would be able to combine the *élan* of the National Socialists with the moderation and conservative tendencies of the Zentrum.

I have been most interested to see that Sir Horace Rumbold, the British Ambassador in Berlin at the time, sent a very clear picture of the situation to his Government in a report dated August 4, 1932, which is reproduced as Document No. 9 in the fourth volume of *Documents on British Foreign Policy*. In a survey of the first two months of my Government, he passes on the comment that Severing's position had become almost untenable. My Government, he said, had created quite a favourable impression in the working-class districts of the Ruhr, who were glad to have a firm hand at the helm in a time of economic crisis. It was clear that in the matter of equality of rights, the foreign policy of the German Government would be conducted with an emphasis foreign to the methods of Stresemann and Brüning. He stated that 'Ministers appear to have worked well together as a team.' He thought that I would rope Hitler and other Nazi leaders into the Cabinet and draw the teeth of the movement by saddling the National Socialists with a certain amount of responsibility.

At the beginning of August I took a few days' respite. The President was due to arrive in Berlin from Neudeck on the 10th, and we would then discuss any necessary alterations in the Cabinet. In spite of all our precautions, political tension in the country showed no sign of abating, and in order to prevent any recurrence of street violence, another decree was promulgated on August 9, which prescribed the death penalty for extreme cases of political acts of violence.

The atmosphere in political circles had not cleared, in spite of the elections. The left wing was demanding my resignation, the Zentrum wanted the Government broadened to include the Nazis – but without Hitler – while the right wing wanted Hitler appointed Chancellor. I had a number of conversations with leading politicians, but achieved little in the way of agreement. The celebration of Constitution Day evoked little enthusiasm in the country. The principles of Weimar served more to divide loyalties than to arouse them, and our formal ceremony in the Reichstag building was chiefly notable for the speech by my Minister of the Interior, Gayl, in which he announced the plans we had worked out for electoral reform.

On the morning of August 12 I was visited by Roehm, the Nazi Brownshirt Chief of Staff, and Count Helldorf, their leader in Berlin.

At this period Roehm, next to Goering, was Hitler's closest associate and the most powerful personality in the Nazi Party, particularly as he had behind him its strongest and most radical faction, the Brownshirts. He was a powerfully-built man, with a big red face scarred with duelling marks, and a disfigured nose, part of which had been shot away. He looked remarkably like a bulldog and provided a considerable contrast to Helldorf, a man of most aristocratic appearance. Helldorf I had known for many years, and between us we monopolized the conversation.

'May I enquire, Herr von Papen, what proposals you intend to make to Hitler when you see him?' I replied that I had no wish to discuss this subject with a third party and preferred to deal with Hitler direct. Roehm was not content with this evasion and interposed a firm demand that Hitler should be made Chancellor. 'The Party will accept no other solution,' he added.

Our interview was inconclusive, and that afternoon Hitler himself called upon me, accompanied by Frick, a Civil servant who was high up in the party before it came to power. I soon realized that I was dealing with a very different man from the one I had met two months earlier. The modest air of deference had gone, and I was faced by a demanding politician who had just won a resounding electoral success. 'The President,' I told him, 'is not prepared to offer you the post of Chancellor, as he feels that he does not yet know you well enough.' I urged upon him the necessity of joining in a coalition government as proof that he and his party were willing to accept their share of responsibility for governing the country. I explained to him that the Nazis had never been in anything but opposition, and their programme contained much that was inacceptable. Their suggestions for social reform, on the other hand, were positive, and there was no reason why we should not reach agreement in matters of economic policy. The President therefore thought that it was Hitler's duty to range the dynamism of his movement behind the present Government for the time being, as the situation demanded the loyal co-operation of all patriotic Germans.

I had referred frequently in public to the necessity of maintaining the Presidential Cabinet, and this suggestion can hardly have come as a surprise to Hitler. I told him he must not think that because I was not prepared to vacate the Chancellorship in his favour, I wanted to exclude his party from their share of responsibility in the affairs of state. I had no great wish to retain the post, but I suggested that for the time being he should join the Government as Vice-Chancellor and that some of his more trusted party colleagues should become ministers. I was prepared to give him my word that if our co-operation in the Cabinet was successful, I would resign the Chancellorship in his favour, once the President had got to know him better.

I had tried to be as serious and straightforward as possible, and I had clearly given Hitler food for thought. But he still tried to convince me how impossible it would be for the leader of such a large movement to play second fiddle to another Chancellor. His movement expected to see him at the head of affairs, and although he did not doubt the honesty of my proposal, it was one that he could not accept. I then tried another tack, and suggested that he should remain outside the Cabinet, as leader of the National Socialist movement, and allow one of his colleagues to become Vice-Chancellor. This would still give the President time to convince himself that the movement intended to co-operate in the general welfare. Hitler would not hear of this idea either. We talked for hours, both of us now and again becoming rather heated. I used every possible argument to convince him that for the moment there was no other practical way of granting him a share of the responsibilities of state. He could not afford to maintain his party in opposition; if he did, their campaign must begin to flag. It was in his own interest to act now.

It was all no use, and I resigned myself to the unpredictable consequences of my failure to reach some understanding. When Hitler asked me whether he was to regard our formal conversations as finished, thus restoring the full freedom of opposition to his movement, I told him that the matter could finally only be settled by a conversation between himself and the President. For my part, I would advise Hindenburg that our conversation had led to no positive result, and the President would have to take the final decision.

I immediately called on the President to make a personal report. He entirely approved of the attitude I had adopted and made it clear that he did not intend to appoint a man of Hitler's type to the responsible post of Chancellor. When Hitler visited him, he intended to make one more appeal to his patriotism, and ask him again to co-operate with the Government, without necessarily taking over its leadership. Schleicher was even more insistent. He felt there could be no question of our relinquishing authority, and considered that if Hitler should refuse all co-operation, his movement must lose strength in the country.

Hitler's interview with the President on August 13 has often been described. It took place in the atmosphere of dignity and respect that the old Field-Marshal's personality automatically imposed. His appeal to Hitler's sense of duty and patriotism caused a very strong impression. But when it became clear that there was no question of Hindenburg accepting Hitler's point of view and appointing him Chancellor, and that Hitler would make no attempt to meet Hindenburg's requests, we knew that our final attempt to ease the internal situation had failed. The atmosphere was icy when Hitler took his leave. The Nazis were now driven into a position of sharp opposition.

Hitler took violent exception to the official communiqué concerning his visit to the President. He declared it to be untrue that he had demanded that the whole power of the State should be placed in his hands, and maintained that he had only asked for unequivocal leadership in the Government. In this he was merely playing on words. Schleicher and I had been very careful in drawing up the communiqué and had very much in mind Hitler's demand that he should be placed in the same position as Mussolini had been after the march on Rome. Hitler had not marched on Berlin, and as long as Schleicher and I were in the Government we did not intend that he should.

The National Socialist press also took up the subject of Hindenburg's reminder to Hitler of his promise to Schleicher that the Nazis would give my Government their tacit support. They now denied that any such undertaking had been given, and I had to ask Schleicher to issue a public statement. In this he confirmed again that the Nazi Party had promised their tacit support to a Presidential Cabinet. Moreover, the undertaking had left no doubt that this support would be forthcoming during the lifetime of the Cabinet. Hitler's reply to this took the form of an interview with an American news agency, in which he declared that this support depended on whether the Government's policies conformed to the National Socialist programme. If I had taken a stronger line at Lausanne, even at the risk of the conference breaking down, the Nazi Party would probably still be prepared to support me. I cannot believe that this was the assurance originally given to Schleicher. It was passed on to me in a much more comprehensive version.

The reaction in the centre and right wing press was principally one of relief at being spared Hitler as Chancellor. They still expressed the hope that some co-operation with the National Socialists would be possible, and the Zentrum seems to have been taken in by discussions they had with the Nazis in an attempt to reach some common policy. An *impasse* had been reached, although for my own part I hoped that the new parliament would come to the only possible conclusion in the circumstances, and provide a majority for my Government on specific measures.

The main issue seemed to be how any reform of the Constitution was to be voted. – 'Herr von Papen is convinced that in some mysterious way, he possesses a popular mandate to govern the country and even to reform the Constitution . . . he is obsessed with the idea that the political parties are in no sense representative of the German people, and that the real desire of the country is for authoritative government, the limitation of parliamentary influence and the reform of the institutions set up at Weimar,' Sir Horace

Rumbold reported to the British Government. This is sharp criticism indeed, but the popular response to the Hitler régime when it finally came to power proved that I was by no means so wide of the mark in interpreting the popular wish to seek in authoritative government an alternative to moribund parliamentary democracy.

In order to reduce unemployment it was now necessary for my Government to meet this situation by some immediate improvement of Germany's economic situation. We intended to present a comprehensive plan of action and invite the nation as a whole to support our measures. On August 26 I announced that I was going to Neudeck for a further conference with the President. In political circles this could only mean one thing: I intended to obtain a decree for the dissolution of the Reichstag, in case this step should prove necessary. The new Chamber was due to meet at the beginning of September and would be asked to vote on our programme of reform. If no majority could be obtained for the necessary measures, I was going to apply the dissolution decree.

In the meantime, we had to deal with a highly controversial event. On August 22, under our decree prescribing the death penalty for acts of political violence, a special court at Beuthen had sentenced five Nazis to death for killing a Communist worker in Potempa. Hitler sent them his famous telegram pledging his support in the face of this 'savage and bloody verdict'. He undertook to 'fight to the end' the Government under which such a thing could happen.

On August 28, I addressed a meeting at Münster of the Westphalian Association of Farmers and Peasants, whose work I had shared for so many years. With Hitler's uncontrolled and demagogic outburst in mind, I laid down my own conceptions of a true conservative policy:

'The work of this Government is not restricted to the mere solution of current economic and political problems. We also want to lay a foundation stone for the rebuilding of the German State. None of us present at this meeting are revolutionaries, nor are we reactionaries. We are bound to the soil and to our Fatherland, and we know that in the last resort the affairs of this world cannot be resolved merely by intellectual processes. We know that we are here to serve God's purposes, and that is the basis of true conservative thought. This requires the State to be organized on a basis of authority. A government must be strong and independent enough to provide a firm foundation for all the manifestations of our social life.

'The verdict at Beuthen has caused a storm of protest from both the right and the left. What these two extremes demand, in effect, is that their political enemies should be dealt with outside the law. It is the duty of any Government to counter this prostitution of political morals. No system of law can be regarded as the servant of one class or one party. That is the Marxist conception, and it has been adopted by the National Socialists. It runs counter to all German and Christian ideals of law. The Prussian tradition has always been to entrust the leadership of the nation only to persons prepared to abide by its laws. The contempt for all these principles, shown in the message that the Nazi leader has just sent, is a poor recommendation for his demands to lead the nation. I do not recognize his right to regard the minority that follows his standards as the nation, and the rest of us as vermin. I am determined to obtain respect for the law and put an end to these conditions of civil war and political violence.'

The death sentences, combined with the firm attitude of my Government, had a salutary effect, and there was a notable decline in street violence. However, the question of carrying out the sentences still remained. The Minister of Justice raised the argument that the emergency decree had only come into force at midnight the day before the Potempa murder occurred. It was therefore possible to claim that the culprits had not been aware of the legal consequences of their action; in which case, it might be proper to commute the sentence to one of life imprisonment.

It was clear that our decision would be more political than legal. I wanted to avoid any impression that we were weakening under Nazi pressure. If I may jump ahead of events for a moment, it had been decided on September 12 to hold new Reichstag elections, and I did not want to provide the more radical National Socialists with unnecessary propaganda material. When it became clear that, following the verdict, the situation had quietened down considerably, the Cabinet decided to recommend to the President that the sentences be commuted. It seemed to us that a display of mercy could only have a further calming effect. It was not long before a Government came to power with ideas very different from those which we tried to express. In the light of later developments, I must now confess that mercy in this case was a grave political error.

★　★　★

Amidst all these difficulties at home, I was still at pains to preserve the thread of our foreign policy. The breakdown of my conversations with Herriot in Lausanne had left the Versailles restrictions on Germany's sovereignty just as they were. The passage of time rendered them increasingly intolerable, and my Government felt that every means must be explored to soothe what had become dangerous national susceptibilities. I instructed Neurath to press at Geneva for equal rights for Germany, and made another attempt to initiate direct negotiations with France. Lausanne had left me still smarting from what I could not help feeling was somewhat cavalier treatment by Herriot, though for this I blamed the British Government. I was still convinced that Herriot shared my interest in improving relations between our two countries, and felt that if we could only reach agreement, the technical work of the disarmament commission would be immensely facilitated.

On August 18 I prepared the ground in an interview with Reuter's News Agency, in which I insisted on the necessity of reaching some agreement on the subject of equal rights for Germany. Three days later Neurath and Schleicher received François-Poncet, the French Ambassador, and handed him a note outlining our feelings, requesting that direct negotiations between the two Governments should be initiated. Our only stipulation was that this approach should remain completely confidential for the time being.

A few days later I received a visit from the British Ambassador, Sir Horace Rumbold, who enquired whether it was true that we were engaged in secret discussions with the French. What had happened was that M. Alphand, the Permanent Secretary of the French Foreign Office, had considered the contents of our note so important that he had undertaken to deliver it personally to Herriot, who was on a holiday cruise in the English Channel with some French journalists. The secret was soon out, and a copy of our memorandum was delivered to the British Foreign Office the next day, with the comment: '*M. Herriot étudie attentivement cette*

grave situation, qui lui inspire de graves inquiétudes.' This remark
referred, I suppose, to our statement that we were not interested in
taking part in the work of the disarmament commission unless our
demands for equality of rights were first met in principle. The indiscreet manner in which our approach was treated is an indication
of the French Government's complete failure to understand that it
was a matter involving the fate of the German Government, in
face of the rising tide of nationalism. In his report to the Foreign
Office after our talk, Sir Horace gives a full account of my arguments and, quotes me as describing our demands as 'imperative'.

In London, our chargé d'affaires, Count Bernstorff, had an interview with Sir John Simon, in which he described our demands as
the logical development of the attitude adopted by Dr Brüning at
Geneva in April. Mr Stimson, the American Secretary of State,
has commented on these discussions as follows:

> '. . . the German Government had declared to the French
> Government that Germany's demands were the natural con-
> sequence of the conversations held at my house at Bessinge
> between the British Prime Minister and the German Chan-
> cellor. . . . I took part in these conversations only as an impartial
> observer, but I can state positively that nothing was said which
> could make the Germans think that their claims to equality of
> rights by way of rearmament had been in any way encouraged
> or approved.' (Mr MacDonald noted on the text: 'What Mr
> Stimson says is absolutely correct.')[1]

The British Ambassador in Washington also records on
September 7:

> 'He [Mr Stimson] read me his record of discussion at
> Bessinge on April 26 at which Brüning and von Bülow had
> explained to Mr MacDonald and himself German desire in
> regard to equality of treatment. His impression was that the
> present German demands went beyond what had then been
> discussed.'[2]

It is only necessary for me to add that these statements dispose
once and for all of Brüning's claims, out of which my political

[1] *Documents on British Foreign Policy 1919–1939.* Second Series, Vol. IV,
No. 136. H.M.S.O. London, 1950.
[2] Op. cit. Vol. IV, No. 74

opponents have made such capital, that he was 'a hundred yards from the winning post' when I succeeded him as Chancellor.

Mr Stimson also emphasized what a bad impression the German demands had caused in Washington, especially as they exceeded anything discussed at Bessinge, and formed an unpleasant and ill-timed sequel to the concessions we had obtained at Lausanne. He remarked also that the restrictions of the Versailles Treaty were not to be lightly cast aside, and 'that stern, blunt methods were effective in bringing the Germans to terms. . . . lack of firmness in dealing with this [demand for equality] would invite further deliberate attacks on the treaty structure. . . . A few sharp words from us [the British] at Berlin would have a salutary effect.'[1] On October 3 a memorandum from Mr Stimson was received in Geneva. It stated: 'Mr Stimson thought it important to avoid treating the matter on the basis of German rights.'[2] Sir John Simon has noted that in a conversation with Herriot, the latter told him that: 'Mr Stimson had conveyed to the French Government a version of the conversation early in the year at Bessinge, which indicated that he had not agreed to anything.'[3]

As soon as the nature of our confidential approach to the French Government had thus been made public, Neurath made a statement, on September 7, in which he explained the purpose of our *démarche*, emphasizing that we demanded equal rights but had no wish to re-arm. We would have been very much better pleased if the other powers had reduced their armaments to our level. Neurath ended by saying: 'No one can expect Germany to tolerate further discrimination that affects our honour and threatens our security.'

The French Government answered our memorandum on September 11 with a blunt rejection. Our demands were described as disguised rearmament. To this we replied that Germany could not see her way clear to attend the session of the disarmament commission, due to begin on September 21. The British Ambassador in Paris reported French reaction to this step in these terms: 'Both M. Herriot and M. Léger, Acting Secretary General of the Ministry of Foreign Affairs, assured me independently, in the most convincing manner, that they regarded the situation as more serious

[1] Op. cit. Vol. IV, No. 100
[2] Op. cit. Vol. IV, No. 126
[3] Op. cit. Vol. IV, No. 134

than at any time since 1919. France will not tolerate that her own armaments should be reduced and Germany's increased. . . . She is incapable of believing that the present spirit in Germany is not directed against her. . . .'

This led to our receiving a few 'sharp words' from the British, as Mr Stimson had suggested. 'In view of Germany's economic difficulties, the initiation of acute controversy in the political field at this moment must be accounted unwise. And, in view of the concessions so recently granted to Germany by her creditors, it must be accounted particularly untimely.' We found the tone of this unnecessarily offensive, and the German press referred to the note as a reminder of the treatment that had been thought suitable in 1919. We made up our minds to answer neither London nor Paris. The paper war was not getting us anywhere. I merely let the British Ambassador know that I was greatly disappointed at his Government's unforthcoming attitude, particularly in view of the assurances the Prime Minister had given me in Lausanne in July, that he would do everything to support my Government. I also told him that Herriot had expressed a wish to continue a friendly exchange of views after our talks on a consultative pact had broken down.

I answered Herriot in an interview that I gave to the German Wolff News Agency: 'The manner in which M. Herriot informed other Governments of our approach, without even the courtesy of consulting the German Government beforehand, seems to prove that France has little interest in reaching any agreement. . . . We have at no time insisted on rearming to the level of France or other States. We desire parity on a basis of a general reduction of armaments.' The French, I am afraid, seemed far from displeased at the check we had suffered. François-Poncet writes in his memoirs, with apparent satisfaction: '. . . et cet échec, loin de rester secret, s'étale en plein jour!'[1]

The British, on the other hand, seemed to realize that rather too much china had already been broken. Two days after my Wolff interview we received another message from the British Government announcing that a new note was on its way, and adding: 'It is clear that consequences of the utmost gravity to the future of the

---

[1] *Souvenirs d'une Ambassade à Berlin, Septembre 1931 – Octobre 1938*. Flammarion, Paris, 1946.

Disarmament Conference, and to prospects of European concord, may result if this situation remains unchanged.' The collection of British Foreign Policy documents from which I have taken all these extracts also shows that Sir Horace Rumbold had been good enough to emphasize to the Foreign Office that the first suggestion for a consultative pact to co-ordinate the policies of the European Governments had come from me in Lausanne.

The new British proposal suggested an immediate meeting in London between the Foreign Ministers of Germany, France, Italy and Great Britain. The French showed little enthusiasm for this. Sir John Simon noted, after another talk with Herriot: 'He described the proposal of the London meeting as "most imprudent", and contended that Germany would claim it as a success, while the proceedings would be "humiliating" to himself and to France.' Nevertheless, Sir John made great efforts to organize the conference, and we were by no means unwilling to find some means of breaking the deadlock. At a Cabinet meeting on October 7 I read again the final communiqué of the Lausanne Conference, emphasizing the task 'of creating a new order which would make possible the establishment and development of confidence between the nations in the mutual spirit of reconciliation, collaboration and justice'. There seemed little point in consigning such fine phrases to the wastepaper basket, so we decided to accept the invitation. Herriot was still looking for some way out, and proposed that the conference should be held in Geneva, and that the Poles and Czechs should be invited as well. This we declined to accept.

The British Government continued its really praiseworthy efforts to bring Herriot round, and I gave what support I could in a speech on November 8 to the Foreign Press Association in Berlin. I referred to the necessity of revising obsolete treaties with the concurrence of all the signatories concerned. 'Other countries should help us in this and meet our aspirations with understanding, for neither by ruses nor by threats will we consent to be bound for all time to observe solutions imposed on us under duress. Our road will be the road of peaceful understanding. We set out on that road at Locarno; we continued along it at Lausanne, and we will continue to follow it in order that those great principles, which we accepted when we laid down our arms in 1918, may prevail in Europe.'

MacDonald and Herriot met in Geneva at the beginning of

December, at the League of Nations Assembly. Neurath was also
there, and a last attempt was made to find some formula which
would enable us to take part in the work of the Disarmament
Conference. This resulted in the famous communiqué published
on December 11, which finally recognized our demands for
equality of treatment: 'The Governments of the United Kingdom,
France and Italy have declared that one of the principles that
should guide the Conference on Disarmament should be the grant
to Germany . . . of equality of rights in a system which would
provide security for all nations . . .'[1] As usual, assistance came too
late. I had been obliged to resign as Chancellor the previous week.
Political events in Germany were taking a course which can only
have made the Western Powers regret that nothing had been done
in time to strengthen my Government's position. My place had
been taken by Schleicher, and that is the next part of my story.

[1] *Documents on British Foreign Policy 1919-1939*. Second Series, Vol. IV,
No. 220. H.M.S.O. London, 1950.

CHAPTER XII

CONSTITUTIONAL CRISIS

The new Reichstag – A disgraceful scene – Parliament dissolved – Economic recovery plan – New elections – The Nazis lose strength – No parliamentary coalition possible – Schleicher's suggestions – The President prepared to break his oath – Schleicher's intrigues – The Army overtaxed – Major Ott's report – I resign

THE newly elected Reichstag met on August 30. Following the normal rules of procedure, the opening formalities were conducted by the oldest member, in this case the Communist deputy, Klara Zetkin. She had just returned from Moscow and was greeted jubilantly by her Communist colleagues. The opening speech was by tradition one of formal welcome, but hers consisted of a violent tirade against capitalism, and against my Government as its servile tool. Her final call for revolution produced an ecstatic reponse from the Communists, but very little reaction from the rest of the House. The next step was the election of the President.[1] The Zentrum and the Bavarian People's Party combined with the Nazis to propose Goering, as the representative of the strongest party. He was quick to draw attention to the fact that this combination represented a strong and workable national majority and that the Government therefore had no cause to insist that a state of national emergency existed. This first formal session was then closed, and the stage set for the next meeting, which was called for September 12.

It was my intention to make a survey of the financial situation and announce the details of an economic recovery programme for discussion by the nation's representatives. We hoped that the parties would apply common sense to the problems involved, and we were fully prepared to adapt our programme to informed and constructive criticism. The Reichstag members had other ideas.

---

[1] The *Reichstagspräsident* is roughly the equivalent of the Speaker in the House of Commons.

Under Goering's leadership, an unholy alliance of Communists, Social Democrats and Nazis had made up their minds to introduce an immediate vote of censure on the Government. I was not even to be allowed to make my report, much less announce any plans for the future.

By tradition, Goering was under an obligation to call on the head of the Government to speak, and then to take a vote on our plans and intentions. But even this elementary rule of democratic procedure was abandoned. The Reichstag was packed, the public galleries filled to overflowing, and the Diplomatic Corps present in full strength. A number of Nazi members were wearing uniform. The atmosphere was tense as Goering declared the session open. Torgler, the Communist, immediately rose to his feet and demanded that before proceeding to the agenda, the Assembly should vote without discussion on the Communist resolution for the repeal of the emergency decrees. He requested that the vote of censure on the Government should also be taken before passing to the agenda. Goering put the question to the House, and asked if there was any objection to the Communist proposal. None was forthcoming and even the German Nationalists remained silent. Frick then jumped up on the Nazi benches and requested that the session be interrupted for half an hour.

The situation was now serious, and I had been caught unawares. I had calculated that the debate on the proposals I intended to make would last several days, and it had not occurred to me to come armed with the dissolution order I had obtained. I sent a messenger off to the Chancellery post-haste, and he returned with the vital document just as the members were reassembling. As the session was reopened, I appeared with the famous red despatch case used for such documents under my arm.

The House became a scene of complete disorder. The session resolved itself into a shouting match, and amidst the tumult Goering refused to recognize my right to speak. He turned ostentatiously to the left side of the House, and pretended not to hear me. Instead he shouted, 'As no objections have come from the floor to the Communist proposal, I intend to proceed with the division.' There was no other solution but for me to march over to the presidential platform, slap the dissolution order on Goering's desk, and walk out of the Reichstag with the members of the Cabinet, to the accompaniment of a positive howl of derision.

Goering pushed the order on one side and continued with the vote, which resulted in a defeat for the Government by 412 to 42. Whereupon he read the dissolution order, commenting that it was now without validity, as it was signed by a minister who had just been ousted by the representatives of the people. He undertook to take the necessary steps to have the order annulled. In this he was unsuccessful, as his own conduct was proved to be contrary to the standing orders. An attempt was made by the left wing parties and the Nazis to accuse me of a breach of the Constitution, but it had no legal basis and soon broke down. When Goering approached the President on the subject he was sharply rebuffed.

The Zentrum Party had little cause to be proud of its part in the day's proceedings. How men like Brüning and Kaas permitted their representatives to join with the Communists and the Nazis against a Government pledged to restore order in the country, I shall never understand. The day had presented the sorry spectacle of the parliamentary discomfiture of the head of the Government, while in the previous session Klara Zetkin, the Communist, had been listened to with respect and attention.

I made a radio appeal to the country the same night, announced some details of our reconstruction plans and called on the nation to stand behind the President in his attempts to secure national unity. The scene in the Reichstag brought an unexpected public response. I received thousands of letters and telegrams the next day from every strata of society, approving of my stand and asking me to continue my efforts. I do not recall any other occasion on which I received such a wide measure of support. Viewing the situation in retrospect, I am now convinced that we would have done better to have governed for a time without the Reichstag.

Our economic recovery programme was introduced in the form of an emergency decree at the beginning of October and provided for the expenditure of 2.2 milliard marks. The Minister of Finance was mainly responsible for its details, but he had had a certain amount of trouble with Dr Luther, the President of the Reichsbank. Luther, a man of great experience, had serious reservations concerning his financial reponsibilities under the plan, and thought we were taking undue risks. However, the need of the moment was for action, and I told Dr Luther that if he was not prepared to accept the risks involved, the Government would be obliged to disregard his advice.

There seemed to be no reason why Germany should not still solve her economic difficulties. In purely mathematical terms, her national debt was one of the lowest in Europe, barely a third that of Great Britain, not an eighth that of France, and only half the pre-war debt. Our main problem was psychological. During the whole of the reparations period, and as a result of inflation, economic pessimism had become endemic. The workers were so bemused by unemployment, and by Communist, Socialist and Nazi propaganda, that they had lost confidence in the power of government to relieve their lot. We had to convince both capital and labour that the solution was largely a matter of confidence.

Our chief instrument was a system of interest-bearing tax-bonds, intended to provide industry with working capital and encourage it to take on workers and increase production. Each new worker employed ensured the employer a reduction of 400 marks in his tax assessment. Other alterations in the tax scale encouraged the introduction of a forty-hour five-day week by the employment of as many workers as possible. We hoped to provide, by the back door, so to speak, not only a powerful impetus to industry, but to combine it with measures of social reform. In spite of this, the Socialist parties opposed every aspect of the plan.

The financial position was desperate enough. It was calculated that 23,500,000 Germans – about 36 per cent of the population – were dependent on public funds. That included the Civil Service, the Army, pensioners, and the unemployed. Such a burden made the free interplay of economic forces almost impossible, but we had made a start. Our 2.2 milliard marks had been provided out of our own resources, without having to apply again for an international loan. It made a call on our last reserves, and the success of our plan depended on whether the sums expended in unemployment pay could now be devoted to more productive enterprises. The first month raised our hopes high, with a reduction during October in the number of unemployed by 123,000.

From the long-term point of view, the reform of the electoral law was equally important. The new Reichstag elections had been set to take place on November 6, and we tried to discover some method of holding them under a new system of voting. But it was not possible to change the electoral law by emergency decree. The proportional system of representation formed part of the Constitution and there was no hope at the time of obtaining the majority necessary for an amendment. Our only hope was to see whether, in the elections, our efforts to oust the Nazis from their key position among the parties would be successful. If we did not succeed, then we would have to persuade the President to break with the Constitution in order to elect a parliament capable of carrying out the business of the nation.

The Government was in no happier position than at the previous elections, and more or less had to let events take their course. We had studied the possibility of forming a new party pledged to support the Government, but I had turned down the idea because it contradicted our intention of maintaining the Cabinet free from and above party political ties. In any case, there was no time to organize a party on a national scale. Our great weakness was, as Sir Horace Rumbold reported to his Government on September 19, that '. . . persons wishing to support the Papen Government, and they are in increasing numbers, will not know how to vote'.

Even Theodor Wolff, who stood at the opposite political pole from me, wrote in the *Berliner Tageblatt* that there was definite sympathy for my Government in moderate and liberal circles. But he also asked how this sympathy was to be transmuted into electoral support. Anyone wishing to vote for me must take a simultaneous bite of the sour nationalist apple, and that, he said, was too much to ask. There is little doubt that he was right. If our Conservative Party had been moderate and progressive, a great many people would have found it easier to support it and provide backing for my Government. But every attempt to modify its character foundered on the rock of Hugenberg's personality. It even seemed likely that the Zentrum would lose votes. Whoever wished to support my Government was obliged to vote for the German Nationalist Party. However, if we succeeded in taking some fifty or sixty seats away from the Nazis, this would deprive them of their key position, and the threat of their possible alliance with the Communists would be removed.

Our efforts were not entirely without success. The Nazis lost 35 seats at the new elections, but the 195 seats they held were still enough to make it impossible to form a majority government without their participation. The situation was now really serious and made any continuation of political life within the framework of the Weimar Constitution more or less hopeless. Had they lost a few more seats, and had it been possible to form a government without them, there might still have been a chance of continuing the policies I had initiated. As it was, the Socialists had 121 seats, the Communists 100, the Zentrum 70 and the German Nationalists 51. The Staatspartei, the former Democrats, returned with only two members.

When these results became known, my first thought was of their effect on other European countries. I held a press conference two days later, at which I repeated once again the points I had failed to get adopted at Lausanne. A strong German Government was not only essential for the country itself, but was the principal factor in maintaining the peace of Europe. As long as the Nazi Party could feed on the resentment caused by the discriminatory clauses of the Versailles Treaty, there would be no hope of normal political life in Germany. Three years later, Hitler organized a strong central authority of another type, one that bore little relation to the principles I was defending. He was able to obtain what the nations had not been prepared to grant to me or those before me. But by that time they were no longer in a position to control the situation.

I embarked on the usual series of discussions with the heads of the political parties. The Socialists were not even prepared to negotiate. Dr Kaas, speaking for the Zentrum, declared: 'The only solution to the present untenable situation is to form a Government which, in protecting the rights of the President, and with full authority, restores contact with the people's representatives and ensures the parliamentary majority the situation demands.' But his party declined to co-operate with me.

Such a majority could only be organized with the Nazis. Hitler, for his part, had made up his mind to do without parliamentary majorities. But historians may care to note that the Zentrum at this juncture regarded a Cabinet led by Hitler as the only way out of the *impasse*. I fail to see how this can be equated with the accusation that I was the person responsible for bringing Hitler to power.

Nevertheless, I was obliged to treat with him. After our contact in August, this required me to leave personal distaste on one side. I wrote to him as follows:

'When I was called upon to head the Presidential Cabinet on June 1, it was on the understanding that an attempt should be made to unite all the patriotic forces in the country. At the time, you welcomed the President's decision and promised your support for such a Cabinet. After the elections on July 31, an attempt was made to combine these forces within the Cabinet itself, but you made it a condition that such a coalition must be formed under your leadership. For reasons known to you, the President did not consider that he could offer you the post of Chancellor . . .

'The recent elections on November 6 have provided a new situation and a new opportunity for uniting the country. . . . The National Socialist press has stated that it would be presumption on my part to enter into discussions with any personalities suited to this work of national concentration. Nevertheless, I consider it my duty to approach you in the course of my present negotiations. I learn from your press that you still maintain your right to the post of Chancellor . . .

'I still think that the leader of a major national movement remains under an obligation to discuss the situation and the measures that have to be taken with the present responsible head of affairs. We must endeavour to put aside the bitterness of the election campaign and place the good of the country, which we both seek to serve, above all other considerations.'

I had hoped to appeal to such statesmanlike qualities as Hitler possessed, but he declined to enter into any discussion. The check his hopes had received in August still seemed to rankle. He was only prepared to consider a written approach, in which I would have had to undertake to abandon my whole political and economic programme. The letter I have quoted was described by the prosecutor at the Nuremberg Trial as 'undignified'; but I do not see how I can have been expected to write in impolite terms when inviting a political opponent to take part in coalition discussions.

The chances of attaining any success in the negotiations with the political parties were extremely small. Those in opposition could not very well retreat from their declared programmes and intentions. The only group on which I could rely was the Bavarian People's Party, influential, but not strong in numbers. A month previously I had visited Munich to reassure the State Government that the arrangement we had been compelled to make in Prussia was only temporary, and to acquaint them with my plans for constitutional reform. The Bavarian Cabinet had expressed itself in full agreement with my plans for ensuring greater stability for the Federal Cabinet and a greater sense of responsibility in the Reichstag. I still hoped that Dr Held, the Bavarian Prime Minister, would use his influence on the Zentrum and German Nationalists.

By November 17, I was compelled to report to the President that my negotiations with the parties had been unsuccessful. Their attitude destroyed any hope of putting my reforms through Parliament. The moment the Reichstag met, the opposition would again introduce a vote of censure, and this would make any further co-operation between Cabinet and Parliament impossible. There was no hope of forming a coalition Government under my leadership. I advised the President to invite the parties to make their own suggestions how to form such a Government. In theory, they were all, with the exception of the Socialists, in favour of such a solution. The best way to ensure that the President had complete freedom of action, and freedom from any atmosphere of personal resentments, was for the whole Cabinet to resign *en bloc*. At the Cabinet meeting immediately preceding my interview, I had suggested that we might do better to remain in office until it was certain that an alternative Government could be formed. However, Schleicher insisted that the President be given a free hand, and in the end I concurred.

The President was more than anxious at the turn things had taken. He seemed to think he would have little better success with the party leaders than I had had. Above all he was determined not to abandon the conception of a Presidential Cabinet and return to the uncertainty of parliamentary methods. I strengthened him in his resolve, convinced that it would teach some of the parliamentarians a sharp lesson when they were faced by the problems of forming a majority Government. When they had all had their say, the President would be in a position to form another Cabinet of his own.

The press of the left and centre was delighted at my resignation. The right wing organs had a few kind things to say about my Government, and insisted chiefly that there must be no retreat from the principle of a Cabinet that stood above the political parties. 'After thirteen years of party warfare, the nation has come to seek its salvation in an authoritative Government to such an extent that even those parties most wedded to parliamentary procedure no longer see in it the solution to our problems,' wrote the

Nazi election slogans, 1932: 'Vote against Papen and the Jews'

Von Papen and Hitler, with Generals von Fritsch and von Rundstedt

The author riding with General von Fritsch, Chief of Staff

Deutsche Tageszeitung on November 18. 'This is a major historical development, and it will have a decisive influence on the future form of the Reich Constitution. The Papen Government can be said to have represented a new departure in German political life.'

Hindenburg received the right and Zentrum Party leaders, Hugenberg, Kaas and Dingeldey, on November 18. The Social Democrats were not invited, as they had made it quite clear in their letters to me that they would not take part in a coalition Government. The next day Hindenburg saw Hitler and requested him, as leader of the strongest party, to examine the possibilities of forming a coalition Government, in which the right and centre party leaders had already declared their willingness to take part. It was made quite clear to him that he was free to occupy the post of Chancellor. Goering brought Hitler's written reply on November 23. This declared that Hitler considered himself unable to solve the Government crisis in purely parliamentary terms, as this would be contrary to his basic convictions.

Hindenburg now turned to Kaas, the Zentrum leader, who told him that Hitler had not even bothered to sound out the other party leaders on the possibility of forming a working majority. Kaas now undertook this task himself, with a view to obtaining agreement on a minimum programme of reform and reconstruction which would command a parliamentary majority. He soon had difficulties with Hugenberg, and the Nazis backed out with the specious excuse that although they were prepared to discuss practical measures, they could see no means of putting them into effect. Kaas was then obliged to tell the President that there was little point in further contact with the party leaders.

Hitler, it is clear, had no intention of being forced into a parliamentary solution. If he was to form a Cabinet, then he would insist on its being a Presidential Cabinet, similar to mine. This was the step Hindenburg was not yet prepared to take, and the situation throws an interesting sidelight on the prosecutor's contention at Nuremberg that Hitler had been invited to take part in these discussions because I had 'warmly recommended the President to make Hitler Chancellor'. By November 26 Hindenburg was, in fact, faced with the problem of forming a new Presidential Cabinet, whose chief dilemma would be how to conduct the affairs of the State in the face of a completely deadlocked Parliament.

This was the situation when Hindenburg called on Schleicher

H

and myself to visit him on the evening of December 1. The results of our discussion were to have a decisive effect on subsequent events. The President turned to me first for my suggestions as to what our next step should be. I gave him a sketch of our two failures to incorporate representatives of the National Socialist Party in the Presidential Cabinet. Hitler had declined to enter into any coalition with other political parties on the basis of forming a Government dependent on a parliamentary majority. Now that this possibility had been exhausted, the only basis on which Hitler was prepared to accept responsibility was as the head of another Presidential Cabinet not subject to party support or affiliations. This raised the question of whether the situation had changed since August 13, when the President had not been prepared to consider this solution. It was my opinion that the President had been given no cause to change his attitude. The unbridled nature of the Nazi Party's behaviour during the intervening months had provided little proof of Hitler's statesmanlike qualities. If the President still maintained the opinions he had held in August – opinions that Schleicher and I had shared – then there was no question but that a state of national emergency existed which called for extraordinary measures. Circumstances had arisen for which the Weimar Constitution found no provision.

I therefore suggested that my Government should remain in office for the time being. We would get our economic programme working and negotiate urgently with the State Parliaments on the subject of the reform of the Constitution. There seemed no reason to suppose that the newly elected Reichstag should not behave in exactly the same way as the previous one. If the Government was not going to be permitted to function, then it must do without the Reichstag altogether for a short period. Our proposed amendments to the Constitution would then be made the subject of a referendum or submitted for approval to a new National Assembly. This procedure, I realized, would involve a breach of the present Constitution by the President.

The situation was so serious that I considered that the President might be justified in placing the welfare of the nation above his oath to the Constitution. I told him I realized that this would be a difficult decision for a man who had always placed the value of his word above everything else, but I reminded him of the manner in which Bismarck had once found it necessary to recommend to the

Prussian monarch that the Constitution should be ignored for the sake of the country. Once the necessary reforms had been voted, it would be possible to return the duties of legislation to the new Parliament.

It was then Schleicher's turn. He said he had a plan which would absolve the President from taking this last drastic step. If he took over the Government himself, he thought he could bring about a split in the National Socialist Party which would ensure a parliamentary majority in the present Reichstag. He then gave a detailed explanation of the differences of opinion within the Nazi movement which made it more than likely that he would be able to attract the support of Gregor Strasser and about sixty Nazi members of the Reichstag. Strasser and one or two of his close supporters would be offered posts in the Government, which would be based upon the support of the Trade Unions, the Social Democrats and the bourgeois parties. This would provide a majority which would make it possible to put through the economic and social programme of the Papen Government.

I interjected here that I had grave doubts whether this plan was feasible. It seemed to me highly unlikely that the left wing of the Nazi Party would split off, as all the members had sworn a personal oath of loyalty to Hitler. However, Schleicher's contacts with the Nazis were much more intimate than mine, and he was probably correct in his assumptions. In any case, the experiment was worth making. My chief objections were of a more fundamental nature. Ever since June 1 the President had been trying to find a remedy for the collapse of parliamentary procedure. An independent Cabinet had been formed for the purpose of devising reforms which would ensure a more satisfactory relationship between administration and Parliament. Schleicher's plan would now mean that this line of action would have to be abandoned. Even if Schleicher obtained his parliamentary majority, it would not be strong enough to put through basic reforms, and therefore would not only be a provisional solution, but a far from satisfactory one.

The President sat in silence, listening with great earnestness to our arguments. He was being called upon to make one of the most fundamental decisions of his long life. He took no part in the discussion, and after we had both presented our views he sat quietly for a moment, then rose and said, 'I intend to follow Herr von Papen's suggestion.' Then, turning to me, he added,

'Herr Reichskanzler, I desire you to undertake immediately the necessary discussions to form a Government, to which I shall entrust the carrying out of your plan.'

Schleicher appeared dumbfounded. He had clearly not expected the old Field-Marshal to take on his broad shoulders the responsibility for a breach of the Constitution. As we both left, I made one last appeal to him. 'I can well understand that you should wish to take over the reins of Government after directing its activities behind the scenes for so long. But I have severe doubts about the advisability of your present plan. Would it not be better to solve the problem once and for all by a reform of the Constitution, rather than resort to yet another temporary expedient? I have been promising the nation for six months that a definite solution would be found and, with your agreement, I might add, we have involved the President's personal prestige in our success or failure to do so. Surely we cannot afford to expose his whole position, the one stable factor in the State, to the confusion that further temporary measures will cause?

'I am ready to hand over the post of Chancellor to you, if you are prepared to carry out the President's wishes. It would probably be the best solution anyway, because in the last resort you will always have the Army at your disposal. This is not a question of personalities, but a matter for immediate action. I still think it would be better to leave me at the head of affairs for a few months, until such time as the Constitution has been amended and parliamentary life restored. I have become such an object of controversy that I might just as well accept this further burden and assume full responsibility for what has to be done. Then I can resign and you will be able to take over the Government with every hope of a good start.'

Schleicher listened to me with undisguised disapproval. For weeks now I had noticed that he was no longer as frank and open with me as previously, and our relationship had become distinctly cool. As we parted, without having reached any understanding, he remarked: '*Mönchlein, Mönchlein, du gehst einen schweren Gang*.'[1]

After this dramatic interview I returned to the Reich Chancellery. I was still amazed at Schleicher's sudden *volte-face*. He had

---

[1] This was the famous remark made to Luther as he was about to leave for the Diet of Worms, and means: 'Little Monk, you have chosen a difficult path.'

always seemed to give the policies of our Cabinet his full support, and in fact he had initiated a number of our measures. He had never given me to suppose for one moment that he had disagreed with the line that I was pursuing. In an interview as recently as September 10, he had declared: 'I am not prepared to abandon the institution of a Presidential Cabinet in favour of a return to party government. I would regard it as a breach of faith with the President to do anything that endangers the present Cabinet's existence.' I had assumed that I could count on his continued support. Our personal relationship had always been close enough for him to have said if he had felt that he could no longer give it.

I felt I must discuss the new situation with some of my Cabinet colleagues, and asked Guertner and Eltz to call on me. I gave them an account of the discussion I had just had and told them of the new directive I had received from the President. When I asked them whether they were prepared to share this new and heavy responsibility, they both agreed without reservation. Both of them considered that a real state of emergency existed and that the suggested solution was the only one. It was a great relief to have a highly respected lawyer like Guertner, and a wise, experienced man like Eltz, on my side, and I was strengthened in my resolve.

They then told me of the discussions Schleicher had had during the preceding two weeks with some of the members of the Cabinet. He had expressed the opinion that if I was entrusted again with the post of Chancellor, the tense situation must deteriorate into civil war. This would oblige the Reichswehr to intervene for the purpose of upholding the authority of the State; a task for which the Army was not organized and which would overtax its strength. A great number of the younger officers were known to sympathize with the National Socialists, and he was not prepared to accept the possible consequences of their intervention.

Both my friends expressed the opinion that Schleicher's views would have had a sufficient effect on most of the members of the Cabinet to prevent them from ranging themselves behind me in this new and difficult task. There was no doubt that the situation must be clarified. To this I replied that Schleicher had at no time expressed any such fears to me and, in my presence at least, had not given the slightest indication to the President that the Reichswehr would not be in a position to guarantee law and order if we were to decree a state of emergency. I then broke off our discussion and called a Cabinet meeting for nine o'clock the next morning, December 2.

At this I gave all my colleagues a full account of my interview with the President and of the new directive I had received. I left them in no doubt that open conflict with the National Socialists would now be unavoidable. I then said that Guertner and Eltz had told me on the previous day of the opinions that Schleicher had been expressing to certain members of the Cabinet, and of which I had been, until that moment, in complete ignorance. In order to clarify the situation, I therefore called on the Minister of Defence to make known his considered view of the situation.

Schleicher rose and declared that there was no possibility of carrying out the directive that the President had given me. Any attempt to do so would reduce the country to chaos. The police and the armed services could not guarantee to maintain transport and supply services in the event of a general strike, nor would they be able to ensure law and order in the event of a civil war. The General Staff had made a study of their obligations in this respect and he had arranged for Major Ott, who had been responsible for drawing up the necessary plans, to place himself at the Cabinet's disposal and present a report. As Minister of Defence, he considered it his duty to keep the Army out of internal political conflicts. It did not exist in order to take part in a civil war.

I answered Schleicher by saying that I shared his view concerning the limitation of the Army's responsibilities in maintaining law and order. I did not agree that either a general strike or civil war was inevitable, or that the police forces were not in a position to keep the peace. The views of the General Staff should certainly be heard, and I requested that Major Ott be admitted to make his report.

Ott, who was later to become Ambassador in Tokio, has written his own account of the report he made. I reproduce it here in full:

'With the increasing deterioration in the internal political situation, the High Command conducted an enquiry into the capacity of the armed forces to carry out their duties against right and left wing extremists in the event of a state of emergency. I was, at the time, head of the Political Division in the

War Ministry, and received orders to prepare a tactical study of the requirements and responsibilities involved. A meeting was called in November 1932 with representatives of every branch of the administration likely to be called upon to implement a decree of emergency. This sat for three days, and investigated the conditions that might be expected to arise in the different parts of the country. A balance was drawn between the measures that appeared necessary and those considered possible. Requirements varied considerably from place to place, but the State's resources appeared in every case to be insufficient.

'In East Prussia, the defence of the national frontiers was the principal consideration. The borders defined in the Versailles Treaty were still under dispute and relations with Poland very strained. There was a distinct possibility that internal conflict in Germany would be used by radical Polish elements as a basis for intervention. Germany's East Prussian garrisons would be cut off from the main body of the country and dependent entirely on their own resources. Even assistance from the militia would only succeed in providing a relatively weak frontier defence force. Most of these reserves would consist of younger elements, among whom the National Socialist movement had made a number of converts, and their co-operation could not necessarily be guaranteed. The double duty of defending the frontier and maintaining internal law and order would almost certainly make it impossible to maintain military discipline.

'The most likely development in Hamburg would be a dock workers' strike. This would bring the work of the port to a standstill and hinder both the importation of food and the delivery of exports. The uniformed and auxiliary forces at the disposal of the State were insufficient to guarantee essential services. In the Ruhr, all work in the mines and in heavy industry could be expected to cease. Shipping on the Rhine would come to a standstill and separatist elements would show their hand again. The absolute prohibition of any intervention by the armed forces in the demilitarized zone presented an additional difficulty. The local *gendarmerie* were the only representatives of law and order, and they had proved themselves completely ineffective in previous disturbances. Experience in recent months had shown that the police could not be relied upon to act decisively against the Communists. No guarantee could therefore be given that the economic life of the country could be protected.

'Similar considerations held in every other part of the country. There was no possibility of providing reserves to be used at the major sources of danger. I therefore informed the Minister of Defence that although administrative measures under a decree of emergency could be set in motion immediately, detailed study had shown that the defence of the frontiers and the maintenance of order against both Nazis and Communists was beyond the strength of the forces at the disposal of the Federal and State Governments. It was therefore recommended that the Reich Government should abstain from declaring a state of emergency.'

It should be noticed how clearly this report proved the limitation of internal action imposed upon us by the restrictions of the Versailles Treaty. However, the problem at the time was a practical one. After Ott had withdrawn, it became clear that most of the Cabinet agreed with his exposition. I declared the meeting closed and announced that in view of the new situation which had arisen, I felt obliged to make an immediate report to the President, particularly as Schleicher had failed to mention these considerations to him the day before.

I went straight to see the President, gave him an account of what had happened, and asked whether the directive I had received was valid. While I did not doubt that there would be local disorders, I was not convinced that there would be a general strike, although the Communists would certainly attempt to organize one. Their attempt to do so in July had met with little success. If the nation as a whole could be convinced that my Government had no other goal but to provide employment and restore a functioning democracy, even if this should involve sharp measures against the Communists and Nazis, then I saw no reason to fear a civil war.

I admitted this was still a matter for conjecture. In the last resort the responsibility for the Army lay with Schleicher, and ultimately with the President. I shared with Schleicher the opinion that we incurred great risks by involving the Army, but at the moment only two solutions were possible. If I was to carry out the previous day's directive, Schleicher would have to be replaced as Minister of Defence, in favour of some other officer pledged to carry out the Government's policies. The other possibility was to follow Schleicher's suggestion and appoint him Chancellor.

The old Field-Marshal listened to me again in silence. When he replied, his voice had lost the confident ring it had had only twenty-four hours earlier. 'My dear Papen,' he said, 'you will not think much of me if I change my mind. But I am too old and have been through too much to accept the responsibility for a civil war. Our only hope is to let Schleicher try his luck.' Two great tears were rolling down his cheeks as I shook his hand and turned to go. Our months of co-operation were at an end. The measure of our mutual trust and confidence can perhaps be judged by the inscription on the photograph he sent me a few hours later as a parting present: '*Ich hatt' einen Kameraden!*'

The next day I received a letter in his own hand:

'I have acceded to your request to be relieved of the posts of Reich Chancellor and Reich Commissioner for Prussia. I do so with a heavy heart and only in response to the arguments you have seen fit to present. My confidence in you, and respect for you and for all you have done, remains unshaken. During your short six months of office I have learnt to appreciate fully the selfless nature of your work, your love of country and your admirable character. I shall never forget our work together, and I would like to express in my own name and that of the country my appreciation of all that you have accomplished in the recent difficult months.

'Please accept my best wishes for the future. With friendly greetings,

von Hindenburg.'

I need hardly add that my final resignation was greeted with joy by the Nazis, the Zentrum and the left wing parties. Only the Liberal and Conservative press found something good to say for my administration. In taking my leave of the Cabinet, I thanked the ministers for their co-operation and requested all who remained at their posts to continue working for their country with my friend and successor. Schleicher, for his part, offered me the post of Ambassador in Paris. I was greatly attracted, because it would have been an admirable opportunity for improving Franco-German

relations. I discussed the idea with the President, but he asked me
not to accept the post for the time being. He would gladly see me
in Paris, but the immediate future was going to be so full of difficulties that he would prefer to have me within reach, so that I
could give him my advice from time to time. I could not bring
myself to resist his request, and stayed in Berlin.

CHAPTER XIII

FROM SCHLEICHER TO HITLER

Schleicher's Government – The Schroeder lunch – The Lippe elections –
Financing the Nazi Party – Schleicher in trouble – The Strasser plot
fails – Schleicher's last fling – Homo regius – An approach to Hitler –
The Hitler Cabinet formed – Thoughts on Schleicher

SCHLEICHER'S first declaration of policy contained little controversial matter. It was clearly his intention to heal the rupture
between the Cabinet and the political parties. There was no
further mention of reforms and the emphasis was on reconciliation.
If his policy was to be successful, it was the only line to adopt. He
made some kind remarks about me and let it be understood that
we had parted on the best of terms. No hint of the dramatic events
of the previous forty-eight hours reached the public.

Most of my intimate friends were highly critical of my having
relinquished office at such a decisive moment. They were probably
right. It was quite true that I felt no personal animosity towards
Schleicher. He was doubtless justified in taking full responsibility
for the political developments he had directed from behind the
scenes for so long. We had come to differ on matters of policy, but
I had no wish to reduce it to a personal issue. A fortnight later I
was guest of honour at a dinner given by the Berlin Herrenklub,
at which I gave a résumé of the six months' work of my Cabinet
and underlined the necessity for reforms, as I saw them. I dated the
real deterioration in the situation, as I have done in these pages,
from Brüning's failure to take the Nazis into coalition before the
Presidential election, at a time when such a possibility still existed.

There were more than three hundred people present, and we
continued our discussion of the political situation long after the
dinner had ended. One of the guests was Schroeder, the Cologne
banker. We spent a few minutes together and had a conversation
so general in character that it required later developments to recall
it. As far as I could make out, he seemed to be of the opinion that
the Government was still under an obligation to reach some

accommodation with Hitler. Perhaps it would still be possible to range the Nazi movement behind the reconstruction work necessary for the country. When he suggested that it might still be possible to make a personal approach to Hitler, I agreed.

There seemed nothing out of the way in this, since Schleicher and I had been seeking for months to devise some way of working with the Nazis. There the matter rested, so far as I was concerned. If I had attached any importance to the episode, I would have mentioned it to Schleicher before I left Berlin. As it was, I left for my home in the Saar just before Christmas without thinking twice about the conversation, and was only reminded of it on December 28. Schroeder rang me up to ask whether I would be free to meet Hitler during the next few days. I told him that I was going to Berlin, via Düsseldorf, on January 4, and could stop at Cologne on the way if he wished.

This was the casual beginning of a meeting which caused as much controversy as anything I have done. At the Nuremberg Trial the prosecution described my lunch with Hitler as the beginning of our plot to bring the Nazis to power. This is an almost unbelievably naïve interpretation; most of the political parties had been prepared at one time or another during 1932 to consider a Cabinet with Hitler as Chancellor. Perhaps I can now put the facts straight once and for all.

I must have been asked dozens of times why this conversation with Hitler ever took place. The answer is simple. The Nazis had 195 Reichstag seats, and remained a major political factor under the Schleicher Government. I still had serious doubts whether Schleicher would ever succeed in splitting the party, and even if he did, he would only command a highly unstable majority. Constitutional reform was still as necessary as it had ever been, and the required majority was still not available. There was evidence to suggest that if the party did split, the non-Government wing would probably team up with the extreme left; which, for tactical purposes, they had often shown themselves prepared to do. Schleicher and I had always shared the opinion that this was a development to be avoided at all costs. It still seemed to me far better that the whole Nazi Party should be saddled with the responsibilities of Government in coalition. By December, Schleicher's plan was already proving itself unworkable. Strasser had, in fact, broken away from the party, after angry scenes with Hitler, but not a single member of importance had followed him. It seemed to me that all the current rumours concerning the weakness of the party were greatly exaggerated. Hitler had restored discipline with his usual ruthlessness. Their finances were supposed to be in a bad state, which was hardly surprising considering the sums that had been spent during the November election. But financially the party had always managed to keep its head above water, whether the funds came from industrial circles or from abroad – a topic that I shall deal with later.

I thought there was still a possibility of persuading Hitler to join the Schleicher Government. A number of leading Nazis were convinced that the losses in the November election meant that the strength of the movement had passed its peak and that they would be well advised to join the Government now. I had not the slightest intention of causing Schleicher difficulties, and thought rather in terms of picking up the threads of my discussions with Hitler in the previous August. I would probably have been less sanguine if I had known of the approach that Schleicher had made to Hitler during the second half of November. Major Ott, whom we have come across before, and who was by way of being in Schleicher's confidence, produced an interesting piece of evidence at the Nuremberg Trial. He said that Schleicher had sent him to Hitler at Weimar with an offer to join the Cabinet he hoped to form when I resigned. Hitler rejected the idea out of hand. However, I knew nothing of this development at the time, and can only assume that Schleicher had a bad conscience about negotiating in this way behind my back.

I arrived at Schroeder's house about midday, and can remember being somewhat surprised as I got out of the taxi at having my photograph taken by a man standing at the entrance. I believe the popular version of this meeting described it as a highly secret affair, with Hitler being smuggled in alone through a back door. In fact, he was not alone at all. I found him in the company of Hess, at that time his secretary, Wilhelm Keppler, his economic adviser, and Himmler. Apart from myself, Schroeder was the only other person present. Hitler and I went off into a room by ourselves and our discussion began badly enough. He broke into a bitter tirade about the way I had treated him on August 13, and then vented his wrath about the Potempa sentences. I told him I could see little purpose in his outburst and said it was certainly not

the sort of thing I had come to hear. I had been given to understand by Schroeder that Hitler wanted to renew some sort of
contact with the Government and discuss immediate future developments with me. Hitler was monopolizing the conversation with
his customary vehemence, until, in the end, I managed to suggest
that it was high time his movement engaged in some sort of
responsible co-operation with the Government. If he would accept
the post of Vice-Chancellor in Schleicher's Cabinet, there was no
reason to suppose that some acceptable division of labour could
not be worked out. I even went so far as to suggest that Schleicher
might be agreeable to some sort of *duum-virat*, and that I would be
prepared to suggest this to him. I wanted to make the idea of
Hitler joining the Government as attractive as possible, in the
circumstances. If he was still not prepared to take office himself,
the suggestion I had made in August, of offering ministerial posts
to some of his colleagues, might yet provide a means of his
becoming Chancellor.

Our conversation turned on this point until Schroeder told us
that lunch was served. As Hitler sat down to his usual vegetarian
meal, I had the impression that he felt we had cleared up certain
misunderstandings and seemed gratified that I still considered he
should take part in the work of government. I promised him that
I would try to influence Schleicher to adopt this solution. We
touched on none of the other topics invented later by the press,
nor did the question even arise of forming a Cabinet with Hitler as
Chancellor, as an alternative to the Schleicher Government.
Schroeder himself has confirmed this, and so has Keppler, in the
correspondence between Schroeder and himself, which has recently
been published. It was Keppler, it seems, who took the initiative in
arranging this meeting, apparently with the intention of renewing
contact with Schleicher and organizing what I believe is called in
these days, a 'pipeline' to Hindenburg. In a note to Schroeder the
next day, he says: 'I had the impression the meeting went very
well, and would be interested to know what the other side [Papen]
feels about it.' He confirms, in other words, that we were only
trying to clear the air, and makes no mention of a Hitler Government. That is all there is to the famous Schroeder lunch. The left
wing press, and a number of organs abroad, have suggested that
the real purpose of our meeting was to devise some means of
bolstering the Nazis' tottering finances. It was even suggested that

if I did not actually place sums at their disposal myself, I induced some of my industrialist friends to do so. All I have to say about this is that neither the Nazi Party, nor any of its organizations, nor Hitler himself, ever got a penny from me. Nor did I at any time arrange for a subsidy from any third party. The finances of the Nazi movement were not even mentioned at the meeting with Schroeder.

The whole question of the finances of the Nazi movement at this period has become one of the most controversial issues connected with Hitler's eventual rise to power. Circumstantial evidence of a compelling nature has led to my name being connected with an elaborate fable which seeks to pin on me the responsibility for furnishing Hitler with urgently needed funds at this critical juncture. I am afraid that I shall once again have to disappoint the rumour-mongers who have so often found me a convenient victim for their inventive imagination. Not a word of the accusation is true.

The most documented account of the National Socialists' sudden acquisition of funds was contained in a book published in Holland in 1933, called *De Geldbronnen van het Nationaal-Socialisme*.[1] The author's name was given as 'Sidney Warburg,' and he gave an exhaustive list of names, dates and payments. The alleged author's thesis was that American financial interests had sought to protect their investments in Europe by placing at the disposal of the Nazi Party, through various intermediaries and banking houses, considerable sums of money to instigate a national revolution and ensure Germany's financial stability. All the copies disappeared soon after publication, although one has come into my possession, together with another book dealing with the same subject, called *Liebet Eure Feinde*,[2] by Werner Zimmermann. This book contains a chapter called *Hitlers geheime Geldgeber* ('Hitler's Secret Financial Supporters') in which the original 'Sidney Warburg' story is repeated with certain variations, one of which is to add my name to the list of contributors.

I have mentioned these publications not only because they summarize, but also because they probably provide the principal basis for the circumstantial account which has attained such currency.

[1] Van Holkema & Warendorf, Amsterdam, 1933.
[2] Fankhauser Verlag, Thielle-Neuchâtel, 1948.

Indeed, the general line of argument was revived again in the German press in 1948. It is therefore particularly gratifying to me to be able to quote for the first time for publication an affidavit made on July 15, 1949, by Mr James P. Warburg, the present head of the family of American bankers, whose name was used to give authenticity to the original fabrication. I have obtained his permission to reproduce this lengthy refutation and it is printed as an appendix to this book.

Mr Warburg's detailed researches have determined that the original 'Sidney Warburg' confession was written by one J. G. Schoup, now dead, and this has since been admitted by his son to have been a forgery. 'Sidney Warburg' was alleged to be the son of the late Paul M. Warburg, but he had no son of this name. His heir, James P. Warburg, is able to refute the whole falsification in his affidavit. He is also able to deal conclusively with the reiterated accusations in the Zimmermann book, together with yet another version contained in a book called *Spanischer Sommer*,[1] written by a Herr René Sonderegger, *alias* Severin Reinhardt, who at one time lived in Zurich.

For my own part, I am most grateful to Mr Warburg for disposing once and for all of this malicious libel. It is almost impossible to refute accusations of this sort by simple negation, and his authoritative denial has enabled me to give body to my own protestations. I can only add the most solemn asseveration that on no occasion did I ever place a single penny at Hitler's disposal or at his party's disposal, either from my own funds or resources or anybody else's.

The financial problems of the Nazi Party were no concern of mine, and I certainly made no approach to Schroeder in the matter. It is a fact that after the Hitler Government had been formed, Dr Schacht collected a campaign chest with subscriptions from various industrial and commercial firms, but then I was not one of Hitler's candidates. At the next election I was standing with my friends on the 'Black-White-Red' list, and we neither contributed to Hitler's fund nor obtained any support from it.

It is high time that some of these 'revelations' about financial support for Hitler were put in their right perspective. What sums were forthcoming to support the Lippe elections I do not know,

[1] Aehren Verlag, Auffoltern, Switzerland.

and it would now be difficult to find out. Schroeder and Thyssen may well have banded together for the purpose, although it seems unlikely that the sum of 200 millions was ever forthcoming.

I had arranged to spend a few days with my mother in Düsseldorf after the Schroeder lunch, and therefore did not go on to Berlin immediately. But first I went to the Excelsior Hotel in Cologne and sent off a long letter to Schleicher, describing my meeting with Hitler and the subject matter of our discussions. It must have been on his desk the next morning. My astonishment can well be imagined, therefore, when the morning papers on January 5 came out with an account of our meeting, accompanied by massive attacks on the 'disloyalty' I had shown to Schleicher. The messages were date-lined from Berlin, and must have been given to the press before Schleicher had any chance of knowing what we had talked about. I hurried to the telephone to give the press my own account of what had passed, and then also discovered that Schroeder had, on his own initiative and without any previous contact with me, stressed to the newspapers that the meeting had taken place at his suggestion. Such totally inaccurate accounts were being published that I even had to ask Hitler to issue a communiqué giving his version of the affair, and this he did.

The background was even more curious and distressing. Schleicher, it seems, had come to regard me with considerable suspicion. He was well aware of my close relations with the President, and knew that Hindenburg had parted company with me very much against his will. The knowledge that I still had access to the Field-Marshal was displeasing to him. He kept a sharp watch on my movements and even had my telephone tapped. He therefore knew all about the proposed meeting in Schroeder's house and was responsible for the presence of the photographer, who turned out to be a detective. In retrospect, I suppose, I must allow for Schleicher's surprise at learning of this development without receiving any information from me. If he had waited a few hours he would not have needed to start such a large political hare. In any case, I cannot really understand why he did not make a perfectly straightforward enquiry, in view of our long personal relationship. At least he would have appreciated that I was completely ignorant of any suggestion of tension between us, and that the idea had not crossed my mind that any attempt to make Hitler see reason would be distasteful to him.

When I finally got to Berlin on the 9th, I went straight to the Chancellery and spent an hour and a half with Schleicher in an attempt to clear up the misunderstanding. He seemed perfectly satisfied, and my wife recorded in her diary that I had reported him as saying, 'It would be the worst day of my life if I lost your friendship.' Some of his comments to mutual acquaintances were much less favourable. 'If Papen lasts the winter, he will be in power for good,' he told one of our friends. However, he put out a communiqué on January 10, which said: 'The conversation between Herr von Papen and the Reich Chancellor gave no ground for assertions in the press that differences had arisen between them as a result of this meeting.' The one point that I want to make absolutely clear is that the developments that were to come on January 30 had nothing whatsoever to do with my discussions on the 4th.

Germany's political fate was being decided during these few weeks of the Schleicher Government. And it may be of interest to record developments in diary form as I noted them down at the time. But first let me add that I went to see Hindenburg immediately after my discussion with Schleicher on the 9th. I assumed he had learnt of the press attacks against me and I wanted to give my own account of what had happened. Instead I learnt, with some repugnance, of Schleicher's manœuvres. To the President he had represented my talk with Hitler as a piece of gross disloyalty, and had demanded that Hindenburg should refrain from seeing me any more; this, moreover, after my explanatory letter of January 4 must have reached him. When I had enlightened Hindenburg about the true state of things, he said, 'That is what I thought all along. I simply could not believe Schleicher's version. In any case, the whole affair makes not the slightest difference to our relations.'

January 11: Hitler passed through Berlin on his way to the regional elections in the State of Lippe. Strasser, who was being mentioned as Vice-Chancellor, had an interview with Hindenburg, but was finding it difficult to reach any measure of agreement with Schleicher. The German Nationalists were proclaiming the necessity of giving the Government a chance, and were suggesting that Hugenberg, the Conservative leader, should be taken into the Cabinet as Minister of Economics. The Government was having difficulties with the Reichslandbund, a farmers' union that included the more well-to-do landowners, which was holding a Congress where protests were made against the Marxist methods of the Government in the agricultural sphere.

January 12: More attacks from the Reichslandbund, which declared that the Government was paying no attention to the plight of agriculture.

January 13: The attitude of the Reichslandbund may well have been concerted with Hugenberg, who went to see Schleicher on this date, and demanded that the German Nationalists should be represented in the Government, with himself as Minister of Economics. Schleicher refused, and was apparently still bent on reaching agreement with Strasser.

January 14: Hugenberg saw Hindenburg, apparently to discuss the possibility of taking the centre and right wing parties into the Cabinet.

January 15: Local elections for the State Assembly had become due in the Principality of Lippe-Detmold. It was a small and unimportant area, and the vote would normally have been without significance. It must not be forgotten, though, that the Nazis had suffered a serious reverse in the national elections of the previous November. The party was in a state of considerable confusion. Many of its members were objecting to Hitler's policy of 'all or nothing', and Schleicher's negotiations with the Strasser wing seemed to indicate that a split in the party was imminent. Schleicher's efforts had been countered for the time being by the decision of the Nazi provincial chiefs to opt for Hitler rather than Strasser, who was now on the point of being ejected from the party. But the Nazis were under an obligation to prove to the electorate that they were not subject to the sort of internal dissension which weakened other parties, and that their leadership was strong and determined. In warning Schleicher on December 1 not to stake all his fortunes on one card, I had been proved only too right.

The possibility still existed that Hitler would succeed in presenting a united front, in spite of widespread disillusionment among the broad mass of his followers. This would only be proved by the results of the next election. Hitler and his entourage therefore exerted their last reserves of energy and influence in order to prove to the nation that the decline in their fortunes had been arrested and that the movement was now stronger than ever. The course of the Lippe elections therefore focused the attention of the whole country, and it acquired the importance of, say, the mid-term elections in the United States, or a critical by-election in Great Britain. The result showed surprisingly high gains for the Nazis and equally surprising losses for the right wing parties, whose total of votes fell by a third. As a result, the general tension in the country increased.

January 16: Schleicher received Kaas, the Zentrum Party leader. The situation was by now very difficult and complicated. The agricultural associations had declared more or less open warfare on the Government. Schleicher recognized this as a critical factor, and threatened to proclaim a state of emergency, if necessary. He seemed to be realizing that his *rapprochement* with Strasser was not having the effect he desired.

January 17: Hitler had a meeting with Hugenberg. He had now finally broken with Strasser. The main point at issue seemed to be whether Hitler and Hugenberg should form a combined opposition or join the Government together.

January 20: The Reichstag Steering Committee decided to postpone the opening of the session from the 24th to the 31st, and agreed to meet again on the 27th to consider the situation. The Nazi committee members were in favour of this postponement, as it gave them more time to decide their attitude in Parliament; the Government welcomed it because their budget proposals were not yet ready. However, Planck, the State Secretary, declared on behalf of the Chancellor, that the Government was no longer interested in possible parliamentary combinations. It was hinted that if, on the 31st, the Government was presented with an impossible situation, a state of emergency would be declared and new elections would be postponed until the autumn. This was indeed a turning point. It was now clear to everybody that Schleicher had given up all hope of splitting the Nazis in order to form a majority Government. He had decided to continue in office, even if this entailed a breach of the Constitution.

January 21: The German Nationalists decided to oppose Schleicher. They declared the need for immediate measures and condemned further delay as harmful. Schleicher had made little headway with the Socialists, and was now tolerated only by the Zentrum. My own Cabinet was based on no party affiliations, but at least it had the tacit support of the right. Yet Schleicher told Hindenburg that a second Papen Government would have no point, because it would only enjoy the support of 10 per cent of the nation. Schleicher was now in the same position himself, and was apparently resuscitating my suggestion that the Reichstag should be adjourned *sine die*.

January 22: The Nazis realized the weakness of Schleicher's position. They were no longer interested in joining the Government after the defection of Hugenberg and the Reichslandbund.

At this juncture I received another approach from Hitler. He sent von Ribbentrop, whom I had known as a young lieutenant in Turkey during the war, to invite me to his house in Dahlem. I asked Hindenburg whether there was any point in my seeing Hitler again. The President thought there was and that I should see what Hitler intended, now that Schleicher had reached an *impasse*. In order to make quite sure of my position, I asked that the President's son, Oscar, and his Secretary of State, Meissner, should accompany me. I was to show myself in a receptive mood and to find out whether, and in what circumstances, Hitler would be prepared to join the Government.

I found both Hitler and Frick at Ribbentrop's house, where we were later joined by Goering, who had just made a speech in Dresden, saying that under no circumstances should Hitler join the present Government. Hitler asked me how the President viewed the situation. I told him that Hindenburg had not changed his mind about offering him the post of Chancellor, but realized that the situation itself had changed. It was now more than ever necessary to integrate the Nazi movement into this or some new Government.

Hitler declined flatly to join the Schleicher Government, and insisted again and again that the only circumstances in which the Nazis would co-operate would be under his Chancellorship. He complained that our communiqué on August 13 had declared that he had demanded exclusive power for the party. That had not been true; nor did he make that demand now. It would be easy to reach agreement on a coalition with members of the bourgeois parties, providing these ministers maintained the institution of a Presidential Cabinet and did not remain responsible to their own parties. During the evening, Hitler repeated all these arguments to Meissner and Oscar Hindenburg, on whom he seemed to make a strong impression.

I wish to make it quite clear that the actual question of forming a cabinet with Hitler as Chancellor was not discussed by Oscar Hindenburg, Meissner or myself. I had had no contact whatever with Hitler between January 4 and 22.

January 23: A decisive development. Schleicher saw the President and told him that his plan to split the Nazi Party could no longer be carried out. There was therefore no possibility of forming a Cabinet with a parliamentary majority, unless Hitler became Chancellor. The only alternative was to declare a state of emergency and dissolve the Reichstag. Schleicher asked for the powers to do this.

I had been right on December 1. Schleicher's plan was now identical with my own, but when he asked the President to countenance a breach of the Constitution, Hindenburg answered: 'On December 2 you declared that such a measure would lead to civil war. The Army and the police, in your opinion, were not strong enough to deal with internal unrest on a large scale. Since then the situation has been worsening for seven weeks. The Nazis consider themselves in a stronger position, and the left wing is more radical in its intentions than ever. If civil war was likely then, it is even more so now, and the Army will be still less capable of coping with it. In these circumstances I cannot possibly accede to your request for dissolution of the Reichstag and *carte blanche* to deal with the situation.'

January 24: The public was still ignorant of Schleicher's rebuff at the hands of the President, but the German Nationalists returned to the attack on the Government. They declared that Schleicher's policy meant the surrender of the authoritarian principles which led to the formation of the Papen Cabinet. Some sections of the press demanded my return as Chancellor. Schleicher declared his intention of refraining from any breach of the Constitution. Yet there was no sign of any parliamentary majority to support him.

January 25: No attempt was made to organize a breathing-space for Schleicher. Hugenberg, presumably offended by Schleicher's refusal on January 13 to take him into the Government, seemed to have made up his mind to oppose him at all costs.

January 26: More confusion and a new set of rumours. The Harzburger Front combination of German Nationalists and Nazis appeared to be finding common ground in their opposition to Schleicher. The possibility of a resignation of the Government was being mooted. One would have thought that the more moderate parties would press for a postponement of the opening of Parliament, to give a little more time for the settlement of the crisis.

January 27: The Reichstag Steering Committee met again, and agreed that the Reichstag should assemble, as arranged, on the 31st. The existence of the Government was now clearly threatened. Many organs of public opinion considered that everything depended on the Chancellor obtaining full powers from the President. It was still not known that this had already been refused. In view of the difficulties involved in granting power to Hitler, there were again suggestions in many quarters that I should form a new Government. The Nazis announced that they would take no part in any plan to declare a state of emergency and govern without either elections or Parliament.

In my report to Hindenburg after the meeting in Ribbentrop's house on the 22nd, I had recommended that Schleicher be given every opportunity to reach some agreement with the Reichstag, and that the President should allow a little more time for this. It was still possible that he might get agreement to a postponement. I had advised against my own reappointment as Chancellor, as I felt that my chances were even slimmer than they had been two months previously. I saw the President again on the 27th and told him there could be no question of my accepting the responsibility; it would simply mean a return to my plan of December 1. I asked him to let Schleicher know that I had no intention of threatening the Government's position in this way.

January 28: Schleicher played one more card. In the *Tägliche Rundschau*, the paper he controlled, an inspired article suggested that a Papen Cabinet with dictatorial powers would threaten the President's own position. The article announced that Schleicher would call on the President to make a formal request for powers to dissolve the Reichstag. If this was not granted, the Cabinet would resign and the President would have to assume sole responsibility for subsequent developments. Three possibilities would then present themselves: a coalition between the Nazis and the Zentrum, which was unlikely in view of Zentrum objections to the Nazis taking over the ministries of defence, transport and the interior; a Cabinet formed from the Harzburger Front, in which the Nazis would meet opposition from Hugenberg to Hitler's

appointment as Chancellor; or, as Hugenberg wanted it, a dictatorial Cabinet under Papen, supported by the German Nationalists
and dependent on the granting of full powers by the President.
The article considered that this last solution would be catastrophic;
such a Cabinet would lead to a crisis in the Presidency, which
should be avoided at all costs.

After this attempt to mobilize public opinion, Schleicher went
to the President, but his demand for full powers for himself again
met the arguments the President had used on the 23rd. Hindenburg refused to grant the dissolution of the Reichstag, and
Schleicher presented the resignation of his whole Cabinet.

He had given up all hope of organizing a parliamentary majority,
and had come round to the opinion that a Presidential Cabinet
under Hitler was the only solution. After Schleicher's resignation,
the Nazis made it clear that they would only settle for a Government with Hitler as Chancellor. During the whole of January their
press had rejected in the sharpest possible terms any idea of a
second Papen Government. The course of events after January 4
makes it impossible to defend the idea that my interview with
Hitler on that date opened the way for his Chancellorship. In later
years the Socialists have also made much play with the accusation
that I prevented Schleicher from basing part of his support on the
Trade Unions. Yet no less an authority than Gustav Noske, the
Socialist leader, makes it quite clear in his memoirs[1] that Leipart,
the Trade Union leader, was instructed by the Social Democrats
not to respond to Schleicher's overtures. The Strasser-Leipart 'axis',
on which Schleicher hoped to build the fortunes of his Government, was therefore doomed to failure.

About midday on January 28 I was called to the President. He
gave me an account of Schleicher's last visit and his resignation.
He had been told at an early hour of the *Tägliche Rundschau* article,
with its threats of a crisis in the Presidency and the possibility of a
breach of the Constitution being regarded as treason. He would
have expected such methods from a politician, he told me, but he
could not forgive an officer for employing them. The possibility
of my forming another Government was barely touched on, and
then only in contrast to what he considered the unpleasant duty of

[1] *Erlebtes aus Aufstieg und Niedergang eine Demokratie*. Bollwerk-Verlag, Karl
Drott, Offenbach, 1947.

calling on Hitler. I made what suggestions I could for keeping the Nazis within bounds. These were adopted when the new Cabinet was formed two days later. The President then asked me, as *homo regius*, to sound out the possibilities of forming a Cabinet under Hitler within the terms of the Constitution. I felt I had to carry out the President's request, because no one else seemed capable of reaching an acceptable compromise with Hitler. If the Defence and Foreign Ministries were given to people in whom the President had confidence, some of the other posts could be given with a clear conscience to the Nazis. Later in the day the Reichstag Steering Committee met again and agreed to postpone the session announced for Monday, the 31st, to give time for the formation of a new Government.

I had my first interview with Hugenberg on the afternoon of January 28. He shared my opinion that Hitler would under no circumstances form a majority Government. There was no point in calling again on Schleicher, who had antagonized all the right wing parties, and only retained the confidence of the Zentrum. We had to reach some agreement with Hitler and seek to limit his prerogatives as much as possible. Hugenberg demanded the Reich and Prussian Ministries of Economics, in return for the support of the German Nationalists.

Thereupon I received Hitler. As I expected, he refused flatly to form a Government based on a parliamentary majority. If the President desired his movement to co-operate in the work of government, then he must be allowed to form a Presidential Cabinet with the same rights as those accorded to Schleicher and myself. On the other hand, he had no intention of making exaggerated ministerial demands, and was perfectly prepared to include certain men from the previous Cabinets who enjoyed the President's confidence.

I told him that the mission I had undertaken on behalf of the President did not permit Hitler discretion in choosing the members of the Cabinet. He replied that the President could fill all the ministerial posts, provided the ministers regarded themselves as independent of the political parties. Hitler desired to be Chancellor and Commissioner for Prussia, and wanted a member of his party to be Minister of the Interior in both the Reich and Prussia.

Later the same evening I saw Dr Schaeffer of the Bavarian

People's Party. He told me that both he and Brüning were prepared to accept ministerial posts under Hitler. I had to reply that there was no question of this. Hitler was not engaged in forming a majority Government, and wanted his Cabinet to consist of people without party affiliations. I expressed my regret that Brüning should have made up his mind to collaborate with Hitler so late in the day, at a time when co-operation was no longer possible. In reply, Schaeffer emphasized that there was no question of himself and Brüning joining a Papen Cabinet.

Dr Schaeffer was to appear as a prosecution witness at my denazification trial in 1947. He confirmed under oath that he had expressed his own and Brüning's willingness to share in the work of a Hitler Cabinet and blamed me for not having taken up the offer. Brüning, on the other hand, has declared that he never had the least intention of joining a Hitler Cabinet. They cannot both be right.

It was late at night before I was able to report progress to the President. He seemed gratified at the moderation Hitler had displayed, and was delighted that men like Neurath, Schwerin-Krosigk, Guertner and Eltz would retain their posts in the new Government. He insisted once again that the Foreign and War Ministries should be put in the hands of completely reliable people. Neurath was to remain Foreign Minister, and we ranged over the list of possible names for the War Ministry. My own suggestion was General von Fritsch, with whom I had spent my early military career and whose capabilities I admired. Hindenburg did not turn him down, but indicated that he would prefer someone with whom he was better acquainted. Finally he came out with the name of General von Blomberg, whom he had known as Commander of the East Prussian military district. Hindenburg considered him a gifted professional soldier, completely apolitical and with a pleasant personality. As head of the German military delegation at the Disarmament Commission, he had shown himself the possessor of all the qualities necessary for a minister. I had only a passing acquaintance with him, but I felt that I could rely on Hindenburg's judgment. If, as the President said, he had kept out of politics, it should be possible to rely on him to turn a deaf ear to the blandishments of the Nazis.

Hindenburg then went on to suggest that I should get Hugenberg to take over the combined Economic posts in one ministry.

He also asked me to get from Hitler the names of the Nazis he wished to appoint to the Cabinet. His final request, right at the end of our conversation, was for me to take on the post of deputy Chancellor, as he particularly wished to retain my services for the time being. I must confess that this request came as no surprise, but I wish to emphasize that I had at no time made any such suggestion myself. It seemed a natural precaution for him to take, once he had finally made up his mind to take the dreaded plunge of appointing Hitler as Chancellor. I felt it was the least service I could give, and I undertook to accept the post if we succeeded in forming the Cabinet.

January 29: Another day of interviews and discussions. My first visitors were Hitler and Goering. They said they wished to appoint Frick as Reich Minister of the Interior, and Goering himself to the same post in Prussia. Frick was known as a senior Civil servant and a man of moderate opinions, who had been a success as head of the State Government of Thuringia. Both my visitors insisted that the Prussian police, which had been in the hands of the Social Democrats for ten years, would have to undergo certain changes in personnel. They declared that this would be necessary if the police were to be relied upon to deal effectively with the Communists, and with my experiences in the previous July in mind, I felt that this was by no means a negligible argument. I told Hitler that the President did not intend to give him powers as Reich Commissioner for Prussia, and that these would remain vested in me as Vice-Chancellor. Hitler accepted this decision with a bad grace, but did not make an issue of it.

My conversations with Hugenberg and some of his Harzburger Front colleagues were chiefly about the measures we should adopt to combat the Nazis' totalitarian tendencies, but we reached no definite plan. I told Hugenberg that the President wished him to act as a co-ordinator of economic affairs, and he seemed to consider this immense task well within his powers. He then introduced Seldte and Duesterberg, the two leaders of the Stahlhelm organization, who undertook to give the new Government their support.

The Stahlhelm, it should be remarked, had always been a conservative and stabilizing factor in the political warfare of the day. It was a well organized association of ex-servicemen, with a very considerable membership, whose activities had always provided a contrast with the excesses of the Brownshirts and the Communist Rotfront. Stahlhelm support would be an important factor in maintaining some sort of balance against the Nazis. We decided that their co-operation should be further assured by appointing Seldte Minister of Labour. The Stahlhelm had always been renowned for the efficiency of its social insurance scheme, which had largely been built up by Seldte himself, and we felt that this was a particularly apt appointment.

My visitors were not all of such an approving turn of mind. A number of my Conservative friends begged me to take no part whatever in forming a Hitler Cabinet. I explained time and again that there was no other solution within the framework of the Constitution. The political parties, and the Socialists in particular, could have given Schleicher one last chance by postponing the meeting of the Reichstag. By failing to do so, they had tacitly acknowledged that the only alternative to Hitler was a breach of the Constitution.

Schleicher, in the meantime, found another card to play. He sent one of his private emissaries, von Alvensleben, to Goering, who immediately hurried over to me with the news. Schleicher had sent a message that my real intention was to deceive the Nazis, and that they would do very much better to combine with Schleicher, who only wished to retain the post of Minister of Defence. Alvensleben had indicated that means could be found to neutralize Hindenburg. Schleicher had apparently even gone so far as to suggest that if the 'old gentleman' should prove difficult, he, Schleicher, would mobilize the Potsdam garrison. Goering told me that he and Hitler had returned a flat negative to the plan and had immediately told Meissner and Oscar von Hindenburg.

This sequel to the *Tägliche Rundschau's* remarks about a crisis in the Presidency seemed highly dangerous. I hurried to see Hindenburg, whose son had told him of this new development. He seemed comparatively unmoved, and declined to believe that a serving general and Chancellor, albeit a provisional one, would lend himself to such a step against the head of the State. We decided, however, that it was absolutely essential to have a new Minister of Defence, and a telegram was sent to Blomberg asking him to leave Geneva immediately and report to the President in Berlin the next day.

The rumour got about that Schleicher was planning a Reichswehr *Putsch* to remove the President. Whether, in fact, he ever really intended to take this step, or discussed it with General von Hammerstein, the Chief of Staff, will probably never be known. But it is interesting to record that when Blomberg arrived at the railway station next day, one of Hammerstein's staff officers was there to greet him with orders to report to the General immediately. The fact that he was returning was known to no one outside Hindenburg's official household and myself, so Schleicher must therefore have been tapping the wires again. This attempt to get Blomberg to Hammerstein failed, because Oscar von Hindenburg was also at the station and escorted him to the President. The whole atmosphere had become so fantastic, with this possible threat of a *coup*, that I made up my mind to get the Cabinet formed as quickly as we could.

January 30: Blomberg saw the President at about nine o'clock in the morning and was given a résumé of the situation. The President impressed upon him most particularly the necessity of reversing Schleicher's course and keeping the Army out of politics. At about half-past ten the members of the proposed Cabinet met in my house and walked across the garden to the Presidential palace, where we waited in Meissner's office. Hitler immediately renewed his complaints about not being appointed Commissioner for Prussia. He felt that this severely restricted his powers. I told him that the President still wished to be convinced that we were all going to co-operate harmoniously, and that the question of the Prussian appointment could be left until later. To this, Hitler replied that if his powers were to be thus limited, he must insist on new Reichstag elections. To our surprise, he produced the argument that the new combination between the Nazi movement and the right wing groups did not command a parliamentary majority, but if they now went to the country, their position would be assured.

This produced a completely new situation and the debate became heated. Hugenberg, in particular, objected to the idea, and Hitler tried to pacify him by stating that he would make no changes in the Cabinet, whatever the result might be. We all took this with a pinch of salt, but Neurath, Schwerin-Krosigk and Eltz did not raise any objections to the idea of new elections. By this time it was long past eleven o'clock, the time that had been appointed for our interview with the President, and Meissner asked me to end our discussion, as Hindenburg was not prepared to wait any longer.

We had had such a sudden clash of opinions that I was afraid our new coalition would break up before it was born. My immediate reaction to the election idea was that it should be possible to organize a strong group of Conservative candidates to provide some counterweight to the Nazis. I still believed that an electoral bloc of this type would appeal to the voters, and begged Hugenberg to withdraw his objections. We decided to ask the President for a dissolution decree, and extracted from Hitler a promise that he would contact the Zentrum and the Bavarian People's Party, in order to ensure the widest possible basis for a parliamentary majority. At last we were shown in to the President and I made the necessary formal introductions. Hindenburg made a short speech about the necessity for full co-operation in the interests of the nation, and we were then sworn in. The Hitler Cabinet had been formed.

★　★　★

We were to learn in the course of time into what hands the fate of Germany had fallen, and I shall try to give as faithful an account of what followed as I have of the events which led up to this development. One thing must be understood. This first Hitler Government was formed in strict accordance with parliamentary procedure and within the framework of the Constitution. The only possible alternative, as I have gone to such pains to explain, would have involved a breach of the Constitution, and although Hindenburg was prepared at one time to consider this solution, he changed his mind when Schleicher told him that he could not answer for the rôle of the Army.

Schleicher is dead, a victim of the Roehm *Putsch* which came a year later. I knew him for many years, and I am not prepared to speak ill of him. But there are one or two points of historical fact that I must clear up, particularly as, after his resignation, he and members of his immediate circle put about a highly inaccurate account of how my 'intrigues' led to his fall from office. This conception has been fostered by the fact that contemporary observers, such as Brüning and François-Poncet, have based their accounts very largely on Schleicher's opinions.

The idea of suggesting my name to Hindenburg as Chancellor seems to have occurred to Schleicher about the beginning of 1932. We often met socially and shared the same views on the measures needed to meet the situation. He knew the attitude I had held for years within the Zentrum Party. When he asked me whether I would accept the Chancellorship, I left him in no doubt as to the reaction that could be expected from my Zentrum colleagues. Their opposition to my Cabinet can therefore have come as no surprise. What he did not seem to realize was that my opposition to the left wing tendencies of my party was due to deep-seated Conservative convictions, based on Christian conceptions of the social order.

He took me for an opportunist, which is what he was in essence himself, and I misunderstood his character in return, assuming that his political ideas were based on fundamental principles. I only realized how wrong I had been at our meeting with Hindenburg on December 1, 1932, when I saw how readily he was prepared to abandon the fundamentals on which I thought we had agreed. He seemed to forget that we were trying, by a process of constitutional and electoral reform, to give new authority to the institution of government, after the Weimar brand of democracy had ceased to function. We had involved the personal authority of Hindenburg in our programme, and had made it clear to the parties that the business of government could no longer be at the mercy of doctrine and the thirst for personal power.

Until the fateful interview with the President, Schleicher at no time indicated his disagreement with any aspect of our pro-gramme. We had even given the Crown Prince to understand that developments must lead logically to a restoration of the monarchy. Both Schleicher and I were convinced monarchists by tradition and upbringing, although we realized that only special circumstances could ensure the return of the institution of the crown, after it had been lost on the field of battle. We both thought that these circumstances might arise after Hindenburg's death, when the nation would feel the need for some permanent repository of authority amid the ephemeral manifestations of political life. In Bavaria the monarchist current was running strong, and we felt that the nation as a whole might come to desire the same course. I assumed that Schleicher welcomed the idea, particularly as he recognized the difficulties of keeping the

Army out of politics, and in view of his concern at the growth of Nazi sympathies among the younger officers.

François-Poncet is quite wrong in maintaining that Schleicher wished to remain in the background, and that I had brought about the situation which compelled him to take over the Chancellorship, in the hope that he would prove a failure. In the latter part of November 1932, he had sent Planck, my State Secretary (who was one of the 'Schleicher men' in important administrative positions), to Paris. This was done without my knowledge, to find out whether the French would object to a general becoming Chancellor. Again behind my back, he had informed members of the Cabinet, in confidence, that the carrying out of our plan for constitutional reform would lead to a civil war, which the Army would be unable to control. He, meanwhile, was the only alternative candidate as Chancellor. As final proof, I need only mention again his action in sending Ott to Hitler in November, to ask whether the Nazi leader would be prepared to join a Schleicher Cabinet. When all this failed, he produced his plan for splitting the Nazi Party and returning to a Government supported by a weak parliamentary majority.

After six months of sharing the work of the Cabinet in complete harmony, he suddenly produced the argument, both to the President and my colleagues, that 'Papen has only 10 per cent of the German people behind him, and his programme means civil war'. I fail to see how he arrived at this figure. There was no such institution as a Gallup Poll available at the time, but public opinion could still be judged quite accurately. Press reaction to the step I took in Prussia, the considerable wave of approval that greeted my speech at Münster on the Potempa affair, my attitude in the scandalous Reichstag session of October 12, and the delight expressed at the Nazis' loss of thirty-five seats in the elections on November 6, were all signs that there was a considerable body of support for my policies, even if they involved a temporary suspension of the Constitution. The Communists and the Nazis enjoyed the support of about half the nation. But Hitler had many differences within his own party, and it is an open question whether its members would have supported a civil war. Certainly it could have had the support of very few Socialists. The lower and middle classes sought only some improvement in their own individual lot. The disturbers of law and order would have been kept within bounds, and our proposed constitutional reforms in no way threatened the rights of the working classes and their Trade Unions. My Cabinet would have had a hard fight, but we would have enjoyed the support of a very strong minority, much stronger than 10 per cent.

I have already mentioned that when I resigned as Chancellor, Schleicher offered me the post of Ambassador in Paris. It seemed a friendly gesture at the time, but it is clear, on reflection, that he was chiefly concerned in removing me from the immediate entourage of the President. I would have been well pleased to accept the post, and turned it down only because of Hindenburg's personal request. My relationship with Schleicher remained, to all outward appearances, cordial, and my only concern was to help him in his difficult task. At no time did I criticize him to the President, but it was clear that the old gentleman found Schleicher's actions at the beginning of December little to his taste. Schleicher had got in touch with the commanders of all the military districts, who had indicated, through him, their unanimous disapproval of Hindenburg's first decision to back my reform programme. The Field-Marshal felt that his prerogatives had been interfered with and that Schleicher had played off the senior officers against him. He was extraordinarily touchy in such matters and objected strongly to involving serving officers in political decisions.

In his first speech as Chancellor, Schleicher expressed appreciation of his predecessor in phrases that went far beyond those of conventional politeness. I was certainly not led to suppose that he regarded me as an embarrassing element in the political scene, to be discredited at every available opportunity. At the Herrenklub dinner I had proclaimed my sympathy and support for Schleicher to a large gathering of important people. In spite of this, he must have instituted a watch on my movements and telephone calls almost immediately. We became used to this sort of thing in the Third Reich, but at this time it was highly unusual.

The meeting with Hitler in Cologne on January 4 gave him the opportunity he had been looking for to fire his full broadside against me. Without demanding or waiting for any explanation from me, he sent Werner von Alvensleben round to the principal Berlin press organs on the evening of the same day, to give a lurid account of my 'disloyalty'. Not content with that, and in spite of having received my letter of explanation, he then went himself to

I

the President to get Hindenburg to forbid me his house once and for all. The President was very sensitive to any attempt to interfere with his personal relationships, and Schleicher's intervention was a psychological error which caused Hindenburg great offence.

The account I received from Hindenburg of this interview finally broke my confidence in Schleicher. From that time on I sought no further contact with him. I was not particularly incensed at his leaving me in the lurch on December 1, because his reasons seemed to be valid. I had not known that he was plotting against me during the whole of November. But I could not forgive him for trying to blacken my reputation with the man under whose banner we had fought for a new conception of State authority. The least he could have done after our own interview was to retract his statements to the President. He did not do so, but even then I took no steps against him while he was in office, and preferred to indulge in no recriminations.

No sequence of events has been more distorted than the alleged results of my meeting with Hitler on January 4. I am accused of having betrayed the Weimar Republic and of having hoisted Hitler into the saddle under a secret pact. I am then supposed to have taken my revenge on Schleicher for having ousted me from power. If any such plot had been formulated at Schroeder's house, there would have been plenty of opportunity for putting it into effect during the next three weeks, but the correct narrative of events proves that there was never any such intention. Schleicher's last manœuvre, of proclaiming a crisis in the Presidency, would make more sense in this context if it had been directed against the appointment of Hitler as Chancellor, rather than against myself.

Schleicher was not well served by his immediate confidants. Werner von Alvensleben, in particular, was a typical conspirator type, for whom intrigue was an end in itself. His brother, Count Bodo, told me that Werner had once confessed that the plan for the Potsdam *Putsch*, which he had mentioned to Goering and Hitler, had been his own idea and he had merely introduced it into the conversation for effect. But in indicating that if they accepted him as Minister of Defence, the Nazis could disregard the influence of Hindenburg, the Army and myself, Schleicher planted the seeds of his own destruction. He had given the impression that he was the one man capable of controlling the Army's intervention. In the days of the Roehm *Putsch* in June 1934, the Nazis probably considered him much more important than he really was.

Although he was a man of outstanding intellect, he finally got his lines of thought confused. He would have been on much safer ground psychologically if, instead of offering his services to Hitler as Minister of Defence, as a protection against Hindenburg and myself, he had said to the President, 'The time has come to try the experiment with Hitler. You know I have always been against it, and am now. If I remain as Minister of Defence in a Hitler Cabinet, I will guarantee the integrity of the Army, and it will be at your disposal if the experiment should fail.' His quarrel with the President was, in the end, a tragedy. He knew the Nazi movement in all its ramifications better than any other man. He should have stayed as Minister of Defence, instead of Blomberg, whom Hindenburg took for a faithful officer of the old school and who, in June 1934, and at the beginning of 1938, displayed such pitiful weakness. Like so many clever men, Schleicher became distrusted, and by the Nazis in particular. The manner of his death was shared by his courageous wife. He had been a bachelor all his life, and only married her in the autumn of 1932. She was a lady of remarkable intelligence and personality, and of inordinate ambition. It may well have been her influence that decided him to abandon his position behind the scenes for the full responsibilities of power.

PART THREE

HITLER IN POWER

CHAPTER XIV

HITLER

Hitler as Chancellor – Responsibilities – A nine-days' wonder – No plot involved – A social policy – Hitler's appeal – His party programme – Coalition problems – My fundamental error – Hitler's strength – His personality – Influence on Hindenburg

WHEN Hitler became Chancellor on January 30, 1933, he had been brought to power by the normal interplay of democratic processes. It must be realized that neither he nor his movement had acquired the character or perpetrated the atrocities for which they were to be execrated fifteen years later. His character doubtless possessed all those traits which have now become familiar, but they were not yet developed in the form in which we know them. Potempa had provided a warning, but it still seemed reasonable to suppose that the responsible head of a government would adopt a different attitude from that he had shown as an irresponsible party chief.

Events and personalities were all to play their part in the crystallizing process. The first stage of this development lasted some nineteen months, and was concerned almost exclusively with events inside Germany. Its course ran from his appointment as the Chancellor of a coalition Cabinet, through the Enabling Law, the dissolution of the political parties, the increasing integration of State and Nazi Party, his assumption of the rights and duties of President and command of the armed forces, to total dictatorship.

I shall try to give an account of this astonishing process against the background of my own experiences and collaboration in the work of government. No account can be final, because it will never be possible to describe in precise terms the inner development of Hitler's personality. Another difficulty is the necessity of

placing oneself again in the mood of the times, after all that has
since happened. Hitler's appointment to the Chancellorship was
greeted either with enthusiasm or scepticism, with indifference or
loathing, depending on the observer's own attitude. Those who
now declare that they knew exactly how things were going to
develop are merely being wise after the event. If they had really
been so far-sighted, many of the events I have now to describe
would have turned out very differently.

During the whole of the eventful January of 1933 the question
whether the President or myself were sympathetic towards a
Hitler Government did not arise. The events of the preceding
months had made all our efforts to forestall such a development
useless, mainly because of the staggering lack of responsibility on
the part of the political parties. As Noske, the Socialist leader, has
said, 'Men who regarded themselves as leaders of public opinion
displayed a degree of bigotry unequalled in the history of political
parties. They opposed every step calculated to preserve the institutions they represented.' Their failure to recognize the demands
of the situation had forced the Brüning Government to rule by
decree from 1930 onwards. My own and Schleicher's Cabinets,
and Hitler's Government, were only part of a logical sequence of
events. However, in insisting on the responsibility of the parties in
this development I wish neither to disclaim nor to diminish my
own. This book is as much a chronicle of my own mistakes as of
the situations with which I had to deal.

It was perfectly clear that a political movement which enjoyed
the support of nearly 40 per cent of the population could no
longer be ignored. It had shown itself perfectly prepared to out-
vote, for tactical purposes, all the bourgeois parties, including the
Social Democrats. I had always maintained that it could only be
neutralized by saddling it with its full share of public responsibility. Our attempts to integrate it in a subordinate position had
failed, and its assumption of the dominant position had become
unavoidable. The tremendous outbursts of mass enthusiasm which
greeted Hitler's appointment showed that it would be no easy task
to direct this force into normal channels. Most of the other party
leaders still thought that this was a change of government like any
other, a nine-days' wonder and an experiment that must soon
break down. Brüning himself remarked on January 30 that he was
glad the decision had finally been taken and was convinced that

the experiment would soon fail. Both he and Dr Kaas, as well as other political personalities who have re-emerged since the war, voted for the Enabling Law. Even Schleicher, who probably knew the Nazi movement better than anyone else, was convinced that Hitler would soon break with the Conservatives, and that the next Government would be formed with Hitler, Brüning and himself.

At the other pole stood the fanatical revolutionaries within the Nazi Party. They regarded this legal assumption of power as the first step towards their final goal. 'The night of the long knives' had not been cancelled: it had only been postponed. The legend that Hitler came to power through the help of a small group of Junkers, generals and industrialists is pure fantasy. He derived his momentum from a heterogeneous mass of support, united in its aims. It had no clear idea of how its aims were to be achieved, but only an instinctive and elementary feeling that 'there has got to be a change. Things cannot go on as they are.'

Certain industrialists, such as Thyssen, Kirdorf and Schroeder, together, it seems with certain parties abroad, had placed considerable funds at the Nazis' disposal because they saw in the movement an ally against the threat of Bolshevism. But industrial circles on the whole were cool in their attitude, as was apparent when Hitler spoke for the first time in the Industrieklub at Düsseldorf. It should also be remembered that then, as now, each party, with the exception of the Communists, received certain subsidies from industry.

The Army was another factor in the situation. It was still organized in the spirit and tradition of Imperial Germany. It regarded the Weimar Republic as something foreign in character, a temporary form of state organization, to which it felt bound by no inner ties. However, it had sworn allegiance to the Republic and the Constitution, and this subconscious conflict of loyalties led to increasing internal stress. Military conceptions of authority, fostered for so long in the Prussian Army, were necessarily unsympathetic to the Weimar system of government, and it is hardly surprising that the younger officers came to regard the Nazi movement with a certain amount of favour. The Leipzig high treason case in the autumn of 1930 had revealed the extent to which the Army was riddled with Nazi cells. Three young officers were accused of encouraging the activities of fourteen of these cells in their regiments. The case caused a considerable stir at the time, as

Hitler, who was called as a witness, was asked to declare whether his party was using illegal means to overthrow the Weimar Republic. His reply was that he and his party intended to use only legal and constitutional methods to achieve their aim, which was nevertheless the overthrow of the Weimar Republic. Ludin, one of the defendants, later became an S.A. leader and Hitler's Minister in Bratislava. Many of the older officers, including Schleicher's General Staff Adjutant, Major Ott, also considered that the Reichswehr could probably make good use of the S.A. stormtroops as part of the eastern frontier defence forces. Here again there was a conflict between the policy of the Government and the Wehrmacht's conception of necessary defence measures. It was not a question of 'certain generals' being partly responsible for the events of January 30, but rather of the officers' corps as a whole hankering for authority and a strong Government. In any case, the Army was only part of the nation, whose psychological mood during this period provides the real explanation of the course of events.

It may be that foreigners, accustomed to think in terms of parliamentary processes, are unable to understand how the nation as a whole could accept Hitler with such docility. But even this does not justify the theory of joint criminal responsibility presented in the Nuremberg indictment, explaining the emergence of Hitler as the result of a vast plot by the German people. This theory completely ignores the mental development of a whole nation in a social and political situation that offered a fertile field for National Socialist ideology. The Weimar conception of democracy had failed to solve the problems of the post-war world. A large number of people had lost faith in the political parties, which tended to judge every situation according to its effect on the fortunes of the party, rather than on the needs of the country. Defeat in war, the inflation, economic collapse in the early 'thirties, increasing unemployment, the proletarianization of the middle class, and the hopeless outlook for the youth of the country, had provided a situation which seemed made to order for the protagonists of Communism. Radical ideas and behaviour began to supplant the old order. Marxist conceptions of materialism had broken the moral resistance of whole sections of the population. Christian ideals, which alone could counterbalance this threat, had lost their appeal. The younger generation, divorced from the tenets of Christianity, sought and found a substitute in Hitler and his programme. His mixture of social and nationalist catch-phrases filled the vacuum. It must not be forgotten that the Nazis' chief support came from this generation, on which the other political parties gradually lost their influence. The Germans are blamed for failing to recognize where Hitler's ideas would lead them. It is easy to forget that Communism was regarded as the principal enemy, and that many people saw in Hitler's movement the best, and probably the only, defence. Gradually the people lost confidence in the ability of the Weimar Parliament and the irresponsible political parties to combat increasing social inequality and the grave distress of the nation.

Every modern country has witnessed the fight of the working classes and their mass organizations for recognition and equal status. In Germany the struggle was particularly bitter, after inflation had condemned the middle classes, and the working man who had bettered himself, to proletarian conditions. This sociological catastrophe, which particularly affected the old Civil Service, played a decisive part in the disruption of bourgeois values. Hitler's chief claim is not only to have recognized the implications of this disruption – many other people did so – but also to have devised a form of demagogy and propaganda which gave expression to the instincts and resentments of this disordered mass.

He demanded that the worker should be regarded as an equal member of society and that everyone should work for the common good. In the whole history of class warfare this was the first attempt of a party that came to power by constitutional means to proclaim some new solution to the social problems of the time. Ever since Pope Leo XIII promulgated his encyclical *Rerum Novarum*, the Papacy had indicated ways of dealing with the problems of capital and labour. But the masses had only been drawn to methods which demanded first of all the overthrow of the State. In the bourgeois camp we had proclaimed, in thousands of speeches and articles, the need for social peace, yet there had been little response. But when these principles were proclaimed by a man from the working class, who had himself experienced the difficulties of earning his daily bread, and now stood at the head of a powerful movement, doubters became really convinced.

Hitler combined with this approach an appeal to nationalist and patriotic feelings which fell on fruitful ground. Our former enemies declined to accept even the gradual loosening of restrictions imposed by the Versailles Treaty. They preferred to reduce Germany permanently to the rank of a second-class nation with inferior rights, and refused to tolerate her gradual assumption of equality. The material effects of reparations, inflation and loss of territory, were not the worst burden the Germans had to bear. Their condition of moral repression proved the more decisive factor, and the longer it lasted, the stronger the reaction became. In spite of the far more drastic ideological conflict of the second world war, Germany is already much further advanced towards equal cooperation with the West than she was nearly fifteen years after the first war. And here I do not overlook the progress that was made with the Locarno Pact. But my own experiences in Lausanne proved the constitutional inability of the Western Powers to consider any arrangement for gradually loosening the fetters of the Versailles Treaty. It is true that material conditions in Germany were so desperate that a great many young people took to the brown shirt not because it was brown, but because it was a shirt, but the moral factor was by far the greater one.

The Weimar parties, including the Conservatives, found no common bond of agreement in this national distress, such as would have occurred in any other country. Hitler's demagogic appeal to nationalist sentiments provided a vivid and acceptable contrast. This psychological background alone helps to explain why many of Hitler's measures, such as the demolition of democratic institutions, the dissolution of the parties, and the increasingly authoritarian nature of his Government met with so little practical opposition. Historical developments are not planned at conference tables. They are born and carried through in an atmosphere which is the product of many diverse factors. I, together with millions of my countrymen, could not remain uninfluenced by this elemental national resurgence and the impersonal impetus which seemed to agitate the masses. The party's methods, and later, Goering's police squads, may have played their part, but the outburst of enthusiasm included a great many people who were not in any way subject to the Nazis' direct influence. I was astonished to see what a high proportion of the nation – and by no means the worst elements – regarded 1933 as the year of national rebirth. It is unnecessary to look further than the reason I advanced at Lausanne: a nation's pride had been wounded and was now on the way to being healed.

Neither Herriot nor MacDonald, nor many other statesmen on either side of the Atlantic, could understand that this was a far more disturbing factor than mere material misery.

Hitler had laid down the 25-point programme of his party in 1920, and these principles were declared to be unalterable in 1926. Like many others, I had come to regard party programmes as having only relative significance. Most of them were means to an end and not much concerned with fundamentals. A lot that Hitler said in his programme had been said before and said better. Moreover, most parties, when they came to power, had found that their principles had to be altered to meet the exigencies of practical politics. It seemed more than likely that the Nazi programme would suffer the same fate. Many of the points that raised the gravest doubts, such as his antipathy to the Jews, seemed to stand little chance of fulfilment, and certainly there was no way of foreseeing that they would lead to the atrocities that were finally committed. The programme spoke of according Jews the rights of aliens. It was no more possible to foresee that this meant their physical liquidation than it was to see that Hitler's demands for revision of the Versailles Treaty meant the waging of aggressive war.

When we formed the Hitler coalition Cabinet, it was in the full knowledge that these demands would have to be countered. We realized it would not be easy to bring Hitler and his party to a sense of statesmanlike responsibility. But we hoped to oppose radical tendencies by the application of Christian principles. I have already described what care was taken to ensure that Nazi influence in the new Government was not too strong. Hitler was Chancellor, but there were only two other Nazis in the Cabinet, as against eight Conservative ministers. I will try to answer the question, how in these circumstances did Nazi influence in the Cabinet increase, until it ended in their dominating the Government?

The fault lay with us – and with Hitler. I will try to explain the process, though I cannot excuse it. My own fundamental error was to underrate the dynamic power which had awakened the national and social instincts of the masses. My conception of State authority, and its function as guardian of the law, was based on the ideals of the Kaiser's time, which many of us had regarded as absolutes. This feeling for law and order had saved the life of the young Republic between 1918 and 1923 against the wave of Bolshevist insurrection. Soldiers had formed themselves into volunteer bands and the old Civil Service had placed itself at the disposal of the new State. As a professional soldier, I should have realized that even in the political field, defensive tactics can never prevail against concentric attacks. The dynamism of a mass movement could only have been met by equal dynamism – never with the doctrinaire ideas of a thin layer of liberals and intellectuals.

In practical terms, the mistake was to consider the apparatus of the State sufficiently intact and independent to assert itself, under Conservative leadership, against the propaganda methods and machinery of the Nazi movement. What had happened was that the long years of party warfare had undermined the apparatus, though none of us realized how far the process had gone. The German middle class in general, insofar as it was not already Nazi, also underrated the revolutionary *élan* of Hitler and his party. They adhered to the old ideas of morality and legality, and believed in law and order, human rights and sober living. The amorality and unscrupulousness of the Nazis were regarded as temporary manifestations, which, it was assumed, would disappear as the revolutionary forces lost their momentum. We believed Hitler when he assured us that once he was in a position of power and responsibility he would steer his movement into more ordered channels. The masses had been so stirred up that it was clear to us that things could not return to normal overnight, and we realized that certain temporary excesses would be unavoidable. We were convinced, foolishly perhaps, that the good elements would triumph. Partnership with such a revolutionary and totalitarian system was a new experience for us, and we lacked the necessary understanding to deal with it. The world of the late 'forties has witnessed a similar process in the coalitions between Socialists and Communists in the countries of Eastern Europe: in each case the smaller and more radical element succeeded in taking over command. In the Hitler coalition Cabinet numbers were on the side of the Conservatives, but in the country at large the support lay with Hitler.

Again, we underrated Hitler's insatiable lust for power as an end in itself, and failed to realize that it could only be combated by employing his own methods. Further, our whole way of thinking and upbringing disqualified us from foreseeing what these methods would lead to. Compared with Hitler's position of power, with his millions of adherents, our own position was extremely weak.

Two important factors, the position and prestige of the President and of the Army, were not under Hitler's control. But time was to show that these two factors were not used either at the right time or in the right way. The appointment to the Cabinet of independent experts, rather than party politicians, was also to prove a mistake. Ministers appointed purely because of their party loyalty had too often proved bad administrators. But the appointment of able administrators, regardless of party, though making for efficiency, deprived them of outside support in the struggle within the coalition. Hugenberg was the only man with a party behind him. The others concentrated on the administrative work of their ministries, and had neither the talent nor the wish to quarrel with Hitler on purely political grounds. I had no ministerial portfolio, and was therefore dependent on my personal influence with Hitler and the President, who retained his full prerogatives, up to the passing of the Enabling Law.

One of the most disastrous early developments was the failure of the Army to maintain an independent position. Blomberg proved himself almost immediately a strong sympathizer with Hitler, and although he was opposed in this by the vast majority of senior officers, the old Prussian conception of obedience and discipline meant that his influence was paramount. The President was ageing fast and gradually ceased to impose his personal authority in day-to-day political developments, although again I must insist that there was no means, as yet, of appreciating the full range of possible consequences. Looking back, I see that there were many times when I should have invoked the President's authority. I can only explain my failure to do so by admitting the error that I and my colleagues made in assuming that radicalism would become more moderate rather than more intense.

In due course I shall describe the failure of our attempt to build up a strong Conservative bloc to counterbalance the Nazis in the elections of March 5, 1933. The middle classes, and particularly those without party representation in the Cabinet, failed to recognize the necessities of the hour. It was clear that there could be no question of a return to the incompetence and instability of the Weimar system, and that a regeneration of the whole apparatus of the State was necessary. As I have tried to explain, in my view a thorough reform of our constitutional and political life was called for, and a more authoritative form of government required for the social and economic problems of the time.

When, a few months later, the political parties dissolved themselves under Hitler's pressure, the Government was faced by a new situation. In the countries of the West, we have come to regard party government as the best means of administering the State in the general interest. As long as the party system existed in Germany, it was the duty of each one of us to remedy, as far as possible, its defects. Once the parties had disappeared, it became necessary to organize the democratic system on another basis, founded on the groups of trades and professions which formed the backbone of the nation. The 'corporate state' has long been an element in Catholic social philosophy, and in many ways represents an improvement on the party system. I was convinced that we would be able to form responsible government and opposition groups, who would alternately exercise the functions of a political democracy. What I did not foresee was that existing institutions and parties, and, in fact, the middle class as a whole, would give up without a fight. It should not be forgotten that both the Trade Unions and the Social Democrats thought, in January 1933, that the Hitler experiment would not last long. This may well have led to their decision not to resort to such methods as a general strike, which they could certainly have set in motion, if they had wished to. However, the general feeling that 'things cannot go on as they are' was so strong that great masses of the working class might well not have heeded a strike call.

The second, and probably the determining, factor in these developments, was Hitler's own personality. Before he came to power, he had been a highly controversial figure. It was widely believed that he merely provided a façade for the real leaders of the Nazi Party. This was to prove a completely false assumption. At the time he became Chancellor, I do not think that Hitler's character was fully developed. It changed and crystallized over the course of the years. But there is no doubt that he was, from the very start, the mainspring of the Nazi movement.

The power of his personality is difficult to describe. There was little hint of either domination or genius in his manner or appearance, but he had immense powers of persuasion and an extraordinary and indefinable capacity for bending individuals and, above all, the masses to his will. He was fully aware of this power and completely convinced of his infallibility. He was able to dominate and impose his opinions on everyone who came in constant contact with him. Even people who differed from him fundamentally became convinced of his sincerity. I was as much a victim as everyone else, and believed all his protestations, until the events leading up to the Roehm *Putsch* in 1934 showed the full measure of his duplicity.

During the first weeks of his Chancellorship he seemed distinctly ill at ease, particularly when he had to appear in a top hat and formal dress. His party colleagues soon persuaded him to abandon these bourgeois trappings in favour of the party uniform. With me he was invariably polite, even modest – at any rate as long as the effect of his first electoral victory lasted. It took me a long time to see through him. At first I had the impression that even though he was not easy to handle, it would still be possible to attract him to my own professed political ideas. In this I was to be grievously disappointed.

In the early stages he gave us reason to believe that he would check the excesses of the Brownshirts and the radical elements in the party. It is impossible to say whether he meant to do so or not. When we protested in the Cabinet at the early offences against the Jews or of political opponents being deprived of their freedom, he often flew into a rage at the lack of discipline among the Brownshirts and their leaders, and issued furious instructions for order to be re-established. I remember on one occasion, when I had protested vigorously against the party's anti-Jewish excesses, he rose suddenly in his seat, beat his fist on the table and shouted at Hess, who was his deputy in party matters: 'See that these *Schweinereien* are stopped! I have had enough of this indiscipline.' Whether these outbursts were genuine or not, we were certainly taken in by them. He kept asking us to be patient and to allow him time to discipline those sections of the party that had got out of hand. I had frequently to discuss with Guertner and Eltz, men whose personal integrity and character were above suspicion, how we were to reconcile Hitler's assurances with actual developments. We all agreed that there was no reason to doubt Hitler's intentions, and hoped that experience in the Cabinet would have a beneficial effect on him.

When I drew Hitler's attention to his Gauleiters' disregard of his own strict orders, he told me that he valued contradictions within the party as a guarantee against complacency. I tried in vain to awaken a more statesmanlike appreciation of his responsibilities. For a long time I hoped, because of his extraordinary gifts and will power, to convert him from a party politician into a statesman. There was, in fact, no ground for such an attempt. I recognized too late that there were too many faults in his character. He had no conception of basic Christian ethics and thought that he could apply the deception and lies of party warfare to the affairs of nations.

I had the impression that in a great many things, especially in his attitude to the established Churches, he was gradually influenced by the radical elements in the party, particularly Goebbels. In our early conversations about Rosenberg and his new 'myth', he used such expressions of ridicule that I could not believe these aberrations presented any danger. He backed up with enthusiasm my efforts to support the rights of the Churches by special treaties, though knowing full well that these privileges would meet with violent opposition from many of his supporters; he must have known also that with the influx of former Socialists and Communists who flocked to his banners, this opposition would grow. To begin with, I believed, mistakenly, that in Church questions it would be possible to wean him away from the radical wing of his party and make him support our own point of view.

I have already mentioned that his strongest characteristic was his almost pathological consciousness of power and his desire to attain it. This was strengthened by his absolute conviction of his own infallibility. As a result, he was deeply suspicious of any opposition. In the Cabinet he used every possible means to avoid being out-voted. When a particular measure met with the opposition of a majority of the ministers, he would always postpone the discussion, rather than be out-voted. For this reason alone, the best way of influencing him was by private conversation, rather than in committee, and I therefore tried from the beginning to establish an atmosphere of mutual confidence and to remove the impression that he was dealing with an opponent. Among those not bound to him by party ties or any other dependent relationship, I was probably the person who most frequently had discussions with him. We talked more of our ideological differences than of actual political problems, and in conversation I found him perfectly normal. He was apt to drift into long monologues, but he was always open to contradiction and took no offence when he was interrupted. I cannot say that I persuaded him to alter his convictions, though it did seem possible to influence him, and in this I saw a ray of hope.

His influence on individuals extended even to the President, whose early suspicions soon gave way to a feeling of confidence. By April, Hindenburg had asked me to discontinue the practice we had agreed upon in January, of being present at his interviews with the Chancellor, which Hitler regarded as an affront to his dignity. Hindenburg agreed to the provision in the Enabling Law, which deprived his office of one of its basic prerogatives – the actual drafting of laws – which was transferred to the Cabinet. This entailed a considerable diminution in his influence, and indeed, in mine, once Hitler had direct access to him.

The developments I have tried to sketch lasted a matter of years, but their framework had been irrevocably laid down during the first nineteen months. The first impulse was given by the result of the Reichstag elections on March 5, 1933, and its impetus can be judged by the fact that from 1937 onwards no further Cabinet meetings took place. Important decisions, whether concerning war or peace, were often taken without the knowledge of individual ministers. But that was four years later.

If Hitler had attempted an immediate revolution such as Lenin brought about, he would have met overwhelming opposition from the nation, which still had a strong feeling for legal processes and would not have tolerated the sudden abolition of its institutions. Germany's history was full of externally imposed tyrannies, but its people had never experienced a form of internal despotism intent on destroying the very foundations of communal existence. The idea of a State authority being hostile to established laws and traditions was foreign to the Germans. They could not grasp the implications. This may help to explain that lack of resistance to Hitler's measures which so astonished the world abroad. But I must make the final point that historians are mistaken in assuming that the details of this process were laid down in advance. Many of the premises already existed in Hitler's mind, but in course of time they were reinforced and strengthened by the seemingly unconditional enthusiasm of his mass of adherents, the idolization of his person, the Byzantine nature of his entourage, his own lust for power, lack of opposition from the bourgeois forces, insufficient resistance from the Conservative members of his first Cabinet and, in the last resort, the fatal consequences of a war instigated on no rational grounds. Perhaps this sketch of later developments will serve as a background to an account of events between January 30, 1933, and my withdrawal from the Reich Cabinet in July 1934.

CHAPTER XV

THE ENABLING LAW

The Coalition programme – The 'Black-White-Red' bloc – My electoral policy – The Reichstag fire – Nazi gains – Zentrum inanition – The Enabling Law – The Vice-Chancellery

ON the evening the new Cabinet was formed, I stood behind Hitler on the balcony of the new Reich Chancellery. We watched an endless procession of hundreds of thousands of delirious people, from every level of society, parading with lighted torches before Hindenburg and the Chancellor. It was a clear, starlit night, and the long columns of uniformed Brownshirts, S.S. and Stahlhelm, with their brass bands, provided an unforgettable picture. As they approached the window at which the old Reich President appeared to the crowd there were respectful shouts. But about a hundred yards further on, Hitler stood on the little balcony of the new Reich Chancellery. As soon as they saw him, the marchers burst into frantic applause. The contrast was most marked and seemed to emphasize the transition from a moribund régime to the new revolutionary forces. I had preferred not to push myself forward and was sitting quietly in the room behind the balcony, leaving Hitler and Goering to take the salute. But every now and then Hitler turned round and beckoned me to join him. The fantastic ovation had put even these hardened party chiefs into a state of ecstasy. It was an extraordinary experience, and the endless repetition of the triumphal cry '*Heil, Heil, Sieg Heil!*' rang in my ears like a tocsin. When Hitler turned round to speak to me, his voice seemed choked with sobs. 'What an immense task we have set ourselves, Herr von Papen – we must never part until our work is accomplished.' I was happy to agree. At that moment he certainly did not sound like a dictator. He seemed a man overwhelmed with humility at the sight of his wishes fulfilled, who sought help and co-operation in the work he had set himself. We parted long after midnight, and agreed to meet early the next day to work out the new Cabinet's declaration of policy.

I experienced much less difficulty than I had expected in formulating a coalition programme. Hitler thought the moral regeneration of the nation to be our principal task. He suggested that economic reconstruction should be accomplished in two four-year plans, and mentioned, for the first time, the necessity of passing an Enabling Law for this purpose. I thought a four-year plan sounded too much like Soviet methods, but agreed that a set programme was necessary. For my part, I laid down those lines of conservative thought which I considered should serve as a framework for our policies, and suggested one or two phrases: 'The Government recognizes the Christian basis of moral existence and regards the family as the basic unit in the nation, requiring the particular protection of the State.' We agreed to strengthen the federal structure of the country by promoting healthy State and Municipal Government, while maintaining sound central direction. In the field of foreign affairs, the Government intended to strive for equal rights in the community of nations, 'fully aware of the responsibilities of a great and free nation in the maintenance and consolidation of peace, more necessary to the world then ever before'. Hitler gave his full approval to these declarations, to which we added the suggestion that a general reduction in armaments would do away with the necessity for any increase in our own.

Our conversation then turned to the new elections, which we agreed should be held on March 5. I told Hitler that I would try to combine all the forces outside his movement into a single electoral bloc, pledged to support the Government's policies. He asked whether we could not find a common programme for the elections, but I told him there was no question of this; he had his ideas and we had ours, but I hoped that we would both emphasize the intention to carry out our tasks in co-operation. He did not seem too happy about this, but did not make an issue of it.

In order to provide some sort of counterweight to the dynamism of the Nazis, it was essential to convince other parties and groups that we were engaged in something more than a normal change of Cabinet. The previous splintering into thirty-two parties had made it impossible for certain principles to be put into practice, and these principles we were now trying to introduce. The task was to organize an opposition group without making this immediately evident. But I had reckoned without the inertia of the existing party organizations. I tried to convince Hugenberg and the leaders of some of the smaller right and centre parties that the time had come for the older members of the Reichstag to stand down and make way for representatives of the new generation. We must make some appeal to the youth of the country, or they would continue to flock to the Nazis, and our position would become hopeless. But it was no use; the party machines were too strong and the old hands clung too closely together.

Some of them did recognize the necessity for concentration of all non-Nazi forces, but they were not prepared to make any sacrifices to achieve this. My only success was to get the agreement of certain factions to support a general declaration of our hopes for the future, and this formed the basis of the 'Black-White-Red' electoral bloc. The results of the poll were to show that this half-hearted initiative was not nearly enough. In the previous chapter I gave some indication of the reasons why it was not possible to bring it home to the German middle class that the momentum of the Nazi movement could only be checked by a solid front of all conservative and Christian-thinking elements. They were too slow to realize all the implications. The best proof lies in the vote of the Stahlhelm members, on which we relied for a large measure of support, and which went mainly to the National Socialists. Our efforts were doomed to failure from the start.

I announced our programme in a number of speeches made in different parts of the country. Our chief statement of policy was made on February 21, at a meeting in the Berlin University of students from every part of Germany and of every shade of political belief. I dwelt at length on the pressing problems of the time:

'Our task [I said] is to combat those who, in the name of truth and freedom, have in recent years destroyed the religious conception of human relationships and brought our society to the verge of chaos. The daily interplay of political events cannot be divorced from the overriding problems of our existence. In previous ages, human society was organized within a framework of belief in God and the hereafter. We have had to watch a process of progressive secularization. Science has replaced religion, and principles of conduct have replaced belief and its code of moral behaviour. This mechanization of the mind, and this travesty of real truth and freedom can only be countered by a spiritual regeneration.

'Social problems cannot be solved by the State alone, although it can sustain the working classes, encourage the development of personality, and halt the present process of bringing everything down to a common level. In our position at the core of Europe, it is our duty to combine the advantages of democracy and true aristocracy. A democracy needs people of intellect and character to conduct its affairs to the best advantage. We want to build a new and better Germany on the ruins of the party state, and must surrender party allegiances to the common good.'

This was my constant theme. Our real task was to rebuild our society on the basis of Christian ethics. This would enable us to counter any dangers that might arise from the heterogeneous nature of Hitler's following, many of whom denied these principles. The collectivization and mechanization of our society could only be countered by a return to the traditional relationship between man and his Maker.

The new Government, and in particular its conservative element had to deal effectively with the social problem. Class hatred and class warfare were a suicidal method of attempting to achieve happiness and prosperity for the working classes. Capital and labour must combine in a true partnership to ensure everyone a worth-while existence. This entailed providing the worker with the full reward for his labours. It was no part of the State's duty to extend its functions to the direct control of great industries, and we intended to combat all forms of socialization. The true duty of the State lay in acting as an arbitrator in the interests of all. Abuses of the capitalist system must be rectified by supporting the weaker bargaining position of the workers and ensuring that social justice prevailed.

Many of us had an instinctive fear of the threat to basic principles of justice and freedom inherent in a revolutionary movement. These dangers were already crystallizing. Our electoral bloc proclaimed the principle that no form of state could be organized that was not based on the overriding authority of the law. A Government had it in its power to restrict personal freedoms, but it was only justified in doing so by legal methods when the general interest demanded it. Such limitations could only be of a temporary nature, and every citizen must retain the right of appeal.

In this we made plain our attitude to the abuses of authority already being practised by Goering's police. We also rejected the racial aspects of Hitler's programme, by pointing out that although there was no objection to the cultivation of pride in our racial homogeneity, this must never develop into hatred of other races. It was Christianity that had made a race out of the German tribes, and there was no need to found a new religion to bolster its existence. There was at this time no indication of the developments which led to the Nuremberg racial laws and ended in the tragedy of the gas chambers.

In our foreign policy we sought only the restoration of our full sovereignty and the maintenance of peace through international co-operation. In our internal organization we sought to end the dualism between Prussia and the Reich, and to assure sufficient power to the Central Government, while maintaining the cultural autonomy of the member States.

This short sketch cannot reproduce the full details of our electoral programme, but at least it indicates that we tried to show clearly where we differed with the Nazis. The weakness of our position was that we were not able to criticize our new coalition partner openly. I could only attempt to convince the electorate of the positive aspects of our programme, in the hope that they would be compared with the negative side of Nazi doctrine. But either through lack of intelligence or because of mental laziness, this hope was never fulfilled. Many people, apparently thinking that Hitler professed the same conservative principles as ourselves, gave their vote to the Nazis.

★ ★ ★

On the evening of February 27 I had arranged a dinner in the President's honour at our club in the Vosstrasse. Suddenly we noticed a red glow through the windows and heard sounds of shouting in the street. One of the club servants came hurrying up to me and whispered in my ear, 'The Reichstag is on fire,' which I repeated to the President. He got up, and from the window we could see the dome of the Reichstag looking as though it were illuminated by searchlights. Every now and again a burst of flame and a swirl of smoke blurred the outline. I suggested to the President that he should return home, and drove him back in my car. I then went straight to the burning building, which had been cordoned off by police. When I finally made my way inside, I found Goering in one of the badly damaged corridors, where, in his capacity as Prussian Minister of the Interior, he was giving orders to the firefighters. With him were his entourage; they were angry and excited. 'This is a Communist crime against the new Government!' Goering shouted at me.

After the fire had been got under control, I left the building, feeling firmly convinced that the cause had not been accidental. That it was a political demonstration of some sort seemed obvious, since it was known that while the building was being searched a foreign Communist had been arrested. I therefore had no reason at the time to doubt the need for sharp measures against the criminal elements of the Communist Party. It seemed to me that the interrogation of Van der Lubbe, and the search of the Communist Party's headquarters, only confirmed this impression.

At one of the next Cabinet meetings, Goering presented some of the documents which had allegedly been found during a raid on the Communist headquarters in the Karl Liebknecht House. I remember they included plans for the liquidation of a number of political leaders, among them most of the Cabinet ministers and myself. I must confess that it did not occur to me that the Nazis, now a responsible government party, would find it necessary to forge such documents in order to bolster up their case. We were all convinced that the Communists had planned an armed uprising and represented a menace to the security of the State.

Even today it is impossible to say with certainty how the fire was started. After the war, when I was detained in the Labour Camp at Regensburg, I found myself in the company of a former police official named Heisig. On the night of the fire he had been the senior police official on duty at the Prussian Ministry of the Interior, and had been the first person to enter the burning Reichstag. Afterwards, he was in charge of Van der Lubbe's interrogation, and also conducted the enquiries into his previous life in Holland. According to Heisig, Lubbe was a fanatical Communist, with a strong grudge against society and also some earlier convictions for arson. There was no doubt that he had actually fired the building, but on his own initiative, not at the instigation either of Communists or Nazis. He had already attempted to start fires in the Labour Ministry, the Schöneberg Town Hall and the Imperial Palace.

Out of this purely criminal act, the Nazis organized a gigantic political scandal, as a means of breaking the power of the Communists. For this purpose they made use of perjured evidence. For instance, a retired Major, named Weberstedt, who worked in the Nazi Party press office, claimed that on the evening of the fire he had seen Van der Lubbe with the Communist leader, Torgler, and also, on an earlier occasion, in the Reichstag. Heisig was able to prove, however, that on the earlier date Van der Lubbe had been serving a prison sentence in Holland. But this did not deter Goering and Goebbels from acting as if a Communist counter-revolution was imminent, and they found a useful ally in a State Attorney named Vogt, whose chief purpose was to ensure himself a position of influence in the Nazi Party.

Rudolf Diels, Chief of Police in Goering's Ministry, who is still alive, has said that about four thousand Communist Party officials were arrested during the police raids that followed the fire. However, many of their leaders, such as Pieck and Ulbricht, succeeded in fleeing to Moscow, where they were able to await more propitious days. The Nazis, having convinced Hindenburg that the fire was intended as the signal for a Communist uprising, prevailed upon him to sign an emergency decree to uphold the nation's security. Although this decree suspended certain basic freedoms, the Communist threat was made to appear strong enough to warrant the temporary introduction of such measures. Hitler wanted to ban the Communist Party altogether, but I objected strongly to such a step just before the elections. I believed also that banned political parties always end as underground resistance movements. When the Communist Party was forbidden in the following April, many of its members underwent an apparent conversion and joined the Brownshirts – which was not the first time that Moscow has adopted fifth-column tactics.

The Nazis succeeded in convincing their Conservative partners that the Communist threat was authentic. Whether or not they themselves were responsible for starting the fire, they certainly gained a great tactical victory over both their political opponents and their allies. Quite frankly, I still have an open mind as to how the fire was caused, although I admit it would have been

impossible for one man to have set fire to so many different parts
of the building in so short a time. It was suggested at Nuremberg
that a final investigation into the responsibility for the Reichstag
fire should be carried out while Goering and his colleagues were
still available, but nothing came of the idea. All we have is Goering's remark to General Donovan, head of the United States Office
of Strategic Services: 'You must at least be convinced that with
death staring me in the face, I have no need to resort to lies. I give
you my word that I had nothing whatever to do with the Reichstag fire.' Rudolf Diels, who knows the background of the early
Nazi years as well as any man, has added: 'From a few weeks after
the fire, until 1945, I was convinced that the Nazis had started it.
Now I have changed my mind.'

* * *

When the results of the vital election on March 5 were counted,
the Nazis had increased their vote from 11.7 million (their figure
in the previous November) to 17.2 million. Their 195 seats had
become 288. The left wing parties obtained very nearly as many
seats as in the previous election. The Socialists were returned
with 119, a loss of 2, the Communists with 81, a loss of 8, while
the Zentrum actually gained 3 seats. The increase in the Nazi
vote came almost exclusively from the right wing and splinter
parties.

It has been suggested that the Nazis achieved this result, if not by
actually tampering with the figures, then at least by suggestive
threats. This is simply not so. An ordinance had been signed on
February 4, 1933, under which permission had to be obtained for
holding political meetings. In Prussia this provision was used by
Goering to limit the electoral campaign of the opposition parties.
But in the other States the Ministers of the Interior were still those
of the Weimar Republic. One important point that should be
recalled is that on March 5 the vote was still secret, and the officials
were drawn in equal numbers from all parties. The pressure
exercised in later elections was largely due to the fact that no one
continued to believe that the ballot was secret. Even if there was
some hint of suggestive influence on March 5, the fact cannot be
denied that two of the most important parties, the Social Democrats and the Zentrum, got roughly the same number of seats as
they had won during the previous thirteen years.

My own electoral bloc obtained 1.3 million votes and 52 seats, but the Nazis, with 47 per cent of the seats, had almost won an absolute majority. The nation as a whole had given Hitler a clear mandate. I had worked to counterbalance his influence, but no one else had recognized this necessity. The Socialist and Zentrum adherents, still obsessed with party doctrine, would not make common cause with us, although we had made it clear that our bloc was not a satellite of Hitler.

The centre parties – the Zentrum and the Bavarian People's Party – were content to rest on their laurels. They saw themselves as the saviours of Germany in the 1919 revolution, as the people who had successfully prevented Socialist experiments and had put the country on its feet again after the wartime collapse. Between February 13, 1919, and June 2, 1932, no fewer than eighty-three ministerial posts in the nineteen Reich Cabinets had been filled by members of the Zentrum Party. In eight years they had provided nine Reich Chancellors. Even the Socialists' record could not compare with this. During this long period of power, the bourgeois centre had lost its sense of realities.

It was hardly astonishing that the Nazis should greet their unexpectedly high support as something like a revolutionary triumph. The result provided the impetus for future revolutionary developments, instigated by the radical wing of the party, and which, though moderated at first by the leadership, were inwardly welcomed.

I do not know what gave Hitler the idea of transferring the opening ceremony of the new Reichstag to the Garrison Church in Potsdam. It was probably his own distorted romanticism, combined with the propaganda value of old traditions. I had no objection to the idea when he raised it. The opening of Parliament had always been accompanied by a religious ceremony in the days of the Prussian Kings and the German Emperors. A return to this tradition, especially in a church that housed the remains of Frederick the Great, and stood as a symbol of all the stern old Prussian virtues, seemed to me to provide a useful contrast to the materialism of the Nazis. To my astonishment, Hitler decided to stay away from the religious part of the ceremony. I told him that he must not mind being criticized within the party, as he was now the representative of the whole nation; but he was not to be moved. This was the first check I received in our relationship, and I could only assume that the fear of criticism within his own ranks was the decisive factor.

Once the elections were over I saw him more often. His delight at the result seemed boundless, and his chief disappointment was the failure of our bloc to formulate a common programme with his party. He tried to talk me out of the independent rôle I had set for myself in the coalition Government. 'You are an old soldier, Herr von Papen,' he said to me, 'and know the old adage about marching with the strongest battalions. If we march together, we are sure of a majority and our success is certain.'

With the basic conservative conceptions recognized in the formal government declaration worked out by Hitler and myself on February 1, it seemed reasonable, in the Cabinet meetings that followed the elections, to adopt a tolerant attitude towards Hitler's plans for economic reform. He insisted that special powers would be needed, and had, in fact, made no secret of this demand since the first moment when the possibility of his joining the Government had been canvassed. Since the previous November at least, the parties must have been aware that some such Enabling Law would be requested. In our discussions, my colleagues and I insisted that if he was to obtain the necessary two-thirds majority, he would have to give the country firm guarantees, such as we had included in the government declaration.

In his speech to the Reichstag on March 21, Hitler met these requirements to the letter. Anyone who reads this speech again today will have to admit that the opposition parties were fully justified in supposing that he would keep his promises. The minutes of the previous day's Cabinet meeting also show that I repeated my demands for a reform of the Constitution, and received from Hitler an undertaking that the position and rights of the President would in no way be tampered with. When, in course of time, the Enabling Law proved to have been a disastrous experiment, all the opposition members who had voted for it sought endless excuses for their action. It is enough to say that Hitler promised never to abuse his powers under the law, and to protect the cultural and economic independence of the German States. He declared it to be our duty to 'ensure a regeneration of religious thinking', and stated that the Government saw in the two main religions 'the most essential factors upholding the life of the nation'. He described Christianity as the firm foundation of the country's life and morals, pledged Government support for the independence of the judiciary, and proclaimed peace as the goal of our foreign policy.

'... After the Chancellor's declaration, Dr Kaas (Zentrum), Ritter von Lex (Bavarian People's Party), Maier (Staatspartei) and Simpfendoerfer (Christian Socialists) undertook that their parties would support the Enabling Law. After a speech by Reichstag President, Goering, the Enabling Law was passed in the Third Reading by 441 to 94; that is, with the necessary two-thirds majority. The Reichstag adjourned *sine die* . . .' So runs the official report.

A whole library has been written about how the Enabling Law helped Hitler towards total dictatorship – most of it written by those who voted for the Law in good faith and now seek some justification for doing so. There is no doubt that Hitler's dictatorship and the self-dissolution of Parliament begins at this point. But those who voted for the Law bear an equal responsibility with the ministers who presented it.

I have already mentioned Brüning's article in the *Deutsche Rundschau* of July 1947. In it he remarks that the Communists should have surrendered their 81 seats to the Socialists, thereby giving them 201 seats and enabling them to play a much more decisive rôle. This is a completely unrealistic suggestion. If the Communists had exhorted their followers to vote for the Socialists in the elections on March 5, the Social Democrats would only have inherited the violent campaign of suppression to which the Communists were subjected. Brüning juggles with figures to prove that Hitler's two-thirds majority could have been prevented. But the Reichstag had 647 seats, two-thirds of which is 431. Hitler obtained 441 votes for the Law, which is nearer three-quarters. The Communists had been banned from the Reichstag and some Socialist members arrested (although I managed to obtain the release of Severing and others), but they still could not have prevented the majority.

Brüning maintained that Hitler was prepared to go on arresting opposition members until he obtained his majority. There is no proof of this, and in any case, the combined opposition parties were always in a position to prevent his getting the necessary vote. It was no doubt alarming to see the Reichstag Building full of Brownshirts, but then Brüning is not a man who lacks physical courage. He would do much better to admit that the opposition was not browbeaten into voting for the Law, but did so out of conviction.

I cannot admit the idea that nothing would have been gained by rejecting the Enabling Law because the Nazis would then have dissolved all opposition parties under the decree of February 28. Brüning forgets that at the time Hitler would not have been able to carry through any such measures. Up to the end of April, I had taken part, at the President's express request, in all his interviews with Hitler. The President and the Conservative members of the Cabinet were always in a position to block such radical measures. It is pure nonsense to suggest that the President could have been brought before the Constitutional Court, had the Nazis made up their minds to overcome his opposition by appointing Hitler in his place. Such a step was neither planned nor possible, and cannot be used as an excuse for voting for the Enabling Law.

At the Nuremberg trial I gave a full account of my own efforts to ensure against dictatorial abuses of the Law. The best weapon was always the President's right of veto, and with my influence on him, I hoped to put this to good use. However, the President soon expressed a wish to dissociate himself from the decisions of the Cabinet and Hitler's measures, and this affected my own influence. It is very convenient for critics to declare that it was obvious from the start that Hitler had no intention of keeping his promises. But they destroy their own case, as the logical conclusion would have been to vote against the Enabling Law, and anyone who failed to do so is hardly in a position to proclaim himself a hero of the resistance.

It was this Law alone that provided the legal basis for Hitler's development as a dictator. Anyone who has been accused, as I have, of underwriting the Nazi despotism, has a right to make this point. No one could possibly foresee the actual course of events, and those now possessed of such hind-sight should ponder their own share of the responsibility. The fact that all the parties, with the exception of the Social Democrats, voted for the Enabling Law, had more effect on developments than the increased electoral support for the Nazis. If the Law had not been passed, it would have been much more difficult to abolish constitutional guarantees and much easier to oppose dictatorial methods.

* * *

The position of the Vice-Chancellor turned out to be anomalous. The post had been created, and I had accepted it, for the purpose of countering the influence of the Nazi ministers in the Cabinet. On the other hand, I held no portfolio and therefore controlled no ministry. My own staff consisted of a few individuals whom I had carefully chosen for their outspoken opposition to the Nazi creed. My ministerial director, Councillor Dr Sabath, was one of the best representatives of the old type of civil servant. My legal adviser, von Savigny, who was also responsible for drafting the laws proposed by other ministries, was an active Catholic with strong connections in the various church organizations. My press councillor, von Bose, was to pay with his life, on June 30, 1934, for his opposition to the régime. He had, as his assistant, Wilhelm von Ketteler, a fanatical anti-Nazi, who met his death at the hands of the Gestapo in Vienna in 1938. My personal adjutant was von Tschirschky, who, in 1935, with the Gestapo after his life, emigrated from Vienna to England. His assistant, and successor, was Count Kageneck. Their heroic and selfless activity on my behalf caused constant friction with the régime, and I shall be referring to them frequently.

The attitude of this small group, evident from its very composition, was realized throughout the country. Before long we became known as the 'Reich Complaints Office', and soon had to deal with a flood of protests from all parts of the community against the measures and the excesses of the Nazi Party. Whenever possible I interceded with Hitler, Goering, Frick, and other responsible authorities, to right these various wrongs. In many cases we were successful; but often, I fear, we were not.

I should like to be able to give details of the work we did, but my files have all been burnt, and my memory for detail is not what it was. However, my *chef de cabinet*, Sabath, gave many examples during my denazification trial. He recalled, for instance, that Gauleiter Wagner and Goebbels had both demanded the dismissal of my chief assistant for Saar affairs, Dr Wingen, on the grounds that he had made disparaging remarks about the party. This was one of the cases in which I intervened successfully with Hitler, and even obtained a letter of apology from Goebbels. We managed also to save numerous other civil servants from dismissal, and in a great many cases to help Jews who had been maltreated. In particular, I remember receiving a letter of thanks from a Herr Feldheim, who lived in my own home town, and whom I had managed to have freed from a concentration camp. We also waged an almost daily battle against Nazi interference in Church affairs.

With the Nazis' increasing control of the press, it became more and more difficult to criticize their measures and give publicity to their abuses of power. We therefore passed on details of the more flagrant cases to the foreign press correspondents, since we found that even the threat of their publication abroad was a useful weapon in dealing with Hitler. Bose and Ketteler were the two people principally responsible for this side of our work, which earned them the special hatred of the Nazis. This attitude to the unpleasant aspects of the party's activities came so naturally to my collaborators that it was never necessary for them to boast of their resistance work. In this they provided a contrast to those who now claim to have opposed the régime, but who preferred, at the time, to keep their criticisms to themselves.

CHAPTER XVI

THE CONCORDAT

I visit Rome – Interview with Pope Pius XI – Radical opposition – Social problems – Elimination of class warfare – The problem of the Jews – The Swastika flag – Blomberg shows his colours – Goebbels joins the Cabinet – Prussia – I resign as Reich Commissioner – Concentration camps – Foreign policy – Germany withdraws from the League – Austria – The Saar problem

M Y chief preoccupation was to devise some practical step for dealing with the declaration of basic Christian principles which the Conservative members of the Cabinet had insisted on including in the Government's statement of policy. If this could be achieved, I felt that we should have a solid basis for future action. I was not content with mere assurances by Hitler. I wanted to establish a legal basis for the rights of the Christian Churches in Germany. The violent anti-clericalism of the Nazi Party's radical wing increased the urgency of the problem. I decided to pay an Easter visit to Rome to study the possibility of reaching some firm agreement.

There had been no Concordat between the Vatican and the Reich since the days of the Reformation. Certain individual States, particularly the predominantly Catholic Bavaria, had signed their own Concordats. Prussia, which was overwhelmingly Protestant, had reached only an unsatisfactory *modus vivendi*, in spite of all the efforts of the Papal Nuncio. During the whole period of the Weimar Republic, the Zentrum Party, which was Catholic by definition, had made repeated efforts to reach a general understanding with Rome, but had never been able to overcome the Social Democrats' opposition to church schools. The new situation in Germany seemed to provide an opportunity for picking up the threads again, and it was my intention to deal not only with the Vatican, but to come to an arrangement with the Evangelical Church as well.

Signing the Concordat. *Centre:* Cardinal Pacelli (now Pope Pius XII)

The old style and the new: the author with Goebbels

Von Hindenburg: *'Ich hatt' einen Kameraden!'*

I was greeted with full state honours from the moment I crossed the Italian frontier. Though my mission was still a private matter, Mussolini, whom I met for the first time, gave it his enthusiastic support. I found the Italian dictator a man of very different calibre to Hitler. Short in stature, but with an air of great authority, his massive head conveyed an impression of great strength of character. He handled people like a man accustomed to having his orders obeyed, but displayed immense charm and did not give the impression of a revolutionary. Hitler always had a slight air of uncertainty, as though feeling his way, whereas Mussolini was calm, dignified, and appeared the complete master of whatever subject was being discussed. I felt he would be a good influence on Hitler; he was much more of a statesman, and reminded one of a diplomat of the old school rather than a dictator. He spoke excellent French and German, and this considerably facilitated the exchange of ideas. He had solved the problem of his own relations with the Vatican by his Lateran treaties, and had proved that a Fascist régime could exist in harmony with the Church. The Vatican Secretary of State was Cardinal Pacelli, the present Pope, who had represented the interests of the Catholic Church in Germany for eleven years, first in Bavaria and then in Berlin. When he left there his departure was much regretted, even in non-Catholic circles, which had come to appreciate his extraordinary personal qualities. He was assisted by Dr Kaas, who had in the meantime changed his leadership of the Zentrum Party for the more peaceful atmosphere of the Holy See.

The Vatican, therefore, had an intimate knowledge of conditions in Germany in 1933. Suggestions that my visit to Rome, and the subsequent signing of the Concordat, were planned by me as a trap are rubbish. Those who repeat this accusation are merely insulting the intelligence of the present Pope and his advisers at the time. Pacelli greeted me warmly and we discussed the situation very fully before arranging for me to have an audience with Pope Pius XI. His Holiness welcomed my wife and myself most graciously, and remarked how pleased he was that the German Government now had at its head a man uncompromisingly opposed to Communism and Russian nihilism in all its forms. Indeed, the atmosphere was so cordial that I was able to settle the details of a draft agreement at a speed quite unusual in Vatican affairs, and I was soon on my way back to Berlin. The Vatican

K

invited the views of the German Episcopate and appointed the Archbishop of Freiburg, Dr Groeber, to represent its interests. He and I worked together in complete harmony.

Hitler accepted my proposals with surprising readiness. This was particularly remarkable, as the Concordat conceded complete freedom to confessional schools throughout the whole country. Only those who had lived through the ceaseless struggle to obtain this concession can realize what a victory it represented in the mind of Germany's Catholics. Was Hitler's agreement pure deceit? This is a question I have often been asked. He was very well aware of the opposition he would meet from important sections of his party, strengthened by the influx of former Socialists and Communists; but he may have felt his position was so strong that he could afford to ignore this sort of criticism. Even now, I am still convinced that although he was completely irreligious, he realized that a conciliatory attitude in Church problems would earn him an invaluable support from all over the country. As the leader of the non-Nazis in the coalition, I felt it my duty to strengthen his position *vis-à-vis* the radical elements in his party. If the new arrangements had the force of law, I felt that Hitler would be better able to neutralize the influence of these elements.

All these aspects of the situation had been freely discussed in Rome, and whatever doubts Cardinal Pacelli and Dr Kaas may have had, the opportunity to strengthen Christian influences in Germany was too good to be missed. We were all well aware of the rôle that Central Europe must play in combating the anti-religious and totalitarian tendencies from the East. In order to speed up the negotiations, Hitler gave me authority to by-pass the normal channels: that is to say, the Foreign Ministry and Herr von Bergen, the German Ambassador to the Holy See. It was not until the final stages, in July, that Ministerial Councillor Dr Buttmann, of the Ministry of the Interior, was brought into the discussions. This judicious and moderate National Socialist official supported me in every way. Just before my second visit to Rome there was a hitch. The party started to raise a host of objections, and Hitler tried to get me to agree to certain modifications; but in the end I talked him out of them.

Mussolini, whom I saw again, insisted on the importance of arranging things as quickly as possible. 'The signing of this agreement with the Vatican will establish the credit of your Government abroad for the first time,' he said. I therefore persuaded him to get his Ambassador in Berlin to impress upon Hitler how necessary it was to reach agreement without further delay. In June, however, some of the Nazi extremists, led by Goebbels and Heydrich, had started a campaign against alleged immorality in Catholic monasteries and convents, and now demanded that certain persons should be brought to trial. It was evidently their intention to inflame public opinion against the Catholic Church and ferment opposition to any agreement. Consequently I became involved, by letter and telephone, in a long series of arguments with Hitler. I pointed out that the Vatican would refuse to recognize him as a possible partner to an agreement unless he immediately put a stop to this sordid campaign. He told me to assure the Papal Secretary of State that he would clamp down on the offenders at once. The final agreement was drafted on July 8, and on the 20th it was signed at a formal ceremony in the Papal Secretariat.

I was delighted at this result and full of hope that the agreement would open a new era of more friendly and solid relations between the Reich and the Holy See. I think I am entitled to say that His Holiness and his Secretary of State both felt the same. The problem of denominational schools seemed to have been settled once and for all, and the general terms of the Concordat were more favourable than any other which the Vatican had signed. It really seemed as if the regeneration of the Christian way of life in the centre of Europe had been placed on a firm basis.

It is hardly surprising that the anti-clericals were roused to counter-attack. Goebbels, as I learned later, had showered Hitler with pleas and arguments against the signing of such a 'diabolical' agreement. But Hitler still had authority to tell his radical colleagues that his reconstruction plans could only be carried out in an atmosphere of harmony in religious matters. He issued orders that all steps that had been taken against Catholic organizations recognized in the agreement were to be immediately rescinded, and all measures against individual priests and Catholic leaders withdrawn. The decree laid down that any repetition of such activity on the part of the provincial Nazi leaders would be prosecuted with the full force of the law. Hitler greeted the Concordat as a major contribution to internal peace and expressed the hope that a similar agreement would soon be signed with the Evangelical Church. Such a warm and unequivocal response was certainly calculated to allay the fears of his coalition partners, if such was his intention.

One of the points which we had not been able to settle in the Concordat concerned the exact definition of the associations which should come under the complete jurisdiction of the Church, and those, such as youth movements, where the State demanded control. This matter was left to later discussions between the Reich Ministry of the Interior and Church leaders. While the Church was irrevocably opposed to abandoning all religious influence over these youth organizations, this influence was precisely what the Hitler Youth Movement sought to exclude. This led to continual friction, but as long as I remained Vice-Chancellor no irrevocable steps were taken.

During the years that followed, the gradual whittling away of the Concordat's provisions was to dash all my hopes. As time went on, I came to be regarded, even by many of my fellow Catholics, as the man who had betrayed my Church to the Nazis. It is a bitter accusation and the one that has caused me most pain. Perhaps I may quote in my own defence the words used by Cardinal Pacelli in 1945, when he had become Pope Pius XII. 'Without the legal protection afforded by the Concordat,' said His Holiness, 'the subsequent persecution of the Church might have taken even more violent forms. The basis of Catholic belief and enough of its institutions had remained intact to permit their survival and resurgence after the war.' I could not wish for a better testimonial.

It only remains to add that as long as I continued to be an active member of the Reich Cabinet, that is to say until June 30, 1934, I retained enough influence on Hitler to see that the terms of the Concordat were honoured as far as possible. He blamed all excesses on irresponsible elements in the provinces. When we parted company I was still able from time to time to get certain cases modified, but after the notorious Bormann became head of the party Chancery, Hitler gradually drifted into the course set by those of his colleagues pledged to eradicate Christianity. An agreement was also reached with the Evangelical Churches, but they presented a far less united front to the later intrigues and attacks of the Party, and suffered even more ill-treatment than the Catholics.

★ ★ ★

Our greatest problem was that of unemployment and the social disruption it caused. Millions of people were out of work, and there was great danger that the youth of the country, with no hope for the future, no work and no dignity, would become infected by the Bolshevist virus. Most of the legislation in this early period was economic rather than political. Employment was organized, agriculture assisted, and the economic structure shorn of its horde of bureaucrats. A system of labour service was instituted which absorbed the young people and employed them in useful public projects. Most of them spent their year's service on the land, which not only eased the shortage of labour, but brought the youth of the big cities into contact with the moral and material values of the countryside. The building of the *Autobahn* network greatly stimulated the transport industry and improved the country's communications. The first stages of rearmament also played their part, although until I left the Cabinet, this was kept within the bounds of what was necessary for the defence of the country. All these measures were successful, and the contrast with the numbed and hopeless apathy of the period of mass-unemployment enhanced the prestige of the new régime, both among employers and employed, to an extent which largely counteracted any dislike of the Party's political methods.

Hitler sought to put an end to class warfare by granting the working class equal rights in the community. It was the best point in his programme, and found favour not only at home but in many countries abroad. Class warfare was a Marxist tool and the socialist Trade Unions were its principal protagonists. The employers' federations manned the opposing front. If class warfare was to be abolished, then the opposing forces would have to be disbanded. Neither in moral law nor in Christian doctrine is it laid down that the interests of the working class may be represented only by the Trade Unions. I do not wish to be misunderstood about this. The Trade Union organizations have made an overwhelming contribution to raising the standards of the workers, but their purely economic functions had been transmuted by the Marxist parties into a weapon of class warfare.

The Government had decided that Labour Day, May 1, should not be celebrated by the Trade Unions alone, but should become a ceremony involving every trade and profession in the State, manual and intellectual workers alike. Ministers, officials, scientists, farmers, peasants and industrial workers, employers and employed, were called upon to take part in the processions on a basis of equality. But this was only a gesture. The problem was far more fundamental. Social justice is not a natural corollary of freedom. Marxism and Bolshevism have shown that a totalitarian state does not provide social justice for the masses. Germany's Government at the time was still a coalition, and our problem was to devise logical means for resolving the conflict between the two embattled groups in the State. The workers' and the employers' organizations were fighting each other at the cost of the community as a whole. On the one hand stood doctrinaire Marxism, and on the other capitalist individualism, long since ripe for reform. Their opposition provides the fundamental schism in society to this day, and the solution to the disastrous alternation of strike and lock-out has yet to be found.

The coalition Government of which I was a member went to great pains to build up a new relationship between worker and employer, and between both and the State. Our principal concern was to eliminate class warfare. To achieve this we were prepared to approve the dissolution of the Trade Unions. There was much in this National Socialist conception which ran parallel to principles familiar to Catholics and enunciated in the Papal Encyclical *Quadragesimo Anno*. In an important speech to the German Workers' Front on May 10, 1933, Hitler declared: 'The new State will no longer represent the sectional interests of a group or a class, but will be the trustee of the nation as a whole.' It was a sentiment much in our minds at the time, and our support for the new Work Law, promulgated on January 29, 1934, was given with the best intentions.

In the end, the experiment failed, although both workers and employers welcomed it because it enabled them for a considerable time to work together in an unexampled spirit of harmony. The Strength Through Joy organization, which provided both relaxation and education for the workers, was an institution that found many foreign admirers. The failure lay not so much in Hitler's socio-political ideas as in the increasing materialism of the Nazi movement, which deified the State and denied all individual freedom. The time may yet come when the principles involved, if put into practice by more moderate and sensible régimes, will prove to contain the germs of a solution.

On August 19, 1932, the *Völkische Beobachter*, the official organ of the Nazi Party, appeared with a banner headline: 'The Papen Government to protect the Jews.' Then followed a long report from their representative in Geneva of proceedings at the Jewish World Congress, at which Herr Kareski, the German representative, had complained about Nazi attacks and praised the attitude of my Government, to which the article referred in the grossest terms.

One would have thought that this attack by the Nazi house organ on Reich Chancellor Papen would have protected Vice-Chancellor Papen from the accusation of being a persecutor of the Jews. The dreadful tragedy which overcame the Jewish race in the later years of Hitler's régime has made people forget the efforts made by the Conservative ministers in the early days of the coalition to stem the anti-Semitic flood which the Nazis had brought with them. There was at the time considerable anti-Jewish feeling in the country as a whole, and as soon as the result of the March elections became known, Nazi extremists began their first attacks on Jewish shops and businesses.

This confronted the Conservative members of the Cabinet with an extremely difficult problem. I had several private conversations with Hitler on the subject, in which I tried to make it clear that both from a social and political point of view the party's anti-Jewish policies must inevitably lead to the most regrettable consequences. While I was able to discuss the policy involved, I always felt there was a certain point beyond which it was impossible to reach a basis of understanding with him.

For years anti-Semitism had been one of the basic tenets of the Nazi Party programme. The loss of the war, the Versailles Treaty, the inflation, and the financial crisis of the early 'thirties were all ascribed to Jewish influences. The whole Party was permeated by the atmosphere of these accusations. Hitler's own anti-Semitic feelings dated back to his early years in Austria, when he seems to have been strongly influenced by the ideas of people like Schönerer.[1] But there was something more than just political conviction. As

[1] In the last decades of the Hapsburg monarchy Georg von Schönerer (1842–1921) was one of the more provocative members of the Vienna Parliament. He gained considerable notoriety by his anticlerical *Los von Rom* movement and, even more, by his vehement anti-Semitism.

with his anticlerical obsessions, one felt there was a pathological hatred resulting from incidents in his youth. He always blamed certain individuals for his early failures as an artist, and later seems to have extended his hatreds to whole groups and races. He often referred to one incident at the age of fourteen, when his religious teacher had slapped his face. He also claimed that his candidature for the Academy of Arts had been blocked by the Jewish directors. He told me once that whenever he had had to do with a court of law, his worst enemies had always been Jewish lawyers and judges. It is a fact that he hated no profession as much as that of the Law.

During the first weeks of the Coalition, as a result of the intervention of Neurath, Guertner and myself, Hitler issued orders to members of the party to restrain themselves, but this seemed to have little effect. To the Conservative members of the Cabinet the only solution seemed to be to draw up some sort of regulations concerning the numbers of Jews allowed to enter the various professions. This, it was hoped, would damp down radical agitation. At the same time we sought some more direct means of bringing pressure to bear on the Nazi extremists.

My own staff in the Vice-Chancellery saw to it that foreign journalists and diplomats were provided with material for publication which would be likely to cause a reaction abroad, and which could then be used to put pressure on Hitler. Even such a man as Rudolf Diels, first head of the Gestapo, and perhaps not a particularly desirable witness to quote to my Anglo-Saxon readers, has paid tribute to the work my people did in this respect. At least he cannot be said to be biased in our favour. The King of Sweden passed through Berlin at this time, and when he expressed a wish to meet Hitler, I asked him particularly to impress on the Chancellor what an unfortunate effect the campaign against the Jews was having abroad. His intervention, however, seemed to have little effect.

At least we were able to ensure that the regulations governing the number of Jews admitted to the professions did not include those Jews who had been civil servants before the war or who had fought in the Army. Retired Jewish civil servants continued to receive their pensions, and Jewish doctors excluded from panel schemes were allowed to retain their private practices. I managed to persuade Hindenburg to insist on these reservations, and Hitler was forced to agree. The association of Jewish ex-servicemen was good enough to write me a letter of thanks for my efforts. As long as I remained an active member of the Reich Cabinet, that is to say until June 30, 1934, we were able to keep the anti-Jewish excesses of the Nazis within bounds.

* * *

On March 11, Hitler told me he intended to ask the President for permission to fly the Nazi flag everywhere on the occasion of the annual ceremony for those who had fallen in the war. He considered that as all patriotic elements in the country had now become united under the party's leadership, it was only natural for the Swastika flag to replace that of the Weimar Republic. I was appalled by the idea, and we walked up and down in the garden of the Chancellery for an hour while I tried to get him to change his mind. I told him it would be an immense psychological mistake to impose his emblem on the vast numbers who did not belong to his movement. The Republic had committed the same error in replacing the old black, white and red flag, under which more than two million of the nation's sons had fallen in the war, with the black, red and gold flag of the 1848 revolution. This had caused great resentment and it would be unwise to repeat the experiment.

Unfortunately, I got very little support from my Cabinet colleagues. So I turned to Blomberg, who I assumed would wish the matter to be arranged so that it would cause as little resentment as possible in the Army. To my complete astonishment, I found his views diametrically opposed to mine. He considered the Nazis were perfectly entitled to convert their flag into the symbol of the Reich. After this, my only hope was Hindenburg. The President fully shared my opinion, but he surrendered to pressure from Hitler and Blomberg. Hitler maintained that a compromise would enable him to keep the more revolutionary elements in his party in check, and in the end Hindenburg agreed that the swastika and the black, white and red flag should have equal status. I made one last attempt in the Cabinet to have the matter submitted to the Reichstag, but nothing came of it, and Hitler announced the new ruling by decree.

Blomberg's disappointing attitude was soon to become apparent again. I have already mentioned the rumours of a possible military *Putsch* on January 29, in which Schleicher and General von

Hammerstein, the Chief of Staff, were said to be implicated. That Hitler should have little confidence in Hammerstein was hardly surprising, in view of his antipathy to the régime; nor did Blomberg feel happy about the relationship. Hitler did not raise the point until he felt sufficiently sure of Blomberg's support, and then made a request to the President that Hammerstein should be replaced by General von Reichenau, who was well known as an active Nazi sympathizer. Moreover, he had been Blomberg's Chief of Staff in Königsberg.

Hindenburg was incensed, as he always was when he thought he detected an effort to interfere with his prerogatives in the military sphere. He discussed the matter with me at length. Hammerstein had been a favourite of his, and he had long admired his soldierly qualities. However, his willing subordination to Schleicher in December and January had changed the President's opinion. He appreciated the need for a change, but for reasons entirely different from Hitler's. Hindenburg did not want the Army to become the satellite of the politicians, and wished to strengthen its independent status. Reichenau he refused to consider. 'He has never even held a divisional command,' Hindenburg said to me, 'and now I am supposed to entrust the whole Army to him. The idea is ridiculous.'

We went through the list of alternatives. Most of them had been promoted at the same time as myself, and during my twenty years as a professional soldier I had been in active association with them. My own choice was General von Fritsch. He and I had sat together with Hammerstein in the War Academy, for three years. I knew him as a man of strong and serious character and a first-class soldier, who could be relied upon to keep the Army free from political influences.

The degree to which Blomberg had become an adherent of Hitler was shown by his statement to me, that if the President did not decide on Reichenau, he would resign. The President, when he heard this, sent for Blomberg and told him that his post was a political one, and that if he wished to do so, he could resign for political reasons. What he was not free to do was to challenge, on political grounds, a Presidential decision in military matters. This, the President said, was tantamount to insubordination. It is a great pity that Hindenburg did not accept Blomberg's resignation. Fritsch was appointed as Hammerstein's successor. His career and his ultimate fate at the hands of the party prove that I had judged him correctly. To get rid of him, the Nazis had to concoct a disgraceful and completely untrue accusation of homosexuality which led to his dismissal. There is every reason to suppose that but for this, he and his colleague Field-Marshal Beck would have warded off the impending war.

* * *

The Conservative majority in the Cabinet received its first set-back when Hitler invented a new post for his friend Goebbels, who was first introduced as a co-ordinator of our foreign propaganda. None of us had a very clear idea what was intended. We were children in the field of propaganda and had no conception of what his diabolical genius would be capable of achieving. Both intellectually and polemically he stood head and shoulders above the rest of us, and individual ministers soon found that in any argument which did not fit into Goebbels' framework they were overruled by Hitler.

At this time, Goebbels was in his early thirties. Below middle height, he had a large head with sharp features, a wide mouth and intelligent eyes. He was so thin as to be almost emaciated and his general appearance was in complete contrast with the Nazi Nordic ideal. Despite the physical disability of a clubfoot, he seemed to suffer no inferiority complex. He had a biting wit and a gift for venomous sarcasm. However, he could be extremely charming when the occasion demanded it. He was a doctor of philosophy and a brilliant intellectual, with an underlying contempt for everything of a traditional nature. I remember on one occasion, while we were paying an official visit to the German Navy in Kiel Harbour, I was wearing, as I was entitled to do, the uniform of the old German Army. 'What a wonderful fancy dress,' he remarked sarcastically.

'Well,' I said, 'two million Germans died in this fancy dress fighting for their Fatherland while you were still wearing diapers.' He turned away without a word.

At this first Cabinet meeting he gave us a lecture on the art and science of propaganda, of which the gist was this: 'During the many years of party struggle, I have learnt how to influence the masses so that they will follow us without question. Whatever decisions we took during those years, we prepared the ground by the incessant repetition of suitable slogans, until the party members believed every word of them. We shall now have to use the same methods to convince the entire German nation of the necessity for the Government's economic and political measures.' The years that followed were to show that he went far beyond this programme, until in the end he dominated the entire intellectual life of the nation.

In my Cabinet we had always proceeded on the basis of majority decisions, but Hitler based his attitude on Article 56 of the Constitution, which stated that the Chancellor was responsible for policy and for the adherence of individual ministers to it. Decisions were therefore a matter between the Chancellor and the responsible minister alone. Hitler took full advantage of this procedure to prevent joint opposition by the Conservative ministers and a possible split in the Cabinet. As soon as differences of opinion became apparent he cut short the discussion and then, in private conversation, sought to impose his will on the minister concerned.

I had no portfolio myself, and was therefore able to express an opinion only in general terms. I was never able to act as Hitler's deputy, since he never allowed himself to be represented. The Constitution contained no provision for the post of Vice-Chancellor, and my position was therefore even weaker than that of my colleagues. They concerned themselves exclusively with the purely administrative work of their departments. Blomberg never spoke, except in connection with military affairs, and I do not remember that he ever contradicted Hitler. Neurath took little part in the general debates and only spoke on matters of foreign policy. Then, however, he usually maintained an independent view. Eltz, Minister of Posts and Transport, was always ready to speak on general problems, and often gave me great support. Seldte had no experience in political affairs and was completely useless as a conservative colleague. The Minister of Justice, Guertner, was always ready to uphold the proper administration of the law, but he invariably argued in strictly legal terms and made little impression on Hitler. He sought actively to protect the rights of the individual, and protested at the attacks on Jewish property by the marauding Brownshirts. But it was always an unequal struggle between a modest provincial judge, with no great powers of self-expression, and the overwhelming tirades of a revolutionary. Schwerin-Krosigk, the Finance Minister, was a considerable master of debate. His interventions were always short, clear and to the point. He had travelled widely, knew England well, and was always able to make an impression on Hitler when the possible attitude of foreign countries to the new régime was under discussion. However, I never felt very confident that he was a man deeply imbued with the idea of applying practical conservatism to the affairs of state. He remained in office until Hitler's collapse, and then became Foreign Minister in the rump government headed by Doenitz. When one of my friends asked him in 1941 how he viewed the progress of the war, he replied: 'Hitler has always been right up to now. Why should he not continue to be so?'

During this early period many of my colleagues were more than sympathetic to the ideas of National Socialism. The children of my friend Eltz regarded Hitler as something of a hero. From a very early stage Blomberg made no secret of his sympathies, and both Seldte and Guertner allowed themselves to be hypnotized by Hitler's personality. None of them had maintained close contact with the Weimar régime.

In the early stages of the Coalition it seemed as if each member of the Cabinet was determined to achieve real personal contact with his new chief and sought to avoid any suggestion of unnecessary criticism. Hugenberg was an exception. There was always something curt and unforthcoming about his attitude. He had no gift for appealing to the human being in a political adversary. He never established any sort of relationship with Hitler, and this deprived the rest of us of his psychological support.

On the Nazi side, Frick was a nonentity. A lifelong civil servant, he had accustomed himself to speaking only when he was spoken to, and it was too late for him to grow out of it. But the eight Conservative ministers more than met their match in the other two personalities, Goering and Goebbels, who can only be compared with the great figures of the French Revolution. They attacked every problem and countered all criticism with the furious *élan* of the rabble-rouser. After one sharp discussion I remember telling Goering that if he did not agree with our ideas he could always resign. He flung himself across the table at me and retorted, 'You will only get me out of this room flat on my back.' If Goering imposed his ideas by the sheer weight of his personality, Goebbels employed the infinitely more subtle methods of the dialectician. He always avoided the root of any matter under discussion and was the complete master of all of us in debate. He adopted the argument that if a revolution was to be avoided we must loosen controls and let things run their course, with the real intention of consolidating the revolution step by step.

When Hugenberg had his final difference of opinion with Hitler over the policies he had maintained at the London Economic Conference, I tried to persuade him not to resign. If he went, the Cabinet would lose the only minister who enjoyed the support of a political party. His resignation would not act as a warning to Hitler, who would be only too pleased to replace him by one of his own people. During the first five decisive months, Hugenberg had never provided a rallying point for his non-Nazi colleagues: he had been far too occupied in the day-to-day work of his two Economic Ministries. I felt that his resignation, which he finally submitted on June 29, 1933, in spite of all my protests, amounted almost to desertion. We could only have put political pressure on Hitler if we had all been prepared to resign *en bloc*. Hugenberg's successor as Minister of Agriculture was Darré, an old party member, and the Economics Ministry was taken over by Dr Schmitt, a well-known insurance expert. He was never happy in the post, and was replaced after the Roehm *Putsch* by Dr Schacht. But by that time the Cabinet had completely lost its 'bourgeois' character.

We received our second check through the conversion to Nazism of Seldte, the Stahlhelm leader. After he became a member of the party on April 27, the internal affairs of the Stahlhelm reached a crisis, which was complicated by a campaign against its joint leader, Duesterberg, whom the Nazis now accused of having Jewish ancestry. This was news to most of us, as Duesterberg had always campaigned against Jewish membership of the Stahlhelm and had been opposed in this by Seldte, Alvensleben, and others. Now the boot was on the other foot and his resignation was demanded. The Stahlhelm became involved in factional disputes between its Conservative and Nazi elements, and in the end Seldte announced that its members were to join the Nazi Party *en bloc*. This removed one of the principal props of the Conservative wing of the Cabinet. This sort of process has become more familiar to-day, with the adherence to Communism of people who appear to be perfectly respectable. But ideological affinities of this sort defy reasonable explanation.

* * *

With our position growing steadily weaker, the responsibility for containing the revolutionary surge which followed the successes of the March election fell largely on my shoulders. More gifted pens than mine have described the extraordinary upheaval in the nation as the Brownshirts, either in their own capacity or as Goering's auxiliary police, roamed the streets, plundered Jewish shops or private residences, and arrested, ill-treated or threw into internment camps anyone whose political opinions they disliked.

During February, and particularly after the Reichstag fire, I agreed with Goering that the Prussian police should take active steps to deal with Communist elements. There was, in fact, good reason to suppose that Moscow had instructed them to engage in open revolt. Goering always excused the excesses of the Brownshirts and the S.S. by claiming that they had been provoked by the Communists. A decree dated February 28 legalized the numerous arrests that had taken place. Hitler and Goering seized the opportunity, while their non-Nazi colleagues were still in the dark about their real intentions, to take complete administrative control of the police, so that they might use them for their own purposes to even greater effect after the Reichstag elections. Prussia was only one State, albeit the largest. In the other States the judiciary and the police were still in the hands of Weimar ministers and officials. But they too were swept up in the current of events, which followed the same pattern throughout the country.

Between March 5 and April 7, I retained my position as Reich Commissioner for Prussia. I had daily disputes with Goering in the Cabinet over his high-handed activities. I insisted that none of the senior posts in the Prussian administration and police should be made the subject of new appointments without my express permission. Goering disregarded my objections whenever he could, but it was possible to ensure that a number of the police commissioner posts went to trustworthy men, such as Admiral von Levetzow in Berlin and Colonel von Heydekampf in the Ruhr. I received less support than I expected from the senior officials in the Prussian Prime Minister's office. Gritzbach, for example, my *chef de cabinet*, very soon joined the 'winning side' and deferred to Goering more than he did to me. His reward was that he continued to remain in office for many years.

Perhaps I should include here a short note on how the situation in Prussia had developed after I became Reich Commissioner. While acknowledging that the steps I had taken as Chancellor lay within the terms of the Constitution, the State Supreme Court, to which the previous Prime Minister, Braun, had appealed, had laid down a division of authority between the Reich and the Prussian Government. This decision was promulgated on October 25, 1932, and acknowledged that this division of sovereignty might well lead to friction. In fact, it proved impossible to have two Governments in the State. My efforts to reach a compromise with Braun in November failed, as did Schleicher's. The leaders in the State Parliament refused flatly either to form a majority government, which would have meant including the Nazis, or to dissolve the Landtag and call fresh elections.

On February 6, 1933, I suggested to the President that a new decree be promulgated, for the 'restoration of normal conditions in Prussia'. This enabled me, in combination with Kerrl, the Nazi Speaker of the Lower House, to out-vote the President of the Upper House, Dr Adenauer, and call new elections. These took place on the same day as the Reich elections, and although I did not like the administrative measures involved, they did make possible a return to what could properly be called normal circumstances. In the Prussian election the Nazis obtained 211 seats, while my own electoral bloc obtained 43, and the other non-Communist and non-Nazi parties 157. I retained my post as Reich Commissioner for the time being, but resigned before the new Landtag assembled on April 7. Goering became the freely elected Prussian Prime Minister, and my influence in Prussian affairs waned.

There were no State concentration camps in Prussia as long as I had any say in the matter. The law permitting the formation of the Gestapo, which, to start with, was Goering's own Prætorian Guard, as it were, was dated April 26, 1933. In the Vice-Chancellery we had, of course, received information about the camps which had been set up by the Brownshirts without the permission of the authorities, and which were presently 'legalized' by Goering. The first chief of the Gestapo, Rudolf Diels, to whom I have referred before, has written a book on this subject,[1] which provides much useful material about the period. Diels, an experienced police official, was chosen in the first place for his administrative capacities,

---

[1] *Lucifer ante Portas*. Deutsche Verlags Anstalt, Stuttgart, 1950.

and although he can hardly be said to have improved his reputation in such employment, he did much to counter Goering's more extreme policies.

I still maintain that it was impossible to imagine that these first concentration camps would ever become the murder factories which were later to disgrace Germany. The disorders of this early period could still be regarded as the aftermath of the unlicensed political warfare which had been going on for years; an arbitrary form of paying off old scores against political opponents of the left. The machinery of justice was still intact and we still believed that Hitler intended to carry out his promises to deal with the excesses of his provincial chiefs. It was not until the war that the Gestapo was granted judiciary powers.

My repeated interventions with Hitler caused him to issue frequent instructions to the party leaders to restore law and order, and it took some time for us to realize that although the official party attitude was to oppose these excesses, they were in fact greeted with private satisfaction. Speaking of some of the few examples of civic courage displayed in those days, Diels writes: 'I remember particularly protests against the Nazis' behaviour by Sauerbruch, the surgeon, Johst, the poet, and certain other people, particularly Schacht and the courageous people on Papen's staff. Most other Germans only joined in the chorus twelve years later.'

In the months that followed, Diels' own attitude to his chief, the continuous intervention of my Vice-Chancellery staff, and my own influence on Hindenburg, whom Hitler did not yet dare to flout, combined to restore a measure of normality. Goering issued an ordinance which required that ministerial approval must be obtained in all cases of political imprisonment, otherwise the prisoner must be freed within a week. Diels states that according to the figures at his disposal, the number of political prisoners in Prussia by Christmas 1933 did not exceed 3,000, and after the amnesty in February, 1,800 prisoners remained in two camps. It was in 1934 that the situation took a turn for the worse, when Himmler and Heydrich took over the Gestapo, and even Goering lost control over it.

★ ★ ★

On matters of foreign policy complete agreement reigned within the Cabinet. We desired a return to full sovereignty, equality of defensive armaments, subject to restrictions common to all powers, and the maintenance of peace by every possible means. Hitler's public declarations adhered faithfully to these principles. In May they were approved by the Reichstag, and it is interesting to recall that even the Socialists voted for them. Such ideas found a response in every German. Severing, who voted with the rest of his Socialist colleagues, declared in 1947 that he was aware from the start that Hitler's foreign policy would lead to war. He is far from being the only one who has allowed second thoughts to colour his recollections of the mood of 1933.

One of the problems we had to deal with was that of national minorities. The purpose of Wilson's Fourteen Points had been to establish the right of national self-determination as a tenet of international law. Unfortunately, this principle was not applied to the national minorities who found themselves included in the new States set up by the Peace Treaty. Newly revived nationalist sentiments led to a considerable restriction of the rights of German minorities in those countries which had previously been minorities themselves. This was not a problem invented by Hitler, although he took full advantage of it in his relations with Czechoslovakia and Poland, which ultimately led to war. There were also national minorities in Germany, and I prevailed upon him to make a reference to their rights in his speech at the Reichstag session, to which I have just referred. He declared that the German Government would not force Germanization upon them, and expected all minorities everywhere to receive similar tolerant treatment. If he had remained true to this principle he would never have broken the undertaking he gave to Chamberlain when, on March 15, 1939, he proceeded to assimilate the Czech nation.

On May 25, 1933, I spoke to forty thousand representatives of European minorities at a festival held on the Iburg, and made an attempt to raise this problem above the level of national susceptibilities. While pointing out that a third of the people of German race lived outside the territories of the Reich, I was at pains to emphasize that the only solution lay in providing a basis of true European co-operation. Wilson's policies had led to a revival of narrow nationalism, whereas standards of living and the interests of peace and co-operation could only be served by organizing Europe within a larger framework. Germany, as the largest ethnic group in Europe, had the duty of providing an example for the future by this co-operation. If we were true to the European responsibilities we had inherited from the Holy Roman Empire, when nationalism was submerged in the universality of the Catholic faith, then all danger of war would pass.

Today, after the tragedy of a second world war, Europe's statesmen are trying to work out a solution along the lines that I advocated. They have realized that Europe can only survive within the framework of a supra-national organization, in which some part of individual sovereignty must be surrendered to the common good. At least the general atmosphere is more conducive to such a solution now than it was in 1933.

I have told how the Great Powers represented in the League of Nations at Geneva acknowledged, in December 1932, Germany's right to equal armaments. We had never demanded anything but the right to defensive armament, and during the period of my Government not a penny had been voted for rearmament purposes. A small sum had, in fact, been set aside in the 1932 budget, but this had been drawn up by Brüning, and I had not made myself familiar with the details. However, the other European countries, and France in particular, were already becoming perturbed at events in Germany. In May, the French Minister of War spoke of sanctions against Germany, in response to our renewed demand for equal rights. In September 1933 the Geneva declaration of the preceding December was suddenly rescinded.

Hitler decided that Germany could no longer tolerate the League of Nations' confused policy towards rearmament and that for the time being it would be better to take no further part in the work of the Disarmament Commission. I agreed; but I opposed with the utmost vehemence his decision to withdraw from the League of Nations at the same time. Neurath was very little help, although I tried to persuade him that such a step would cause an immense loss in prestige and confidence. He told me had been unable to convince Hitler of this, but had no objection to my taking up the matter with him again. Hitler, in the meantime, had left for a week-end visit to Munich.

I followed him there the same night, and the next morning spent several hours with him in the bourgeois surroundings of his flat. My objections that a withdrawal from the League of Nations would deprive us of personal contacts essential to the conduct of our foreign policy seemed at first to impress him. But, as on many other occasions, I felt the whole time that he had a deep mistrust of diplomatic exchanges which were not under his personal control, just as he had of relationships outside his own immediate sphere. But at least I obtained an undertaking that he would sleep on the matter and let me know his decision in the morning. On Sunday he came to see me in the Vier Jahreszeiten Hotel. He walked into my room in a state approaching exaltation. 'It is all quite clear to me now, my dear Herr von Papen,' he said. 'There is only one solution, and that is to withdraw from the League. We must make a clean break. All other considerations are completely irrelevant.' I realized with despair that his mind was made up and there was no way left to reopen the argument.

He had also decided to submit this decision to the nation on November 12 in the form of a referendum. He hoped by this means to convince the outside world of the wide nature of his support within the country, but he also wished to make it clear that the decision had been taken from peaceful motives only. He therefore issued, in combination with the President and Neurath, a formal pronouncement of the peaceful intentions of the German Government. Once the decisive step had been taken, I felt that this aspect must at all costs be stressed. I therefore made a point of appearing with him at a mass public meeting in the Ruhr for the purpose of pledging my support for his foreign policy. The fact that I was highly critical of many National Socialist measures was already fully realized in Germany. Although I had opposed the withdrawal from the League of Nations, I wished to act as witness for the peaceful intentions of the Government as a whole. At that time my opposition to the course that the Nazis were following had not yet got to the point it reached six months later, when in a speech at Marburg I publicly proclaimed the Government's sins and errors. At the end of 1933 I still retained the hope that it would be possible to neutralize the party's radical elements and proceed in accordance with our combined declaration of policy.

One of the most disturbing elements in foreign affairs was the progressive deterioration of our relations with Austria. In due course I shall devote a section of this book to the problem, but coming events were already casting their shadows. The responsible Minister was again Neurath, a man of measured opinions and no fanatic. In his personal relationships he was accustomed to reinforce his opinions with that degree of argument which is normal among sensible, civilized people. But such tactics were of little use against Hitler – most particularly in the case of Austria, which was his birthplace, and where there was a strong National Socialist movement. Reason was of no avail on a subject which he dealt with on purely emotional grounds.

Hitler's assumption of power had given a tremendous fillip to the Nazi Party in Austria. In order to co-ordinate their work with that of the party in Germany, Hitler had appointed a man named Habicht as a sort of 'inspector' of the Austrian party, with head-quarters in Munich. His office was responsible for issuing the orders and planning the subversive campaign to bring the Nazis to power in Austria. The Federal Chancellor, Dollfuss, countered their methods by imposing a ban on the party and its activities. Hitler reacted to this by forbidding Germans to travel to Austria unless they posted a thousand-mark bond, thereby ruining our small southern neighbour's tourist industry and severely affecting its economy. Although Neurath can hardly have appreciated my constant intervention, I seized every opportunity to protest in the Cabinet at this intolerable interference in the affairs of a friendly neighbouring State. I was firmly opposed to the travel restrictions and the methods employed by Habicht. My efforts to convince Hitler of the deplorable effect these measures were having on foreign public opinion would only have been effective if Neurath had threatened to resign over the question. This he made no attempt to do.

On September 10, 1933, the Austrians were due to celebrate the 350th anniversary of their liberation from the Turks. I suggested to Hitler that I should be sent as special German delegate to the festivities in Vienna, as a sign of our friendly intentions and our desire to return to normal relations. The Cabinet showed very little interest in the proposal, and as the Austrian Nazis were opposed to it, nothing came of the idea. However, at a public meeting in the Berlin Sportpalast on September 10 I was able to proclaim my regret that the Cabinet had been too short-sighted to make this friendly gesture.

In September 1933, Austrian Social Democrats made an un-successful attempt on the life of their Chancellor, Dr Dollfuss. Certain of my friends and I decided we would try to persuade Hitler to send the Chancellor a message of congratulation on his escape. Relations between the two countries were at a low ebb, as a result of the illegal Nazi Party's activities and the various economic sanctions imposed by Germany. We felt that such a telegram would ease the atmosphere and strengthen the position of Dollfuss, and we hoped to sugar the pill for Hitler by emphasizing the need for a combined front against the forces of the left. What was more, Neurath, the Foreign Minister, was on holiday, and would not be in a position to make his usual objections against what he considered outside interference in his own exclusive sphere.

Hoping to strengthen our case, I got in touch with Blomberg, who immediately supported the idea and said he would be ready to visit Hitler with me. When we rang up Berchtesgaden, Hitler said his programme for the day was full, but that he would be able to see us the next day at Stuttgart, where he was attending the national athletics tournament. The next day, therefore, I flew to Stuttgart with Tschirschky, Blomberg and his adjutant. Amidst the general holiday atmosphere there seemed little hope of getting Hitler on one side, and in any case, surrounded as he was by party leaders, the opportunity hardly seemed a favourable one. However, time was pressing, and as he intended to take the salute at an interminable march past, we asked him to find time for a private conversation. Finally he agreed, and we drove out to Untertürkheim, one of the suburbs. Neurath, who had been spending his leave on his estate not far from the town, had also turned up at the tournament, and at Hitler's request he came with us.

Blomberg and I told Hitler our plan and he accepted it. He was just going to dictate the telegram to Dr Dollfuss when he suddenly remembered the Foreign Minister. 'Herr von Neurath,' he said, 'you have not spoken so far. Have you any opinion?' Neurath said that the proposal was completely new to him. He would approve any attempt to improve relations with Austria, but he added, 'You must not overlook the fact, Herr Reichskanzler, that this would be a stab in the back for the Austrian party.' Hitler stopped short. With an angry look he turned to Blomberg and myself and said, 'Gentlemen, the Foreign Minister is perfectly right. You could well have thought of this for yourselves.' It was impossible to argue with him. He got up and left the room in a rage.

★   ★   ★

The problem of the Saar territory occupied an important position in our relationships with France. As a result of my close family connections with this area, Hitler appointed me Reich Commissioner for Saar Affairs. This at least provided me with a post in which I was independent of my ministerial colleagues and able to deal once again with my favourite subject of Franco-German relations. My first concern was to put an end to the dubious and embarrassing activity of the Nazi Party there. The Zentrum was the largest party in the area, the Socialists were also strongly represented, and the Communists were weak; but like all the other parties, the Nazis were permitted full political activity. However, the local Gauleiter had made no attempt to adhere to the tacit agreement between all the other parties, not to make a political issue of the referendum, which was due to take place in 1935. To the accompaniment of their usual threats and pressure, the Nazis were engaged in organizing support for the referendum. I was never in any doubt as to what the result would be, and I wished to avoid at all costs the accusation that a vote for the return to Germany had been obtained as a result of the Nazis' terror tactics. I therefore got Hitler to withdraw his Gauleiter and suspend party activity until January 1935.

It was also clear to me that we must come to some arrangement with France which would spare her the psychological disappointment of a defeat in the plebiscite, and decide the future of the territory on a basis of mutual interests. I suggested either that a treaty to this effect should be drawn up, thereby rendering the plebiscite unnecessary, or that the vote should take place immediately. The Quai d'Orsay seemed, however, to be completely ignorant of the Saarlanders' general mood, and hoped that they would either vote for France or agree to a prolongation of their status as an autonomous area under international administration. My suggestions were sharply rebuffed. When Mr Eden visited Berlin in January 1934, I tried to interest him in my plan, as a sure means of avoiding the increase in Franco-German tension which an overwhelming vote for Germany must cause. My efforts to get him to intercede with the French Government brought the somewhat naïve reply that the British Government had no influence in Saar affairs, which came exclusively under the ægis of the League of Nations. When the referendum was held, only 4 per cent of the population voted for France. I still think it would have been better to have reached a friendly arrangement beforehand.

Nevertheless, I was able to arrange for certain guarantees to be given by both countries, whatever the result of the referendum. Property rights, bank credits, pensions and personal rights of all kind were protected. Moreover, the Reich Government, as a result of my preliminary work, kept strictly to the terms of this agreement. Nor must it be forgotten that in spite of the overwhelming victory in the plebiscite, we paid 900 million francs for our rights in the Saar mines. This was done as the result of my proposal that such a gesture would soften some of the bitterness of defeat.

CHAPTER XVII

THE NIGHT OF THE LONG KNIVES

Dissolution of the parties – Nazi attacks on the judiciary – I protest publicly – Hindenburg leaves Berlin – Roehm and the Army – I take issue with Hitler at Marburg – Goebbels bans publication – The Roehm Putsch – Jung and Bose murdered – Hindenburg – My responsibility

'WHO among us thought it possible that the irresistible force of National Socialism would completely subdue the whole German Reich in four short months?', I declared in a speech at Dresden on July 13, 1933. 'The political parties have been dissolved, the institutions of a parliamentary democracy have been abolished by a stroke of the pen, and the Chancellor possesses powers accorded not even to the German Kaisers.'

The dissolution of the political parties was without doubt the hardest blow for those who thought in purely parliamentary terms. While I was in a position to do so, I had tried to bring about some improvement in the prevailing system of party government. I had criticized Brüning for his failure to enrol the Opposition in the work of government as a means of enabling them to make some constructive contribution to the conduct of our affairs. I had always pressed for a reform of the Constitution as a means of making a working entity out of the Weimar conception of democracy. Now the pillars of that particular political system – the parties – had disappeared. Those of us who were Catholics were less nonplussed than some of our colleagues. The social teachings of the Church had already envisaged a type of state organization based on trades and professions. The 'corporate state' had succeeded the party state in Italy and Austria, and there seemed no reason why this form of government should not provide a substitute in Germany too, once the political parties had failed to ensure stability. When we discussed the measure in the Cabinet, there was practically no opposition. Hugenberg, the only party representative, had already resigned, and the other ministers were experts without party ties. I put to Hitler the fundamental question: 'In what form do you intend that citizens of the new State should co-operate with and control the work of the Government?' I then developed my theory of a democratically controlled corporate state. 'If the parties are to disappear in this process, then it would be logical to dissolve the Nazi Party as well. Otherwise it would lose its *raison d'être*, once the rest had disappeared. If you want to continue your political activity, then the party will have to exist as a movement only.'

Hitler objected vehemently. 'There is no question of my dispensing with the party,' he said. 'It has now become the main prop and support of the State. Whether the apparatus of Government assumes the form described by Herr von Papen is not a question we can decide today. The time is not yet ripe and we must not make hasty decisions.' The only member of the Cabinet who supported me was the Prussian Minister of Finance, Dr Popitz, who took part in all our meetings. But even his incisive and determined opinions had no effect on Hitler.

The complete collapse of the 'bourgeois' camp is best exemplified by their attitude to this development. The Zentrum and the Bavarian People's Party told their members to place themselves under Hitler's leadership for the reconstruction of the country. The Socialists, in a resolution passed in Wuerttemberg-Baden on May 10, had already recommended that Socialist Reichstag members should proclaim their support for National Socialist reconstruction.

I have often been asked why I did not appeal to public opinion when I found so little support for my plans in the Cabinet. In a speech at Dresden I made very clear my conviction that the time had come to turn the Nazi movement into more orderly channels. 'A permanent condition of revolution carries with it the danger of anarchy,' I declared. The pressure of the Nazi Party's radical elements was forcing the Chancellor to make more and more concessions to them. Yet no real opposition emerged. In these early months, a counter-revolution was still a practical possibility, if only Hitler's opponents had realized what was really at stake. But too many of us, and I include myself, still continued to believe that his protestations were made in good faith. In the meantime, the influence of Goebbels, Himmler, Heydrich and their like was increasing.

Whether my detractors like it or not, the fact remains that in the flood of excesses committed by the Nazi radicals, the focal point of normality in the Government was my Vice-Chancellery and its staff. The other ministers were happily engaged in the technicalities of administration. But right up to the Roehm *Putsch* on June 30, 1934, my staff received thousands of complaints, protests and warnings, which were sifted and, where necessary, brought to the attention of the responsible ministers. In party circles we soon acquired the reputation of being a 'nest of reactionaries' and our names were included in the lists of those ripe for liquidation. If a few of the Germans now engaged in flooding the market with resistance legends had spent half their energy at the time in such real opposition, things might have been different.

By the autumn the radical elements in the party had started their campaign against 'outmoded' theories of individual freedom, of equality before the law, and the independence of the judiciary. In a speech at Bonn at the end of May, I had already given a warning against this development. By December I considered it necessary to be more explicit. The 150th anniversary of the founding of the Bremen Club gave me an opportunity to speak my mind to two thousand people, including leading members of the party, in this ancient Hanseatic city. I dwelt on the things that Hitler least wished to hear: the growing unrest in the nation at the attacks on the principles of law, and the restrictions placed on the churches and the free development of individual personality. 'The nation is becoming divided into two camps,' I declared. 'Those who deny a personal existence to the individual, and those who see in individual personality the fundamental basis of existence.'

In a violent attack on the Nazis' terror methods I stated, 'Non-members of the party are not second-class citizens with inferior rights.' Every revolution was faced by the problem of harnessing its dynamics to orderly administration. If it failed to do this, the basic values on which national life had been built up would be destroyed. I compared the Party's anticlerical tendencies with the methods of the Bolsheviks. Their campaign against the judiciary I described as a campaign against the very conception of law. My statements were greeted with frenzied applause, and it was clear that I had expressed the thoughts of a vast majority of my audience. The Party leaders present drew their own conclusions. While they had turned up in full panoply to greet my arrival, not a single uniform was to be seen at my departure from the station, and there was not a single Hitler salute. Senator Bernhard, who accompanied me to the train, thanked me for my speech, saying that such criticism had become only too rare now that the press had ceased to be an organ of true public opinion.

The President left Berlin in May 1934 to seek quiet and convalescence at his country estate at Neudeck. He was already a sick man, and this was the last time I saw him alive. I went to see him off, and his last remark, in that strong, commanding voice was, 'Things are going badly, Papen. See what you can do to put them right.'

Things had indeed gone from bad to worse. Instead of giving the nation a respite, the radical elements of the party were increasing the revolutionary tempo. They complained that they had been cheated out of final victory and that there were still too many conservative elements in leading positions in the Government, the Civil Service and the Army. The measures the coalition Government had taken up till now were much less radical than these people had expected or had probably been promised by their leaders. They now started to press for the fulfilment of these promises, particularly with a view to dominating the Army.

There is no doubt that the Nazi leaders were greatly exercised about the Army's attitude. There had been a time when Schleicher actively supported the idea of a militia system to reinforce the Army, and while he was in office Roehm, the Brownshirts Chief of Staff, had supported him. For months now, Roehm had been pressing Hitler to introduce this militia system as part of a plan for rearmament, in defiance of the terms of the Versailles Treaty. This would give the Brownshirts military status, and would presumably provide Roehm with the post of their commander-in-chief. Hitler would then be able to rely absolutely on the loyalty of the Army. During May and June Hitler must have been toying constantly with the idea. He knew that most of the active generals were rigidly opposed to it. Even Schleicher would not have agreed to his original plan being modified to make the Army a docile instrument of the party, while Blomberg's attitude was that he would answer for the Army's loyalty provided this step was not taken.

Whenever I drew Hitler's attention to the dangerous consequences of conceding Roehm's demands, he always made light of them and described them as an aberration of individual party leaders. I found it difficult to appreciate what might happen if the Brownshirts continued in their demands and Hitler remained completely passive. As far as I could make out, neither Goebbels nor Himmler had any clearer idea of what decision Hitler would make. When he finally made up his mind to break with the radical wing of the party, it must not be assumed that he did so to win the support of the Conservatives, the industrialists or the generals. No return to moderation was involved. As a political opportunist he chose the easiest way to secure the loyalty of the Army and to confirm and consolidate his absolute power.

By June I had made up my mind that the time had come to make a public issue of the situation. Argument, private pressure and discussions in the Cabinet had been useless. I decided to make a public appeal to Hitler's conscience.

I had been asked to give an address in the Auditorium Maximum of the old university of Marburg on June 17. I prepared my speech with great care, knowing that the leaders of Germany's intellectual life would be present. This was the best way of reaching the ears of the nation. A public challenge in such circumstances could only have two consequences. Either I would prevail on Hitler to make a last-minute change of course, or, if this failed, I must resign from the Cabinet. I was not prepared to accept further responsibility for things as they were. I had no wish to avoid my share of the responsibility for the events of January 30, 1933, and my repeated hopes that the Hitler experiment would succeed put me under an obligation to give an account of the part I had played.

Every seat in the hall was filled. I began by saying:

'I am told that my share in events in Prussia, and in the formation of the present Government, has had such an important effect on developments in Germany that I am under an obligation to view them more critically than most people. I am so convinced of the need for the regeneration of our public life that I would fail in my duty both as a private citizen and a statesman if I did not give expression at this point in the German revolution to what it is now necessary to say . . . If other organs of public opinion fail in this task, then it is the duty of the statesman himself to call things by their right names . . . The Reich Minister of Propaganda seems pleased with the

present uniformity and docility of the press . . . He forgets that
it has always been its duty to call attention to injustices, errors
and the failings of individuals. An anonymous or secret information service, however well organized, can never replace these
functions.'

After this introduction I gave an account of the situation I had
encountered in 1932, and the developments which had led to the
democratic assumption of power by the Nazis. The coalition
Government had been formed on conservative principles to replace
an unworkable party political system by a State organized on
corporate lines. It had been our desire to solve the social problem
and to restore equilibrium, both moral and material, in the
country's internal affairs. What we had not foreseen was that the
dissolution of the parties would lead to dictatorship at every level,
open revolution against law, human rights and the Church, and
that anyone who protested against these methods would be stigma-
tized as a reactionary.

If democracy were to be saved by unification of the previous
parties under the National Socialist banner, then this could only be
regarded as a temporary expedient, pending the emergence of a
new intellectual and political *élite*. I reminded my audience of the
conclusions drawn by Count de Tocqueville, the French Foreign
Minister, a hundred years earlier from the results of the French
Revolution. He had regarded the principles of equality and equal
opportunity for every citizen as a self-cancelling paradox and had
questioned whether modern ideas of democracy represented the
only solution to the social problem. If everyone was given an
equal chance, differences in personal characteristics would soon
result in a new aristocracy, call it what you will, occupying a
dominating rôle. This aristocracy would then seek to bolster this
form of 'equality' by tyrannical methods. The only result would
be a change in the leadership. Events in Soviet Russia had proved
the correctness of this thesis. Czars had been replaced by Com-
missars, but the lot of the common people had not improved. It
had never been our intention to follow this example by installing a
permanent dictatorship. We had wished, with the assistance of the
National Socialist movement, to replace a system which had
become unworkable by something better.

Statesmen might change the form of the State, but the real

problem was to give form and character to individual lives. The nation looked for just, responsible government. I mentioned my hopes of a restoration of the monarchy. 'Germany will only find her aspirations fulfilled in an ultimate authority which stands above political warfare and the demagogues, and is independent of industrial strife,' I said. The country would have to make up its mind whether to base its corporate life on the Christian principles that had provided its foundation for centuries, or whether to accept the destruction of those principles as advocated by the Nazis. I was convinced that the Nazis' methods would lead only to destruction. At one time they had insisted that personal accomplishment was a prerequisite to party membership. Now we were faced by a situation in which party intellectuals disputed the right of internationally recognized experts to practise their professions unless they were party members. The party was seeking to shatter all previous beliefs in a hierarchy of values by suppressing individual security and freedom. They wished the law to become a servant of party doctrine, and regarded equality before the law and an independent judiciary as obsolete conceptions. 'Men do not become great by propaganda alone, but by the historical acknowledgment of their achievements. The integration and the form of the body politic cannot be determined by terroristic methods. The suppression of individual thought indicates confusion between vitality and brutality, and reveals a respect for naked force which is a danger to the nation.'

I ended with an appeal to Hitler to break once and for all with those members of his party who were distorting his policies. Any truly great man called upon to play a decisive rôle in historical developments had the obligation of controlling the revolutionary forces that brought him to the top. 'No nation can live in a continuous state of revolution, if it wishes to justify itself before history. Permanent dynamism permits no solid foundations to be laid. Germany cannot live in a continuous state of unrest, to which no one sees an end.'

At first both professors and students seemed astounded and almost unbelieving as they listened to my catalogue of accusations, but I soon sensed that they were all gripped by the freedom of my criticisms: 'If we are false to our cultural tradition, ignore the lessons of our long history and disregard the obligations of our position in Europe, then we will lose the best opportunity this

century is likely to offer us. If this continent of ours is to maintain
its leadership in the world, then there is not a moment to be lost.
We must all turn our energies to the work of moral regeneration
and forget our petty quarrels. The world is in a state of transition,
and leadership can be assumed only by a nation fully conscious
of its traditional responsibilities.'

The roar of applause that greeted me, completely drowning the
shouts of protest from some of the Nazis present, was as if the very
soul of the German people had given tongue. I felt I had expressed
certain basic truths which were as valid then as they had always
been. The only question was whether Hitler would be persuaded
to adjust himself to the public mood.

I felt an immense sense of relief at having unburdened myself in
this way, and was prepared to accept whatever personal consequences might follow. Goebbels reacted even more quickly than
I expected. We had agreed that a recording of my speech should
be broadcast on the radio that same evening. He must have realized
very quickly the political implications of what I had said. The
broadcast was banned and the press instructed to avoid all mention
of the speech. Only the *Frankfurter Zeitung* had time to publish a
few extracts the same afternoon.

As soon as I realized that a ban had been imposed, I went
straight to see Hitler. I told him that I had considered it my duty
to take a firm stand in a situation which had become critical. I
hoped he realized what great value I still attached to our partnership and begged him to give serious consideration to the points I
had raised. It was, I told him, a time for decision. The Vice-
Chancellor of the Reich Government could not tolerate a ban by a
junior minister on the publication of an official speech. I had
spoken as a trustee for the President and had given an account of
the developments of the previous eighteen months. I told him that
Goebbels' action left me no alternative but to submit my resignation from the Government. I would advise Hindenburg of this
immediately, unless the Goebbels' ban was lifted and Hitler
declared himself prepared to adopt the policy I had outlined.

Hitler tried to calm me. He admitted that Goebbels had blundered,
and assumed that he had been trying to avoid an increase in the
prevailing tension. Hitler then launched into a tirade against the
general insubordination of the S.A. They were making life increasingly intolerable for him and they would have to be dealt

Conversation piece at Berchtesgaden

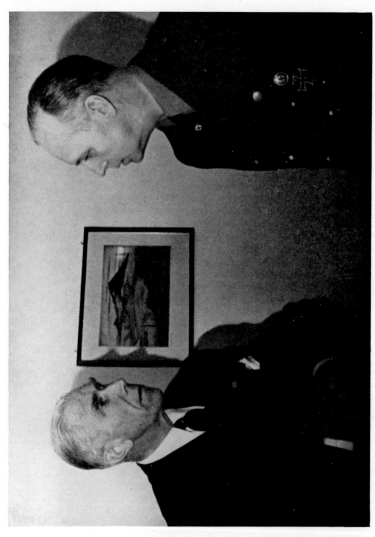

At Hitler's headquarters with Ribbentrop. 1942

with. He said that he would instruct Goebbels to lift his ban, and asked me to withhold my resignation until he himself had gone with me to Neudeck to see the President. He suggested a joint interview. Any discussion with the President could clearly not be restricted to the ban on the publication of my Marburg speech. The whole situation would have to be discussed, and concrete results could only be achieved if the head of the Government was present. I saw no point at this time in seeing the President alone, but Hitler kept putting off this visit quite deliberately.

Had Hitler set a trap for me? It was difficult to say. At the time I assumed that he meant what he said, and I agreed to await the result of our interview with Hindenburg. But we never started on our journey. Goebbels could not prevent public opinion abroad learning of my speech with genuine interest and considerable pleasure. Several heads of foreign missions visited me to enquire what was now likely to happen, but I felt I could say little without prejudicing Hitler's and my discussion with the President. My collaborators in the Vice-Chancellery saw to it that the text of my speech was run off at the *Germania* press, and copies were given to all the diplomatic representatives and foreign correspondents. We posted further copies to friends throughout the country, but I learned later that the Gestapo had tried to put a stop to this and had confiscated many of the letters in the post. One of my friends, Count Westphalen, was arrested for distributing copies and spent some time in one of the Nazi camps.

Five days after the Marburg speech I was in Hamburg, where I had been invited to attend the German Derby. I have been a passionate follower of horses all my life, but this was the first time in my experience that a race meeting acquired a political character. No sooner had I appeared in the grandstand than thousands of people flocked towards me with shouts of welcome and cries of '*Heil Marburg!*'. This was an extraordinary demonstration for the normally somewhat phlegmatic Hamburgers, especially on a purely sporting occasion. I could hardly take a step without being hemmed in by hundreds of people, and I found the whole thing a little embarrassing.

However, my reaction was as nothing compared with that of Goebbels, who was also invited. As an unwilling witness of this demonstration, he tried to draw some attention to himself, and at one point came with me through the crowd in order to enjoy a

L

little reflected glory. When people failed to take any notice of him, he decided to abandon the hated 'bourgeois' in the grandstand and stage a demonstration in the popular seats. There he was greeted with a few handclaps – the Hamburgers are always polite – but that was all.

By this time I had made up my mind that if people wanted to show their feelings, I would take advantage of it. I might as well find out whether my speech at Marburg had appealed only to the 'grandstand' classes, or whether poorer people had also approved of it. I followed Goebbels into the public enclosures. Here my reception was even more remarkable. Dock workers, students, in fact all the working classes of the community, gave me a tremendous ovation. This was too much for Goebbels. In a thoroughly bad humour he decided not to attend the official dinner that evening and – so I was told by friends – told Goerlitzer, the deputy Berlin Gauleiter, 'This fellow Papen is much too popular. See if you can make him look ridiculous in the newspapers.' For myself, I was delighted to realize that my attitude had found so much public support, and considered it some compensation for all the disappointments of the previous months. A week later Goebbels tried to take his revenge.

During the days that followed, tension rose visibly. It was impossible to discover what was going on behind the scenes, but I was obviously being boycotted by the leaders of the party and most of my ministerial colleagues. Marburg had opened a breach. In any case, I had to leave Berlin on June 25 to attend my niece's wedding in Westphalia.

Not until the Nuremberg trial did I hear what had really happened. Funk, Reich Press Chief at the time, and later Minister of Economics, stated in evidence that he had been instructed by Hitler to go to see Hindenburg and inform him that my 'deviations' at Marburg had made it impossible for Hitler to co-operate with me any further. In other words, Hitler did the exact opposite of what he had undertaken to do. Presumably, he wanted to make it clear to Hindenburg that he wished my resignation to be accepted.

★   ★   ★

On June 26, the day of the wedding, Tschirschky told me by telephone that Edgar Jung, one of my unofficial collaborators, had been arrested by the Gestapo and that I must return at once. I flew back to Berlin the next day, and as I could not get at either Hitler or Goering, I protested vehemently to Himmler about Jung's arrest. I was told that alleged illegal contacts with foreign countries were being investigated. He could give me no further information for the time being, but undertook that Jung would soon be released. Three days later the storm broke.

The story of the Roehm *Putsch* has been told and re-told from every point of view, and as I was being held more or less *incommunicado* at the time, there is not much that I can add. Whether Roehm and his entourage really intended to obtain control of the Army through a *coup d'état* will probably never be known. What must be realized is that those of us who were involved in the affair had every reason to suppose that such a *Putsch* had been planned and that the interests of the State demanded that it should be suppressed.

It was a more or less open secret that the Brownshirt Chief of Staff coveted the post of War Minister. Once in possession of this key post, it was apparently his intention to infiltrate members of the S.A. right through the Army chain of command, and to supplant the Army officer corps by his own cadres. Hitler had been very chary of supporting this plan. It was always a principle with him to prevent any person or organization in the State from acquiring a degree of power that might threaten his own position. In any case, his early relations with Blomberg were most cordial and he had no desire to make a change in the post of War Minister. Roehm, on the other hand, considered that his S.A. had played the principal part in bringing the Party to power, and felt that although its political leaders had been more than suitably rewarded, the stormtroops had obtained little recognition.

Things started to come to a head in the spring of 1934. Roehm put up a demand to Hitler that the President's permission should be obtained for the incorporation of Brownshirt leaders into the Army as officers and N.C.O.s. I recall that the figure of five hundred of the former and two thousand of the latter was bandied about at the time. In the end Hitler agreed and approached Hindenburg, who rejected the idea out of hand. This must have taken place about the time when Hindenburg held his first official reception of the new régime. Those who attended noticed a distinct air of coolness between Roehm and Hitler.

From this point on, Roehm must gradually have turned to the possibility of gaining his ends by force. During the preceding months there had been a growing spate of rumours of an S.A. plot against Hitler and the Army, and reports of illegal arms shipments from abroad – principally from Belgium – to reinforce the Brownshirts' strength. General von Bock, commander of the Stettin military district, seized one such shipment with a false declaration of contents, made up of Belgian rifles and machine-guns. Hitler, Goering and the Army all had their own information about these developments, and the Army began quietly to take precautions. Rumours of a second revolution began, and I remember Bose telling me one day that it was set for the end of June, to coincide with a congress of Brownshirt leaders.

The S.A. cannot have remained ignorant of the measures that were being taken to counter any steps they might be planning. About June 26, Bose heard that an attempt planned for the 30th had been postponed. The Brownshirts apparently intended to mislead the Army and the police, and hoped to carry out their plan when those organizing the counter-measures had been lulled into a sense of security. They also calculated that if the Army took independent action on June 30 the Brownshirts would be able to strengthen their position by protesting about unnecessary provocation.

On June 29 Hitler was in Essen, where he seems to have made up his mind to deal with the S.A. leaders once and for all, whether they had postponed their plan or not. Goebbels flew in on the same day. The rumour long persisted that he was playing with both sides in order to ensure his own position, whatever the outcome. Roehm's orders cancelling his preparations apparently did not reach all his subordinates and there were a number of local conflicts between the S.A. and the Army. On the evening of the 29th, the S.A. in Berlin were ordered to report armed to their local headquarters. On the 30th Hitler flew to Munich, where he caught the S.A. leaders in their beds. All of this, of course, only came out later.

Early that morning Tschirschky rang me up from the Vice-Chancellery, and asked me to come to the office as soon as possible. He had been rung up at his own home before dawn by an anonymous enquirer who was trying to find out where he was. This had aroused his suspicions, and he had immediately got in touch with

Bose to see if he had any news, but Bose had nothing to report. I got to the office at nine o'clock, to find that Goering's adjutant, Bodenschatz, had already rung several times asking me to call on Goering immediately. Still without any hint as to what was going on, I hurried over to his home in the garden of the Air Transport Ministry, and I remember being amazed to find that the whole area was full of S.S. guards armed with machine-guns.

Goering was in his study with Himmler. He told me that Hitler had had to fly to Munich to put down a revolt headed by Roehm, and that he himself had been given powers to deal with the insurgents in the capital. I protested immediately at this, and pointed out that as I was the Chancellor's deputy, in his absence such powers could only be granted to me. Goering would not hear of this, and declined flatly to delegate his authority. With the police and the air force troops under his command, he was certainly in the stronger position. I then said that it was essential to tell the President what was happening, declare a state of emergency, and bring in the Reichswehr to restore law and order. Again Goering refused. There was no need to disturb Hindenburg, he said, since, with the help of the S.S., he was in complete control of the situation.

Tschirschky, who was outside in the waiting-room, told me afterwards that while I was with Goering, Himmler had gone to the telephone and had spoken to someone very quietly. Tschirschky could only distinguish the words, 'You can go ahead now.' This was apparently the signal for a raid on the Vice-Chancellery.

Our discussion became distinctly heated, and Goering cut it short by stating that my own safety demanded I should return to my home immediately and not leave it again without his knowledge. I told him that I would accept full responsibility for my own safety and was not prepared to submit to what amounted to arrest. While this was going on, Himmler kept passing messages to Goering. I did not understand them at the time, but later realized that they were reports of the occupation of my Vice-Chancellery by the S.S. and the Gestapo. Presumably Himmler had made Goering call me to his office, assuming – rightly, I may add – that I would have refused to permit this occupation, and that his thugs would have had to deal with me on the spot. My presence would, no doubt, have been an additional embarrassment.

In the Vice-Chancellery – and all this had to be pieced together later – Bose had been shot out of hand, for 'offering resistance'. My secretary, Baroness Stotzingen, Savigny and Hummelsheim had been arrested and carted off to gaol or concentration camps. This was a backhanded way of making my own position impossible, although I could not understand the arrest of Hummelsheim, who had never been a member of our inner circle. The offices were searched for secret documents and then sealed. A row of safes in the basement – the building had been a bank – were blown open and found to be empty.

In the end, Goering, who had a flood of incoming messages to deal with, more or less threw me out. When Tschirschky and I tried to leave, the S.S. guard at first refused to allow us out of the building. Tschirschky went back to Bodenschatz, who came down and ordered the guard to open the door. This he refused to do, until Bodenschatz shouted at him, 'We'll see who is in command here, Minister President Goering or the S.S.!' Whereupon the gate was opened, and we drove off to the Vice-Chancellery in the Vosstrasse, so that I could pick up my files. I found it occupied by Himmler's people and a guard with a machine-gun prevented me from entering. One of the clerks managed to whisper to me that Bose had been shot, then we were parted and I was told to get back into my car. We were surrounded by representatives of the S.S. and of Goering's own secret police, both of whom were trying to arrest Tschirschky. Things became so heated that they nearly started shooting at each other. This was an interesting indication of the prevailing confusion. Clearly there were at least two groups at work, one of them led by Goering and the other by Himmler and Heydrich.

My home was surrounded by an S.S. detachment armed to the teeth. The telephone was cut off, and in my reception room I found a police captain, who had had orders that I was to have no contact with the outside world and that no one was to be allowed to see me. Later he told me that he was responsible with his own life for preventing any Brownshirts or Gestapo from attempting to abduct me, unless he received direct orders from Goering. I must say it would have been nice to have known this a little earlier. My unfortunate wife and two of our daughters had accepted an invitation to visit friends in Bremen, and I could well imagine what her state of mind must have been when she heard reports of what was happening.

I spent the next three days completely alone. I had no idea what was going on in Berlin or in the country as a whole, and expected to be arrested and probably shot at any moment. I had no doubt that Goebbels, Himmler and Heydrich had made up their minds that it was time for the Marburg reactionary to be liquidated. As I learnt later, the only man who stood between me and this fate was Goering. He probably felt that my liquidation would only complicate matters still more.

My chief preoccupation was how to get some word through to Hindenburg to declare a state of emergency. This would have placed the Reichswehr in command of the situation and enabled us to hold an investigation into what was really going on. Ketteler, one of my most trusted friends and assistants, apparently had the same idea. He had escaped arrest and had set off alone to Neudeck to see the President, but when he reached Oldenburg-Januschau's neighbouring estate he was told that the President's condition made a visit impossible. The telegram sent in Hindenburg's name, congratulating Hitler on his suppression of the revolt, made it clear that he had no real idea of what was going on. I do not know whether Hitler and Goering had contrived to isolate him. If this is so, then Meissner, his *chef de cabinet*, was the man to blame.

During these three days I had one tenuous link with the outside world. Certain good friends managed to walk past my windows to convince themselves that I was still alive. One of these was the American Ambassador, Mr Dodd, and another a courageous and well-known medical consultant, Professor Munk, who refused flatly to be turned away by the guard until he had received a note in my own handwriting proving that I was still alive. On the fourth day, July 3, I managed to get some news of what had been going on, and was given confirmation that Bose had been shot and many of my associates arrested. The *Putsch* had apparently been dealt with. My son, who had been shut up with me, was allowed to leave and sit for his law examination, although he can hardly have felt very well prepared for it. My wife and daughters, who had arrived in Berlin the day before from Bremerhaven, were also allowed to come home and were thankful to find me alive.

When the telephone was reconnected, I received a call from Goering. He had the effrontery to ask why I had failed to appear at that day's meeting of the Cabinet. For once I replied in highly undiplomatic terms. He expressed astonishment that I was still

more or less under arrest and apologized for the 'oversight'. Shortly
after this the guards were removed, and I was able to leave immediately for the Chancellery. At this time I was still under the
impression that Himmler had conducted the operation against the
Vice-Chancellery, on the pretext that we might have been involved in the Roehm affair, and I was still foolish enough to think
that Hitler had had no part in it.

I found him on the point of holding a Cabinet meeting, at
which he intended to give an account of the previous days' events.
He asked me to take my place, but I declined to do so, and
demanded to see him alone. In a neighbouring room I explained
angrily what had happened, and asked for an immediate judicial
enquiry into the measures taken against my officials. I told him to
regard the resignation I had submitted on June 18 as final, and that
I refused to take any further part in the work of the Government.
I also insisted that my resignation be announced immediately, but
this he refused. 'The situation is serious enough,' he said, 'and I can
only announce your resignation when things have quietened
down. In the meantime, I would thank you to attend the meeting
of the Reichstag, at which I shall give a public account of my
actions.' I told him that there was no question of my sitting on
the ministerial benches.

On this note we parted and I drove straight to see my friend,
Fritsch, at the strongly-guarded War Office in the Bendlerstrasse.
His adjutant, an old steeplechasing acquaintance of mine, looked
as if he were seeing a ghost. 'Good heavens, sir, what has been
happening to you?' he asked. 'As you can see, I am still alive,' I
said, 'but this *Schweinerei* has got to be stopped.'

Fritsch appeared most depressed. He told me that Schleicher
and his wife had been shot, that the Army was being held in
readiness, but that the danger of an S.A. *Putsch* seemed to be over.
I asked him why the Army had not intervened and declared a
state of emergency. Two of their generals had been murdered and
hundreds of people shot or arrested who were certainly in no way
connected with the alleged Brownshirt plot. Whether or not a
real danger to the State existed, the Army and the police, as the
forces of law and order, were certainly strong enough to put
down any revolt. It seemed impossible that in a civilized State the
Army could sit by and watch a campaign of murder. I asked
Fritsch direct why he had not assumed the duties of Commander-

in-Chief. Neither the S.S. nor the Brownshirts would have been a match for the Army. He replied that this was exactly what he and most people in the Army had wanted, but they could not move without explicit orders from Blomberg or Hindenburg. However, Blomberg had rigidly opposed any intervention, and Hindenburg, the Commander-in-Chief, could not be reached and seemed to be wrongly informed.

Later on I realized that the Army as a whole had been against intervention. It is true that a number of the senior and more thoughtful generals, such as Fritsch, Beck, Hammerstein, Bock, Adam, Kluge and Kleist, were alarmed by the *Putsch*, and disliked it. The manner in which Roehm's plans had been suppressed and the high death-roll among the innocent were an affront to these men's ideas of law and propriety, and they knew that if the leaders of one group could be stood up against a wall and shot, the same fate might await those of another. But this trend of thought was not strong enough to counterbalance the general feeling.

When Hitler came to power he did much to improve the Army's material situation, and it is not surprizing that this won him a greater degree of loyalty than had been given to the Weimar Republic. By training and tradition the officers were conditioned to keeping out of politics. Brought up on the old Prussian precepts, they disliked moving without orders from above, even when their convictions seemed to justify insubordination; a fact that caused other tragic situations later, especially during the war. Some of the generals saw in Blomberg's support for Hitler a means of furthering the Army's interests. To these considerations was added the undeniable fact that the Army emerged from the *Putsch* much strengthened by the neutralization of the Brownshirts.

One incident that may have further influenced the Army's attitude took place a short time before the actual Roehm purge. I cannot give chapter and verse for this, but the account came to me from a reliable source. Roehm and General von Fritsch were said to have held a meeting at a hunting lodge in Mecklenburg belonging to Werner von Alvensleben. They were supposed to have reached an agreement that soldiers who had completed their military service would be incorporated into a militia, under Roehm's command, for further training. This would provide a reserve of manpower on which the Army could call in case of need. At the same time, Roehm gave an undertaking not to interfere in the Army's internal affairs. Hitler was most annoyed when he heard of this arrangement. He saw in it an alliance between reactionary generals and the leader of a body which, in many respects, was becoming increasingly obstructive.

If the Army had chosen to intervene, it would have met with very little resistance. Hitler's actions had completely demoralized the S.A. The older members, embittered at the murder of most of their leaders, were now hostile to him. The S.S. was still relatively weak.

Years later, when we were in prison in Nuremberg, I discussed the Roehm *Putsch* with Keitel and Goering. The German newspapers had never reported the circumstances of Schleicher's death, and I asked Keitel whether he knew exactly how Schleicher had been shot. He replied that he had been told by Blomberg that Schleicher had been supporting Roehm in his plans to dominate the Army by a Nazi militia. He was also said to have been in touch with certain quarters in France. At this point Goering broke in to say that the Gestapo had received direct orders from Hitler to arrest Schleicher. But when they broke into his home Schleicher had drawn his pistol. His wife, coming into the room at that moment, had flung herself between them and been mortally wounded by a shot from one of the Gestapo. A fusillade then broke out, in which Schleicher was killed.

Goering also claimed that on the evening of June 30 he had begged Hitler to put an end to the arrests and shootings, as otherwise the situation would get out of hand. In the end Hitler had agreed to this, although he insisted that there were still a lot of people who deserved to be shot. Frank, who was imprisoned with us at Nuremberg, and who had been Bavarian Minister of Justice at the time, said that in the course of a discussion lasting some hours, he had persuaded Hitler to reduce the number of people due to be shot in the Stadelheim prison from two hundred to about sixty. When I asked Goering whether he thought that the President had ever seen the congratulatory telegram that was sent in his name, Goering replied that Meissner had often made a point of asking, half-jokingly, whether Goering had been 'satisfied with its text'.

★   ★   ★

It is difficult to recall one's personal reactions at the time. I was shocked and disgusted at the cowardly murder of Bose and Jung. For the first time one had the impression, later to become only too common in the Third Reich, that the individual stood completely helpless in the face of some great criminal conspiracy. A general atmosphere of hysteria reigned. Hitler was in a completely unpredictable mood and was prepared to adopt the slightest excuse for starting the purge again. My chief concern was for the safety of those of my officials who had been arrested and whose relatives besieged me with requests to intercede for them. I was still under the impression that Roehm's alleged plot had represented a real threat. Most of the Brownshirt leaders who had been murdered were highly undesirable characters, and in some cases criminals, who in more normal times would probably have ended their lives in gaol. But the manner in which the purge had been carried out was a negation of the normal processes of law, and no one could foresee the consequences.

In the days that followed I wrote a number of letters to Hitler, which were of considerable importance in the prosecution's case against me at Nuremberg. These letters can only be properly understood if related to the times in which they were written. I was prepared to make almost any concession, and even to agree to the announcement of my resignation again being postponed, if this would result in the release of my associates, four of whom were still in gaol. The Gestapo was searching the Vice-Chancellery high and low for evidence of our implication in the *Putsch* as grounds for liquidating us, and our files were so full of complaints against the régime and the records of our own attitude to the leaders of the party that there would have been no great difficulty in faking a case against us. My ministerial colleagues were no help. The only chance seemed to be to convince Hitler of the loyalty of my officials. If I could do this, perhaps they would be released. If some of the phrases in these letters now seem open to criticism, it should be remembered that I wrote them while I was at my wits' end. When I wrote to Hitler on July 4, it was chiefly to clear myself and my collaborators of any suspicion of being involved in the plot. I protested against their continued imprisonment and the seizure of my papers, and asked for an immediate judicial enquiry. A short extract from this letter was published in the press, but Hitler did nothing to follow it up. On the 10th I wrote to him again, demanding that our reputation, and particularly that of

poor Bose, should be cleared by a public declaration that we had
in no way been involved in the plot. I also told him that all my
attempts to get in touch with the President had met with the reply
that he was still badly in need of rest and that I would do better to
postpone my visit for a few days. I therefore asked Hitler to
arrange for my resignation to be announced.

Next day, the 11th, I managed to see him. He told me that a
meeting of the Reichstag was to be called two days later, and that
he would accept full responsibility for everything that had happened,
including certain unfortunate acts committed 'in an excess of zeal'.
He was not prepared to deal with Bose's death as a special case,
and accused me of putting my personal interests before those of
the country. The situation was still too serious to dwell on individual incidents. On the 12th I wrote him another letter. I told
him that although I appreciated his courage in accepting responsibility for 'certain actions carried out without his knowledge', I
considered that he would be unwise to identify himself with them.
I asked again for a judicial enquiry into Bose's death. On the
morning of the 13th I sent him a note stating that I was not prepared to attend the Reichstag session.

In the meantime, my officials had been released one by one. But
we also received the terrible news that Edgar Jung had been killed.
Up to this moment we hoped that my intervention with Himmler
on June 29 would have had some effect and that perhaps Jung was
hiding somewhere. In spite of Goering's and Hitler's express instructions, none of my archives were returned. They contained
nothing but our ordinary office records, covering the stream of
complaints which had reached us, and the steps we had taken to
deal with them. Bose's personal files, however, must have contained an immense amount of material on the activities of the Nazi
Party and the excesses of Himmler and Heydrich. This had been
collected for possible publication, as a means of halting these
excesses, and the total of evidence must have been extremely
damaging. The Vice-Chancellery remained sealed, although it
seemed that Speer and his architects had access to it for the purpose
of rebuilding it as a new wing of the Reich Chancellery.

I wrote three more letters, on the 14th, 15th and 17th, all insisting yet again on the complete innocence of anyone in my office of
any complicity in Roehm's plans. I considered that our personal
honour was involved in this. I repeated my readiness to withhold

the announcement of my resignation until Bose's death had been properly investigated. None of the letters had any effect, and I continued to be made the object of defamatory and scurrilous attacks by the wild men of the party.

At one point Hitler, in order to spare himself the further complication of my resignation, had suggested that I should take up one of the foreign diplomatic posts. I had made it clear that my acceptance of any such offer was dependent on the release and rehabilitation of my officials. It was a difficult position. If Bose was declared innocent, then Hitler and the Gestapo would be responsible for a murder. If I rejected all further Government employment, there was always the risk that a 'case' would be concocted out of my files to prove the complicity of the Vice-Chancellery in Roehm's alleged plot.

Hitler's methods in this case were nothing if not direct. On July 6 or 7 he had sent his State Secretary, Dr Lammers, to me to suggest that I should take up the post of Ambassador to the Vatican. If I considered that the emoluments of the post were too low, I was at liberty to name any arrangement I thought suitable. I am a naturally polite person and very seldom lose my temper. But when Lammers put this suggestion to me, I shouted at him, 'Do you and the Führer think I can be bought? This is the most brazen piece of impudence I have ever heard. Tell the Führer that.' And thereupon I showed him to the door.

I never succeeded in my efforts to get in touch with Hindenburg at Neudeck, so that I could give him a personal account of all that had happened. Every time, I got the same answer from Meissner and the adjutants: the President's health would not permit it. It was impossible to see the situation clearly. Public opinion was so confused that some of my Conservative friends pressed me to remain in office at all costs, as the only man still capable of ensuring some return to law and order.

The Cabinet, in whose work I had taken no further part, agreed to *post-facto* legalization on the executions. Here Guertner, the Minister of Justice, made one last stand. Although he was prepared to by-pass the normal method of judicial enquiry into the executions of seventeen of the most unsavoury S.A. leaders, he insisted that all the other known deaths should be properly investigated. Hitler agreed to this, but the actual work of investigation was made impossible by the refusal of Himmler and the Gestapo to give any assistance. It was some days before I obtained final confirmation that Jung had been shot in the underground cells of the Gestapo prison in the Prinz Albrechtstrasse. I persuaded Guertner to issue a writ for murder against persons unknown. An enquiry was instituted but uncovered no evidence, and after Guertner's death nothing more was heard of it.

I lost in Jung a friend and close associate. He was a lawyer with a practice in Munich, and had become known as one of the most active and gifted Conservatives of the younger generation. He had published many original works, in which he tried to present a practical alternative to the mechanistic and materialistic doctrines of Rousseau, Marx, Engels and Lenin. Our ideas ran parallel, and I had expressed them when I took over the Chancellorship, in demanding a new conception of State authority.

My many duties made it essential that I should have someone to help me formulate these ideas. It was my old friend Humann who suggested I should approach Jung. When I asked him if he would be prepared to act as an unpaid adviser, he agreed with enthusiasm. Together we worked out our tactics for the first Hitler elections. We would agree on a theme, and Jung would suggest the draft of a speech. We would then discuss it for days, or, in the case of the Marburg speech, for weeks. Jung was a Protestant, and was less obsessed than I was with the necessity of basing all reconstruction on the renewal of Christian ethics in day-to-day life. He left it to me to integrate the teachings of the Catholic Church with our political thought.

He was responsible for many of my speeches on the 'national revolution'. When the Enabling Law was being discussed, he acted as my liaison with the German National Party and the Bavarian People's Party in our attempt to retain the President's right to promulgate laws. When, in the latter half of 1933, it seemed as if some return to normality was still possible, Jung and I saw less of each other. It was only in May 1934, when Himmler and the Gestapo had achieved such a powerful position in Prussia, and Hindenburg's health began to fail, that we came together again to work out the final appeal that I had made at Marburg.

Bose used to say to me jokingly, 'Write your own speeches, sir, they are always the best.' I mention this because whenever my detractors find themselves at a loss, they suggest that Jung was entirely responsible for my speeches. I was much too unintelligent, they say, to have thought them up myself. Sabath, who had been my *chef de cabinet*, was good enough to say at my denazification trial that none of my officials in the Vice-Chancellery were in any doubt that the Marburg speech represented exactly the opinions I held at the time. There is nothing unusual in a man in the position I then held drawing on the best possible advice and assistance. Some of President Roosevelt's best speeches were the result of similar teamwork.

While I was serving my labour camp sentence at Garmisch, in 1948, I had a conversation with a former S.S. general. He had been a police official and had been seconded to the Gestapo in 1933. He believed that Hitler had used the *Sicherheitsdienst* under Heydrich, rather than the Gestapo, as his chief instrument in putting down the Roehm *Putsch*. The Berlin detachment was commanded by a man called Behrens. This general told me that he had been instructed to interrogate Edgar Jung, with a view to finding out whether he had written the Marburg speech. Jung had denied this, and the interrogation had then been taken over by Behrens. It must have been shortly after this that Jung was shot.

At the end of February 1948, I was called as witness at one of the later Nuremberg trials (although I did not actually give evidence). There I had another short conversation with a former police official, whom I will call G., and learnt a few more details of the death of my other friend, Bose. He had been killed, so G. was told, while offering resistance. G. said that on the evening of June 30, 1934, he received orders to remove Bose's corpse to the mortuary. The post-mortem report showed that he had been shot several times in the heart, and five or six cartridge cases were picked up in the Vice-Chancellery. G. remained for a week with instructions to examine my archives for evidence of complicity in the Roehm plot. However, he found this task too much for one man, and handed all the files over to the Gestapo.

Bose, as I have said, had been building up a file on the activities of Himmler and Heydrich. He had as his assistant in matters concerning the press a man named Bochow, who later served for a period as a *Sicherheitsdienst* agent. I have not the slightest doubt that it was Bochow who disclosed this side of Bose's work to the Gestapo, and was therefore directly responsible for his death. Bochow turned up later in Vienna, when I was Ambassador there, and I shall have more to say about him, in connection with the murder of another of my officials, von Ketteler, which occurred at the end of my term of office there.

Bose's wife, who had two young children, had a nervous break-down when she heard of her husband's death. The Gestapo refused to surrender his body. All the victims of the purge were hurriedly cremated to prevent any awkward enquiries into the manner of their death. A week after he was shot, the Gestapo responded to my insistent demands by handing over an urn containing his ashes, and in spite of Himmler's warnings against provoking any public demonstration, I arranged for them to be given a proper burial in Berlin's Schöneberg cemetery. I felt that the least I could do was to give a suitable funeral oration. I spoke of his high services to the nation, proclaiming that we buried him as a man of truth and honour. Every word of what I said was taken down by sour-looking Gestapo stool-pigeons, who mingled with the mourners.

My little speech did not go unnoticed. Mussolini sent a message through the German Ambassador in Rome, von Hassell, saying that it was a bold gesture, and expressing surprise that the members of the coalition Cabinet had shown so little resistance. Perhaps I have given some explanation of this in describing the extra-ordinary state of confusion in our minds at the time.

The real tragedy of June 30 and its consequences lies in the fact that if the situation had been slightly different in only one or two ways, it would have been possible to end the revolutionary trend of the National Socialist Movement. If only the President's health had held out for another few months, his sense of duty would have kept him in Berlin. It would have been possible to keep in touch with him, and he would not have received such a distorted account of events. He would have been able to appreciate the very real effect of my speech at Marburg, and would have learnt what had happened to his former Defence Minister and Chancellor Schleicher. Nor would it have been possible to suppress news of the mass executions.

Without doubt, he would have immediately decreed a state of emergency and used the Army to restore order. There would have been a proper investigation into the whole affair, the guilt and innocence of plotters and executioners alike would have been determined, and the rule of law would have been re-established. Hitler would have been stripped of the fascination he had for the masses, and the nation would then have returned to normal.

For the vacuum caused by Hindenburg's absence, Blomberg must take his full share of responsibility. Schleicher's murder should have given him the signal to act. Instead, he was watching with satisfaction the arrangements for Roehm, the Army's rival, to be put out of the way. I too must shoulder some responsibility. For seventeen months I had believed, mistakenly, that it would be possible to regulate Hitler's conduct of affairs. I may have lacked political judgment, but the accusation made at Nuremberg that I had deliberately delivered up my country and its people to a rule of violence that would lead to chaos only betrays complete ignorance of the facts. The shape of things to come was not immediately apparent. Unfortunately, there is no 'if only' in history.

Sir David Maxwell Fyfe, the British prosecutor at Nuremberg, maintained that I should have regarded it as my duty, in the days after my release, to make a public protest against the events of June 30 and proclaim my resignation. This would have caught the attention of the outside world and would probably have altered the course of events. To this I would reply that Goebbels' complete control over the press and radio made the idea of a public protest, in the normal sense, illusory. Moreover, although counter-charge is a poor answer to any accusation, I feel entitled to make this point: at the time when all this was happening, the world outside was better informed of events in Germany than were most Germans. Neither June 30, nor Hitler's constant disregard of international treaties – the remilitarization of the Rhineland, the reintroduction of conscription, the rejection of the Versailles Treaty, and the annexation of Austria – prevented foreign countries from concluding pacts with him, as long as they saw in him a defence against the threat of Bolshevism. 'Appeasement' was not a German policy. The actions of one man, whatever position he occupied, could have had little effect. The rest of the world has very real responsibilities in the matter.

CHAPTER XVIII

THE HINDENBURG TESTAMENT

*Attempts to restore the monarchy – Hitler agrees in principle – Hinden-
burg persuaded to recommend its return – Hitler sees Mussolini – Death
of the President – The Presidency passes to Hitler – The Army's oath
of loyalty*

THE death of Hindenburg on August 2 removed the last
barrier to Hitler's assumption of complete power. We had
all been aware of the danger inherent in re-electing so old a
President. Brüning, who was in power at the time, must have
given much thought to the question of the Field-Marshal's candidature. It is difficult to understand why he recommended him for
the office of Chief of State, if the statements he has made in recent
years are true. He maintains that Hindenburg suffered a breakdown in September 1931 which impaired his faculties for about
ten days. Meissner, the President's *chef de cabinet*, has denied this, as
has Herr von der Schulenberg, Hindenburg's military A.D.C. The
old gentleman often had attacks of faintness, but his intellect
remained unimpaired. When I became Chancellor in June 1932,
the President still had all his wits about him, and his powers of
decision did not fail during this critical period. It was not until the
end of 1933 that his physical condition started to deteriorate, but
even then there was no sign of any intellectual decay.

It was clear, however, that he could not last for ever, and with
so critical a situation in the country I realized that his death would
have serious consequences. The fury of the National Socialist
revolution was increasing steadily, and Hitler either could not or
would not control the hotheads in the party. If the President
should die, it was highly undesirable that his mantle should fall on
Hitler or one of his party colleagues. Quite apart from the dangers
of fusing the offices of Head of the State and Head of the Government, it seemed vital to keep out of Hitler's hands the one non-
Nazi instrument of power, the Reichswehr. I therefore took up
the matter with some of my coalition Cabinet colleagues. They

were chary of broaching the subject with Hitler, although I was convinced that the issue could not be avoided.

A restoration of the monarchy seemed the only practical solution. Hitler would never have allowed the election of any individual, to whom he would nominally be subordinate, but there was a possibility that he might respect the institution of the Crown. There was still a strong current of monarchist sentiment in the country. For my own part, I had always supported the idea of a constitutional monarchy on the British model, to serve as an ultimate and impartial authority amid the more ephemeral manifestations of public life. Somehow I had to bring Hitler round to this idea. We had a long conversation on the subject in March 1934. I argued that it would be difficult for him to surrender his leadership of the party, in order to become a non-political Chief of State. I suggested that it was too much to expect him to hand over his political position to others, and that a return of the monarchy provided the only real solution.

I was surprised how willingly he fell in with the idea. He was full of praise for some of the great Prussian kings, especially Frederick-William I, the father of Frederick the Great, one of the ablest administrators in our history. He felt that in order to prepare the ground, the attention of the public should again be drawn to their great services. He even gave instructions for a film to be made of Frederick-William's life, in which Emil Jannings was to play the part of the King. But Hitler insisted that the internal situation must first be consolidated and all treaty limitations on sovereignty removed before a monarch could hope to maintain his position.

He had no objections to the Hohenzollern dynasty, although he felt that a new Kaiser might be handicapped by no longer being King of Prussia. At the beginning of the previous January the Reichstag, in spite of my opposition in the Cabinet, had drastically reduced the autonomy of the German States. There could be no question of any revival of the Principalities or the Kingdom of Bavaria. Hitler did not consider the Crown Prince a suitable candidate, nor his brother, Prince August Wilhelm, although he had joined the Nazi Party. We decided that one of the sons of the Crown Prince should be given first consideration. Hitler was much impressed by the fact that one of them had taken a job in the Ford works at Detroit. I felt that the youngest son, Prince Friedrich, would probably be the best choice, and it was decided that whoever we chose should be found employment in the Chancellery, in order to get some insight into the affairs of State.

When we had reached agreement, I went to see Hindenburg and discussed with him quite openly the problem of his succession, should he be taken from us. The Weimar Constitution laid down that in the event of the President's death his duties devolved on the Chancellor, until a new Presidential election had taken place. It was not clear whether the Nazis would adhere to the electoral obligation, but in any case Hitler would be able to command the necessary majority. A wise precaution would be for Hindenburg to leave a political testament to the nation, recommending the return of the monarchy. Hindenburg still enjoyed immense influence throughout the country and a last wish of this sort might well enable Hitler to overcome the radical wing of his party in their opposition to the monarchy. Hindenburg thought well of the idea and asked me to draft a suitable document. He also told me that, as a prologue to his autobiography, he had prepared an account of his lifelong service and would use this as the basis for the testament I suggested.

My draft recommended that after his death a constitutional monarchy should be adopted as the form of government, and I made a point of the inadvisability of combining the offices of President and Chancellor. In order to avoid giving any offence to Hitler, there were also certain approving references to some of the positive accomplishments of the Nazi movement. I laid it before the President in April 1934. He read it and locked it in a drawer of his desk, with the remark that he would give the final version his full attention. A few days later he asked me to call on him again, and told me that he had decided not to approve the document in the form I had suggested. He felt that the time was not yet ripe for such a proposal, and considered that the nation as a whole should make up its mind as to the form of State it desired. He therefore intended to regard the account of his service as a testament, and his recommendations concerning the return of the monarchy would be expressed, as his last wish, in a private letter to Hitler. This meant, of course, that the whole point of my original suggestion had been lost, as the recommendation concerning the monarchy was no longer addressed to the nation; a fact of which Hitler later took full advantage.

Herr von der Schulenburg, Hindenburg's military aide, giving evidence at my denazification trial, explained what happened after this. In the latter half of April 1934, the President handed him two manuscripts containing certain alterations and deletions, and instructed him to have fair copies of each document made by hand. These were the testament and his last wishes. Hindenburg signed the fair copies, which were sealed up in separate envelopes, one addressed to 'The German People', and the other to 'Reich Chancellor Adolf Hitler'. Both were placed in the President's safe, and when Hindenburg left on his last journey to Neudeck, Schulenburg took them with him. All this was unknown to me at the time.

In 1934, I spent three weeks' Easter holiday in Italy. My chief object was relaxation, but I wrote a long letter to Hassell, our Ambassador to Rome, in which I expressed my fears that our hopes of a return to normal conditions would be dashed by the increasing radicalism of the Nazis. He invited my wife and me to stay with him on our way home, and we spent a couple of days in his handsome Villa Wolkonski. He told me I had been most indiscreet to put so much on paper, but when I got him alone in his study I found that we were in full agreement.

He had taken a box at the opera that evening, and I was surprized to find Mussolini in the one next door. Hassell had told him about my incognito visit, and during the interval, as well as at the end of the performance, I had a long discussion with the Duce who was most disturbed at the behaviour of the Nazis in Austria and at the way things were shaping in Germany. I told him of our efforts to check the revolutionaries and of my despair at the deterioration in our foreign relations. I asked the Duce if he would be prepared to invite Hitler for a State visit, in an attempt to make him mend his ways and to convince him of the need for a peaceful foreign policy. I knew that Hitler had great admiration for Mussolini's personality and achievements, and I hoped that he would be able to bring some pressure to bear. Mussolini agreed wholeheartedly with this suggestion and asked me to convey an official invitation.

When I told Neurath of this on my return, he seemed most put out by my intervention in his affairs. He considered such a visit would be premature and thought that Hitler should first be left to deal with the growing-pains of his movement – a turn of phrase which seemed to me rather unfortunate.

Nevertheless, it was arranged that the meeting should take place in Venice in the middle of June. It was, of course, Neurath's duty, not mine, to accompany Hitler. In any case, Neurath knew the Duce well, from his period as Ambassador in Rome. What he lacked was the ability to break into Hitler's long monologues and allow the person he was talking to to get a word in. I could do this, and had always found it most necessary. Neurath's standards of diplomatic politeness made him think it rather ill-mannered, and I was afraid that the Duce might never be able to put over the ideas I had suggested.

I therefore decided to send my friend Lersner to see the Duce about the beginning of June. Lersner will be known to my readers by now. We had been friends before the first world war, had served in the United States and Mexico together, and had been in touch on the Western Front, when he was the Foreign Office liaison officer to the General Staff. His independent attitude on the German delegation at Versailles had put an end to his diplomatic career, but while I was Reich Commissioner for the Saar, he had served me well as my representative at Geneva. I told him to impress on the Duce the necessity of persuading Hitler to restore the monarchy after Hindenburg's death. The Duce assured him that he would do his best.

The meeting was not a success. Hitler had not as yet any resounding achievements to his name, and probably wished to prove to the Duce that he was not to be imposed upon. Members of their entourage told me that the two chiefs spent most of their time talking at each other, rather than to each other. Hitler, in particular, kept up an almost uninterrupted flow of words which made any discussion impossible. On his return – I remember it was on the day of my Marburg speech – he was full of sarcasm about the 'monarchist meddlings' in Italy and said to me, 'If I have never been anti-monarchist before, I am now.' It appeared he was offended at what he considered the snobbish attitude of the Italian Court. The meeting with Mussolini did not even alter his policy in Austria, which was to culminate four weeks later in the murder of Dollfuss.

In order to complete the episode of Hindenburg's testament I must jump ahead in time. When I returned to Berlin after Hindenburg's funeral at Tannenberg, Hitler rang me up. He asked me if a political testament by Hindenburg existed, and if I knew where it was. I said that I would ask Oscar von Hindenburg. 'I should be obliged,' said Hitler, 'if you would ensure that this document comes into my possession as soon as possible.' I therefore told Kageneck, my private secretary, to go to Neudeck and ask Hindenburg's son if the testament still existed, and whether I could have it to pass it on to Hitler. As I had not seen Hindenburg after he left Berlin at the end of May, I had no idea whether he had destroyed the testament or not. Kageneck was given both the envelopes, still sealed, and brought them back to me in Berlin. Three days later I had to call on Hitler in Berchtesgaden, before taking up the post of Ambassador in Vienna, and I took the two envelopes with me.

I handed them over on August 15, in the presence of my other secretary, Tschirschky. Hitler read both documents with great care and discussed the contents with us. It was obvious that Hindenburg's recommendations in the document expressing his last wishes were contrary to Hitler's intentions. He therefore took advantage of the fact that the envelope bore the address 'Reich Chancellor Adolf Hitler'. 'These recommendations of the late President,' he said, 'are given to me personally. Later I shall decide if and when I shall permit their publication.' In vain I begged him to publish both documents. The only one handed to his press chief for publication was Hindenburg's account of his service, in which he included praise of Hitler.

Even if Hitler had published both documents, it would not have altered the course of events, as he had already decided the problem in his own way. On August 1, a few hours before Hindenburg died, the Cabinet had agreed to a law combining the offices of President and Chancellor, which was to come into force on Hindenburg's death. The legal position was, in fact, rather complicated. Article 51 of the Weimar Constitution, as I have said, laid down that the duties of President devolved on the Chancellor until such time as new Presidential elections could be held. However, on December 17, 1932, the Schleicher Government had introduced an amendment, which was accepted by the necessary two-thirds majority of the Reichstag, providing that the President of the High Court of Justice should enjoy the interim prerogatives. The Enabling Law passed on March 24, 1933, gave Hitler certain powers to deviate from the Constitution, provided that neither the institution of the Reichstag nor the Presidency suffered any diminution of their rights. Hitler had declared at the time that he would use these powers sparingly, and it is difficult to see how they could legally be applied to the question of Presidential succession.

Nevertheless, the Cabinet agreed to the law of August 1, and Hitler went to see the President that day. Hindenburg was already dying and hardly recognized him. Certainly they had no sort of discussion, as was subsequently maintained. When Hitler returned from this visit, he described how Oscar von Hindenburg had accompanied him into the old gentleman's bedroom, where he was lying with his eyes closed. 'Father,' said Oscar, 'the Reich Chancellor is here.' At first, the President did not react, so Oscar repeated the words; whereupon Hindenburg said, without opening his eyes, 'Why did you not come earlier?' Hitler then asked Oscar, 'What does the President mean?'

'The Reich Chancellor could not get here until now,' Oscar told his father. 'Oh, I see,' said the President, and lapsed into silence again. Oscar made another attempt. 'Father, Reich Chancellor Hitler has one or two matters to discuss.' When the President heard this, he opened his eyes with a start, looked at Hitler, then shut his eyes again and did not say another word. He had apparently been under the impression that it was I who had arrived. Hitler was quite shaken by this episode, but made no attempt to conceal it.

For me it was tragic to realize that my wish to see the President had corresponded with his own desires, and that for reasons outside my control we had been prevented from meeting. Now it was too late to give him my own account of the difficult days through which we were passing. The day after he died, I arrived at Neudeck at the invitation of his family. I was overcome at the memory of the many private and official conversations I had had there with Hindenburg, who had become almost as much a father to me as a friend. It was a solemn and unforgettable moment when Oscar von Hindenburg left me alone to take my farewell of the President. He was laid out on an iron camp bed in his spartan little bedroom, with a Bible clasped in his hands, and on his face the expression of wisdom, kindliness and determination that I had known so well. I had honoured him and given him the best years of my life, and now I had to say good-bye. He represented a whole era of German history. He had fought at Sadowa, and had attended the coronation of the German Kaiser at Versailles. In his declining years his sense of duty had led him to take over the leadership of his country. Now, when the whole weight of his authority was most needed to guide future developments, he had been taken from us.

Hindenburg had left instructions that he was to be buried next to his wife, near his own home at Neudeck. Hitler had other ideas – of a grand state funeral. The family was subjected to a storm of requests that the burial should take place inside the great Tannenberg memorial, and the President's body be laid to rest in one of its towers. In the end they gave way. It was, I must confess, highly impressive to see the old Field-Marshal surrounded for the last time by the flags and standards of his regiments, spoilt only by the appalling tactlessness of Hitler in wishing such a devout Christian 'entry into Valhalla'. Hindenburg belonged to an era which had in fact ended with the first world war and the penalties of the peace. He was the last imposing representative of a world that had disappeared, and he could no longer halt the avalanche which descended on us. Only eleven years later his East Prussian home had become part of Asia, the Tannenberg memorial had been razed to the ground, and the fate of Europe was in the balance.

* * *

Immediately after the President's death the Cabinet approved a second law, confirming that Hitler had taken over the rights and powers of the Presidency. In the circumstances, it bore all the characteristics of a *coup d'état*.

For some reason both these laws, as published in the official gazette, bore my signature. This was only brought to my attention at the Nuremberg trial. I can only say that I neither signed the laws nor had any part in their composition. My signature was either forged or the stationery office had committed an 'error'. I had taken part in no Cabinet meeting since June 16. If it was indeed a forgery, to persuade the nation that everything had been done legally, then it compares with Goebbels' efforts to hide the fact that the law of August 1 had been agreed upon before Hindenburg's death.

After this piece of legal chicanery, Hitler's first move was to demand that the armed forces should take a new oath of loyalty to him. This must have been arranged beforehand with Blomberg, otherwise it would have been impossible for the new swearing-in to take place so quickly at every garrison in the country. This was the point at which Blomberg bowed to Hitler for the second time. The previous oath had demanded loyalty and obedience to the Constitution and the President. The new oath was given to Hitler in person. Germany's masters had not even bothered to use the Enabling Law to amend Article 176 of the Constitution, so as to allow this to be done. Apart from this, it was a most unusual procedure, the oath normally being taken only by new entrants. It was not until August 20 that the law to cover the new oath was passed. Hitler might well send a personal letter of thanks to Blomberg for his co-operation. Though he fell out of favour later, he was the man responsible for this development. Hitler's own person had now become the focus of the Army's loyalty. Only those nurtured in the Prussian tradition of loyalty and obedience can realize what fatal effects this step had on future events. Any general who thought of playing an independent rôle was faced by a breach of what he had been taught all his life to regard as an absolute – loyalty to his oath.

Hitler had indeed good reason to suppress the second part of Hindenburg's testament. In making up his mind to deal with Roehm, he had already taken his decision about the monarchy. He realized that Hindenburg and the Army could have made his conduct of the purge look very different. With Blomberg on his side, and the President kept in isolation, he had managed to bluff his way out of danger for the time being. He had no intention of facing the same risk again. From his point of view, the laws of August 1 and 2, and the Army's new oath of loyalty, were the logical means of confirming him in his position.

PART FOUR

MISSION TO AUSTRIA

CHAPTER XIX

A NEW TASK

*A visit from the Gestapo – Hitler offers me the Vienna post – Our agree-
ment in Bayreuth – The Austrian problem – Tradition of union –
Completing Bismarck's work – The political situation in Austria – My
arrival in Vienna*

I was in Berlin at the end of July 1934, packing up the contents
of my town house before removing them to our home at
Wallerfangen. At two o'clock in the morning my son and I
were woken up by a thunderous knocking on the door. We were
both convinced that it was a visit from the Gestapo, and while my
son, pistol in hand, went to the door, I hurriedly put on some
clothes. The three men outside were indeed from the S.S. They
had been sent, they said, from the Chancellery, with an urgent
message for me to ring up Hitler in Bayreuth. He had been trying
to get me for hours. My son and I wondered whether this might
be an attempt to hustle us into another room and there fill us with
bullets: such was the incredible tension of those days, with the
almost complete collapse of the rule of law. However, what the
men had said was true, and when I spoke to the Chancellery I was
put straight through to Hitler.

He was in a state of tremendous agitation. 'Herr von Papen, you
must go immediately as Minister to Vienna,' he said. 'The situation
is extremely serious. You must accept the post.'

'I don't understand this offer,' I said, 'after everything that has
happened between us. Why is the situation suddenly so serious?'

'You don't know what has happened, then?'

'I know nothing at all,' I said. 'I have just arrived from the
country, and am in the process of packing up my house.'

Hitler then went into a long explanation: Dollfuss, the Austrian
Chancellor, had been murdered, and Mussolini was massing

divisions on the Brenner Pass. The German Minister in Vienna
Dr Rieth, had behaved in an impossible manner and would have
to be court-martialled – the expression was Hitler's. In short, I wa
the only man who could restore such an appalling and dangerou
situation. 'We are faced,' he said, and I can still hear his hysterica
voice, 'with a second Sarajevo.'

When he had finished, I told him that all this was news to me
but by no means surprising. For months I had been warning hin
to change his Austrian policy, and I was appalled that Germany
had been placed in such a situation in this vital area. In any case
after the Roehm affair, he could hardly expect me to take up
another post in the service of his Government. However, he insisted. He could understand my reluctance, but the situation wa
serious and he appealed to my patriotism. The least I could do
would be to talk the matter over with him personally. It was impossible to present all the arguments on the telephone, and he
would place his private plane at my disposal for me to fly to Bayreuth. In the end I agreed.

At about eight o'clock the next morning we set off from
Tempelhof Aerodrome – my son, my two personal assistants
Wilhelm von Ketteler and Count Kageneck, and myself. The
morning papers were full of the news from Vienna – in a carefully
prepared Nazi version, but even this could not disguise from the
initiated the full tragedy of the Dollfuss affair. It must now be
clear to the outside world that the rule of law had vanished not
only from within Germany, but was also being attacked beyond
her frontiers. Even though the German Nazi Party denied all complicity in the Vienna *Putsch*, no one doubted for a moment that the
Austrian Nazis danced entirely to the tune of Gauleiter Habicht
whom the German Nazi Party had appointed as their unofficia
head. The other Great Powers, particularly France, could be
expected to react violently. Even if the Roehm *Putsch*, apparently
a purely internal crisis, had provided no grounds for intervention
against the new dictatorship springing up in their midst, the same
could hardly be said of the Vienna *Putsch*. Germany was in no
condition to defend herself, and Mussolini was already indicating
that he was prepared to intervene.

In the period since my Marburg speech and the Roehm *Putsch*
I had seen the destruction of all my hopes of guiding the Nationa
Socialist revolution into more orthodox channels. Now Germany

was faced with a complete breakdown in her international relations. My mind was in a turmoil as we flew over the sunlit countryside, for I knew I was faced by a difficult decision. I could not understand why Hitler had turned to me, of all people, when even the talents of Dr Goebbels were obviously insufficient to clear Germany of responsibility for the killing of Dollfuss. I had closed my accounts with Hitler in my letter of July 17. Perhaps he thought that my opposition in the Cabinet to his Austrian policy indicated me as the proper person to repair the damage he had caused. Most people in Government circles were aware of my protests against the terrorist methods of the Nazi underground in Austria, supported as they were by their party colleagues in Germany. I had objected strongly to the imposition of the thousand-mark bond on Germans wishing to visit Austria, which had had such disastrous consequences on Austria's tourist trade and her economic welfare. I had also protested against providing Habicht with cover as press attaché at our Vienna Legation, where he used his diplomatic immunity in order to direct the nefarious activities of the Austrian Nazi Party. Hitler knew that I had been a personal friend of Dollfuss, and that I must feel his murder demanded the re-establishment of some measure of goodwill for Germany in Austria. Perhaps he thought my reputation abroad was still good enough for him to pin his hopes on to it. But I made up my mind to have things out with him before coming to any decision.

Hitler had gone, with Goering, Goebbels and Hess, to the Wagner festival at Bayreuth. I found him in a state of hysterical agitation, denouncing feverishly the rashness and stupidity of the Austrian Nazi Party for having involved him in such an appalling situation. After he had given his own account of the affair, I had a look at the foreign press reports to get some idea of the reaction abroad. My worst fears were fulfilled. Not only were Hitler and Germany regarded as responsible for the crime, but Mussolini's action in concentrating troops in the Brenner Pass had met with universal satisfaction. The governments of the victorious powers were discussing what measures should be taken to maintain Austrian independence and how Germany was to be held to her international obligations. The situation was indeed threatening, and Hitler certainly appreciated this.

It was soon clear that the most urgent task was to prevent, if possible, a complete breakdown in Germany's relations with the outside world, with everything that this implied. I discussed with my own associates what decision I should make. They agreed with me that to re-enter the service of the Nazi Government, after the disgraceful events of June 30, would be to many people an incomprehensible act. Another factor to be considered was the general belief that, in spite of the murder of Jung and Bose, I had resigned myself to continuing to work for Hitler. Only my close acquaintances were in a position to know that Hitler had persistently refused to announce my resignation or publish letters of protest. But a statesman with a true sense of responsibility must sometimes be ready to face the unjust censure of his friends. Ketteler and Kageneck, who had shared all my experiences, were equally convinced that I must not let personal resentment influence my decision, and thought that I might still render some service by agreeing to Hitler's request, providing he would give certain specific guarantees.

The Roehm affair had confirmed all the fears I had expressed in my Marburg speech. Disillusioned as we were by internal developments, it seemed all the more necessary to prevent a catastrophe in our international relations. I cannot admit the argument that it would have been better for foreign intervention to put an end to Hitler. If a régime can only be overthrown by war, it is the nation to which that régime belongs that suffers in the end. I felt it my duty to salvage something from the wreck, whatever criticisms and misunderstandings might be directed at me personally. There was no way of proclaiming effective public opposition to the Nazis' policies, so the next best thing to do was to work quietly in the background and risk the odium of one's friends.

We therefore sat down together to work out the text of a written list of conditions which I was to present to Hitler. This document was unfortunately lost during the war, but its main points were:

(1) Habicht was to be dismissed from his position immediately, and steps were to be taken to ensure that his contacts with Austria and Austrian National Socialists were completely broken.

(2) The German Nazi Party was to be forbidden to interfere in internal Austrian affairs.

(3) The problem of Austrian union with Germany must never be resolved by force, but only by evolutionary methods.

(4) My mission was to end as soon as normal, friendly relations had been restored between Austria and Germany. For this purpose I was to receive the appointment of a 'Minister on special mission'.

(5) I was not to come under the jurisdiction of the German Foreign Office, but was to be responsible to Hitler alone. The Foreign Office, however, would get copies of my reports to him.

Armed with this document, I then had a formal interview with Hitler. 'The first condition is quite impossible,' he said. 'If I now dismiss Habicht, it would be tantamount to admitting participation in the *Putsch*.'

'Then you must choose between him and me,' I said. 'I decline to discuss the matter. Whether you dismiss him or not, the outside world already places the moral responsibility for what has happened on the party.'

I then went on to emphasize that far and away the most important aspect of my demands was the question of eventual Austro-German union. Hitler raised no objection to my insistence that any solution to this problem by force was absolutely out of the question. The disastrous consequences of the Dollfuss murder had made this clear to him, and he fully agreed that this delicate problem must be handled with the greatest caution on the German side. Only thus would it be possible to obtain international recognition of the idea of granting the rights of self-determination to the defeated powers, as well as to the former minorities in the defunct Hapsburg empire. I told him his acceptance of this approach was a prerequisite to my acceptance of the mission.

Our conversation lasted several hours. In order to show that I was in earnest, I finally insisted that Habicht was to be brought to Bayreuth in person and dismissed in my presence. For a character such as Hitler's, it required an almost superhuman effort to admit an error, particularly as in this case, to repeat Talleyrand's remark, we were faced by something worse than a crime – a really appalling piece of political stupidity. However, I intended to drive the lesson home. In the end Habicht appeared, and after being severely reprimanded, was dismissed on the spot.

After that, the other conditions presented little difficulty. Hitler even agreed to announce my resignation from the Cabinet and allow publication of my reasons for this step. He also accepted formally my proposals concerning a possible union between Austria and Germany. Such a union, I pointed out, would strengthen Germany's position as a bulwark against the threat from the East, but it must never be achieved by force. Enough blood had already been spilt in this fratricidal strife. It would be my endeavour, I told him, to make the Austro-German question no longer a matter for decision by other foreign powers or international organizations. The desires of the two nations themselves should be the determining factor. It was a purely Austro-German affair, and gradually the Great Powers would have to get used to the idea. The best way of achieving this would be to prove in the course of time that Germany had no aggressive intentions in consummating such a union, but only sought to strengthen her position in the interests of Europe as a whole. For this reason, the manner in which the Austro-German problem was handled would have a decisive influence, not only on the two countries directly involved, but on the whole European community. It would, in fact, form the touchstone of German policy.

Once I had obtained acknowledgment of the vital importance of this problem in Germany's foreign policy I tried, as my account will show, to exercise an influence on that policy as a whole. As far as I could make out, it was handled by the Foreign Ministry on a day-to-day basis, rather than with the long view in mind, and I considered Neurath too open to party influence. Hitler's signature at the bottom of our agreement seemed to me the best guarantee of his future behaviour that I should get. At least I had cleared my conscience by accepting the post, whatever the general impression might be. Nor do I think the later accusations of my love for office were justified. After all, from being German Chancellor, I was now accepting the post of a Minister at a minor Legation.

There was a short interval before the Austrian Government accepted my appointment. I took great pains to make sure they should not get the impression that I was being got rid of as a result of the events of June 30, that I enjoyed the full confidence of the Chancellor in my mission, and that the policy I intended to pursue was the policy of the Reich Government. I therefore asked Hitler to write me a letter in this sense. But unfortunately there was a further hitch. In his haste to pour oil on troubled waters, he had announced on July 27 that he was sending me as Minister to Vienna. The normal diplomatic procedure would have been first to obtain Austria's approval of my appointment, but Hitler could hardly have been expected to have the necessary knowledge of diplomatic forms. The required apologies took up a little time, but by August 7 the Austrian Government had signified its agreement.

My letter of appointment had in fact been signed by Hindenburg at his home in Neudeck, on July 28. It was the last document to which he put his signature. Professor Sauerbruch, the well-known surgeon, who attended him during his last weeks, told me later that Hindenburg had asked him, when the document was presented to him, 'Is this really what Papen wants?'

* * *

The Anschluss question must be difficult for any non-German observer to understand. The thousand years' history of the German Empire is probably as foreign to the general reader as the rôle of Scotland or Ireland in the history of Great Britain is to the Continental observer. In the Middle Ages, after the time of the Saxon Kings and the Hohenstaufen, the centre of gravity of the 'Holy Roman Empire of German Nations' moved to Vienna. Under the Hapsburgs it was for many centuries a decisive factor in European and world politics. But while other nations began gradually to forge their national unity, the German Empire was much less fortunate in this respect. Several member States, such as Switzerland, Alsace-Lorraine, Luxembourg and the Netherlands, acquired their own independence or came within the French sphere of influence, while religious conflicts and the Reformation weakened the Empire's strength at a critical period. Nevertheless, the German people's desire for unity remained strong, in spite of their collective weakness.

The campaigns of Napoleon finally broke the loose bonds of the German Empire under the Hapsburg Kaiser Francis I, who rescued the Austro-Hungarian monarchy by renouncing the title of German Emperor. The Union of German Princes, of which he remained the head, was no substitute for the Empire's lost unity, and it was no longer able to act as a stabilizer in European politics. Bismarck devised a partial solution, which served in some measure

M

to strengthen the rôle of the German peoples in Central Europe, but the union of Germany under Prussian leadership only included the northern Germans. After the fall of Napoleon III, Bismarck saw that Russian imperialism remained the principal threat to European security. He tried to convince the Austrian monarch that the existing alliance of the three Emperors no longer provided a real guarantee against Russian intervention, and sought a defensive alliance between Austria and the German Reich. He was careful to avoid any suggestion of supporting the 'Greater Germans', who envisaged the incorporation of the German-speaking part of the Dual Monarchy into the Reich. Rather did he seek to bolster the strength of the Hapsburg Empire, to enable it to fulfil its rôle in South-Eastern Europe, and saw in close co-operation between Berlin and Vienna the best means of sustaining Europe's political equilibrium.

Germany entered the first world war to assist her ally, Austria-Hungary, against Slav aggression. When the war ended, the victorious powers failed to re-establish the equilibrium of the European continent. In accordance with the rights of self-determination laid down by President Wilson, the Danube Monarchy was split up into new countries, Czechoslovakia, Poland and Yugoslavia. The Balkanization of Central Europe was one of the principal elements in the decay of European stability and an invitation to the rivalries of newly-founded nationalism. The German part of the Hapsburg Monarchy – that is to say, the Austrian part – had assumed that Wilson's principles would apply to themselves as well, and that the inhabitants would be able to decide their own future. But this was to prove an error. The Austrian National Assembly, which met on November 12, 1918, decided unanimously to give their country the constitution of a democratic republic within the framework of a Greater Germany, and to revive the centuries'-old conception of a formal union with Germany. In a letter to President Wilson four days later, the Assembly demanded the same rights for Austria as had been granted to the other members of the disbanded Empire. On March 12, 1919, the newly elected Constituent Assembly passed a law in which the decisions of the Provisional Assembly were repeated and strengthened.

The Allied Powers answered this unanimous decision by Article 88 of the Peace Treaty of St Germain, which laid it down that: 'The independence of Austria is inviolable, and may only be modified by a decision of the Council of the League of Nations. The Austrian Government therefore pledges itself to engage in no negotiations without the permission of the Council which might directly, indirectly or in any other way, endanger its independence.' On September 6, 1919, the Austrian National Assembly protested unanimously against this ban on union with Germany and the withholding of the right of self-determination. A formal note to the victorious powers protested against the ban on the vital aspirations of the German-Austrian nation to fulfil its 'heart's desire, the economic, cultural and political union, with the German motherland'. This call for union was taken up on both sides of the frontier. In Austria the Socialists, under the leadership of the late President, Dr Karl Renner, led the struggle, and in Germany, on March 21, 1919, the Weimar Assembly accepted the proposal that 'German Austria should enter the German Reich as a member State'. This paragraph could not be included in the new Constitution, as the Versailles Treaty placed on Germany the obligation to recognize and maintain Austria's independence. The chief opponents of the idea of union were France, and the Czechs, Masaryk and Benes.

In 1921 the Austrian National Assembly organized a referendum on the subject of the Anschluss. To avoid infringing the terms of the Treaty of St Germain, the question to be answered read thus: 'Should the Federal Government request the permission of the Council of the League of Nations for the union of the Austrian Republic with the German Reich?' Strong political pressure was brought to bear by the victorious powers to prevent the holding of the plebiscite. Economic conditions were already approaching bankruptcy, and the Government could not risk the withholding of financial assistance from abroad. The ballot was therefore organized on a provincial basis, and on April 24, 1921, a vote was held in the Tyrol which showed 145,302 people to be in favour of the request and 1,805 against. Salzburg and Upper Austria were due to vote three days later, but faced with threats that Carinthia would be occupied by Yugoslavia and other intimidations of the same sort, the Federal Government banned further provincial plebiscites. However, a privately organized vote in Salzburg showed 98,546 for and 877 against.

Austria's complete economic dependence on the victorious powers enabled them to impose the conditions of the Geneva

Protocol of October 4, 1922, in which Austria, in exchange for an international loan, was required to declare that her independence would never be abandoned. Nevertheless, a strong current of public opinion in both countries continued to press for the union, with such protagonists as Dr Seipel in Austria and Paul Loebe, the Socialist President of the Reichstag, in Germany, who declared in 1926 that the right of the German peoples to reunite should be made a condition of Germany's entry into the League of Nations.

This bare sketch may perhaps enlighten the events which in 1938 culminated in Germany's 'rape' of Austria. I am not speaking now of Hitler's methods, but of the Anschluss problem in its historical perspective. What had been attempted before Hitler's action was a peaceful correction of the catastrophic error of the Versailles Treaty in preventing Germany from reassuming her historic rôle as the main dyke holding back the Slav flood. If the victorious powers had recognized this function, and if an attempt had been made to lay the foundation stone of a truly European policy, by removing the differences between France and Germany, some sort of arrangement for the integration of Austria could certainly have been devised. Instead, we were not even allowed to enter into a Customs union with Austria. The rôle that Germany had played in Europe for over a thousand years received no recognition.

* * *

When I undertook to relieve the tension between Austria and Germany after the abortive Nazi *Putsch* and the murder of Dr Dollfuss, it was clear that the only long-term policy I could follow was the historical path of eventual union. In spite of the personal circumstances involved, I freely admit that I was fascinated by the magnitude of the task and the possibility of providing a modern interpretation of Bismarck's policies. It seemed to me a task of European importance. The increasing threat from Communist underground movements in every Western European country, and their unmistakable intention of disrupting the whole social order by world revolution, made it seem to me imperative to rebuild the Central European dyke. That was the decisive factor in my acceptance of the Vienna post.

Even if we admit the idea of eventual union as a tenet of German foreign policy, this did not mean that any immediate positive action was possible, and it certainly did not include the conception of an 'Anschluss' which would really be no more than a unilateral procedure. My duty, as I saw it, was to prevent radical elements in the Nazi Party, both in Germany and Austria, from pursuing any policy which would be likely to lead to international complications. As long as Austria felt threatened by Germany, she would seek help abroad and make any hope of eventual union illusory. My first task was therefore to remove this fear. Equally important was the more positive obligation of encouraging mutual co-operation in the cultural and economic fields, so that the two countries could reach a condition of harmony in their affairs. In such an atmosphere Austria might, by her own free choice, take the initiative towards full union.

It may be objected that a policy of furthering union by evolutionary methods might have been justified if normal conditions had still reigned in Germany, but that it was unforgivable to expose Austria to the methods of Hitlerite Germany. This question has been put to me often enough and discussed over and over again with my closest associates. I can only answer that the desire of the two countries for union could not be set aside merely because a certain man and a certain party ruled Germany, whatever reservations one might have had about their internal policies. I say internal policies, because until 1938 there were no indications that Hitler intended to conduct his foreign policy on the basis of risking a European war, in order to rectify the clauses of the Versailles Treaty. Authentic documentary evidence of his warlike intentions first became available at the Nuremberg trial in what has now become known as the Hossbach Protocol. This was only drawn up in November 1937, and its contents were known to not more than five people in the whole of Germany.

No one doubted Hitler's fanatical opposition to Bolshevism. The acceptance by the Western Powers of his measures for the internal consolidation of Germany, in spite of the revolutionary methods employed, and the manner in which they tolerated his unilateral revision of several of the Versailles Treaty clauses, strengthened my conviction that it would be possible to achieve a solution of the Austrian problem without endangering the peace. Moreover, it was still possible to regard a régime as a short-term manifestation in the life of a people and therefore subject to change. Certainly there was no reason to abandon the sense of historical continuity in the vital question of Austro-German relations.

Austria was then no more capable of independent economic existence than she is today. Close co-operation with Germany could only benefit both partners. Her seven million Catholics would provide a powerful reinforcement of the Catholic element in Germany and strengthen the section of the population immune to Communist infiltration. Moreover, a considerable proportion of the people in Austria had been attracted and impressed by Hitler's solutions of social problems and the success he seemed to have obtained in raising the standards and self-confidence of the working class. No German statesman was prepared to renounce the Anschluss idea, and the principal problem was to ensure that its achievement by evolutionary methods was not disturbed by the intervention of the Nazi Party. I had received written guarantees to this effect. It remained to be seen how they would work out in practice.

*   *   *

The Nazi Party which had grown up in Austria recognized Hitler, himself an Austrian by birth, as its head. On March 6, 1933, the three presidents of the Austrian Houses of Parliament resigned their offices under Dollfuss because, in their view, the number of splinter parties had made the continuation of parliamentary democracy impossible. Thereupon, the Austrian Chancellor installed an authoritarian régime, similar to that in Germany. However, he based it on different forces and attempted rather to form a Catholic 'corporate state'. In June 1933, he disbanded the Nazi Party in Austria. To ban a political party is to issue an open invitation to underground activity. The example of the Communist Party offers very clear evidence of this. A great many Austrians believed that if the Nazi Party had not been banned, the attempted *Putsch* of July 25, 1934, would never have taken place and Dollfuss would not have been assassinated.

Attempts to improve relations between Germany and Austria had come to nothing, and amid the increasing intransigeance shown by members of the Nazi Party in both countries, the position of Dollfuss was becoming untenable. On the day of his death an intermediary was on his way to Hitler. He carried a suggestion from Dollfuss that the Nazi Party should be legalized again, providing it gave up, for the time being, its campaign for union with Germany. This was not to be abandoned as a matter of principle, but only until such time as the European situation provided a more suitable background to the solution of the problem.

Through his death Dollfuss had become a martyr in the Austrian cause. The difficulty now was that German policies towards Austria were represented in both countries by groups whose methods offended most people, yet whose activities must somehow be fitted into a framework of normal political methods. The head of the German diplomatic mission in Austria would be in no position to intervene in internal Austrian affairs. This would make it very difficult to counteract the influence of the radical elements of the Nazi Party on Hitler as well as within Austria. The difficulties were tremendous, and sometimes I had to adapt my reports and criticisms to the prevailing psychological situation. It should be remembered that I had to be careful not to lose the confidence of either party, so as to be able to act in the best interests of both.

Political ideals cannot be countered by police measures alone. I hoped to be able to convince Chancellor Schuschnigg, who had succeeded Dollfuss, of this axiom, and help him enlist the intelligent and constructive co-operation of the National Socialists, rather than see them engaged in fruitless opposition and soured by the frequent threat of concentration camps. I could see no reason why a legalized Austrian Nazi Party should not advocate German interests with in the framework of European needs; provided, that is, that Hitler kept his promise not to interfere. Dr Schuschnigg, as we shall see, chose another road. He continued Dollfuss' authoritarian policy and banned all political parties with the exception of the 'Fatherland Front', the organization entrusted with the leadership of the State. The backbone of the Fatherland Front was formed by the Heimwehr units, of which we shall hear more later. It was nevertheless his policy to attract his opponents into this Front. The Trade Unions had been disbanded and their members were invited to join the *Soziale Arbeitsgemeinschaft* (Workers' Social Association), but the former Socialists refused to co-operate. Most of the workers were Catholics and many of them belonged to the *Freiheitsbund* (Freedom Union), which in due course was to play its part. This was, in fact, a forbidden organization, but was tolerated and assisted by Schuschnigg. For those who favoured the Greater German solution, but were not members of the Nazi Party, he set up the *Volkspolitisches Referat* (Office for Greater German Affairs) whose cumbersome name was in itself almost a guarantee of its ineffectiveness.

★ ★ ★

Many of my ancestors had through the centuries devoted their services to the Emperor in Vienna, rather than suffer the Prussianization of the western part of Germany. Many historical and family ties bound Catholic circles in Austria with those in Westphalia and the Rhineland. The happy-go-lucky atmosphere in Austria made it easy to understand the obstacles in the way of union with the Reich, founded as they were largely on the fear of the militant Protestantism of Prussia and her anti-clerical policies. I had sought to strengthen religious rights in Germany with the Concordat I had signed at Rome in 1933, and I hoped that this agreement would serve to allay many Austrian fears. However, I was well aware of the unceasing and underhand attacks of the German Nazi Party against the Concordat, and I knew I should have to try to convince Hitler from Vienna that there was no hope of solving the Anschluss problem as long as he allowed free play to the radical and anti-Christian views of his friends in the party. I hoped to appeal to his sense of tradition and arouse his enthusiasm for making Germany the cultural successor of the old Danube monarchy in Central Europe.

I arrived in Vienna by air on August 15, 1934. It was a grey, drizzling day. The empty streets along my route were cordoned off, and the city had a sad, neglected air. At the old German Embassy in the Metternichgasse, so often the scene of meetings between the German and Austrian rulers, their portraits had all been banished to the attics. I felt that the honour due to tradition demanded their replacement, and I had them all hung up again. I intended that everyone should know where I stood. The Legation staff consisted of trustworthy people. My Counsellor was Prince Victor Erbach, who knew everyone in Viennese society, and the principal secretaries were Herr von Heinz and Herr von Haeften, a strong antagonist of the National Socialist régime. For this reason attempts were soon made to have him removed from Vienna, and I had a hard struggle to retain his services. He was executed after the plot against Hitler on July 20, 1944.

My principal diplomatic colleagues were M. Puaux, the French

Minister, known, because of his close connections with the Austrian Cabinet, as *Le Ministre Plénipotentiaire d'Autriche*, and Sir Walford Selby, the British Minister, who was succeeded in due course by Sir Arthur Palairet. They and their colleagues of the Little Entente, including Herr Fierlinger, who has attained another reputation in Czechoslovakia since the war, could hardly be regarded as allies in my task. Nor could Mr Messersmith, the American Minister, about whom I shall have more to say in connection with the Nuremberg trial.

The presentation of my letters of credence gave me a taste of what was to come. The Ballhaus Platz was ringed round with machine-gun posts like a fortress, and the famous old palace, in which the Congress of Vienna had met, provided an icy reception. Dollfuss' death mask decorated the window-ledge in the room in which I was received, and the message of goodwill which I brought evoked no response. The Nazi grip on newspapers and the normal channels of communication had prevented any true picture of the events in Germany from reaching Vienna. The Austrians had no conception of the stand I had taken in the Cabinet on various matters, particularly the Austrian question itself. They were as ill-informed about the course of events that ended in my Marburg speech and the Roehm purge, leading to my resignation from the German Cabinet, as they were about the motives which had led me to accept this new post – that of avoiding at all costs the outbreak of a European war. Instead, it seemed, I was regarded as the man who had broken the back of Germany's Zentrum Party, who had plotted the downfall of Brüning, and raised Hitler to power. I was suspected of having trapped the Vatican into signing the Concordat and of being a 'Catholic in wolf's clothing', against whom everyone must be on their guard. I realized that I had set myself an almost superhuman task.

CHAPTER XX

RELATIONS IMPROVE

Austria after Dollfuss – Starhemberg and the Heimwehr – Innitzer and the Nazis – The Hapsburgs – The European situation – Stresa – Mussolini and Starhemberg – Hitler's Reichstag speech – A draft treaty – Austrian counter-proposals – Starhemberg loses influence – Tschirschky and the Gestapo

THE internal political situation in Austria at the time I took over my post as Minister, was one of chaos. I therefore considered it advisable, once I had presented my letters of credence and made formal contact with the members of the Austrian Government, not to show too much *empressement* for my new task; and so until October I retired to my home at Wallerfangen.

After the murder of Dollfuss, most of the better-known National Socialists in Austria had been sent to prisons or internment camps, but the movement continued in existence as an underground organization. A number of its adherents fled to Germany, where they were housed in camps and organized into an Austrian Legion. When I told Hitler of the Austrian Government's complaints about this procedure, he replied that the party was only concerned with the subsistence of these people and was making no attempt to organize them politically. However, they were free as citizens to organize themselves, and the State had no intention of forbidding such activity. This Legion was made up principally of the more radical Austrian party members and it was clear that there was little hope of controlling them. They maintained an intricate system of communications across the border and constantly urged their German party colleagues to get Hitler to adopt a more radical policy towards the Austrian Government.

In this early period their influence was not great, and I could only guess at its extent. But as time went on their activity increased, although I was seldom able to get proof of their intervention in

Austrian internal affairs which would have enabled me to take counter-measures. In any case, the Austrian National Socialists lay low for a time after the failure of the Dollfuss *Putsch*, and this allowed me to begin more or less undisturbed the work of improving relations between Germany and Austria. The principal activity of the National Socialists consisted in combating the Heimwehr movement, which had become the dominating factor in Austrian affairs.

This movement was led by young Prince Starhemberg. The bearer of a great and historic name, he had an aristocratic appearance and dashing manner which gave him the outward aspect of a true leader of men. Unfortunately, his political ability did not match his appearance. I first met Starhemberg in 1932, when he attended the great Stahlhelm Congress in Berlin as the head of a group of Austrian ex-servicemen. He had taken part in the fight for freedom in Silesia in the years after the first world war, and was greeted in the German capital with great enthusiasm. At a lunch given in his honour in the Chancellery I had proposed a toast in which I expressed the hope that the unification of our two countries would be brought about by the generation which had fought side by side for a common cause in the war. It was only when I arrived in Vienna that I discovered that most Austrians of that generation had been organized into a political movement whose aim was to block the unification we had discussed.

Starhemberg's principal adjutant in the Heimwehr was Major Fey, a much more unscrupulous *condottiere* type, who was alleged to have been concerned in the plot against Dollfuss, of whose Government he had been a member. Other personalities were constantly appearing and disappearing in the upper hierarchy of the Heimwehr, with the result that it lacked any clearly defined policy. Above all, it had no programme for the unification of the German-speaking peoples. If the Heimwehr wished to become the core of a popular movement, to which the Austrian Chancellor could look for support in his policies, then it was useless to ignore the question of union with Germany. Political problems are not solved by purely negative methods. Starhemberg lacked the long view of affairs and found it easier to deal with events as they arose. In the years to come I often tried to discuss this problem with him. However justified his criticisms and dislike of National Socialist methods might be, founded as they were on the assassination of Dollfuss, he should still have attempted to devise some positive approach to the problem that would be to the mutual advantage of both countries. There was a strong body of opinion, both in Austria and Germany, which favoured the union of the German-speaking peoples. But Starhemberg never took this feeling into account, and in the end it caused the collapse of his movement.

The possibility of a Hapsburg restoration also played its part in Austrian affairs. I do not mean to suggest that the monarchist movement ever attained the importance of a decisive political factor. But it complicated the peaceful settlement of the union question because of the strong influence of monarchist circles on Schuschnigg. Moreover, the States which had been formed out of the former Austro-Hungarian Empire lived in constant fear of a restoration. The Imperial family was unpopular in Germany because of the part that Kaiser Karl and his wife, the Empress Zita, had played at the end of the first world war. However, there was no personal resentment against the young Archduke Otto, and I told Schuschnigg on a number of occasions that the German Government regarded the restoration problem as purely an Austrian affair. If union was achieved, we asked only that Germany should be assigned the leadership which had belonged to the House of Hapsburg until 1806. I had in mind the arrangement which had governed the relationship between the Bavarian Royal House and the Central Government until 1918. Schuschnigg showed no positive reaction to these suggestions.

Most of the older officers of the former Imperial Army, under the leadership of Colonel-General Prince Schönburg-Waldenburg-Hartenstein, a former War Minister, remained true to monarchist ideals, but the new generation of officers sympathized largely with the revolutionary movement which had achieved such successes in Germany. The split that this caused in the old aristocratic families was clearly indicated by the fact that Prince Schönburg's son and heir was one of the most fanatical Austrian Nazis.

Outside Nazi Party circles the main body of opinion in favour of a Greater Germany was led by Field-Marshal von Bardolff, who had been personal aide-de-camp to Archduke Franz-Ferdinand, heir to the Austrian crown, who was assassinated at Sarajevo. Baron Bardolff was President of the 'German Club', an association of those who favoured the idea of union with Germany. I was careful to avoid giving the Austrian Government the impression that I was actively supporting this group, so although Bardolff and I used to meet socially, I visited the Club only two or three times.

Another important group that I had to take into account were the German citizens living in Austria, of whom there were no less than 30,000 in Vienna alone. Their acknowledged leader was Professor Paul Krüger, head of the Zoological Institute. They had their own recognized association, and my chief concern was to make sure that those who were members of the Nazi Party did not exercise an undue influence in Austrian affairs.

Here I had to deal with Herr Bohle's *Auslandsorganisation*. This was a completely superfluous institution, since the German Foreign Office had always managed perfectly well to protect the interests of Germans living abroad. Bohle was an ambitious young man, born incidentally in Bradford, who apparently regarded his organization as a step towards his being appointed Foreign Secretary or at least Colonial Minister. He tried to find favour within the party by undertaking to organize these groups of Germans living abroad into Nazi cells, whose duty was to sing the praises of the Third Reich. It had long been a habit of these Germans to organize themselves into clubs and associations for the purpose of maintaining contact with their homeland. In the United States alone there were over a thousand German choral societies, which kept alive the tradition of German music and song. Other countries had German schools for their children. But none of these various organizations acquired a political complexion, nor did they attempt to influence the internal politics of their adopted countries. The leaders were invariably men of ripe judgment and good faith.

As they stood, these organizations were of no use to Herr Bohle. Most of the committees he considered too old, too reactionary, and lacking in understanding of the Third Reich. So the older men were gradually ousted and replaced by younger ones whose enthusiasm for National Socialism was in most cases matched by their failure to become successful members of the community. Vienna provided no exception to this process, and I could soon detect the danger of a Bohle-organized clique intent on torpedoing my attempts to find a peaceful solution to the problem of Austro-

German relations. I therefore went to some pains to ensure that this association should be governed on more orthodox lines. At my instigation, new regulations were voted which laid down that the association should remain outside politics and should exist only to further good relations between Austria and Germany. It was also laid down that any German who accepted this provision could become a member. This met with stiff opposition from the party members, who wanted at all costs to exclude the membership of Jews. Nevertheless, in April 1935 this new constitution was approved and recognized by the Austrian Ministry of the Interior. I received a number of grateful letters from Jewish members of the association, and Vienna was probably the only German diplomatic mission which refused to apply the Aryan laws[1] in the German organizations for which it was responsible.

Another influential association in Vienna at this time was the *Kulturbund*, most of whose members, which included the *élite* of Viennese society, were opposed to union with Germany. Their main social activity was to invite distinguished guests of all nationalities to lecture on the arts and sciences and also on political questions. My influence here was restricted chiefly to ensuring that the leading German scientists appeared in their programme. Bohle's *Auslandsorganisation* tried to interfere even here. The *Kulturband* had an extremely efficient secretary, who was always a welcome guest in my house. But she was a Jewess. Bohle therefore circulated an order to the members of the German colony to boycott the *Kulturbund's* meetings. I wrote to Neurath saying that it was an impossible situation for an Ambassador of the Reich to invite leading German representatives like Professor Sauerbruch to a meeting which was boycotted by the German colony. I asked him to call Bohle to order, but without effect. However, in spite of the party's intervention, I maintained my own connection with the *Kulturbund* until the end of my mission.

Most of the Austrian aristocracy had been left in greatly reduced circumstances as a result of the war and had lost their hereditary

---

[1] The 'Nuremberg Laws' – so called because they were announced at a Nuremberg Party Rally – legalized discrimination against the Jews, depriving them of practically all civic rights. Among the measures legalized were orders to wear the yellow badge, to use only certain park benches and certain parts of public vehicles, and so on.

positions with the fall of the monarchy. Their long tradition of cosmopolitan thought induced little sympathy for Germany under the Nazi régime. Nevertheless, many of them, such as Prince Windischgrätz, the son-in-law of Emperor Franz Joseph, Prince Karl Kinsky, Count Dubsky, and others, gave me considerable support in my efforts to establish more harmonious relations between the two countries.

One of my main difficulties in Germany had been to overcome the repugnance of the higher clergy to the National Socialist régime, and to any attempt to improve relations with it, which was hardly to be wondered at after its attacks on the Catholic Church. But it was certainly not my intention to expose the Austrian clergy to the same danger. In spite of the manner in which Hitler was failing in his obligations under the Concordat, I never gave up hope of convincing him that the anti-clerical policy of the Nazi Party was not only fraught with danger, but was one of the greatest barriers to any hopes of an Anschluss.

From the beginning I tried to find some way of making this clear to the head of the Church in Austria, Cardinal Innitzer. I did not want to be suspected of advocating union with Germany until the Nazi attacks on the Church ceased. In the light of later developments, it may be thought that I was a good deal too optimistic about this. At any rate, I did my best to show Hitler the folly of Rosenberg's scheme for supplanting the Catholic Church with a new religion. For a considerable time he sympathized with my ideas. But later, under the influence of such people as Goebbels and Bormann, he gradually changed his mind.

For two years after our first formal exchange of greetings, the Cardinal refused to receive me or accept any of my invitations. This attitude, so I was told, was dictated by a decision at a conference of his bishops. The negative attitude of Chancellor Schuschnigg was also probably due largely to the influence of the higher clergy, and I knew that news of the way in which I was boycotted by religious circles would be bound to encourage the intransigeant attitude of the party leaders in Berlin.

★ ★ ★

It may be as well for me to summarize as briefly as I can the political situation in Europe at this period – that is, between July

1934 and May 1935 – since it had a direct bearing on affairs in Austria.

Germany's withdrawal from the League of Nations and the Disarmament Conference had placed her in a position of isolation. I have already described my conflict with Hitler over these decisions and how I tried to make it clear that our absence from Geneva would deprive Germany of valuable contacts with the world's leading statesmen. Such contacts are always worth infinitely more than any number of diplomatic notes. The new German Government was threatened by the same sort of isolation as were the post-war Cabinets of the early 'twenties. This involved the danger of conducting foreign policy in a vacuum, with no possibility of appreciating the political factors determining the behaviour of the other great powers. Our continued presence at the Disarmament Conference had been made impossible by the plan put forward by Sir John Simon on October 9, 1934, which sought to exclude Germany for a further four years from the equality of rights which my own Government had obtained in principle in December 1932. If we had remained a member of the League of Nations it would always have been possible to present new proposals on the subject of disarmament during the course of the debates. The fault was to slam both doors at the same time.

The world outside Germany was now obliged to seek other security measures against the revolutionary movement which had sprung up in its midst. Every Cabinet sought the panacea of 'collective security', the political password of the time, in a ring of alliances surrounding Germany. The first step was to end the long ostracism of Soviet Russia by granting her membership of the League of Nations. This occurred in September 1934, shortly after the assassination of Chancellor Dollfuss had shown Nazi contempt for the normal conduct of international relations. Mussolini was maintaining additional divisions on the Brenner Pass, France sought security in multilateral pacts, and Great Britain, with Mr Baldwin's cry, 'our frontiers lie on the Rhine', countered the threat of Hitler by a programme of rearmament. The Saar plebiscite, with its overwhelming majority for a return to Germany, played its own, if considerably misunderstood, part in heightening the tension. This vote, in which I and thousands of Saarlanders from all over the world took part, was a gesture of confidence in Germany rather than in Hitler.

French suggestions, after the meeting of M. Laval, M. Flandin and British ministers, that non-aggression and assistance pacts should be negotiated with countries to the east and south of Germany, did not finally preclude the possibility of coming to some agreement with Germany. While the German Government was prepared to discuss the limitation of air forces – providing Germany had an air force – it could hardly be expected to participate in pacts directed primarily against itself. The German counter-proposal of bilateral talks were taken up by the British Government which announced its intention of sending Sir John Simon and Mr Anthony Eden to Berlin for discussions to begin on March 6, 1935. Two days beforehand, a British White Paper was issued justifying the Government's rearmament proposals and accusing Germany of breaking the rearmament clauses of the Versailles Treaty. This was regarded in Germany as a deliberate attempt to remove any basis for negotiation, and Hitler advised the British Ambassador that he was too unwell to receive the British ministers.

Ten days later Hitler proclaimed the reintroduction of conscription in Germany. How much truth there was at this time in the allegations that German rearmament threatened the peace of the world will always be open to question. It is my opinion, reinforced by the numerous documents presented at the Nuremberg Tribunal, that it is not possible to apply the term rearmament to the period between the fall of my own Government and the end of 1934. No heavy weapons were available, and the strengthening of the Army's cadres, and the purely theoretical studies of what measures should be taken to increase its effectiveness, could hardly be called rearmament.

Foreign opinion reacted violently to Hitler's announcement, but no positive steps were taken, and the various notes of protest soon began to show marked discrepancies. The British Government enquired again whether Germany was now prepared to negotiate, and Hitler seized this opportunity with both hands. French indignation continued strong, and insisted that the visit of the British ministers should be of an informative character only. Mr Eden was therefore to continue his journey to Moscow, Warsaw and Prague, thus destroying the psychological atmosphere for his talks in Germany. Nevertheless, the talks with Hitler were friendly, although, in view of the basic differences between Bolshevism and National Socialism, he declined flatly to take part in any eastern pact. Nor would he consider the idea of a Danube non-aggression pact without some definition of the term 'intervention', which he requested in view of the special relationship between Germany and Austria. It was at this conference that Hitler first suggested the idea of a naval pact with Great Britain. This was one of his major diplomatic successes, in that it sowed discord between France and Great Britain.

The tension increased when, on April 11, 1935, the Western Powers met for their conference in Stresa. The British and French Prime Ministers, Mr Ramsay MacDonald and M. Laval, accompanied by their Foreign Ministers, joined forces with the leader of Fascism, for whom they had little sympathy, in an attempt to close the ring round Germany. Strange bedfellows indeed. How much better it would have been to hold a general meeting of all the Heads of State to discuss the unification of Europe, with the member countries freed from the restrictions of out-of-date treaties. Instead, the three powers declared their intention 'to oppose by all means in their power the unilateral abrogation of treaties'.

Strong words, but did they indicate a united front? Hitler had sufficient political intuition to realize that the divergent interests of the three powers militated against a united policy. On May 2 the French Government signed a pact of mutual assistance with the Soviet Union. The cause of European solidarity would have been better served if the historic mission of Germany as a barrier to Slav aspirations had been recognized, and her reasonable demands met.

* * *

The result of the Saar plebiscite, with its overwhelming majority in favour of Germany, gave considerable encouragement to the various groups in Austria who favoured union with the Reich. The painfully forged ring of alliances round Germany, and Hitler's rejection of the military clauses of the Versailles Treaty, were matters of vital concern to Austria. During the whole of this period Mussolini's influence on the Austrian Government continued to be strong. At his suggestion legislation was discussed for increasing the size of the Austrian Army and reorganizing the

Heimwehr as its reserve formations. Mussolini seems to have assumed that the suggested Danube Pact would be simply a loose organization of States, and he intended to increase their strength, in order to secure Austria's position against Germany, by installing Prince Starhemberg as a sort of Regent, rather in the manner of Admiral Horthy in Hungary.

The idea of a Heimwehr dictatorship made little appeal to Schuschnigg or his Foreign Minister, Herr von Berger, who asked me on one occasion to obtain some guarantee from the German Government that Austria was recognized as a second German State, with its own sovereignty. If this assurance was forthcoming, he told me, he would abandon Austria's present foreign policy and come to an arrangement with Germany. These considerations caused me to press Hitler further to intervene in the Mussolini-Starhemberg plot. The mutual interests of Austria and Germany, I wrote, would best be served by replacing the totalitarian intentions of the Nazi Party in Austria by a combination with the body of Christian Socialists, who favoured agreement between the German-speaking peoples. A pact between the two countries would make possible Germany's participation in the Danube Pact and remove entirely its anti-German connotation. Such a step would have a beneficial influence on the European situation and, particularly, on our relations with Great Britain.

Whatever Mussolini's or Starhemberg's final ambitions may have been, my last appeal to Hitler, sent shortly before his Reichstag speech of May 21, 1935, proves that my major preoccupation was to obtain his public recognition of Austrian independence and sovereignty. This was not merely a tactical move on my part, and I insisted that such a declaration would have to be made sincerely, if Schuschnigg was not to regard it as a trap. In his speech Hitler stated that Germany had neither the intention or the wish to interfere in Austrian internal affairs or to force the annexation or incorporation of Austria into Germany. This was the assurance he had given me at Bayreuth in July 1934, before I would undertake the Vienna mission. But he had always refused obstinately to repeat it publicly. Now he had done so, and I had a solid basis for reaching a peaceful settlement between the two countries.

This new approach found a warm welcome. A week later the Austrian Chancellor declared before Parliament: 'Austria recognizes herself as a German State.' In my constant attempts to counter

Hitler's contemptuous tirades against the 'un-German policy of the Austrian Government', I had always insisted that the first step – recognition of Austrian sovereignty – must come from Hitler. It would then be possible for Schuschnigg to show whether it was his intention to regard Austria as a member of the German group and direct his policies accordingly. Now that Hitler had made a precise and unmistakable declaration, I tried to persuade Schuschnigg to define his own position at the earliest possible opportunity. Naturally enough, the new trend was little to the liking of the French Government and I attempted to soothe the suspicions of their Minister in Vienna, M. Puaux, by telling him: '*Y'a-t-il une différence entres les intérêts de Berlin, Vienne ou Paris de former une zone de sécurité contre l'invasion du bolchévisme? Si vous n'y arrivez pas par la création d'une fédération danubienne, ce sera la mission de nous autres allemands y compris l'Autriche. En soutenant cette tâche, elle – en tant qu'Etat souvérain et allemand – n'éprouvera aucune difficulté à observer ses obligations envers vous.*'

On July 11, 1935, exactly a year before the final conclusion of our treaty with Austria, I called on Herr von Berger at the Austrian Foreign Ministry with the first draft of a proposed agreement. I called it a 'personal study', and when he asked whether my Government had authorized me to negotiate on this basis, I confined myself to saying that the German Government had been informed of its contents. I had no means of telling what use Herr von Berger would make of the document. Before I told him that I had agreed the text with Hitler, I wanted to be sure that it would not be rejected. Herr von Berger, who understood very well my reasons for caution, immediately adopted evasive tactics. He replied that in his position as Minister he could take no official cognizance of private expressions of opinion and would place my memorandum in the hands of his experts.

Dust gathered on the document for some months, until on September 9 I returned to the attack and informed the Foreign Minister that Hitler had expressed his approval of my proposals. This obliged Herr von Berger to make some reply, but it took another three weeks before he handed me counter-proposals drawn up by his Ministry, with the remark that the matter had not yet been discussed by the Cabinet. A comparison of these two documents is essential to an appreciation of the situation. Their main points were:

My proposals:

With a view to restoring relations between the two countries on a normal and friendly basis, and in the conviction that the maintenance of peace is essential to the general development of Europe, the Governments of the German Reich and Austria have agreed:

(1) The Austrian Government has noted the declaration of the Führer and Reich Chancellor on May 21, 1935: 'Germany has neither the intention nor the wish to interfere in Austrian internal affairs or to force the annexation or incorporation of Austria into Germany.' This declaration shows that the German Government does not seek to influence political parties or groups within Austria. The present ban in Austria of the National Socialist Party is therefore a purely internal affair.

(2) As a result of the Austrian Chancellor's declaration on May 29, 1935, that Austria regards herself as a German State, the Austrian Government will adapt their policy to the peaceful requirements of the German peoples as a whole.

(3) Separate agreements are to be made on questions concerning the press, the partial lifting of the ban on newspapers, radio and cultural matters, the emigré problem, national emblems and anthems, the rights of German citizens, and restrictions on the movement of capital.

Austrian counter-proposals:

[The preamble is the same, with the omission of the words 'and friendly'.]

(1) The German Government recognizes the present Constitution of the Austrian régime. The declaration of the German Führer on May 21, 1935, indicates that the Reich Government seeks no direct or indirect influence in internal Austrian affairs, and recognizes that the National Socialist movement in Austria, whose activities are at present forbidden, is an internal Austrian matter. It is understood that the provisions in this Article will be observed by the German National Socialist Party and all its organizations.

(2) The Austrian Government recognizes the present régime in Germany, and will conform in its policies in general, and its relations with Germany in particular, to the declaration of the Austrian Chancellor on May 29, 1935, recognizing Austria as a German State.

(3) Individual agreements on the matters mentioned in the German proposals to be worked out, together with the formation of a mixed commission, to meet regularly to consider grievances and necessary modifications.

It will be appreciated that my proposals were accepted almost in their entirety by the Austrian Foreign Ministry.

In the meantime, on June 27, 1935, I had written a long report to Hitler, in which I tried to summarize the results of his Austrian policy. Dollfuss had become a martyr to the 'Austrian idea' of an independent country, able to secure its own political future. This conception was what kept together the Heimwehr movement, the principal factor in Austrian political life. On the other hand, I said, Hitler must realize that most members of the Austrian National Socialist movement, whose activities were now banned, had joined the party less out of belief in Nazi doctrine than in desperation at Austria's hopeless economic plight and her dependence on the victorious powers. When Dollfuss broke the revolt of the Socialists in February 1934, some of the Nazis had fought on their side. A great many Austrians regarded their deliverance from extreme left wing radicalism as due to the intervention of Dollfuss and the Heimwehr. The Nazis were therefore regarded with double suspicion. Since the murder of Dollfuss the Austrian Government had made considerable progress in reorganizing their country along corporate lines, and their position was now sufficiently strong to render any idea of another *Putsch* hopeless. If Austria was to be persuaded to align herself with Greater German interests, the German Nazi Party would have to curb its tendencies towards centralization. Hitler's desire for a common policy for the German-speaking peoples could best be achieved by allowing a strong opposition in Austria to be built up as a matter of Austrian internal policy alone.

In the summer and autumn Austria's policy of close co-operation with the Italian Government was subjected to a further strain. Mussolini's Abyssinian adventure caused an open rift with his two Western allies and placed Austria in a most difficult position. On October 18, the Austrian Cabinet was reshuffled, with Prince Starhemberg and his Heimwehr gaining considerably in influence. While some of the former ministers had appeared anxious to improve Austria's relations with Britain and France, Starhemberg seems to have been convinced that Mussolini would emerge victorious from the international tussle over the Abyssinian affair, and was therefore determined to carry out the Italian dictator's wish for an authoritarian strengthening of the Austrian Government.

However, in a conversation with Starhemberg on the possibility of reaching some understanding between Germany and Austria, I found his reactions much more German in sentiment than Herr von Berger's had ever been. 'The hardening of the situation on both sides makes it appear difficult to Starhemberg to consider such an agreement in terms of detail,' I reported to Hitler. 'The whole question of Austro-German relations must form part of a larger conception. He considers that the countries with authoritarian régimes are open to the same sort of attack as is now being made on Fascism. The principal problem is to form a common front between Italy, Austria, Germany and Hungary.'

I asked Starhemberg whether he thought Mussolini, in view of his ties with France, would be prepared to enter such discussions. Starhemberg replied that he could win Mussolini over. I told him that the German Government had made no secret in Italy of their attempts to bring about an Austro-German understanding and I would be grateful for any influence that Mussolini might bring to bear. Our conversation was marked by an open friendliness which was in striking contrast with the tone of most of the discussions I had with the Chancellor and the Foreign Minister. Starhemberg had a natural vivacity and much personal charm, and if his intel-lectual qualities had been in proportion he would have played a much more considerable rôle in the history of these years.

* * *

Before I end my account of this period of my activity, perhaps I can indicate the lengths to which the Nazi Party and the Gestapo went in interfering with my work. As early as October 1934 the same groups in the Nazi Party that had sought to liquidate me and my associates in the Roehm affair began a violent campaign against two of the oldest and most trusted members of my staff in the Vice-Chancellery in Berlin, Tschirschky and Ketteler, who had accompanied me as members of the special mission to Vienna. As I had no intention whatever of dispensing with their services, the Nazi extremists had to find other ways of getting rid of these two men. The Gestapo decided to deal first with Tschirschky, and resorted to the same sort of totally unwarranted accusation of homo-sexual activities against him that was to prove so successful later in the case of Colonel-General von Fritsch.

Tschirschky was one of my most valuable assistants. In the tur-bulent days of 1934 he had been largely responsible for preventing interference by the party in the affairs of the Vice-Chancellery, and all his work since had made him indispensable. In November and December 1934, Tschirschky had been asked several times to report to the Gestapo headquarters in Berlin in order to make statements or be a witness in cases which were allegedly connected with the Roehm affair. He had always answered these 'invitations' by saying that he was quite willing to give evidence but could not leave Vienna because I often had to be absent myself and he, Tschirschky, therefore had to remain in Vienna to watch the day-to-day developments of the delicate Austrian situation.

In December 1934, at a meeting at Berchtesgaden, Hitler told me of the accusations the Gestapo had drawn up as a means of getting rid of Tschirschky. In my opinion there was only one way to deal with this, and that was to ask for a proper trial in a court of law. I therefore asked Hitler to give instructions to this effect. I hoped this would spike the Gestapo's guns, because the wicked attack on Tschirschky's reputation made me particularly angry. Early in January 1935 I again wrote to Hitler. I told him that I had good reason to suppose that if Tschirschky appeared at the Gestapo headquarters he would be detained in Berlin and probably liquidated. Any such action by the Gestapo would be contrary to the interests of Germany and do great harm to my work, and I asked Hitler once again to have the matter dealt with – if any charge could be formulated – in a court of law.

On February 2, 1935, von Neurath, the Foreign Minister, sent me a coded telegram saying that Hitler would personally guarantee Tschirschky's safety, but as head of the State ordered his appearance for interrogation by the Gestapo. Tschirschky declined to go. Instead, he handed me his resignation in the form of a long document in which he gave his reasons for refusing to obey Hitler's order, and declared his intention of leaving Austria. I sent Hitler a letter by special courier, giving Tschirschky's reasons, and from this document, which still exists and which was widely publicized in 1946, it is clear that he had good cause for his feelings of mistrust and insecurity; but as the head of the State himself intervened, no other action was open to him but to leave Austria. I made a last attempt to persuade Tschirschky not to aggravate his and my critical situation by openly disobeying Hitler's orders, but the attempt failed. 'Even though I am disobeying the order of the head of the State,' said Tschirschky, 'I cannot accept Hitler's instructions, because I know that even he has not the power to prevent the Gestapo from liquidating me. I can no longer consider Hitler's Germany a State where justice and law exist. I would rather live as an emigré in a foreign land and earn an honest living as a labourer, than live in an atmosphere where lies and dishonesty prevail.'

I can well understand why Tschirschky preferred to emigrate. It was a great break for me to have to say good-bye to such a true friend and collaborator, together with his charming wife and children, and I did all I could to help to ease their problems. In 1947, when I appeared before the denazification tribunal, he braved every obstacle to appear as a witness in my case. Two months earlier, the Russian judge at the Nuremberg Tribunal had opposed my acquittal, on the grounds that Tschirschky had met his death in a concentration camp because of me, and that I should hang for it.

Thus another of my associates was taken from me. Ketteler remained until the end of my mission, and then at the time of the Anschluss was brutally assassinated.

CHAPTER XXI

AGREEMENT AND AFTERMATH

The July Agreement – Hitler's reaction – I am offered the London Embassy –
The Ribbentrop Bureau – Hitler sees Leopold – Schuschnigg's intentions
– Cabinet reshuffle – Guido Schmidt in Germany – Schuschnigg's speech –
The Committee of Seven – A banned book

AUSTRIA's international position had not been improved by events. The Italian attack on Abyssinia had broken the united front of the Stresa powers, and Mussolini advised Schuschnigg that he would welcome a better understanding with Germany. Schuschnigg's visits to Paris, London and Geneva had met with little success and he had obtained no guarantee of Austrian independence. He therefore judged the time opportune to take up the matter of Austro-German relations at the point where von Berger and I had left them the previous autumn.

On May 1, 1936, Dr Guido Schmidt, the Austrian President's *chef de cabinet*, brought me an official message of good wishes on the occasion of the German national holiday, and asked on Schuschnigg's behalf how I would view the resumption of talks for a peaceful solution of relations with Germany. I replied that I was prepared to take up the matter at any time and encouraged Schmidt to impress on the Chancellor my conviction that the need for a speedy solution was becoming increasingly urgent. I gathered from Schmidt that Schuschnigg shared this opinion.

I immediately informed Hitler that the tension which had arisen over his reoccupation of the Rhineland would lessen notably if a peaceful solution could be found to the Austrian problem. I also told him that such a step would improve German relations with Italy and would do much to nullify the dangers implicit in any Central European collective security pacts.

It must be recalled that after the reoccupation of the Rhineland the British Government addressed a questionnaire to Hitler making some point-blank enquiries as to his future intentions. I told Hitler at the time that the best way of answering this enquiry would be to give a demonstration of his peaceful intentions towards Austria. He accepted the proposition, and agreed with me that it was a suitable occasion to legalize the Austrian Nazi Party, so that it would be able to work, within the framework of Austrian internal policy, towards the goal of eventual union.

Berger and Starhemberg left the Austrian Cabinet on May 13, and Guido Schmidt took over the affairs of the Foreign Office. This change made my own work much easier. On the 18th I had my first confidential meeting with Schuschnigg, who undertook, in return for an assurance that the German Nazi Party would cease to interfere in Austrian affairs, that he would accept members of the 'National Opposition' into the Fatherland Front. He emphasized, however, that he would only accept those representatives who acknowledged Austrian independence, although there would be no objection to their entertaining ideas of eventual union, which might become possible as the international situation improved. This is an important point to note. It meant that the Chancellor acknowledged the idea of union as a possible goal.

In the days that followed, we had several meetings to determine the exact nature of the agreement. Schuschnigg asked that each country should officially recognize the régime of the other. I talked him out of this, however, because I considered that as each of our countries maintained diplomatic relations with the other, such recognition was automatically understood. Schuschnigg, for his part, turned down a suggestion of mine that Germany should be kept informed if the question of restoring the monarchy came under active consideration.

At the beginning of July, when we had reached agreement on details, I flew to Berlin to get Hitler's final approval. In order to convince Schuschnigg of the sincerity of our intentions I suggested he should arrange for some person in his confidence to accompany me, who could be present at my discussions with Hitler. But he did not respond to this suggestion. He did, however, specifically ask that only the general terms of the agreement should be published and that details concerning the settlement of press questions, the lifting of the thousand-mark travel bond, amnesty for the Austrian Nazis, and so on, should be included in a secret 'gentlemen's agreement'. The published agreement would contain Hitler's recognition of Austrian sovereignty and his undertaking not to intervene in her internal affairs, together with

Schuschnigg's declaration recognizing Austria as a German State and proclaiming his readiness to formulate policies within such a framework.

Schuschnigg had written to me on June 20 requesting that complete secrecy should be observed during the course of the negotiations. This was exactly in accordance with my own wishes, because I was afraid that any leakage of information would lead to desperate attempts by the party extremists in both countries to bring pressure on Hitler not to sign the agreement. He and Neurath were the only two people in Berlin who knew about it, except Tauschitz, the Austrian Minister. Austrian representatives elsewhere throughout the world were only to be advised of the agreement on the day it was signed. Only one other person was kept fully informed of what was going on, and that was Salata, the Italian Minister in Vienna. The result was that when Schuschnigg and I signed the agreement on July 11, the announcement came as a complete surprise.

A remarkable light is thrown on Schuschnigg's relationship with Archduke Otto by the fact that in spite of the undertaking he had extracted from me to keep the affair secret, he sent the director of the Government Information Service, Herr Weber, at three hours' notice to Belgium to obtain the Pretender's approval of the agreement. This Otto refused to give, and besought the Chancellor not to sign the agreement under any circumstances. This incident is the more curious in view of the fact that even the Austrian President was only advised of the details of the agreement on the day it was signed. Weber, who was called as a witness at the trial of Guido Schmidt after the war, stated in evidence that Schuschnigg had told him to inform the Archduke that the agreement was only being signed 'under German pressure'. This is hardly in accordance with the initiative that Schuschnigg took to reopen negotiations.

When I returned to the German Legation after signing the agreement, I telephoned Hitler to advise him of its completion. His reaction astonished me. Instead of expressing his gratification at the result of nearly two years' hard work on my part, he broke into a flood of abuse. I had misled him, he said, into making exaggerated concessions in return for purely platonic undertakings by the Austrian Government, which they would probably never fulfil. The whole thing was a trap. All I could say in reply was that if he had such a poor opinion of my work, he could accept my resignation. He was in one of those hysterical rages which I had experienced before, though never on the telephone. As I replaced the receiver, I wondered what could have caused this sudden change of mind. Some of the party leaders must have got hold of the terms of the agreement, which by then had been announced over the radio without any commentary, and must have criticized him for making too many concessions. My perplexity can well be imagined as I dictated a formal note of resignation to my secretary. I intended to send it off within a day or two, but first I wanted to see what would be the reaction abroad.

As I had hoped, the world's press described the agreement as a major contribution to the relief of European tension, and Schuschnigg and Hitler were congratulated on defining their respective attitudes so clearly. Even the French press found little to object to in the recognition of Austria as a German State and the proposal for co-ordinating German and Austrian foreign policy. General satisfaction was expressed that only two years after the death of Dollfuss, Germany had agreed to recognize Austria's sovereignty and independence. The union question had thereby become a matter of historical evolution, and the common aim of the German peoples more or less a family matter.

In Germany the radical wing of the Nazi Party was by no means satisfied with the agreement. They blamed it on to Habicht, the Gauleiter whom I had insisted that Hitler should remove before I went to Vienna, but who nevertheless remained leader of the Austrian party *in absentia*. They seemed to feel he should not have bowed so easily to Hitler's wishes. Former members of the more moderate parties were particularly pleased, regarding the agreement as a reverse for the Nazi Party, or at least as a sign of the weakening of its radical wing. Church circles and former members of the Zentrum Party, particularly in the south of Germany, were delighted with the whole affair. The Army, too, was especially pleased, and I was told that an early opportunity would be found for establishing friendly relations with the Austrian armed forces.

As soon as Hitler saw how public opinion had reacted, he realized that he had been wiser than he thought. I was invited as his guest to the Festival at Bayreuth. However, I told Lammers, the secretary of the Chancellery, who forwarded the message, that my recent discussion with Hitler hardly encouraged me to accept the invitation. Lammers tried for several days to talk me over, until in the end Hitler sent a message saying that he sincerely regretted the tone of his previous criticism and asked me once again to be his guest.

I flew to Bayreuth and found him in the best of spirits. As an expression of his thanks, and presumably in an effort to make me forget his behaviour on July 11, he granted me the personal rank of Ambassador. It was a doubtful honour. He promptly rejected my suggestion that to mark our new friendship the Austrian Government should be asked to raise the Legations in the two countries to the level of Embassies. This he regarded as going too far, and my promotion remained empty of significance, since the Austrian Government took no official notice of it.

In the middle of my talks with Hitler he surprised me by a sudden offer to send me as Ambassador to London. Herr von Hoesch had just died and the question of his successor was under discussion. I reminded him immediately that we had already agreed I should occupy the Vienna post only until relations with Austria had resumed their normal course: this they had now done. London was without any question our most important point of contact with the outside world, and our representation there clearly took precedence over our representation in Austria. It was perhaps the decisive point during a shift in the European balance of power and the search for European security. French policy had become far too inelastic and doctrinaire, and the problems of the remaining shackles of the Versailles Treaty – the Danzig Corridor, the problem of union with Austria, and the level of armaments – could only be solved in intimate contact with Downing Street. I told Hitler that if his offer was made in earnest I would give it my most serious consideration.

'The whole matter is under discussion at the moment,' he said, 'but I would like you to consider the possibility seriously.' 'I would only accept the appointment under one condition,' I said. 'And what is that?' he asked, somewhat sharply. 'You must give me an undertaking that the Ribbentrop Bureau shall not interfere in my activities in any way.' 'And why not?' Hitler asked with some heat.

I had apparently raised a hornet's nest. The Ribbentrop Bureau was in high favour at this time, following the conclusion of the

Naval Treaty with Great Britain, and Hitler was most impressed by the organization's work and effectiveness. I therefore confined myself to saying that in such a post there could be only one channel for reports, one policy to follow, and one responsible authority, and I was afraid there were many matters on which I did not see eye to eye with Ribbentrop.

It is probably instructive at this point to give some account of the manner in which Hitler determined foreign policy, with particular reference to the Ribbentrop Bureau. Shortly after January 30, 1933, Ribbentrop approached me with the request that he should be appointed Permanent Secretary of the Foreign Office, a post to which he apparently considered himself entitled because of his services to the Nazi Party. I tried in vain to convince him that the post of Permanent Secretary was the cornerstone of a Ministry whose political head changed with the vicissitudes of the parties in parliament. The Secretary must therefore be a man of long experience, familiar with the whole routine of the department. Obviously, someone outside the service could not be considered for the post. In any case, it was a question for Herr von Neurath, then Foreign Minister, to whom he should make further application. The ambitions disclosed in this conversation were to be pursued in other ways.

Ribbentrop was a man of markedly elegant appearance, always impeccably dressed, who spoke perfect English and French. Unfortunately these qualities did not suffice to make him a statesman. In normal circumstances, a man of his education and background could have been expected to be a success in high office. In Ribbentrop's case there were insurmountable obstacles. He was immensely industrious, but devoid of intelligence; having an incurable inferiority complex, his social qualities never matured as they should have done. It was a tragedy that such a man came to occupy a vital position affecting the history of our time.

Hitler, who had a natural distrust for all Foreign Office reports, was suspicious of anyone whom he did not know personally or who was not a member of the Nazi Party. He had no opinion of the abilities of Ambassadors or Ministers who came from reactionary aristocratic families and who had, in his view, no conception of the National Socialist outlook. Ribbentrop was always eager to oblige with additional reports to correct or supplement those of the Foreign Ministry or, if necessary, prove them to be false.

Considerable sums of money were voted from Party funds to found the Ribbentrop Bureau, which set up its offices in the Wilhelmstrasse, opposite the Foreign Office. An information network was organized all over the world, and the Bureau soon had more employees than the Foreign Office itself. They were made up largely of out-of-work journalists, young commercial travellers who had had no success abroad, and young Nazis who sought a short cut to a diplomatic career. Foreigners arriving in Berlin, whether they were important or not, journalists, businessmen, bankers and industrialists, were visited by members of the Ribbentrop Bureau and asked for information. If any of them had anything of interest to say, they were asked if they would like to have an interview with Hitler. Many of them, particularly the more avid type of journalist, thought this an excellent idea. Hitler was then told that a certain influential person or some well-known journalist was available, and that a long interview would serve to popularize the National Socialist cause.

The Foreign Office never produced such interesting people; in fact, there seemed to be a certain distaste there for the type of journalists who published long and inaccurate articles, which in the end only caused trouble. The Ribbentrop Bureau always found it possible to reverse the Foreign Office evaluation of certain foreign governments or statesmen, nothing being easier than to obtain an entirely contradictory version from members of the opposition. Carefully selected excerpts from the foreign press were also presented to Hitler, who, having no knowledge of languages, was unable to draw direct conclusions. The one conclusion he did favour was that he was better served by the Ribbentrop Bureau than by the Foreign Office. The career diplomats took good care to authenticate and check all their reports. The Ribbentrop Bureau, however, ignoring this responsibility, usually submitted reports of a much more sensational nature, which they managed to send in considerably sooner. This pseudo-Ministry had no official responsibility, and doubtless gave great satisfaction to its founder and employees; but I could never understand why Neurath, in defence of his own interests, did not have this sort of nonsense stopped.

This digression into the conduct of foreign affairs gives the proper perspective to my request to Hitler at Bayreuth. In Vienna I had been mercifully free from interference by the Ribbentrop

Bureau, having insisted on placing myself directly under Hitler's orders. The day after the offer of the London post was made, Neurath arrived in Bayreuth. We discussed the Austrian situation and I told him of my talk with Hitler on the subject of the London post. He raised both hands in horror and said, 'No, no – we must send Ribbentrop there. It is the only way of getting rid of him and his Bureau.'

'I can well understand that you want to get this uncontrollable institution out of the way,' I said. 'But what would Ribbentrop make of this important post?' A broad smile spread over Neurath's jovial face. 'After three months in London he will be done for. They can't stand him there, and we shall be rid of him for good and all.'

I told him I had heard that Ribbentrop was resisting the idea of going to London because he was afraid of losing his close contact with Hitler, and feared that some other party member would take over his position of influence. 'That is more than likely,' Neurath agreed. 'But we shall never have another opportunity like this of letting him make a fool of himself.' I was by no means so sure, and I told Neurath that it might prove to be a very expensive experiment. In any case, Hitler made no further mention of his offer to me, and I can only assume that Neurath gave Ribbentrop's candidature his full support.

The course of history was to show how mistaken Neurath had been. In spite of Ribbentrop's deplorable behaviour in London, he lost no favour with Hitler, and Neurath continued to be saddled with the Bureau, which still followed the directives of its absent chief in discrediting the Foreign Office on every possible occasion. In Hitler's eyes, Ribbentrop became an expert on the affairs of the British Commonwealth and 'at long last, one Ambassador with a bit of sense'.

In the archives of the German Foreign Office which were captured by the Allies after the war there is a memorandum from Ribbentrop to the Führer (January 2, 1938), in which he recommends '(1) Outwardly, continued understanding with England. . . . (2) Quiet but determined establishment of alliances against England. . . .'[1]

It would be interesting to know what Neurath's opinion of such

[1] *Documents on German Foreign Policy 1918–1945*. Series D, Vol. I. No. 93. H.M.S.O. London, 1949.

N

a policy was, and who the partners in this anti-British coalition were to be. Seldom can so much wanton nonsense have been expressed in so few words.

Ribbentrop's opinion that the British Empire had passed its peak, and would no longer take military steps to restore the balance of power in Europe, formed the basis for Hitler's aggressive plans against Czechoslovakia and Poland. This ludicrously false evaluation of the British was to involve Hitler and all the rest of us in catastrophe – simply because Ribbentrop's counsel was preferred to that of more intelligent and moderate advisers.

★ ★ ★

Shortly after the signing of the Austro-German Treaty, on July 11, Hitler received at Berchtesgaden the leader of the Austrian Nazis, Captain Leopold. Hitler told him that the new agreement was to be taken seriously, and that the Austrian Nazis must behave in a disciplined fashion and regard the Anschluss problem as an internal Austrian affair, only to be solved within the framework of Austrian politics. After the first surprise of the signing of the agreement, this further development was little to Leopold's taste. However, no criticism of the Führer's orders was possible.

Giving evidence at the Guido Schmidt treason trial after the war, Schuschnigg revealed that he regarded the July agreement with Germany as providing a breathing space, after his unsuccessful attempts to persuade the three Stresa powers to guarantee Austrian independence. 'Its terms,' he said, 'represented the limit of the concessions we were prepared to make to Germany. Normal relations between the two countries would have made it possible to mitigate some aspects of the state of emergency that still existed in Austria, but no major step, such as the legalization of the National Socialist Party, could have been undertaken if Austria was to maintain her liberty and independence. The wording of the agreement and the interpretation placed upon it by the Austrian Government at the time, made it quite clear that it was not to be regarded as the first step towards union with Germany. It was on this point that the Austrian and the Nazi interpretation diverged.'

There was also no reason for Germany to interpret the terms of the treaty as preparatory to union. No provision had been made for the reconstitution of the Nazi Party, but it must have been clear to both sides that the spirit of the agreement allowed those with Greater German sympathies to exercise their normal democratic right of pursuing their aims by open and legal means.

Hitler did not give up the idea of eventual union with his recognition of Austrian independence. That was too much to demand of any German statesman with a feeling for history. However, in 1936 he sought to avoid further international complications, and the agreement with Austria was signed in good faith. His instructions to Leopold and the latter's adherents provided the only solution for both sides. Yet, as a native of Austria, he felt a special obligation for developments there, and this obsession was to cloud the whole of my efforts. He regarded the restrictions placed on the Austrian Nazis as a personal affront.

Schuschnigg either could not or would not understand this. He declared at Guido Schmidt's trial: 'I have known a number of German Nationalists over the course of the years, and I have admired many for their personal qualities, but politically I did not trust any of them. Glaise-Horstenau was probably the only exception; but then I trusted his assurances that he was not a National Socialist; and in any case, I made sure that he enjoyed no political independence.' It may well be asked which of the two partners to the agreement had signed it with a view to future deception.

* * *

Once the agreement had been signed, the Austrian Government declared an amnesty for political prisoners. The numbers involved gave an indication of the extent to which police methods were used to silence the opposition. During the last six months of 1936, 15,583 prisoners were released, and only forty held for trial. In my reports to Hitler I drew attention to these measures as a sign that the Austrian Government genuinely desired peaceful relations.

In October, Schuschnigg's relations with the Heimwehr and its armed formations reached another crisis. Ever since the death of Dollfuss, Starhemberg had been trying to create an independent position for himself. Once the armed Socialist formations had been abolished, the Heimwehr and the Army became the only organizations able to resort to arms, particularly since Starhemberg's rival, Major Fey, had been ousted from his position as chief of police. The Heimwehr thus became the dominant political force, and in 1935, as I have already mentioned, Starhemberg hoped that with Mussolini's support he would be able to acquire the position of a Regent, similar to that of Admiral Horthy in Hungary.

His exaggerated dependence on Italy brought him into conflict with Schuschnigg, who himself had close contacts with Mussolini, but who wished to associate himself with the Western Powers rather than organize a slavish copy of the Fascist system. The Heimwehr's attitude in foreign affairs had always seemed to me one of the chief obstacles in the way of Austria attaining a policy more friendly to Germany. In the spring of 1935 I hoped for a time that a coalition between the Christian Socialists and Greater German sympathizers might provide a counter to the Heimwehr's policies, especially as I knew that the Austrian Chancellor viewed Starhemberg's increase of strength with considerable disfavour. However, Schuschnigg preferred to meet the situation by strengthening the Army and incorporating the armed Heimwehr formations.

Starhemberg was also a legitimist, in the sense that he sought to attract those circles advocating a restoration of the monarchy. However, the monarchists regarded both Schuschnigg and Starhemberg with considerable mistrust, and an attempt by Starhemberg in December 1935 to enter into closer relations with Archduke Otto brought him no positive result. He only succeeded in retaining his monarchist adherents by abandoning his plans for a regency and acknowledging the primacy of the House of Hapsburg. When his friend Berger resigned from the post of Foreign Minister, Starhemberg sought to strengthen his position by demanding a greater measure of control in the affairs of the Army. This Schuschnigg resisted, since his remilitarization plans were designed to reduce the power of the Heimwehr, not to increase it. In the spring of 1936 the Chancellor started to deprive the Heimwehr formations of their weapons, by that time feeling himself sufficiently well established in office to oppose Starhemberg openly. With the isolation of Mussolini, following the Abyssinian war, and the move towards better understanding with Germany, not to mention the July Agreement, Schuschnigg was able to neutralize Starhemberg completely. The Prince made one last effort to regain influence in the Cabinet, but this was rejected by Schuschnigg, who had decided finally to disband the Heimwehr formations. His order to this effect caused very little stir. The country as a whole wanted peaceful relations with Germany and believed that this was his policy. For his break with Starhemberg, Fey and company, he had chosen just the right psychological moment.

A further reshuffle of the Cabinet took place on November 3. To outward appearances, at least, ministers known to have strong anti-German feelings were replaced by men more sympathetic to the idea of Austro-German co-operation. The new Security Minister was Herr von Neustaedter-Stuermer, whom I represented to Hitler as a man of German nationalist sympathies. It was not clear to me whether this was so, but I was at pains to give evidence of Schuschnigg's good faith. The Chancellor had assured me that the police would be instructed to adopt a different attitude to those who favoured union with Germany, but had asked me to make it clear to Hitler that it would take time to establish better relations. Glaise-Horstenau became Minister of the Interior on the understanding that he would use his influence to establish a more normal atmosphere.

★ ★ ★

In the second fortnight of November the new Foreign Minister, Dr Guido Schmidt, paid an official visit to Germany. I had suggested this step myself, to enable him to make personal contact with Hitler and Neurath, and discuss Austria's pressing economic problems. Austria's chief interest was in a revival of the tourist trade, which could only be effected if Germany's lack of Austrian schillings could be corrected by an increase in exports. I also advised Berlin that Schmidt desired still further to improve relations between the two countries by the exchange of friendly declarations. He was willing to praise the achievements of the National Socialist régime and its leader, but hoped that Germany would make some reciprocal statement concerning the Austrian Chancellor. I was sure that Schuschnigg was only looking for a favourable opportunity to make some friendly public comment, and I suggested to Neurath that Schmidt should be given cause, after his conversations with Hitler, to make an announcement to the Austrian press. I suggested this text: 'In my conversations with the Führer, which dealt with our outstanding problems, he expressed warm approval for the efforts of the Austrian Chancellor to improve the internal and external situation of Austria. He remembered with particular gratitude the years during which the Austrian Chancellor fought as a soldier in the former Austro-Hungarian Army in the common cause of the German peoples.' This suggestion was duly approved by Hitler.

I accompanied Schmidt to Berlin, where he had private conversations with Hitler and Goering, which seemed to give him complete satisfaction. In the course of numerous festivities and official dinners, all of a very cordial nature, he spoke to most of the ministers and party leaders and obtained a clear idea of their opinions on the world situation in general and the Austrian problem in particular. The protocol agreed as a result of the visit was not published. It contained the following points:

(a) A common front of both Governments against the Communist threat to the freedom and security of Europe.

(b) Both Governments agreed to co-operate in Central European affairs and undertook not to sign economic agreements with the Danube countries without previous consultation.

(c) The implementation of the July Agreement: settlement of the standing of German citizens in Austria; mutual cultural exchanges, and a gradual lifting of restrictions on the press on both sides; a settlement of the problem of Austrian emigrés in Germany; and the expansion of commercial relations and the tourist trade.

Neurath added that he was anxious for the speedy inclusion of men with Greater German sympathies in the work of the Austrian Government, and gave an assurance that the Nazi Party in Germany would be told to ensure that its members carried out the terms of the agreement loyally.

Schmidt's visit had only just ended when the Austrian Chancellor made a speech in Klagenfurt to the members of his Fatherland Front. This movement, he said, had three potential enemies: Communism, which was not greatly to be feared, National Socialism, and defeatism in its own ranks. He declared that Austrian Nazism must be regarded as an enemy of the Austrian Government and people.

The next day I received a telegram from Neurath with instructions to express to Schuschnigg his astonishment that the satisfactory result of Schmidt's visit should have such a sequel. 'Does the Chancellor really think that he can proceed with ruthless measures against National Socialism in Austria and still steer a common

course with the Reich in matters affecting the German peoples?'
He added that this speech made a return visit by him to Vienna
quite out of the question.

In my reply to Hitler I tried to give plausible reasons for the
sharp tone the Chancellor had taken, and explained that, in fact,
his speech had been directed to all Greater German partisans who
were not prepared to accept the idea of an independent Austria.
Schuschnigg told me that he regretted the misunderstanding, and
I informed Hitler that I had made it quite clear to Schuschnigg
that the expected development of our relations was only likely to
be realized by an understanding between the Austrian Government and its chief source of support, the Fatherland Front, on the
one hand, and the partisans of the Greater Germany idea on the
other. I had asked Schuschnigg not to regard this as an intervention in Austrian affairs, but rather to view it in the spirit of the
July agreement. It would be a disservice to the common cause, I
told him, to regard the agreement merely as a façade behind which
to continue more parochial Austrian policies. Schuschnigg replied
that he fully recognized Austria's historical mission within the
framework of the new German bloc. He was prepared to draw the
necessary conclusions from Austria's changed situation in the post-
war world. I then went on to say to Hitler that I was much disturbed
at the continued underground activity of the illegal Nazi Party,
and distressed that Leopold, out of some sort of inferiority complex, was doing his best to keep reliable people of moderate views
from occupying any position of influence.

About this time the Counsellor of my Legation, Prince zu
Erbach, was sent as Minister to Athens. As his successor I received
Freiherr von Stein, who up to that time had been Counsellor in
Prague. He was soon to reveal himself as an ardent Nazi who gave
every possible support to the members of the party in Austria and
made many difficulties for me.

It is interesting in this context to consider a memorandum on
the subject of Leopold which Stein sent to the German Foreign
Office at this period. Its contents have only come to my notice
since the war, as part of the collection of German Foreign Office
documents published by the Stationery Office in London. In it he
refers to Leopold's character in glowing terms, and mentions that
he had recommended him to Schuschnigg as a reliable person.
Apparently Stein had remarked to Schuschnigg that it was not

easy to resolve the conflict between Church and State in Germany, because such a large proportion of the German population was anti-clerical in its sympathies.

These observations show not only that my closest collaborator was engaged, without my knowledge, in making a series of independent reports to the German Foreign Office, but that he was following a policy diametrically opposed to my own. This intrigue was continued until February 1938, apparently with the full encouragement of the German Foreign Office, whose officials presumably resented my direct contact with Hitler. Yet in their communications to me there was never any indication of a difference of opinion between us on matters of policy.

I have often referred to the manner in which the Church felt itself threatened by the National Socialist movement, and I constantly drew Hitler's attention to the dangers of such a policy. The problem was of particular importance in Austria because the Vatican feared that although union might strengthen the Christian front in a Greater Germany, Austrian Catholics might be exposed to the same sort of persecution as those in the Reich. I often had cause to discuss this problem with Bishop Dr Aloys Hudal, head of the German religious foundation 'Anima' in Rome. Born in Bohemia, he had devoted great attention to the whole problem of religious affairs in Austria and Germany under the Nazi régime. In 1936 he wrote a book[1] on the foundations of National Socialism, which dealt with every aspect of the question. While approving the Nazi régime's efforts to find a new basis for the relationships between capital and labour, and its fierce opposition to the nihilistic tendencies of Bolshevism, Dr Hudal criticized the Nazi movement's infringements of natural law, and expressed the opinion that it could succeed in its aim only if its programme was shorn of everything that conflicted with the theory and practice of Christian ethics.

The book was published in Austria, and at Dr Hudal's request I presented the first signed copy to Hitler. He accepted it with pleasure and undertook to read it with interest. What is more, he gave an order for it to be imported freely into Germany, where I hoped it would have a sobering effect. Goebbels and, above all,

[1] Aloys Hudal: *Die Grundlagen des Nationalsozialismus*. Johannes Günther Verlag, Leipzig-Vienna, 1936.

Bormann reacted swiftly. They told Hitler that the book would have a most unfortunate effect on the party, and all my attempts to convince him that open discussion of the problems involved was essential, were nullified by the mere suggestion that the debate raised by the book might endanger the party. Dr Hudal was bitterly disappointed that his attempt to solve the differences by bringing them into the open had failed. He has been criticized for assuming in 1936 that some change in the character of the National Socialist régime was still possible, but the Pope himself, in an encyclical in 1937, still expressed the hope that such a change was possible. As far as I was concerned, with my knowledge of the growing opposition of the Austrian Catholic hierarchy to any idea of a closer relation with Germany, this was a new blow.

*　　*　　*

My report to Hitler on the events of the year 1936, written on January 12, 1937, consisted largely of another attempt to place the Austrian problem in its European perspective. I insisted once again on the familiar arguments. Germany's principal mission lay in building up a strong position in Central Europe. Schuschnigg, realizing that his Fatherland Front was proving a weak organ for the prosecution of an independent policy, had assured me, towards the end of the year, that Austria's political and moral strength would be devoted to ensuring that the German peoples regained their historical position in the world. This, I insisted to Hitler, could only be achieved within a federalistic framework, and not as the result of a centralized system imposed by Berlin. Moreover, Austria was a Christian and Catholic country, and he could not expect any enthusiasm for the idea of exposing its people to the ideological disputes between Church and State which constantly occurred in Germany. If only he would bear these conditions in mind, it would not be difficult to find a constitutional formula for uniting Austria with Germany. The common front of the Stresa powers had been broken by the Italian adventure in Abyssinia, and the resultant weakening of foreign support for Austria's independence must, in the end, bring Austria into Germany's orbit. Once again I stressed in the clearest terms the necessity for the peaceful and evolutionary development of relations between the two countries.

However, it seemed impossible to bring home to the Austrian Nazis that the July Agreement signed by Hitler provided the best framework for the policy of the two countries. With each increase in the power of the Reich, they pressed for action. They found evolutionary methods far too slow, and above all mistrusted Schuschnigg's desire to give them his support. One section of the party preferred to concentrate on illegal activities, while the more moderate elements contented themselves with pursuing the goal of union within the terms of the Agreement.

Here we may consider for a moment the character of the man who contributed so much to Austria's internal unrest. In the first world war Leopold had been promoted from the ranks for conspicuous bravery. His education was limited and he was stubborn and dogmatic in character – a typical unintelligent non-commissioned officer. After the Nazi Party had acquired power in Germany, through a freely elected majority, Leopold, hoping to achieve the same result in Austria, insisted loudly on new elections. One of the senior officials in the Austrian Chancellery, a man with Greater German sympathies, used to tell me how Leopold was always coming to him for advice. When the Presidents of the Austrian Houses of Parliament resigned under Dollfuss, this official had advised Leopold to join forces with the Chancellor, instead of continuing to fight him. Dollfuss clearly intended to follow the precedent of setting up an authoritarian régime on German lines. This ruled out the possibility of an election, and so frustrated Leopold's hope of acquiring power by this means. But Leopold refused to see reason. If he had collaborated with Dollfuss, the whole history of Austro-German relations might have taken another course.

He was too obstinate to see a solution in supporting the more moderate elements in his party. His own position was none too secure, and he sought popularity by supporting the more radical wing. Some of the Party members, such as In der Maur, Tavs and Rainer, had at one time the reputation of being moderates, but they could not afford to offend the radical wing and risk being denied the fruits of office, should Austria and Germany ever be united. They therefore tended to support whichever methods seemed most likely to bring about a quick result. It was for this reason that I interceded frequently with the Chancellor to permit members of this 'National Opposition' to be given posts of responsibility in his corporate State, in order to encourage the more moderate elements.

By February 1937 I was able to report to Hitler a notable step towards the political re-emergence of the opposition. Schuschnigg had made up his mind to form a committee of seven members of the opposition, to organize their adherents and ensure their representation in the administration. Dr Jury, a moderate National Socialist, was appointed chairman. After an interview with Schuschnigg, he announced on behalf of the committee: 'We acknowledge the independence of Austria, and undertake to conduct our affairs in accordance with the 1934 Constitution and the law concerning the Fatherland Front, and undertake to build no political party outside this organization.' This was at least a start, though I made it clear to Hitler that the Austrian Chancellor would still have to overcome considerable difficulties in the ranks of his own supporters.

CHAPTER XXII

THE SITUATION DETERIORATES

Preliminary hopes – International visits – Neurath in Vienna – Austrian police seize documents – Trouble in Pinkafeld – Hitler calls me to Berlin – I have it out with the Führer – Schuschnigg apologizes – Hapsburg prince in an incident – Trouble in the Committee of Seven – Seyss-Inquart becomes Under-Secretary – A joint commission meets – The demonstration at Wels – Mussolini in Germany – A hunting story – Schmidt and Goering – I visit Paris – Schuschnigg becomes difficult – I forbid Leopold to enter the Legation – Another police raid – Crisis in the Wehrmacht

IT seemed for a time that in the year 1937 a new spirit of harmony was abroad in Europe. Statesmen in every country were eagerly pursuing the cause of peace, and the success of the Berlin Olympiad seemed to indicate that even the Third Reich would not seek to disturb the general atmosphere by discordant demands. On January 30, the anniversary of his advent to power, Hitler announced: 'The period of surprises is over, peace is our highest aim.' Friendly international intercourse received a powerful stimulus from European participation at the Paris Exhibition, the International Workers' Congress in Hamburg, and the Coronation of George VI in London. Here the only jarring note was the refusal by Ribbentrop to allow the German delegation to be led by Neurath and his insistence that Field-Marshal von Blomberg would be a more suitable representative of Germany's growing might. Ribbentrop drew entirely false conclusions from the Abdication crisis, which – because of the close relations he claimed to have established with King Edward VIII – he seemed to take as a personal affront. With ever increasing insistence he reiterated to Hitler his belief that the British Empire was going into a rapid decline, and that Hitler could wreak his will in Europe without any fear of intervention by the British Government. Hitler was already beginning to give more credit to reports of this sort, which pandered to his own preconceptions, than to the opinions of serious and competent advisers. It was a failing that became increasingly apparent as the years went by.

In April Goering paid a state visit to Rome. In his insatiable ambition to secure his position as 'crown prince' of the Nazi régime, he had acquired the posts of Prussian Prime Minister, Air Minister, State Game Warden, President of the Reichstag, and Director of the Four Year Plan. But all this did not suffice. The most interesting sphere of activity, discussed by all and understood by few, was that of foreign policy. It offered opportunities for travel, entertainment and the acquisition of decorations, and Goering soon had his finger deep in the pie. He had already visited Warsaw, Belgrade and Budapest, but so far had kept out of my way in Austria. The apparent reason for his visit to Rome was to discuss the Spanish Civil War, but his conversations with Mussolini, as Schmidt, the interpreter, tells us in his book,[1] soon turned to German-Italian relations. Goering remarked that the Anschluss problem need provide no cause for conflict between the two countries. However, instead of stating any intention to adhere to the terms of the July Agreement, his chief comment was, 'The Anschluss must and will be effected.' Mussolini seems to have been astonished by this frank remark, and asked Schmidt to repeat the translation in French, although he understood the German original perfectly well. His only reaction was a shake of the head. Between the massing of his divisions on the Brenner Pass and this speechless gesture, two and a half years had gone by. Hitler, when the conversation was reported to him, doubtless drew his own conclusions.

It has been maintained, and I think rightly, that the sanctions against Italy demanded by Britain at the League of Nations, would have brought Mussolini's whole Abyssinian adventure to an end. Moreover, they would have given Hitler the sharpest possible warning, short of war. Laval's intervention not only prevented sanctions, but was interpreted by Hitler as a sign of weakness, the worst possible psychological impression that could be given to a man of his character.

In May, Dr Schacht travelled to Paris for the opening of the German pavilion at the Exhibition. Here he made a remarkable speech, in which he appealed for a scheme of international economic security as the best basis for world peace. Schacht and I were on

---

[1] Paul Schmidt: *Hitler's Interpreter*. Heinemann, London, 1951.

friendly terms, and on my frequent trips to Berlin from Vienna, I always tried to have at least one lunch with him at the Reichsbank. He had the only clear head in the whole Cabinet, and never hesitated to speak of his doubts and problems. Before his journey to Paris we discussed the general lines of his speech, and I particularly asked him to make contact with Léon Blum and other leading French political personalities. Our plan was to see if it would be possible to devise, in collaboration with the French, some means of controlling Hitler's restless ambition. If some settlement of the colonial problem could be achieved, and a means of access to raw materials devised, we felt that he might become sufficiently engrossed in world economic affairs to modify his rearmament programme.

Schacht often told me that Hitler's grasp of economic matters was that of a sixth-form schoolboy. When Schacht tried to explain to him the danger of inflation inherent in the rearmament programme, and begged him to keep to the financial limits prescribed, Hitler merely shrugged his shoulders. Nor was Blomberg any help, but in the many conversations that Schacht and I had with Fritsch, Adam, Kluge, Gienanth, Bock, and other leading generals, we found them most disturbed at the over-rapid expansion of the Army. They all realized that the Army represented the only stable factor in the German internal balance of power. Most of them were old service colleagues of mine, and were in full agreement with me that if Hitler attempted to embark on any exaggerated enterprises, they must act as a restraining influence.

While in all outward aspects the possibilities of peace appeared to grow, Hitler's intentions seem to have crystallized in quite another direction. Nine years later, at the Nuremberg Tribunal, we were to learn of the Hossbach protocol concerning Hitler's secret conference, on November 5, 1937, with Neurath and the heads of the three armed services. For the first time war was described as necessary and inevitable, and approximate dates were laid down for armed intervention in Austria and Czechoslovakia. I have just mentioned one reason for this psychological transformation. Up to a point Hitler had always been afraid of the reaction of the Western nations to his unilateral abrogation of the Versailles Treaty clauses. But Mussolini's Abyssinian adventure had broken the façade of union achieved at the Stresa Conference, and the Italian leader was adopting a benevolent attitude towards

Germany. The League of Nations had proved itself incapable of applying sanctions to Italy, to the extent of cutting off her supplies of oil, and Axis intervention in the Spanish conflict had evoked only a feeble veto from the Western Powers. The dissolution of the anti-Nazi coalition caused Hitler to adopt an increasingly uncompromising attitude in his foreign policy.

* * *

But I have been getting ahead of events and must return to Austrian affairs.

In February I had persuaded Neurath, in spite of his previous reluctance, to return Guido Schmidt's visit. I assumed that the jovial and moderate personality of Hitler's Foreign Minister would help to make my own task in Austria considerably easier. Unfortunately, the result was to be quite different. The Austrian Nazis made up their minds to greet Neurath's arrival in Vienna with a mass demonstration in favour of an Anschluss. On February 22, as we drove from the station through the Mariahilferstrasse to the Legation, the line of cars was suddenly surrounded by thousands of men and women of all ages shouting 'Heil Deutschland!' and 'Heil Hitler!' The numerous police and security forces completely lost control of the crowd, and our cars were only able to advance at walking pace. However, there were no incidents, and the police apparently felt that the presence of an official guest precluded the normal use of their truncheons. Guido Schmidt was himself in the leading car, but the Chancellor, who had been present at the station, had returned to the Chancellery by another route. However, he saw part of the demonstration and made up his mind to have his revenge in due course.

One of the chief topics of the conversations was the question of a Hapsburg restoration, which had been occupying public opinion for some time. Neurath emphasized that this was an internal Austrian affair, but asked that the German Government should be informed on all points of common interest, should any decision be taken in this matter. He drew attention to the considerable complications that would arise, particularly in the Danube States which had formed part of the Austro-Hungarian Empire, if Austria became Hapsburg again. Schuschnigg pointed out that the ruling house still had much support in Austria and that a return of the monarchy might be a good means of relieving the internal tension; whereupon Neurath made it quite clear that Germany could not accept such a solution, which, he considered, would be disastrous for Austria. Czechoslovakia and Yugoslavia would view such a development as a possible threat, and this might well oblige Germany to engage in a conflict which was not of her seeking. Schuschnigg would give no undertaking to obtain Germany's agreement to a restoration, but expressed his willingness to consult with the German Government. However, this provided the only important difference of opinion between the two statesmen, and the talks on the whole were successful.

Then came the incident which was to destroy the main purpose of the visit. An hour before Neurath was due to leave, I was informed that all roads leading to the station had been sealed off by the police and were full of thousands of Heimwehr adherents. Schuschnigg had made up his mind to show Neurath that there were other people besides Nazis and Greater Germany sympathizers in Vienna. The Fatherland Front had been ordered to parade *en masse* and the police had been instructed to deal with any pro-German demonstrations. It was an appalling situation, and it seemed more than likely that the rival demonstrations would end in riots. This would not only nullify all my efforts in Austria, but might have unforeseeable results for Austro-German relations. I therefore suggested to Neurath that he should start his journey from a station outside Vienna and avoid the official route. This he declined to do. It would have given the appearance of yielding to political pressure, and he had no intention of leaving Vienna by the back door. I found both Neurath's stubbornness and Schuschnigg's theatricals little to my taste. However, in the end we drove to the station in the midst of tumult, with the immense crowd crying 'Heil Oesterreich!' 'Heil Schuschnigg!' and 'Nieder mit Hitler!' Fortunately, there were only a few minor incidents. Schuschnigg seemed thoroughly pleased at the result of his arrangements and I was left to reflect on the possible consequences.

A fortnight later I went to Berlin myself to discuss the whole European situation, as seen from my vantage point in Vienna. Great Britain's decision to re-arm, and Mussolini's threat to her position in the Mediterranean must, I felt, lead to some attempt to weaken the Berlin-Rome Axis. Austria seemed to provide a suitable point at which to apply pressure, since a considerable body of Austrian opinion would be prepared to accept an offer to join the

Little Entente of the Danube Powers, providing guarantees were forthcoming from Britain and France.

I pointed out to Hitler that the only way to strengthen Germany's position was to support Schuschnigg's régime, whether we liked it or not. Schuschnigg had made up his mind to come to some arrangement with the Greater Germany sympathizers. It was therefore in Germany's interest to make this task easy, to tone down the criticism of Austria in the German press, and cease bedevilling the Austrian Chancellor with pinpricks. The illegal Austrian Nazi Party must be told once again to regard an Anschluss as an internal Austrian affair and cease activities which would only make Germany's international position more difficult. At the same time, Germany must take more decisive steps to strengthen commercial relations with Austria.

My efforts to have the Austrian Nazis restrained had little effect. In May the Austrian police raided an illegal headquarters in Vienna and found a quantity of incriminating documents. These provided evidence of contacts between the German and Austrian Nazis, the supply of funds for underground organization, and propaganda material attacking the Austrian Government and members of the Cabinet. Although the Austrian Government made no official protest, I sent Hitler a full report of these insubordinate acts by his adherents.

The smallest incident seemed to aggravate the situation. On May 1, which had become an official holiday in Germany, German citizens in Austria were allowed to fly their national flag, a right accorded them in the July Agreement. In Pinkafeld, a small town in Styria, a young lieutenant of the Austrian Army, on duty with the garrison, had his attention drawn to a German flag flying from the attic window of one of the little houses. This officer, under suspicion of Nazi sympathies, had just been posted to Pinkafeld from a larger garrison, and had been told that he would be cashiered if any further evidence was produced against him. His first reaction was therefore to cover himself by ordering an N.C.O. and two soldiers to take down the flag, which they promptly did by breaking into the house.

Within a few hours I was presented with a violent protest from the German colony at this insult to the flag. I feared the worst. It was not the first time I had experienced this sort of thing. In Tampico, in 1914, a Mexican mob had hauled down an

American flag; an incident which so inflamed public opinion in the United States that President Wilson declared war. What had been good enough for Wilson might well be good enough for Hitler, and I immediately sent off a telegram saying that I was investigating this unfortunate incident and would demand satisfaction from the Austrian Government, adding, however, that the whole matter seemed due to a misunderstanding. But Bohle's *Auslandsorganisation* was already in action and sent Hitler a highly coloured account of the affair.

The following day I received urgent instructions to report personally to Hitler in Berlin. I arrived the same evening and went immediately to the Chancellery. However, as I had received no appointment by the next day, I went to see Neurath, to whom I gave an account of the affair and expressed my fears of its possible consequences. I asked him to request Hitler to receive me before making any decisions, but his intervention seemed to have little effect. The next day I had still received no appointment, so I sent Hitler a note, saying: 'You ordered me to Berlin on May 2 to discuss the unfortunate incident in Pinkafeld. I have now been waiting for two days to make my report and suggest some way of settling the affair. As you have not received me, I can only assume that I have lost your confidence as Minister in Vienna, and must therefore ask you to accept my resignation forthwith.'

Twenty minutes after sending off this note by special messenger, I received a telephone call from the Chancellery saying that Hitler wished to see me immediately. I found him red in the face, pacing up and down the main reception room in Bismarck's old palace. 'This is outrageous!' he shouted. 'These people cannot go on treating Germany in this cavalier fashion. This business of dragging our flag through the mud is too much!' With these words he began a tirade of abuse against Austria, which I will not attempt to repeat. In accordance with my usual practice, I let him work off this outburst of rage, and for about half an hour made no attempt to say a word. Then I began to talk.

'In July 1934,' I said, 'we came to a written understanding – that the union of the two German peoples was only to be sought by evolutionary methods. Nine months ago you signed an agreement in this sense with Austria, an agreement which lays down a specific procedure for the settlement of disputes. This incident with the flag is simply due to a lieutenant's lack of judgment. It cannot possibly be attributed to any higher authority. It can be settled at once without the slightest difficulty in no time at all. However, if you wish to use it as an excuse for severe measures against Austria, I must remind you that this would be a breach of our personal agreement. The whole German question has been the cause of far too much fratricide in the course of history, and never again must it cause a drop of blood to be spilt. If you are looking for a representative who will organize flag incidents and play them up to the point where you find it necessary to march into Austria, well, I don't doubt you will find any number of idiots willing to take over the job. But I am certainly not prepared to do any such thing, and you may therefore consider my post at your disposal.'

He listened to all I said with astonishment, and our conversation then continued on somewhat quieter lines. Now that his rage had subsided, I felt he was more open to reasoned argument. As we rose, he said to me, 'You are quite right. Please go back to Vienna and deal with the matter as you have suggested.' I left feeling exhausted but considerably relieved.

The next day I was back in Vienna and had an audience with Schuschnigg. He immediately agreed to my suggestion of an apologetic note to the German Foreign Office and a suitable release to the press. The whole affair was settled in ten minutes.

It was not long before I had to deal with a similar incident. In the window of a German travel agency, on a corner of the Kaerntnerstrasse, the usual display of travel brochures was relieved by a few publications bearing a picture of Hitler. One evening the younger of the two Hohenberg brothers, sons of the Archduke Franz-Ferdinand, who was killed at Sarajevo, was passing along the street in a somewhat elated condition. The pictures of Hitler seemed to cause him some offence and he therefore smashed the plate-glass window with his walking-stick. Another tremendous outcry arose from the Austrian Nazis. They could hardly have found a better subject for their propaganda than attacks on a prominent member of the House of Hapsburg. However, the young man's family informed me how deeply they regretted the incident, and I decided to settle the matter, if possible without recourse to the Austrian Government. This time Hitler showed more understanding, still apparently under the influence of my protestations after the Pinkafeld affair. He agreed that I should have a private talk with the young prince. A call at the Legation could hardly have been an easy one for him to make, but I let it be known through friends that the interview would be as painless as possible. When he arrived we talked about the weather, and Vienna, and mutual acquaintances, but not a single word about the incident was mentioned. Then, when I rose to accompany him to the door, I said I was sure he would approve of my expressing his regret to Hitler about this undergraduate prank. To this he eagerly agreed, adding how pleased he was to have settled the matter, which had been weighing on his mind more heavily than a visit to the dentist. In later years he was sent, during the war, to Dachau concentration camp. In 1944, as a result of repeated representations to Himmler, I was able to secure his release.

* * *

With Schuschnigg's formation of the Committee of Seven, it became possible for me to give some attention to the personalities within Austria who favoured the Anschluss idea. From my point of view, the only group of any value was made up of about six or seven men who stood outside the illegal Nazi Party and its leader, Leopold. Chief among them was Professor Menghin, Rector of the University, and a man who enjoyed the confidence of Schuschnigg. Then came Dr Jury, an elderly man of firm character, Dr Seyss-Inquart, a lawyer with conservative political leanings and an active Catholic, and Reinthaller, well known in agricultural circles and devoid of any political extremism. All these men were known to me personally. Their group also included an intelligent young doctor named Rainer, and a Dr Muehlmann, who was a close personal friend of Goering's two sisters, Frau Huber and Frau Riegele.

I had obtained in January a copy of a circular sent by Leopold to his party colleagues, in which he warned them not to indulge in illegal activity, but ordered all members of the party to hold themselves ready to take up the fight again as soon as Hitler gave the word. It was clear to me that his hope that Schuschnigg would soon lift the ban on the Nazi Party would not be fulfilled for some time. His order to the party people to hold themselves in readiness could therefore only mean that they would soon become active again. I decided I would do all I could to prevent this.

On the other hand, Schuschnigg gave little encouragement to the members of the Committee of Seven, apart from suggesting that they should draw up a list of suitable men for appointments in the State administration. The Chancellor seemed to think that he had fulfilled his part of the July Agreement by putting Guido Schmidt in the Foreign Ministry and appointing Glaise-Horstenau as a minister without portfolio. The few moderate people in the Committee were still deprived of any influence on affairs, and Leopold soon lost patience with them, especially as they were not his nominees. He therefore tried, by infiltrating their headquarters in the Teinfaltstrasse with his own adherents, to turn the place into a centre for illegal party activities. The Austrian police were well aware of this move, but made no attempt to close the office down, since it made it considerably easier for them to keep a watch on the party's illegal activities.

Professor Menghin came to see me in June to express his dissatisfaction with the work of the Committee, and I strongly recommended him to resign, unless he wanted to be branded as a Nazi. Schuschnigg, in the meantime, made up his mind to allow at least one minor ministerial change, as a step towards including suitable outside personalities in the Fatherland Front. He asked Seyss-Inquart to join the administration, with the rank of State Secretary, so as to act as intermediary between the Government and the Opposition. This appointment was vehemently opposed by Leopold because Seyss-Inquart was not a Nazi. Seyss-Inquart, for his part, planned to organize the more moderate Greater German sympathizers into an opposition group to Leopold's Nazis, and in this he counted particularly on the country people, who owed allegiance to Reinthaller.

All the Austrians who knew Seyss-Inquart regarded him as conscientious, prudent, tolerant and unlikely to indulge in any wild adventures. Although convinced that the reunion of the German peoples was a desirable ideal, he recognized the necessity for maintaining Austria's independence. If Schuschnigg had made up his mind to take Seyss-Inquart into his confidence, all might have been well. As it was, Seyss-Inquart was not allowed a free hand, and Leopold was left far too much liberty. Complaints that Schuschnigg was making no attempt to carry out the terms of the July Agreement became more insistent. While I studied the possibility of again bringing Austrian and German statesmen together, in an effort to clarify the situation, Hitler, apparently making a genuine effort to curb the Austrian Nazis, sent one of his Under-

Secretaries, named Keppler, to Austria. Readers will remember him as a member of the famous luncheon party at Baron von Schroeder's house in Cologne in 1933. In Austria, Keppler seems to have given way far too much to the radical wing of the party, although for a time the Austrian Government's complaints concerning its illegal activities ceased. It is perhaps interesting to note that a long letter written by Leopold to Hitler on August 22, 1937, described me as the greatest enemy of Austrian National Socialism and demanded my removal.

The plan to incorporate members of the opposition in the structure of the Government made practically no progress during the whole of this year. The Committee of Seven drowned itself in oceans of paper, and the radical elements of the illegal Nazi Party derived strength from Schuschnigg's dilatory behaviour. They sent a constant stream of protests and requests for intervention to the party in Germany, yet Schuschnigg made no attempt to dispel their discontent by granting any of the expected concessions. Several times I tried to rouse him from his passive attitude. In an interview towards the end of May I impressed upon him how serious the situation was becoming. The increasing number of incidents, and the fact that so little was being done to carry out the July Agreement, must raise the question in Hitler's mind whether there was any further point in maintaining an ambassador on special mission to Austria. Almost any incident could result in a situation which might have quite unforeseeable consequences, and although Hitler was at pains to maintain peaceful relations, he must nevertheless insist that the Austrian Government carry out its obligations.

Schuschnigg replied that he was well aware of the seriousness of the situation. If no progress had been made in the establishment of more friendly relations with Germany, it was largely the fault of the radical members of the illegal Austrian Nazi Party and the reaction in the Fatherland Front. He mentioned the unfortunate effect of the activities against the Church in Germany, and said that Leopold, who had been received by Hitler and Goering, had been encouraged in his aggressive tactics. This accusation I rejected, pointing out that Hitler had assured me that any breach of the July Agreement was against his wish. If the Austrian Government would give chapter and verse of any intervention from Germany, I would recommend the necessary steps to be taken. Schuschnigg's principal complaint was that any members of the opposition who were given ministerial posts thereby ceased to be regarded by the opposition as reliable representatives.

The commission which had been set up under the July Agreement had its first meeting in Vienna in July 1937. The German delegation was headed by Herr von Weizsäcker. I had hoped that the Austrian delegation would be led by Herr Hoffinger, the head of the German section of the Foreign Office, who was an experienced and conciliatory official; but Schuschnigg preferred to appoint Dr von Hornbostel, who could be relied upon to make not the slightest concession.

The negotiations became a test of patience. The chief difficulty resulted from our wish that the amnesty envisaged in the July Agreement should be extended to cover Austrian Nazis who had fled to Germany. I laid great emphasis on this myself, as these refugees had formed themselves into an 'Austrian Legion' and were a constantly disturbing factor. They continually put pressure on Hitler and other Party leaders to effect an Anschluss with Austria by force, and, through the colleagues they had left behind, were perpetually interfering in Austrian affairs. In the end, agreement was reached on this point, against the bitter opposition of Hornbostel, who was, however, overruled by Schuschnigg. In a long conversation with the Chancellor, Weizsäcker came to the conclusion that although he was not actively opposing the inclusion of Greater Germany sympathizers in the administration, he was only prepared to proceed in the matter very warily, until he was sure of his ground. However, it appeared that Seyss-Inquart had to a certain extent gained Schuschnigg's confidence, and at the end of the conference I was able to tell Hitler that while Schuschnigg was still not prepared to allow the reconstitution of the Nazi Party in Austria, he would not forbid the discussion of National Socialist ideology. The Fatherland Front was also showing much greater tolerance to the idea of admitting members of the opposition, and I begged Hitler again to give Seyss-Inquart every chance and to see that the Austrian Nazis gave him their support, instead of constantly seeking to sabotage his work.

Relations between the two countries took a turn for the worse during July, following a demonstration which took place at Wels during a parade of ex-servicemen from both countries. These demonstrations had been forbidden for a number of years, but the

Austrian Government apparently felt that little harm could come from their revival, since most of the people taking part were older men without strong political affinities. I had been invited to attend and was delighted by the enthusiasm shown by the large crowd of spectators at the march past of representatives of famous German and Austrian regiments. But what had been planned as a purely non-political meeting acquired quite a different aspect when the military band played the Austrian national anthem. The immense crowd sang to this the words 'Deutschland, Deutschland über alles' – the tunes are the same – and I could see that all the Austrian Government representatives were appalled at what had become a political demonstration. I made my own speech as short as possible, excusing myself by saying that I was expected in Munich for the gala opening of the Academy of Arts, and must leave immediately because the weather looked as if it might interfere with my flight.

Hitler was also in Munich for the occasion, and greeted me in a rage. 'What has been going on in Wels?' he asked. 'Police with carbines have been turned loose on our people there. A disgraceful business!' I was quite unable to answer, and could only assure him that as long as I had been there everything had gone smoothly. Apparently the Austrian police had considered that the crowd was getting out of hand, and in an attempt to disperse the demonstrators, they had come to blows. There is little doubt that Leopold's Nazis had a hand in the demonstration and had sent off a grossly exaggerated report to Hitler. On the other hand, the whole crowd was not made up of Nazis, and the enthusiasm shown for the German contingents was genuine enough, however distasteful it might be to the Austrian Government. The general effect of the incident was most unfortunate and led to a stiffening of attitudes on both sides which, regrettably, increased with time.

* * *

The general situation in Europe changed little during the summer of 1937. But it must have become clear to the Austrian Government that Mussolini was an uncertain prop for any Austrian policies directed against Germany. On September 25 the Duce arrived in Germany with Count Ciano on an official visit. He had a long conversation with Hitler in Munich and – to the secret delight of a great many people – made Hitler an honorary corporal in the Fascist militia. At last it seemed that Hitler, who had never risen higher than a lance-corporal in the German Army, had earned his promotion. Then came a long series of official visits to the Ruhr and attendance at the autumn manœuvres in Mecklenburg. At the invitation of my old friend Colonel-General von Fritsch, I attended the last phase of these manœuvres, and was present when he summarized the results to the Führer and the Duce. The contrast between them was most marked. Mussolini, with his sharply limned Roman head, powerful dome and strong chin, was much more the Cæsar than his curiously sunken and characterless counterpart. As Fritsch summed up the qualities of the new Army, and gave a warning of the danger of over-estimating its still untrained strength, and of its inability to carry out anything in the nature of a war on two fronts, Hitler scowled, while Mussolini nodded his expressive head in affirmation. It seemed to me that in this new friendship the strong character of Mussolini might well dominate the partnership and have a good influence on Hitler's unstable temperament.

Another guest at the manœuvres was Lord Londonderry, who stayed on for a few days at Goering's invitation to take part in a stag and bison shoot at Darss, the Government hunting estate on the Baltic coast. Goering asked me if I would care to accompany our English guest, and I accepted at once. I always found that hunting parties and the long evenings round an open fire provided an admirable opportunity for making the real, human contact rendered so difficult by the formality of diplomatic life. Lord Londonderry was deeply interested in obtaining a true picture of the new Germany and had been most impressed by the exhibition of her military power.

I told him that the best way of dealing with outstanding problems would be to negotiate directly with Hitler. The Nazi Party's exaggerated nationalism would have the wind taken out of its sails if the remaining shackles of the Versailles Treaty could be loosened. If this were done, I should have little fear for the future, I said, adding that I regarded Hitler's new friendship with the Duce as providing a sobering influence. 'As long as the generation that went through the first world war has any say in the conduct of affairs, there will be no second outbreak,' I assured him. This, indeed, was my firm conviction. Lord Londonderry accepted my statements at their face value, and I found it an immense pleasure to talk to a man of his honourable and open nature. He was the perfect type of old-world aristocrat. How much easier it must have been to deal with international problems when effective power in each country was exclusively in the hands of such people, each forming part of a world-wide family.

Before his visit ended there was an amusing incident. Goering had gone to great pains to resuscitate the strain of bison which formerly roamed all over Northern Europe, and kept a herd in semi-captivity at his shooting lodge at Karinhall. He was very fond of boasting to his guests that at last he could provide them with a type of game which it required cunning and personal courage to shoot. Lord Londonderry had greeted the idea of shooting bison with great enthusiasm. He did not know that there were no bison at Darss – nor that Goering, to make good this lack, had given orders for a suitable bull to be sent from Karinhall. The head gamekeeper at Karinhall saw little point in sending one of his few sound bulls to be shot at by an English lord, and sent off a decrepit beast which, as far as he was concerned, might just as well be shot as not. The head gamekeeper at Darss let it loose in a part of the forest, surrounded by a ring of beaters, and although he noticed that the beast was in poor shape, gave a graphic account to Lord Londonderry of having coralled a magnificent animal, which would provide him with splendid sport the next day.

At four o'clock in the morning an agitated messenger burst into the hunting lodge to say that the beast had escaped, after attacking one of the beaters, and that after trailing it for several hours they had lost it. Lord Londonderry was greatly disappointed, but was propitiated by an offer of a first-class stag. What he never learnt was that all the gamekeeper's efforts to see the bison through the night on its feet had failed, and it simply keeled over and died from the rigours of the journey. In his distress the head game-keeper had had to invent a plausible story. Lord Londonderry would have been most surprised to learn, I am sure, that the Third Reich carried its theatricals into the depths of the North European forest.

★   ★   ★

Guido Schmidt still derived a certain amount of pleasure from playing on his connections with Paris and London, but opinion in these two countries had undergone a considerable change. M. Delbos, the French Foreign Minister, even expressed the opinion that in the last resort Austria's salvation lay in union with Germany. Schmidt was invited to Berlin by Goering for the hunting exhibition. During his visit Schmidt was shown a map of Europe which omitted the frontiers of Austria; good huntsmen knew no frontiers, Goering told him with a grin. Whatever the impression this incident caused, the visit gave rise to a long correspondence between the two men, which first became known to the public at Schmidt's trial for high treason after the war, but which is of distinct historical interest in this context.

In his first letter, dated January 29, 1937, Schmidt complained of certain remarks made by Goering to the Austrian Minister in Rome, during his state visit to Italy. Apparently he had expressed the opinion that 'saboteurs' were trying to wreck the July Agreement. Schmidt rejected this accusation and drew attention to the real efforts of the Austrian Government. It was evident from Goering's answer, which was couched in very friendly terms, that he was trying to gain Schmidt's confidence. Goering emphasized that the German Government had made up its mind to co-operate with the Austrian Chancellor and would ensure that possible causes of discord were removed. He spoke of evolutionary methods and Austria's right to independence.

Schmidt was prepared to follow up these overtures, but Schuschnigg showed little interest. Nothing happened until the end of June, when Goering invited Schmidt to visit him again. But another two months went by before Schmidt finally appeared at Karinhall. In the meantime the international situation had undergone a change and Hitler had become more intransigent. Schmidt suggested that the best thing would be for Goering to discuss matters with Schuschnigg, and that he should arrange a hunting party for this purpose. A letter from Goering on November 11 took a much sharper tone and made it clear that such an invitation could only be accepted if some positive result was to be expected from the visit. Friendly relations between the two countries, he wrote, could only be based on close co-operation in a common German policy; their military forces must be integrated, a trade pact agreed, and a financial and customs union signed. He also made it clear that these suggestions had Hitler's approval. This letter of Goering's was a pretty direct *avis au lecteur*, and it is incomprehensible to me how Schuschnigg and Schmidt could maintain at Nuremberg that Hitler's demands, presented two and

a half months later at his meeting with Schuschnigg in Berchtesgaden, came as a complete surprise. All the demands made then
were included in this letter of Goering's on November 11, 1937.

★ ★ ★

After the international hunting exhibition in Berlin, I paid a short
visit to Paris, where the World Exhibition provided me with a
suitable opportunity for political conversations without having
undue attention drawn to my presence. I had interviews with the
Prime Minister, M. Chautemps, and with MM. Reynaud, Bonnet,
Pietri, Daladier, and other leading personalities. I attached particular importance to seeing M. Léon Blum, the Socialist leader,
on the question of Austria. He held no ministerial post at the time,
but his party was one of the principal supports of the Government.
I was compelled to keep our meeting a secret in order to prevent
the Nazis making political capital out of my interview with one
of the chief targets of their anti-Jewish propaganda.

M. Blum received me in his tastefully decorated apartment and
listened with great interest to what I had to say. I asked him to
convince party colleagues that an autonomous Austria within an
overall German federation was a step towards the goal of European federation sought by the Socialists themselves. If Richelieu's
old divide-and-rule policies towards Austria and Germany were
finally abandoned, the effort would be amply repaid by the
improvement in relations between France and Germany, the basic
prerequisite of European peace and security. Only thus would
Germany be in a position to play her old part in Central Europe
and act as a bulwark against the western march of Communism.
I would therefore be most grateful, I told him, if France could
abandon her opposition to any change in Austria's status and view
evolutionary developments with a benevolent eye. Blum could
make no promises, but he undertook to discuss the matter with
the members of his party and the various ministers.

Almost everyone to whom I spoke expressed the opinion that
some evolutionary method must be devised for solving the problem
of Austro-German relations. M. Bonnet, the Minister of Finance,
showed complete understanding of my efforts in Austria, and
when he arranged for me to see M. Chautemps, I found the Prime
Minister fully prepared to discuss a new approach to Central
European problems. He also expressed the hope that France and

Germany would be able to reach a general settlement for the purpose of ensuring European peace. I sent a long report to Hitler and Neurath insisting that now, if ever, was the time to make an approach to the French, and I had every reason to suppose that my suggestion would be taken up. Unfortunately I found on my return to Vienna that Schuschnigg took a very jaundiced view of my Paris visit.

In November Schuschnigg decided to stop the entry of any new members into the Fatherland Front, thereby more or less putting an end to the policy of seeking some understanding with the opposition. The struggle between the two camps flared up again and Leopold's gift for trouble-making took on new and original forms. One morning my Counsellor, Freiherr von Stein, showed me a letter he had received from the headquarters of the illegal Nazi Party, in which it was alleged that I had advised the head of the Austrian police to keep a sharp watch on Stein. As I have pointed out earlier, Stein's whole attitude and personality was little to my taste, but I could not allow this accusation to go unanswered and gave instructions for Leopold to be brought before me.

We had a stormy meeting in which he accused me of such constant opposition and intervention in the affairs of the Nazi Party that Schuschnigg had been strengthened in his intentions not to carry out the terms of the July Agreement. The opposition was therefore under no further obligation to respect its own part of the agreement. I told Leopold that it was not his business to decide when an agreement between our two countries was to be abrogated. I wished to have nothing further to do with the members of an organization which employed such unpleasant and questionable methods and disregarded so completely Hitler's specific instructions. 'Your behaviour is intolerable and I wish to have nothing further to do with you,' I told him. 'I forbid you from now on to enter the Legation compound, and I shall give the members of my staff instructions to see that you are kept out.' I knew that this action would bring a storm of protest about my ears from the party on both sides of the border, but I intended to show Schuschnigg how I stood in the matter. However, it was not until January 1938 that the Chancellor authorized me to make representations to Hitler on his behalf to have Leopold expelled to Germany, and remove him, at least territorially, from the leadership of the illegal party. I was astonished at how willingly Hitler accepted this request. I can only assume that Leopold was too much of a bull in a china shop, even for him.

On January 25 the Vienna police raided the offices of the Committee of Seven. This body had long since ceased to bear any resemblance to the organization set up by the Chancellor, and had become merely the headquarters of the Nazi underground. A considerable quantity of incriminating material was found, which became known as the Tavs papers, after the name of one of the leading Austrian Nazis. One memorandum from this gentleman, written to party headquarters in Germany, pressed for the Wehrmacht to march into Austria as there was no further hope of co-operation with the Schuschnigg régime. It would then be possible to form a Government under Leopold's leadership. One of the documents even made the suggestion that I, or my military attaché, should be assassinated in order to provide an excuse for German intervention. The Austrian Government made no immediate protest and apparently preferred to retain the material as a bargaining counter in any future talks with Germany. However, Dr Tavs was arrested and charged with high treason.

It was this incident that finally decided me to press for Leopold's removal to Germany. On January 27 I travelled to Garmisch to watch the ski races between Austria and Germany. There I met, by chance, Dr Seyss-Inquart, and on a trip up the Kreuzeck we discussed our mutual worries. He asked me to impress upon Hitler that the intervention of German Nazis in Austrian affairs must at all costs be avoided. If Schuschnigg was to offer him a full ministerial post, he would have to be accepted as the trustee of the opposition as a whole, with no obligation to accept orders from Germany. The problem could only be solved if the opposition were to form a party entirely independent of leadership from Berlin. I agreed with him wholeheartedly and repeated his arguments word for word to Hitler a few days later, pressing at the same time for the removal of Leopold, and suggesting that it was high time Hitler and Schuschnigg discussed the whole situation personally.

In Berlin I learnt from my old colleagues in the Army of the struggle for power and influence that was going on in the Wehrmacht. Most of the Army had remained true to its old traditions and to the type of personality who normally served in the General

Staff or achieved general's rank. With re-armament, the Army had come to occupy an increasingly important place in the State, and it had become a matter of concern to Hitler and the party to ensure its loyalty. We now know from the Hossbach protocol, which was drawn up at the beginning of November 1937, that the Commander-in-Chief, General von Fritsch, and the Chief of Staff, General Beck, opposed Hitler's plans bitterly. They could not be relied upon to carry out any Nazi-inspired adventures.

On the other hand, Hitler was faced by the truly Byzantine intrigues of Goering and Himmler to obtain control of this power-ful instrument. Himmler was gathering his alleged proofs of Fritsch's immoral behaviour, and Goering was taking an open part in encouraging Field-Marshal von Blomberg to enter into his fateful second marriage.[1] The whole plot was designed not only to remove the key figures, but also to discredit their characters in the eyes of the public and their fellow officers.

All this is written after the event. At the time, there was only the general feeling of tension. I found Hitler sullen and touchy. Even the normal celebrations on January 30, the anniversary of his coming to power, did not take place. Yet when I returned to Vienna, it was without any inkling of the storm that was about to break.

---

[1] Blomberg's registry office wedding was witnessed by Hitler and Goering, but very soon afterwards Himmler cast discreditable aspersions on the lady's past.

CHAPTER XXIII

ANSCHLUSS

I am dismissed – Hitler persuaded to see Schuschnigg – The invitation in retrospect – The meeting in Berchtesgaden – Hitler's demands – The Keppler Protocol – Agreement reached – Hitler's Reichstag speech – Leopold replaced – Pressure from France – Schuschnigg proposes a plebiscite – Goering intervenes – The Army marches – Reflections – Ketteler missing – I return home

THE Wehrmacht crisis came to a head on February 4, 1938. In order to distract attention from its effects, Hitler touched off another crisis, which was to have even more far-reaching consequences for the German people. That evening I was sitting quietly in my office at the Legation, when the telephone rang. Lammers, Secretary of the Berlin Chancellery, was on the line. 'The Führer wishes me to inform you that your mission in Vienna has ended. I wanted to tell you this before you read about it in the newspapers.'

I was almost speechless with astonishment.

'Can you give me some reason for this sudden decision?' I asked. 'Surely the Führer could have told me of it last week when I was in Berlin?'

'The decision has just been taken,' he replied. 'Herr von Neurath [the Foreign Secretary], Hassell and Dircksen [the Ambassadors in Rome and Tokio] have also been relieved. I am sorry I cannot give you any further information at the moment.'

I simply did not know what to think. I had now been in Vienna nearly four years, and in spite of all the difficulties and setbacks, I had come to love the work. I went to Vienna originally to deal with a problem of vital importance to Germany, and I had put all personal considerations aside. The first few months had been thoroughly depressing, but now I had the feeling that something substantial had been accomplished. The results of a patient, steady, open and loyal policy were just beginning to show. I had won a number of friends in Austria who believed that I sought a solution to the problem which was not only in the interests of Germany. The Austrian problem no longer excited international passions and had come to be regarded more or less as a private quarrel between cousins. Even Mussolini had abandoned his original objections to the idea of union. Now everything was at an end, and for no apparent reason.

When I discussed this development with my family, we could only conclude that Hitler had had enough of my policy and intended to replace me by some radical member of the Nazi Party. I assumed he would choose someone readier to yield to his wishes, who was not in possession of a written undertaking that union was only to be achieved by evolutionary methods and that no blood must be spilt. I was chiefly distressed at the probable undoing of all my work, and made up my mind that the outside world should in due course know that I had had no part in this new turn of events. The defamatory campaigns of the Third Reich were only too well known to me, and I decided to adopt the somewhat unusual course for a diplomatic representative of depositing copies of all my correspondence with Hitler in a safe place, so that they could not be destroyed by the Gestapo. At least I would then be able to prove what my policy in Austria had been.

Wilhelm von Ketteler, my assistant and friend for many years, was with us that evening and undertook to find a place of safety for the documents. He felt, as I did, that if anything should happen to me, and relations with Austria should reach a crisis, I should probably be blamed posthumously for the whole train of events. If the documents were in safe custody, it would still be possible for the truth to be known.

Ribbentrop's appointment as Foreign Minister, Hitler's assumption of the rank of Commander-in-Chief, and the dismissal of a number of older generals, most of whom I knew personally, were unmistakable portents. I had served my purpose, it seemed, and could now go. However, I wanted to obtain some picture of what was going on, so I decided to go to see Hitler. I reached Berchtesgaden on February 5, and there found Hitler exhausted and distrait. I said I regretted that he had found it necessary to dispense with my services, as I had always assumed that we had been in full agreement on our Austrian policy. His eyes seemed unable to focus on anything, and his thoughts seemed elsewhere. He sought to explain my dismissal with empty excuses. It was only when I

O

made it clear that I had not come to Berchtesgaden to complain of
the loss of my post, or to ask for a new one – I was much happier
at home in Wallerfangen than anywhere else in the world – it was
only then, and when I reminded him that four years earlier in
Bayreuth he had undertaken to conduct a moderate and responsible
policy towards Austria, that he seemed to understand what I was
talking about.

My successor, I said, would have a difficult time. It had been
hard enough to build up a foundation of mutual confidence which,
although it did not include the Austrian Chancellor, extended to a
great number of influential Austrians. Since December, however,
Schuschnigg had been expressing a wish to meet the Führer personally, in an attempt to solve the many problems outstanding. I
had welcomed the idea, which at least showed that the Austrian
Chancellor was now convinced that a free exchange of views, on
the basis of the July Agreement, could do no harm. I therefore
wished, as my last official act, to recommend again such a meeting
before Hitler chose to adopt other methods.

The idea seemed to capture Hitler's attention. He had apparently
forgotten that I had already made this suggestion when the
Austrian police confiscated the Tavs papers. It seemed to me even
then that direct conversations between the leaders of the two
countries provided the only means of lessening the tension caused
by Leopold's activities. Now I felt that a discussion was even more
necessary, since I had been relieved of my duties and was no longer
in a position to prevent Hitler adopting more radical measures.
Suddenly he seemed to grasp the fact that Schuschnigg was ready
to meet him half way, and he became all enthusiasm. 'That is an
excellent idea,' he said, 'please go back to Vienna immediately and
arrange for us to meet within the next few days. I should be very
pleased to invite Herr Schuschnigg here and talk everything over
with him.'

'I am hardly in a position to do that,' I said. 'I have already told
the Austrian Government of my recall. You will have to put this
matter in the hands of the chargé d'affaires. Moreover,' I added,
'the press all over the world has already reported my dismissal and
has drawn all sorts of unpleasant conclusions from it.'

'That makes no difference,' Hitler replied. 'I beg you, Herr von
Papen, to take over the affairs of the Legation again, until the
meeting with Schuschnigg has been arranged.'

Hitler certainly had curious ideas of diplomacy. Nevertheless, I considered the proposal. Perhaps such a conversation might bear fruit and prevent Germany adopting a policy of naked threats. I realized I should look somewhat foolish returning to Vienna again, but I felt that the opportunity to render one last service to the solution of the Austro-German problem was not to be lightly dismissed. I therefore agreed. If I had known at the time of Goering's correspondence with Schmidt, I would probably have refused. At least I would have made my agreement dependent on a guarantee that the Austrian Chancellor was not to be presented with demands which contradicted the spirit of the July Agreement. As it was, I thought there was a good chance of reaching a friendly understanding. I assumed that the echo abroad of the Fritsch and Blomberg affairs would cause Hitler to make some gesture showing that his becoming Commander-in-Chief did not signify the introduction of more aggressive policies. To the general astonishment of my family and colleagues, I arrived back in Vienna on February 7 and immediately got in touch with Schuschnigg.

★　★　★

In the interests of historical accuracy I must deal at this point with the accusation made at Nuremberg, that I enticed Schuschnigg to Berchtesgaden under false pretences, so that Hitler could present him with a series of demands which I had known about all along. This is quite untrue.

It had become clear to me that relations between the two countries could only be restored outside the usual diplomatic channels. I had already suggested to Schuschnigg in December that he should have a meeting with Hitler in order to clear up all the points under dispute. I made the same suggestion to Neurath and Hitler. In my conversation with Schuschnigg I also suggested that a new ministerial post should be created to deal with the opposition's problems, and with complaints from both sides about breaches of the July Agreement. The new minister, I said, would have to be someone in whom Hitler had confidence. Such an appointment would ease our difficulties considerably.

On January 7 I repeated to Guido Schmidt the suggestion for a meeting between the two Chancellors, adding that Hitler had proposed a date towards the end of the month. Schmidt, after discussing the matter with Schuschnigg, informed me in writing that the date was suitable. He insisted, however, that the matter should be kept secret. On January 26 I saw Schmidt again, and told him that Hitler would like to invite Schuschnigg to Berchtesgaden on February 15. Would the Austrian Chancellor still be interested? At this meeting Schmidt made a number of complaints about the activities of the Nazi opposition, based again on the evidence of the confiscated Tavs papers. He also insisted that he would regard the removal of Leopold, Tavs and In der Maur to Germany as the best indication of Germany's wish to improve relations between the two countries. I made a note of all this and undertook to forward the complaints to Berlin. It is therefore perfectly clear that the meeting between the two Chancellors was not a sudden suggestion made by me at the last moment, but something which had been under consideration for a couple of months.

My sudden dismissal on February 4 came as a complete surprise, both to the Austrians and myself. It was taken as an indication that Germany no longer intended to follow the lines of the agreement I had signed on July 11, 1936. It was even rumoured that I was to be replaced by Buerckel, who had gained such an unsavoury reputation as Gauleiter in the Saar. The crisis in the Wehrmacht, the dismissal of Neurath, and the appointment of such a prominent Nazi as Ribbentrop to the post of Foreign Minister, made Schuschnigg even more anxious to discuss things with Hitler before matters took a turn for the worse.

At his trial after the war, Guido Schmidt declared that on my return to Vienna on February 7, Schuschnigg told the Cabinet that he intended to go through with the arrangement to meet Hitler. Mussolini was informed and expressed approval of the idea, and Schmidt told the British and French Ministers and the Papal Nuncio of the Chancellor's plans. I must confess it is not quite clear to me how he reconciled this with his request that the matter should be kept secret. Schmidt also mentioned in evidence the letter I had sent to him on February 10. 'In this note von Papen drew attention to the serious view taken by Germany of the way relations were deteriorating. Von Papen feared that the Chancellor had no clear idea of the serious consequences that might result from failure to deal with the situation. Germany, he said, was going through an internal crisis, and this would be the best opportunity for Austria to obtain concessions.'

I think it is also only fair to quote a statement by the Secretary-

General of the Austrian Foreign Ministry, who was certainly no Germanophile. Giving evidence at Schmidt's trial, he said: 'I had the impression that the visit to Berchtesgaden had been a favourite idea of Schuschnigg's for some time. In conversation with me, the Chancellor had often suggested that the best solution would be for him to discuss the situation with the man [Hitler] himself.'

Schuschnigg has also accused me of failing to keep my word to provide an agenda for the meeting. In fact, I had declined this request straight away, because I felt there should be no limit to the matters discussed. The head of the German Department in the Austrian Foreign Office, Hoffinger, confirmed this at the Schmidt trial. 'The German side,' he said, 'would not agree to the drawing up of an agenda.' It was clearly necessary, however, for the Austrians to decide what attitude they should adopt to Hitler's demands, providing always that these did not exceed the terms of the July Agreement.

Schuschnigg and I had decided that no demands should be made or accepted which transgressed the independence and sovereignty of Austria, as recognized by the agreement. I had therefore arranged with him that a combined Austro-German communiqué should be published after the talks, which would make this point quite clear. We could not decide the exact wording of the communiqué, of course, until the talks had taken place; but the fact remains that this communiqué was published, as agreed.

Schuschnigg took the preparatory step of instructing Zernatto, the Secretary-General of the Fatherland Front, to work out, in conjunction with Seyss-Inquart, a list of proposals and possible concessions. As questions of internal policy alone were involved, Schmidt was excluded, and it was only on his way to Berchtesgaden with the Chancellor that he was told what had been agreed. These proposals, which have become known as the *Punktationen*, went on record during Schmidt's trial after the war. They show to what extent Zernatto, the watchdog of Schuschnigg's policy, and indeed Schuschnigg himself, were prepared to make concessions without feeling that they were departing from the terms of the July Agreement. At the time, I had no knowledge whatsoever of this document.

A study of these *Punktationen* shows that Schuschnigg was ready to instal Seyss-Inquart as the arbiter of all matters concerning the opposition. His ministry was to provide the channel for all communications on this subject with the German Government. The censorship on books and the press was to be lifted, and the armed forces of the two countries were to be closely co-ordinated, with the same system of training and weapons. Any Nazis still under arrest were to be released, and members of the opposition who joined the Fatherland Front were to receive their share of posts in the ministries, local government offices and town councils. A list of suitable persons was prepared, which included the names of Dr Jury, Reinthaller, Professor Menghin, and others.

Giving evidence at his trial, Schmidt referred to the drawing up of these proposals as a great misfortune. He suggested that Keppler, Hitler's right-hand man in everything that concerned Austria, was in close contact with Seyss-Inquart and had obtained either a copy or at least some indication of the contents of these proposals. 'Every demand made by Hitler at Berchtesgaden was based on this document,' said Schmidt.

It will be seen that there was great similarity between these proposals and the terms presented by Hitler at the Berchtesgaden meeting. There is therefore absolutely no foundation for Schuschnigg's claim that Hitler's terms came as a surprise. Even less truth is there in his accusation that I tricked him into meeting Hitler, knowing full well the demands with which he was to be presented. If Seyss-Inquart did, in fact, pass on the details of the proposals to Keppler, this was a gross breach of confidence. Though Schuschnigg may have come to believe in later years that I shared this knowledge, I can only say that this is completely untrue.

In 1943 Gauleiter Rainer, in a speech to Austrian Nazi leaders, gave an account of the part he and certain others had taken in the events leading up to the Anschluss. He made a point of stating that I had been ignorant of the whole affair. 'The Party was informed of every detail discussed by the Austrian Cabinet,' he said, 'our channels of information extended right into Schuschnigg's bedroom.'

★ ★ ★

The meeting between the two leaders was arranged for February 12, and on the previous day I went to Berchtesgaden, where I spent the night, in order to be ready to welcome our Austrian guests at the frontier and accompany them to Hitler. In the hotel I met one of Ribbentrop's secretaries, who told me that Ribbentrop was staying with Hitler and would be present at the meeting next day. General Keitel, who had become a fixture in Hitler's entourage, was also there, and had arranged for General Reichenau, Commander of the Munich military district, and General Sperrle, the senior German Air Force officer in Bavaria, to be present. I assumed that Hitler had asked them to be there in order to discuss one of his favourite themes – the integration of the Austrian and German armed forces.

At breakfast next morning in my hotel I was somewhat surprised to see a well-known Austrian National Socialist, Dr Muehlmann. I was still more astonished to find that he was fully informed about Schuschnigg's visit, and that this was the reason for his own journey. We spoke of our hopes for a reasonable solution of the many misunderstandings on both sides. I told him how much easier life would be for my successor in Vienna if Schuschnigg could make up his mind to take into his Cabinet someone in whom he had confidence, such as Seyss-Inquart, who could deal with the problems of the opposition. 'Do you think Hitler would be prepared to accept the appointment of Seyss-Inquart for this purpose?' Dr Muehlmann asked. 'That I do not know,' I said, 'but I consider him the best person for the job, in spite of not being a member of the party.' I knew that Hitler might be even further prejudiced against Seyss-Inquart because of his being in Schuschnigg's confidence. I therefore suggested to Muehlmann that if Hitler should oppose Seyss-Inquart's nomination, it might be a good idea for Muehlmann himself to put in a word for him. 'That I am fully prepared to do,' he said; and as we shall see, it later became necessary for him to intervene.

At about eleven o'clock I was on the frontier at Salzburg to receive our guests. The Austrian Chancellor, accompanied by Guido Schmidt and an adjutant, had spent the night in Salzburg and appeared cheerful and confident. They asked me for news and enquired whom they would meet in Hitler's mountain retreat. I told them what I knew and mentioned that the party included three generals, a piece of information that seemed little to their taste.

Half an hour later we were at the entrance to the Berghof. Hitler received his guests with great politeness and personally conducted Schuschnigg to his study, where they had a private conversation until lunch time. The rest of us spoke in general terms about the problems under discussion, and presently I took Ribbentrop and Schmidt into a corner for a private talk. So far there was no sign of the three generals.

This was Ribbentrop's first official appearance since his appointment as Foreign Minister on February 4, and he was still sufficiently unsure of himself to put on his most forbidding manner. I was able to break the ice a little, because as a result of my determination to keep his Bureau out of my province, Ribbentrop was completely uninformed about Austrian affairs, and had to keep turning to me for information. After a few empty exchanges, he produced a document which he handed to Schmidt, saying that it contained the German suggestions for a final settlement of relations with Austria. The contents had been approved by the Führer, who would insist on their acceptance. It only remained to discuss details. This presentation of what amounted to an ultimatum seemed an unusual act of diplomacy, and I began to despair when I saw the astonishment on Schmidt's face, as he quickly ran through the text. Not having been advised of any specific demands, I asked to be allowed to see the document, so as to guide the conversation into more normal channels. With amazement I read that the Austrian Government was called upon to recognize National Socialism as compatible with Austrian aspirations; that Seyss-Inquart should be appointed Minister of the Interior, and Glaise-Horstenau War Minister; that a Dr Fischboeck should be appointed Minister of Finance, for the purpose of integrating the economies of the two countries, and that two Austrian officials, who were responsible for control of the press, should be replaced.

It was clear that these demands represented unwarrantable interference in questions of Austrian sovereignty. The suggestions concerning Seyss-Inquart and Glaise-Horstenau could have been made in an entirely different form. Both of them already enjoyed Schuschnigg's confidence to a considerable degree, and in any case, Glaise-Horstenau was already Minister of the Interior. But the document that was presented read: 'The Federal Chancellor will implement by February 18 the following measures . . .' This infamous method of presenting an ultimatum in matters which might perfectly well be solved by friendly negotiation was one of the Nazi habits which destroyed any hope of peaceful compromise.

Dr Schmidt immediately raised all the objections I expected. I gave him as much support as I could and pointed out that the

Austrian constitution, of which Ribbentrop seemed to be completely ignorant, did not allow the Chancellor to name or dismiss ministers. This was exclusively the right of the Federal President. The conversation became exceedingly difficult because Ribbentrop had practically no idea of the persons or considerations involved. When lunch came to our rescue, Schuschnigg took Schmidt on one side to give him an account of the discussions with Hitler. The Führer had apparently monopolized the conversation and had accused Schuschnigg in gross terms of un-German behaviour and of sabotaging the July Agreement. He had threatened that if Schuschnigg's policy was not altered, other methods would be used. The Austrian Chancellor has given a detailed account of this conversation in his book,[1] and although he may be guilty of some exaggeration, I have no doubt that Hitler brought all his heavy guns to bear. Certainly Schuschnigg appeared worried and preoccupied.

At lunch the generals appeared and were presented to the guests. Hitler was polite and calm, and the main topics of conversation were the war in Spain, in which General Sperrle had taken part, new types of aircraft, and political gossip. The generals, who kept more or less in the background, made no attempt to impress Schuschnigg with details of German rearmament. They told Schmidt they had no idea why they had been invited. After lunch the conversation concentrated on Hitler's demands, which have become known, and were referred to at the Nuremberg trial, as the 'Keppler Protocol'. The main provisions were as follows:

I. As a result of the thorough exchange of views between the Führer and Reich Chancellor and Federal Chancellor, Dr Schuschnigg, the following communiqué has been agreed for publication in the press of both countries . . .

II. In view of the agreement expressed in the above-mentioned communiqué, the Federal Chancellor undertakes to introduce the following measures by February 18:

(1) The Austrian Federal Government undertakes to consult with the Reich Government on all matters of foreign policy concerning the two States. The Reich Government gives the same undertaking to the Federal Government.

[1] Kurt von Schuschnigg: *Austrian Requiem*. Gollancz, London, 1947.

(2) The Austrian Federal Government recognizes that National Socialism is compatible with Austrian sovereignty, providing its aspirations are fulfilled within the framework of the Austrian Constitution. In this context the Austrian Government will introduce no measures which could be interpreted as a ban on the National Socialist movement. The Federal Chancellor agrees to the extension of the work of the Office for Greater German Affairs.

(3) Under-Secretary Dr Seyss-Inquart is to be appointed Minister of the Interior, with control over the security forces. It will be his right and responsibility to ensure that the National Socialist movement may conduct its activities in accordance with the provisions of Article 2.

(4) The Federal Chancellor will declare a general amnesty for all persons arrested or imprisoned for National Socialist activity. Such persons, whose continued residence in Austria might endanger relations between the two countries, may, after each individual case has been examined by both Governments, take up residence in the Reich.

(5) The withholding or reducing of pension, public assistance and education rights from persons who have engaged in National Socialist activity will cease and be made good retrospectively.

(6) All commercial discrimination against National Socialists will cease.

(7) The implementation of the press agreement between the two Governments will be assured by the replacement of Minister Dr Ludwig and Federal Commissioner Colonel Adam.

(8) Relations between the German and Austrian Armies will be regulated as follows:

    (a) Federal Minister Glaise-Horstenau will be appointed Federal War Minister.

    (b) A regular exchange of officers (100 from each army in the first instance).

    (c) Regular consultations between the General Staffs.

    (d) A planned reorganization of personal and technical contacts.

(9) All discrimination against National Socialists, especially with regard to service in the armed forces, will be raised.

(10) The integration of the Austrian economic system with that of Germany will be started, and to this end Dr Fischboeck will be appointed Austrian Minister of Finance.

III. The Reich Government recognizes that Dr Seyss-Inquart, in his capacity as Minister of the Interior, alone becomes responsible for the implementation of Article II, Section 2, of this protocol. The Reich Government will take steps to prevent intervention by German party officers in internal Austrian affairs. Should differences of opinion arise concerning the implementation of Article II, Section 2, negotiations shall be conducted only through Minister Seyss-Inquart.

After Schuschnigg had conferred with Schmidt, his conversation with Hitler began again. This second talk, during which Schuschnigg refused to meet Hitler's demands, led to angry scenes. Hitler finally presented an ultimatum and threatened to march into Austria if his demands were not accepted. When Schuschnigg left the study in order to confer again with Schmidt, Hitler could be heard shouting behind the open door: 'General Keitel! Where is Keitel? Tell him to come here at once!' Keitel came hurrying up. He told us later that when he presented himself and asked for orders, Hitler grinned and said, 'There are no orders. I just wanted to have you here.' In fact nothing was discussed between them, and Hitler had apparently put on this little pantomime in order to convince Schuschnigg that things were getting serious. This was the only active part that the generals played in the whole affair.

A deadlock having been reached, Schuschnigg and Schmidt asked me to intervene, and I decided to do so. I went in to see Hitler and told him that this was no way to deal with the matter. Some of his demands were obviously unacceptable and all that he would get in the end would be a declaration by Schuschnigg that the Austrian Constitution did not permit him to make the changes suggested, and that he must discuss the matter with the Federal President. Would it not be better to obtain the Chancellor's agreement to as many measures as possible, so that the meeting should result in some progress? I undertook to try to win over Schuschnigg and Schmidt to this view, and Hitler agreed to my doing so. For several hours Schuschnigg, Schmidt and I thrashed the matter out, and finally we agreed on a text. This laid down that the only

measures to be carried through by February 18 were the appointment of Seyss-Inquart; the admission of National Socialists to the
Fatherland Front; the amnesty; financial arrangements; and the
agreement on the press. Section 2 of Article II was rejected and in
its place an undertaking was given to admit individual National
Socialists into the Fatherland Front, the Government, and other
organizations. The amnesty was to cover only National Socialists
living in Austria and would not refer to those who had sought
refuge in Germany, whom Schuschnigg regarded as completely
untrustworthy. No undertaking was given to appoint Glaise-
Horstenau as War Minister, although a change in the Chief of the
General Staff was proposed. Dr Fischboeck was not to be appointed
Minister of Finance, but only to be given a position of influence in
the financial administration.

The main concession concerned the appointment of Seyss-
Inquart. This was no great sacrifice on Schuschnigg's part, as the
post was already held by Glaise-Horstenau. What did provoke
much argument was the extension of Seyss-Inquart's powers to
include control of the police. Schuschnigg might well have doubted
the advisability of handing over to him the security services, in
case he should use them to favour the radical elements in the
country. In fact, nothing of the sort occurred. The Vienna Chief
of Police, Skubl, a man who enjoyed Schuschnigg's confidence,
remained at his post as head of the security services. Many years
later, at the Nuremberg trial he declared on oath that no attempt
had been made to interfere with his authority.

After our long conversation, the Chancellor went in to see
Hitler again. I could soon hear that the tone of the discussion was
not what it should have been, and I therefore took it upon myself
to break in. Entering the study, I found Hitler launched on a tirade
about Schuschnigg having no feeling for German history and joint
responsibility. 'I have now known the Chancellor for four years,'
I said, interrupting Hitler, 'and I can guarantee that he is as German
in his way of thinking as you are. Your differences are not based
on divergent ideas of patriotism, but rather on your own attitude
to the outside world. The representative of a sovereign state has
the right and the duty to make his views known.'

Hitler seemed surprised. 'That is so. But Herr von Papen, you
proved yourself to be a great German on another occasion – when
Hindenburg asked you to form a Cabinet under my leadership. If

Herr von Schuschnigg were to offer me his hand today and enter into a new relationship between Austria and the Reich, he would also be known to history as a great German.'

'I agree,' I said, 'that the position of Germany in Central Europe can only be restored in close association with Austria. Up till now you have always said that this situation must be reached not by force, but by gradually interweaving the two countries' affairs. I don't understand this sudden urgency. Give the Chancellor time. Do not demand measures which he is not able to carry out by himself.'

Thereupon the two leaders parted again, in order that Schuschnigg should have time for further reflection.

In his book Schuschnigg gives only a fragmentary account of this conversation, in which I, as German Ambassador, took his part against Hitler. However, he admits that when he rejoined Hitler about half an hour later, the Führer said, 'For the first time in my life I have made up my mind to reconsider a final decision.' The ice was broken and the way clear for an agreed solution. The chief difficulty remained the appointment of Seyss-Inquart. The Austrians had finally agreed to accept him, but Hitler now began to object to him. He called for me again and shouted, 'What sort of a man is this Seyss-Inquart? I don't know him, he's not even a party member.' This was simply a tactical device. He knew perfectly well who Seyss-Inquart was, but having made certain concessions himself, he apparently wanted to get someone of more radical views appointed as Minister of the Interior.

I tried to represent Seyss-Inquart as a man of National Socialist sympathies, although my chief reason for favouring him was that I considered him a person of conservative leanings. I then remembered my early-morning conversation with Dr Muehlmann. 'I met a well-known Austrian National Socialist this morning,' I said, 'Dr Muehlmann. You will find his opinion of Seyss-Inquart a better guide than anything I can say.' Dr Muehlmann was then sent for, and Hitler, apparently satisfied by his remarks, renounced his opposition to the appointment.

Schuschnigg and Schmidt, content with his agreement on this point, were nevertheless astonished at Muehlmann's intervention. They seemed to think that I was responsible for his presence and had engineered the whole episode. It was made clear at Nuremberg that he had been sent as a sort of spy by Zernatto, and had been told about the proposed conference by Keppler. Schuschnigg's later accusation, that I broke our agreement to preserve the secrecy of his meeting with Hitler, is therefore completely unfounded.

It was late at night before the various differences were resolved and the agreed text signed by Schuschnigg and Hitler. All of us were worn out, and I could well understand why Schuschnigg and Schmidt declined Hitler's invitation to dinner. His pressure tactics, which had overshadowed the results, made his concessions seem more negative than they were. The return journey to Salzburg started about eleven o'clock at night in an oppressive silence. Schuschnigg clearly did not wish to enter into any discussion of the day's events. However, I could not refrain from saying to him, 'Now you have some idea, *Herr Bundeskanzler*, how difficult it is to deal with such an unstable person.'

Having been relieved of my post in Vienna, I had had no official reason for taking part in the discussion at all. I had wished only to be of some service in the matter. If Schuschnigg had known Hitler better, and had answered his insults in kind or shown the same determination, events might have taken a less dramatic turn. He was not yet bound to the agreement. If he had felt convinced that the draft they had signed meant the eclipse of Austria, he could still have sheltered behind the provision that the final decisions could only be taken by the Federal President, and he could then have offered his resignation.

It only remains to add that a comparison of the signed agreement with the *Punktationen* worked out before he left Vienna, shows that the new appointment to the Ministry of the Interior, and the inclusion of control of the police in its provisions, were the only important concession not planned by Schuschnigg in advance. It was easy to blame me later on and to say that he had been surprised by all the demands that were presented.

Hitler still had publicly to explain the Wehrmacht crisis and its solution. He had therefore called a meeting of the Reichstag for February 20. He had told Schuschnigg that he wanted to deal with the Austro-German problem in his speech, and had therefore asked that certain measures they had agreed upon should be carried out by February 18. No doubt he wished to divert attention from the rather ugly picture of intrigue in the Wehrmacht by providing some outstanding success in the field of foreign policy. This may well explain the pressure he had brought to bear on Schuschnigg, although it certainly does not excuse it. His request gave the Austrians five days' grace.

If the Austrians wished to present themselves to the world as the injured party, and were already thinking of a plebiscite, this, rather than three weeks later, was surely the moment for an international showdown with Germany? The Cabinet, having told the world that the new agreement had been signed under duress and was inconsistent with the guarantees of sovereignty in the July Agreement, could have resigned. However, the Chancellor could not make up his mind. Foreign reaction showed that Italy supported Hitler, that Great Britain did not feel herself directly affected, and that only France, in the opinion of Herr Vollgruber, the Austrian Minister in Paris, was likely to fight for Austria. The Austrian President decided in the meantime to give the agreement his support. Berlin was advised on February 15 that it had been accepted, and on the 18th that the political clauses had been dealt with. The agreed communiqué was then published in both countries.

The meeting in Berchtesgaden and the acceptance of the agreement had brought my mission to an end, and the President and the Austrian Cabinet now invited me to a farewell luncheon. If the 'accepted' version of my part in all that had happened were true, this function would surely have been a very stiff and formal affair. The President and his ministers, however, were quite exceptionally kind and friendly. I was given the highest Austrian decoration, and at the moment of the President's toast in my honour, Guido Schmidt shouted, to the amusement of the whole company, 'How about going to Berlin now as our Ambassador?' In the course of the last few days, my wife and I were overwhelmed with handsome presents, each of them an appreciation of the efforts I had made in the last four years to improve the relations between the two countries.

* * *

Hitler's speech to the Reichstag aroused feverish expectations. In his main reference to Austria, he declared:

'I am happy to be able to announce that during the last few days it has been possible to reach a further measure of agreement with a country which, for a variety of reasons, is particularly near to us. The Reich and German Austria belong together, not only because they are inhabited by the same people, but because they share a common history and culture.

'The difficulties that became apparent in carrying out the agreement of July 11, 1936, compelled us to attempt the removal of the misunderstandings and obstacles to a final settlement. If we had not taken this step, it is certain that one day, whether by accident or design, an impossible situation would have arisen that would have had catastrophic results.

'I am happy to be able to tell you that this view is fully shared by the Austrian Federal Chancellor, whom I invited to visit me. Our main aim was to relieve the tension by granting to those Austrian citizens who support National Socialist ideas, the same rights as those accorded to every other citizen. A general amnesty is to be proclaimed, and friendly co-operation between the two countries in every field has been assured by an agreement which fulfils the spirit of that of July 11.

'I would like to thank the Austrian Chancellor in my own name, and in that of the German people, for his understanding and kindness in accepting my invitation to devise a way of serving the best interests of our two countries – the interests, rather, of the German peoples as a whole, whose sons we all are, wherever we may have been born.'

I still contend that in speaking thus Hitler meant what he said. He was pleased at the success he had gained and wished to reach his goal without the use of force. By speaking in such friendly terms he certainly wished to make things easier for the Austrian Chancellor. Guido Schmidt found the speech completely satisfactory, and felt it created an atmosphere which would give time for the working out of normal relations.

Four days later Schuschnigg made a public reply in the Austrian Parliament. Still smarting under the treatment he had received at Berchtesgaden, he made little attempt to respond to Hitler's friendly overtures. Though he referred to the agreement that had just been signed as a milestone in the history of the relations between the two countries, he still went to great pains to emphasize the need for Austrian independence. In my report to Hitler the next day – the last I was to write from Austria – I tried to excuse Schuschnigg's tone by explaining that in view of considerable opposition to some of the concessions that had been granted, he was finding it necessary to secure his position within the Fatherland Front. Thus, my last official act was to try to remove the sting from this psychologically unfortunate speech.

In the meantime there had been a meeting on February 21 between Hitler, Goering, Keppler and Leopold. I had insisted that Leopold should be forbidden residence in Austria. Hitler accused him of having pursued a thoroughly irresponsible policy, which had included plans for an uprising and an invasion by German troops. Most of the difficulties of the situation had now been removed by negotiation, and Leopold was told that his actions could very well have placed Hitler in a highly embarrassing situation. Relations with Austria must now be organized on an entirely different basis, and Hitler had therefore finally made up his mind that Leopold and his chief collaborators must live in Germany. The leadership of the party in Austria would devolve upon Klausner, who would have to understand that all illegal activities would be forbidden. Hitler pointed out that Seyss-Inquart had a very difficult task and must be fully supported by the Party, which must seek expression of its ideals within the framework of the Fatherland Front. The radical elements had got to be kept in check and it must be realized that from time to time Seyss-Inquart might even have to order the arrest of certain Nazis. These measures hardly confirm the arguments of those who suggest that Hitler was already plotting the Anschluss by force.

On February 26 I paid my final visit to Herr Schuschnigg. During the years I had spent in Austria, my efforts to establish any sort of warm personal contact with him had failed. Intellectually he was a highly gifted man with great academic knowledge. But I had always found him difficult to negotiate with and to talk to. Perhaps he was particularly careful what he said in my presence. In any case, I had always found it impossible to obtain from him any firm opinion on political subjects. As an ambassador taking his leave, I could have restricted my conversation to a pure exchange of formalities. Instead, I preferred to dwell once again on the dangers inherent in the situation, and made a last appeal for his co-operation in relieving the tension. While his speech had contained warm words for Austria's German mission, his dramatic references to Austrian independence, even if they were only designed for internal consumption, had had a decisive effect on the previous day's debate in the French Chamber of Deputies. For four years I had striven to remove the Austrian problem from the field of European discussion, and had tried to turn it into a domestic question between our two countries. I much regretted that it had again become a matter for European concern, and I made it clear that any form of Austrian independence which rested on French and Czech assistance would arouse new passions in Germany and give rise to arguments which might easily threaten the agreement we had just signed. I asked the Chancellor to bear in mind the dangers of trying to bolster Austria's position with help from outside Germany, and he assured me that this thought was uppermost in his mind.

That same evening I left for Kitzbühl to enjoy a few days skiing and rest before returning home. There I met Count Kageneck, who had been one of my principal assistants in Berlin when I was Vice-Chancellor, and we were joined shortly by Wilhelm von Ketteler, my faithful assistant in Vienna. With my imminent departure, the future of Austro-German relations might well become influenced by radical elements which I would no longer be in a position to restrain, and we still felt that the plan we had devised when I was first dismissed should be carried out and that some evidence of my four years' work in Vienna should be preserved. Ketteler had therefore brought copies of my reports to Hitler, as well as of all my important correspondence with the Austrian Government. These copies we intended to deposit in a place of safety, in case they should ever be required as proof of my policy. After two days' ski-ing, Ketteler and Kageneck drove off together to Switzerland, where they were to arrange for the documents to be placed in a safe deposit. On March 8 I returned to Vienna to pack up my furniture. The next day Schuschnigg sprang his plebiscite surprise.

* * *

Herr Vollgrubber, the Austrian Minister in Paris, had already sent a long report to Schuschnigg on February 26, giving a résumé of the foreign affairs debate in the French Chamber. Most of the speakers had expressed their conviction that France must show a positive attitude on the question of Austrian independence, as the only means of maintaining peace and French influence in Europe. The Berchtesgaden agreement was not regarded as a likely instrument for the preservation of peace. On March 7, Vollgruber sent another report, this time on a conversation he had had with M. Léger, the Permanent Secretary of the Foreign Ministry, and one of the principal arbiters of French foreign policy.

M. Léger had made it clear that France had no intention of allowing her position in Europe to be threatened by Germany. The defence of Austrian independence was one of the principal aims of her foreign policy, though France could take no positive action unless there was an open threat from Germany against which Austria reacted. The French Parliament had been much exercised by reports of the pressure that Hitler had brought to bear on the Austrian Federal Chancellor, and the French Government, Vollgruber insisted, would be able to obtain almost any mandate it might require, should the situation develop unfavourably.

This despatch can only be taken to mean that if Schuschnigg felt himself threatened, and was able to prove that the majority of the Austrian people stood behind him, France would be prepared to intervene. The French Minister in Vienna, M. Puaux, a close friend and adviser of Schuschnigg, is said to have been the father of the plebiscite idea. Schuschnigg certainly adopted it on his own responsibility, but the French Government of the day must bear its share for the events which now followed.

The Austrian Chancellor had gone to a meeting of the Fatherland Front at Innsbruck, where he had decided to announce the holding of a plebiscite on the question of Austrian independence. The population was to be asked to answer 'yes' or 'no' to the question whether they desired Austria to remain independent. This announcement was made on a Wednesday night, and the referendum was due to take place on the following Sunday; that is to say, three days were available for its organization. For years the electoral register had not been kept up to date, there would be no time to organize the ballot properly in the more isolated mountain regions (where, incidentally, the National Socialists were strongly represented) and the younger generation had not been registered as voters at all. Moreover, the Austrian Constitution made no provision for such a referendum, and neither the Government nor the President had promulgated any ordinance which would make it legal. It was obvious to me that Hitler's reaction to this would be violent. He would regard this decision of Schuschnigg's simply as a propaganda manœuvre designed to annul the

results of the Berchtesgaden conference. My first thought, therefore, was to obtain a postponement of the plebiscite, so as to allow
proper time for its preparation and to have the question phrased
more objectively.

I suggested a new form of words which, while including all
Schuschnigg's points, was drafted in a manner likely to cause
Hitler less offence. 'We want a free and German Austria, an independent and socially just Austria, a Christian and united Austria;
an Austria which will pursue its German mission in close accord-'
ance with the Reich.'

This would have been the best way of meeting Hitler's objections
without calling on the Austrian Chancellor to make undue concessions. I no longer held any official post and could only act as a
private person. I made the above suggestions to Schuschnigg, but
they were turned down flat. There was little else for me to do.
Guido Schmidt had told von Stein, the chargé d'affaires and my
successor, that it was a purely internal matter and did not concern
him. In spite of the fact that Mussolini warned Schuschnigg that
he had prepared a bomb which would explode in his hand, the
Chancellor's mind seemed to be made up.

Schuschnigg, after all, was the responsible leader of a sovereign
State. No one could deny him the right to defend its sovereignty
by every means at his disposal. Moreover, the Austrian Nazis,
encouraged by the concessions which the Chancellor had been
obliged to make in Berchtesgaden, had started a new campaign to
weaken his position, not only in the Fatherland Front but in the
country as a whole. His decision to adopt this new measure is
therefore understandable, particularly in view of his determined
efforts during the preceding four years to secure his country's
international position. His honourable defence of a principle he
believed to be right is all the more praiseworthy when set beside
the inexcusable treatment he had received at Berchtesgaden. If I
venture to criticize his decision to hold a plebiscite, I do so not in
any personal sense. Where we differed was in our conceptions of
Austria's rôle within the framework of the future of the German
peoples: a conception with which Schuschnigg's international
policies seemed to me irreconcilable.

On March 11, as I was to learn later, a message arrived for
Seyss-Inquart from Hitler asking him to intervene with the
Austrian Chancellor to postpone the plebiscite. This request was

presented in the form of an ultimatum accompanied by threats. Seyss-Inquart went to see Schuschnigg, who again refused to consider the idea. Hitler's action in addressing himself directly to the Austrian Minister of the Interior was in fact in accordance with the terms of the Berchtesgaden agreement; but the developments of the next day or two were to show how unfortunate it was that there was no German diplomatic representative in Vienna able to act as an intermediary in the affair. Stein was not known to Hitler personally and was much disliked by the Austrian Cabinet for his Nazi sentiments. He was therefore in no position to mediate, nor to prevent the intervention of Goering, who now took a leading part in the affair, using General Muff, the German military attaché in Vienna, as his representative.

Late on the Thursday evening I received a telephone call from Hitler ordering me to go immediately to Berlin. A night flight seemed to me somewhat unnecessary, and I therefore told the Chancellery that I would be in Berlin at nine o'clock the next morning. I was at a loss to understand the reason for this order. Either Hitler wished to remove me from the centre of events, fearing perhaps that I might intervene in some way contrary to his plans, or he wished to seek my advice about the crisis; in which case there was still some chance of my attempting to find a compromise, whereas in Vienna I had no rôle whatsoever to play.

I drove to the airport at six o'clock on a drizzling March morning, the beginning of a day I shall never forget. I reached the Reich Chancellery at about nine o'clock, and found the main salon already full of people. There was that tension in the air that I had so often noticed as an accompaniment to Hitler's actions. In the days of my own Chancellorship, and before, whenever grave decisions were to be taken, the persons consulted were the responsible ministers and their immediate advisers. Now everyone, who by reason of duty, curiosity, employment or intrigue, had any connection with the subject discussed, seemed to be present. Neurath was there, representing Ribbentrop, who at this moment was making his official farewells in London. Frick, the Minister of the Interior, was there with several of his officials. Goebbels was there with his cohorts from the Propaganda Ministry. Himmler was there, surrounded by a dozen giant S.S. officers, and Brauchitsch, Keitel and their adjutants were there as representatives of the armed forces. I was immediately pounced upon by everyone for news of the situation in Vienna. I could only report that both the Fatherland Front and the opposition seemed to be carrying their parades and propaganda to a climax and that it was difficult to tell which side was being the more offensive.

I was then ushered in to Hitler, who was in a state bordering on hysteria. I let him have his say, as usual, and then tried to explain why Schuschnigg had found it necessary, in his speech of February 24, to speak so sharply. This, I said, had aroused passions in both the Austrian camps. But it would still be possible, I thought, to persuade him to postpone the plebiscite if we were to point out that it would be not only unconstitutional but quite impossible to organize it on a fair and free basis within a space of three days. At the same time, I warned Hitler against taking any military measures. There was no way of telling how the other Great Powers would react, and the idea of a European war over the German question, or of the shedding of blood between the two brother nations, was equally appalling. The only solution which could have any historical justification would be one arrived at by peaceful means, not by the use of the sword. I thought my words had some effect. He certainly became quieter and more thoughtful. After our interview I spent the rest of the time in the ante-roon of the Chancellery without playing any part in the dramatic events of the day. In fact, it was extremely difficult to find out what was going on.

Seyss-Inquart had got his message from Hitler that morning, and Goering had the first of his many telephone conversations with Seyss-Inquart at three o'clock the same afternoon. I am still convinced that any counter-proposal from Schuschnigg during this period would have entirely changed the situation.

The world now knows, from records of the telephone conversations between Berlin and Vienna that afternoon – presented as evidence at Nuremberg – how the fate of Austria was decided during the next few hours. Goering ordered Seyss-Inquart to resign, thereby obliging Schuschnigg to do the same, and required the Austrian Federal President to call on Seyss-Inquart to form a new Cabinet favourable to the opposition. About five o'clock there came a report that this was being done. Most of us had had little to do during the intervening hours. We were conscious only that vital decisions were being taken, in which most of those in the salons and waiting-rooms had no part to play.

When the news of Schuschnigg's resignation came through, I

went immediately to Hitler and begged him to give up the idea of sending troops into Austria. The whole matter was in the process of being solved and there was no need for further risks. Hitler agreed and, turning to Keitel, said: 'Tell Brauchitsch immediately that the orders for the troops to march have been cancelled.' I had been spending some hours in conversation with the military leaders. All of them were earnestly hoping that Hitler's threat of invasion was a bluff and that they would not have to deal with Italian or Czech intervention, not to mention the possible effects of the reaction in France. Now, as Brauchitsch came into the room again to receive Keitel's message, he heaved a sigh of relief and said, 'Thank God we have been spared that.'

However, the ordeal was not at an end. When the news came through that the Austrian President was refusing to entrust Seyss-Inquart with the formation of a new Cabinet, Seyss-Inquart was prevailed upon to say he would send a telegram asking for the intervention of German troops to maintain law and order. Where-upon the orders to march were given again. Seyss-Inquart, in fact, had been more than unwilling to meet Goering's demands. The situation in Vienna in no way made German intervention necessary. We now know that he sent no such telegram, but that the German Minister of Posts and Telegraphs had a suitable telegram concocted after the event and deposited in the files. I remember that at the time Neurath came out into one of the ante-rooms and told us that Seyss-Inquart was about to send a telegram asking for armed intervention. 'For heaven's sake,' I said, 'see that it does not turn out to be a second Ems Telegram.[1] The request must be genuine and in black and white.' Neurath agreed nervously and hurried off to a telephone booth.

Goering had been responsible for all the telephone conversations with Vienna, and the rest of us in the ante-rooms were dependent entirely on rumour for news of the way things were going. The situation in Vienna was described to us as completely out of hand. Street clashes were taking place and civil war seemed imminent.

[1] In 1870 the French Foreign Office sent a telegram to King Wilhelm of Prussia who was taking the waters at Ems. In it they added humiliating conditions to the settlement of the Franco-Prussian crisis. Bismarck published the telegram in a shortened form, making the French demands appear even more insulting. This 'editing' helped to precipitate the Franco-Prussian war.

When, at a quarter to nine that night, Hitler handed Brauchitsch the written order to begin military operations at dawn the next morning, I felt the whole world of my hopes had collapsed. Armed intervention could only lead to war and the shedding of blood between two brother nations. It would probably mean a European conflict. When I left the Chancellery I was in despair. Even Bismarck did not succeed in re-establishing the Holy Roman Empire of German nations. The circumstances had obliged him to go no further than forming a close alliance with the Danube Monarchy. It had always been a cardinal point of his policy never to endanger friendly relations between Berlin and Vienna. Now, when it had seemed that we were on the point of establishing between the German part of the Danube Monarchy and the Reich a relationship analogous to the old Empire, Hitler appeared to have ruined the opportunity by a single act of criminal irresponsibility. His decision seemed to me a betrayal of German history.

* * *

The march into Austria spared the German people, for the time being, from harvesting the bitter fruits of their leader's dilettantist policies. Contrary to my fears, not a shot was fired, and the German Army was greeted with jubilation and bouquets. Though Hitler's methods were a disgrace to our history, for the moment they were overshadowed by the extraordinary enthusiasm with which the majority of Austrians greeted this act of union. Historians who still speak of the rape of Austria would do well to study the press reports of those days – not merely those published in Germany, but by foreign correspondents from all countries who either worked in Vienna or were attracted there by the crisis. Even those who were most critical of the political developments could not disguise the enthusiasm with which the German troops were greeted on their way to Vienna. The inner meaning of those historic days fired an immense number of people who had never at any time belonged to the illegal opposition. The ties of kinship and a common history lasting more than a thousand years proved stronger than political expediency. None of this excuses Hitler's methods, but it shows how ill-advised were all those who, since 1918, had done their best to prevent the union of the two countries.

The referendum on April 10 approved the Anschluss law by an overwhelming majority. National Socialist electoral methods may have increased the percentage in favour of union, but there is no doubt whatever that the general feeling of relief and enthusiasm would have assured a strong majority.

Like everyone else, I was caught up in the general enthusiasm and overwhelmed by the historical magnitude of the occasion – the union of the two German peoples. I was still in Berlin on March 13, when I received a telegram from Hitler ordering me to go to Vienna the next morning. The same day the German radio announced that I had been awarded the Gold Medal of the Party. This I was to learn for the first time when I arrived in Vienna. At the Tempelhof aerodrome in Berlin I met Lammers, the State Secretary of the Reichs Chancellery, who travelled with me in the plane. Our conversation turned to the future. Reports from the other European capitals showed that there was no fear of an international conflict. Everything now depended on statesmanlike handling of the German problem and the reconciliation of the opposing camps. Lammers, following the same line of thought, suggested that the best solution would be for me to become *Reichsstatthalter* (Federal Governor) of Austria. I knew the problem better than anyone, he said, and would be able to protect Austria's traditions, while building a cultural bridge between Northern and Southern Germany. It occurred to me that this was perhaps the reason for my being invited to Vienna, so I told Lammers to let Hitler know that in view of my experiences over the last few weeks, and his breach of the undertaking he had given me at Bayreuth, I should not be able to accept such a post.

Friends and critics alike have questioned my motives in returning to Vienna. I can only say that I shared the general intoxication resulting from the great event which had just taken place, but I was ready to impress upon Hitler once again to what degree future developments would depend on his handling of the Austrian problem, now that the act of union had been accomplished without bloodshed.

We landed at Aspern aerodrome, near Vienna. Driving into the city, I felt quite overcome by the extraordinary atmosphere of jubilation. Nazi flags, which had no doubt been brought in thousands from Germany, were flying everywhere. But it would have been useless to pretend that the immense waves of people thronging Vienna's wide streets were there by order, or that their high spirits were not completely spontaneous. Hitler, whom I found at the saluting base opposite the Hofburg, I can only describe as being in a state of ecstasy. I introduced the foreign diplomatic representatives to him, including the Ministers of Poland, Hungary, Bulgaria, Yugoslavia and Italy. We then settled down to watch the parade, in which Austrian units, some of them in colourful Hussar uniforms, also took part.

During a pause in the parade I managed to get in a few words with Hitler about the tremendous task which still lay ahead in Austria. Above all, I told him, he must come to terms with the Church. Austria was a Catholic country, and if the Church was to be subjected to the sort of attacks it had suffered in Germany, all this enthusiasm for the Anschluss would evaporate within a few weeks. Delight at the union with Germany could only be maintained if Austria was administered according to Austrian lights, with all her traditions duly respected.

'Have no fear,' he told me, 'I know that better than anyone.'

'In that case,' I said, 'it is surely essential that you give some immediate sign of your intentions. Why don't you see Cardinal Innitzer as soon as this parade is finished, and give him an assurance to this effect?'

'Certainly,' Hitler answered. 'Tell him that I will be delighted to see him in the Hotel Imperial.'

I was more than relieved by this spontaneous reaction, especially as the Concordat which I had signed, and which was still in force, did not extend its provisions to Austria. I sent an Austrian friend of mine to the Cardinal's residence with Hitler's invitation, and expressed my satisfaction at being able to render this last service before I left Vienna.

Pope Pius XI, in his encyclical *With Burning Anxiety* of March 14, 1937, had condemned in strong words the National Socialist doctrine of religious persecution. Even so, he still expressed the desire that some understanding might yet be arrived at. In spite of their breaches of the Concordat, he sought to bring the National Socialists to reason, and hoped for a return to the terms of the agreement. He did not want to break with the Reich Government or to recall the Papal Nuncio. Am I then open to such strict criticism for considering it my duty to press for the application of the Concordat terms to Austria?

I was not present at the hour's conversation between Hitler and the Cardinal, but Innitzer seemed gratified and content as I con-

ducted him back to his palace. He had assured Hitler of the loyalty
of Austria's Catholics, providing the religious freedom laid down
in the Concordat was guaranteed. He expressed a particular wish
that Austria's youth should not be prevented from playing their
part in the work of the Church and its associations. All this Hitler
had agreed to, he told me, remarking that, as an Austrian himself,
he desired the best possible relations between the country of his
birth and the Reich. This was the last time I saw the Cardinal. As
we parted, he thanked me for having arranged the meeting.

★   ★   ★

All these demonstrations soon acquired a bitter taste for me.
Directly I arrived in Vienna I was told that my friend and colleague,
Wilhelm von Ketteler, had disappeared on Sunday night, March 13.
He had spent the evening with my secretary, Fräulein Rose, who
lived not far from the Legation, and had left her flat shortly before
midnight. Having previously parked his car in the Legation compound, he set off to collect it. Fräulein Rose had noticed as he
walked away that there were three men behind him. On Monday
morning his car was still where he had left it, his flat was empty,
and he had apparently not returned there. He was never seen alive
again. In view of his strained relations with the party, it was
reasonable to suppose that he might have left Vienna secretly and
made his way to friends in the country or in Hungary. He must
certainly have known that the first Gestapo units had arrived in
Vienna on Friday, because some of them had been billeted in the
Legation. However, enquiries among his friends produced no clue
as to what had happened to him. Nor had he given any indication
to my secretary, with whom he had worked for many years and
who was on terms of complete mutual confidence with him, that
he had reason to doubt his safety or that he felt it wise to leave
Vienna. Anxiety over his disappearance overshadowed all the
other emotions of those days. The mere thought that he might
have met the same fate as Bose filled me with horror and despair.

As it now seemed possible that there had been foul play, I
decided to get in touch with the Gestapo, which had taken over
the direction of all police duties in Vienna, although there seemed
little point in asking for the assistance of the agency which in all
probability was responsible for Ketteler's disappearance. On Tuesday morning, however, I went to see Heydrich. I gave him an

account of Ketteler's disappearance and asked if he had any news of his whereabouts. Heydrich assumed an air of astonishment and undertook to start a search immediately. That same evening I met Himmler by chance in front of the Imperial Hotel and gave him a description of the affair. Baroness Stotzingen, my other secretary, was with me. She was an impulsive and courageous young person who, like the rest of us, was in a state of great agitation over the Ketteler business. Suddenly she turned to Himmler and said, 'Herr Himmler, no doubt all this is some new Gestapo *Schweinerei*. I know you have been after him for some time, and your people have probably already carried him off to a concentration camp.' Himmler denied this heatedly and promised that immediate enquiries would be made. The next few days brought no results, so I went again to Heydrich, who had by now taken over control of the Austrian police, and asked him to announce in the press that I would offer a reward of 20,000 marks for any information leading to the discovery of Ketteler. There was always the hope that he might have fled abroad, and on my return to Germany I tried to comfort his mother with this idea.

As soon as I got back to Germany I wrote to Hitler, giving him details of the affair and asking for his help, especially if it should turn out that the Gestapo had, after all, had a hand in the matter and Ketteler was now in some concentration camp. To this letter I received no reply. I therefore asked for a personal interview, but this was refused on some specious excuse. The whole affair began to look extremely suspicious. On such occasions Hitler always became evasive. In the meantime, one of Ketteler's younger brothers had gone to Vienna to carry out further investigations with the help of a private detective.

The Gestapo and the Nazi extremists were clearly in the ascendant, but as long as there was any hope of finding Ketteler alive it was essential for me to maintain some sort of contact with the leading members of the party. Although it had been my intention to hand back the Gold Medal of the Party which had been awarded me, this seemed hardly the moment for such a gesture.

In searching Ketteler's flat, the Gestapo had found some Swiss money and also evidence of his recent journey to Switzerland on my behalf. They then started to interrogate his friends, including, one must assume, a man named Bochow who had worked on my

staff as a foreign press monitor when I was Vice-Chancellor.
Bochow had been at one time a foreign correspondent in England
and spoke perfect English. His immediate chief on my staff had
been Bose, who was shot by the Gestapo on June 30, 1934, when
they occupied the Vice-Chancellery. Soon after I had taken up my
post in Vienna, Bochow had appeared, and had told Ketteler,
whom he knew, that he had got away from the Gestapo and was
settling down in Vienna as part-time correspondent for certain
newspapers. Ketteler had no suspicions, and in course of time they
became close friends. Without any real reason for doing so, I constantly warned him against associating too closely with Bochow,
who was, I am convinced, a Gestapo spy sent to Vienna to keep an
eye on me.

As I was getting nowhere with Hitler, I turned to Goering. His
adjutant, General Bodenschatz, told me that his chief, who had
little doubt that Ketteler had been murdered on Heydrich's orders,
had flown into a rage, and told Bodenschatz that he would get
Hitler to deal with Heydrich. Goering sent for the Gestapo files on
the case and told me he would give me full support in clearing it
up. But when I visited him a second time his mood was very
different. He greeted me with the accusation that it was now
known that in February Ketteler had taken all my secret files to
Switzerland. This, he said, was a very serious crime, involving
heavy penalties. From a voluminous file he then read out details of
alleged treasonable activities by Ketteler, including a plan to
assassinate Hitler.

Ketteler had always had the idea that the only way to get rid of
Hitler would be to kill him, and we had had many conversations
on the subject. I remember him once suggesting that it should be
possible to shoot Hitler with a long-range rifle, equipped with a
silencer, from one of the windows in the Kaiserhof Hotel in Berlin,
which was only 150 yards from the balcony of the Reich Chancellery. I told him that I did not believe in such methods, that they
were rather childish, and tried to laugh him out of it by telling
him he was not going to mix me up in any such Wild West
escapades. I still do not believe that Ketteler committed any of this
to paper. The Gestapo can have learnt of his plans only from someone else with whom he must have discussed them. Who this must
have been, I have already said.

At first, I was speechless. Still, there was little point in denying

I had sent the files abroad, so I said to Goering: 'I sent my papers to Switzerland after my dismissal from Vienna, so as to be able to prove that my policy in Austria had been one of peaceful evolution, and that at no time had I envisaged an Anschluss by force. My dismissal showed clearly that this policy was no longer to the Führer's liking. He wanted to solve the Austrian problem by other methods, in which I wished to have no part. I am fully aware of the seriousness of my action, and if I am to be tried for treason, I shall make it clear that the responsibility was entirely mine, and that Ketteler was merely carrying out my orders.' As for the other accusations against Ketteler, I told Goering that they were pure invention, intended by the Gestapo to justify his liquidation, if this should ever come to light.

My situation was now exceedingly difficult. I expected to be arrested any day on a charge of high treason. The investigation in Vienna was producing no results, except that Bochow had now disappeared as well. By this time there was no doubt in my mind that he was the villain of the piece. One of the accusations that Goering had read out from the file concerned certain plans of Ketteler's to set up a private transmitting station near Salzburg during the year 1937. This was to be manned by friends who would keep us informed of any unusual military preparations on the German side of the frontier. This proposition had seemed to me fantastic, and I had declined to provide funds for it. The only other person with whom Ketteler could possibly have discussed it was Bochow, whom he regarded as a refugee from the Gestapo. The evening I was dismissed, his first request was to pass on the news to Bochow, so that 'the poor devil' could earn a few extra shillings for his exclusive information. No doubt he must have told Bochow at some time or other about the business of my secret files.

The only clue which our detective obtained in Vienna was that on the evening when Ketteler left Fräulein Rose's flat, a motor car with a German number plate had been parked nearby for some time. It was noticed by one of the Embassy employees, who took the number. Yet when I asked Himmler to find out to whom this car belonged, the only reply I got was that the car with this registration number had never left Germany. The matter became hopeless. The public prosecutor in Vienna refused to move because he said that the Gestapo had taken over the case, and an appeal to

Kaltenbrunner, who was now in charge of the Vienna police, produced no results. When I raised the reward for information to 50,000 marks, I found that no newspaper was prepared to carry the advertisement.

At the end of April we received news that a corpse had been fished out of the Danube at Hainburg, well below Vienna. Ketteler's brother dashed to the place and identified the body, which was taken over by the Gestapo, in spite of our attempts to have a post-mortem carried out. In the end, we received official intimation that there was no indication of foul play, and that certain wounds on the body must have been caused by the propellers of river steamers. There was no doubt in my mind that Ketteler was killed by the Gestapo and thrown into the Danube.

We had his remains brought back to Germany and he was buried at his parents' home in Westphalia. After four years I was again under the obligation of saying a few last words about an old friend. In Berlin, in 1934, it had been Bose, and now it was another of my faithful and devoted colleagues. On both occasions we stood under the shadow of brutal force that was prepared to strangle any sign of opposition at birth and cared little what methods it used. Ketteler had survived the affair of June 30, 1934. After the failure of his efforts to intercede with Hindenburg to restore law and order, he had carried on the fight. After the murder of Dollfuss, when we decided that an effort should be made to reintroduce decent standards into Germany's policy in Austria, it was Ketteler who finally convinced me that the best interests of our country demanded my presence there. He became my closest and dearest friend.

* * *

Looking back on my four years in Austria, I can only say this: the task I undertook at Bayreuth in 1934, of improving relations between the two countries and fostering the idea of union between them by evolutionary methods, could only have been accomplished if the Austrian Nazi Party had been completely divorced from the party in Germany. The question of union, although it affected the German peoples as a whole, was one that could only be solved on Austrian initiative. This was the path I set myself to tread.

However, the connection between the two parties, and the fact that they both recognized the same head, were to prove stronger than I was. There was, in the last resort, no way of making Hitler see reason. By pressing home the point at every opportunity, I was able to convince him on certain occasions that violent methods would lead to no satisfactory conclusion. But although, while I retained my appointment in Vienna, I was sometimes able to check the designs of his radical party colleagues, they always prevailed in the end.

From the middle of 1937 onwards, the overall direction of Austro-German affairs was taken more and more out of my hands. Goering's insatiable ambition for more influence in the international field had succeeded to an extent which I underrated at the time; this success being largely due to corresponence with Guido Schmidt and his visit to Mussolini in Rome. Schuschnigg and Schmidt came to regard him as the second most powerful personality in the Reich, and seemed to think that they would reach a better compromise with him than they would through me.

The course of events in the Reich Chancellery on March 11, 1938, revealed the extent to which Goering had become the dominating personality among those who advocated the 'total' solution. It is not generally realized that Hitler at first ordered the military occupation authorities to draft a law in which the two countries were to be united in his person, as head of both States, with Austria retaining an autonomous administration. It was only as a result of the fantastic welcome he received between Linz and Vienna that, on Goering's insistence, he made up his mind to incorporate Austria into the Reich.

In spite of all his assurances to me, and disregarding the fruits of my four years' work, Hitler had brought about the Anschluss by force; in spite of all warnings and prophecies, his own methods had proved the most direct and successful. Not only had there been no armed conflict between the two countries, but no foreign power had seen fit to intervene. They adopted the same passive attitude as they had shown towards the reintroduction of conscription in Germany and the reoccupation of the Rhineland. The result was that Hitler became impervious to the advice of all those who wished him to exercise moderation in his foreign policy.

If Schuschnigg had shown more understanding for my line of thought, and if he had advised me in good time of the exchange of correspondence with Goering, events might perhaps have been steered into much more moderate channels. If I had seen what influence the radical wing of the party had gained, and if I had known that the question of my dismissal was under debate, I could have taken fresh steps again to counter the radical wing's influence on Hitler. When I was relieved of my duties on February 4, it proved at least that Hitler had realized he would not be able to conduct any policy of aggression with my support.

PART FIVE

FROM ANKARA TO NUREMBERG

CHAPTER XXIV

WAR BREAKS OUT

Return to Germany – Ribbentrop is difficult – Request to King of Sweden – Italy invades Albania – Offer of Ankara post – My conditions – Hitler revokes Naval Pact – Arrival in Istanbul – Turkish fears – I intercede with Ribbentrop and Ciano – I see Hitler again – Ribbentrop flies to Moscow – War with Poland – Germany's defeat inevitable – My three choices

BACK in Germany from Austria, I retired to our home at Wallerfangen. The estate lay in the middle of a section of the Siegfried Line, and my pleasure at being able to devote some of my time to family and personal affairs, after six years' ceaseless labour, was overshadowed by the sight of all these preparations for a new war. Besides this, I still fully expected to be brought to trial on a charge of high treason, for having sent to Switzerland the files of my reports to Hitler.

Ketteler and Kageneck had deposited them in a bank safe at Zurich, which belonged to one of Ketteler's cousins. Ketteler's death, incidentally, had no connection with this operation, he having 'disappeared' before the Gestapo had had any opportunity of instituting enquiries. However, their subsequent investigations had probably revealed enough clues for them to have discovered the place where the documents had been hidden. If they had once got possession of them, they would have given Heydrich a very useful means of justifying Ketteler's 'disappearance' to Hitler and Goering, besides providing an excuse for squaring accounts with me. Walter Hagen, a particularly well-informed member of the Abwehr organization, states in his book, *Die Geheime Front*,[1] which was published after the war, that Heydrich had never for-

[1] Nibelungen Verlag, Linz-Vienna, 1950.

given himself for allowing me to escape at the time of the Roehm *Putsch*. 'Right up to Heydrich's death, one member of his secret service was under standing instructions to liquidate Papen at all costs,' says Hagen.

I had sent nothing to Switzerland which could have given the Gestapo any material from which to fabricate a case against me. My original draft of the Hindenburg Testament, contrary to certain rumours that have gained circulation, was not included in the material. But I could not tell whether some of Ketteler's own notes about his plans for dealing with Hitler, and of our conversations on the subject, might not have been included. I therefore decided to send Kageneck to Zurich, armed with a pass from the Foreign Office courier service, to bring the files back to Germany before he could be subpœnaed to produce them himself. Kageneck found it impossible to put this mass of files – it was the accumulation of four years' work – in a diplomatic courier's bag without the risk of attracting attention from the Gestapo agents at the frontier. He therefore burnt most of them and brought the rest back to me.

In the meantime, the Gestapo had got wind of our activities. I received a warning from the head of the Foreign Office courier section that Kageneck was about to be arrested. However, he managed to escape to Sweden. I now decided that the best thing to do would be to return the remaining files to Hitler, asking that he should read them again, and if he considered them treasonable, that I should be brought to trial. I repeated that after my unexpected dismissal I had sent them to Switzerland only so that I should be able to prove what policies I had pursued in Austria. Meanwhile, the Gestapo had been following up the scent in Zurich, but in the end they were shown only the empty safe. This tension lasted several weeks, until more important events caused Hitler and Goering to tell Himmler and Heydrich to drop the matter.

I first learnt of the Sudeten crisis through the press. My only intervention in the Godesberg talks consisted of a telegram to Hitler and a letter, written after the Munich affair was over, to Mr Neville Chamberlain. In my telegram I reminded Hitler of his solemn promise to bring peace to the German people and begged him not to miss the opportunity of reaching an agreement with Great Britain. Mr Chamberlain has been much criticized, most unfairly, it seems to me, for his visits to Germany and for the

Munich Agreement. He had two objects in view: time in which to complete the British rearmament programme and, above all, peace at an honourable price. The unrestrained joy of the ordinary people in Germany when war had apparently been averted was sufficient tribute to his courage in making the journeys. I told Mr Chamberlain something of this in a long letter. His reply was lost during the war, but I remember one sentence, in which he said, 'I was so glad to have reached the heart of Germany.' We were to be quickly disillusioned. Hitler's speech in Saarbruecken at the beginning of November showed his anger at Britain's plans for rearmament. While Ribbentrop signed a consultative pact in Paris, such as I had long advocated, Hitler's unstable temperament was already undermining the hopes of a European settlement.

We were to learn at Nuremberg that Hitler by this time had made up his mind to wage war. The meeting described in the Hossbach Protocol between Hitler, Goering and the service chiefs, had taken place on November 5, 1937. Hitler was in fact extremely displeased at Mr Chamberlain's intervention, which did not meet with his aggressive plans. However, the warmth of the British Prime Minister's reception in Germany, and the attitude of Mussolini and Daladier, forced him to accept the compromise for the time being.

It was about this time that I had another encounter with Ribbentrop. I had received an invitation to address the Swedish-German Society in Stockholm, which, with Ribbentrop's permission, I gladly accepted. I had many friends in Sweden, and the King had often shown a personal interest in my political activity. So it seemed an admirable opportunity to present some of my views on the German situation from a country beyond its borders.

On my way through Berlin I called on Ribbentrop, who demanded to see the manuscript of my proposed speech. I told him this was impossible as I never spoke from a script, and that even if I had had one, I would not have submitted it to him. 'You have already made one speech that was hostile to the State,' said Ribbentrop angrily. 'I cannot risk such a danger again.' Then, seeing my look of astonishment, he added, 'That was at Marburg.'

'That speech was made in my official capacity as Vice-Chancellor,' I said. 'You are not in a position to judge or criticize it. If you don't wish me to speak in Stockholm, I shall have to send a telegram to the King, because he intends to be there.' With that I left the room. As I was to find on other occasions, this was the only way to deal with a man so obsessed with prejudice and with his own inferiority complex. He hurried after me and apologized. In the end he expressed his pleasure that someone, in an effort to promote international goodwill, should attempt to explain Germany's slightly confused foreign policy abroad.

My speech appealed to the nations of Europe to combine in defence of peace. The King, in his usual manner, was gracious and understanding, and I suggested to him that as doyen of European monarchs, he should make it clear to Hitler that Germany's present foreign policy could only end in war, and that now, after the Munich Agreement and Ribbentrop's visit to Paris, the way was open for a peaceful solution. The King undertook to consider the matter, but I heard later that he had been overruled by Sweden's Socialist Government.

On my way back through Berlin an unusually polite Ribbentrop offered me the post of Ambassador in Ankara, which had been vacant for three months. I declined it. In February 1939 he renewed the offer, but again I refused it. Some idea of the speed with which the Army was now being built up came to me when I received a request to serve again as commanding officer of an infantry regiment stationed in Wiesbaden. This regiment was to form part of a reserve division to man the Siegfried Line if mobilization was ordered.

In the political sphere, events followed thick and fast. The interview between Hitler and President Hacha of Czechoslovakia, and the march into Prague, finally destroyed Hitler's reputation as an honourable statesman. Everything that had happened up till now could somehow have been explained, but here he stood convicted of breaking the formal promise which he had given Mr Chamberlain, who after going to extremes in attempting to maintain peace, was thus rebuffed. The consequences must have been clear to anyone with the slightest political insight.

I was discussing the situation with friends in Dresden, where I was taking a cure at the Weisse Hirsch Sanatorium, when I got an urgent telephone call from the Foreign Office in Berlin. Ribbentrop was on the line, declaring excitedly that I could no longer refuse the offer of the Turkish post. I asked him what had caused him to make this third offer. He told me that Italy had just invaded Albania – apparently unexpectedly, and with as little reference to

her Axis partner as Hitler had shown in his recent exploits. The
Italian invasion, Ribbentrop said, threatened to complicate the
European situation even further. It seemed an astonishing statement from a man whose recent actions had borne so little relation
to the need for European solidarity. It was obviously impossible to
get a clear picture of the situation on the telephone, so I broke off
my stay in Dresden and set out for Berlin.

It was Good Friday, April 7, 1939, a date I shall always remember.
Once again I had to consider whether to accept, against my will, a
post that was to cause me another five years of inner conflict. I
soon summed up the situation. From my previous knowledge of
Turkey I knew that Kemal Atatürk had solemnly enjoined his
successors always to be on their guard against possible attacks on
the Dardanelles, the major threat to which could be expected
from Fascist Italy. The attack on Albania, and the vainglorious
announcement by Count Ciano that Italy intended to station thirty
divisions there, could only be regarded as a crystallization of this
threat. Atatürk and his successor, Ismet Inönü, had concluded
agreements with the Balkan States which appeared to provide a
first line of defence. But Rumania had just signed a commercial
agreement with Germany, which seemed to indicate a *rapprochement* with the Axis Powers. Bulgaria also had steadfastly refused to
join the Balkan Federation, and the Germanophile and anti-
Turkish sentiments of the Government were a constant source of
apprehension to the Turkish territories on the European mainland. The *Mare Nostrum* fantasies of the Duce must have seemed a
very real threat.

The situation in Europe was now even more complicated than
it had been before Munich. British and French military missions
were negotiating in Moscow for mutual aid pacts with Poland and
Rumania as a deterrent against further aggression by Hitler. The
British Government had greatly increased its defence estimates and
was considering guarantees to Poland, Rumania, Greece and Turkey. In a talk I had with Sir Nevile Henderson, the British
Ambassador in Berlin, he confirmed my opinion that the situation
could yet be saved if it were made clear to Hitler that any new
aggression would automatically mean war. It still seemed possible
to cancel the last unfortunate legacy of the Versailles Treaty, the
question of the Danzig Corridor, without a general conflict.

Once more I was haunted by the reflections that had plagued

me at Bayreuth in 1934 when, after the murder of Dollfuss, I had been called upon to undertake the difficult mission to Vienna. At that time many of my friends had failed to understand my decision, in view of my experiences with the Nazi régime. Of those who had supported me, one of my closest associates, Wilhelm von Ketteler, had already been murdered. After taking much advice I now came to the same conclusion – that a final effort, in which I would do my utmost to save Germany and the outside world from the threatening catastrophe, would be better than to put on my old uniform and fight a hopeless war in the Siegfried Line.

Ribbentrop could add little to my appreciation of the situation. He and Hitler apparently still hoped to resolve the Polish Corridor question without a general war, it still being Ribbentrop's conviction that Great Britain was only bluffing. I felt, nevertheless, that he and Hitler might well shrink before the final consequences, and that it might be possible to bring Mussolini to some sense of the requirements of European stability. I decided to do what I could to avert the conflict – 'to lend anew my services to this diabolic system', as this action was described in the indictment against me at Nuremberg.

In view of my previous experiences, I asked to be placed directly under Hitler's orders, and to be given a guarantee that the Gestapo would be instructed to regard me and my work as outside their domain. To all this Hitler agreed. His only stipulation was that in order to ensure a better co-ordination of foreign policy I should come under the Foreign Office, though I would be free at any time to refer to him personally. Typically, he blamed the Duce for the way the situation had deteriorated, without apparently appreciating that his own march into Czechoslovakia had been *pire qu'un crime – une bêtise*. Any impression I may have got that he could be swayed by argument was dispelled, however, by his Reichstag speech of April 28, in which he dealt in the most cavalier fashion with President Roosevelt's request for guarantees against further aggression, and announced the revocation of the Naval Agreement with Great Britain. The Franco-British guarantee to Poland was answered by his cancellation of the non-aggression pact he had signed with Marshal Pilsudski, which still had five years to run.

The errors of psychology at this time were not entirely on Hitler's side. The British guarantee could only have acted as a deterrent if the help that it promised could have been provided effectively. The war was to show that it was no more than a paper promise. It would only have been valid if Mr Chamberlain had succeeded in persuading the Soviet Union to underwrite the guarantee, even at the expense of permitting some revision of her frontier with Poland. Hitler would not have attacked Poland if he had been faced by a war on two fronts. But the fact that Great Britain made the guarantee to Poland while her negotiations with Russia were still deadlocked, revived in Russia the old fear of a *cordon sanitaire* and drove Stalin into Hitler's arms.

★   ★   ★

Late in April, I climbed into the Orient Express filled with gloomy thoughts. I had told Ribbentrop emphatically that I would regard it as my duty in Ankara to keep the peace and to quell the rising political passions in Europe. He had agreed with me completely and my task seemed perfectly clear: to assure the Turks that we would do our utmost to avoid a European conflict. We would demand from our Italian friends convincing proofs that no general threat to Balkan and Turkish interests was intended. Our primary object was the maintenance of the *status quo*, and we would regret any move by Turkey to enter into alliances directed against us. This policy had been confirmed by Hitler.

On my arrival in Istanbul, where I was received by our Consul-General and the large German colony, I was disturbed by the news that a personal emissary from Stalin had just arrived in Ankara for important talks with the Turkish Government. I therefore continued my journey the same evening and was able to present my letters of credence to President Inönü the next day. We had a long conversation, in which the President told me that in view of the close alliance between Italy and Germany the invasion of Albania had given rise to grave concern. He accepted with satisfaction my assurance of our peaceful intentions, but pointed out that Italy had often made the same protestations without in any way altering her actions. The stationing of so many divisions in a country which only needed a small body of *gendarmerie*, and the activities of the Italians in the heavily fortified Dodecanese Islands, were highly provocative. Did Germany intend to give these policies her support? I denied this vigorously, and repeated the assurances that Hitler and Ribbentrop had given me. The President said the agreement with Great Britain and France had yet to be ratified. I therefore asked him to give me an opportunity of returning to Berlin, so that I could persuade Hitler to use his influence on Mussolini with a view to easing the situation. The President promised to await the results of my intervention.

I immediately sent off a long telegram to Hitler and Ribbentrop, giving an account of Turkey's fears, and suggesting that pressure be put on the Italians to reduce their Albanian garrison to the minimum required for maintaining law and order. I also suggested the cession to Turkey of two small and unimportant islands in the Dodecanese which actually lay within Turkish territorial waters. These gestures would have convinced the Turks of Italy's goodwill. I also sent off a long written memorandum, with copies to the chiefs of the armed services, in which I sought to impress upon them that Turkey's participation in the ring of alliances round Germany was a natural result of her fears and a reflection of her military position commanding the Eastern Mediterranean. I ended by saying:

'The disturbed equilibrium in the south-east is only part of the tense world situation. But the position adopted by the Turks and their participation in the political encirclement of Germany is of fundamental importance to German policy. If the Albanian affair or the problem of the Polish Corridor should lead to armed conflict, then, in the present grouping of the powers, this can only result in a new world war.

'The 1914–18 war proved that the British Empire cannot be defeated unless its main arteries can be cut. These are the lines of communication to the Far East and the oil supplies essential to modern warfare. In other words, the Suez Canal and the Persian Gulf. Although Turkey was our ally in the last war, our combined efforts did not succeed in achieving this result. With Turkey in the opposite camp, there is infinitely less possibility of carrying out such an operation. Turkey is the key to the military situation in the Near East. Whichever side is denied the use of her territory as a base for operations can rule out the idea of dominating the Middle East. It is therefore more than ever necessary for Germany to concentrate on the maintenance of peace. Any war forced on us by Italian imperialist policies or brought on by our own, would be lost the day it began.'

A passage in Count Ciano's diary[1] refers to what appears to have been the only immediate result of my démarche. Ciano received representations from Herr von Mackensen, the German Ambassador in Rome, and Signor Attolico, the Italian Ambassador in Berlin, drawing attention to Turkish fears and suggesting certain assurances. He quotes Mussolini as remarking that the Turks deserve to be attacked, if only because they are afraid. This memorandum of mine, incidentally, caused another argument with Ribbentrop, who said that I had no right to send such documents to anyone but himself. However, my interest lay in convincing the service chiefs that a European war would be suicide for Germany, and giving them arguments to back up this opinion. I had in my time fought in the Syrian desert and in Palestine, and had some appreciation of the problems that would face them.

When I arrived back in Berlin I found myself caught up in the festivities that marked the signing of the German-Italian alliance. The details had been arranged between Ribbentrop and Ciano in the first week of May, and the announcement of the pact was to be used by Hitler as an answer to the activities of the Western Powers. The evening after the signing a grand reception was arranged in the Chancellery, and I decided to take advantage of the occasion to have a frank talk with Ciano. In spite of everything, I still hoped that Mussolini would act as a brake, and would use his influence on Hitler to prevent any worsening of the situation. I therefore repeated to Ciano in strong terms the fears that had been expressed to me in Turkey, and tried to impress upon him the absolute necessity of some gesture to ease the situation. He listened to everything I had to say, but became increasingly irritable. When I had finished speaking, he excused himself curtly and stormed over to Ribbentrop with a shower of gesticulations.

Later in the evening Ribbentrop came over to me: his face was red with anger. 'What do you mean by giving advice to Ciano on the conduct of Italian policy?' he asked. 'Such a thing is unheard of. Who is responsible here for German policy, you or I? What do you mean by interfering in matters concerning our friendship with Italy? Ciano is furious and has complained bitterly to me.'

'I do not question your responsibility for foreign policy,' I said.

---

[1] *Ciano's Diaries 1939-1942*. Heinemann, London, 1947.

'But that in no way deprives me of the right to hold a conversation with the Italian Foreign Minister on the seriousness of the situation. Three weeks ago you sent me to Ankara to find out whether the situation in the south-east could still be saved. I have given Count Ciano my opinions in the same terms as I have given them to you. If you consider this to be wrong, then I would thank you to accept my resignation immediately. Moreover, I would like to add that I find your tone most unsuitable. Please remember that I am not accustomed to it.' Whereupon I turned away and left him.

The following morning, while I was considering what the next move might be, a messenger arrived with a letter from Ribbentrop in which he expressed his regret at the sharpness of our encounter the night before, and excused it on the grounds of Ciano's state of excitement. He invited me to the dinner and reception he was holding in his house in Dahlem in Ciano's honour, and suggested that we could continue our conversation there.

During the course of this reception personal relationships were somewhat restored, although it can hardly be said that Ciano took my advice to heart. He advised his Ambassador in Ankara, Signor de Peppo, to keep a sharp eye on me, and seemed to regard my 'intrigues', as he called them, chiefly as a weapon in his armoury when taking up a debating position with Ribbentrop.

On my return to Turkey I occupied myself with constant exchanges of visits with the Turkish ministers and my diplomatic colleagues. Chief among these, from my point of view, was M. Saracoglu, the Foreign Minister. He was a man with an open and charming manner, with whom I found it easy to establish close personal contact and to discuss every problem with complete freedom. In the five years I spent in Ankara I was in constant touch with him and he earned my very highest regard, both as a person and as a minister.

I soon learnt to appreciate also the worth of the Permanent Secretary at the Foreign Office, Numan Menemencioglu, an immensely capable official, who rendered great service to his country. He had a truly remarkable feeling for the nuances of diplomatic activity and had firm opinions on European political questions. He liked plain speaking and his word was his bond. He made no secret from the beginning that Hitler's Germany was a constant source of disquiet. Turkey needed a balanced situation in Europe. She also needed a strong Germany in the centre of Europe to counterbalance the imperialistic tendencies of the Soviet Union and Russian designs on the Dardanelles. This balance of power was being disturbed by the aggressive policies of the Axis nations, in which each partner seemed to be encouraging the other. Turkey must look to her own security, especially as her obligations under the Balkan Pact required her to come to the assistance of any member subject to attack. I was in no position to quarrel with these arguments, and made no defence of the events leading up to the march into Czechoslovakia. My only concern, I assured him, was to maintain peace, and it was for this reason alone that I had undertaken my mission, in spite of my unpleasant experiences with the Nazi régime.

At one of our early meetings I described to M. Menemencioglu the personalities of Hitler and Ribbentrop, whom I urged him to visit during his coming holiday in France. This I did in the hope that he would impress Ribbentrop with the need for moderation. Later, Menemencioglu described his visit to me. He and Ribbentrop had paced up and down the garden of the latter's country estate, while Ribbentrop tried to persuade him to abandon his policy of alliance with the Western Powers and join the Axis countries. He treated Menemencioglu to a vivid and repetitive account of the combined strength of Germany and Italy, and their 'will for peace'. Germany's only wish was to correct the anomalies of the Versailles Treaty. All this was accompanied by a highly-coloured picture of British decadence. However, Menemencioglu, far from being persuaded, was somewhat surprised at the terms in which this invitation to join the Axis had been presented.

Of my diplomatic colleagues, by far the most interesting to me was the British Ambassador, Sir Hughe Knatchbull-Hugessen, a man of charming and open character. He would have remained in my memory as a typical example of the old type of English aristocrat, if he had not written certain blatant untruths about me in his memoirs, *Diplomat in Peace and War*.[1] Of my arrival in Ankara he says: 'His Government had for something like a year been pressing the Turks to accept him. Up to that date [I arrived in April] they had resisted, and even then he was received with

---

[1] John Murray, London, 1949.

scant enthusiasm.' I do not understand this interpretation. I only agreed to accept the post on April 11, 1939. The request to the Turkish Government to accept me as Ambassador can only have been sent on April 12 at the earliest, fourteen days before my arrival. An affirmative reply was received almost immediately.

There is much more misrepresentation of this nature, but there is one personal matter on which I should like to correct Sir Hughe, even at this late date. About the middle of August I entertained him and his wife to lunch. It was an unlucky day. Just before they arrived I had received a telegram telling me of the death of my mother. It was too late to cancel the engagement and I preferred to keep this sad news to myself until our guests had left. I was probably not at my best, and Sir Hughe's comment was: 'There was something terribly professional about his charm.' I would like to think that I can now offer this belated excuse.

I left for Germany again the next day to attend my mother's funeral, and found the political situation had reached a point of crisis. I decided to seek an interview with Hitler at once. On my way to Berchtesgaden, where I arrived on August 20, I found every road full of marching columns. Mobilization seemed to be in full swing. Hitler smiled when I asked him about the state of the dispute with Poland and the obvious preparations for war. He seemed to be in the best of spirits. 'In strictest confidence,' he said, 'I will tell you of a major event that is just about to happen.' He then gave me a detailed account of his efforts to torpedo the British and French negotiations for a pact with Russia. 'To-morrow Herr von Ribbentrop is flying to Moscow to sign a non-aggression pact with the Soviet Union.' I was astounded at the news.

My first reaction was that peace was now secure. With Russia allied to Germany, Poland would be obliged to come to some reasonable agreement on the Corridor problem. With only the British guarantee, and no assurance of Russian neutrality, they would not dare to persist in obstinate refusal. I breathed a sigh of relief and congratulated Hitler on his immense diplomatic victory. It seemed that we had returned to the conceptions of Bismarck, who, while regarding Russia as the principal threat to European freedom, had always sought to check her aspirations by seeking some understanding with her. I told Hitler that this pact had made Germany's position in Central Europe far stronger than any resort to arms. At this he smiled again. There was no attempt to damp my enthusiasm. Nor, of course, was there a single word of his Machiavellian plans to overrun Poland and divide the booty with the Russians. I do not know to what extent he had already made up his mind to sacrifice the Baltic States as part of the non-aggression pact, or whether this definition of 'mutual spheres of interest' was a result of the conversations which Ribbentrop had had with Stalin and Molotov on August 23. In any case, the secret clauses of the pact signed on that day consigned this problem to the future, when it was to be solved amicably between the two partners. It is now obvious that this aspect of the talks had been thoroughly discussed by Hitler and Ribbentrop before the latter's departure. Equally obvious is the fact that in my interview with Hitler I was grossly misled about his real plans.

In the early morning of August 21 I went to the aerodrome to see Ribbentrop off. Later the *Völkische Beobachter* published a picture of us together. This was doubtless what started the story that I had played an important rôle in the negotiations leading to the signing of the Russo-German Pact. It was even reported that three days later, on a ship in the Bosphorus, I met the Russian Ambassador to Turkey, with whom I discussed details of the newly established friendship. In fact, I returned to Istanbul, still convinced that the worst was over, and expressed the opinion to the Turkish Government that the new agreement would contribute to a peaceful settlement of the German-Polish question.

I was only a distant and ill-informed spectator of the dramatic developments in the last days of August. Like everyone else, I pinned my hopes on Hitler's final offer for the solution of the Corridor problem, without suspecting that this was only a cover for his long and meticulously prepared attack. The die was cast. It was reliably reported that Hitler believed till the very last moment that the British and French threats were only a bluff and that he would be left to apply his solution of the Polish question alone. For my own part, I was certain that his attack meant the beginning of the second world war, and when Britain declared war on September 3 I knew that it meant the eventual downfall of Germany.

This is not merely being wise after the event. My trusted personal secretary, Fräulein Maria Rose, noted in her diary at the time: 'I listened to the announcement of the outbreak of war on the radio at the Embassy in Ankara, together with the Ambassador and all the other members of the staff, and then went out with Herr von Papen into the garden. He was extraordinarily agitated and seemed quite shattered. I had never seen him in such a state, even in the worst days at the end of June 1934, nor even after the assassination of his friend Ketteler. I remember every word he said – "Mark my words; this war is the worst crime and the greatest madness that Hitler and his clique have ever committed. Germany can never win this war. Nothing will be left but ruins." '

I had now to ask myself the question that was to be put to me six years later at Nuremberg: 'What did I intend to do?' Even without the documentary proofs which later became available, it was clear that Hitler had provoked the war and plunged Germany into nameless catastrophe. It seemed that I had three choices. I could direct a fierce protest to the world in general, which would indicate a moral weakening within Germany. To do this I would have had to seek asylum in Turkey and not return to Germany. Moreover, it seemed useless. The war has proved that even the most burning patriots, once they became emigrés, were able to do nothing for their country which served to shorten the war and restore peace. I could have resigned. This would have meant my putting on uniform again and leading my regiment. My third choice was to remain at my post in Ankara, which seemed to offer the best chance of deflecting the coming catastrophe. The question whether I would be more use as a Colonel or as an Ambassador was easy to answer. Ankara would be the key post for anyone engaged in an attempt to limit the conflict. I decided to remain where I was, and in doing so accepted odds far higher than any I would have encountered as a refugee.

CHAPTER XXV

HITLER'S FATEFUL DECISION

War changes our lives – Russia and Turkish neutrality – The Balkan Pact – Efforts to include Bulgaria – Dutch mediation in the conflict – A formula for peace – Trouble with Ribbentrop in Berlin – Conversation with Witzleben – Hitler and the Peace of Westphalia – Queen Wilhelmina's offer rejected – Peace offensive collapses – Conversation with King Boris – Memorandum to Hitler – Denmark and Norway invaded – Italy enters the war – Anxiety of the Turks – Their lack of modern arms – British and German policy – I see Hitler again – His anger at Britain's attitude – A final plea – Reichstag speech and its answer – M. Massigli's despatch – Italy attacks Greece – Turkey's obligations – I reassure Inönü – Berlin – Molotov's visit – Russia and the Dardanelles – Balkan spheres of interest – Operation Barbarossa

THE war unleashed by Hitler changed the pattern of our lives at a single stroke. In Ankara there is only one main street, the Cankaya Avenue, and we found ourselves living in this city with our new enemies and having to pretend every day that we did not see each other during our many involuntary meetings. There was only one exception, Sir Hughe Knatchbull-Hugessen, the British Ambassador, who always raised his hat to us whenever he met my wife or myself. I found this act of politeness a pleasant relief from the day's strain, and naturally I responded.

The number of neutral diplomats was limited and most of them, although charming to meet personally, had little time for Hitler's Germany. I was to have many conversations in the years to come with M. Lardy, the Swiss Minister, who served as a useful channel for transmitting my views to the British Ambassador. His own sympathies lay entirely on the other side, but he was a man of such probity that in 1944, when relations between Germany and Turkey were broken off, I had no hesitation in requesting him to take over our interests. Any failings in this capacity were probably due to his bureaucratic nature. The most charming representative of the neutral states during the early months was the explorer-diplomat,

454

Philips Christiaan Visser, Holland's representative. I had many conversations with him, and later we were to work together on a plan for restoring peace.

With the Polish campaign running its expected course, Count Schulenburg, the German Ambassador in Moscow, sent a report on September 2 concerning Russian negotiations with the Turks, designed to ensure Turkish neutrality. Ribbentrop, at my request, had suggested this step in Moscow, since it appeared to me necessary to ensure that as many states as possible should remain neutral, if the conflict was to be limited. Great Britain was trying to persuade the Rumanians to give military assistance to the Poles, and these attempts could only be nullified by our efforts to preserve Turkish neutrality, and thus, in accordance with the Treaty of Montreux, keep the Dardanelles closed to the transport of military supplies.

On September 17 Schulenburg advised us that Turkey had suggested to Russia the signing of a pact of mutual assistance which was, however, to contain the clause that such assistance must not be directed against France or England. This seemed to indicate another attempt by the Western Powers to build up a solid Balkan bloc against German aggression. Its members had included for some time Rumania, Yugoslavia, Greece and Turkey, but not Bulgaria. It now became one of the chief objects of the Western Allies' policy to obtain Bulgaria's inclusion. If the Turks and the Russians then came to an agreement, the latter would be obliged to render military assistance if the Balkan Union, or one of its members, was attacked by Germany.

I thought it my first duty, when peace feelers were being put out after the end of the Polish campaign, to prevent as far as possible the division of Europe into two hostile camps. There would be no reason for us to attack the Balkans, providing no attempt was made to hinder our commercial relations with these countries. I therefore did my utmost to influence the Bulgarians and the Russians not to enter into any further alliance. My Bulgarian colleagues in Ankara fully supported me. The Russians made enquiries in Berlin about the attitude they should adopt towards the Turkish proposal. For my part, I recommended its rejection, or at least the inclusion of a clause relieving Russia of any obligation to fight against Bulgaria and ourselves.

In the end no agreement was signed, although the Western

Allies still tried vigorously to persuade Bulgaria to join the Balkan Union. My British colleague himself travelled to Sofia to try to persuade King Boris to do so; while the treaty of alliance between Turkey and the Western Powers, signed on October 19, 1939, placed upon Turkey the obligation of winning over Bulgaria. I am still astonished at the lack of understanding of the Balkan situation that was shown by the Western Allies. They seemed to have forgotten that the peace of 1918 removed from Bulgaria, as a former ally of the Central Powers, some of her most essential territories. Macedonia had been ceded to Yugoslavia, the Dobrudja to Rumania, and the vital outlet to the Aegean Sea, the harbour of Dedeagach, to Greece. No wonder this rump Bulgaria showed little enthusiasm for an alliance with her despoilers. Moreover, the centuries-old history of Bulgarian-Turkish relations left little love between the two countries. The winning of Bulgaria to the Western Allies' cause was a forlorn hope, although even after the fall of France in 1940, pressure was still brought on the Turks to effect a *rapprochement*.

In the meantime I had several conversations with my Dutch colleague, M. Visser, in order to determine how peace could be restored after the end of the Polish campaign on the Western Front. There was a stalemate. The German armies had hoisted banners proclaiming their intention not to start the shooting, to which the French soldiers had replied with the same assurance. On both sides there was strong aversion to starting the fight, and the time seemed ripe for diplomatic steps. My formula was this: an independent Poland must be restored, with the cession to Germany of her former western provinces. Czechoslovakia, within the frontiers of the then protectorate, must regain her sovereignty, being bound to Germany only by an alliance. Any threat of an attack on the Balkans or the Eastern Mediterranean must be excluded by specific German guarantees. I would have preferred to discuss the matter with Hitler, and to have tried to win him over before contacting Ribbentrop. I hoped I would be able to persuade him that a Polish buffer state would only be an advantage, and that an allied Czechoslovakia would be sufficient guarantee for Germany's security. M. Visser undertook to ask the Netherlands Government whether they would be willing to act as intermediaries in presenting this plan to the British Government. He also told the British Ambassador of this step, as soon as the Dutch Government had signified its agreement. The matter then became official and I was obliged to inform Ribbentrop. Whereupon he turned down the whole project.

On October 18 I went to Berlin. Ribbentrop was ill, but sent a message to say that under no circumstances was I to talk to Hitler about any peace plans. However, this did not prevent me having a long conversation with Hitler two days later, in which I outlined my picture of the general situation and the possibility of initiating peace moves through the mediation of the Dutch Government. I kept for a second conversation the details upon which Visser and I had agreed. Hitler showed no immediate reaction, either positive or negative, but asked me to continue our talk as soon as I had returned from a two-day visit to my home in the Saar.

The effect on Ribbentrop of this conversation was staggering. He could not dismiss me, so he circulated an order forbidding any official in his Ministry to receive me or engage in any political discussion with me. It must be unique in the history of diplomacy for a Foreign Minister to seek in this way to cripple an Ambassador in the course of his duties. I still have a copy of this amazing document.

My short visit to the Saar was chiefly memorable for a conversation I had at Kreuznach, the local Army headquarters, with the Commander-in-Chief, General von Witzleben. He was already known for his aversion to the régime – he was one of the principal victims of the purge after the attempt on Hitler's life in July 1944 – and I exchanged views with him very frankly on the possibilities of ending the war, if necessary against the wishes of Hitler and Ribbentrop. Witzleben hoped even then that it would be possible to persuade Hitler of the uselessness of trying to wage a world war. He was waiting to see whether the objections of the General Staff would be overruled. I still have a vivid impression of his determination to do everything possible to avert the coming catastrophe.

On my return to Berlin I had a second interview with Hitler, to whom I complained immediately about Ribbentrop's ridiculous order to his staff. I told him it was impossible to continue working with a Foreign Minister who employed such methods. He replied that Ribbentrop was extremely nervous and that I was not to take the matter too seriously. I then gave him an account of my impressions on the Western Front, the complete lack of enthusiasm among the soldiers I had seen, and the general air

of apathy. I impressed on him the necessity of putting an end to
the conflict immediately, in view of the prevailing psychological
atmosphere. My suggestions concerning Poland and Czechoslovakia he answered with a shrug of the shoulders. I told him
that the Foreign Minister could not forbid me to express opinions
held by every German. There must still be a way of preventing
the second world war breaking out in full force.

Hitler did not interrupt me, but I had the impression that he
was less open to reasoned argument than he had been three days
earlier. Putting his hands on my shoulders in a friendly way, he
said: 'No, my dear Herr von Papen, such an opportunity to revise
the Peace of Westphalia will never present itself again. We must
not be deterred now.' The Peace of Westphalia? Hurriedly I
searched my recollections of history to put this reference in perspective; but I need not have bothered. In a stream of words,
Hitler sought to prove that now was the chance to secure for
Germany the position in Central Europe from which she had been
cast out by the Thirty Years' War and the Treaty of Münster in
1648. There is no point here in reproducing my objections. It was
clear that Hitler had taken one of those decisions resulting from
the pressure of certain unstable advisers. Every member of his
entourage considered himself an expert in foreign policy, from
Bohle, Rosenberg, Bormann and Goebbels to Hoffmann, the
court photographer, and the various ladies who visited headquarters. Only one thing was certain: the more stupid and unrealistic the suggestion, the more likelihood there was of Hitler
acting upon it. Every attempt to expostulate was useless. I had
never left the Chancellery in a more disillusioned frame of mind.

Ribbentrop's instructions were carried out to the letter. I was
unable to make a single appointment with any official, all of
whom were afraid of compromising themselves. He informed me
that the letter which the Queen of the Netherlands had sent to
Hitler, offering to serve as mediator in peace talks, would not even
be answered. When I turned to Goering for support, he told me
that he personally was very much in favour of ending the war, but
that Hitler and Ribbentrop had made up their minds to have it
out with Britain, and he was unable to influence their decision.
When I left, he advised me that I should be a little more careful in
my remarks to foreign diplomats about changes in the régime or
the possibility of restoring the monarchy. Their reports were all

tapped and deciphered, and I might be preparing some un-pleasantness for myself.

The peace offensive had therefore collapsed. The only hope remaining was that the General Staff would succeed in convincing Hitler that he was in no situation to fight a world war. Their attempts to postpone the offensive in the West are well known.

I travelled back to Ankara disillusioned and dispirited. In Sofia I had a long conversation with King Boris. I could not tell him that I had given up all hope of localizing the conflict, but I assured him that I would do everything possible to ensure Turkish neutrality and thus lighten some of his fears. The King was per-fectly open about the problems of his own country. He sought no alliances in any direction, but was sympathetic towards Germany's efforts to nullify the worst features of the Versailles Treaty. The future would show whether Bulgaria was to derive any benefits from this policy. Instinctively he was opposed to the Turks and begged me not to take their protestations of neutrality too seriously. However, he shared my opinion that any further building up of alliances was to be avoided, if possible.

Back in Ankara I found my Dutch colleague, M. Visser, as dis-turbed over the failure of our plans as I was myself, but our personal relationship did not suffer. He repeated some of my experiences in Berlin to Sir Hughe Knatchbull-Hugessen, who records them in his memoirs.

At the end of December I sent Hitler another memorandum in which I developed the argument that the Western Allies' strongest weapon was their propaganda. By describing the dictatorial methods of the Nazi régime in stifling every form of free opinion, they were trying to convince the neutral nations how much it lay in the general interest to stamp out such methods. There was only one way to answer this propaganda: Germany must cease to be a police state and return to constitutional methods, by once again granting the German people the right to decide their own fate without the threat of concentration camps and executions. Hitler should carry out his previous undertaking to give the Germans a constitution and a real parliament in which all questions of national importance could be freely discussed and decided by democratic procedure. I quoted the example of parliamentary institutions in Great Britain during the war, and the manner in which a free nation had rallied round its Government in a common cause, and

I expressed my conviction that the German nation, if given the same opportunity, would come to the right decisions. The restoration of constitutional rights would place the German Government in a stronger position than it had ever held. I never learnt the fate of this document, but I was told later that the former Gauleiter for Austria, Habicht, whom Ribbentrop had installed as an undersecretary in the Foreign Office, expressed the opinion that it was the best and most sensible report that he had ever read. Apparently Habicht, whom, it will be recalled, I had had dismissed from his post in July 1934, had managed to learn something with time. He was later to be killed on the Russian Front.

Events now moved fast. In April came the invasion of Denmark and Norway. On May 10 Hitler's obsession with the Peace of Westphalia culminated in the attack on Belgium, Holland and France. It was a bitter moment for me. I sent off a personal letter to my friend Visser, deploring the event and our failure to avert the cataclysm that had now descended upon us. I could only hope, I added, that our personal friendship would remain intact if we survived the war.

On June 10 Italy entered the war, thus facing Turkey with the problem of her obligations under the terms of her alliance with the Western Powers which now required her to declare war on the Axis. However, one clause exempted her from this obligation – if a declaration of war should place Turkey in danger of attack by a third power.

After the signing of the Russo-German Pact in Moscow, Turkish relations with Soviet Russia had become distinctly cool. It seemed likely that if Turkey became a fighting partner of the Western Allies, the Russians would revive their old claims on the Dardanelles. I did not hesitate to present this powerful argument to Saracoglu and Menemencioglu, although to impute such intentions to our Russian friends ran completely counter to Ribbentrop's instructions. However, I knew from numerous conversations with the Soviet Ambassador, M. Terentiev, how anxious his Government was to obtain, peacefully or by force, some revision of the Treaty of Montreux.

It is interesting to read in Sir Hughe Knatchbull-Hugessen's memoirs that he considers the chief reason for the Turks not fulfilling their apparent treaty obligations lay in the inadequate equipment of the Turkish Army. Where they were expected to fight is not clear. There were no ships to take them to Italy or Greece, and it seemed a lot to ask of Turkey to expect her to enter the war at the time of France's *débâcle* and the disaster to the British Expeditionary Force at Dunkirk. However, there is no doubt that such a step would have had a great moral effect, and Sir Hughe and M. Massigli, the French Ambassador, redoubled their efforts to induce the Turks to join in. They found, however, that the Turks' sense of realities was not to be deflected.

The magnificent soldiers of the Turkish Army completely lacked modern technical weapons, tanks and, above all, a suitable air force. Their British allies had lost most of their own material at Dunkirk and were in no position to fulfil Turkey's needs. Marshal Çakmak, the Turkish Chief of Staff, and President Inönü both had a very clear conception of the requirements of modern warfare, and I saw to it that my military attaché, General Rohde, himself a former instructor in the Turkish Army, kept them fully informed of our tactical experiences in the Polish and French campaigns.

A few weeks after the end of the French campaign, a British military mission arrived in Ankara to discuss Turkey's requirements. I therefore invited some of my Turkish military acquaintances to see a film in the Embassy. Most of the major operations had been filmed by front-line photographers, whose efforts provided a highly realistic picture of the techniques of modern warfare and the use of the latest weapons. My friends were greatly impressed, and were thus well prepared for the reception of their British visitors. The difference between the British reaction and my own to Turkey's wish to modernize and equip her army, was that the British tried for four years, by every possible means to bring Turkey into the war, while I endeavoured to make her so strong that she would be in a position to defend her neutrality against any attack, from whatever direction.

I was back in Germany again three days before Hitler's Reichstag speech of July 19, and called on him at Berchtesgaden. His curt refusal to meet Italy's territorial demands, and the manner in which he had soothed French pride to the extent of allowing them to keep their fleet, seemed to me a sign that he was attempting to restore some sort of equilibrium on the European mainland. The British Government would have been well advised to take advantage of this change of mood; but instead they announced their intention of resisting any peace feelers. I found Hitler in a state of

angry indignation over the campaign in the foreign press, which
was rejecting, in advance, offers he had not yet made. I impressed
upon him the necessity of paying immediate attention to the reorganization of Europe. History would never again offer such an
opportunity, providing it was carried out with wisdom and
moderation. I tried to convince him that Britain's curt rejection of
any idea of reconciliation was a sign of weakness. If France,
Belgium, Holland and the Scandinavian countries could be won
over to the idea of co-operation, without imposing on them territorial and economic demands, then in due course Great Britain
would have to join in.

On the other hand, to continue the war would spell disaster.
Even if the invasion of England should succeed, the British Empire
would continue to fight from America. Moreover, I asked him,
what was the Russians' neutrality really worth? All they were
hoping was that there would be no peace and that finally Europe
would reach a stage of exhaustion from which their own goal of
revolution could be more easily reached. Hitler listened to me
attentively and without interruption. He agreed fully with my
arguments, but asked how the expenses of the war were to be
covered if a peace were signed which did not include reparations
clauses. I told him that a stable Europe, with extensive bilateral
trade agreements, would amortize Germany's debts far more
quickly than any imposed reparations. The last war had proved
this. If Britain continued to fight, Europe could still be defended,
even if Germany had to evacuate the Channel coast, Holland and
Belgium. Providing there was unity on overall policy, it would be
possible to sign defence pacts with the various countries concerned, and, if necessary, still keep German covering troops in
those countries until their military strength had been built up. I
got the impression that Hitler was giving this idea his close
attention. He seemed convinced that France could be won over to
the idea of European co-operation, and he seemed to have little
interest in pulling chestnuts out of the fire for his Italian partners.
Their contribution so far roused him only to sarcasm. 'They have
become insatiable,' he said.

However, in spite of my hopes, his Reichstag speech gave the
anxious German people little cause for encouragement. 'I see no
reason why this war should continue,' he said. 'The sacrifices involved are frightening . . . Mr Churchill may very well disregard

my evidence; he may contend that it is only the result of fear and of doubt in the possibility of final victory. But whatever is to come, my conscience is clear.'

But Mr Churchill's attitude was already well known. He had repeatedly declared his Government's resolve to fight on, 'if necessary for years, if necessary alone'. Europe's fate was sealed.

In view of post-war developments, it is interesting to note here that Sir Stafford Cripps, who had arrived in Moscow as British Ambassador, was presenting new arguments for the purpose of getting Russia to change sides. Schulenburg, the German Ambassador to Russia, advised us on July 13 that Molotov had told him of an attempt by the British to convince the Russian Government that Germany sought hegemony over the whole of Europe, and that Russia should intervene to restore the European balance of power. Schulenburg also reported Molotov as saying that for this purpose the British had declared themselves ready to recognize the Balkans as a Russian sphere of interest, and acknowledged Russian aspirations in the Dardanelles.

It is interesting to observe this act of British diplomacy at a time when Turkey was her formal ally. Now that the Russians have, in fact, established themselves in the Balkans, perhaps the idea seems less attractive.

I stayed on in Berlin to watch the course of events, but on August 1 I went to Berchtesgaden again to take my leave of the Chancellor. His idea now seemed to be to win over the French to the idea of a military pact against Great Britain. From what I had learnt in Berlin about the plans of his crazy band of Gauleiters, this seemed to be an utterly unrealizable project. Their main obsession seemed to be to split up France's territory, annex the northern departments to Germany, and resurrect the Burgundy of Charles the Bold.

Ribbentrop succeeded in playing one more underhand trick on me. In the archives seized at the French Foreign Office, his people had found a report from M. Massigli, the French Ambassador in Ankara. In it he described an interview with the Turkish Foreign Minister, in which M. Saracoglu had suggested the idea of an air attack on the Russian oil wells at Baku. The publication of this document caused consternation in Moscow and considerable embarrassment in Ankara. M. Massigli issued an immediate contradiction – there was nothing else he could do – and M. Saracoglu, in order to calm the Russians, sent an uncoded telegram to his Ambassador in Moscow drawing attention to the contradiction and describing it as a complete invention. However, Ribbentrop could not leave well alone, and made another announcement to the effect that M. Massigli's statement was not in accordance with the facts. It seemed to be his intention to weaken Saracoglu's position and get him replaced by someone with greater German sympathies. I found all this most awkward, having always maintained friendly relations with Saracoglu, in spite of his Anglophile tendencies. My British colleague in Ankara lost no time in proclaiming *urbi et orbi* that I was the author of this incident. I therefore told Ribbentrop that his attack had made any further contact with the Foreign Minister impossible, and that he must authorize me to say that he regretted the incident and that the official responsible in his press department had been dismissed. This was arranged, and from that time on there was no further friction in my relationship with M. Saracoglu.

★ ★ ★

On October 28, the Italian Army which was based on Albania attacked Greece. For Turkey, the warning of Kemal Atatürk's political testament had become a reality. Hitler, who understood immediately the crass stupidity of this new development, was too late to restrain the Duce. His own system of presenting his partner with a *fait accompli* had turned into a boomerang. There was little doubt that the whole Balkans would now be drawn into the war, involving a dispersal of German strength in the confused situation of Central Europe where its concentration should have been the paramount consideration. The shock to the Turks was immense. If their contractual obligations had been called into question when Italy entered the war, how much more seriously were they questioned now, with Turkey's commitments to Greece under the terms of the Balkan Pact? There was no way for them to tell in Ankara that this sudden blow of Mussolini's had not been carried out in full agreement with Hitler or that the next step would not be a German invasion of the Balkans. The tension rose, and the Western Allies put great pressure on the Turks to remind them of their double treaty obligations.

The next day was the anniversary of the founding of the Turkish Republic, and the whole diplomatic corps assembled in Parliament to congratulate the head of the State. The representatives of the two European camps gathered in separate salons, but the heads of mission were called out with their staffs in alphabetical order to greet the President. I entered the reception-room just after Sir Hughe Knatchbull-Hugessen had taken his leave of the President. M. Inönü's face was grave and he showed none of the amiability with which he usually greeted me as a colleague from the first world war.

I congratulated him on behalf of the German Government, and then added, 'I know, Mr President, what misgivings affect you and your country at this time, and I am fully aware of the great seriousness of the decisions you may be called upon to make. Allow me to say one thing, here and now. You may have little trust in diplomatic assurances, but I stand here as a man who loves Turkey as his second home, and who has had the honour of being your comrade-in-arms. As long as I occupy this post, I undertake that my country will not break the peace with yours. Please consider this the contribution of an old friend and ally to the decisions which you now have to take.' Looking at me with his luminous eyes, Ismet Inönü grasped my hand. I knew that we had understood each other.

A few days after this I was called to Berlin. I assumed that Ribbentrop wished to discuss with me the tension which had arisen over the Italian attack on Greece. In fact, the talks on November 12 and 13 were to cover a much larger field and were designed to determine the fate of the European continent. When I saw Ribbentrop on the 10th he gave me a rough sketch of the subjects to be discussed with M. Molotov two days later. It was time, he said, to come to an overall agreement with the Russians and to determine our mutual spheres of interest. One of the requirements would be to provide them with a warm-water exit to the world's oceans, and he wanted to hear my opinions on the attitude of Turkey and the problem of the Dardanelles. I repeated the arguments I had used to him many times. For Turkey, the question of maintaining her sovereignty over the Straits was one of life and death, but it would be possible to suggest to the Russians that the Montreux Treaty might be revised to permit the passage of her warships under certain conditions. An alteration of the Treaty's conditions by force was out of the question, as this would involve Turkey's entry into the war.

Hitler, whom I also saw, was more precise. He wanted to know what we could offer the Russians in order to keep them on our side. This, he said, was the most urgent question of the hour and must be clarified. No other combination in the world would be able to withstand the partnership of Germany and Russia. The only question was the price he must pay. He was prepared to suggest sharing the British Empire. An interest in the Persian Gulf with its oil reserves would, he hoped, deflect Russian ambitions from Rumania, which was economically essential to Germany. But how far could he go where Turkey and the Dardanelles were concerned?

I endeavoured to explain to him the background of the Turkish position, knowing that he had a sharply developed sense for events in their historical perspective. The Turks had dominated the Dardanelles for some six hundred years, and the first breach in their hold on the Straits had come in 1700 when, under the Treaty of Istanbul, Peter the Great had succeeded in obtaining the right of passage for his fleet. From that time, it had been a constant aim of Russian policy to obtain control of the Dardanelles and the territory on either side, in order to become a Mediterranean power and turn the Black Sea into a Russian lake. The question of including Russia in the Mediterranean orbit had exercised succeeding generations. If Russia had been a State on the European pattern, it would have been possible to discuss the matter. That condition did not exist. Nor was it possible to cut off Turkey entirely from Europe and place her long Black Sea coast at the mercy of the Soviet Union. The effect of advancing Russian influence to the Gulf of Izmit and the communications between Ankara, Brussa and Izmir could only be understood by a student of the geography of Asia Minor.

It would be possible, I suggested, to meet Russian demands by altering certain clauses in the Treaty of Montreux, in agreement with the Turks and other interested powers. On the other hand, the *status quo* did not threaten Russian interests in the Black Sea as long as Turkey, as a neutral power, closed the Dardanelles to all vessels of war. The best way out would therefore be to impress on M. Molotov the desirability of maintaining Turkish neutrality. I also expressed to Hitler my doubts whether, in fact, any concessions would satisfy the Russians, and reminded him of their offer of an assistance pact to Bulgaria. This clearly showed the

cloven hoof. Russia's chief preoccupation was to increase her influence in the Balkans. But as the regrettable decision of Mussolini
to extend the war to Greece would automatically oblige Germany
to take military measures against possible British intervention on
our southern flank, it was essential, at least for the duration of the
war, to parry Russian intentions in the Balkans.

Molotov arrived in Berlin on November 12, in company with
the Deputy Commissar for Foreign Affairs, Dekanozov. I took no
part in the conversations, but was presented to Molotov at a
reception given by Ribbentrop in the Kaiserhof Hotel. Molotov
remarked that I was not exactly unknown to him. At dinner I sat
between Dekanozov and the notorious Gestapo chief, Heydrich.
It was never quite clear to me who had thought up this particular
honour, but as Dr Meissner was nominally responsible for questions
of protocol, I caused him to be advised that after this experience I
had no interest in taking part in any further official banquets.
Dekanozov, a man of small stature with an intelligent and mobile
face, spoke only Russian, and my attempts to work up a conversation in any other language failed completely. No interpreter
seemed to be available at our end of the table. Heydrich, however,
sought to restore the balance, and seemed to be in high good
humour at finding himself sitting next to the man whom he had
so often sought to liquidate. He explained that, although he was no
churchgoer like myself, he considered himself a very religious
man. Every time he took an aeroplane journey he felt very much
nearer to the Almighty than in a church. 'Your materialism has
the advantage,' I replied, 'that you can always prove by the alti-
meter how much nearer you are to God than the rest of us here on
earth. However, have you any proof that you are that much
further removed from Hell?' This seemed to exhaust our topics of
conversation.

The Russian guests departed after agreeing to continue their
discussions at ambassadorial level. Hitler received me for a short
interview before I left, and gave a somewhat dissatisfied answer to
my question concerning the progress of negotiations with the
Russians on the subject of Turkey. He said that he had gained the
impression that the Russians were not really concerned with
important post-war problems, but were looking for immediate
advantages in Finland and the Baltic. He was not happy about the
proposed Russian guarantee to Bulgaria, but remarked in a some-

what distrait fashion that small matters must clearly be subordinated to the major issues. A coalition between Germany and the Soviet Union would present an irresistible force and must mean complete victory. I was not able to deny this particular point, but I felt that I had to say something. 'What is to be gained,' I asked, 'by dividing up the world with the Russians? If Bulgaria and the Dardanelles are to be surrendered to them, do you think that we can prevent the whole Balkans from being swallowed on the Baltic model? Germany has given a guarantee to Rumania and stands on terms of friendship with Bulgaria. Hungary was always part of the old Empire and the best bulwark against Asiatic influence. How can you surrender all this? Moreover, the Turks would fight to the last against dividing their sovereignty in the Dardanelles with Russia. You would then certainly have war on this front and the Russians on the Mediterranean.' He looked at me thoughtfully but said nothing.

The disclosure of Molotov's proposed guarantee to Bulgaria gave me a sufficiently clear insight into the price that would have to be paid for a full alliance with the Russians. We stood at a crossroads of history. I could feel how attractive Hitler must find the idea of facing the British Empire and the United States with a Russian alliance. His decision could alter the face of the world. It was with this thought that I said to him as I left, 'Do not forget that you and I joined forces in January 1933 in order to protect Germany – and Europe with her – from Communism.'

★ ★ ★

Back in Ankara, I was unable to give the Turks any proper information about the true content of the talks with Molotov. Ribbentrop saw to it that only the barest details were available. If the truth had seeped through, we would only have bound Turkey even more closely to her Western Allies. Count Schulenburg, in Moscow, had already advised Ribbentrop on October 30 not to announce the proposed adherence of Hungary, Rumania, Slovakia and Bulgaria to the Axis Powers before Molotov's journey and to discuss the matter first with the Russian Foreign Minister. Although the importance of this grew, as the conversations concentrated more and more on the Balkans, neither Ribbentrop nor Hitler brought the matter up. When, however, the Hungarian ministers Count Teleki and Count Csaky, visited Vienna on November 20 to announce their alliance with the Axis Powers, I breathed a sigh of relief. If it had been intended to smooth the way for a full alliance with Russia, the declaration of this new German sphere of interest in the Balkans would not have been made. We now know that Hitler told the Hungarians that Russia, whether in her Czarist-Imperialist or international Communist guise, was 'a threatening cloud on the horizon. If Germany deserts the Balkans, then the Russians will march in, just as they have done in the Baltic'.

Rumania joined the Axis on November 24, and two days later Molotov's first detailed reply to Ribbentrop's alliance proposals arrived in Berlin. It laid down as prerequisites the immediate withdrawal of German troops from Finland, the signing of a pact of assistance between Bulgaria and the Soviet Union, the granting of facilities for Russian land and sea forces in the Bosphorus and Dardanelles, and the recognition of the territories south of Batum and Baku in the direction of the Persian Gulf as the main sphere of Russian interests. A secret clause was to provide for joint military action, should the Turks refuse to join the alliance.

Hitler answered this by instructing his Chiefs of Staff to prepare for 'Operation Barbarossa' – the organization of war against the Soviet Union must start immediately and be completed by May 15, 1941.

I have no means of judging whether my personal opposition to Russian desires or the policies I had recommended in Berlin had any effect on Hitler's decision to reject the Russian demands in the Balkans. I knew nothing at the time of the resolution that had already been taken to abandon the invasion of England and to concentrate all available forces against the Soviet Union. As a soldier, it did not occur to me that Hitler would risk war on two fronts, which I assumed would be prevented by the General Staff. At least it eased my conscience to think that the alternative decision, with its betrayal of Europe, had not been taken.

CHAPTER XXVI

DUEL FOR TURKEY

War on two fronts – Dangers of attacking Turkey – Competing offers by Hitler and Churchill – Peace feelers through Sweden – Eden and Dill in Ankara – Hitler's assurances – Campaign in Yugoslavia – Russian apprehensions – Talks in Hitler's headquarters – King Boris's demands – Chromium from Turkey – Ankara in ferment – Revolt in Iraq – M. Inönü offers mediation – Turko-German friendship pact – Germany invades Russia – At Hitler's headquarters – Another clash with Ribbentrop – War with America

THE heroic resistance of Greece had brought the Italian offensive to a halt. It was clear from the reports of our Minister in Athens, my old colleague Prince Erbach, that British intervention was to be expected. This would present Hitler in his turn with the question of assistance, and serve to bring the whole Balkan problem to a head. It was a classic example of the difficulties of fighting a war in coalition, when one partner destroys the other's conceptions because there is no basic agreement on ends and means.

The instructors and training units which Germany had sent to Rumania were followed in January 1941 by a number of divisions. If this Army Group was to be sent to Greece, it would have to march through Bulgaria. This would undoubtedly involve the entry of Turkey into the war. Her obligations under the Balkan Pact would become so clear that she would no longer be able to withstand British pressure to fulfil them.

At the same time the General Staff had prepared, at Hitler's request, a memorandum on the best methods of continuing the war against Britain, now that the air offensive had failed to prepare the way for an invasion. This memorandum reiterated the view that the British Empire could only be dealt a mortal blow by an attack on its essential lifelines – the Suez Canal and the Persian oil-fields. For Germany the only lines of approach lay along the North African desert or through Syria. Without command of the sea in the Eastern Mediterranean, this route must pass through Turkey.

Confidence in the Italians had sunk to zero after the failure of their offensive in Cyrenaica, and the only alternative route seemed to lie along the historical line of advance through Syria to the Nile delta.

With Turkey in the opposite camp, this possibility was ruled out. Ribbentrop, to whom treaties did not mean very much, plied me with orders to persuade the Turks to denounce the pact with Britain, now that France could no longer be counted as an active partner, and get them to join the German side. My usual reply, that Turkey would stand by her obligations, seemed to him not only incomprehensible but also evidence that my diplomatic ability was insufficient to prevail upon the Turks. Hitler was much more realistic. I was able to make it clear to him that although a German attack could reach the narrow seas and traverse them without undue difficulty, the next stage would be suicide. The defence of Anatolia, with the invading troops restricted to one single supply line through Eskişehir and the high Taurus, a line with innumerable bridges and tunnels, would be a simple matter for the brave and determined Turks. My military attaché gave me the fullest support by drawing for the General Staff a graphic picture of what such an operation would involve. Also, on one of my visits to Germany I had managed to convince General Halder, the German Chief of Staff, how completely impossible such an operation would be, and all this now had its effect on Hitler. The German Foreign Office was fond of decrying the usefulness of any diplomat with a military background, but in some cases such a background was found to have its merits.

On January 28 I sent Hitler another long report on the situation in south-eastern Europe, with special reference to the dangers inherent in including Bulgaria in the theatre of war. I recommended that should he find it necessary to send troops to Greece to meet the threat of British landings, he would be well advised to send a personal letter to the Turkish President. In this he should specify the limited nature of such an operation, guarantee the inviolability of Turkish territory, and undertake to order that all German troops should be kept at least twenty miles away from the Turkish-Bulgarian border.

It was at this time, as we now know, that Mr Churchill sent an urgent personal letter to the Turkish President, drawing his attention to the dangers inherent in the occupation of Bulgarian airfields by the Luftwaffe, and inviting Turkey to take defensive measures

Q

before it was too late. Mr Churchill suggested that ten British fighter and bomber squadrons should be placed at the disposal of the Turks, to be followed by the five already operating in Greece. He also offered a hundred anti-aircraft guns. It was indeed a proof of Turkish realism that in spite of such overwhelming pressure and such munificent offers, her ministers decided to trust Germany's assurances and remained out of the war.

The fear of such an enlargement of the conflict was now so acute that at the end of January I made up my mind to explore once again the possibilities of peace. Relying on the confidence I enjoyed with the King of Sweden, I sent him a personal letter describing the situation, and asked whether he did not feel that it might be possible for him to approach the King of England with a view to initiating peace talks. This letter I sent by the Swedish chargé d'affaires, M. Thyberg, who gave my efforts his sympathetic support. I did not know at the time that Mr Churchill had reacted in a negative fashion to a similar suggestion by the Swedish King the previous summer. I had repeated to M. Thyberg the terms of the plan which I had outlined to my friend M. Visser when the Dutch Government played a similar rôle, and I hoped that this would add weight to any suggestions made by King Gustav. He did not care, however, to risk a second rejection of his aid, and informed me through his chargé d'affaires that he did not consider the time suitable for such a step.

The situation soon became even more tense. On February 26 Mr Anthony Eden and Field-Marshal Sir John Dill arrived in Ankara to explore the possibilities of building up a Balkan front with Greece, Yugoslavia and Turkey, for the purpose of pinning down important German forces. The day before their arrival I entertained the Turkish Prime Minister, M. Refik Saydam, and his Cabinet, at dinner, which provided me with an admirable opportunity to reiterate my arguments in favour of continued Turkish neutrality. The exchange of correspondence between Mr Eden and Mr Churchill shows that Mr Eden did not find the Turkish attitude encouraging. The Turks were determined to fight if they were attacked, but did not consider their army sufficiently equipped for offensive enterprises.

It was on the first day of their visit that Bulgaria announced her adherence to the Axis Powers. A few days later I was able to subdue some of my worst fears by presenting the Turkish President with the letter that I had suggested Hitler should write. M. Inönü was surprised and clearly grateful. The assurance that German troops would stay at least twenty miles from the Turkish frontier, if British intervention in Greece obliged Hitler to send troops through Bulgaria, enabled the President to justify, both to his own country and the world, Turkey's policy of neutrality.

The immediate danger seemed to have passed, and I managed to dispel doubts of the value of Hitler's assurances by stating that I would not retain my post for another hour, if I were not convinced that on this occasion he intended to keep his word. When the contents of his letter were published I received many congratulations from my Turkish friends, who felt they had escaped the rigours of war without failing in their obligations as honourable allies.

Next came the campaign in Yugoslavia. In view of our later knowledge of Hitler's intentions concerning Russia, his desperate need for speed becomes apparent. It was no surprise to me that Russo-German relations continued to grow worse. The Russian Ambassador in Ankara, M. Vinogradov, called on me on April 1 and asked for an explanation of Germany's declared intention to defend the Rumanian and Bulgarian Black Sea ports against any attack. I could only reply that he must accept it as a warning to the British Fleet; but I sent a message to Ribbentrop that the Russians had taken this totally unnecessary warning as directed against themselves.

As the fighting in Yugoslavia drew to an end, I was asked by Hitler to visit him at his headquarters, where I arrived by air on April 18. In his special train I found the King of Bulgaria.

Bulgarian troops had taken part in the attack on Yugoslavia, and now the King had come to present his demands to Hitler. I was asked to give my opinion as to how far they could be granted without harming Turkish and Greek interests. King Boris was chiefly interested in Macedonia, although there was some difficulty here with the Italians over certain chromium deposits in the Ochrida region, in which Ciano was supposed to have some personal interest. The King also required, as an exit to the Aegean Sea, not only the harbour of Dedeagach, which had been taken away from Bulgaria in 1918, but also Salonika and its hinterland. I told Hitler that I considered this an impossible demand and that it would be most unwise to mutilate Greece in this fashion. Without Salonika, the country's economy would be completely out of balance and its cession would only start a new chain of difficulties. Even more complicated was the question of the Greek corridor which ran along the Maritza between Turkey and Bulgaria as far as Svilengrad. This had deprived the Turks of the essential field of manœuvre before their frontier fortress of Adrianople, which had thereby lost almost all military importance. It also hindered international rail traffic, since the only line between Turkey and Europe had to go through this narrow corridor before entering Bulgaria. I therefore suggested that this portion of the permanent way should be placed under temporary Turkish administration and that in any final peace treaty Turkey should receive that part of the corridor in front of the Adrianople fortress.

The delight of the Turkish Government at this arrangement – it was announced in June – was only matched by the displeasure of King Boris. He thought that Bulgaria, as an active ally, was entitled to more consideration than a country allied to the enemy. In a number of conversations I endeavoured to explain to him that moderation in this matter would prove advantageous in the long run. Once the war was won, Bulgaria would hold the key position in the Balkans. On the other hand, Turkey was growing as a European power from day to day. The cementing of good relations between the two countries and the dissipation of historical antipathies would be a most important contribution to a stable situation in south-eastern Europe. He criticized my policy as being too friendly to the Turks and expressed grave doubts that I would ever be able to include Turkey in a friendship pact with the Axis Powers. It would be the constant aim of Britain to turn Turkey into a base for an offensive against the Balkans. I fully appreciated the King's difficult situation *vis-à-vis* Russia, in view of the lively Slav sympathies of his people. He had succeeded most astutely, in spite of joining the Axis Powers and taking part in the war against Yugoslavia, in maintaining friendly relations with Russia. The large Russian mission in Sofia, which remained until 1944, was a thorn in Hitler's side and quite the best information-gathering centre in the Moscow network. Hitler wanted to have it closed, but I managed to persuade him that this would cause great difficulties for the King.

My aim was to get back to Ankara as soon as possible, but as Ribbentrop wanted to take up a number of questions with me, I went on to Berlin. Ribbentrop's main preoccupation was how to ensure from Turkey a continuing supply of the chromium essential to the armament industry. Germany had always been the principal purchaser from this source, but Great Britain had made it a condition of her alliance with Turkey that further sales to the Axis Powers must be stopped. This condition applied only until the beginning of 1942, but the Western Allies had an option to continue their exclusive purchases. As this was Germany's only available source, it was urgently necessary to try and arrange for further shipments. This tussle with the British caused me endless trouble. At the beginning of the war, Germany had more or less let counter-deliveries to Turkey go by default, and the exchange of trade was at a low ebb. I therefore had to find some new basis which would be of interest to the Turks. After the friendship pact was signed in June, I succeeded in obtaining for Germany a considerable proportion of Turkey's chromium exports; a situation which lasted until the summer of 1944, when the Western Allies were again able to prevent any Turkish exports to Germany.

Ankara, on my return, was in a state of ferment. My prolonged absence had given rise to a thousand speculations. Would Germany present an ultimatum to Turkey, demanding adherence to the Axis, now that the Balkans and Greece had been overrun? Or would Turkey be invited to join in the revolt of the Government of Iraq against Britain? There had indeed seemed every reason for the Turkish Government's disquiet, although the fact that my daughter had remained in Ankara was apparently reassuring, since it seemed unlikely that I would have left her there if Germany had had aggressive intentions.

The affair in Iraq was to plague my existence for the next three weeks. As the result of a treaty signed in 1930, Iraq had become a sort of British protectorate, with Royal Air Force bases in Basra and Habbaniya. In March 1941 an Arabian freedom movement, headed by Rashid Ali el Gailani, had ousted the former Anglophile government and the Regent had fled the country. Faced by this threat to their oil supplies and pipelines, the British Government had sent an Indian brigade to Basra, which compelled Rashid Ali to institute military measures before he had time to concert his activities with the Axis Powers. Iraqi forces attacked the British air base at Habbaniya, but were unable to capture it and were routed by greatly inferior British forces.

Hitler and his General Staff appreciated what an opportunity was being offered to them, now that the campaign in Greece had been successfully concluded and air superiority assured in the Eastern Mediterranean. In Greece an airborne corps was stationed ready for the assault on Crete. They must have been greatly tempted to divert it for capturing Baghdad and Basra, throwing the Indian brigade into the sea and thus becoming at one blow master of the oilfields and the Persian Gulf. It was a plan with every prospect of success. The French commander-in-chief in Syria, General Dentz, was loyal to Vichy, and the British maintained only weak forces in Palestine. Such an operation would have cut the British Empire's lifeline and caused the most violent reaction.

However, there was no means of securing the German lines of communication through Syria, since no shipping was available in the Eastern Mediterranean and the Axis Powers did not command the seas. The land route through Turkey was closed and would remain so, as long as Hitler adhered to my arguments. The only possibility was for the apparently overwhelming strength of the Italian Fleet to open the sea way. But its defeat in the Battle of Matapan at the end of March had exposed its combat morale, and later developments in Crete showed only too clearly that it would be of no use to us.

Our unprotected convoys to Crete were sunk and dispersed by the Royal Navy more or less at will, without a single Italian destroyer showing itself. While the British Mediterranean Fleet, under Admiral Cunningham, engaged in an heroic battle with severe losses in defence of their troops on the island, the Italians made not one single attempt to take advantage of this favourable opportunity. There was no hope of establishing a line of communication through Syria without the help of Turkey, and this meant that in fact no real attempt could be made to assist the revolutionary movement in Baghdad and Basra.

The exploits of Herr Rahn[1] (later to become Ambassador to Mussolini's rump Government in Northern Italy) and his consorts were merely an amateur adventure. Rahn had been ordered, more or less on the spur of the moment, to fly to Beirut, obtain the support of General Dentz, and bring some assistance to Rashid Ali,

[1] R. Rahn: *Ruheloses Leben*. Eugen Diederichs Verlag, Jena, 1950.

who had been joined in the meantime by the Grand Mufti of Jerusalem. In fact, a few German aircraft landed on May 13 in Mosul, but provided little help. Another German emissary, Herr von Blomberg, the son of the general, who had been sent on to Baghdad to study the situation, was shot down in error by the Iraqis themselves. His successor, General Felmy, arrived with instructions from Hitler to assist the Arab freedom movement in any possible way. The terms of these instructions were vague: 'whether it will be possible to destroy the British position between the Persian Gulf and the Mediterranean by a combined attack on the Suez Canal is a matter for the future.'

Rahn in the meantime was busily trying to collect arms for Iraqi divisions which either did not exist or had already been dispersed. He needed petrol for the German aircraft, and the only way to get it was through Turkey. Ribbentrop was bombarding me with telegrams, insisting that I get the Turks to permit the passage of every sort of war material. Naturally, they declined, although they did allow the transport of petrol, which could not be defined exclusively as war material. I tried to get Ribbentrop to appreciate the Turkish position and disregarded his insistent demands to seek interviews with M. Saracoglu. Whereupon Rahn himself appeared in Ankara to solve the transport problems. He describes angrily in his book how I kept him waiting for an hour and a half because I wanted to finish a game of tennis. In spite of his considerable knowledge of the country, he apparently had not learnt the Turkish proverb, 'Haste belongs to the Devil.' In any case, the revolt in Iraq ended on May 30 with the appearance of Indian troops in front of Baghdad, and the flight of Rashid Ali and the Grand Mufti into Persia. The adventure ended for Herr Rahn soon afterwards. With General Catroux marching his Free French forces north into Syria, he too had to flee. He consoles himself with the thought that he provided Field-Marshal Rommel with a breathing space. In fact, his activities did not have the slightest effect on the operations in North Africa, for the British High Command did not move a single man from the Nile Delta.

* * *

The Turkish President, in his turn, advised me during this period that he was prepared to act as mediator in peace talks, if the German Government felt able to suggest practical and acceptable terms. It was clear that it was in Turkey's interest to arrange a peace. German armies were in close proximity to her northern and western frontiers, and the possibility of active British assistance was declining. It would only have been possible for me to interest Hitler in M. Inönü's plan if the war against England had entered a decisive phase. I was completely in the dark concerning 'Operation Barbarossa' and expected hostilities to flare up in Libya. In any case, I would have been unable to approach Ribbentrop with such an offer because he had officially forbidden any peace feelers. 'You do not seem to have grasped the fact that we have won the war,' he had said to me in Berlin. I had answered that this was a fact of which I was indeed ignorant.

For some weeks, however, I had been working, with the full knowledge of Berlin, to convert Turco-German relations from their attitude of mere non-belligerence into a condition of true neutrality and friendship. I suggested to M. Saracoglu and M. Menemencioglu that the two countries should sign a pact of friendship, to which they were agreeable, providing that such a treaty did not conflict with their other obligations. Such a condition came naturally enough to the Turks, but to convince Ribbentrop of its relevance was quite another matter. He continued to insist that no agreement could be signed which mentioned in any way Turkey's obligations to Great Britain. He was left in no doubt that the Turks intended, out of loyalty to their allies, to keep the British Ambassador fully informed of each phase of our negotiations, and that I had agreed to their so doing. When, about the middle of June, Ribbentrop again refused to consider any agreement which mentioned Turkish obligations elsewhere, I sent him a cable saying that he must accustom himself to the idea that the Turks were gentlemen and that gentlemen had the habit of keeping their word. That went home. He withdrew his objections, and on June 18 we were able to sign a document in which the following provisions were set out:

'With a view to placing their relations on a basis of mutual confidence and friendship, the German Reich and the Turkish Republic, reserving their rights under current obligations, have agreed . . .

(1) The German Reich and the Turkish Republic undertake to respect the integrity and inviolability of their respective

territories, and to take no measures aimed, directly or indirectly, against the other partner to this agreement.

(2) The German Reich and the Turkish Republic undertake to
discuss all matters of mutual interest in a spirit of friendship
with a view to reaching a compromise agreement.

(3) This treaty enters into force on the day of its signature and
is valid for ten years.'

The announcement of this agreement caused general astonishment, as the negotiations had been carried on in great secrecy, and
the British did not disclose their previous knowledge of it. My
Turkish friends were delighted to have renewed such a long-
standing friendship.

Six days later, in the early morning of June 22, German and
Rumanian forces crossed the Russian border on a wide front
between the Baltic and the Black Sea. I had become increasingly
aware of the rising tension. But although news of the massive
build-up of German forces on the Russian frontier had filtered
through, I assumed this to be a form of political pressure to compel
Russia to maintain her attitude of benevolent neutrality. The event
surprised me as much as it did the Turkish public. I was awakened
in the middle of the night to receive an urgent telegram from
Ribbentrop ordering me to notify the Turkish Government of the
reasons for this new assault. My British colleague's suggestion that
I had only signed the agreement with Turkey because of this impending attack, is completely false. In the detailed correspondence
with the German Foreign Office concerning my preliminary
negotiations there is no mention whatsoever of the possibility of
war with Russia.

I found M. Saracoglu in a state of great excitement – an understandable state, in view of his constant concern at Russia's hostile
attitude and the possibility of a joint Russo-German operation
against the Dardanelles. This weight was now lifted from his
mind. 'Ce n'est pas une guerre, c'est une croisade,' he cried. M.
Menemencioglu, head of the Turkish Government's 'Brains' Trust',
who had never hidden from me his opinion that Germany was
becoming too strong for the European balance of power, shared
this relief, but was afraid that a successful campaign would remove
the brake on Germany's ambitions.

We were under no illusions as to the far-reaching effects of

Hitler's latest decision. Without any instructions from my Government, and prompted only by my own intuition, I suggested to M. Saracoglu that the time was now ripe to approach the British Ambassador with the request to ask his Government whether they did not consider the time had come to abandon the conflict in Western Europe and combine against the Power whose policy envisaged the destruction of the western world. M. Saracoglu endeavoured to get in touch immediately with Sir Hughe Knatchbull-Hugessen, but the British Ambassador was aboard his yacht on the Sea of Marmora and could not be reached. By the time they met the next day, Mr Churchill had already made his broadcast pledging help to Russia, and Sir Hughe informed M. Saracoglu that there was no point in his making any such approach.

In view of the accusation that Turkey was pressed to sign the friendship pact as part of Germany's preparations for the attack on Russia, I feel I must quote one or two sentences from M. Saracoglu's speech to the Turkish National Assembly on June 25. 'This treaty is a pillar of peace amid the storms and destruction of war. It benefits the Turkish people, the German people and the whole of humanity. It has been exposed for a week now to the judgment of public opinion abroad, and I can only record that it has met with universal approval. The whole world is now bound by treaties and alliances to maintain peace with Turkey.'

The entire future now lay under the shadow of the tremendous battle in the east. Relations between Turkey and Great Britain had reached their nadir. On July 17, Schulenburg, the German Ambassador in Moscow, arrived in Ankara with his staff. He told me of his desperate efforts to prevent Hitler and Ribbentrop from declaring war. In September our staff from Teheran also arrived, as the Persians, under combined English and Russian pressure, had been obliged to sever relations with Germany. The Minister, Herr Ettel, was one of Ribbentrop's party diplomats, and had made his name as organizer of the Germans living in Italy. He revealed to one of my colleagues the secret of professional success in the eyes of Hitler. Reports to the Chancellor must always be 'interesting', whether accurate or not. Hitler's first question when reports were brought to him was: 'Is the report negative or positive?' 'Negative' documents were not even read, but were filed straight away.

At my summer residence in Therapia I also saw Admiral Canaris, head of the Abwehr. He was duly grateful for the information which my staff had been able to give, and which he said had always seemed to him more objective than any reports from the occupied capitals or the few other countries that were still neutral. About the Russian campaign he was deeply pessimistic, as indeed were most of the experienced regular officers. Between us, and with the help of the Turkish Government, we organized a large-scale assistance programme to relieve distress in Greece.

I had known Canaris for thirty years. In my difficulties with the Party, and particularly after the murders of Bose and Ketteler, I had turned to him for assistance. I knew that he was an outspoken opponent of the régime and I had often admired the dexterity with which he maintained his position in the face of Heydrich, the Gestapo, and even Hitler himself. I was always able to express my thoughts to him quite openly.

His Abwehr was only one of a number of competing and overlapping agencies. The *Sicherheitsdienst*, which the Gestapo had formed under Heydrich's command, was originally an internal German organization, although its information services were expanded as soon as war broke out. Bohle's *Auslandsorganisation* also maintained its own intelligence service. The work of these agencies, however, was unco-ordinated, and they were always getting in each other's way. In Turkey their rivalry went so far that they denounced each other's agents to the Turkish police.

Canaris was unable to put an end to this ridiculous situation. I knew him as a true patriot who would never have done anything to harm the interests of his country. The suggestion that he might have been a British spy is ludicrous. But he was always struggling to reconcile his desire to curb the excesses of the régime with the wish to avoid harming his country's cause.

In September I returned to Berlin on sick leave, accompanied by my wife and the senior surgeon of the German hospital at Istanbul. After my convalescence, I paid a visit to Hitler in his East Prussian headquarters. My many friends in Berlin had begged me to give Hitler an account of the country's sinking morale. It did, indeed, seem grotesque at this particular time, when the nation was being called upon for even greater efforts, to have begun another campaign against the churches. The sermons of the Bishop of Münster, Count Galen, protesting against this development, were being passed from hand to hand, and I learnt from Lammers, the

Secretary of the Chancellery, that they had been shown to Hitler. This at least provided me with an opportunity to broach the subject. Hitler seemed to appreciate my arguments but, as on a number of previous occasions, placed the whole blame on the hotheads of the party. He had given instructions to the party chief, Martin Bormann, that this 'nonsense' was to stop; he would brook no conflicts in the internal situation. It appears that Bormann told his Gauleiters that these instructions were not to be taken too seriously. Before leaving for Ankara I learnt that my son, who had taken part in the Yugoslav campaign and whose unit had been in reserve while their equipment was repaired, had joined the Army Group marching on Moscow.

Before my visit ended, I had another brush with Ribbentrop. One of the handicaps under which his Ambassadors suffered was the fact that our interception services were able to decode all enemy and neutral messages, with the exception of the British and American ciphers. It was, therefore, impossible to converse with neutral friends who might be likely to report one's conversation to their own governments, without risking that the details would be on Ribbentrop's desk the next morning. I knew, for instance, that we had broken the secret Italian cipher, and I told Ribbentrop on one occasion that there was no reason to suppose that the British interception service was any less expert than our own. We would therefore be well advised to tell the Italians to change their system. To this he would not agree, as then he would not know what was going on in Rome. Apparently it was of no consequence to him if the British knew every time the Italian Fleet left harbour, what our plans in Africa were, or whether our own troops risked being sunk with greater ease, providing he knew what his friend Ciano was up to. It is impossible to calculate the cost of such cynicism.

The following telegram, dated September 26, which I received from Ribbentrop, not only underlines this difficulty, but gives a remarkable insight into his opinions and capacity as Foreign Minister:

'From the secret source known to you, it appears that you recently had a conversation with M. Gerede [the Turkish Ambassador in Berlin] on which he based a long report to his Government in Ankara. This mentions various military details, such as an estimate of Russian forces in the Crimea at one and a half divisions, and a statement that the German Army will have occupied the industrial centres of European Russia, including the Moscow area, by the end of October. Another part of the report alleges that you stated to M. Gerede that "favourable conditions and opportunity for peace would arise after the destruction of the Russian Army". There is little doubt that the contents of this report will have been communicated to the British and, through them, to the Russians.

'Such statements as this might lead the enemy to certain tactical conclusions and, as I mentioned to you in our recent discussion, an assumption that there was a movement towards peace in Germany. This they might take as a sign of weakness, which, as you know, does not exist. Although I am prepared to assume that your conversation with M. Gerede has been wrongly reported, and therefore do not choose to attach great importance to the matter, I must ask you to exercise particular care in your statements at the present time, particularly in view of present military operations. More especially I must ask you not to divulge any knowledge of operations that you may have gained at headquarters, but rather to indicate that the Russian Army is, to a large extent, destroyed, and that the remaining forces will be scientifically and systematically wiped out by the end of this year. Once in possession of the main industrial, food-producing and raw material resources – and I would ask you to make special mention of the Moscow area – Germany will have won the Russian campaign and will be in a position to maintain a thirty years' war, if the British still have the stomach for it.

'Concerning that part of the report which deals with the possibility of peace, I can only remark that should we appear to fail to reject immediately any suggestion of peace coming from outside, the impression might be gained that we were in fact interested in the idea of peace. The British Government, who are doubtless kept informed of such matters by the Turks, might therefore assume that we would be prepared to negotiate after the collapse of Russia. I can only repeat that the suspicion of any such intention on our part would have a precisely opposite effect on the British mentality and would serve rather to prolong the war. If the British can be made to understand that, far from concluding peace after the end of the Russian campaign, it is our intention to organize the territorial and economic basis for a prolonged war against Great Britain and, if necessary, America, and that we shall turn this whole vast war potential against the Anglo-Saxon powers, the will to peace in Britain may rise and the British Government may sue for terms. I must therefore request you to make it quite clear that we shall never take the first step towards a negotiated peace and that the only correct policy is to avoid all discussion on the subject until the British take the initiative.

Ribbentrop'

★ ★ ★

The disaster that fell upon the German armies in front of Moscow needs no further description from me. The effect on German public opinion was calamitous. Then on December 7 came the news of the Japanese attack on Pearl Harbour. It seems clear that the Japanese statesmen had no idea of the military catastrophe suffered by their German partners. Needless to state, Hitler seemed to regard this new development as a deliverance. Four days later, Germany herself declared war on the United States. I was faced by a whole set of problems. Was there any way of freeing the German people from the régime which was leading their country and Europe to disaster? This fateful problem was to occupy me for the next three years.

CHAPTER XXVII

AN APPROACH TO ROOSEVELT

Attempted assassination – Hitler offers arms to Turkey – Approach to the Vatican – Nazi Party intrigues in Turkey – Axis Powers lack co-ordination – A shooting incident – Saracoglu Prime Minister – Stalingrad the turning point – The Russian threat – 'Unconditional surrender' – Inönü and Churchill meet – My Istanbul speech – Ribbentrop's anger – The German underground – An approach to Roosevelt – Cardinal Spellman visits Turkey – German P.o.W.'s letters – Italy capitulates – Trouble with two Gauleiters – A mysterious emissary

THE winter in Ankara during 1941–42 was positively Siberian. Although the capital lies in about the same latitude as Naples, and therefore gives promise of hot summers and reasonably mild winters, the climate is influenced by the high Anatolian plateau. Summer temperatures are abnormally high, with sand-storms and a sirocco from the south, but winter temperatures sink to twenty degrees below zero and the whole region lies under deep snow. While we were collecting clothing for the German troops on the Eastern Front, wolves were penetrating the outer suburbs of Ankara. There was very little social life, few theatrical performances or concerts, and most members of the diplomatic corps spent their evenings playing bridge or poker. In spite of the cold, I found it a pleasant change from bridge to go out hunting wolves in the bright moonlight.

Amid these minor pleasures, by which we sought for a few hours to forget the nagging worries of the day's work, one event exploded like a bomb – in the literal sense of the word. On February 24, at about ten o'clock in the morning, I was walking as usual with my wife from our house to the Embassy. The Atatürk Boulevard was almost deserted. Suddenly we were both hurled to the ground by a violent explosion.

I picked myself up immediately, then helped my wife, who was somewhat shaken, to her feet, noting with some satisfaction that no bones seemed to be broken. 'Don't go a step further,' I shouted.

I could only assume that we had set off a mine – this was my first reaction, for when I looked round there was not a soul to be seen – or that one had been exploded from a neighbouring house, and that another might follow. At this moment a taxi stopped near us. I shouted to the driver to go to the Embassy and ring up the police. This, however, was no longer necessary, as the explosion had broken all the windows for a couple of hundred yards and a crowd had quickly begun to gather. Members of the excellent Turkish security service were soon on the spot and began a detailed investigation. Communications with the outside world were cut off for the time being, with the result that Istanbul was flooded with rumours which were transmitted all over the world.

My wife and I made our way to the Embassy. Apart from a cut knee and a torn trouser leg, I was unhurt, although my eardrums had suffered from the noise and the force of the explosion. My wife was completely unhurt, but the back of her dress was stained with blood, presumably that of the vanished assailant. Within twenty-four hours the Turkish police had solved the riddle. Human remains, including a shoe hanging in a tree, had been found at the scene of the explosion. These clues led the police to a Macedonian student at the University of Istanbul, who had taken lodgings in a small hotel in Ankara. From there the trail led to the Russian Consulate-General in Istanbul, which was immediately surrounded by the police. In spite of the outraged protests of the Russian Ambassador, it remained surrounded until the Russians responded to an ultimatum to surrender another student, suspected of complicity, who had taken refuge there.

The Turkish Prime Minister announced that the incident would be fully investigated, whatever the political consequences might be. He would not allow Turkey to become the scene of a political assassination. The investigations and the trial lasted several months, and the accomplice was eventually sentenced for his part in the affair. It was proved that for several weeks the would-be assassin and his accomplices had been practising pistol shooting at the Russian Consulate-General in Istanbul. They had found out that it was my habit to walk to the office at a certain hour every morning, and that at that time of day the empty street gave the best opportunity for attack. In case the student found himself unable to make a get-away after the shooting, he was to pull out the pin of a bomb with which he had been provided. This, he was told, would emit a smoke screen, under cover of which he would be able to escape. The young man must have been over-cautious, and presumably decided to shoot with one hand and set off his bomb with the other. It may be that he exploded it a fraction of a second before firing the shot. At any rate, I have no recollection of hearing a bullet. However, the 'smoke' bomb proved more effective than he had expected, and he was blown to pieces. The wonder was that my wife and I had remained unhurt. The investigation also showed that the prime mover in the plot left the Russian Consulate-General in Istanbul so speedily that the frontier guards at Erzerum could not be warned soon enough to detain him.

Until the investigation got under way, Ankara was full of rumours as to the reason for the attack. At first it was not clear whether it had been directed against me or Marshal Çakmak, who passed down the Boulevard Atatürk in his car a few minutes earlier. The Russians, the British Secret Service and the Gestapo were all suspected of having organized the affair. The fact that the assassin was obviously well informed about my morning walk was at first thought to be due to the British Intelligence, which had set up headquarters in a house opposite my private residence, which was kept under continual observation with field glasses. This rumour also reached the British Ambassador, who immediately asked some of our neutral colleagues to assure me that his people had had nothing to do with the affair. The Gestapo seemed a distinct possibility, and this suggestion was reinforced by accounts of mysterious telephone calls that various people claimed to have heard. However, all this speculation came to an end very soon, as the Turks pinned the guilt on the Russians: I myself had had very little doubt as to who the real culprits were. My Turkish friends showered me with congratulations, and the President and his wife presented my wife with a magnificent bouquet of flowers and expressed their regret at this murderous attempt on our lives.

About the middle of March, when the inflammation of my inner ear, resulting from the explosion, had been cured, I flew to Berlin again. I wanted to get from Hitler some further guarantee of the Turkish position. The immediate Russian threat to the Dardanelles had lessened, but British pressure on Turkey to enter the war would increase as soon as the German forces suffered some new setback in Russia or North Africa. It was therefore in our interest to make the Turks as independent of their British allies as possible. Great Britain had sent a military mission to Ankara to study Turkish requirements, but made no move to provide weapons as long as Turkey appeared chary of active intervention. If, however, we were to provide the Turks with their most urgent needs – the equipment for one or two armoured divisions – they would be able to pursue a much more independent policy between the two camps.

Hitler's immediate reaction to this suggestion was: 'What happens if the Turks use these armoured divisions one day to attack us?'

'I assure you that such a thing will not happen,' I answered. 'The Turks must be given the feeling that they can defend themselves against Russian attack without finding it necessary to rely on the assistance of the British Government.' I was astonished at Hitler's compliance. No doubt he was under the impression that the provision of arms would attract Turkey to join the Axis Powers, although I had left him no illusions about such a possibility. He authorized me to begin preliminary discussions, which were concluded in the summer when Herr Clodius, the German trade expert, visited Ankara. We signed an agreement with the Turks, under which we granted a loan of 100 million Reichsmarks to finance the arms shipments, which were to be paid for over a period of time by the export of Turkish goods, particularly chromium.

I assume that the British were duly astonished to find that it was the Germans who were arming the Turks. At any rate, the discovery prevented my British colleague from using his favourite argument that Hitler was about to attack Turkey. The Turks were naturally interested to learn something of modern methods of war at first hand, and I asked Hitler's permission for a Turkish military mission to visit the Eastern Front. This mission was headed by an old friend of mine, Colonel-General Ali Fuad Erden. He and his officers saw not only the actual fighting on the Southern Russian front and in the Crimea, but also made a tour of inspection of the Atlantic Wall.

From the military situation it was now clear that Hitler had no hope of reaching a decision on the field of battle against the combined forces of Britain, America and the Soviet Union. Local successes, even if they included reaching Moscow and the Volga, would not lead to final victory. I therefore arranged with my friend, Baron Lersner, that he should visit Rome and enquire through the Vatican whether there was any hope of beginning talks with the Western Allies. Lersner, whom my readers will remember, had got in touch with me shortly after I had arrived in Turkey and expressed the fear that for racial reasons he was in the Gestapo's bad graces. There was Jewish blood in his family. I therefore arranged for him to join me in Turkey as President of the Orient Association, a body formed to encourage cultural and economic relations between Germany and the countries of the Middle East. At the same time Admiral Canaris gained a wise old diplomatist for his Abwehr organization.

It was clear that Hitler would not be acceptable as a partner in any discussions with the Western Allies, and I told Lersner to suggest that if a real possibility of negotiations existed, steps would have to be taken to ensure that they were conducted with a different German régime. Lersner saw a number of important people at the Vatican, including the State Secretary, Monsignor Maglione, and his deputy Monsignor Montini. Both told him that they saw little likelihood of interesting the Western Allies in such a proposal. The war situation was such that there were strong fears that Stalin, who was already demanding a second front, might reach some compromise with Hitler. For this reason alone, no thought of peace talks could be entertained. Our efforts were therefore to no purpose.

During the whole of this period the Nazi Party continued to meddle with my work in Ankara. In November 1939 I had asked the Foreign Office to stop the flow of reports from the Istanbul party office to Bohle's *Auslandsorganisation*. The author of these reports, which often touched on political matters, was not in a position to obtain reliable information, and the whole business involved an unnecessary and often harmful duplication of work. At the end of the year, because of a Turkish ordinance forbidding foreigners to indulge in party political work, I gave orders that all activities of the party in Turkey were to cease. The only exception I made was to allow the Winter Aid collections. Needless to say, I received a tart telegram from Bohle protesting against my decision and pointing out that my position as Ambassador did not entitle me to issue such an order. But his complaints that his organization could not do without the information from their representative in Ankara were disallowed by Ribbentrop, who supported me in putting an end to this duplication of work. I felt that I could not run the risk of intrigues which would damage our political credit, and by ignoring Bohle's repeated protests I managed to maintain my ban on the party's activities.

In the summer of 1942 matters were brought to a head. My Embassy Counsellor came to me one morning to say that all the Party members in Ankara had held a private meeting at which the Party head in Turkey, a man named Friede, had said it was high time I was shot or put into a concentration camp. This meeting had been attended by almost all the members of the Embassy staff, who were, with one exception, Party members. I gave orders that Friede should be brought before me immediately. As soon as he appeared, I asked him whether he had expressed the view that had been reported to me. Upon his admitting that he had, I gave him forty-eight hours in which to leave the office that he occupied in one of the Embassy buildings, where he handled the problems of German nationals in Turkey. I also refused him further right of entry into the Embassy compound or any communication with members of the diplomatic staff, and circulated an order to this effect within the Embassy.

But Friede had his own wireless transmitter, although such apparatus had been forbidden by Ribbentrop in all the Party bureaux abroad, and he immediately sent off a message of protest to Bohle and asked for an investigation into the affair. Before I could compose my own report to Ribbentrop, I received his instructions to reinstate Friede and place myself at the disposal of a committee of investigation. This I refused to do, and instead offered my resignation. The affair was to drag on for another year before I finally managed to get Friede sent home. The Party sent out its own committee of investigation, and Ribbentrop instructed the head of his personnel division to make a personal report. Fortunately this man was an old civil servant and had no hesitation in composing a report unfavourable to Friede. My colleagues in the opposite camp may consider themselves lucky not to have had to deal with such internal difficulties.

During June, both Sebastopol and Tobruk were captured. In spite of Hitler's failure to support Rommel, which was due to his inability to appreciate the strategic significance of the campaign, it seemed that his initiative and daring were likely to open a route to the Suez Canal. By July he stood at El Alamein. If he should succeed in reaching the Nile Delta, I felt that this would provide a situation which would make peace talks possible. My Japanese colleague in Ankara never ceased to insist that Germany's strength must not be sapped by a long war with Russia and that some means must be found of reaching a compromise between the two nations. This point of view was also put forward in Tokyo, but Ribbentrop refused even to consider it.

The lack of co-ordination in the military effort of the Axis was thrown into sharp relief when Rommel stood at the gates of Cairo. Now, if ever, was the time to combine the full available strength of the German and Italian forces. Every unit of the Italian Fleet should have been committed to securing Rommel's supply lines; air force units should have been concentrated from other fronts, and full use should have been made of airborne troops. But Hitler had never learnt that military strategy was a matter of improvisation and that it is necessary to make decisions when they are least expected.

At my suggestion the Italian, Japanese and German Ambassadors in Ankara, with their service attachés, met once a month to reach some agreement on common policy for transmission to their respective Governments. My Japanese colleague, Kurihara, had a very decisive mind on military matters. Japan, he said on one occasion, was too busy organizing her conquered territories to help in relieving the pressure on Germany. Lack of resources made any attack on Russia out of the question. No impression was made by my warning that we would have to gain a combined victory over the enemy before proceeding to any plans of territorial organization, and that independent policies could only result in our piecemeal defeat. When I asked if Japan could not at least send some submarines to break the ring of the blockade, he answered with an enigmatic smile, 'We have only a few submarines and we need them all ourselves.' This particular meeting I closed by remarking that I knew of no coalition war in the whole of history in which there was such a complete lack of co-ordination on ends and means as in this one.

* * *

Wartime provided us with very little opportunity for social distractions, but the constant strain demanded some sort of relaxation and whenever possible I tried to get a day's shooting. One story which became current in Ankara, of an unwilling encounter with some of my diplomatic colleagues in the opposite camp, has been somewhat exaggerated, but is not unamusing. I had gone off one day to take a shot at some duck on one of the local lakes. I had just put out a few live decoys and had settled down in my blind, when I was startled by two shots fired from close by. Pellets churned up the water in front of me, and my decoys paddled round in a frenzy. I sprang up and saw two figures turn away and run. I thought I recognized one of them as a member of the British Embassy and shouted after them: 'It's a shame to kill my decoys. There is no war yet in Ankara!' Fortunately, my tame ducks were unhurt. One of my young attachés, who was shooting nearby, told me that one of the interlopers was the American Ambassador, Mr Laurence Steinhardt. I have always regretted that I met this outstanding diplomat only in 1946 when he visited me in Nuremberg gaol. It was then too late to talk about politics or to organize a better duck shoot. I must protest, incidentally, against gossip in the diplomatic corps that in my anger I had fired at the two retreating figures. This is a complete invention.

It was soon after this incident that the Turkish Prime Minister, M. Refik Saydam, died, following a short illness. M. Saracoglu, the Foreign Minister, succeeded him, and M. Menemencioglu took over the Foreign Ministry. In his first speech the new Prime Minister emphasized Turkey's intention of maintaining her neutrality. This autumn brought new worries. German losses on the Eastern Front were enormous, and in spite of the warning to Hitler that it would be impossible to mount simultaneous offensives against Stalingrad and the Caucasus, he persisted in this policy. The Russians soon found the weak points on this long front, and their first counter-attack was directed chiefly against the Italian divisions, which broke under the pressure, and the battle for Stalingrad began.

In September I flew to Budapest at the invitation of Admiral Horthy. He had just lost his eldest and favourite son, and was gravely preoccupied about the fate of the Hungarian divisions fighting north of Stalingrad. I promised to tell Hitler and the General Staff of his concern. I went on to Vienna to visit my son, who had just been wounded for the second time, but I declined to comply with an order from Ribbentrop to proceed to Berlin. His recent telegrams after my breach with the party had been too insolent.

October brought the successful British counter-offensive at El Alamein, and Rommel started his retreat. This news was greeted with relief by Turkish statesmen, who had never been happy at the proximity of German forces to the north, west and south. Thus the year ended with serious defeats in Russia and North Africa. For the first time the initiative seemed to have passed to the enemy. Only Hitler failed to recognize the portents. It was the turning point of the war.

Germany's fate was sealed during the campaign of 1943. Some of us could foresee the future, though not those who were directly responsible for it. For those who no longer had illusions it was a tragic epoch, and was accompanied by a growing feeling that it was no longer possible to influence the course of events. On January 7 I had a long conversation with M. Menemencioglu. His view of the world situation was the same as mine. The destruction of the German 6th Army at Stalingrad had already begun. The chief problems now were what the reaction of the Western Allies was likely to be, and whether the Russians could be prevented from becoming masters of the fate of Europe. This was also the dominant question in Turkish minds, and M. Menemencioglu was more than ever determined to keep his country out of the conflict. Each new Allied success would make it more difficult to withstand the pressure placed on Turkey to fulfil her treaty obligations to the Allies. Financial problems were also increasing, and M. Saracoglu had devised a new tax which fell on the incomes and property of all foreigners living in Turkey. I tried to ease the strain on a number of German concerns by a subsidy from German official funds. My English colleague was obliged to do the same, and we found ourselves in the curious position of both subsidizing the Turkish budget.

The Casablanca Conference between President Roosevelt and Mr Churchill began on January 23. It was here that we heard for the first time the formula of 'unconditional surrender', which was to prove a fatal stumbling block for those Germans who placed the fate of Europe above that of their own country and concerned themselves with the idea of making peace. We now know that the phrase was first suggested by President Roosevelt, more or less on the spur of the moment, and without any deep consideration of its possible psychological effects. A comparison between this devastating demand and the benevolent terms of the Atlantic

Charter leaves one astonished that this first conception was maintained to its uttermost limit. The Atlantic Charter, with its
guarantees of freedom, possessed all the elements for the conclusion of a just peace, whereas the Casablanca decisions merely
entailed war à l'outrance and the destruction of Europe. When I
made an approach to President Roosevelt a few months later, it
was in the hope that the formula of unconditional surrender had
been chiefly devised as a propaganda weapon, and that it would be
possible to negotiate. I had assumed that the President had sufficient
political flair to measure its effects. Unfortunately I was wrong.

While he was in Casablanca Mr Churchill apparently decided
to invite the Turks once again to enter the war. He expressed a
wish to see the Turkish President and Prime Minister, and asked
them to join him in Cyprus. M. Inönü replied that the constitution did not permit him to leave the country, but that Mr
Churchill would be welcome to pay a state visit to Ankara.
Eventually it was agreed that they should meet in Adana. At this
conference Mr Churchill submitted a memorandum to President
Inönü in which he warned the Turks against Germany's historical
Drang nach Osten: 'They may in the summer try to force their way
through the centre . . .' He offered the Turks, immediately on
their being drawn into war, twenty-five British and American air
squadrons, and urged them to push forward with the construction
of new aerodromes 'with frantic energy'.[1]

In the discussion which followed, the Turks expressed themselves as more concerned about their future relations with Russia
than about participation in the war. 'All the defeated countries,'
said M. Saracoglu, 'would become bolshevized if Germany was
beaten.' The Turkish delegation did not seem to think that the
country was threatened by Germany, and Marshal Çakmak, the
Turkish Chief of Staff, made it clear that the Turkish Army was
insufficiently equipped to be of real use to the Allies, and would
only become the target of envious Russian designs if preparations
were made to join in the war. It was agreed that an Allied military
commission should study Turkey's needs and that an effort should
be made to meet them.

I was told that President Inönü took advantage of the occasion

[1] Winston S. Churchill: *The Second World War*, Vol. IV, pp. 631–5. Cassell,
London, 1951.

to impress Mr Churchill with the need for bringing the war promptly to an end. The complete defeat of Germany, he said, would give Russia the chance of becoming a great danger to Turkey and Europe. He asked Mr Churchill whether he would not like to discuss the possibility of peace with me, whom he described as representing a school of thought which would prefer to accept even an unfavourable peace for Germany if this would guarantee the prosperity of Europe. In spite of the President's insistence, Mr Churchill declined. I was told he felt that such a conversation would be treasonable.

The results of this conference have been correctly described in the memoirs of the British Ambassador in Turkey[1]: '. . . much friendly intercourse . . . Menu papers were signed and exchanged.' Nor is it surprising that he was able to state: 'The German reactions were surprisingly mild. The Ambassador actually went so far as to express some degree of satisfaction!' But when Sir Hughe continues: 'A certain degree of mystery did in fact surround the question of the calmness with which the Germans accepted not only the Adana Conference but the subsequent visits to Ankara of our Air, Army and Navy Commanders', I can assure him that the reason I remained completely unperturbed by all this activity was because I seem to have understood the basic Turkish conception better than our enemies. During this period I had been able to give the Turkish Government a renewed assurance from Hitler that he harboured no aggressive intentions towards Turkey. I had a perfect understanding with the Turkish statesmen; our friendship pact took second place to the Anglo-Turkish alliance, but the obligation in the latter to enter the war would only be fulfilled in extreme circumstances.

My next approach to the problem of peace took the form of a speech at Istanbul on March 21, 1943, at a ceremony for those who had fallen in the service of their country. The final disaster at Stalingrad provided a grim background to this occasion, as I called on the Western World to come to the rescue of Europe. I asked the Western Powers to study again the history of the Continent in order to understand the rôle that Germany must play, an historic mission with its roots deep in the sands of time. They would then

[1] Sir Hughe Knatchbull-Hugessen: *Diplomat in Peace and War*. John Murray, London, 1949.

be better able to appreciate that if the Russian giant succeeded in subduing Western Europe, Communist doctrine would continue its victorious campaign overseas. I appealed to British and American statesmen to take decisions which would result in a new organization of Europe, in which each nation would have an honourable place in the service of freedom and progress. Feeling that such an initiative would have to come first from President Roosevelt, I made pointed reference to the stature of certain American statesmen and their services to humanity.

My remarks were widely reported in the enemy press and my conception of European solidarity was widely commented on. It remained for President Roosevelt to pick up the threads. The reaction in Germany was curious. I expected a violent outburst from Ribbentrop because I had again disregarded his instructions not to mention the subject of peace; but nothing of the sort occurred. Perhaps they were afraid to disavow me before the whole world. It was only when I paid my next visit to Hitler's headquarters that I appreciated how furious the hardbitten core of fanatics were, while those of more moderate views pressed me to follow up my line of thought.

I travelled to Berlin about the middle of April, and Ribbentrop took me in his special train to Hitler's headquarters in East Prussia. During the journey we had our first conversation on the situation that had arisen since the Stalingrad disaster. He placed the blame for this military catastrophe on the completely unreliable generals and the 'bourgeois clique' still responsible for the affairs of the Army. 'If Hitler had had the same opportunities as Stalin to purge his Army of such rabble, we should never have suffered this misfortune. Now we have to make up for lost time – ruthlessly. This whole bourgeois clique must disappear, and the sooner the better.' It was quite clear that he was using Hitler's words. This, then, was the point that we had reached. There was no practical difference between the Bolshevism they decried and the Nazi régime. There was no point in my arguing with Ribbentrop, and I merely remarked that it was quite clear that my generation had no further part to play under such a system of government.

The *Wolfsschanze*, or Wolf's Lair, as Hitler's headquarters was commonly called, was built in a thick pine wood near Rastenburg in East Prussia. The barrack buildings consisted of prefabricated cement huts, and Hitler's block was indistinguishable from the rest. It included a private suite with a number of offices and a dining-room. The buildings had very small windows because of the danger of air attack, and with their close curtain of trees, were always dark and depressing. Electric lights burnt day and night, and the whole place gave the impression of being sunk in a swamp. The entire area was surrounded by a triple barrier of barbed wire, and as the war progressed, it became possible to enter only with special passes. Most visitors had to undergo a search by the guards. On this occasion my conversation with Hitler added nothing to what I had already heard from Ribbentrop.

He had taken over the field duties of Commander-in-Chief in December 1941, after the first serious setback of the German armies, when he had dismissed the former C.-in-C., Field-Marshal von Brauchitsch. From then on, the entire system of command in the Army changed completely. Until that time the normal procedure had been to give army commanders overall directives and leave them to work out the details. The moment Hitler took over, no senior officer was allowed to determine his own tactics. Hitler supervised every detail himself, and the longer the war lasted, the worse this became. Towards the end, his headquarters in East Prussia determined the movement of troops at battalion level. The effect of this on military operations was disastrous. The orders usually arrived forty-eight hours late and were often wrongly conceived. The military genius attributed to him by his entourage, and which he himself came to believe in, never really existed. His strategic and technical abilities, such as they were, were completely untrained and he was incapable of making correct decisions. It was characteristic of him that after 1941 he always refused to visit the front lines or any of the bombed-out cities of Germany.

He did, however, have a certain technical flair. Although he could not drive a car, he had an exceptional capacity for understanding and grasping mechanical points, and officers who came in contact with him over the development of new weapons and equipment were sometimes amazed at the intuition which often enabled him to see a solution that the technician himself had not yet reached. He could explain in detail the construction of some new weapon about which he himself had only been informed once. He even found occasion from time to time to discuss his favourite hobby, architecture, with Speer, who had succeeded Todt as his chief adviser in this field. Every detail of the possible construction had to be discussed before the plans were approved.

I remember Speer telling a story about this to Furtwängler, the conductor, who had remarked how pleasant it must be for a relatively young man like Speer to be given a free hand to develop his own ideas. 'That is true,' said Speer, 'but sometimes it is as though you had started conducting a Beethoven symphony and your impresario walks in and says: "It is my irrevocable decision to play the accordion in this orchestra."'

Back in Berlin, morale was at zero. I was struck by the attitude of two National Socialists of long standing, both with an aristocratic background – Count Helldorf, the capital's chief of police, and Count Gottfried Bismarck, the local government head in Potsdam. They had both joined the party in its early days from idealistic motives and had reached high positions which gave them a clear view of the situation. Both were now convinced that the Bolshevist methods introduced by Hitler could only result in the complete collapse of Germany. Helldorf described the unbelievable conditions in the prisons, in which hundreds of people were being held under sentence of death for minor offences. The People's Courts and the recently formed 'Special Courts' had practically taken over the work of the ordinary courts and were passing sentences against which there was no appeal. I was greatly shocked by this information, which made me realize that not only had Germany's external situation become desperate, but that conditions within the country had reached a stage which required desperate counter-measures.

Helldorf, Bismarck and I had dinner one evening at the Union Club and afterwards retired to a private room. They then disclosed to me the plans of a small group, headed by the former Chief of Staff, Colonel-General Beck, who had made up their minds to remove Hitler. Great care would have to be taken to avoid this leading to an internal revolution affecting the front, and it was intended to take him prisoner rather than kill him. The command of the armed forces would then be transferred to someone else and Hitler would be given a properly conducted trial. A well-known cavalry officer named Freiherr von Boeselager was prepared to surround Hitler's headquarters with his cavalry brigade and capture not only Hitler, but Himmler and Bormann as well. But before setting anything in motion it was essential to know what attitude the Western Powers would adopt towards a Germany liberated from Hitler's leadership and seeking just peace terms. I was asked if I was prepared to sound the Western Allies.

This was the first occasion on which I had received concrete information about the resistance movement within the country. From what I had seen and heard in Berlin and at headquarters, I was in no doubt as to what my attitude should be. The fate not only of Germany but of Europe was at stake. I have never seen any justification for political assassination. Murder remains murder. But Hitler's arrest and trial would answer any subsequent 'stab in the back' stories much more effectively than his assassination. However, the tension and unrest inherent in changing the régime at such a critical time could only be risked if we had certain guarantees from the enemy powers concerning Germany's future. We needed to know whether they were prepared to abandon the formula of unconditional surrender; and whether they would grant, to a German Government which met democratic requirements, the rights to which Germany's history and position entitled her. This must be the decisive factor in any further step.

I promised to contact President Roosevelt as soon as I returned to Ankara, and we agreed that Herr von Trott zu Solz, who often came to Ankara on behalf of the Foreign Office, should act as our courier. As soon as I got back I asked my friend Lersner to get into touch with Mr George H. Earle, who was by way of being President Roosevelt's personal representative in Turkey. Mr Earle had left the Republican Party in 1932 to join President Roosevelt and had been the first Democratic Governor of Pennsylvania for fifty years. He had served as Minister in Vienna and had been President Roosevelt's representative in Sofia from 1940 to 1942. When he had to leave Bulgaria, the President had sent him as naval attaché to Istanbul, where he continued to keep the President informed on all matters affecting the Balkans. It seemed to me that he was the right man to entrust with a personal message to the President.

A member of the United States war information service stationed in Istanbul had already contacted me through Dr Leverkuehn, a member of our Abwehr, with the information that Cardinal Spellman, the Archbishop of New York, intended to visit Turkey shortly. In fact, the Turkish Government had advised me as early as March that if the German Government would provide a representative with whom the Cardinal could exchange views, he would be prepared to include Turkey in the journey that he was making abroad. While in Berlin I had suggested to Ribbentrop that Dr Leverkuehn would be a suitable representative. Ribbentrop had refused to entertain the idea, but now I raised the matter again. I was given to understand that the Cardinal had undertaken his journey at the request of President Roosevelt. However, the war information service representative advised me that Cardinal Spellman was not travelling in any official capacity and merely wished to obtain a picture of the situation in the Balkans and the Middle East. Ribbentrop had by now given a second flat refusal to any idea of such a contact and I was unable to arrange for any conversation with the Cardinal. In his interviews with the press he declined to make any reference to the possibilities of peace, and M. Menemencioglu told me that his chief interest had been to enlist the help of the Turkish Government in the emigration of Jewish refugees from Europe. In the meantime I was still without any indication of what had happened about the approach that I had made to Mr Earle.

The military situation went from bad to worse. On May 7 my old comrade and orderly officer in the first world war, Colonel-General von Arnim, capitulated in Tunisia. I do not understand to this day why a man of his standing and record was not accorded the honours due to a defeated enemy, and at least received by General Eisenhower. In Germany itself the Allied air offensive was becoming more effective each day, and the destruction of German cities reached an intensity which no one had thought possible. One of the worst aspects was the fate of our prisoners of war in Russia, whose parents and relations were left without the slightest indication of what had become of them. By chance, the Swiss Red Cross representative in Ankara told me one day that he had received about 400 postcards from prisoners, which he intended to forward to the German Government. I asked him to let me have an alphabetical list of their names to send to Berlin. Among them figured the son of the owner of the little bookshop in my home town of Werl. I immediately sent him a personal letter telling him that his son was alive.

This note had the most extraordinary consequences. The rumour seems to have spread immediately that I kept a list of prisoners of war, and I was soon receiving thousands of letters a month from distracted relatives asking me to enquire into the fate of their menfolk. Hitler, it appears, had given orders that P.o.W. postcards were not to be delivered. Even the 400 forwarded by my Swiss friend had been kept back. The reason apparently was the fear that if it should become known that the Russians were treating their prisoners in a humane fashion, the number of deserters would increase. I protested against this inhuman regulation, but the only result was that Ribbentrop ordered me to discontinue my efforts to get information about missing soldiers.

This I refused to do. I passed on all the enquiries to the Red Cross representative and asked him to try to obtain further details from the Russians. The volume of correspondence became immense, and although in many cases we were able to give no help, I had the consolation of receiving numerous letters from anxious mothers and wives expressing their gratitude and saying that my Embassy was the first official organization to show any sympathy for their plight. Ribbentrop tried to put a stop to this by ordering me to forward all such requests for information to Berlin and prohibiting any further private correspondence on the subject. I replied that although I had no influence on the inexplicable manner in which this matter was being handled, it was outside the competence of a Foreign Minister to forbid an Ambassador to write private letters. I continued this small service of mercy right up to the moment that diplomatic relations between Turkey and Germany were broken off.

★ ★ ★

On August 28, King Boris of Bulgaria died suddenly in Sofia, in mysterious circumstances. A week earlier he had paid a visit to Hitler. The loss of this intelligent monarch was to have unforeseen effects on his kingdom. The infant Crown Prince, Simeon, was unable to ensure the succession. His mother, a daughter of the King of Italy, had always been an opponent of the King's policies, particularly after the fall of Italy. The threat of a German defeat exposed the nation to the revenge of their Slavonic brothers from the East. Only the determined and adroit personality of the King could have guided the future course of affairs. It must have been a long-term aim of the enemy rather than of Hitler to obtain his removal from the scene, yet enemy propaganda tried to pin the responsibility for his mysterious death on the National Socialist régime.

Queen Giovanna has stated that the pilot who flew the King

back from Berchtesgaden to Sofia received orders from Hitler to fly in alternate swift climbs and descents. He took his machine up to heights of over 30,000 feet and then power-dived. The oxygen masks were allegedly defective, resulting in considerable damage to the King's internal organs. The Regent, Prince Cyril, also professed this theory and maintained that Hitler wanted to liquidate Boris because the King had refused to declare war on the Soviet Union.

The facts seem to contradict this version. The King returned from Berchtesgaden in perfectly good health, and had climbed the highest mountain in the country, the Mussala Peak, only three days before his final illness. He retired to bed on August 23, and on the 26th a medical bulletin was issued, specifying an affection of the lungs, heart and brain. The German air attaché in Sofia, General von Schoenebeck, who was on terms of personal friendship with the King, was a leading figure in the events of the next few days. I have seen the diary he kept at the time, but as he reserves the right to publish its details himself, I can only refer to what was general knowledge in court circles.

The King asked Schoenebeck to arrange for certain well-known German specialists to be flown to Sofia. These included Dr Sauerbruch, and the renowned Viennese physician Dr Eppinger. However, the King's immediate entourage prevented them from carrying out any clinical examination, and when the King died a few days later, they were not permitted to conduct an autopsy. From the cursory examination they were able to make, they were convinced that the King's death could not possibly be due to any of the causes suggested by the Queen. They noted signs of a complete decomposition of the internal organs, which could only be due to some form of poison.

Hitler, who had long since conceived a hatred against the Italian Royal Family, was convinced that the Queen herself had poisoned Boris. He ordered Ribbentrop to instruct Beckerle, the German Minister in Sofia, to have the Queen and the heir to the throne arrested by the S.S. and brought to Berlin. However, Schoenebeck and some of his colleagues were successful in preventing this. It was all a most mysterious affair, and Sofia was full of rumours at the time, but from the evidence I have seen I am convinced that this was one crime of which Hitler was not guilty.

★ ★ ★

A last talk with King Boris

A discussion with M. Saracoglu, Turkish Prime Minister, at the German Embassy in Ankara

Nuremberg: a cell

On September 8 Italy capitulated. This led to the British occupying the Dodecanese islands of Samos, Cos and Leros, apparently with the purpose of showing the Turks that they could now join the war against Germany without risk. This was to prove another psychological error. The German Air Force completely stopped the flow of supplies to the islands and the British forces had to evacuate them. This happened right under the noses of the Turks, and they could hardly be blamed for continuing in their policy of neutrality. They could see little likelihood of protection in the event of German raids on Smyrna and Istanbul. At this period in the war neither side was showing much psychological insight. The Allies decided at a conference in Moscow during October that Turkey must finally be made to see reason; while Hitler, for his part, freed Mussolini from his mountain prison and tried to set him up as the head of a Fascist Republic in Northern Italy. There was as little hope of bringing him back to political life as there had been for Napoleon when he left Elba.

Some aspects of the war almost belonged to the realm of fantasy. One day in Ankara two high party officials from Berlin called on me. They had been picked by Hitler as the Gauleiters for Georgia and Azerbaijan, and wanted to make a study of the ethnological and economic structure of these two provinces. Their presence was soon the talk of the town, for they had no hesitation in telling everyone of their important missions. The first question from one of them was about the salary and perquisites of the Viceroy of India. When I said in astonishment that I had not the slightest idea what these were, he said that he merely wanted some idea of the sort of income necessary to maintain himself with the dignity due to his position. I was appalled to think of the howl of laughter that would greet this sort of anecdote if the enemy propaganda service got wind of it, and I arranged with Berlin for the speedy recall of these two gentlemen.

★ ★ ★

It was not until October 4 that there came what I assumed was a reaction to the approach we had made to Mr Earle. The manager of the Orient Bank, Herr Posth, rang me up to say that a mysterious foreigner wanted to talk to me on a highly important matter. He had been introduced by Professor Rüstow and it was suggested that I should ask the Professor for further details. Rüstow was an

R

emigré and not a man with whom I had any official contact. Nevertheless, I asked him to visit me. A person of high character, who still retained a warm feeling for his native land, he had considered it his duty to facilitate the interview with this mysterious person, whom he described as an American citizen with a Portuguese passport, who wished to speak to me urgently on behalf of President Roosevelt.

I weighed the risks involved in receiving such a person, who might, for all I knew, be an *agent provocateur*. Herr von Trott zu Solz, my contact with the German opposition group, had visited me in July and I had then had to tell him that Mr Earle had received no answer from the American President. This stranger might well be the messenger we were expecting, and I decided to receive him.

Next morning, a gentleman in his late thirties was shown into my room and identified himself by a Portuguese passport. I soon found that he knew nothing of Mr Earle's mission. Nevertheless, he claimed to have been entrusted by President Roosevelt with the task of discussing with me personally the possibility of an early peace. The President had read with great interest about my Istanbul speech in March and wanted to get a picture of the personalities in Germany with whom it might be possible to negotiate. For this purpose Hitler and his whole clique were out of the question. My visitor did not come empty handed. He took out of his brief-case a roll of microfilm about two inches long which showed the conditions that might serve as a basis for peace with Germany. The only prerequisite was the arrest of Hitler and his surrender to the Allies, who undertook to give him a fair trial. It was suggested that it might be possible to kidnap Hitler on one of his flights to the front, by landing his aircraft in Allied territory. My visitor made an excellent impression. I undertook to study his proposals and arranged for another rendezvous the next day, somewhere outside the Embassy.

I must add here that all the notes I so carefully made, together with the microfilm, were brought back to Germany in August 1944, but they were later confiscated by the French authorities in Gemünden and I have not seen them since. I am therefore giving these details from memory.

I arranged with Posth the next day that he should take our mutual friend to his country house at Büyük Ada and that I would make my own way there in a motor launch. I had read the details on the microfilm through a magnifying glass and had learnt that it was not intended to deprive Germany of her rôle in Central Europe. The former frontiers were to be restored in the West, and Poland must be assured of an independent existence in the East. The film also said that the Allies realized Germany was not self-sufficient, and therefore suggested that the Ukraine should be made an independent State, though associated somehow or other with Germany. I told our emissary that these conditions seemed to provide a solid basis for peace talks. But I advised him to inform whoever had sent him that Germany would do much better to decline any association with the Ukraine. Such a scheme would cause unending conflict with Russia and make our position in the east untenable. We then went into further details of a peace settle-ment in which I presented again my propositions for European unity.

I made it quite clear that I could not take any further step until I had written proof from President Roosevelt that he would under-take to negotiate on the basis of the terms we had discussed. He must understand that no one on the German side could take responsibility for the drastic steps involved merely on the basis of vague generalizations, such as President Wilson's fourteen points. My visitor was fully in sympathy with this demand, but thought it very unlikely that the President would commit himself to paper. Why should I not fly to Cairo, he asked, where the President would shortly be paying a visit? He could then arrange for an interview between us. I told him that such a plan was impossible without news of it leaking out, and as an emigré I would be of little service. We parted on the understanding that he would come to see me again as soon as he had got in touch with the President.

This curious incident had no sequel, and I can only assume that the President considered it too risky to be more specific. Another possibility is that the whole affair was organized by a third party for some unspecified purpose. But if this were so, it seems curious that no attempt was made to make capital out of our conversation. I was left entirely in the dark as to whether there was any alterna-tive to 'unconditional surrender' as a basis for peace.

CHAPTER XXVIII

'OPERATION CICERO'

Menemencioglu sees Eden in Cairo – Allied pressure grows – Germany's desperate military situation – Bombing raid on Berlin – Interlude with Horthy –'Operation Cicero' – Marshal Çakmak dismissed – Dr Vermehren deserts to the British – Allied Balkan plans collapse – German commercial agreement lapses – Emigrés protected – Deportation of Jews in France stopped – Final approach to Roosevelt – Mr Earle's report on its failure – Chromium shipments stopped – Recalled, but permitted to return – Visit to Paris – Lunch with Laval – Menemencioglu resigns over naval incident – 'Overlord' succeeds – Turkey severs relations with Germany

THE decision taken at the Allied Foreign Ministers' conference in Moscow, to bring Turkey into the war before the end of 1943, led to M. Menemencioglu being invited to a conference in Cairo with Mr Anthony Eden. Although M. Menemencioglu was ill at the time, he made the journey and heard Mr Eden use every conceivable argument for an immediate declaration of war by Turkey. M. Menemencioglu replied that Turkey had little inclination to come in at the eleventh hour merely to help in dividing the spoils, and reminded Mr Eden of the general disgust at Mussolini's entry into the war against France in 1940. He also insisted that Turkey would have to be given specific duties to perform if she were to join the fight, so that her Government would remain in political and military control of such an intervention. It was finally agreed that the Turkish Government would make a formal reply as soon as possible. If the reply was affirmative, further conversations would be necessary; if negative, then the matter would be dropped. But it was made clear to him that a refusal could only lead to complete disillusionment on the British side and a serious worsening of relations.

My report at the time shows how grave the situation had become:

'At a reception for M. Menemencioglu, he gave me a long

account of the serious situation in which Turkey now found herself. . . . Since his return from Cairo the British Ambassador has more or less broken off relations with the Turks, no longer invites them to his residence, and intends to remove the seat of his Embassy to Istanbul, a reminder of the period in which the great powers regarded the régime of Kemal Atatürk as having no official existence. The British Ambassador has presented a note in the name of his Government which has all the characteristics of an ultimatum. It demands *inter alia* the complete ruption of commercial relations between Turkey and the Axis Powers. The tone and commentaries in the Allied press make it clear that this is agreed common policy. M. Menemencioglu has emphasized that the Turks cannot surrender their independence in trade matters, but feel obliged, and fully intend, to fulfil their present agreements.

'When I asked M. Menemencioglu what means the enemy could use to bring pressure on Turkey, he replied that the Western Allies were their sole source of certain essential raw materials, such as rubber, tin, textiles, a certain amount of bread grains and, above all, oil. He told me that he had done his utmost to keep Turkey out of the war, but was not prepared to permit the present situation to develop into a breach with Great Britain. If Turkey's economic position was to be threatened, then he would rather declare war. In spite of his determination to honour all current agreements, he must take some steps to ease the pressure. For this reason it would not be possible to receive a German delegation to discuss the renewal of our commercial agreement. . . . It would need a radical change in the military situation in Germany's favour to strengthen his position *vis-à-vis* the Western Allies.'

We had now arrived at a situation in which the Turks were prepared to declare war under the final threat of British political and economic pressure. I decided I must fly immediately to Berlin.

At Hitler's headquarters I gave him a full report on the situation. I also gave details of a new source of information which was to prove of the greatest possible value to us in the coming months, and about which I shall have more to say later. At one of the headquarters' briefings I was able to appreciate how desperate the situation had become on every front and how little confidence was placed in Hitler's conduct of the war. It had reached the point where he was giving orders at battalion level, dissipating his energies in seeing to unnecessary details and making every move-ment of troops a matter for his personal approval. As a result, one of the essential requirements for efficient manœuvre – the exercise of independent command by junior officers – was being com-pletely stifled. Hitler merely laughed at my suggestion that the war should be brought to an end. It seemed that our cities were to be reduced night after night to rubble and ashes, and thousands of innocent civilians condemned to a horrible death, merely because of the nihilism of this one man. It was clear that I must somehow try to get an answer from President Roosevelt to the enquiry I had sent him.

In Berlin I experienced at first hand the full horror of the raids. During one of the worst attacks I was sitting with my son and daughters in the cellar of our house. Everything in the neighbour-hood was reduced to rubble, and although we managed to put out incendiary bombs which had fallen through into my study, the house became uninhabitable, with its doors and windows blown out and the roof destroyed. The rest of the night we spent in the nearby Hotel Esplanade, the only building which remained intact amid the huge conflagration all round it. There was no question of sleep: we spent the night fighting fires.

Next morning I found that practically the whole of the Wilhelm-strasse, the Whitehall of Berlin – including the Foreign Office – lay in ruins. All the railway stations had been severely damaged and no one could tell me whether it would be possible to start my return journey that afternoon. We waited on the station platform from midday onwards, and then towards evening the air-raid alarm sounded again. The crowd of would-be travellers made no attempt to seek shelter, and in the middle of the raid a train made its way into the station in complete darkness. I was full of admira-tion for the miracle performed by the faithful railway workers.

On my way back to Turkey I accepted Admiral Horthy's invitation to break my journey at Budapest. He took me off to Mezöhegyes, the famous state stud farm, where he had invited the members of his Cabinet to a hunting party. There I was presented by his Minister of the Interior, M. Keresztes Fischer, with a truly astonishing document. This was a report of conversations between certain Nazi Party emissaries and a group of Hungarian nationalists, in which they had discussed the possibility of breaking up Hungary into its constituent provinces and incorporating them into German territory. Admiral Horthy and his Cabinet were referred to in the grossest terms.

I agreed to make representations to Berlin, which I did on the spot, as the Hungarian Prime Minister, M. Kallay, had no contact with the German Minister. Admiral Horthy told me it was clear to him that from a military point of view there was no further hope of winning the war, and that he had already put out certain feelers in order to ascertain the intention of the Western Powers. It seemed to me that as the head of a sovereign state, subjected to such treatment and kept completely in the dark concerning the course of events, he was undoubtedly entitled to make such a move. The only apparent result of my intervention was that Veesenmayer, one of the chief Nazi intriguers in Budapest, was appointed German Minister.

* * *

The new source of information I had mentioned to Hitler has now become world famous under the name of 'Operation Cicero'. Most of the details have been described by my former attaché, Moyzisch, in his book of the same name.[1]

At first I objected to the publication of this story because I wished to spare my British colleague in Ankara, Sir Hughe Knatchbull-Hugessen, any embarrassment. At one time, in Peking, my son had become a good friend of the family, and during the war, when my son visited me in Ankara, after making his way to Europe from the Argentine, Sir Hughe went out of his way to take him on one side at a diplomatic reception and have a friendly talk with him. I was much touched by this act of politeness, and would have preferred to make some belated acknowledgment by having the 'Cicero' manuscript suppressed. However, as Moyzisch agreed to submit his manuscript to me, I was able to prove to my satisfaction that he had described the case with complete fairness. In a postscript to the English edition I stated that in due course, and in the interests of historical accuracy, I would make my own comments on the matter.

The whole business began in a rather puzzling way. Herr Jenke,

[1] *Operation Cicero*. Allan Wingate, London, 1950.

one of my two ministers, came to me one day to say that a man-servant whom he had employed at one time had rung him up on the telephone with an offer to provide us with important in-formation. Jenke was Ribbentrop's brother-in-law, and for many years before the war had lived in Turkey as a businessman. His former servant was using the name of Diello, although I under-stand his real name was Elias. I refused at first to have anything to do with the matter. It seemed to me that a spy who offered his wares by telephone was hardly worth taking seriously. However, Diello became insistent, so I gave instructions for Moyzisch to look into the matter.

Moyzisch, it should be explained, was attached to my Embassy in the nominal capacity of commercial attaché, but was really the representative of the Gestapo and the *Sicherheitsdienst*. It may be asked how such an appointment came to be made after my insistence, before coming to Turkey, that the Gestapo should not be allowed to meddle in my affairs. Once war had broken out, it was difficult to resist demands that the intelligence service of the secret state police should be represented in Ankara, and in the end I had to give way. Moyzisch was under my orders for adminis-trative purposes, but I did not see his reports, nor would they have interested me. He took no part in the diplomatic affairs of the Embassy.

If I had treated Diello's first approach at all seriously, I should have arranged for the Abwehr people, who worked under the orders of my military attaché, to investigate the matter. But for all I knew the fellow was an *agent provocateur*, and if anyone was going to be made to look foolish, I preferred it to be the Gestapo rather than the Abwehr. I should have been spared much sub-sequent trouble if the Abwehr had been in charge, but once Moyzisch had taken over the matter it was too late to make any change. In spite of his dual allegiance, Moyzisch played very fairly with me, and himself handled Diello quite as skilfully as anyone in the Abwehr could have done.

I shall never forget the morning when Moyzisch showed me the first examples of Cicero's work. He had worked all night to obtain prints of the rolls of film which our informant had given him, and came into my office pale and unshaven and laid a folder of photo-graphs on my desk. 'What do they consist of?' I asked. Moyzisch shrugged his shoulders. It was clear that his knowledge of English was insufficient for him to have grasped the value of the contents. I picked up the first one and must have given a visible start, such was my surprise. 'Good heavens, Moyzisch!' I said, 'I hope we have nobody in our Embassy who is photographing this sort of thing.'

It needed only one glance to tell me that I was looking at a photograph of a telegram from the British Foreign Office to the Ambassador in Ankara. Form, content and phraseology left no doubt that this was the genuine article. It consisted of a series of answers from the Foreign Secretary, Mr Eden, to questions which Sir Hughe Knatchbull-Hugessen had asked in another telegram, requesting guidance on certain aspects of his country's policy, particularly as regards Turkey. I realized that we had come upon a priceless source of information. For purposes of internal security I thereupon asked Moyzisch always to refer to our informant as Cicero. It seemed a happy nickname.

When eventually Moyzisch's chief, Kaltenbrunner, recognized the importance of the source, he claimed exclusive rights to it and instructed Moyzisch to send further material direct to him without showing it to me. As soon as Moyzisch told me of this, I said to him: 'Tell your superiors that as long as I am Ambassador here in Ankara, I refuse to tolerate such a procedure. You are my subordinate, and I require you to show me in the first instance all the material that passes through your hands.' I intended to subject all the material to my own political evaluation, even if Ribbentrop chose to support Kaltenbrunner's demand.

Not until I read for the first time in Moyzisch's book about the telegrams referring to the bombardment of Sofia did I realize that I had not after all been allowed to see the whole of the material, and that some of it must have been sent direct to Kaltenbrunner. It would be possible to check this only if the complete details were ever published.

In his book, Moyzisch refers to 'indiscretions' which might have betrayed our source, and this requires some comment on my part. Many of the British telegrams contained information which made it necessary for me to intervene with M. Menemencioglu. There was one which referred to the possibility of setting up radar stations in Turkish Thrace, for the guidance of Allied bombers in their attacks on the Rumanian oil wells. Thinking it necessary to make an immediate protest about this to the Turkish Foreign Minister, I had to say I had heard that the British air attaché or one of his colleagues had mentioned such plans to certain neutrals. I drew attention to the serious danger of German reprisals, such as a bombing raid on Istanbul, which I would be unable to prevent if Berlin reacted violently to this information. M. Menemencioglu was astounded at the extent of my knowledge and gave an account of our conversation to the British Ambassador.

The next day the photograph of another telegram from Sir Hughe to the Foreign Office lay on my desk. In it he made the remark, 'Papen knows more than is good for him.' Ribbentrop soon saw a copy of this, and assumed that there must have been some indiscretion and that our source had been endangered. It was only when I had given him the reasons for my intervention that he understood that if any use was to be made of this information, certain risks would have to be taken.

The whole of 'Operation Cicero' was naturally carried out with the greatest discretion. Jenke, the Counsellor, was the only other member of the Embassy in the secret, and even the military attaché and his Abwehr personnel knew nothing. Fräulein Rose, who had been my personal secretary for several years, came to me one day in a state of great agitation and asked to be transferred. It was obvious, she said, that certain material was being withheld from her, and she could only assume that this meant a loss of confidence on my part. I myself wrote all the telegrams to Berlin on the subject. However, it was clear that information such as this, which from time to time required counter-measures, could not continue indefinitely, whatever precautions were taken. It is interesting that Moyzisch's own secretary, also an employee of the Gestapo, deserted to the British.

What I do reject most emphatically is Moyzisch's assertion in his book that practically no use was made of the information obtained. During the period of the Foreign Ministers' meetings in Moscow, of the Teheran and Cairo Conferences, and, indeed, right up to February 1944, the flow of Cicero's information was of priceless value. I was fully informed of the Moscow decision to compel Turkey to declare war by the end of the year (communicated to Sir Hughe in Foreign Office telegram No. 1594 of November 19) and of Sir Hughe's reply (in telegram No. 875) which said, in part:

'M. Menemencioglu assures me that the Turkish Government

will be prepared to take part as soon as it is clear that Allied landings in the West have been successful; that is to say, about a fortnight after the invasion.... If we are unable to agree on an earlier date, it might be well worth our while to fall in with M. Menemencioglu's suggestion. At least this would permit us to prolong the enemy's present state of uncertainty. The Foreign Minister expressed himself in very definite terms and said that he was prepared to discuss the matter with his Prime Minister with a view to confirming this undertaking.'[1]

Cicero also kept us informed of the conversations between the Turkish President, Mr Churchill and President Roosevelt in Cairo, and of the manner in which the Turkish Government managed to meet the increasing pressure placed upon them to enter the war.

After the Roosevelt-Churchill-Stalin meeting in Teheran at the beginning of December, the British Ambassador in Ankara was requested to invite the Turkish President to a conference with the three heads of state in Cairo. President Inönü replied that if he was being invited to conversations which merely presented him with a series of decisions taken at Teheran, he was not prepared to accept; but if the meeting would provide an opportunity for full and free discussions on the manner in which Turkey could best serve the common interest, then he would go. This assurance was given, although in view of the decisions taken in Moscow and Teheran, it is not clear to me on what grounds it was forthcoming.

The President left Ankara on December 3, accompanied by M. Menemencioglu and his advisers. At Adana he was met by President Roosevelt's private aircraft. The Turkish statesmen made it quite clear at the beginning of the conversations that they were not prepared to fall in with the requirements laid down in Moscow and Teheran, and would not allow their country to become a pawn to be moved at will on the Allied military chessboard. They had the impression that it was intended to make use of Turkish air and naval bases without regard to the reprisals this might involve. They suspected also that there was no intention of giving any specific rôle to the Turkish forces. Their principal concern, how-

[1] [As Herr von Papen has already explained, his own files were lost during the war. This quotation was taken by him from an incomplete photostat copy of an article by Dr Paul Schwarz, which he was given to understand appeared in the *New Yorker Staats-Zeitung*.]

ever, was Stalin's expressed intention of declaring war on Bulgaria as soon as Turkey joined the Allied side.

After long and difficult negotiations, in which the Allies attempted to dispel Turkey's fears, it was finally agreed that as no further postponement of the Allied war plans was possible, the Turkish Government would make its intentions clear during December. Turkish demands for military equipment would be given full consideration and the Turks were asked to outline specific requirements. In the meantime her air bases should be prepared for possible use.

'Even if we could use the Turkish bases, we did not necessarily expect Turkey to join in actual hostilities,' Sir Hughe writes in his memoirs.[1] But the Turks saw the matter in a very different light. Their General Staff in Ankara knew it would be impossible for the Allies to use Turkish airfields without either a declaration of war or the inevitable consequences. 'No blame was to attach to Turkey if she decided to answer in the negative,' Sir Hughe remarks. This again is being wise after the event. From the British Ambassador's telegrams at the time it was clear that he had lost patience with Turkey's obstructive methods and was suggesting that relations with Ankara should be broken off.

The Turks had been informed that Allied plans for 1944 included operations against German positions in the Balkans with the landing of Allied forces at Salonika. For this purpose it was asked that certain air bases near Smyrna should be made ready for use by February 15, so that the bomber and fighter squadrons needed to cover the landing operations could be stationed there.

The Cicero telegrams showed that the main political debate between the Big Three at Teheran concerned the 'unconditional surrender' formula. There was considerable difference of opinion, and although a joint statement on the subject was proposed, it was never issued. Churchill and Stalin regarded the demand as bad tactics, likely to encourage the Germans – and Hitler in particular – to fight until the last moment, but they were unable to convince Roosevelt. For this reason his declaration[2] on December 24, 1943, made a considerable impression at Hitler's headquarters. 'The United Nations have no intention to enslave the German people,' he said. 'We wish them to have a normal chance to develop, in

---

[1] *Diplomat in Peace and War.* John Murray, London, 1949.
[2] In a Fireside Chat.

peace, as useful and respectable members of the European family.'
This seemed to represent a change in his opinions and was probably
the main reason why Himmler was allowed to empower a Swedish
intermediary in London to ask for a final definition of the
'unconditional surrender' formula. However, this approach led
nowhere.

The differences of opinion between the service chiefs at Teheran
were even more interesting. Churchill's stubborn insistence on a
Balkan offensive through Salonika and the Adriatic was rejected in
favour of the invasion of Northern France. A secondary operation
was to be carried out through Salonika, but the main weight of
the attack was to be made across the English Channel. This was
'Operation Overlord', often referred to in the Cicero telegrams.
While Churchill wished to free the Balkan satellites from German
domination, and still prevent them from coming under Russian
influence, Stalin regarded their liberation as his task alone.

At no time did I receive from either Hitler or Ribbentrop any
instructions on the general policy to be pursued. Any other Foreign
Ministry would tell an Ambassador forwarding such priceless
information what they thought of it and what steps they expected
him to take. As it was, I was left entirely to my own devices. It has
often been argued since the war that Churchill's plan for a Balkan
invasion would have shortened the conflict and all its sufferings.
On this point alone, the decision I had to take was one of very
great responsibility. From the military point of view it seemed
that any offensive through Greece, Macedonia and Yugoslavia
would be extremely difficult because of the mountainous terrain
and sparse communications. If it took the Allies until the spring of
1945 to reach the Alps through Italy, it can well be imagined how
much longer their advance through the Balkans would have taken.
It seemed to me, therefore, that the factor of ending the war more
quickly did not really enter into the question.

It has also been suggested that Allied intervention in the Balkans
would have prevented Russia's occupation of Bulgaria, Yugoslavia and Hungary. I cannot agree with this. In view of the
confidence that Stalin still enjoyed, at least with President Roosevelt,
Russia would certainly have been invited to share in the task of
occupation. As far as I was concerned, the overriding consideration
was Russia's known ambitions concerning the Dardanelles. I
remembered Molotov's suggestions in November 1940. If Turkey

and the Dardanelles were to be abandoned to the Russians, they would gain control of the Eastern Mediterranean and would be able to threaten Western Europe from the south. I therefore maintain that I was right in doing what I could to influence the Turks as far as possible in preventing the Allied operation at Salonika, especially in view of the evidence now available: that the Western Allies were prepared to make considerable concessions to Stalin because of their fear that he might conclude a separate peace with Hitler.

In any case, it was clear to the Turkish Foreign Minister and General Staff that Allied use of Turkish air and naval bases would inevitably lead to German reprisals, which I would not be able to prevent. The least consequence would be the complete destruction of Istanbul and Smyrna. One of the ways by which the Turkish military leaders sought to avert the final step was by making considerable demands for anti-aircraft weapons. Lists of the necessary material were drawn up and handed to the British mission. From the British telegrams I learnt that these demands were regarded as highly extravagant. The only ports where this material could be landed, according to the Turks, were Alexandretta and Mersin, and the British calculated that its transport on the single-track Taurus railway would take at least a year.

Thanks to Cicero, the Turkish Government's reply to the Allies, dated December 12, lay on my desk a few days later. M. Menemencioglu declared that in view of the totally insufficient flow of supplies to the Turkish forces it would be quite impossible to complete the preparations for the Salonika operation by the middle of February. This note proved a grave disappointment to the Western Allies, and Sir Hughe even suggested that in view of the Turks' grossly exaggerated demands, it would be better to break off negotiations and put an end to friendly relations. Mr Eden replied that no such step could be taken in the tense situation that still existed, and there was no alternative but to make the best of a bad job. All this was passed on to Hitler, who thus realized that the Balkan offensive would not now take place.

Turkey's exaggerated demands for material, made simply to avoid a declaration of war, seemed to me perfectly justified. I still hoped that it would be possible, by reaching some agreement with President Roosevelt and Mr Churchill, to halt the Russian advance at the frontiers of Europe, even if this involved our capitulation to the Western Allies. During the whole of this period Mr Earle continued to assure my friend Lersner that this possibility was being actively presented to President Roosevelt, and that he still hoped to excite his interest.

Hitler and Ribbentrop, knowing the decisions taken at Teheran and Cairo, had a vivid picture of what was in store for Germany, but their mental attitude prevented them from drawing the necessary conclusions. I knew that Hitler was not shown any reports that mentioned the possibility of losing the war, nor any that Ribbentrop thought might have a defeatist effect. There was therefore little point in engaging in a long correspondence concerning the decisions taken at Teheran and Cairo. This I had to leave until my next visit to Hitler's headquarters. However, the first months of 1944 brought me so much work, accompanied by a decline in my relationships with Hitler and his entourage, that I was unable to make this visit until April. It had become absolutely clear to me, as a result of reading all the Cicero telegrams, that I must do everything I could to hasten the end of the war. I needed to find out once and for all whether President Roosevelt was prepared to consider some mitigation of the unconditional surrender clause, and whether, by our capitulation in the west, the Russian armies could be held on Germany's eastern frontiers. This branch of my activity was not known to the *Sicherheitsdienst* and therefore formed no part of Moyzisch's reports.

* * *

Cicero's information was immensely valuable for two reasons. A résumé of the decisions taken at the Teheran Conference was sent to the British Ambassador. This revealed the Allies' intentions concerning the political treatment of Germany after her defeat, and showed us where the differences between the Allies lay. But what was of even greater and more immediate importance was the intimate knowledge it gave us of the enemy's operational plans.

We obtained indisputable evidence of Turkey's attitude to increasing Allied pressure. We also learnt that the possibility of an Allied attack on the Balkans through Salonika could be ruled out. This was of great importance, because it meant there was no need for the considerable dispersal of our defensive forces which the indifferent communications in this region would otherwise have made necessary. The Supreme Command now realized that the only real threat with which it had to contend was the invasion of France, although our knowledge of Operation Overlord was limited to the name. (I repeatedly suggested that in order to deceive the enemy into thinking that we knew its details, our propaganda should give the impression that we possessed considerable knowledge of Overlord. However, for some reason Hitler declined to allow this.)

We were thus able to appreciate the intentions of our enemies in a way that can hardly have a parallel in military history. Moyzisch is right only up to a point when he says that this flood of information caused nothing but sceptical head-shakings in Hitler's headquarters. It is true that for some time the whole thing was regarded as a clever ruse on the enemy's part. These doubts were probably a result of Ribbentrop's habit of keeping bad news from Hitler as much as he could, and describing the source of all such reports as untrustworthy. It was only after the Allied air attack on Sofia, which had been accurately foretold in a Cicero telegram, that doubts were removed as to the validity of the information.

Since then a great deal has been written about this feat of espionage. One article in the German weekly *Die Zeit*, of December 14, 1950, contends that Diello, the 'Cicero' of the story, had been placed in the British Embassy by the German *Sicherheitsdienst*. I can only assume that the author of this article shares with Kaltenbrunner, its former chief, an obsession with the virtues of the S.D. If 'Cicero' had been an S.D. man, Berlin would hardly have remained convinced for so many months that the whole business was a trap laid for us by the British Secret Service, and I certainly would not have had the trouble I had in convincing Ribbentrop that the source was reliable and the information of such vital importance.

I can only give a fragmentary account of what happened to Cicero, alias Diello, or Elias, or whatever his name was. After Moyzisch's secretary had deserted to the Allies on April 4, 1944, the British can have been under no illusions as to the extent of Cicero's activities. Yet he was seen several times round Ankara, and once by Moyzisch in Istanbul as late as August 1944. At various times, Egyptian newspapers reported that he was being sought by the police. There have also been reports from Turkey that batches of forged British Treasury notes 'made in Germany' have been seized, and that they formed part of the sums paid to him by Moyzisch.

When I revisited Istanbul myself at the end of 1951 for the purpose of arranging at long last for the transfer to Germany of all the furniture and personal belongings I had left behind, I was able to confirm a few more details. Apparently Cicero had spent part of the intervening period in Egypt, but when he heard that the Twentieth Century-Fox Film Company was making a film of his story on the spot, he hurried to Istanbul to offer his services. However, his offer to play his part in person was not accepted. Since then he has disappeared from circulation again, although there was one report that he had been arrested by the Turkish police. When Ribbentrop's brother-in-law, Jenke, was accidentally drowned in the Bosphorus in July 1951, the Turkish newspaper, *Vatan*, had a further anecdote in their news story of his tragic death. A week earlier one of their reporters had interviewed Jenke and asked him whether Cicero was still in Turkey. 'I think so,' Jenke was reported as saying. 'Last year he sent his daughter to me with a demand for £15,000. Naturally, I sent her back empty-handed. I saw him a couple of times in Pera, but all he did was to raise his hat politely and pass by.'

* * *

In spite of M. Menemencioglu's cool response to the Western Allied overtures, the various British missions in Ankara did not give up hope. On the Turkish General Staff there was a group of officers, supported by a section of the press, who believed a declaration of war to be inevitable. On the other hand another group, which included M. Hüsrev Gerede, who had recently returned to Turkey from his post as Ambassador in Berlin, assured me that an overwhelming majority of the Government party and the Army wished to avoid a breach with Germany. My personal relations with the Government continued on a basis of complete confidence, and as a New Year present for 1944 my wife and I received from M. Menemencioglu a magnificent set of hand-beaten Turkish silver.

The British reaction to what they considered the grossly exaggerated Turkish demands for military equipment led to caustic attacks on the Army staff and particularly on the Chief of Staff, Marshal Çakmak. They maintained the Marshal was too old, had no understanding of the requirements of modern warfare, and had adopted an obstructive and pro-German attitude. The President apparently made up his mind to give way where necessary and decided to part company with the Marshal, his friend and colleague for many years. He was succeeded by General Kâzim Orbay and General Salih Omurtak, who were presumably more acceptable to the Western Allies.

Fevzi Pasha, Marshal Çakmak, with whom I had fought on the River Jordan in 1918, and who was one of the chief architects of the Atatürk revolution, was in fact very much more than the simple title Chief of Staff implies. He was the absolute authority on all matters concerning the armed services and probably the most trusted man in modern Turkey. His replacement was therefore greeted with very mixed feelings. It was an error to label this great soldier, or any of his leading generals, pro-German or pro-British. They were Turkish patriots, and their first concern was the safety and well-being of their nation.

I left Istanbul for a few days' stay at Brussa, where I hoped the mineral baths would relieve my rheumatism. My visit was soon broken by the news brought to me by a member of my staff that one of our principal Abwehr agents in Istanbul, Dr Vermehren, had deserted to the British. Dr Vermehren had married a Countess Plettenberg, who was a distant relation of mine. She was a devout Catholic and had converted her husband to this faith. Her religious convictions had, moreover, led to a profound distaste for the Nazi régime, which they shared. However much one might admire their sentiments (and in fact I had myself obtained permission from Berlin for her to join her husband) there was little doubt that the British now had an intimate knowledge of the ramifications of our Abwehr organization, or so Berlin chose to assume. The incident caused consternation in Germany, and party circles were quick to accuse me of having organized the whole affair. The most important repercussion was Hitler's decision to remove control of the Abwehr from Admiral Canaris and the Army, and place it under the orders of Himmler. I hurried to Istanbul, but was unable to obtain a reversal of Hitler's decision. My own position in Berlin had been considerably weakened and the party was clamouring for me to be brought to trial. I was to learn later that the Gestapo made plans about this time to send a plane-load of reliable S.S. men in plain clothes to Ankara for the purpose of kidnapping me and taking me back to Berlin. Apparently Hitler did not permit this in the end, although Ribbentrop had already signified his approval of the scheme.

On February 3 the British military missions left Turkey. There was no longer any hope of carrying out the planned operation on Salonika on the 15th of the month. The British had realized at last that there was no way of overcoming Turkish opposition to taking part in the war, and the whole Balkan operation had to be abandoned. In England there was severe criticism in the press at this diplomatic and military failure, and British relations with Turkey reached their lowest point. On February 8 I had the pleasure of entertaining the Turkish Cabinet in the Embassy to hear a concert by the famous pianist Gieseking. M. Menemencioglu made no attempt to disguise his disquiet at the situation and told me that Turkey could not allow her relations with her British and American allies to get any worse. He would have to seek some means of *rapprochement*, and I understood that he was thinking in terms of our commercial relations.

The Berlin Government made things no easier for the Turks. German relations with Hungary had reached such an acute stage that the Prime Minister, M. Kallay, feared an attempt on his life and took refuge one night in the Turkish Legation. Highly incensed, Ribbentrop requested me by telegram to press the Turkish Government to deny the right of asylum to M. Kallay. I had no wish to see this statesman's life endangered, and in a conversation with M. Menemencioglu ascertained that the Turks had no intention of abandoning the extra-territorial rights of their Legation. I therefore informed Ribbentrop that there was no question of denying asylum.

The Nazi campaign against the Jews caused me further difficulties. Hitler ordered me to withdraw passports from all the German emigrés in Turkey and deprive them of German citizenship. I resisted this order and informed Ribbentrop that the majority of the emigrés had left Germany with the full permission of the Government, and many of them had taken up posts in Turkish universities and other institutions. They had engaged in no political activities and remained loyal to Germany, even though they found the Nazi régime unacceptable. I could not see my way to carry out his instructions, and told him that the Turkish Government would consider such a step inexplicable. Not a single emigré was molested in any way. I came in for renewed criticism from the party, which demanded a boycott of all Jewish firms in Turkey. I pointed out that such a restriction had no validity in a neutral country and, to underline the point, made most of my own purchases in Jewish shops.

I was able to render another service to the victims of Hitler's anti-Semitic campaign. I learnt through one of the German emigré professors that the Secretary of the Jewish Agency had asked me to intervene in the matter of the threatened deportation to camps in Poland of 10,000 Jews living in Southern France. Most of them were former Turkish citizens of Levantine origin. I promised my help and discussed the matter with M. Menemencioglu. There was no legal basis to warrant any official action on his part, but he authorized me to inform Hitler that the deportation of these former Turkish citizens would cause a sensation in Turkey and endanger friendly relations between the two countries. This démarche succeeded in quashing the whole affair.

I mention these incidents only to demonstrate that it was possible, even in the final stages of the régime of terror in Germany, for a person in my position to exercise normal human instincts and refuse to obey such unprincipled orders.

* * *

With final catastrophe looming ahead, I made another attempt to find out whether there was any possible way of coming to agreement with President Roosevelt which would not involve the German people in a surrender of all their rights. In March I asked Lersner once again to renew contact with Mr George Earle. He was to make concrete proposals and obtain some definite response from the American President. I was prepared to arrange for Mr Earle to be flown secretly to some convenient place for a meeting with my friends, Helldorf and Bismarck, and decide with them what steps were necessary for the neutralization of Hitler and his eventual surrender to a properly constituted international court. The offer to the American President specified that the 'unconditional surrender' formula must be modified to permit an armistice in the West and the transportation of German troops to the Eastern Front to prevent Russian troops occupying territory within the borders of Germany and her Balkan allies. This provision would have to be recognized in any peace negotiations.

Mr Earle gave an account of this matter in an interview with the *Philadelphia Enquirer* on January 30, 1949. 'This offer was explained to President Roosevelt at once, by courier, and rejected: the President ruled that all such attempts at negotiations must be made through the Supreme Commander, General Eisenhower.' That meant, of course, the end of my intervention. I had no contact with General Eisenhower, nor was he in a position to make a decision of a purely political nature. Mr Earle states in the article that this rejection caused him to fly to Washington to take up the matter further with the President, to whom he expressed the conviction that with Germany's inevitable defeat, the victorious Russian armies would threaten the whole of the Western World. He quotes President Roosevelt as replying: 'The Normandy invasion would soon be launched, that the Germans would be beaten "in a few months" and that Russia, made up of so many peoples speaking so many languages, need not be worried about and would, in fact, fall apart after the war.' Whereupon he told the President that unless he was specifically forbidden within a week to do so, he would make a public announcement that the President's foreign policy was false and that Russia presented the main threat to the American continent.

'The President at once wrote in stern terms,' Mr Earle's article continues, ' "I specifically forbid you to make public any information or opinion about an ally that you may have acquired while in office or in the service of the U.S. Navy." The President also revoked our agreement; I was to resign my commission as Commander and [be] turned over to the Navy Department, which sent me to Samoa as Deputy Governor of 16,000 natives.'

Mr Earle's insistence on making his views known personally to the President is worthy of recognition. His fall from grace reminds me of my own experience in 1916, when the German Chancellor, Bethmann-Hollweg, asked me to give my views on submarine warfare to the German press: whereupon General Falkenhayn ordered me to report to my battalion on the Western Front within twenty-four hours. 'Suppose . . . . we had accepted Papen's offer?' says Mr Earle at the end of his interview. That indeed is a leading question. President Roosevelt's rejection destroyed our last hope of an agreement in the best interests of Europe.

* * *

My wife and I spent Easter in Istanbul. Odessa had fallen, the siege of the Crimea had begun, and we were greatly worried about my daughter, Isabelle, who had just left for Bucharest on her way back to nursing duties in a field hospital in the area. The Papal delegate, Monsignor Roncalli, who had arrived in Istanbul for a Confirmation service, tried to assuage our fears. He could see no alternative to a German defeat, but he had confidence in the judgment of the Western Allied statesmen and their intention of taking all the measures necessary for European security. At my request he forwarded to the Vatican my pleas that the Allies should realize the difference between the Hitler régime and the German people.

On April 20 M. Menemencioglu informed me, to his great regret, that the Turkish Government felt obliged to suspend all further deliveries of chromium to Germany from May 1. I had long expected this decision. Allied representations on the subject of Turkish exports to Germany had reached a crescendo, and their success dealt the German economy a heavy blow. The production of high-grade armour plate depended entirely on these deliveries, and their cessation affected the whole conduct of the war. Additional locomotives and rolling stock had just been provided for increased shipments of chromium. This did, at least, make it possible to transport every available ton up to the stipulated date.

Ribbentrop reacted with a sharp message which spoke of reprisals, and ordered me to report to Berlin immediately. It was an unpleasant journey, flying over the Black Sea, Bulgaria and Yugoslavia more or less at ground level, in order to avoid Allied air attacks. On April 27, the day before my arrival, the German Government issued a communiqué stating that the Ambassador in Ankara would not return to his post for the time being. When Ribbentrop told me of this decision in Berlin, adding that a sharp note was to be sent to Turkey threatening counter-measures, I told him that such a communication would have no effect, except to cause pleasure to the Western Allies. I deplored his practice of recalling an Ambassador whenever relations with a particular country became strained. It was just such situations which demanded the Ambassador's presence. If he intended to send me on a diplomatic holiday, then I would prefer him to accept my resignation. This annoyed Ribbentrop, who said it was a matter for Hitler to decide.

At our combined interview with Hitler, I found him again

open to reasoned argument and prepared to overrule his Foreign
Minister. After we had both presented our points of view, Hitler
declared that it was nonsense to send off a sharp note threatening
counter-measures if we were in no position to carry them out. He
agreed that it was essential to have an Ambassador back at his post
in such a situation and asked me to return immediately. In our conversations on the general situation I spoke of the information that the
Cicero telegrams had provided concerning the Teheran decisions.
Hitler replied sharply that the Allied intention of destroying Germany was best appreciated from their demand for unconditional
surrender. Everything else was merely propaganda to soften up
Germany and inject the idea of capitulation. He rejected flatly any
idea of a compromise and was still convinced that his Atlantic
Wall was impregnable. When the British and Americans had
stubbed their toes on it, he would soon bring the Russians to a halt.
Ribbentrop nodded in agreement. There was clearly little point in
going on with the conversation.

On the same day I received the news that my son, serving with
an armoured reconnaissance unit in Rennes, had been wounded in
an air raid and was in hospital in Paris. I asked Hitler's permission
to visit him, and this was granted. The rail journey took me
through Saarbrücken, Metz and Châlons, and I was shocked to
see the destruction caused by Allied air attacks in the large towns
along this route. It was only just possible to keep trains circulating,
and in France the Allied air forces had for weeks been bombing
bridges, cuttings and marshalling yards. In Metz, for example, it
had been possible to maintain only a single line for the passage of
trains. On the train I met my old friend Count Schulenburg, our
Ambassador in Moscow, who was also travelling to Paris for a
few days. It was our last meeting before he fell a victim to the
purge that followed the attempt on Hitler's life on July 20.

After I had satisfied myself that my son was on the way to
recovery, I spent a few days studying the situation in France. I
visited Field-Marshal von Rundstedt at his headquarters, in order
to obtain a picture of the defence measures being organized against
the daily awaited Allied invasion of France. Rundstedt was
desperate. The systematic destruction of the railway network was
making the rapid movement of his reserves impossible. He had
informed Hitler of this and expressed the opinion that a landing on
a major scale could not be contested. I had no chance of speaking

to him alone, so my attempts to find out whether he had been initiated into any plans for removing Hitler, and his opinions on the desirability of prolonging the war, were fruitless. I also visited General von Stülpnagel, the Commander of the Paris District. He was even more pessimistic than von Rundstedt, but did not respond at all to my suggestion that some other way must be found of ending the war.

Abetz, the German Ambassador in France, invited me to lunch with M. Laval and other leading Frenchmen. In a private conversation Laval assured me that after the fall of France it had always been his wish to co-operate with Hitler in the reorganization of Europe, but that Hitler had always prevented this. The threatened invasion, if successful, would mean the end of the war and the end of Hitler. It could be resisted only with the co-operation of the French, whom Hitler had so cruelly deceived. He asked me to impress on Hitler that this was the last chance of establishing Franco-German relations on a new basis. If Hitler wanted French assistance in repelling the invasion, then he must demonstrate his full confidence in the French people and agree to the measures which had for so long been necessary.

Immediately after this talk I went to Salzburg for another talk with Hitler. As I had prophesied to Laval, his complaints and requests made not the slightest impression on Hitler. They were all brusquely rejected. Hitler now harboured grandiose illusions which bore no relation to reality.

No sooner was I back in Ankara than Operation Overlord began. Ten days later Menemencioglu had to resign as Turkish Foreign Minister. To a certain extent this was our fault. The German Naval High Command had asked for permission for a number of small vessels to proceed from Rumanian ports through the Dardanelles into the Aegean. My naval attaché, Admiral von der Marwitz, gave assurances that these were not warships or auxiliaries, and carried neither naval personnel nor arms. Permission was given for their passage, but a strong Western Allied protest greeted the arrival of the first ship.

Menemencioglu informed me that he could only allow the remaining vessels to proceed if I gave him my personal assurance that they were not auxiliary naval vessels, as the Allies claimed. I ordered Admiral von der Marwitz to make a personal investigation and report. After I had passed his further assurances to the

Foreign Minister, the Turkish harbour authorities carried out their own inspection of the second ship. They found in the hold a quantity of small arms, radar equipment and uniforms for the crew, who were wearing civilian clothes. As a result, their further passage was forbidden. I can only assume that my naval attaché had himself been deceived. As an old political hand, he would never have deliberately put me in such a situation with the Turkish Government. Menemencioglu, too, was placed in an embarrassing position and was obliged to bear the consequences. No one regretted his resignation more than I did, and my only consolation was that our personal relationship was not affected by this incident.

In Europe there was no holding the invasion of the Allies, and their successes led to a further intensification of their pressure on Turkey. It was made quite clear that if Turkey wished to take part in the peace settlement, the Government must make up its mind to sever relations with Germany. The growing power of Russia made it impossible for Turkey to risk falling finally into the Allies' bad graces. They alone would be in a position to check Russian ambitions in the Dardanelles and the Eastern Mediterranean. There was still a strong current of opinion which deplored the termination of friendly relations with Germany, but the future of the nation was at stake, and on August 2 the National Assembly approved the severing of diplomatic relations.

This was a sorry end to my mission, and my final audience with the Turkish President was difficult for us both. He found few words to mitigate the situation and we contented ourselves with general conversation on the world's troubles. His final words to me were, 'If I can serve in any way as mediator in this conflict, I am entirely at your disposal. Our personal relationship is in no way affected by the historical events which have made this step necessary.'

Ribbentrop sent me orders to return to Germany within twenty-four hours. The purge following the attempt on Hitler's life on July 20 had been in full flood for more than a week. Ley had made a bloodthirsty speech about liquidating the officers corps and the whole aristocracy. My friends Helldorf and Bismarck had been arrested as accomplices.

The details that reached us were fragmentary and confusing. Only one thing was certain – Hitler had survived the assassination attempt. It seemed an extraordinary trick of fate that this man, now intent on involving Germany in his own ruin, should have survived. There was no doubt that he would order brutal counter-measures, and that a number of my own friends would be included among those to be liquidated. My own fate was by no means certain. Jenke, the Embassy Counsellor, who was Ribbentrop's brother-in-law, overwhelmed me with demands that I should send a telegram to Hitler on behalf of the Embassy personnel, congratulating him on the fact that his valuable life had been spared to the nation. In the end he and the other members of the party in the Embassy grew so insistent that I was unable to with-stand their demands without it appearing that my sympathies lay with the other side. Jenke was much disappointed with my draft, which he considered far too formal in the circumstances.

On August 2 Mr Churchill made a speech in the House of Commons, describing the continued successes of the Allies, the coming German defeat and the consequences of the unsuccessful assassination plot. He noted with satisfaction the severance of Turco-German relations. He added: 'Herr von Papen may be sent back to Germany to meet the blood bath he so narrowly escaped at Hitler's hands in 1934. I can take no responsibility for that.'

President Inönü had told Mr Churchill of my efforts to end the war, and President Roosevelt must also have informed him of the approach I had made. He must have assumed that this time Hitler's revenge would know no bounds.

In Ankara the head of one of the neutral missions told me that he had been asked by the Allies to warn me not to leave Turkey in any circumstances. My fate was certain and it would be foolhardy to return to Germany. The Allies undertook to offer me protection and support if I would announce publicly my breach with the Nazi régime. I asked him to thank his friends for their offer, but to reply that I was unable to fall in with their suggestion. There were still some Germans who considered it unworthy to save their own skins and abandon their country in her hour of need. Two days later I left Ankara for home.

CHAPTER XXIX

ARREST

Return to Germany – My last sight of Hitler – Back in Wallerfangen – We become refugees – The Allies break through – Arrest by the Americans – The death of Roosevelt – The Concentration Camps – At Eisenhower's headquarters – Reunion with Horthy – Imprisonment at Mondorf – Colonel Andrus – Horthy writes to Churchill – Arrival at Nuremberg

I LEFT Turkey on August 5, 1944. The Turkish Foreign Minister had placed his private railway coach at my disposal, but the train only went as far as the frontier. The coach should have been detached at the Bulgarian border station of Svilengrad, but as the Bulgarians had none with which to replace it, I had to get in touch with the Turkish Foreign Ministry and ask permission to continue my journey in their coach as far as Sofia.

The situation in Bulgaria was already becoming very difficult. With the diplomatic breach between Germany and Turkey, and the inexorable advance of the Russian armies, the Slav sympathies of the Bulgarians were beginning to stir. Surprisingly enough, I was welcomed at every stop across the country with gifts of flowers, fruit and the local plum brandy; but the German Legation staff were treated very differently only shortly afterwards, when they tried to escape the Russian advance amid the general collapse. Perhaps, after all, the Bulgarians had got some inkling of all the efforts I had made to keep the peace in South-Eastern Europe.

The train passed through Belgrade just after a massive Allied air attack, but when we got to Budapest the beautiful city on the Danube lay unharmed in the August sunlight, with no sign of the terrible calamity that was shortly to befall it. I approached the German frontier with mixed thoughts. For one thing, I fully expected to be arrested by the Gestapo. My name might well have been given by some of those arrested after the July 20 attempt on Hitler's life, and I probably figured in their lists as a likely person to negotiate with the Allied Powers, or as Foreign Minister in any Government destined to take Hitler's place. My granddaughter was travelling with me, and in case anything unpleasant should occur I entrusted her with final messages to my wife, who had preceded me home.

However, at the border everything was normal. In Dresden I parted company with my granddaughter and sent off all my luggage in the chauffeur's care to our house at Wallerfangen. Perhaps they were going to deal with me when I got to Berlin, I thought, and I made the last stages of the journey in a state of some trepidation. But instead of the Gestapo, I found waiting for me a delegation from the Foreign Office, led by Doernberg, the chief of protocol. I learnt that I had no reason to fear arrest, although tension in the capital was at breaking point. Doernberg whispered to me that a number of Foreign Office officials, including Haeften, who had been in the Vienna Legation with me, and von Trott zu Solz, had been arrested. Schulenburg, the former Ambassador to Moscow, was also thought to be on the list. I was expected to report to the Führer's headquarters in East Prussia the next day.

One of my first calls came from Prince Otto Bismarck, Counsellor of the German Embassy in London before the war, and I arranged to have dinner with him and the Princess in the Adlon Hotel that evening. They were both in great distress at the arrest of his brother, Gottfried, one of the earliest members of the party and administrative head of the Potsdam area. They could not believe that he was in any way implicated in the plot, and begged me to intercede with Hitler on his behalf. It can be imagined what a difficult situation I was in. I had learnt from Gottfried Bismarck's own mouth of his plans, but I could not tell his brother this, and undertook to do what I could.

I took the special night train, and arrived at Hitler's headquarters the next morning. Two people on whom I had always relied for information, von Schmieden and Dr Megerle, were in a state of acute depression and had no idea which way events were leading. Ribbentrop was full of assumed indignation at the 'perfidy' of the Turks in breaking off relations, and in a bloodthirsty rage at the 'bourgeois traitors' of July 20. He was incensed that members of his own ministry were implicated, and talked of the necessity for a wholesale purge. He was quite incapable of conducting a logical conversation concerning the general situation after our breach with Turkey.

That afternoon I saw Hitler. I was taken to his barracks through a dense screen of security precautions. The number of check points had been doubled, and at the last of them visitors had to surrender their hats, coats, brief-cases and anything else they were carrying. In spite of this, I was not asked if I were carrying a weapon, and was escorted by two guards into his ante-room. After I had waited a few minutes Hitler came in, ashen pale, one arm in a sling, trembling in every limb. The man was a nervous wreck. He tried to greet me in a hearty fashion. His first remark referred to the plot. As far as I could distinguish from his disconnected sentences, he was trying to minimize the whole affair. But while he spoke with a deprecatory gesture of the 'traitors', bitter hatred shone from his sunken eyes. However, he soon pulled himself together. 'And what is your news, Herr von Papen?'

I told him briefly about final developments in Turkey, the increasing pressure of the Allies and their threat to exclude Turkey from all peace negotiations if she did not break off relations with the Reich. I gave an account of my final audience with the Turkish President, and how Inönü had offered, in spite of the breach in our relations, to act as mediator should Germany ever wish him to do so. I emphasized the President's readiness not because I thought Hitler would be likely to take advantage of it, but because I wanted to prevent any attempt by Ribbentrop to instigate some act of revenge, such as bombing Istanbul. Hitler seemed completely satisfied with my account and, far from echoing Ribbentrop's accusations of Turkey's perfidy, said that he had been reckoning with Turkey's defection ever since the loss of the Crimea.

Encouraged by this sane approach, I tried to turn the conversation to the general situation. I sought to impress upon him that if both jaws of the vice were closing in on Germany, a decision would have to be made as to how best to employ our strategic advantage of interior lines of communication. The only real solution, I said, was to concentrate all our forces on keeping the Russians as far away from Germany's frontiers as possible. Although this would ultimately benefit the Western Allies, it might be possible to reach some form of agreement with them. From what we had learned from the Cicero documents, we were still in a position to rescue what was left of Europe.

Hitler reacted violently to this. Such a compromise, he said, was impossible, and he made no response whatever to a suggestion of mine that I should go to Madrid and sound out the Western Allies. Instead, his face hardened, and he said in staccato sentences: 'This war must be fought without compromise to its end. When our new weapons are ready, we will show the British where they get off. With such people there can be no compromise.'

Livid patches appeared in his white and haggard face, and again he broke into a bitter tirade about the plot. 'I have always known that there was a small faction intent on getting rid of me. But they will not be successful. I shall continue with my task to the end. What these people forget is that almost the whole of the officer class is behind me and that the youth of the country is solid in its support.'

When the flood of words came to an end, I interjected, 'I hear that even some of your close party associates, Count Gottfried Bismarck, for instance, are said to have been mixed up in the affair. I have no means of forming an opinion, but I know one thing: you must never present the world abroad with the spectacle of the Iron Chancellor's grandson on the gallows. If he is found guilty, sentence him to life imprisonment, but do not give our enemies an opportunity to make capital out of such an incident.'

Hitler narrowed his glaucous eyes as he looked at me, then forced out the words, 'This bunch of aristocrats! – they don't deserve anything better.' Nevertheless, I had the impression that my words had found their mark and that Bismarck's life would be spared.

Just as I was about to leave, Hitler took me by surprise by handing me a little case containing the Knight's Cross of the Military Merit Order. 'You have rendered many services to your country, and it is certainly no fault of yours that your mission in Turkey has come to an end. You have been serving in the front line there, as the attempt on your life has shown.' And he held out his hand. Our last meeting was at an end.

As I left his quarters the press wanted to take a photograph of me with my new decoration, and were somewhat surprised when I declined by saying that I did not feel that I had deserved such an honour. I was still bemused by the episode, and can only suppose that Hitler had done it quite deliberately to counter the supposition abroad – to which even Mr Churchill had given expression in the House of Commons – that I would be included on the July 20 death list. In his arbitrary fashion Hitler had made up his mind to prove the opposite. As I left the headquarters area I noticed that a new pyramid-shaped concrete bunker was being built for Hitler's personal protection. He can never have used it, because shortly afterwards his headquarters had to be hurriedly evacuated.

When I got back to Berlin I tried to use such influence as I had regained in the party, as a result of my new decoration, to intercede with Himmler for the lives of some of those arrested after the July plot. Fifteen members of the Union Club, whose President I had been for eleven years, were among them, and several had already received death sentences. Of my old regimental comrades, von Colmar, von Boehn and the Braunschweig brothers had also been arrested, together with Pastor Bonhoeffer, the son-in-law of my old friend Hans Wedemeyer. Several members of well-known Silesian, Pomeranian and Westphalian families had also been caught in the net, although they can have had little connection with the plot. This correspondence with Himmler dragged on until the following January without any noticeable result.

I was only too happy to get back to my home in Wallerfangen, where I arrived at the beginning of September. But its normal quiet was shattered by the sudden flood of units of the broken army of occupation retreating from Northern France and making their way to the Rhine. The hopelessly confused columns showed what ludicrously swollen staffs we had built up during four years of occupation. There seemed to be no order and no plan, only the panic-stricken rush of those who were trying to save their skins. Most numerous were the ground formations of the Luftwaffe, with columns of lorries carrying pianos, furniture, cattle, and an unbelievable collection of women. Some of them were doubtless admirable girls who had been doing their duty to their country as members of the auxiliary women's services, but the eyes of an old soldier saw much else besides.

The High Command seemed completely unprepared for this influx. One evening the deputy Commanding General for the Saarlouis section of the West Wall appeared from Wiesbaden. He told me that leading units of the United States Army had reached the Moselle on both sides of Metz and were marching on Trier through Luxembourg. Hitler had given orders for the retreat – it was more like a rout – to be halted on the Saar at all costs. The only reserve available in the fifty-mile sector between Trier and Saarbrücken consisted of the non-commissioned officers' school at Saarlouis. The famous West Wall existed only in the imagination.

All its complicated barbed wire entanglements had been re-moved to the Atlantic Wall, none of its bunkers were manned, and not a single machine-gun or piece of artillery was in position. If the Allied Command had followed the classic prescription of harrying a beaten enemy by every available means, they could have been across the Saar and on the Rhine overnight. I naturally assumed that this was what would occur, and the General shared my opinion. I comforted him by saying that the war would be over all the sooner and its ravages finally at an end. At least the Western Allies would be able to occupy the whole of Germany before the Russians crossed her eastern frontier. But, as often occurs in war, the unexpected happened. The Allied forces paused to regroup on the Moselle. They too had come to a standstill, in spite of their immense services of supply. A handful of young cadets held the great fortress of Metz and the German armies were given time to re-form.

In the meantime, the pounding of Germany's cities from the air went on. Hitler, it seemed, was oblivious to this senseless destruc-tion, which could only end by making it impossible for Germany to take any part in the work of European recovery. In view of the hopeless position on the Western Front, which Government circles in Berlin either ignored or knew nothing about, I decided to make one last attempt to stop the conflict. I thought that if we could come to some agreement with the Western Powers it would be possible to halt the Russians on our eastern frontiers. Although Hitler had made no response to my suggestions at my last visit to his headquarters in August, I decided to make another appeal, through Baron Steengracht, the Secretary of State at the Foreign Office. I told him that I was prepared to go to Madrid to contact the Western Allies with a plan for them to occupy Germany step by step while we held fast in the east. But the reply came back from Ribbentrop that anyone who weakened Germany's power of resistance by engaging in such discussions would be shot as a defeatist. The local Army command received orders that under no circumstances was I to fall into the hands of the enemy, and was instructed to evacuate me and my family to the rear. I declined to go, saying that an old soldier like myself could not possibly set such a bad example. I intended to stay where I was until orders came through to blow the bridges over the Saar.

Towards the end of November instructions were, in fact, given

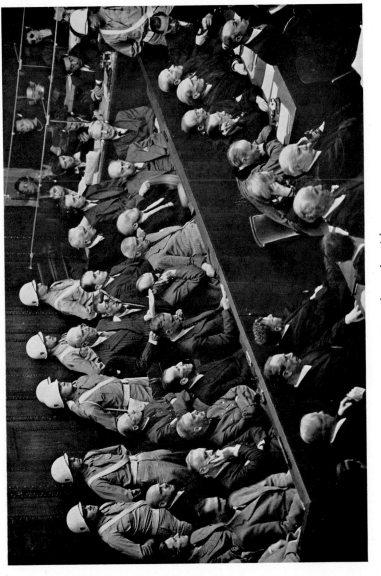

Nuremberg: the trial

The denazification trial

to evacuate all the German villages west of the Saar, but after a conference with the local Gauleiter, I intervened again and sent a telegram to Hitler requesting that all those not of military age be allowed to remain with their livestock for the purpose of protecting their property and homes. The original order was rescinded and most of the farmers were able to stay where they were. However, the Allies had started to advance again, and this time we had to go. We took only bare necessities, and left all our furniture, family heirlooms and my valuable collection of books and pictures in the cellars, as I did not wish to take up transport space that could be used by others. Baron Salis, who had a country house at Gemünden, near Coblenz, had offered us a temporary home. We had become refugees, like so many of our countrymen.

When Rundstedt began his hopeless Ardennes offensive, we learned that the United States Army had removed everything of value from our Wallerfangen house and the place had been burned to the ground. Just before Christmas my daughter Isabelle's short leave ended, and although I told her that to return to the Eastern Front would be extremely risky because of the chaotic transport situation, she made up her mind to go back to her post as a nurse at a field hospital in the Tatra mountains. She had served in this capacity right through the Russian campaign, and although it meant that we should not spend Christmas together, I could only be proud of her sense of duty.

In the meantime the Gestapo had established a post in the village to keep an eye on my movements. The local postman told me in secret that all my incoming and outgoing mail passed through their hands. By March 1945, the Americans had reached the Rhine at Remagen, and had crossed the Moselle on a broad front. Their armoured spearheads were already in Simmern, only a short distance away from Gemünden. On the 15th, I was awakened at three o'clock in the morning by an officer from the Army High Command, who told me that he had received orders to accompany me and my family across the Rhine. I could have refused, and would then have become an American prisoner the next day. But my other three daughters and son were back in Germany at the mercy of the Gestapo, and I was not prepared to risk them being taken as hostages. I decided to comply, but declined to expose my wife and remaining daughter to the rigours of a second flight, and they stayed where they were.

S

The country's defence had ceased to be organized along any logical lines. From his distant headquarters, Hitler was now determining the movement of companies, and any deviation from his orders was punishable by death. Corps commanders were being forced to sacrifice whole divisions because they were left no discretion as to when to order a retreat. The armies in the Saar positions were left to be surrounded when they could have been brought back across the Rhine and used to form a new line. The Allied spearheads surged forward relentlessly.

I made my way through the confusion of defeat to my married daughter's home at Stockhausen in Westphalia, but this was only to be a temporary refuge. I had hardly arrived there before the Allies surrounded the entire Ruhr. While my son, who was still convalescing from a wound, and my son-in-law remained in the house, my daughter, with her children, and myself, retired to a small lodge in the woods as the battle crept ever nearer. On April 9 the main house was surrounded and searched from top to bottom, and my son and son-in-law were carried off as prisoners of war. About noon the next day an American platoon arrived at the lodge and the sergeant challenged my identity. When I admitted who I was, he said I was under arrest, although I protested that I held no military command and was already over sixty-five years old. We invited him to sit down while I finished a plate of stew with the children; then I packed a few things into a rucksack and went off with him in his jeep.

*　　*　　*

I was to spend the next four years of my life under guard, either in prison or in a labour camp. The first stages gave no foretaste of what was to come. I was treated with military punctilio by my American captors, who took me first to the divisional headquarters in Ruethen, where I was rejoined by my son and son-in-law. We travelled together through Werl, Dülmen and Haltern to the Army headquarters, and then by plane to Wiesbaden, headquarters of the army group. My emotions on passing through my birthplace at Werl can be imagined. Fortunately the little town was relatively undamaged, unlike Dülmen – I had been its honorary mayor – where every building had been reduced to rubble. At my request, the Americans in Wiesbaden were kind enough to send a young officer to pick up some more clothing from Baron Salis' house at Gemünden. He was also able to bring back something infinitely more precious – the news that my wife and daughter were safe.

In Wiesbaden we learned of the death of President Roosevelt. Although we knew that he had hated Hitler's Germany and was advocating harsh terms for the beaten enemy, his death was a great blow. The Treaty of Versailles had initiated a bad peace and had sown the seeds of another war because our most powerful enemy, President Wilson, with all his humanitarian ideas, had retired from the European scene. We wondered whether this tragedy would be repeated. Roosevelt was not a dreamer like Wilson, but a man of action. His intervention had saved both Britain and Europe, and his dominating influence among the Allies would have made him the principal agent in the reconstruction of the Continent. We had always hoped that he would use a strong hand to abolish the narrow nationalism of the European powers, and would take them into partnership with the United States as a defence against the totalitarian doctrines of his Russian partner. We had no means of knowing the extent to which Roosevelt had convinced himself that it would be possible to integrate the Soviet Union as an honourable member into the concert of the United Nations. We had no knowledge of what had passed in Yalta or of the concessions that had been made to keep Stalin in the Allied camp – concessions which rendered the maintenance of a true balance of power in Europe impossible.

At the time, Roosevelt's death seemed a disaster. It seemed impossible that any successor would have the same knowledge of the world's problems. Roosevelt's extraordinary qualities, his lively, penetrating intelligence, his powers of decision and his gift for imposing his ideas on others, are seldom given to more than one man in a generation. Now it seemed that Churchill would make the peace. He had also joined in unnecessary concessions to Stalin, but he knew the true needs of Europe better. His whole strategic conception throughout the war showed his correct appreciation of Russia's intentions. His idea of building up a second front in the Balkans instead of France was the one way of keeping the Russians out of this disputed sphere of interest. Even if American influence was still paramount, there seemed good reason to suppose that Churchill would be able to impose his strategic designs. It was impossible to foresee that this statesman, whose genius and energy had saved the Western world, would soon be dismissed from all conduct of affairs by the verdict of his own people.

Fortunately our fears at the time have proved unfounded. Roosevelt's successor, President Truman, little known to the outside world when he assumed office, appreciated the true nature of Russia's policies probably even more quickly than Roosevelt would have done. The trend observable at Yalta and Potsdam has been reversed, and we have to thank President Truman and his advisers, above all General Marshall, for placing Europe on its feet again. Under American guidance, economic recovery has taken the place of apathy and narrow nationalism has been recognized as an out-of-date conception. Moreover, British foreign policy has shown once again that whichever government is in power, the true interests of the country prevail. Under Mr Bevin, the Labour Government's foreign policy remained true to the overriding conceptions which Mr Churchill had always professed.

* * *

An even worse shock greeted us in Wiesbaden, when our escorting officers told us of the unbelievable conditions encountered in the German concentration camps. At first we found their accounts impossible to believe, but some of them had actually visited these death camps. For their part they found our genuine ignorance – and indeed that of most of the German people – of conditions in these camps equally unlikely, and met our astonishment and disgust with disbelief. It can be imagined how these disclosures added to our existing depression.

Both then and ever since, those who live in western countries have found it impossible to believe that people in Germany were ignorant of what was going on in these camps. I can hardly blame them. In Great Britain and America even minor brutalities find their way into the courts and the full glare of newspaper publicity. They cannot imagine a state of affairs which could hide the evidence of such atrocities from the vast majority of a nation.

Perhaps I may here insert a word, if not of explanation, at least of comment. That concentration camps existed was, of course, known in Germany. Some of them had been set up as early as 1933, long before they became death camps. The names of places such as Oranienburg, Sachsenhausen and Dachau were even treated with slight irreverence in the catch-phrases of the day. There was a children's couplet which ran: '*Lieber Gott, mach' mich fromm, dass ich nicht nach Dachau komm!*' To all outward appearances these camps were properly conducted. They were visited from time to time by foreign police experts and others, who saw nothing to complain of as far as accommodation, food and medical services were concerned. It was not possible during such brief visits to decide what degree of moral or physical pressure was brought to bear on the inmates. The security precautions were already so well organized that even people who only spent a short period as prisoners, refused to divulge any information when they were released, because this would have led automatically to their re-arrest, probably for good.

After the outbreak of war, the number of these camps was considerably increased. At the same time, other camps were set up for workers transported from the East, and for the outsider it became almost impossible to distinguish between labour camps, prisoner-of-war camps, and concentration camps. Security precautions were redoubled, and increased with the general reign of terror which extended as the war drew to a close. The conditions found in these camps as they were captured by the Allies must not be assumed to be those current during the whole of their existence. With defeat near, the Gestapo gave orders for large numbers of the inmates to be liquidated. At the same time the camps became hopelessly overcrowded, and with the increase of hunger and endemic diseases, the number of corpses exceeded the capacity of the burial parties. The rupture of communications due to the invasion and the air war also gravely increased the problem of feeding these thousands of unfortunate people. This was true of the country as a whole, but at least the people outside the camps were able to seek additional food for themselves.

Any comment on conditions in the concentration camps or criticism of their existence, led in the latter years of the war to automatic arrest for defeatism. Those with real knowledge did not dare to speak, and everyone else preferred not to hear. It must not be forgotten that even in the foreign press such camps as Belsen, Ravensbrück, Flossenburg and Natzweiler became known only after the war. I can give a personal example of the general state of ignorance. My son spent six months during the war at a training centre near Gotha, in Thuringia. Buchenwald was only fifteen miles away, about five miles from Weimar. During the whole of this period my son knew nothing of the existence of a concentration camp there. If the name Buchenwald was mentioned, it was always described as the headquarters of an S.S. unit.

★ ★ ★

At the end of April we were transported with an air of mystery to Rheims, which had become General Eisenhower's headquarters. There I was interrogated by a commission of four generals, led by General Strong. It included the American General Batts and two Russians. I was still completely in the dark as to the reason for my continued arrest, and was given no explanation in answer to my enquiry. We engaged in a general high-level discussion, at which I was able to give little of the military information they required, but offered to lend my name to any appeal to the German nation which might serve to conclude hostilities immediately. I said that I could do this only as a free agent, and could not engage in any negotiations within the framework of unconditional surrender. I suggested that I should be taken to a sector of the front where I could get in touch with the German Army command in the west. General Strong then asked, 'Which of the German generals do you think would be prepared to consider proposals for an armistice?' After deliberating for a minute or two, I suggested the names of Colonel-General Blaskowitz and General Count Schwerin. Our discussion was broken off at this point, presumably to enable the generals to consult with the Supreme Commander. However, at a second conversation the next day I was told that my suggestion had not been taken up.

Shortly afterwards I was taken away again, and after a long car journey, deposited at the Chateau de Lesbioles, near Spa, where comfortable accommodation had been arranged for us and where we came under the charge of a United States major named Seeger and a Captain Robertshaw of the British Army. They behaved at all times with great correctness, and we were able to live a normal and civilized life. I was soon separated from my son, who was taken off to a prison at Révin. My son-in-law, Max von Stock-hausen, was permitted to return home. In return, I received a distinguished companion – Admiral Horthy, the former Regent of Hungary.

I had last seen him in December 1943, at a shooting party in Mezöhegyes, and have already described the conversation we then had. He had aged greatly since that time. The loss of his eldest son, an air force pilot, had hit him hard, and the disgraceful treatment he had received at the hands of Hitler and the Gestapo had worn him down. They had behaved like gangsters, finally extorting his abdication in return for a promise that he would be allowed to see his second son, who had already been carried off by the Gestapo. They met again only after the war. Horthy was incensed at being treated as a prisoner by the Americans. He had been Hitler's prisoner in a Bavarian castle for over six months and had regarded the Allied armies as liberators. At Lesbioles he was treated with great respect and had no inkling of what was yet to befall him.

Our comfortable existence did not last long. In May we were taken on another journey which ended at a small hotel in the little town of Mondorf, near Luxembourg. To our astonishment, it was not only surrounded by two high barbed-wire palisades with watchtowers and armed guards, but completely devoid of all furniture except for camp beds and trestle tables. Horthy was aghast. 'Is this the way you treat a head of state, even of a defeated country?' he asked. Our unfortunate escorting officers seemed somewhat nonplussed, and promised to ask whether there was not some misunderstanding.

We soon learnt that the Grand Hotel, a thousand yards away, housed all the principal surviving German Government personalities, who were being held to answer for war crimes. It had not previously occurred to me that I might be included in their number, and I became greatly dispirited. We received no newspapers and were completely cut off from the outside world. Our food, such as it was, was brought in an old tin can from the other hotel and always arrived cold. Horthy was quite unable to eat it, and his condition soon deteriorated to the point where a breakdown seemed inevitable.

We came under the authority of an American colonel named Burton C. Andrus. At first we remained under the care of our two conducting officers, who did all they could to improve our lot. But it was not long before Horthy had a complete collapse, and I forced one of the American orderlies to hurry to the Grand Hotel for a doctor, who soon arrived, accompanied by Colonel Andrus. The Colonel was a plump man of medium height, with a smooth-shaven face and what I believe is called a crew-cut hairstyle. Behind rimless spectacles shone a pair of angry brown eyes. The buttons and belt of his uniform and his steel helmet were highly polished, and he carried a riding crop, which I soon learnt was his usual custom. This was the first time I had seen him, and I was so angry at the conditions in which we were being kept that I lost my temper.

'What do you mean by treating the head of a state in this disgraceful fashion?' I shouted. 'Are you not aware that the United States has signed the Hague Convention which lays down rules for the treatment of prisoners of war? How can you possibly treat an old gentleman well over seventy in such a scandalous fashion as to bring him to death's door?'

The Colonel seemed completely taken aback. 'I have no idea who is shut up here,' he said. 'I know nothing about a head of a state. I am responsible for the guards and nothing else concerns me.'

'Then get in touch with your headquarters and tell them that something has to be done about conditions here,' I replied heatedly.

I had not complained about my own treatment at all, but might have done so. Although the food became more abundant and was better served, all the windows were replaced by wire netting, and straw mattresses substituted for the beds. A number of other prisoners were brought over from the Grand Hotel, including Schwerin-Krosigk, the former Finance Minister, and Baron Steengracht, the last Secretary of State at the Foreign Office. We were now packed six in a room and although I asked that Horthy should be given a room to himself, this was curtly refused. His personal servant, who had volunteered to remain with him, was sent off to a prison camp, although he had never been a soldier. Most of our clothes were taken away, and the best I could do for the unfortunate Horthy was to have myself put in the same room with him, where I was able to get a few extra blankets for his bed and look after him a little.

I soon had another brush with Andrus, when I asked him to declare whether we were civilian prisoners or prisoners-of-war. 'You are prisoners-of-war,' he said.

'In that case we have the right under the Hague Convention to write to our families,' I answered. 'Or am I then to assume that the United States did not sign the Hague Convention?'

'That does not interest me in the least.'

'But it interests us,' I retorted. 'We do not consider that the

American Army can deprive us of rights accorded to us under international law.'

The next day a notice was hung up stating the conditions under which we might write letters.

Horthy wished to take advantage of this to communicate with the Allies on the subject of his unfortunate country, and he asked me to draft a letter to Mr Churchill. In it he appealed to the Western countries to permit Hungary to retain her natural frontiers and to ensure that her Western traditions remained alive. Hungary, he said, was a country in which Christianity was deeply rooted and which for centuries had acted as a 'warden of the European bequest' in the Balkan area. If her economic stability was guaranteed by being given some sort of trusteeship over Croatia, with access to the Mediterranean, the country would prove a powerful bulwark against Bolshevism. Stressing the fact that in the hour of need he had remained at his post, and did not leave his country as Benes had left Czechoslovakia after the Munich Agreement, Horthy asked that his action should be given due recognition. He also sent an appeal to the King of England, while I sent a letter to the King of Sweden on his behalf and wrote a personal letter to General Eisenhower, rejecting the theory of collective responsibility for the war and asking for some indication of the war crimes with which I was to be charged. There was no reply to any of these communications.

At the beginning of August, all the people in our hotel were moved into a separate wing of the Grand Hotel at Mondorf. We were informed that most of us would shortly be transferred elsewhere, and Horthy left the next day with my own best wishes for his future welfare. Two days later I was roused at dawn, taken out and pushed into a lorry, where to my horror I found myself in the company of Goering, Ribbentrop, Rosenberg and their satellites. All communication was forbidden, and we greeted each other in icy fashion. Goering no longer wore one of his pompous uniforms, and the remainder had a confused and shabby air. In most cases they had been wearing the same clothes or uniforms for months, and their ties and shoelaces had been taken away. It made me think of the last time I had seen them all together at the party rally in Nuremberg in 1937, when its leaders were at the height of their glory.

We were taken to Luxembourg aerodrome and put on two

transport planes. I went, under a heavily armed guard, with Streicher, Rosenberg, Frank, and others. Colonel Andrus brought up the rear. We seemed to be going east, but there was much cloud and it was not until after we had landed and were driving through a ruined town that I recognized it as Nuremberg.

CHAPTER XXX

PRISON

Prisoner behind bars – Interrogation – Chaplains and psychiatrists – The indictment – Choice of defence counsel – Conditions in the gaol – Schacht and the photographer – A sketch of my co-defendants

WITH an armed guard on each side I was taken into a building of a type which I had never entered in my life. Its purpose was only too clear. On either side of a long corridor three storeys high there were endless barred cells connected by narrow gangways. In case anyone should have the idea of jumping to his death from the top gangway, they were each closed off with wire netting. The air was damp and icy, and the building smelt of long disuse. *Lascia ogni speranza!* Hell as Dante described it could not have had a greater effect on me than thus finding myself, at the end of a long and industrious life – lived according to the best of my ability in the service of God and my country – a prisoner behind bars.

Colonel Andrus conducted me personally to cell No. 47. The door clanged, and I was alone with my thoughts.

The prison was very roughly equipped. Instead of the cell window, high in the wall, there were thick iron bars, and the lighting installation in the ceiling had been removed. In one corner there was a collapsible wooden bed with a grey blanket. The only other furniture was a small table and stool. The hatch in the door, through which the meals were passed, was kept open, so that the guards outside could keep us continually under observation. This meant that there was always a draught, but a wire-mesh outside window was installed before the weather got cold. We were told that the food we were getting, which was far from sufficient, represented German rations. Without any light, we were obliged to go to bed at dusk, and as the days got shorter I often spent long hours sitting glumly on the edge of my bed, not even able to read.

The worst thing was not knowing why we were in prison or what we were being charged with. In addition, I was in great distress over the possible fate of my two daughters, who had been serving as nurses on the Russian front. There had been no news of them since Christmas 1944, and I had not received a single letter since my arrest. I could only hope and pray that they had survived the collapse and found their way home. Not until September did I learn, from the United States Army Catholic Chaplain, that my wife and daughters had arrived in Nuremberg, and I could breathe a sigh of relief.

At the end of August I was returning from our weekly visit to the shower-room in the basement when, to my great astonishment, I came face to face with Admiral Horthy. We were unable to speak, but I was amazed that he should be in prison. He did not look well, but still retained his air of authority, in spite of the sly remarks of the guards.

Detailed interrogation started at the beginning of September. Mr Dodd, my American questioner, was polite, correct, even kind. I tried to explain the course of my political career. After I had given my account of Hitler's appointment as Chancellor, Mr Dodd interjected: 'And immediately after February 1933 you organized the notorious People's Courts, which turned the whole judicial system of Germany into a farce.' 'There you are in error,' I replied. 'There were no People's Courts as long as I was Chancellor or Vice-Chancellor. They were formed much later.' It transpired that Mr Dodd was referring to the emergency decree signed by the President after the Reichstag fire. This authorized three judges to sit as a special court, and bore no relation to Hitler's People's Courts, where the judges were laymen and not members of the legal profession.

In the course of our discussions, it became clear that he had only a very superficial knowledge of events and the internal developments in Germany. Speaking of the Roehm *Putsch*, he remarked that it was completely baffling to him how anyone could have accepted another post under such a Government after the treatment I had received. I tried to explain the situation at the time, and how I had accepted the Vienna appointment after the murder of Dollfuss only in order to prevent a general European conflict. Mr Dodd refused to accept this argument, and insisted that I had submitted myself entirely to Hitler. Our discussion became heated, and I said with some asperity, 'I am sorry that you cannot understand a situation in which duty to one's country comes before personal considerations.' Mr Dodd then showed himself at his best. He said that he had not wished to impute any dishonourable intentions to me. After that we understood each other much better, although even then I was unable to find out what was being held against me. After the trial he acknowledged my acquittal with a box of Havana cigars. I still think of him warmly.

Mr Dodd and the two admirable Catholic chaplains, Father Flynn and his successor, Father Sixtus O'Connor, were a great solace to me during this difficult period. Much less agreeable were the visits of the gentlemen who called themselves psychiatrists. It was their duty, apparently, to determine our sanity, though few of them gave the impression of having any genuine scientific qualifications. If they had, people like Goering and Ribbentrop would certainly have been fascinating subjects. Instead we were called upon to undergo intelligence tests, together with silly problems like explaining what we saw in certain abstract splodges of ink. This was above my head and I asked to be excused. I told one of our questioners that if he wanted to satisfy himself of my sanity I was prepared to answer any question in the spheres of history, geography, politics or economics, but apparently this was a type of conversation for which he was less well prepared. These investigations did, however, provide one lighter moment, when our marks were added up and announced. Top of the class was Dr Schacht – a result that surprised none of us. Speer, as I recall it, was second, and I was third, in spite of my obstinacy about the pictures. Streicher came last, a position which could have been occupied by almost any of the other Gauleiters.

To keep some account of the passage of time I had marked up a calendar on the wall of my cell. The prison doors had closed behind me on August 12. My first interrogation took place on September 3 and the second on the 19th. It was not until October 19 that I received a copy of the indictment. I saw that the start of my trial had been set for November 20, and observed with a feeling of relief that there were no charges against me under the heading of war crimes or crimes against humanity. I was charged with having conspired to wage war. In my ignorance of the new judicial procedure to be adopted, I imagined it would be easy to prove my complete innocence and my strong opposition to the declaration of war. Moreover, I still thought that each of us would have an individual trial, and I wrote a cheerful letter to my wife, saying

that I expected the proceedings to last two or three days and that
I would be with her by the end of November. I was soon to be disillusioned; but it gives an indication of the strict nature of our
solitary confinement that no one had hinted to me that all twenty-
one 'war criminals' were to be given a mass trial. We had no
reason to suppose that it would last nearly a year and would have
as its object the pinning of collective responsibility on the whole
German nation.

With the indictment each of us was handed a list of German
lawyers, from whom we were free to name one as our personal
defence counsel. The only name known to me was that of Dr Dix.
When I asked if he could be appointed to my defence, I was told
that he had already undertaken that of Dr Schacht. I therefore sent
Schacht a letter asking if Dix could defend both of us, or that Dix
should recommend one of the other lawyers for the purpose. This
letter Schacht never received. The result was that by November 10
I was still without a defence counsel, but chance came to my aid.
An old friend of mine, Count Schaffgotsch, had heard of a well-
known Breslau lawyer, Dr Kubuschok, who was prepared to
accept my case. It was indeed a fortunate choice. Kubuschok was
an excellent defence counsel, with a keen intelligence which
enabled him to master every situation. But even he found that the
procedure adopted at the trial taxed the qualities of the most expert
counsel. As I did not know Kubuschok personally, I asked that my
son, who had studied law, should be allowed to assist him, as he
knew the whole of my political career. In the end, he was released
from a prisoner-of-war camp at Stenay for the duration of the
trial. Without wishing to minimize Kubuschok's services in any
way, it is only fair to say that without my son's help the verdict in
my case might have been very different.

★ ★ ★

I intend to deal in the next chapter with the legal and judicial
aspects of the trial, both as it affected me and against its historical
and political background. But it may interest my readers to have
an account of how my co-defendants and I reacted to the long
strain of the next eleven months.

Arthur Koestler, in his book *Darkness at Noon*,[1] has given us a

[1] Jonathan Cape, London, 1940.

vivid description of the methods used in the mass Soviet trials to obtain confessions from the accused. In the Nuremberg trial the prosecution had thousands of documents on which to base their case and none of us were required to sign confessions, but we were subjected to a prison régime which bore many resemblances to Koestler's description. A system had been devised by which our resistance was gradually lowered, through sleepless nights with a light shining in our faces. By the time the trial ended, although my mind was still working, I was physically a broken man.

Under the pretence of preventing an attempt at suicide by any of the prisoners, a guard was stationed outside each door and was changed every two hours, night and day. These guards were required to keep us under continuous observation through the hatch in the cell door. In the corridors and gangways there was a blinding light, and a reflector was mounted on the outside of every door to illuminate each prisoner. It depended on the whim of the individual guard whether this light was directed on to our faces or slightly to one side. We had to sleep on our right sides so that our faces were always visible. If I turned over during my snatches of sleep, the guard would put his arm through the hatch, shake me by the shoulder, and shout: 'Turn around! I can't see your face!'

It is hardly surprising that real sleep became impossible, and we woke up in the morning with aching limbs. Every time the guards were changed, they made a tremendous clatter which was magnified a hundred times in the echoing corridors of the prison building. Before the reflectors were fixed, the night guards were provided with powerful electric torches which they shone in our faces. When I complained one morning to the officer of the guard that this lamp had been switched on in my face 127 times in half an hour, he shrugged his shoulders and said, 'He is on duty.' If I had not been in good physical trim after a life of outdoor exercise, I do not think I could have stayed the course.

We were forbidden to have any communication with the guards, but many of them found it difficult to contain themselves, particularly in their thirst for autographs. I always refused their requests by saying, 'You can have as many of my signatures as you want the day I am acquitted.' This always roused their indignation. 'Everyone except you has given us their autograph,' they would say, 'and they'll string you up first of all.' 'That will be your bad luck,' I used to answer, 'because then you'll get no autograph at all.' They often took their revenge by unnecessary noise during the night.

We were not allowed to see any newspapers, and were forbidden to receive any sort of parcel from outside. When I asked that my wife be allowed to send in a hand towel to put over my fur coat, which I was using as a pillow, this was refused. At Christmas time, the prisoners-of-war who ran the kitchen saved a small amount of our meagre rations, intending to give us a more substantial meal than our ordinary dinner. They were forbidden, however, to serve anything but the usual rations.

Sometimes things occurred which passed, in our circumstances, for light relief. At luncheon we used to sit four in a room, each at individual tables, one against each wall. I usually ate with Neurath, Doenitz and Schacht. One day an American photographer came into the room and took up his stand next to me just as I was eating the soup out of my tin can. I was very angry. I told him I considered this an unwarranted intrusion, and turned my back. He then turned to Schacht, who, even angrier than I, picked up his cup of coffee and threw it in the photographer's face. The fellow shouted for the guard. For soiling a United States uniform, Schacht was forbidden his exercise period for four weeks, during which time he was given no coffee. The fact that the incident set us in high good humour gives some idea of the state we had reached.

Our defence lawyers protested to the Court several times during the trial at the conditions in which we were kept. These protests had very little effect, as the prison itself did not come under the Court's jurisdiction, but was purely a matter for the local U.S. Army command. Colonel Andrus was not responsible to the Secretary-General of the Tribunal but to the American General commanding the Nuremberg district.

Most of the security precautions were designed to prevent attempts at suicide. The regulations were considerably tightened before the trial, as two of the prisoners, Dr Conti, leader of the Nazi medical association, and Dr Ley, the former head of the *Arbeitsfront*, had succeeded in killing themselves. Ley, who was due to figure as a major war criminal, had hung himself with a towel attached to the lever of the water closet in his cell. This was situated in a small recess in the near right-hand corner, and therefore was not under the immediate observation of the guard, who could see only the prisoner's legs. After the principal trial was over, General Blaskowitz managed to kill himself by jumping from the third storey of the prison block.

After Goering had committed suicide an investigation was held in an attempt to ascertain how he had come by the poison. His wife, his lawyer and the German personnel in the kitchen were closely interrogated without result. But there were other possibilities. I can report from my own experience that on two occasions American guards offered me means of killing myself in order, as they put it, to escape certain hanging. The first one offered me a few pills which he claimed were poisonous, although they were not cyanide capsules, of which Goering availed himself. On another occasion a different guard offered me a pocket knife, with the suggestion that I should cut the arteries in my wrists. I declined both these offers and told my kindly guardians that I did not expect a death sentence. However, the second one was so insistent that in the end I had to call the officer in charge in order to get rid of him.

When the trial started we were each given a decent suit every morning in which to appear before the Court, together with ties and shoelaces. These had to be given up again at the end of each day's session. My fellow prisoners made an interesting psychological study. We sat together in the dock for nearly a year, and within limits it was possible to converse with those next to us and to send notes to each other.

On my right sat Jodl, with whom I had few points of contact. The case against him was a purely military one. Logical and clipped in speech, he conducted himself in a soldierly manner and awaited his fate with calm resignation.

Seyss-Inquart, on my left, was very different. We had our Austrian experiences in common. Although I had recommended him to Hitler as a mediator between the two governments, I had avoided him after the Anschluss because I felt that he had surrendered Austria, first to Hitler and then to Buerckel, the Gauleiter, and the Nazi extremists. I now heard his full story for the first time, and had to make allowances. He had behaved correctly, but had given way too much to the extremists. I told the Court that some of my past comments about him had been made on false premises. We discussed our joint defence on the Austrian section of the indictment, and I asked that he should be heard before me.

He was by nature the complete Austrian, cheerful, relaxed, often telling Viennese stories, and he counted with certainty on his acquittal. He had only recently learnt that Hitler had named him in his testament as the next Foreign Minister and was most unhappy about it.

In front of me sat Frank. Between 1933 and 1945 I do not suppose I exchanged ten words with him. His reputation as an extremist and his behaviour in Poland were well known. I had always found him antipathetic, yet as his end approached, he showed himself more of a man than he had done in his whole life. Father O'Connor, the Catholic chaplain, told me that Frank was convinced from the start that his fate was sealed, that he deserved it, and that his defence was unnecessary. He spent his days in meditation, embraced the Catholic faith, and prepared himself for his Maker. He used to hear Mass with Seyss-Inquart, Kaltenbrunner and myself, and I had several conversations with him. He told me he could not understand how he had come so completely under Hitler's influence, or become a willing tool in the criminal persecution of the Jews. In his new-found faith he looked death unwaveringly in the eye for over a year, and one could only admire the new strength of character he had acquired. His conduct was in marked contrast with that of many of his fellow prisoners.

Ribbentrop had his place in the front row. I was told that he spent all his spare time writing long justificatory letters, while overwhelming his defence counsel with accusations of crass incapacity. When he came under cross-examination, he attempted no measured defence of Hitler's policies, whose most determined advocate he had been for more than twelve years. He revealed himself to the world as what some of us already knew him to be, a husk with no kernel, and an empty façade for a mind. It was an unwritten law among the defendants that each was to conduct his own defence without implicating any of the others. On this score even Ribbentrop escaped criticism.

I had no interest in people like Rosenberg and Streicher. The former spent his time making pencil sketches of the witnesses. They seemed to be as devoid of content as his 'Mythos'. Streicher used to break into loud cries and shouts during the night. I do not know whether he was being ill-treated, or whether he suffered from attacks of frenzy. His co-defendants had little to do with him.

Among the service chiefs, I had most sympathy for Raeder and Doenitz. Keitel had always been an office general, but these two always carried with them the pride of their profession. They defended themselves in a measured and dignified fashion, with Doenitz often going over to the offensive. I found their whole attitude admirable.

Neurath was, as always, calm and collected. His Swabian temperament never allowed him to get flustered. Unfortunately, he was indifferently defended and himself lacked the gift of clear exposition which might have balanced the scales. Speer and Baldur von Schirach were the two youngest defendants. Schirach seemed to have had second thoughts about the ideals he had impregnated into Hitler's younger generation. On one occasion he remarked to me that he regretted having applied principles which conflicted to such an extent with those of Christianity. Speer was full of hope for the future. He expected a sentence of imprisonment, and thought that the Americans would then call on him to assist in the development of Alaska, which he regarded as a territory with a great future, especially in view of its strategic position between the two rival continents.

Frick, Hitler's Minister of the Interior, showed, even in this fight for his existence, that he was only a minor official. He had never been called upon to make a decision of his own and had never attempted to bring influence to bear on Hitler. He was the only one of us who declined to appear as a witness in his own defence – he might have had to answer some awkward questions – and thus deprived himself of any attempt at a real defence of his actions, yet he still paid the maximum penalty.

None of us really knew whether Hess was mad or not. I think he was sane when he flew to England, and could have made a telling point out of this attempt to atone for his previous misdeeds by warning the British that Hitler's attack on Russia must lead to the ruin of Europe. Incidentally, it is still a mystery to me why there is no indication in Mr Churchill's memoirs that this warning was ever passed on to President Roosevelt. Hess's behaviour, both in court and in prison, was not that of a normal person. In the dock he seemed completely removed from what was going on and read Bavarian novels by Ganghofer. He refused to have any communication with his defence counsel, who had pressed for a medical commission to enquire into his fitness to plead. The commission was unable to reach a conclusion, but at the moment when the Court was preparing to consider a decision on the matter, Hess stood up and declared he was perfectly normal, that he had only been simulating madness, and desired to be tried in the same manner as the other defendants. His intervention caused something of a sensation, but he retired once again into his previous state of complete indifference to the proceedings. I am personally convinced that Hess was insane, although he may have had lucid moments.

At the end of one row sat Schacht. His sense of humour and opportunism never deserted him. He had not changed one iota, and was just as I had always remembered him: highly intelligent, sarcastic and full of biting irony when it came to correcting some of the prosecution's statements. He remained the egoist he always had been. He called as his principal witness Herr Gisevius, who had been a Gestapo official before he joined Canaris' Abwehr, had afterwards worked for the United States Secret Service, and represented himself as the resistance worker *par excellence*. However, in an effort to underline Schacht's resistance work, he suggested that all the other twenty defendants should be hanged.

With Goebbels dead, the Propaganda Ministry was represented by Hans Fritzsche. It was a pity in a way. The dialectical ability of the satanically gifted little doctor would have given the Tribunal some hard nuts to crack. He could not properly be represented by one of his subordinates. However, Fritzsche defended himself skilfully by insisting that he had only been 'his master's voice', even if his opinions differed.

This leaves me with Goering. He was probably the outstanding personality of the whole trial. Hitler, the principal actor, had committed suicide. So had his main supporters, Goebbels and Himmler. Those who now appeared to answer for their actions were, with the exception of Goering, not of the first rank. He completely outclassed these *dei minores*, and was the only one who had the courage to defend what he had done and what he had tried to do. 'Not a word against Hitler,' he said to us on one occasion when the guards' attention was elsewhere. He seemed to think that loyalty to the régime should continue even within the walls of a prison; or it may have been pride which prevented him from admitting to the enemy what his own intelligence had probably grasped in the meanwhile. At least it was to his credit that he was the one man who really tried to defend his beliefs.

Goering's co-defendants ignored his injunction not to speak ill of Hitler. For some peculiar reason the Court was more punctilious in this respect. One of the most grotesque aspects of the trial was that no accusation was levelled at Hitler, either in the indictment or the verdict. When it became increasingly clear during the proceedings that Hitler, far from being a figurehead manipulated by intriguers behind the scenes, was himself the instigator of almost every measure that had been introduced, the Court made practically no attempt to place this on record. Hitler should have been the chief defendant in the trial, even though he was dead. That no attempt was made to arraign him was one of the major psychological failures of the trial and will yet have repercussions in history.

In the conversations I had with Goering during the period between the end of the trial and the pronouncement of the sentences, I found him the same uninhibited and jovial character I had always known. Completely unconcerned at his certain fate, he often discussed with Neurath, Keitel and myself certain phases of the past. At one period I had tried to find out why this 'crown prince' of the Third Reich had not intervened when he saw that Hitler's policies must lead to war and the collapse of Germany. Now I tried again, but on this point it was still not possible to pin him down. 'I have accepted full responsibility for everything that happened,' he answered. 'I could not prevent the war, even though I regarded it as a great mistake. You or Neurath could probably have made peace, but Ribbentrop was incapable. All he did was to blabber what he thought was in Hitler's mind.' He told me that in the latter years of the war he felt that Hitler was probably insane, but he was unable to do anything about it. As a person, Goering had many virtues. He was a man of open, masculine nature, with great personal charm. This he retained to the end.

CHAPTER XXXI

THE TRIAL

The Statute – The procedure – The Court – The judges – The indictment against me – Difficulties with witnesses – Documents withheld – The Austrian case – Guido Schmidt's evidence – My cross-examination by Sir David Maxwell Fyfe – The verdict – I am acquitted – Thoughts on the trial

THE Nuremberg Tribunal represented something absolutely new in the history of jurisprudence and international intercourse. I shall make no attempt to give a detailed account of the hearings – the official record of speeches by the defence and prosecution, and of the documents produced as exhibits, fills no less than forty-two volumes. I can only give a short account of the indictment as it affected me personally, together with some general remarks on the nature of the Tribunal itself in its historical and juridical aspects.

As an instrument of international law the Tribunal laboured from the start under the terms of its own Statute. This had been drawn up by the four victorious powers in London on August 8, 1945, for the purpose of trying those considered responsible for unleashing the war and the events leading up to it. The draft on procedure had been worked out by Mr Justice Jackson for the United States, Sir David Maxwell Fyfe for Great Britain, Professor Gros for France and General Nikitchenko for the Soviet Union. Mr Justice Jackson and Sir David became their country's chief prosecutors at Nuremberg, and General Nikitchenko was one of the judges. It is hardly to be wondered at that the rules of procedure seemed to favour the prosecution. Article 3 denied both prosecution and defence the right to challenge the jurisdiction either of the Court or its members. This ruled out from the start the possibility of questioning the competence of the Tribunal to deal with the various matters brought before it. Article 6 established the right of the Court to condemn persons, whether as individuals or as members of an organization, for crimes against peace and conspiracy to wage war, war crimes and crimes against humanity. Article 8 referred particularly to defendants from the armed services and laid down that the carrying out of superior orders did not absolve them from responsibility, although it could be regarded as a mitigating circumstance. One of the most difficult points of law was involved in Article 9, which granted the Court the right to declare a given organization to be a criminal one. Proven charges against individual members of an organization could be adduced as evidence of the criminal nature of the organization itself.

Whenever the defence protested against the unfair advantages which the charter seemed to accord the prosecution, we were reminded that we were lucky to get any trial at all, and that the Allies would have been justified in summarily shooting those whom they considered as war criminals as a retaliation for the methods employed by the Third Reich. This attitude had a certain logic. However, in the same breath we were told that we were being subjected to normal legal procedure, the nations whose captives we were believing in the due processes of law. The trial was praised as a model of Anglo-Saxon justice. Had this been true, we should have been accorded all the rights of prisoners in those countries. The choice was between legal procedure and the old cry of 'an eye for an eye . . .' You cannot have it both ways.

Before the Court met it was impossible to obtain a clear idea of the procedure to be adopted. Anglo-Saxon criminal law is entirely different from that on the Continent, not only in substance but in procedure. Two of the judges and their deputies came from Anglo-Saxon countries and one from a Continental power. The fourth member, the Russian, represented a dictatorship, which, like the Third Reich, had abandoned the conception of an independent judiciary. Article 13 granted the Court power to devise its own rules of procedure, and Article 14 required the four principal prosecutors to present a draft scheme of procedure to be accepted or rejected by the Court – surely a most curious innovation. Article 16 granted the accused the right to call witnesses and produce documents in their own defence, and also to cross-examine the prosecution's witnesses. Article 19 gave the Court wide latitude in the interpretation of what constituted evidence. In practice, this was found to include hearsay evidence so tenuous that not another ourt in the world would have listened to it for a moment. Then Article 26 came a particularly important provision: no appeal could be made against any verdict, which must be considered final.

I have already mentioned the four main heads of the general indictment, of which we all received a copy, with an appendix listing that particular part of it which referred to each individual defendant. No accusation was made against me of war crimes or crimes against humanity. My responsibility as party to a conspiracy to wage aggressive war was based on assertions that I had been a member of the Nazi Party from 1932 to 1945 (I was never a member), had been a member of the Reichstag, Reich Chancellor, Vice-Chancellor, Special Commissioner for the Saar, Plenipotentiary for the Concordat, and Ambassador in Vienna and Turkey. In these appointments I was said to have used my personal influence and my close association with Hitler to facilitate the Nazis' assumption of power and their subsequent dictatorship, and thus their active preparation for war.

The reader who has come thus far with me in the account of my life will, I hope, have obtained some conception of where I stood in the matter of peace and war. He will appreciate my failure to understand how I could be accused of fomenting war. German law does not include the conception of conspiracy in this sense, and I had no idea what use could be made of it by those trained in Anglo-Saxon procedure. In due course I was to be greatly enlightened.

The day before the trial began, the combined defence lawyers submitted a memorandum in which they claimed that the first point of the indictment, that of crimes against peace, had no foundation in international law and therefore contravened the first requirement of jurisprudence: that no punishment could be exacted if no law existed at the time the crime in question was committed. The memorandum then pointed out that the Court was made up of representatives of states who were a party to the dispute, and requested that its constitution should first be examined by a body of undisputed authority in international law. These requests were turned down by the Court under Article 3 of the Statute, which forbade its competence to be questioned. All subsequent attempts by the defence to raise this question met with the same rebuff.

The trial opened on November 20, 1945, at ten o'clock in the morning. For the first time we entered the hall in which we were to hear every day for a year the accusations against us and the German nation. It was much too small for its purpose. The defendants sat in two rows against one of the longer walls, flanked by American military police in their polished white helmets. In front of us, three rows of benches accommodated our defence counsel. To our left, along one of the shorter walls, sat the judges; opposite us, at four long tables, the prosecution representatives of the four nations. At the other end was the press gallery, with up to two hundred journalists and cameramen from every country in the world, and above them the spectators' gallery. This presented an endless kaleidoscope of uniforms. The only nation missing were the Germans, whom one would have thought to be those most affected by the proceedings.

As the marshal called for silence for the members of the Court, the hum of conversation died away. We all stood up in our places and saw for the first time the men in whose hands our fate rested. Their personalities soon defined themselves. The President, Lord Justice Lawrence, was a man of great dignity and authority. I often had the feeling that a man of his reputation must have felt uneasy at the restrictions placed upon him by the Statute, but he did not deviate from its prescriptions by a hairbreadth. He seldom intervened personally in the proceedings.

His neighbour on the left, Mr Biddle, seemed the most intelligent of the judges. He followed every word with great attention, and his questions to both defendants and witnesses always hit the nail on the head. What impressed us most was his completely objective attitude, particularly when his American colleague, the chief United States prosecutor, Mr Justice Jackson, was involved. In Mr Biddle and his deputy, Mr Parker, we saw the best guarantee of an unprejudiced verdict. It was impossible to reach any conclusion concerning the French member, Professor Donnedieu de Vabres. He never addressed a single question to anyone. All he did was write, for days, weeks and months on end. His notes must have filled countless volumes. General Nikitchenko, the Soviet judge, we regarded with complete disinterest. We knew what his verdict would be, with or without a trial. The only time when any expression crossed his youthful face was when the Russian prosecutor, General Rudenko, got into difficulties. This happened when the Katyn forest affair was brought up. The defence attempted to submit in evidence the agreement providing for the joint partition of Poland which was signed by Stalin and Hitler a week before war broke out. Both Nikitchenko and Rudenko seemed to regard this 'bourgeois' procedure as a completely superfluous form of Western comedy.

The details of the indictment had been divided up more or less arbitrarily among the prosecution teams. The case against me was presented on January 23 by Major J. Harcourt-Barrington, a British assistant prosecutor. My share of the responsibility was delimited to the period between June 1, 1932, and the Anschluss in March 1938. It was alleged that in spite of my knowledge of the Nazi programme and Nazi methods I had used my personal influence to facilitate Hitler's assumption of power. By lifting the ban on the S.A. and the S.S. in 1932 I had rendered the party an invaluable service, and I had paved the way for Hitler's appointment as Chancellor at a discussion with Herr von Schroeder in Cologne on January 4, 1933.

Major Barrington attempted to introduce here a long affidavit signed by Schroeder, to which my defence counsel immediately objected. He pointed out that Schroeder was a possible defendant in a later trial and was therefore an interested party, and insisted that if the affidavit was admitted, the witness should be produced by the prosecution for cross-examination. The Court ruled in his favour, whereupon the prosecution withdrew the affidavit as they did not choose to produce Schroeder. The prosecution then alleged that I had helped to consolidate the Nazis in power by sharing in such legislation as the setting up of special courts, amnesty decrees, the integration of individual states into the Reich and responsibility for the April 1933 boycott of the Jews, which they alleged had been previously approved by the Cabinet. I had signed the Concordat, but was now said to have helped to sabotage it. After speaking of my uncritical co-operation in the Nazis' power politics, the prosecution then referred, rather surprisingly, to my Marburg speech, which was described as openly critical of the Nazis. Then came the comment: 'If he had stopped then, he might have saved the world much suffering. Suppose that Hitler's own Vice-Chancellor, just released from arrest, had defied the Nazis and told the world the truth. There might never have been a reoccupation of the Rhineland; there might never have been a war.'

My activities in Austria were considered under the heading of conspiracy to wage aggressive war, and this was taken to include the Anschluss. Here the prosecution based its case on my reports to Hitler and a truly astonishing affidavit signed by the former American Minister in Vienna, Mr George Messersmith. In this he alleged that I had told him in 1934 that I had come to Austria only in order to undermine the Government and enable Germany to extend her influence as far as the Turkish frontier. In a second affidavit he alleged that I had used my reputation as a Catholic to influence people like Cardinal Innitzer. The prosecution maintained that the July Agreement between Austria and Germany was signed as a deliberate deception, and that I had forced the Austrian Government to appoint Nazis to key posts in the Cabinet. The fact that (at Schuschnigg's request, it will be remembered) part of the agreement had been kept secret, was regarded by the prosecution as particularly damning.

I was faced by the problem of how best to counter these accusations. To all intents and purposes, there were two main points: first of all, I had to prove that my activities between 1932 and 1934 had not served to bring Hitler to power or strengthen his position. Secondly, I had to show that I had not attempted to undermine the Schuschnigg Government by subversive methods but, on the contrary, had done all I could to combat the Nazis' plans for a forcible Anschluss, while seeking evolutionary methods of bringing about union between Austria and Germany. How was I to set about it? There was the method, completely unknown to our own legal processes, of a defendant appearing as witness in his own defence under oath. I felt that this provided the best opportunity of rejecting the accusation of my evil intentions and explaining my true thoughts. However, I was under no illusions as to how much belief was likely to be given to my protestations. The general atmosphere in the months after Germany's collapse was such that the victorious powers regarded almost any German who had held an official appointment in the Third Reich as a criminal whose word was not likely to be accepted. The problem was to obtain objective proofs.

I had no archives or documents at my disposal. The files of the German Government had either been destroyed or were in the hands of the occupying powers. Almost all my own private files in Wallerfangen and Berlin had been lost or destroyed in the war.

Germany's transport and communication systems had practically ceased to exist. There was no way of discovering the whereabouts of friends or acquaintances, or even of ascertaining if they were still alive. Some of my closest collaborators were dead, and we were not permitted to get in direct touch with foreigners. There was, in any case, the question of whether they would be prepared to testify in favour of a German. According to the rules of procedure, all our requests for witnesses had to be made through the prosecution, who then forwarded them to the Court with their own comments. Under the system, again outside our experience, of differentiating between prosecution and defence witnesses, most of Germany's leading personalities had been arrested and were being held as possible prosecution witnesses, and were therefore not at our disposal.

We had no means of knowing exactly what documents the prosecution possessed. In my own case, for example, they presented a series of my reports concerning my activities in Austria, covering the period from August 1934 to the spring of 1938. I could only assume that they had a complete set, but our repeated requests that these reports should be placed at our disposal – I knew that they provided me with a complete defence – were rejected on the grounds that the prosecution had no further documents in their possession. I will leave it to the reader to judge whether it is likely that the prosecution had come by chance on only those particular documents which supported their own case. This shabby manœuvre was shown up later when the very reports I had been asking for, which provided incontrovertible evidence of my continual fight with the illegal Nazi Party in Austria, were produced by the prosecution in a later trial, as part of their case against Hitler's former emissary there, Wilhelm Keppler. We met with the same treatment over the minutes of the Cabinet meetings in 1933 and 1934. Only a few were presented by the prosecution, and our requests for the remainder were again rejected on the grounds that the prosecution did not have them.

I have referred more than once to our unfamiliarity with the procedure adopted by the Court, which caused the German defence counsel much difficulty. The prosecution was at all times the dominating factor. To those accustomed to Continental methods, the Court played only a minor rôle. In any German criminal trial, it is above all the duty of the judge, by interrogation and enquiry, to extract the truth. Here it was a contest between the prosecution and the defence, in which the Court acted as a sort of umpire. According to the Statute, both prosecution and defence had the same rights, but this equality existed only on paper. As I have described, the prosecution held all the trumps and the defence had nothing, being entirely dependent on the goodwill of the prosecution for the production of their evidence. The defence was greatly restricted in its efforts, whilst the prosecution could surprise them at any time with new witnesses and documents. The defence had to make all its requests for evidence weeks beforehand, thus providing the prosecution with ample time to counter their arguments. A request for a witness led in almost every case to that person being arrested and brought to Nuremberg, where they were first interrogated by the prosecution. Even if the defence finally obtained access to them, it was only in the presence of a representative of the prosecution. The result was that it became an imposition to require anyone to undergo this ordeal. Those who were produced did not know whether they might not be incriminating themselves, and in most cases tried to pin on other people the responsibility for anything that had happened.

There was also another fundamental point – the presence in the Court of a Russian member. Relations between the Soviet Union and the Western Powers still preserved a façade of amicable cooperation. The result was that any attempt to refer to Russian policies, such as, for example, their joint attack on Poland in 1939, was forbidden. Today it would seem grotesque to have a Russian sitting in judgment on charges of waging aggressive war. In any normal criminal trial the fact that a judge himself participated in the crime before the court would act as an immediate disqualification. But at Nuremberg any attempt to suggest that the Russians or, in specific circumstances, the Allies, had employed methods with which the Germans were now charged, was immediately ruled out of order. 'We are not interested in what the Allies may have done,' Lord Justice Lawrence used to say.

It is true that the *tu quoque* is a bad defence. But in a case like this, when what was at stake was to decide whether certain tenets of international law had been binding at a given time, the *tu quoque* argument was not without significance. Its use by the defence was completely invalidated. There was only one exception – the conduct of the U-boat war. The sinking of ships without warning formed part of the war crimes indictment. However, Admiral Nimitz, the American Fleet Commander in the Pacific, gave evidence in writing that American submarines had also received orders to sink all enemy ships at sight. This led to a pronouncement by the Court that such a procedure contravened international law, but as it had been adopted by both sides, it would be struck out of the indictment against Grand Admiral Doenitz.

The prosecution's efforts to restrict the evidence of the defence can be better understood if one takes into consideration the opinions voiced by the same gentlemen during their discussions on the subject at the London conference in June 1945, which have since been published by the United States State Department[1]:

Discussing the presentation of evidence, Sir David Maxwell Fyfe explained that the defendants might be compelled to put in writing the purposes for which evidence was going to be called, 'in order to prevent mere political speeches being put in under the guise of evidence. Otherwise a witness may suddenly be called into the box; we do not know what he is going to say, and he starts making political speeches in defence of German activities'.

At another session, Mr Justice Jackson said:

'I really think that this trial, if it should get into an argument over the political and economic causes of this war, could do infinite harm, both in Europe, which I don't know well, and in America, which I know fairly well. If we should have a prolonged controversy over whether Germany invaded Norway a few jumps ahead of a British invasion of Norway, or whether France in declaring war was the real aggressor, this trial can do infinite harm for those countries with the people of the United States. And the same is true of our Russian relationships.'

Later, he repeated: 'I don't want to be in a position where the United States is obliged to enter into a discussion at this trial of the acts or policies of our allies . . .' and '. . . it seems to me this trial is likely to take a very unfortunate course if we don't so limit it that it does not get into the remote causes of the war.'

General Nikitchenko said at one point:

'Is it supposed [sic], then, to condemn aggression or initiation of war in general, or to condemn specifically aggressions started

[1] *International Conference on Military Trials, London, 1945.* Department of State, U.S.A., Publication 3080.

by the Nazis in this war? If the attempt is to have a general definition, that would not be agreeable.'

I make no comment.

★ ★ ★

In view of the obstacles placed in the way of calling witnesses, I took advantage of one facility provided by the Court, to address questionnaires to certain persons whose information might be of use to my defence counsel. I sent these to the former Apostolic Delegate in Turkey, Monsignor Roncalli; the Dutch Minister there, M. Visser; the Hungarian Regent, Admiral Horthy; my life-long friend, Lersner; my former colleague in the Vice-Chancellery and in Vienna, von Tschirschky; the Legation Counsellor in my Vienna days, Prince Erbach; and others. The only witnesses I asked to appear personally were Dr Kroll, my Embassy Counsellor in Ankara, and Count Kageneck, my personal secretary for many years.

As far as the Austrian episode was concerned, things were made considerably easier for me by Goering's free affirmation under cross-examination that he had been the driving force in the events that led up to the Anschluss, and that in March 1938 he had insisted that Hitler should end the dispute by force. The situation was further clarified by the evidence of the former Austrian Foreign Secretary, Dr Guido Schmidt, who was called to testify in the case against my neighbour in the dock, Seyss-Inquart. Schmidt was instrumental in completely refuting the assertions to which I have referred in the affidavit signed by the former American Minister, Mr Messersmith.

Schmidt made it quite clear that the negotiations leading up to the signing of the July Agreement had been entered into as much on Austrian initiative as on mine, and that its terms were fully approved by Schuschnigg. He also confirmed that certain details were kept secret at Schuschnigg's express request. In his description of the meeting between Schuschnigg and Hitler at Berchtesgaden on February 12, 1938, he confirmed that I had exerted no pressure on the Austrian Chancellor, and had sought rather to act as mediator. He also proved conclusively that I had no knowledge of the *Punktationen* that Schuschnigg had worked out with Zernatto before his journey, and that I had been as much surprised when their terms were revealed at Berchtesgaden as Schmidt himself had been. I should like to quote two more of his answers verbatim, as they not only gave a clear indication of the situation in Austria at the time, but also completely clarify my own participation in events.

Asked if he regarded as correct the prosecution's accusation that the July Agreement had been signed with intent to deceive, Schmidt replied: 'No, I have no reason to disbelieve that he considered this agreement a serious attempt to create a *modus vivendi* between Austria and the Reich. The fact that it resulted in a *modus mal vivendi* does not alter this.'

He was then asked if the German Government had not complained that Austria's internal policies had undergone no modification, even after the signing of the Agreement. Schmidt's answer was: 'Yes, many reproaches were made, and thus we came to the last and the real cause of the conflict with the Reich. The struggle against National Socialism within the country in the interests of maintaining the independence of the country and, on the basis of the Agreement of July 11 the co-operation with the German Reich – the leaders of which were National Socialists – these were the two imperative demands which, after a time, the Austrian Government found so irreconcilable. This also explains the difficulties encountered by all persons entrusted with carrying out this agreement in Vienna, including the German Minister.'

Schmidt, it will be recalled, was himself under arrest at the time, and was later tried in Austria on a charge of high treason. He was acquitted on every charge. Other Austrian witnesses called in Seyss-Inquart's case were Glaise-Horstenau, and the former Gauleiter, Rainer. They both testified to my endless struggle with the illegal party in Austria. It therefore became quite unnecessary to call any further Austrian witnesses in my own defence.

My own examination began on June 14, 1946, and was to some extent complicated by the fact that the Court, after agreeing that no time limit should be placed on Goering's evidence concerning the rise of the Nazis, then declined to hear other evidence of this general nature from the other defendants. This was a considerable hindrance, as my own participation in the events he had described was based on premises which were almost diametrically opposed to those of the Nazis. I was therefore continually being called to order and asked to make my evidence brief. I found this a great strain, because it was quite impossible to accept the provision in

the indictment which took up my case at June 2, 1932. The
historical processes I felt obliged to describe dated back much
earlier than that. The only passage during which I was not interrupted was that describing the contents and reasons for my speech
at Marburg. I spoke on the witness stand in my own defence for
the best part of three days – a Saturday and a Sunday intervened –
and on the afternoon of the 18th came under cross-examination by
Sir David Maxwell Fyfe.

In my opinion, he was by far the most able jurist in the whole
prosecution. He was a complete master of the art of cross-
examination, so important in Anglo-Saxon law. Himself a politician
and Member of Parliament, he had a much clearer view of the
political developments at stake than had his American colleagues.
He employed towards me a much sharper tone than he had used
with any of the other defendants, and it occurred to me later that
he probably sought thus to make up for the distinctly meagre case
which the prosecution had been able to make out against me. At
the time I had to be too much on the *qui vive* for such reflections.

His questions followed what had now become a familiar line of
reasoning. He accused me of having helped to bring Hitler to
power, in spite of my knowledge of the true nature of the Nazi
movement. He was able to make little capital out of my period
as Vice-Chancellor, but sought to implicate me rather in the later
developments, or because I had accepted further employment after
the Roehm *Putsch*. Again the hypothesis was advanced that developments might have been halted if I had gone into open opposition.
To all this I could only answer that the rise of the Nazi movement
was a long historical process and that its existence could not simply
be ignored. I also tried to show that people were probably better
informed abroad about events in Germany than we had been ourselves, but that this had not prevented Great Britain from making
the first *de facto* acknowledgment of Hitler's régime with the Naval
Agreement, which was a direct contravention of the Treaty of
Versailles.

My correspondence with Hitler after the Roehm *Putsch* was
also referred to at length. I could only explain again that my concern at the time was to remain in contact with those in power, in
order to protect the members of my staff who had been arrested or
who had disappeared. My efforts to prove that the Vice-Chancellery
had been in no way connected with the Roehm affair were directed

T

solely to protecting my staff from further injury. I was also able to prove that I had attended no further Cabinet meetings after I had been released from house-arrest. Sir David's attempts to read into my reports from Vienna confirmation of the indictment that I had acted throughout with intent to deceive, were not difficult to refute from their very context.

In his peroration, Sir David made no real attempt to claim that I had been guilty of crimes against peace or conspiracy to wage aggressive war: 'What I am putting to you is that the only reason that could have kept you in the service of the Nazi Government, when you knew all these crimes, was that you sympathized and wanted to carry on with the Nazis' work. That is what I am putting to you – that you had this express knowledge; you had seen your own friends, your own servants, murdered around you. You had the detailed knowledge of it, and the only reason which could have dominated you and made you take one job after another from the Nazis was, that you sympathized with their work. That is what I am putting against you, Herr von Papen.'

To this I replied: 'That, Sir David, is perhaps your opinion; my opinion is that I am responsible only to my conscience and to the German people for my decision to work for my fatherland; and I shall accept their verdict.'

Then followed my re-examination by my own counsel, and the evidence of the only witness I finally called, Dr Kroll. Although the indictment in my case took no account of events after the Anschluss, the matter of my alleged part in the conspiracy to wage war still remained open, and we considered it essential to prove that I had done everything in my power, while acting as Ambassador in Turkey, either to shorten the war or prevent its extension. I was satisfied that nothing had been brought up in Court to substantiate any individual charges against me. My fate therefore depended largely on whether the Court accepted the prosecution's theory of a general conspiracy dating back to the beginnings of the Nazi Party. If so, there was almost no limit to the number of people who could be included, especially if it were accepted that anyone who had played a major part in the events that led to the assumption of power by Hitler was particularly concerned. Most of my co-defendants, and indeed many of the defence counsel, were convinced that this had become a political trial with a preconceived verdict and that therefore no acquittals were possible.

This belief was strengthened by the concluding speeches by the prosecution, which were to all intents and purposes a repetition of those at the beginning of the trial, and seemed to take no account of all the evidence heard in between. Both the French and the Russian prosecutors demanded the death sentence in my case. I could hardly believe that people of the reputation of Lord Justice Lawrence or Mr Biddle would lend themselves to such a procedure, but there were four judges and one of them was a Russian. The trial dragged on till the end of August, with the presentation of much documentary material, and then adjourned for a month.

It reassembled on September 30 to hear the verdict. We had no idea what the final result would be. Security precautions were so strict that even the interpreters were held incommunicado in the Court building. The atmosphere in the Court was, if anything, more tense than it had been at the beginning of the trial as Lord Justice Lawrence began the long presentation of the Court's findings.

The Court was packed. Press representatives from all parts of the world had gathered to send colourful accounts of the fate of this band of 'war criminals'. Even at this juncture, the only nationality missing among the spectators were the Germans themselves, although one would have thought that they were chiefly concerned. Different parts of the verdict were read in turn by the four judges. It began with a long description of developments in the Third Reich, went on to give an account of the internal political situation, and described in detail the preparation and carrying out of individual warlike acts.

For my own part, I was prepared for the worst. It seemed to me that there was little hope of acquittal in what had become a purely political trial. If the Court accepted the definition of conspiracy formulated by the prosecution, we could all expect the death sentence. The atmosphere became electric as Lord Justice Lawrence started to deal with this point. He pronounced that the beginning of the conspiracy would be dated at November 5, 1937, when the Hossbach Protocol of Hitler's war plans was drawn up after his secret meeting with Neurath and the service chiefs. This could only mean that I was freed of complicity, unless it was held that I had participated actively in the march of German troops into Austria.

The reading of the verdict lasted all that day and part of the next, before it dealt individually with the fate of each defendant. However, by the end of the first day each of us had a clearer idea of the fate that awaited us. There seemed a reasonable hope that the Court would prove more objective than we had feared. Still, I doubt if any of us slept very much that night; certainly, I did not even close my eyes.

When Lord Justice Lawrence finally came to the individual verdicts, the whole court became absolutely still. He began with Goering, and continued in the order in which we were sitting. I was fifth from the end. None of the defendants in the front row moved a muscle as they heard what their fate was to be. At the end of the row came Schacht. He was acquitted. An astonished hum rose from the spectators in the packed court. My own feelings can be imagined. If Schacht could be acquitted, there was still hope for me. I tried to keep my face expressionless, but it was an effort for me to do so.

I heard Lord Justice Lawrence order the Court Marshal to release Schacht at the end of the session. Then came the verdicts on Raeder, Doenitz and those who preceded me on the second bench. When my turn came, I was acquitted and also ordered to be released at the end of the session. I only learnt later that the press had known these details for at least an hour, they having received a list of the individual verdicts before the Court started to read them. Several journalists apparently attempted to advise me by signs that I was free, but I noticed nothing. However, someone had been kind enough to ring up my daughters, who were in Nuremberg awaiting the result, and had told them the good news.

As we were taken out separately by the military police, several of my co-defendants turned round to give us their good wishes, including Goering, who said to me, 'Congratulations. You are free – I did not doubt it for a moment.' I could not utter a word. I shook the hands of those I could reach, including Jodl and Seyss-Inquart, between whom I had sat for so many agonizing months.

* * *

It is now possible to look back on the trial as a whole somewhat more dispassionately. We now know that at the Yalta Conference Stalin and Roosevelt proposed at first that some fifty thousand of the leading personalities in Hitler Germany should be subjected to summary proceedings. Churchill immediately objected to this plan, which he said the British Government would never support. We have him to thank that there was any trial at all. Whether the cause of international justice was thereby strengthened is another matter.

In his opening speech for the prosecution, Mr Justice Jackson declared that the defendants had no right to a fair trial, as they had for years abandoned all pretence of normal legal procedure both inside and outside Germany, and if they had won, would certainly have made no concession to their enemies. From the purely legal standpoint this argument is not acceptable. The very fact that the judiciary in the Third Reich had been deprived of the independence normal in civilized countries was one of the main points of the Nuremberg indictment. If the Allies wished to prove their superiority in this respect, they could not subject to the same procedures those held responsible for such a development. .

It is open to question whether any objective and independent trial was possible at the time in any circumstances. When the Nuremberg Tribunal assembled, both Germany and the world were still recoiling from a series of crimes and atrocities which militated against any clarity of thought or moderation. No one was prepared to recognize that although Germany had been the principal instigator, the effect had not been confined to Germany. The events themselves were still too recent to permit any acknowledgment of the fact that in total war, crimes had been committed on both sides.

The Nuremberg Tribunal was an instrument of the victorious powers. It included neither German nor neutral judges. In Germany, as in every other country, the necessity of determining the guilty parties was acknowledged. The unilateral composition of the Court overshadowed the whole trial, and it was asking too much of any judge to submit the conduct of the war by both sides to objective legal scrutiny.

The Court accepted the theory that at the time of the outbreak of war in 1939, a war of aggression was not only a crime under international law, but that individual leaders in the State could be made responsible for its declaration. I do not think that calmer afterthoughts will sustain the validity of this theory. Aggressive war is condemned in a number of international agreements, but it is nowhere laid down that individual statesmen can be held personally responsible for the declaration of war by their country.

Even if this is accepted, the question still remains of how to delimit the number of people to be included in such a charge, especially in a totalitarian state like the Third Reich. There is no shadow of doubt that Hitler was the supreme power in Germany, and that all major decisions were taken by him. This does not exclude the responsibility of his immediate advisers, but the question of the extent to which the heads of the armed services can be held responsible for political decisions is much more open to question. On the one hand, the individual soldier is bound by the laws of his own land and the orders of the head of the state; on the other, he is faced by a singularly imprecise situation in international law, which does not, in any case, form part of the legislation of his own country.

I am not speaking here of the ordinary criminal code which covers such matters as murder, assault, theft, and so on, and therefore covers the charges brought up under the heading of war crimes and crimes against humanity. The majority of the defendants brought before the Nuremberg Tribunal were guilty by German law and would have been sentenced. It was not necessary to refer to doubtful points of international law in order to obtain their conviction. I hold that one of the greatest errors in the Nuremberg trials was to rely on a new interpretation of international law, rather than to depend on the clearly defined criminal codes of the individual nations.

This dependence on international law raised the question whether its provisions should be imposed unilaterally by the victors, or whether they were also subject to its interpretation. This aspect, as I have remarked more than once, the Court resolutely refused to discuss. One of the nations represented, Soviet Russia, not only maintains concentration camps but was as guilty of waging aggressive war as Germany. The Russo-German Treaty for the division of Poland, Russian methods there, the attack on Finland, and Russian occupation of parts of Rumania, were as much aggression as Germany's attacks on her neighbours. The expulsion of millions of Germans from Czechoslovakia and the territories occupied by Russia and Poland were as much crimes against humanity as Hitlerite Germany's measures in Russia and Poland.

Total war rendered the provisions of the Hague Convention in 1907 completely out of date. There had been no conception at the time of the rôle to be played by bombers and atomic weapons.

The question must be asked whether the appalling effects of air warfare on the civilian population are to be considered in a different light from the conscription of the population of a defeated country for slave labour. I do not wish to be misunderstood in this. I am not trying for one instant to excuse the atrocities committed by Hitler against the civil populations of the lands he occupied in a war for which he was solely responsible. I only pose the question whether international law today is defined clearly enough to determine what is permitted in total war and what is not. I am afraid that the situation has only been complicated by the Nuremberg trial. The measures that have had to be adopted against the partisans in the Korean war are the same as those adopted by the German High Command in Russia, which formed part of the Nuremberg indictment.

Until some such body as the United Nations is able to achieve the acceptance by each individual nation of rules of international conduct, there can be no basis for true international law. The Nuremberg Tribunal was set up in answer to a universal demand that certain things that had happened should not go unpunished, for fear they should be repeated in even worse form. But the trials affected only one side and therefore undermined the basic conception of law – that it must be universal and binding on all. Its sequel should have been the drawing up of a code of international criminal law to be accepted by every member state as binding in national law. The second step would then have been to apply its provisions wherever necessary. So far, no step in this direction has been taken.

Nuremberg had one positive result, in that it awakened the conscience of the world and drew its attention to the problem. Perhaps in due course the nations will surrender enough of their national sovereignty to permit a solution. On the other hand, it established the conception of the collective guilt of certain organizations. Under the aegis of the occupying powers this led to the formation of denazification courts, which have probably done more damage to the general conception of law than can yet be appreciated. Millions of people in Germany have been placed under an assumption of guilt which they have had to disprove individually in totally inadequate hearings. This has led to a form of juridical chaos, the moral and political effects of which will weigh on the German people for years to come. The very same methods were employed as those which the Nuremberg Tribunal condemned so roundly in the Third Reich. If the conception of true international law is to be given a firm foundation, respect for the law on a national plane will first have to be re-established.

Another point which should not be overlooked is that the reports of the proceedings did not have the effect on the German population which was probably desired. Quite apart from the extraordinary duration of the trial, which caused outsiders gradually to lose interest, the reports, to all intents and purposes, were restricted to the case for the prosecution. The official report on the German radio was given every evening at eight o'clock by a gentleman named Gaston Oulman, who concentrated almost entirely on the more sensational aspects of the prosecution's case. The result was that listeners began to lose all faith in the truth of his reports. He made no mention of any points made by the defence which rebutted any of the charges, and his listeners consequently assumed that it was purely a show trial with a predetermined verdict. Herr Oulman, who wore American uniform, and was therefore assumed to be an official spokesman of the occupying powers, did a disservice both to them and the Germans.

Many of the reports in the German press were very little better, and many reporters who endeavoured to send objective accounts complained that their editors usually struck out anything favourable to the defence. In any case, the ability of German journalists at the time was neither what it had been nor what it has now become again. Most of them were young men with very little knowledge of the political and historical backgrounds involved. The papers themselves were very small and usually came out only two or three times a week; consequently, their reports were often so truncated as to be incomprehensible.

CHAPTER XXXII

ENVOI

Last days at Nuremberg – Rearrested – Denazification – Labour camp –
Beaten up by an S.S. man – My appeal – Final reflections

SCHACHT, Fritzsche and I were separated from our co-defendants before sentence was passed. One would have thought that our acquittal, irrespective of personal sympathy or antipathy, would have been greeted with relief by the German people. At least it indicated that the theory of the collective guilt of the whole nation had not been upheld. But Herr Hoegner, the acting Bavarian Minister President, who, unlike some of his Social Democrat colleagues, had preferred security in Switzerland to underground opposition in Germany, had different views. He announced that he regarded our acquittal as a miscarriage of justice, and instructed his police to arrest us the moment we left the prison. For the time being, there was no alternative but to taste our new-found freedom in our former cells.

I wrote to the British and French Military Governments asking permission to live either at Gemünden, where I had left my wife, or in Westphalia, where I had been arrested. I also asked the American Military Government to grant me safe conduct to my destination. It was weeks before I received an answer. The local authorities in Westphalia were asked to ascertain from the population whether they would welcome my return. The local *Landrat*, although he was a Socialist, reported that my old neighbours raised no objection. However, the British Military Government regarded the matter as one of such political importance that they declined to make a decision and referred the matter to London.

Schacht and Fritzsche had less patience. They left the prison on the strength of completely informal assurances from Colonel Andrus, and were soon rearrested. I had to move from my cell between Jodl and Seyss-Inquart and was allocated another on the top floor. There I could observe how those under sentence, dressed in convict uniforms, with shaved heads, and often handcuffed, were led out for their daily exercise. On October 14 I was suddenly moved into another wing of the prison. The final act was drawing near. In spite of the security precautions, we knew from the prison grape-vine that the night of the 15th would see the end. Sleep was impossible. For fifteen long months I had shared with my co-defendants all the humiliations and unbearable tension of imprisonment and trial. Some of them I had hardly known, but in our common misery, something like a personal bond had been formed. Some had maintained a dignified attitude in the face of certain death. Others had tried to excuse themselves by pleading their obligation to obey Hitler's orders. A third category had possessed neither the intelligence nor the character to face their accusers with an attitude which would have seemed consistent either to a psychologist or a judge.

Now that they were about to pay the price for their misdeeds, I tried to summarize in my own mind what these Nazi leaders had stood for. Were they true revolutionaries, who had really believed that National Socialism was a new epoch-making ideology which could supplant two thousand years of Christian tradition and impose a new social order, under Hitler and his Gestapo, on a united Europe? One might almost have hoped that at least one of Hitler's closest associates would have stood before this world tribunal and proclaimed unreservedly the convictions which had guided them in their actions. Danton's oration to the French revolutionary tribunal came to my mind. But the French were true revolutionaries, something the Germans have never been. They remain – and only the German word will do – *Spiessbürger*, who had adopted an idea without applying any real critical faculties. The majority had succumbed to Hitler's and Goebbels' flaming rhetoric and embarked on a course from which in the end they were unable to deviate. Some had been attracted by the splendour of high office, by the feeling of power and the fruits of power. But they were not revolutionaries. When the time came for a final gesture it was too late. It was no longer possible to exchange the prisoner's dock for the revolutionary's rostrum.

Of them all, only Goering made the attempt, but even he made no lasting impression, as he also sought to excuse himself. But at the last moment he made his final gesture, and departed in his own way from the world scene where he had been in turn admired and loathed. The others paid the price. Those who were not hanged were moved to the Spandau prison in Berlin, and as long as this remains partly under Russian control it is doubtful whether we shall ever see them again. Those of us who had been spared had once more to come to grips with life. I made up my mind to leave the prison, whatever the consequences might be.

★　★　★

The Nazis had instituted the system of rearresting a man if his acquittal by a regular court did not meet with their approval. These methods were continued by the Bavarian police under the nose of the occupation authorities. I was not at first taken physically into custody, but placed under police surveillance and ordered not to leave Nuremberg. An old friend from my Uhlan days, a former chief of police named Adam, had offered me a room in his house in the shattered and overcrowded city. He was married to a Jewess who had survived all the Nazi pogroms and who now devoted herself to the care of my wife, one of my daughters and myself. We were under continual police guard.

My health was so undermined that I asked to be allowed to go to a nursing home just outside Nuremberg. When the local Communists heard of this they threatened to correct the Nuremberg verdict and string me up. Although I professed complete unconcern, the president of the local denazification court, Herr Sachs, forbade me to move. I was sent to the city hospital. The committee of hospital employees then met and demanded my immediate removal. A hospital, they said, did not exist to treat such criminals. The senior doctor protested, but in the end I had to go, and finally found refuge in the hospital of St Theresa, where the Catholic sisters were mistresses in their own house and could ignore the clamour of the outside world. But a policeman continued to be stationed at the entrance.

I will not go into detail concerning my subsequent vicissitudes. About the middle of January 1947 I was informed that the Bavarian Denazification Minister, Loritz, had given orders that my trial should begin immediately. The Court was composed of seven members, of which two, both Social Democrats, were members of the legal profession, while the other five were representatives of the democratic parties – one Communist, two Social Democrats, one Liberal and one Christian Democrat. The President, Dr Sachs, and his deputy, were Jews who had been deprived of their appointments by the Nazis.

The prosecution sought chiefly to prove, largely on the basis of the Hindenburg testament, that I came in the top category of those who had assisted and profited from the Nazi movement. While the trial was in progress, Loritz, in a public speech in his capacity as Denazification Minister, demanded that I should be given the maximum sentence of ten years in a labour camp. The court finally condemned me to eight years in a labour camp, the confiscation of all my property, with the exception of five thousand marks, and lifelong deprivation of civic rights. The costs of the trial, in any case, absorbed almost the whole of my remaining fortune.

My state of health was still so bad that I was at first sent to the labour camp hospital at Fuerth. When this was closed I was sent to another camp at Garmisch, but the authorities soon discovered that a hospital was too good a place for me and I was transferred to another camp of notorious reputation at Regensburg. There I was soon sent to hospital again, with a heart ailment, but I recovered under the devoted care of the nurses. One morning, in the communal wash-house, I was suddenly set upon by a fellow prisoner who had been an S.S. man. He beat me almost to death; my nose and cheekbone were fractured, my lips and eyelids split, and I was carried more or less unconscious into the operating theatre to be sewn up again. This fellow had apparently attacked a number of people in another camp and had been kept in solitary confinement before being transferred to Regensburg. The camp doctors had simply not bothered to read his medical history on arrival. Now he was hurriedly packed off to a lunatic asylum, although this was little comfort to me. However, another prisoner was an outstanding nose surgeon and I was soon more or less back in shape again.

The camp hospital at Regensburg was closed in 1948 and once more I was sent back to Garmisch, where the beautiful scenery made the barbed wire seem a little less depressing. The Garmisch camp was closed down in August and I finally ended up in the Langwasser camp, near Nuremberg. All these camps were under the supervision of American officers of what was called the Special Branch. Their chief duty, I believe, was to see to the political re-education of the prisoners. I have particularly unpleasant memories of some of these gentlemen, most of whom were first-generation Americans, not of Anglo-Saxon origin, and with strong leftist leanings. They did everything they could to make my life more miserable than it was already. In January 1949 the appeal for which my counsel had been fighting all this time, and which Herr Sachs was in no hurry to arrange, was at last heard. The conditions this time were very different. The hysterical atmosphere of the first trial had been replaced by a calm attitude on the part of the judge, who sought only to arrive at the truth.

It should be explained here that the Denazification Minister had the power to quash any verdict reached either in the first hearing or on appeal. One of the members of the court left my lawyers in no doubt that an acquittal would immediately be appealed against by Dr Sachs, who had in the meantime become acting De-nazification Minister, and that I would therefore be immediately rearrested. The only means of getting out of my labour camp was to be content with a mere reduction of the original sentence. We were therefore placed in the extraordinary situation of pleading only for some remission of sentence, otherwise I would be obliged to return to the labour camp and probably wait years for a new trial. The court was hard put to it to avoid pronouncing my complete acquittal, and although I regained my freedom I was still placed in the second of the five categories applied to those appearing before these courts, deprived of civic rights for my lifetime, and placed under certain restrictions for five years. The time I had already served in the labour camps was adjudged to have met the original sentence.

Much has been written, and remains to be written, about the legal chaos of these denazification trials. Their statutes were drawn up at a time when the Morgenthau plan formed the basis of Allied policy towards Germany. Contrary to the normal practice in any civilized country, the accused was presumed guilty until he had proved himself innocent. Again the traditional theory of *nulla poena sine lege* was abandoned, since at the time the crimes were alleged to have been committed, no legislation had existed which would have allowed charges to be formulated. Clearly defined and provable offences were not involved, but only membership of political organizations. The courts were often composed of political opponents without legal training, and procedure differed in each of the four zones of occupation. What brought the law into further disrepute were the countless cases in which prosecutors and members of the court were suspended or removed for accepting bribes and other corrupt behaviour. The whole process, which retarded the recovery of normal justice from all that it had suffered under the Hitler régime, is still having far-reaching effects.

* * *

Shortly before I put the final touches to this manuscript my family and I went to Burg Hohenzollern to attend the funeral of the last representative of the German Crown, the former Crown Prince of the Reich and Prussia. With him died the last vestiges of an era of German history. The tapestry of the events of my seventy years passed before my eyes. I thought back on the majesty of the vanished Empire and remembered the struggle to maintain its values and its traditions. In my mind's eye I saw once again the battlefields of the first war, in which so many millions had offered their lives, and found it difficult to believe that their efforts had been so ill rewarded.

The Crown and all it had represented for over a thousand years had been swept away. Civil war had shaken the country to its foundations. All that remained to us was our honour and our sense of duty. One task seemed paramount. Germany's historical mission in the centre of Europe had to be carried on, even in the midst of political chaos. With countless contemporaries from every class and profession, I had dedicated myself to this goal, both as a parliamentarian of no great importance and in high public office.

The result had been failure, but I had still retained faith in my country's mission. Some way had had to be found of relieving social distress, mass unemployment and the despair of the younger generation, while building up Germany as a bulwark against the threat from the East. We were to be disillusioned once again. Germany's resurgence, only to be explained by her inner belief in some great future, was diverted and twisted by evil forces whose representatives squandered her patrimony and reputation. More than that, we had broken faith with the Western ideals that it was our duty to defend. A tragic end indeed.

When I first sat down to write this account of my life, I had just finished reading the Confessions of St Augustine. Unfortunately, the courage he displayed in tracing his own errors is a gift denied to most ordinary men. Perhaps my critics will bear this thought in mind. Autobiographies can never be truly objective. They can only be a personal contribution to the mosaic of contemporary history, and our sins of omission and commission must be viewed against the events of the time. Although I have criticized my opponents, I have not sought to excuse myself.

The short span of one human life has seldom covered such an epoch-making series of events as those I have been called upon to witness. We are still too close to them to give an unbiased verdict on cause and responsibility. Europe is no longer the leading factor in world affairs, a far-reaching and complex development which cannot be attributed only to the results of Hitler's policies. Oversimplification renders a disservice to true historical understanding. Unless we make a deep study of the social conflict of our times, with its class warfare between capital and labour, and the restriction of individual responsibilities by the anonymity of the mass, we shall never understand the present ideological schism in the world.

I have described the hopes and plans that filled our minds between the end of the first world war and the emergence of Hitler. The period provides a sorry study of European statesmanship. French fear of Germany, combined with outmoded conceptions of nationalism, led first to attempts to annex the Rhine provinces of the Ruhr and the Saar. Treaties with Poland and the attempt to organize a Confederation of the Danube to encircle Germany found their echo in British policy, which regarded a strong France as a better guarantor of peace than a reconstituted Germany. Both Locarno and Lausanne told the same sad story of failure to reach a solution on a true European basis.

But, it will be argued, this still does not explain the growth of a movement which came to enjoy the support of nearly half the German nation. The Nazi movement was born in 1920 out of despair, and had its roots in the widespread desire to counter the Weimar Republic's policy – that of fulfilling all the victors' demands to the letter – by devising some new form of social and national ethos. Its later aberrations would never have developed if the Western Powers had shown some psychological understanding of the needs of a nation conscious of its contributions to history.

Very well, these nations may say, perhaps the Versailles Treaty was a bad peace and our subsequent policies shortsighted. But is it not true that Germany greeted every concession with demands for more? Did the Germans not show their contempt for treaties?

Were our suspicions not confirmed a thousand times by the combination of lies and deception which brought catastrophe on the world, with results that still threaten its existence?

Thus phrased, such questions cannot be answered. But the premises are false. It must first be asked why so little was done to encourage those Governments in Germany which still adhered to Western ideals and long-standing traditions. It must then be explained why a dictator was granted concessions and recognition which were denied to the bourgeois Governments that preceded him.

Once these questions have been answered without prejudice, it may be possible to understand a point that is otherwise difficult to explain psychologically: how it was possible, not only for an *élite* of civil servants, officers, economists and scientists, but also for the vast majority of the German nation, inwardly to reject the methods of the Hitler régime, and yet to make no public protest against these methods being used to attain political ends which were believed to be desirable.

I can well understand the disdain and disbelief of those abroad when they read memoirs and articles on life in the Third Reich which proclaim that nobody was really a National Socialist, that everyone was secretly in opposition to Hitler and that he therefore attained his ends against the resistance of the whole German nation. This picture is, of course, false.

I am one of the few people still alive who held high office during the whole transition from a parliamentary democracy to an increasingly unfettered dictatorship. I have already tried to explain how impossible the Germans found it to appreciate the phenomenon of a state authority which was itself opposed to normal conceptions of religion and law. No previous ruler had set out to undermine the rule of law. Right up to the outbreak of war, nobody could quite grasp where it all was leading. When Hitler formed his first coalition Government, both his Conservative colleagues and the nation as a whole hoped to assimilate his movement into the normal framework of our existence. The Roehm *Putsch* was to shatter our illusions. Even so, this was not brought home to the great mass of the people. Some were relieved that the Army had been saved from infiltration by the Brownshirts, and others approved the disappearance, whatever the methods employed, of so many morally corrupt individuals. Nevertheless, murder was murder. It must also be remembered that in the general improvement of their social and material position, the masses were prepared to disregard the inroads on their political and legal freedom.

In any case, it was still a long step to the methods that came to be employed from 1938 onwards. During the intervening period, the recognition which Hitler obtained abroad may not have relieved the Germans from their own internal responsibilities, but it had a very powerful psychological effect. The reassumption of our sovereign rights, whether in the Rhineland, or later in the Danzig Corridor, combined with what we believed to be defensive rearmament, were goals of which every patriotic German could not but approve. There seemed every likelihood that a strong Government would attain them by peaceful means more easily than by the wearisome negotiations of concessions which had characterized Hitler's predecessors. Our satisfaction, it is true, was increasingly overshadowed by moral doubts. During my Vienna years, I often discussed with my closest friends whether we could answer to our consciences for working towards union between the two countries under a régime which we inwardly rejected. Our conclusion was that Hitler was a temporary manifestation. He might die suddenly or be assassinated and his movement would break up. But the union of the two countries, if achieved by evolutionary methods, would not be a temporary manifestation; it would be a real contribution to our history.

In this we were in error. Hitler, and what he stood for, was no temporary manifestation. After the breach of the Munich Agreement even his reputation abroad became worthless. For those of us who recognized the signs, it became from then on a question of rescuing something from the impending chaos. Anyone who held high office during the following years knew the dreadful dichotomy which affected every honourable patriot. It was felt by both politicians and serving soldiers, of whatever rank, who tried to forge a path between duty and treason. To attempt the removal by internal means of a Government or the head of a State whose activities are damaging the nation is one thing. But what I cannot understand is how people calling themselves patriots can lend their services to an enemy to ensure the downfall of a Government by contributing to the nation's military defeat.

Germany was entirely responsible for the second world war.

We have no excuse to offer. Those who seek to do so by proclaiming that Hitler marched on Russia as part of a European crusade are doing us a disservice. The protagonists of this argument have failed to grasp that Hitler did not invade Russia to free the country from the Bolshevist yoke, but only as part of his brutal plan to subject the continent of Europe to his Greater German Empire. The Bolshevist methods which he had once execrated had long since been introduced into the Reich, and the difference between the two systems had become negligible. This legend must be exposed if people are to believe that we stand ranged with the lovers of freedom and are determined to fight in defence of Western ideals.

One thing must be recognized. In spite of the chaos in individual minds, there was in Germany a resistance movement which reduced to absurdity the theory of the whole German nation's corporate responsibility. Post-war propaganda endeavoured to elevate Germany's Communists and Socialists as the only resistance forces and guardians of democracy. The Morgenthau Plan, even in its modified application, provided the basis for appointing Communists to administrative positions, as prosecutors and judges in the denazification courts and as licencees of the reborn newspapers. It took some time for the occupation authorities to realize what sort of democracy these people professed. The Plan fertilized the economic and decartelization policies, which were only reversed when it was realized that they were leading not only to the ruin of Germany but of Europe. The working classes were regarded as the embodiment of resistance to Hitler. The truth is that as long as peace reigned and as long as they – the great mass of the workers – were assured of employment and the possibility of social betterment, they solidly supported Hitler's still undefined ends. This does not in any way detract from the courage of individual representatives.

When they found themselves at war, this otherwise peaceful mass came under the discipline of the Army and a war economy. Those with Marxist tendencies became victims of their own theories of the superiority of the State over individual minds. Modern war permits of no individualism, and everyone is submerged in an amorphous mass directed anonymously along totalitarian lines. It was therefore impossible for the masses to form part of the resistance movement. Whatever share of the blame for

Hitler's rise to power can be placed on the professional and educated classes, the fact remains that they provided 90 per cent of the resistance to Hitler. The leaders of the left had largely been put out of action during the early years of the Hitler régime, not necessarily because of active resistance work, but because of their political convictions. Thereafter, and particularly towards the end of the war, the evidence shows that active resistance came far more from representatives of the right than from the left.

We have seen how the theory of Germany's exclusive guilt for the first world war and the resulting moral repression of the German nation provided a key to the developments of the 'twenties. Let us hope that our former enemies will have the courage this time to abandon the theory of collective guilt and the defamation of everyone who occupied a position of authority in the troubled years of the Hitler régime. We shall never be able to play our part in the defence of Western ideals in a condition of enforced inferiority complex.

Where does our path now lead? We must first of all clear our minds about our true situation in the world. Whether we recognize it or not, Europe is no longer the arbiter of the world's affairs. While the individual countries were tearing each other to pieces, the balance of power gravitated to two new centres – the Asiatic bloc with Russia and China, and the American with the Western world. A new development of this magnitude is not completed in a day.

One thing is certain. The British Commonwealth is no longer the power it once was. The drive for independence in its component parts has broken its former unifying influence. Nor can other European nations hope to maintain their hold over the parts of Asia they once governed. The era of colonialism has gone for good. In the Middle East and elsewhere, peoples are rejecting European tutelage and must shortly become independent. This process cannot be halted by American subsidies to raise the standard of living, and this form of aid is only a subsidiary weapon in the overall battle of ideologies. It might have been possible to prevent the attachment of the Chinese to the Soviet bloc if the European nations had recognized more quickly the forces at work in Asia. The time for such a decision is now past. We now have to reckon with the stark reality of a Communist empire of eight hundred million people, under central direction, stretching from the Elbe to Shanghai and from the Arctic to the tropics. In spite of our successful holding operations in Korea, Indo-China and elsewhere, the fact remains that the Communists hold the initiative.

The leadership which one belonged to Europe has now passed to the United States. This young and ebullient nation is faced by one of the most onerous responsibilities in history. It might seem as if Europe was a mere onlooker, but that depends on whether we heed the call of the hour. It is no exaggeration to say that the battle cannot be fought without our help. Our reservoir of scientific ability, technical knowledge and centuries-old political experience make Western Europe still the most vital factor in the Western Hemisphere. Its two hundred and seventy million people have a production index twice that of the Soviet Union and they are the repository of the world's ideals of freedom.

America is aware of this. The Marshall Plan and its successors were devised to place the Old World physically and morally on its feet again, in preparation for the great ideological struggle to come. There has seldom been a more magnificent political gesture, but it places upon Europe the obligation not only of gratitude, but of action. The way to unity and reconstruction is full of obstacles. The basic impulse is there in every country, but the practical results are slim and take little account of the urgency of the danger. Out-dated conceptions of nationalism still play too great a part, and mutual fears and suspicions, inherited over generations, still obscure recognition of the fact that we are all in the same boat and must sink or swim together.

The greatest obstacle to European union lies in the sphere of Franco-German relations. We understand only too well the reservations of our Gallic neighbours, even though we do not accept the popular historical conception of 'three attacks on a peaceful France in the last seventy years'. But these fears can be overcome only if goodwill exists on both sides. The Schuman Plan provides a wise and statesmanlike basis for future co-operation. The unification of Western Europe's productive capacity in the sphere of heavy industry is a highly desirable development, which has been warmly greeted in Germany as a first step towards general integration. If Europe cannot be defended without our help, then let us have a common general staff and high command, as I suggested at Lausanne in 1932. But these forces must be raised on a basis of equality, if all its members are to be prepared to sacrifice their lives in the common cause. One more point must be observed. One of the most disastrous aspects of the policies of the last fifty years was the playing off of France against Germany, which the British regarded as a means of securing their position as *arbiter mundi*. This has now become out of date. The whole influence of the Commonwealth must now be used to encourage the integration of French and German interests.

The best start that could be made would be a solution of the Saar problem. At this stage in the history of Europe, it should be recognized that annexations represent a projection into modern times of the nationalistic obsessions of a past age. France and Germany should regard the Saar as a bridge between the two countries, and its natural resources should be exploited in the interests of both. The economic organization of such a condominium could be achieved without altering the basically German character of the territory. The Saar was for decades my home – although the present Government forbids me to return there – and I earnestly hope that a bilateral solution of its future status will form the first step towards the reunification of Europe. This should be accomplished without waiting for any formal peace treaty, which may, for one reason or another, continue to be postponed. Such an action would enable us to prove to the United States and the world that we had overcome our former nationalistic differences and had turned together a new page in the history of Europe.

Germany too must play her part in producing the atmosphere necessary for European integration. We must forego all ideas of exaggerated pride and seek to appreciate the part that other nations have played in our common Western heritage. Above all, the younger generation must be given hope and faith in the future. Never again must hopelessness lead them to seek extreme solutions. The new Bonn Republic must provide a surge of democratic ideals to counter the false promises to which the nation's youth is daily subjected by the rival Government on the other side of the Elbe. The Western Powers must appreciate that economic restrictions on Germany can only lead to unemployment and the renewed spiritual degeneration of Germany's youth.

After a life full of incident, great hopes and even greater disappointments, I have become convinced of the impossibility of saving the Western world by purely rationalistic and materialistic methods. It is the crisis in our spiritual existence which has brought us to the brink of disaster. Unless I have misread the signs, the catastrophe that has overcome Germany has uncovered strong forces which had become submerged during the decades of materialistic thinking. There is now a return to belief in the Power that stands above our terrestial affairs and first gave our life its true meaning.

The deification of matter, of the machine, of the masses and of human authority is slowly making way for the old spiritual conceptions: that God gave man a mind with which to organize the affairs of the world according to His precepts. The enslavement of mind by matter must be eradicated and the value of the individual personality restored. We cannot halt the discoveries of science, but we can bring them once again under the authority of the mind. Only then will it be possible to combat the totalitarian states, which have become the slaves of science and materialism. We must embark on a new crusade to restore belief in God to its rightful place in the centre of our affairs. That is the ultimate duty to which we must all consecrate ourselves, whatever our place in the scheme of things may be.

APPENDIX I

In 1933, the Dutch publishing house of Holkema and Warendorf published a short book entitled *De Geldbronnen van het Nationaal-Socialisme—Drie Gesprekken met Hitler* ('The Financial Sources of National Socialism – Three Talks with Hitler'). This book was allegedly written by 'Sidney Warburg', described as 'a partner in the influential American banking house of Warburg & Co.' It purported to be a confession by 'Sidney Warburg', stating circumstantially how he, acting for a group of American bankers, had procured some $8,500,000 for Hitler and the Nazi Party before and after its accession to power. It attempted to show that the National Socialists actually came into power in Germany through the machinations of American capitalists who thought that, by backing a Nazi counter-revolution, they could protect their German investments against a Communist revolution.

I was informed at the time about the appearance of the book by one of the partners of the then existing firm of Warburg & Co., Amsterdam. This same individual shortly thereafter informed Messrs Holkema and Warendorf that no such person as 'Sidney Warburg' was known to exist in the United States, that no banking firm of Warburg & Co. existed in the United States, and that the book was obviously a complete forgery. The publishers promptly withdrew the book from circulation, realizing that they had been hoaxed by a mysterious Mr J. G. Schoup of Antwerp, who had brought them what he described as a Dutch translation by himself of an English manuscript which he claimed had been given to him for publication in the previous year (1933) by 'Sidney Warburg'. These facts have been recently confirmed by Holkema and Warendorf in a letter dated January 6, 1949.

Since it appeared that the publishers had acted in good faith, no further action seemed indicated at the time, even though the book contained a mass of libellous material against various members of my family and against a number of prominent banking houses and individuals in New York. I have never to this day seen a copy of the book. Apparently only a handful of copies escaped the publisher's withdrawal.

The original purpose of the forgery remains somewhat obscure even today. Its obvious anti-Semitism made it appear as part of the then current flood of anti-Semitic propaganda emanating from Berlin. On the other hand, the alleged proof that Hitler owed his chief support to American Jews made it seem doubtful whether this forgery could have been the product of the Nazi propaganda machine, although examples of such double finessing are not uncommon in the history of Nazi propaganda.

In any case, it now appears that one of the few outstanding copies came into the hands of the Schuschnigg Government in Austria at the time when it was under pressure from the Nazis – probably in 1937. I shall pick up the thread of the story at this point as soon as I have filled in the necessary background as it has developed since that time.

In September 1946, I received a letter from a Mrs Hertha Sonderegger of Zurich, Switzerland, who described herself as the widow of René Sonderegger, a student of contemporary history. Mrs Sonderegger offered to sell me for $3,000 the original 'Sidney Warburg' manuscript and certain 'interesting' supporting documents in her deceased husband's collection.

I did not reply to, or even acknowledge the letter, but sent it immediately to General Clay, the then American Military Governor in Germany, expressing the opinion that this allegedly deceased Sonderegger might well be alive and the actual perpetrator of the original forgery, in which case the authorities might be interested to lay their hands on one of the slickest propagandists of the Nazi era; and that, even if Sonderegger were actually dead, his widow might merit some attention because of the obvious implications of her attempt to sell me these documents.

Apparently the inquiries made by the Swiss authorities at the request of General Clay sufficiently frightened Sonderegger so that he quite shamelessly emerged from his alleged grave and wrote to me himself, repudiating any possible implication that his wife's letter, admittedly written at his behest, had in fact been an attempt at blackmail. He urgently renewed his 'friendly offer' to sell me the 'Sidney Warburg' papers. This letter was likewise transmitted by me, unanswered, to General Clay's Chief of Intelligence. In addition, Sonderegger tried to approach me indirectly through at least two other channels. The evidence concerning these approaches was likewise transmitted by me to Berlin. Owing to Sonderegger's Swiss nationality and residence, the American Military Authorities were hampered in their investigations but, nevertheless, came to certain conclusions which, I feel sure, they would be willing to disclose to properly constituted authorities at the appropriate time.

Having failed to sell his wares, and probably feeling safe because there was no apparent further investigation, Sonderegger now undertook a second phase in his campaign. This phase falls into two – possibly three – parts: (1) the publication in 1948 by the Aehren Verlag, Auffoltern, Switzerland, of a book called *Spanischer Sommer* ('Spanish Summer') by Severin Reinhardt; (2) a campaign to revive the original 'Sidney Warburg' myth in the German press, also in 1948; and (3) the publication, also in 1948, by the Eduard Fankhauser Verlag, Thielle, Switzerland, of a book called *Liebet Eure Feinde* ('Love Your Enemies') by Werner Zimmermann.

'Severin Reinhardt', the author of *Spanischer Sommer*, has since been publicly identified in the Swiss press as René Sonderegger. *Spanischer Sommer* is a vicious concoction of falsehood and libel. The false and libellous statements concern not only my father, several of my uncles, the firm of Kuhn Loeb & Co. (founded by my grandfather), the Hamburg firm of M. M. Warburg & Co., but a large number of American firms and individuals, among whom are J. P. Morgan & Co., Thomas L. Lamont, the Rockefeller family, Winthrop Aldrich, the Guaranty Trust Co., William Potter, Justice Barndeis, Bernard M. Baruch, etc., etc.

The central theme of the book is an alleged Jewish conspiracy to dominate the world. (There are strong overtones and echoes of the discredited 'Elders of Zion' forgeries.) To bolster this theme there are such fantastic allegations as: that J. P. Morgan & Co. is controlled by Kuhn Loeb & Co.; that Kuhn Loeb & Co. is 'the most powerful of the five Federal Reserve Banks'; that Jacob H. Schiff and Thomas Lamont financed the Bolshevik Revolution in Russia; that my father, Paul M. Warburg, 'seized control' of the American currency system, etc., etc.

The *pièce de résistance* in this galaxy of malicious fabrication is the 'Sidney Warburg' confession, rehashed complete with new

embellishments. The capstone of the climax is Reinhardt's circumstantial 'proof' that the solution of the 'Sidney Warburg myth' is
to be found in the simple fact that I, James P. Warburg, was and
am the man who wrote the book and who did the things that
Sidney confesses.

The story, as now 'revealed', is that the whole Sidney confession is actually true; that I made the confession because I had a
change of heart after I saw what I had done in bringing Hitler to
power; that I gave my diaries, cables and notes to J. G. Schoup for
translation and publication in Holland some time during the
London Economic Conference. The 'proof' of this fantastic story
is roughly as follows:

At an unspecified time, probably in 1937, Sonderegger was, or
says he was, approached by a member of the Austrian Secret Service and asked to come to Vienna. There he was given by a high
official in the Schuschnigg Government (there are hints in another
document that it was Minister of Information Adam) one of the
few outstanding copies of the 'Sidney Warburg' book, with the
suggestion that he do something about it. (Schuschnigg – so runs
the story – and this part of it may be true – wanted to use the
material to discredit the Nazis, but was afraid to have it come out
under Austrian auspices.) Sonderegger was chosen for this job
apparently because, as an original supporter of the Hitler movement, he had followed Gregor Strasser in his break with Hitler
after the blood purge, had written a preface for Strasser's book,
and had published in Switzerland some sort of a little-noticed
rehash of the 'Sidney Warburg' story under the title *Finanzielle
Weltgeschichte* ('History of World Finance') brought out by the
Resoverlag in 1936.

And now we get the 'proof' of my identity. Reinhardt (Sonderegger) goes to a party in Prague to celebrate the promotion of the
Swiss chargé d'affaires, Dr Bruggmann, to the rank of Minister.
There he tells the story he heard in Vienna. And there Dr Bruggmann's wife, of all people, identifies 'Sidney' with 'Shimmy
Warburg', explaining that, in America, both Sidney and James
are commonly abbreviated as 'Shimmy'. But that is not all. Mrs
Bruggmann says that she happens to be an intimate friend of mine,
that we were playmates in our youth and went to school together.
She gives definite proof that Sidney and James P. are one and
the same. She even says that 'Shimmy' looks a little bit like

Sonderegger! And all this – says Sonderegger – is made doubly interesting because Mrs Bruggmann happens to be the sister of Henry Wallace and is now the wife of the Swiss Ambassador to the United States.

Further 'proof' of my identity is offered by Sonderegger in the report of an alleged telephone conversation between Roger Baldwin of New York and myself, in which Baldwin is supposed to have called me up in Sonderegger's presence and I am supposed to have said that Baldwin should tell Sonderegger to 'go to hell'.

Now for the second item in the 1948 campaign. In 1948 there suddenly appeared in the German press a spate of stories dishing up as new the publication in Amsterdam of the original 'Sidney Warburg' book. These stories did not identify me with 'Sidney'. They made no mention of the fact that the publishers had withdrawn the book when they found that there was no 'Sidney'. They played up the 'confessions' as a new revelation.

My cousin, Eric M. Warburg of New York, who has many friends and connections in Germany, heard about these newspaper stories, energetically pursued the matter and obtained formal retractions from a number of German newspapers. In the course of his investigations, a number of interesting facts as to the origin of the material came to light which indicate that more is afoot than the malicious and perhaps psychopathic enterprise of one individual. There are clear indications that certain anti-democratic and chauvinistic groups in Germany are involved in what appears to be a systematic effort to clear the German conscience of all guilt for Nazism by proving that Hitler was put into power by foreign capital and especially by a Jewish conspiracy.

How does Sonderegger come into this? The editor of one of the German papers which printed the 'Sidney' story and subsequently printed a disavowal of the same, received a lengthy letter of protest from none other than René Sonderegger, dated April 27, 1949. In this letter Sonderegger states that, while it is true that there was no 'Sidney Warburg', the 'confessions' are nevertheless authentic because 'Sidney Warburg' was merely the pseudonym under which I, James P. Warburg, had masqueraded. The letter then repeats the fictitious circumstantial 'proof' of identity much as stated in *Spanischer Sommer*, including the story of Mrs Bruggmann and the Roger Baldwin tale. (Among other things this letter would clearly identify 'Severin Reinhardt' and René Sonderegger, if that identity were not already established.) The letter proposes to the German editor a systematic campaign of 'investigation and exposure of the Warburg Secret' and gives some extremely interesting hints as to the nature and background of the Sonderegger undertaking.

The third item in the recent campaign is the Zimmermann book previously mentioned. This contains a chapter called *Hitler's Geheime Geldgeber* ('Hitler's Secret Financial Supporters') in which the original 'Sidney Warburg' story is rehashed, with certain perhaps intentional discrepancies. There is, as yet, no evidence of any direct connection with Sonderegger, but the rest of the book is suggestive of certain tie-ups with the group in Germany, which sponsored the recent newspaper stories.

The following is a translation of a release put out by the *Deutsches Zeit Archiv* on November 20, 1948. This contains the substance of the newspaper campaign above referred to.

'*U.S.A. Bankers helped Hitler into the Saddle.* (The Amsterdam firm of Holkema and Van Warendorfs Uitg. Mij. NV, has published, under the title "The Monetary Sources of National Socialism – Three Conversations with Hitler", a book about the foreign financial sources of support for National Socialism. The author is Sidney Warburg, partner in the influential American banking house of Warburg & Co.)

'When in 1929, so reports Warburg, dangerous downward trends became manifest in the American economy, one began to worry about money invested abroad. At the time Warburg was asked by the President of the Guaranty Trust to go to Europe to find out to what extent capital invested in Germany might be jeopardized by the danger of a Communist revolution. Warburg went to Europe in 1929. On his return he confirmed what had already been considered in high American financial circles – there was only one way – Hitler! And as Hearst, the owner of the greatest American newspaper concern, believed, Hitler would show himself to be not unapproachable. Warburg had to go to Europe again – this time via Italy – in order to visit the Banca Italiana in Rome for this purpose. At the same time he dined with Gregor Strasser and Goering at Balbo's house. The money, which had recently been made available, flowed through foreign banks: five millions through the Rotterdamsche Bankvereiniging and five millions through Mendelssohn & Co., Amsterdam. But the Party needed more. Another 15 millions were contributed to lift the Party into power. Nevertheless, the course of events did not go fast enough to suit Warburg's principals. In January, 1933, Warburg is in Germany again. This time Goering received him and Goebbels is also present. Again millions were placed at Hitler's disposal. Now the sum with which he allowed his road to power to be paved had risen to 34 millions.

'These revelations show how little one does justice to fact if one blames the Germans alone for the coming into power of National Socialism.'

WHAT SHOULD BE DONE?

There is, of course, the obvious procedure of instituting libel actions against Sonderegger (*alias* Reinhardt), the Aehren Verlag, Zimmermann, the Fankhauser Verlag, and perhaps others, including the Resoverlag. I am not familiar with Swiss law, but I should think that it would not be too difficult to win such libel actions. They would, however, probably entail considerable expense with small chances of recovery and – worse – a tremendous amount of time and energy. Far more important than these considerations, however, is the fact – clearly indicated in Sonderegger's letters – that he would welcome a libel action for the sake of the publicity he would thus obtain. Judging from his rather modest demand of $3,000 – modest, that is, for an attempt at blackmail – he would not be bothered by the certainty of losing the verdict and having damages assessed against him. This may, however, not be true of the Swiss publishing firms involved. The question of libel action should be studied further but it does not constitute the only method of procedure.

At this time I have decided to do two things:

First, to bring this whole matter to the official attention of the Swiss Government, the Government of the United States, and the British and French High Commissioners in Germany.

Second, to provide for those who may wish to use it, a formal affidavit in which I state the essential facts concerning both the original 'Sidney Warburg' forgery and the spurious identification of James P. Warburg with the non-existent 'Sidney Warburg'. This formal affidavit follows as part two of this statement.

FORMAL AFFIDAVIT BY JAMES P. WARBURG

Concerning the wholly false and malicious allegations made by René Sonderegger of Zurich, Switzerland, *et al.*, as set forth in the foregoing part of this statement, I, James Paul Warburg, of Greenwich, Connecticut, U.S.A., depose as follows:

1. No such person as 'Sidney Warburg' existed in New York City in 1933, nor elsewhere, so far as I know, then or at any other time.

2. I have never at any time used the name, 'Sidney Warburg', in writing or otherwise.

3. I never gave any manuscript, diary, notes, cables, or any other documents to any person for translation and publication in Holland, and, specifically, I never gave any such documents to the alleged J. G. Schoup of Antwerp. To the best of my knowledge and recollection I never at any time met any such person.

4. I was not an intimate friend of Madame Bruggmann at any time, was not her childhood playmate, did not go to school with her, and, to the best of my knowledge and recollection, have never had the pleasure of meeting her at all, in Europe or in the United States. Her alleged identification of me with 'Sidney' is a complete fabrication.

5. The telephone conversation between Roger Baldwin and myself, reported by Sonderegger, never took place at all and is pure invention. I never heard of Sonderegger until September 1946, when I received the hereinbefore described letter from his 'widow'. Baldwin has confirmed to me in writing that he has 'no recollection whatever of a man named Sonderegger nor of the incidents referred to'.

6. With respect to the actions specifically ascribed to 'Sidney Warburg' in the sample press release quoted in the foregoing part of this statement, which actions are attributed to me by René Sonderegger, *alias* Severin Reinhardt, as hereinbefore stated, I depose as follows:

(*a*) I did not go to Germany at the request of the President of the Guaranty Trust Company in 1929, or at any other time.

(*b*) I did go to Germany on business for my own bank, The International Acceptance Bank, Inc., of New York, in both 1929 and 1930. On neither of these occasions did I have anything to do with investigating the possible prevention of a Communist revolution in Germany by the promotion of a Nazi counter-revolution.

As a matter of recorded fact, my opinion at the time was that there was relatively little danger of a Communist revolution in Germany and a considerable danger of a Nazi seizure of power. I am in a position to prove that, on my return from Germany after the Reichstag elections of 1930, I warned my associates that Hitler would very likely come to power in Germany and that the result would be either a Nazi-dominated Europe or a second world war – perhaps both. This can be corroborated as well as the fact that, as a consequence of my warning, my bank proceeded to reduce its German commitments as rapidly as possible.

(c) I did not 'return to Germany via Italy' in 1929, 1930, or at any other time. I never at any time in my life visited any bank in Rome.

(d) I never met Balbo, never went to his house, and never met Strasser or Goering there or anywhere else.

(e) I had no discussions anywhere, at any time, with Hitler, with any Nazi officials or with anyone else about providing funds for the Nazi Party. Specifically, I had no dealings of this sort with Mendelssohn & Co., or the Rotterdamsche Bankvereiniging or the Banca Italiana. (The latter is probably meant to read Banca d'Italia, with which I likewise had no such dealings.)

(f) In February 1933 (see pages 191 and 192 of Spanischer Sommer) when I am alleged to have brought Hitler the last instalment of American funds and to have been received by Goering and Goebbels as well as by Hitler himself, I can prove that I was not in Germany at all. I never set foot in Germany after the Nazis had come to power in January 1933. In January and February I was in New York and Washington, working both with my bank and with President-elect Roosevelt on the then acute banking crisis. After Mr Roosevelt's inauguration, on March 3, 1933, I was working with him continuously helping to prepare the agenda for the World Economic Conference, to which I was sent as Financial Adviser in early June. This is a matter of public record.

The foregoing statements should suffice to demonstrate that the whole 'Sidney Warburg' myth and the subsequent spurious identification of myself with the non-existent 'Sidney' are fabrications of malicious falsehood without the slightest foundation in truth. The fact that I have dealt only with what appeared to me to be the heart of Sonderegger's campaign of wilful and malicious libel does not in any way imply that a vast mass of slanderous falsehood against myself and others, which has not here been dealt with, is thereby admitted to be true. It would require a full-length book to deal with all the untrue and criminally libellous material contained in Sonderegger's book, *Spanischer Sommer*. Should any further information be desired, which I am in a position to supply, I should be glad to co-operate with any duly authorized groups or individuals whose purpose is to ascertain and expose the truth.

(Signed) James P. Warburg

New York City
July 15, 1949

APPENDIX II

THE PAPEN CABINET ON 1 JUNE 1932

Chancellor	von Papen
Foreign Minister	von Neurath
Minister of the Interior	von Gayl
Minister of Defence	von Schleicher
Minister of Economics	Prof. Warmbold
Minister of Finance	Count Schwerin-Krosigk
Minister of Justice	Dr Guertner
Minister of Food and Agriculture	von Braun
Minister of Labour	*For a short period the permanent secretary, Dr Syrup, took charge of the Ministry, without Ministerial rank.*
Minister of Transport and Post	von Eltz-Rübenach

THE HITLER CABINET ON 30 JANUARY 1933

Chancellor	Hitler
Vice-Chancellor and Reich Commissioner for Prussia	von Papen
Foreign Minister	von Neurath
Minister of the Interior	Dr Frick
Minister of Defence	von Blomberg
Minister without portfolio and Reich Commissioner for Aviation	Goering
Minister of Economics and Food and Agriculture	Dr Hugenberg
Minister of Finance	Count Schwerin-Krosigk
Minister of Justice	Dr Guertner
Minister of Labour	Seldte
Minister of Transport and Post	von Eltz-Rübenach
Reich Commissioner for Employment	Dr Gereke

INDEX

Abbeville, 31

Abegg, 189

Abetz, Heinrich Otto, 526

Abraham, oasis of, 73

Abu Chuff, 74

Abwehr, 481, 489, 510, 512, 554; Hitler places under Himmler, 520

Abyssinia, Italian adventure in, 23, 364, 368, 387; breaks façade of union achieved at Stresa, 388–9

Acre, 88

Adam, Federal-Commissioner, 416

Adam, General, 319, 388

Adana, 83, 88, 513; Conference at (1943), 494–5

Adenauer, Dr Konrad, 101, 164, 191, 294

Adige Valley, 88

Adrianople, 25, 474

Adriatic Coast, 25, 515

Aegean Sea, 456; Bulgaria and, 25, 473

Aetna Powder Company, 37, 38

Afghanistan, 22

Africa, North, French expansionist policies in, 23; campaign in, 477, 482, 490–1, 493

Agadir, 12, 24

Aix la Chapelle, Treaty of, 89

Alaska, 553

Albania, becomes independent State (1913), 25; Prince zu Wied's reign, 25; invasion by Italy, 443–4, 445, 446, 447, 448; Italian Army attacks Greeks from, 464

Albert, —, 39, 40, 44–5, 50, 51, 56

'Albert papers', 50, 51

Aleppo, 69, 71, 72, 74

Alexander the Great, 71

Alexandretta, 516

Algeciras, Treaty of, 24

Ali Fuad, General. See Erden, Ali Fuad,

Allenby, General, 68; Palestine offensive, 70, 71, 72, 75, 76, 77, 79, 80, 81, 82

Allied Powers (Second World War). See Western Allies

Allies (First World War), propaganda to bring U.S. intervention, 29; atrocity propaganda against Germany, 31–2; campaign against Papen in U.S., 51; efforts to persuade America to enter war, 60; naval blockade of Germany, 62; threaten break-through on Western Front, 66; operations in Palestine, 70–5; dismiss Central Powers' offer to declare

war aims (1916), 87; secret pacts signed by, 87; draw up Balfour Declaration, 88; and unity of Germany, 89; hysteria engendered by propaganda of, 94; fear of Germany, 94; arrange Reparations Conference, 162. *See also* Western Allies

Alphand, —, 201

Alsace-Lorraine, 28, 343

Alvensleben, Count Bodo von, 113, 248

Alvensleben, Werner von, 162, 242, 247, 248, 292, 319

Amanus tunnel, the, 70

Ame des Peuples, L', 128

America. *See* United States of America

American Military Government, in Germany, 575

Amman, 77, 78, 79, 81

Amnesty, in Germany (1933), 295; Austrian, 416

Am Tage Danach, 166

Anatolia, 70–1; defence of, 471

Ancre, 66

Andrus, Colonel Burton C., 541, 542, 544, 545, 550, 575

Anglo-French-American loan, 137–8

Anglo-French-Turkish Alliance (1939), 24, 495

Anglo-Russian Convention (1907), 22, 23

Anglo-Saxon countries, two-party system in, 168; criminal law in, 557, 558, 567

'Anima', German religious foundation in Rome, 382

Ankara, Papen offered post as German Ambassador in, 443; Papen's task in, 446; Papen's work during five years in, 449; Papen's arrival in, 450; Papen decides to remain in, 453; British military missions in, 461, 488, 495, 519; Eden and Dill arrive in, 472; Rahn arrives in, 477; Schulenburg arrives from Moscow, 480; attempted assassination of Papen, 485–7; Clodius visits, 488; meetings between Axis Ambassadors in, 491; 'Operation Cicero', 509–17; Cicero seen in (1944), 518; Papen's mission ends, 528

Annaly, Lord, 9

Annie Larsen, S.S., 40

Anschluss, Papen accused of organizing, 2; Hitler agrees to possibility of, 342; Allied Powers' ban on, 344–5; 1921 referendum, 345–6; Papen's attitude to,

346-8; Austrian group favouring, 354; *Kulturbund's* opposition to, 356; Saar plebiscite encourages supporters of, 360; Austro-German discussions, 397-8; French attitude to, 400-1; final events leading to, 406-39; Mussolini abandons objections to, 407; foreign attitude to, 421, 438; approved by Austrian referendum, 430-1

Anti-clericalism, Socialist, 104, 129; Nazi, 278, 281, 350, 357, 383; Hitler's, 286

Anti-Semitism, 402; Goebbels' campaign, 113; Papen accused of, 285; basic tenet of Nazi Party, 285; Hitler's, 285-6. *See also* Jews

Anzac cavalry units, 78

'Appeasement', not a German policy, 327

Arabian freedom movement, in Iraq, 475, 477

Arabs, 78; Lawrence and, 77, 80; autonomy for,81; offended by Balfour Declaration, 88

Archibald, —, 49-50

Argentine, 509

Armistice (1918), the, 83

Army, British. *See* British Army

Army, German. *See* German Army

Arnim, General Juergen von, 500

Arras, 67, 74, 75; battle of, 116

Artois, 67

Aryan Laws. *See* Nuremberg Laws

Asia, 335; Germany's position in, 88; threat to Europe from, 129; rejects European tutelage, 585

Asia Minor, 88, 466

Asim Bey, 76

Associated Press, Papen gives interview to, 193

Association for the Encouragement of Industrial Co-operation, 118-19

Association for the Maintenance of Western Culture, 129

Atatürk, Mustafa Kemal, 72-3; Papen meets, 74; enjoins successors to be on guard against attacks on Dardanelles, 444; his political testament, 464

Atlanta, 47, 58

Atlantic Charter, the, 493

Atlantic Wall, 533-4; Turkish mission tours, 488; Hitler's belief in, 525

Attolico, Count Bernardo, 448

Audja, the, 75

Augustine, St, 580

August Wilhelm, Prince, 329

Auslandsorganisation, 355-6, 392, 481, 489

Austria, Papen arraigned as architect of rape of, 2; Germany's plans for Customs Union with, 136 (*See also* Anschluss); on verge of disintegration, 136; French objection to Customs

Union with Germany, 178; deterioration of relations with Germany, 298-300; Social Democrats attempt to kill Dollfuss, 299-300; Mussolini perturbed by Nazis in, 331; Hitler orders Papen to go as Minister, 337-9; Papen's conditions for mission to, 340-1; 1918 Constitution, 344; political parties banned in, 348-9; Fatherland Front, 349, 380, 381, 383, 390, 396, 403, 412, 423, 426; Socialists' refusal to join Workers' Social Association, 349; Papen's arrival in, 350-1; internal political situation in, 352-3; Heimwehr, 353, 361, 364, 377-8, 390; possible Hapsburg restoration in, 354, 389-90; German citizens in, 355-6, 391-3; Mussolini's influence in, 360-1; Schuschnigg's declaration on Austria as German State, 361; Papen's appeal to Hitler for recognition of independence, 361-2; text of Papen's proposals for Austrian question, 363; relations with Italy, 364; Papen's reports to Hitler on, 365, 368, 382, 385; Cabinet changes, 369, 379; Papen's discussions with Schuschnigg, 369-70; July agreement with Germany, 369-72, 376-7, 383, 387, 391, 395, 396, 397, 401, 403, 408, 409, 411, 415, 421; Schuschnigg's relations with Heimwehr, 377-8; Foreign Minister visits Berlin, 379-80; protocol as result of Foreign Minister's visit to Berlin, 380; Nazi Party leader's policy, 384; plans to incorporate Opposition in Government, 384-5, 394-6; Committee of Seven, 385, 394-6, 404; Neurath's visits, 389-90; demonstrations against union with Germany, 390; Papen's reports to Hitler on Nazis, 391; German flag incident, 391-3; Hitler sends Under-Secretary, 396; Schuschnigg's accusations against Nazi Party, 396; Austro-German commission meeting, 397; ex-servicemen's political demonstration in, 397-8; Foreign Minister visits Berlin, 401; correspondence between Goering and Austrian Foreign Minister, 401-2; Papen's discussions on, with French political leaders, 402-3; Schuschnigg stops entry of members into Fatherland Front, 403; Papen's representations for expulsion of Austrian Nazi leader, 403-4; police raid offices of Committee of Seven, 404; Papen's discussions with Seyss-Inquart on German Nazi intervention, 404; Hitler dismisses Papen, 406; Hitler requests Papen to resume duties, 408; Papen's discussions with Schuschnigg and Schmidt, 409–11; proposals for discussion by Hitler and Schuschnigg, 411–2; Berchtesgaden meeting between Hitler and Schuschnigg, 412–21; Papen's wishes for inclusion of Seyss-Inquart in Cabinet, 413; German proposals, 414–7; foreign reactions to German proposals, 421, 438; Hitler's speech to Reichstag on, 421–2; appreciation of Papen's efforts, 421; Papen's report to Hitler on, 422–3; Nazi leader's meeting with Hitler, Goering and Keppler, 423; Papen's Vienna papers taken to Switzerland, 424, 435–6, 440–1; Schuschnigg decides on plebiscite, 424; French share in plebiscite idea, 425; Papen's suggestions for changes in wording of plebiscite rejected by Schuschnigg, 426; Mussolini warns Schuschnigg about plebiscite, 426; new Nazi campaign in, 426; Goering orders Seyss-Inquart to form new Cabinet, 428; Schuschnigg's resignation, 428; Papen advises against sending of German troops, 429; President Miklas refuses to entrust Seyss-Inquart with formation of Cabinet, 429; Hitler orders march into, 430; referendum approves Anschluss, 430–1; Papen returns to Vienna, 431–2; Gestapo in, 433, 434, 435, 436–7; disappearance of Ketteler in, 433–7, 440; police under control of Heydrich, 434; Goering's increased domination of Austro-German affairs, 438. *See also* Anschluss *and* Nazi Party, Austrian

Austria-Hungary, and Balkan crisis (1913), 12–3; extends influence in Balkans, 24; threat of war with Russia, 25, 26; conflict with Serbia, 26; Germany declares war to aid against Slav menace, 61; call for German divisions, 83; dissolution of, 89; divided into its component parts, 95. *See also* Austria

Austrian Legion, 352, 397

Austrian Nazi Party. *See* Nazi Party, Austrian

Autobahn network, the, 283

Axis Powers, 460; Hungary joins, 468–9; Rumania joins, 469; Bulgaria joins, 472; Iraq and, 475; lack of military coordination between, 491

Azerbaijan, Hitler's Gauleiter for, 503

Baden, S.A. ban never lifted in, 163

Badger, Admiral, 17

Bad Harzburg, right wing front devised at, 143

Baghdad, Turks lose, 68; plans for recapture of, 69, 71–2, 117; revolutionary movement in, 476–7

Baghdad railway, 25, 26, 69, 83

Baku, 117, 469; Saracoglu suggests air attack on, 463

Balance of power, 177; German General Staff and, 21; decisive shift after 1907, 22, 23, 24; Russian threat to, 26; neither side true to in 1914, 86; Germany too strong for, 479; concessions to Stalin destroy, 537

Baldwin, Stanley, 358

Balfour Declaration, the, disastrous consequences of, 88

Balkan Federation, 450, 470; Bulgarian refusal to join, 444, 455–6

Balkans, conflict in (1913), 12–3; Wars (1911–13), 22, 25–6; as Russian sphere of interest, 463; Hitler rejects Russian demands in, 469; Eden and Dill explore possibility of front in, 472; Bulgaria's key position in, 474; Churchill's plan for offensive in, 515; Allied attack ruled out, 516, 517, 521

Ballin, —, 64

Baltic States, the, 102, 444; Papen's anxiety over Germany's intentions in, 452

Bardolff, Field-Marshal von, 354–5

Basra, 475, 476

Batotzki, —, 165

Batts, General, 540

Batum, 469

Bavaria, 213; Soviet government in, 95; Zentrum Party in, 97; and Rhine Republic movement, 120; ban on S.A. not lifted, 163; strong monarchist current in, 245; Concordat with Vatican, 278; Royal House, 354

Bavarian People's Party, 166, 194, 207, 213, 239–40, 244, 272, 324; supports Enabling Law, 274; places itself under Hitler's leadership, 304

Bayreuth, 337, 338, 341, 361, 372, 408, 431, 437, 445; Festivals at, 339, 371

Beck, Field-Marshal Ludwig, 281, 319, 405, 498

Beckerle, —, 502

Bedouins, 80

Beersheba, 70, 73, 74

Behrens, —, 325

Beirut, 477

Belgium, 54, 92, 370, 462; Schlieffen plan necessitated invasion of, 28; Bethmann-Hollweg's desire to respect neutrality of, 28; German invasion of, 32, 181;

illegal shipments to S.A. from, 314; Hitler's attack on, 460

Belgrade, 387; Allied air attack on, 529

Belmont, August, 32

Belsen, concentration camp, 539

Belvoir meet, 8

Benedict XV, Pope, 87

Benes, Edouard, 345, 543

Benkendorf, Aleksandr Konstantinovich, 20

Bennigsen, Rudolf von, 6

Berchtesgaden, 300, 502; Papen's visits to, 333, 366, 376, 451, 461, 463; Schuschnigg's conference with Hitler at, 402, 409–10, 412–21; agreement between Hitler and Schuschnigg at, 415–21, 424, 426, 427, 565

Berckheim, —, 16

Bergen, — von, 280

Berger, —, 361, 365; presented with first draft of agreement with Germany, 362; resigns as Austrian Foreign Minister, 369, 378

Berlin, 5, 6, 11; Papen reports to, 68, 69; torn by revolution, 86; threatened French march on, 119–20; Catholic Bishop of, 128; state of emergency in, 190–1; University, 266; Hindenburg should have stayed in, 326; Stalhelm Congress in, 353; Ribbentrop Bureau's activities in, 374; Olympiad, 386; morale at zero, 498; air raids on, 508

Berliner Tageblatt, 165, 211

Berlin-Rome Axis. *See* Axis Powers

Berne, 185

Bernhard, Senator, 306

Bernstorff, Count Albrecht von, 202

Bernstorff, Count Johann Heinrich, German Ambassador at Washington, 15, 30, 32, 42, 43, 45, 46, 47, 50, 55, 64, 76, 81

Bessinge, near Geneva, 140, 171, 202, 203

Bethmann-Hollweg, Theobald von, 28, 62, 64, 523

Beuthen, 199–200

Bevin, Ernest, 538

Biddle, Francis, 559, 569

Bismarck, Count Gottfried von, local government head in Potsdam, 498; and Roosevelt's peace plan, 522; arrested after July plot, 527, 530; Papen pleads with Hitler for life of, 532

Bismarck, Prince Otto von, policies of, 4, 22, 26, 87, 97, 344, 346, 430, 451; solution for Federal and State Government relations, 99–100, 152; his recommendation that Constitution be ignored, 216–7; Ems telegram, 429n

Bismarck-Schönhausen, Prince Otto von, Counsellor of German Embassy, London, 530

Bismarck-Schönhausen, Princess Otto von, 530

'Black Reichswehr', 119, 120, 121

Black Sea, 466, 524

Black Tom Case, Papen and, 55–9

'Black-White-Red' electoral bloc, 230, 266

Blanquet, General, 16–7

Blaskowitz, General Johannes, 540, 551

Blomberg, Field-Marshal Werner von, 300, 306, 388; Hindenburg proposes as War Minister, 240, 242, 243; as War Minister, 249; Nazi sympathies, 287, 288, 291; in Hitler's Cabinet, 290; cordial relations with Hitler, 313; and Roehm *Putsch*, 319, 320, 327; allows new oath of loyalty to Hitler, 335–6; represents Germany at George VI's Coronation, 386; his fateful second marriage, 405, 409; his son shot in Iraq, 477

Blum, Léon, 104, 177; Schacht advised to visit, 388; Papen's secret meeting with, 402

Boch-Galhau, Privy Councillor von, 9, 92

Bochow, —, 325, 434–5, 436

Bock, Field-Marshal Fedor von, 11, 314, 319; disturbed at over-rapid expansion of the Army, 388

Bodenschatz, General Karl, 315, 316, 435

Boecklin, Arnold, 7

Boehn, — von, 533

Boer War, 23

Boeselager, — von, 498

Bohle, Ernst Wilhelm, organizer of the *Auslandsorganisation*, 355–6, 392, 481, 491; influence on Hitler, 458; protests against Papen, 489

Bolshevism, 27, 252, 256, 283, 284, 305, 327, 360, 382; Hungary bulwark against, 543

Bonhoeffer, Pastor, 533

Bonn, 164, 305

Bonnet, Georges, 402

Bonn Republic, the, 99, 101, 587

Boris, King of Bulgaria, 456, 459; demands to Hitler, 473–4; death of, 501–2

Bormann, Martin, head of Nazi Party Chancery, 282; influence on Hitler, 357, 458; reaction to Hudal's book, 383; continues persecution of Churches, 482; plot to capture, 498

Bose, — von, 276, 277, 314, 315; murder of, 316, 317, 321–3, 324, 325–6, 340, 433, 435, 437, 481

Bosphorus, 452; Russia granted facilities in, 469; Jenke drowned in, 519

Boy-Ed, Captain, 15, 42, 47, 50, 56

Bracht, Dr, 190

Bradford, Bohle born in, 355

Brandenburg, Province, emergency in, 190

Brauchitsch, General Walter von, 427, 429

Braun, Otto, 164, 166, 190, 191, 192, 294

Braunschweig brothers, 533

Braun-Severing State Government, 110

Bremen, 185, 316

Bremen Club, the, 305

Brenner Pass, the, Mussolini masses divisions on, 338, 339, 358, 387

Brest-Litovsk, Peace of, 87

Briand, Aristide, 105, 127, 138

Bridgeman-Taylor, *alias* Horst von der Goltz *and* Wachendorf, 34, 53

Bridgeport Projectile Company, 38, 43

Britain. *See* Great Britain

British Army, expeditionary corps at Abbeville, 31; surrenders to Turks at Kut el Amara, 68; attacks on Gaza beaten off, 70; attack on Gaza, 74; captures Beersheba, 74; enters Jerusalem after German evacuation, 76; offensive against Jerusalem-Nablus road, 77; attack on Jordan line, 78-9; offensive on Palestine front (1918), 81-2; at Dunkirk, 461; in North Africa, 477

British Commonwealth, Ribbentrop and, 375; no longer the power it was, 585

British Empire, at the turn of the century, 8; Papen impressed with vitality of, 13; Anglo-Russian Convention gives precedence to its interests, 22; Ribbentrop's opinion of, 376, 386; Papen's report on lines of communication of, 447; Hitler prepared to share with Russia, 466; German High Command's memorandum on its essential lifelines, 470

British Military Government, in Germany, 575

British Navy, command of sea in 1914, 30; blockade of Germany, 34, 35, 37, 40-1; Mediterranean Fleet, 476

Brockdorff-Rantzau, Count Ulrich von, 118

Brogan, Prof. D. W., 92

Broglie, Maurice, Duc de, 128

Brownshirts (S.A.), 193, 253, 264; excesses of, 242; lack of discipline in, 260; Communists join, 270; attacks on Jews, 290, 293; concentration camps set up by, 294; Roehm demands military status for, 306-7; Hitler's tirade against excesses, 310; and Roehm *Putsch*, 313-4, 318, 319, 320, 321, 323; illegal arms shipments to, 314

Brüning, Dr Heinrich, reputation and character, 108-9, 133, 170; Papen supports, 109; downfall of, 113; forms 'Presidential Cabinet', 132-3; and the Socialists, 133, 134-5, 136, 144-5; emergency measures, 134-6, 139, 143, 145; visits London, 137; visits France, 138; deflationary measures, 139; resists co-operation with the right, 141; and Presidential Election, 143; failure to reach agreement with the right, 143, 144-5; and Harzburger Front, 144; and National Socialists, 147, 151, 161, 225; attempts to ensure Hindenburg's re-election, 146, 147, 328; his *Deutsche Rundschau* article, 149, 274; plan to suppress Nazis, 149; differences with Hindenburg, 148, 150; *Osthilfe* affair and fall of, 164-5, 167; domestic policy of, 170; and Lausanne Conference, 171-2, 202-3; prepared to accept post under Hitler, 240; and Papen, 244; conviction that Nazi experiment would fail, 251-2; on the Enabling Law, 274-5

Brunswick, Nazi coalition in, 141

Brussa, 466, 520

Bryan, William Jennings, 32, 43

Bucharest, Treaty of, 25

Buchenwald concentration camp, 539-40

Budapest, 387; Papen visits, 492, 508, 529; Nazi intrigues in, 509

Buerckel, Josef, 410, 551

Bulgaria, in anti-Turkish alliance, 25; obtains Thrace and Aegean coast, 25; attacks Serbia and Greece, 25; loses Macedonia, 25; cedes Dobrudja, 25; Central Powers' front breaks in, 82; refuses to join Balkan Federation, 444, 455-6; Western Allies' policy for inclusion in Balkan bloc, 455-6; relations with Turkey, 456, 459, 470, 474; Russian offer of assistance pact to, 466, 467, 468; Papen on dangers of bringing into war, 471; adheres to Axis, 472; takes part in attack on Yugoslavia, 473, 474; interest in Macedonia and Salonika, 473-4; key position in Balkans, 474; Russian mission in Sofia, 474; King Boris' death, 501-2; Stalin's intention to declare war on, 514; Russia's occupation, 515; difficult situation in, 529; Papen passes through, 529

Bülow, Bernhard Wilhelm von, 175, 178, 202

Burg Hohenzollern, 580

Burgundy, Hitler's plans for, 463

Busche, General, 118

Buttmann, Dr, 280

Büyük Ada, 504

Caernarvon, 75, 76

Cairo, 70; Rommel at the gates of, 491; suggestion of a meeting between Roosevelt and Papen at, 505; Menemencioglu meets Eden at, 506–7; Cicero's information during conference at, 512, 513; Hitler and Ribbentrop told of decisions taken at, 517

Çakmak, Marshal Fevzi, 74, 461, 487; considers Turkish Army insufficiently equipped, 494; British attacks on, 519–20; Inönü dismisses, 520

California, 40

Canada, Papen promotes sabotage in, 33–5, 54; divisions on Western Front, 66, 67

Canadian Car and Foundry Company, 55

Canadian Pacific Railway, 33, 34, 35

Canaris, Admiral Wilhelm, 18; head of Abwehr, 480, 481, 489; replaced by Himmler, 520

Cankaya Avenue, Ankara, 454

Carinthia, Yugoslav threat to, 345

Carp family, 7

Casablanca Conference, 493–4

Casement, Sir Roger, 35, 36, 46, 56

Caserta, —, 53

Caspar, —, 189

Catholics. See Roman Catholic Church

Catroux, General Georges, quells Arab revolt in Syria, 477

Caucasus, 492; Turkish front in, 69, 77, 117

Cemal Pasha, General, 77, 78, 80, 81

Cemal Pasha, Governor-General of Syria, 70, 72, 77

Central Europe, Germany's position in, 2; as bulwark of the West, 6–7, 9; Germany's rôle in, 94; rôle in combating totalitarianism from East, 280; Balkanization of, 344

Central Powers, 88; position weakened by Italian rapprochement with Triple Entente, 25; protests in America against 'inhumanity' of, 42; limitation of resources, 61; effect of Allied naval blockade on, 62, 63; not true to balance of power in 1914, 87; offer to declare war aims (1916), 87; victors' hatred of, 94

Cevad Pasha, General, 76

Châlons, 525,

Chamberlain, Neville, 183; Hitler's undertaking to, 296, 443; and the Munich Agreement, 441–2; Papen's letter to, 441–2; and the guarantee to Poland, 446

Chapultepec Castle, 18

Château Thierry, 81

Chaulnes, 66

Chautemps, Camille, 402

Chevy Chase Club, 15

Chiang Kai-Shek, Generalissimo, 76

Chicherin, Grigori Vasilievich, 119

China, 22, 585

Christian Democratic Union, 101

Christian Democrats, German, 99

Christianity, 96; collapse of, 3; German duty to defend in Central Europe, 27; overthrow of, 91; basis for government, 91; spread by Germany, 94; Prussian defence of, 128; denial of, 129; loses appeal under Weimar, 253; Hitler and, 273–4, 280; Nazi extremists against, 282

Christian Socialists, support Enabling Law, 274; Austrian, 378

Churches, the, Hitler's attitude to, 261; Nazis interference with, 277, 382, 396; attempt to establish legal basis for, 278

Churchill, Winston S., 102; Hitler's comment on his war policy, 462–3; invites Turkey to take defensive measures, 471; turns down Swedish King's peace approach, 472; pledges support for Russia, 480; Casablanca Conference, 493–4; visits Turkey, 494, 495; at Cairo and Teheran, 513; and 'unconditional surrender', 514; insistence on Balkan offensive, 515; Papen hopes to interest in preventing Russian advance in Europe, 516; on Papen, 527, 532; and severance of Turco-German relations, 528; and the making of peace, 537; Horthy's appeal to, 543; and Hess's flight to England, 553; objects to Stalin-Roosevelt proposal about Nazi leaders, 570–1

Church of St Paul, Frankfurt, Liberal Democratic ideas proclaimed at, 166

Ciano, Count Galeazzo, accompanies Mussolini to Germany, 398; announces Italy's attack on Albania, 444; attention drawn to Turkish fears, 448; works out details of German-Italian alliance with Ribbentrop, 448; personal interests in Macedonia, 473; Ribbentrop intercepts communications of, 482

'Cicero,' 510, 511, 512, 513, 514, 515, 516, 517, 518, 525, 531

Ciphers, Italian, 482

Class warfare, 92–3, 254, 267; Hitler seeks to put an end to, 283

Clemenceau, Georges, 101

Clodius, Karl, 488

Colmar, — von, 533

Cologne, 101, 156, 247, 560

Committee of Seven, the, 394, 396, 404

Committee for Un-American Activities, 38

Communism, 13; triumph of Moscow brand of, 91; Lenin on hopes of, in Germany, 103; ground ripe for, in Germany, 253; holds initiative today, 585–6

Communist Manifesto, 92

Communists, German, 95, 129; in Prussia, 110, 189, 192; in Saxony, 120; suppression of uprisings of, 123; gains in 1930 Election, 135; threat to German security, 141; negotiations with Social Democrats and Nazis, 189; revolutionary intentions of, 192; call for revolution by, 207; co-operation with Nazis, 208; resolution for repeal of emergency decrees (1932), 208; workers bemused by propaganda of, 210; in November (1932) Election, 212; excesses of Rotfront, 242; influx into Nazi Party, 261, 280; and Reichstag Fire, 269–71; Nazi arrests of, 270; leaders flee to Moscow, 270; banned, 270; join Brownshirts, 270; in Election of March, 1933, 271, 274; banned from Reichstag, 274

Concentration camps, 294–5; threat of, 349; unbelievable conditions in, 538–40

Concordats, Vatican, 127, 278, 281, 350, 351, 357, 432

Confederation of the Danube, 581

Confessions of St Augustine, 580

Congress, United States, 64, 87, 193

Congress of Vienna, the, 89

Conservatives, German, 104, 105, 211, 255; Papen out of sympathy with, 90, 97; beg Papen not to take part in Hitler's Cabinet, 242; failure to build bloc to counterbalance Nazis, 258; in Hitler's Cabinet, 278, 289, 290, 291

Constantinople, Russian aspirations towards, 26. *See also* Istanbul

Constitution Day, 195

Conti, Dr, 550

Contrat Social, the, 92

Cornelius, Peter, 7

Coronel, Battle of, 18

Cos, British occupation of, 503

Council of Europe, 128

Covenant of the League of Nations, 186–7

Cradock, Admiral Sir Christopher, 18, 19

Cravath de Gersdorff, Swaine and Wood, 58

Crete, 25; German General Staff prepares for assault on, 476

Crimea, 531; Russian forces in, 482–3; Turkish military mission see fighting in, 488; the siege of, 524

Cripps, Sir Stafford, in Moscow, 463

Croatia, 543

Croats, 95

Csaky, Count Istvan, 468

Cuba, 16

Cunningham, Viscount, Admiral of the Fleet, 476

Cuno, Wilhelm, 118

Curtius, Julius, 137, 143

Customs Union, Austro-German, proposed, 136, 137. *See also* Anschluss

Cyprus, 494

Cyrenaica, 471

Cyril, Prince Regent of Bulgaria, 502

Cyrus, 71

Czechoslovakia, German minority in, 296; Germany assimilates, 296; opposition to union of Austria and Germany, 345; Hitler's interview with Hacha, 443; German march into, 443, 445; Papen's plan for Dutch mediation, 456–7

Czechs, 49, 95, 205

Dachau, concentration camp, 538–9; Prince Hohenberg sent to, 394

Dahlem, 235, 449

Daily Mail, the, 194

Daily Telegraph, the, 194

Daladier, Edouard, 402, 442

Dalmatia, given to Italy, 88

Damascus, 71, 72, 78, 80, 81, 82

Danton, Georges Jacques, 576

Danube Monarchy. *See* Austria-Hungary

Danube Powers, 360–1; Little Entente of, 391

Danzig Corridor, 372, 444, 445, 451, 452

Dardanelles, the, 69, 88; Atatürk's warning of possible attacks on, 444; Turkey's fear of Russian ambitions in, 450, 465, 527; attempts to keep closed to military traffic, 455; Russian aspirations, 460, 463, 487, 515–6; political history of, 466; Molotov's demands, 469; Turkish fear of Russo-German operation in, 479, 515–6; German ships pass through, 526

Dark Invader, The, 46

Darkness at Noon, 548

Darré, Dr Richard Walther, 292

Darss, 399, 400

Dawes Plan, the, 131

Dead Sea, 77

Dedeagach, 456; King Boris asks for return of, 473

Dekanozov, Vladimir Georgevich, 467

Delbos, Yvon, 400

Democratic Party (State Party), German. *See* German State Party

Denazification courts, 573, 577–80; Papen's trial, 367, 577–9

Denmark, invasion of, 460

Dentz, General, 476

Deutsche Rundschau, Brüning's article in, 149, 161, 274

Deutsche Tageszeitung, 215

Devoy, John, 35

'Dictatorship of the proletariat,' 104

Dictatorship or Parliament? Papen's pamphlet, 103

Diello. *See* Cicero

Diels, Rudolf, 270, 271, 286, 294–5

Dill, Field-Marshal Sir John, in Ankara, 472

Dingeldey, —, 215

Diplomat in Peace and War, Knatchbull-Hugessen's memoirs, 450

Dircksen, Herbert von, 406

Disarmament Commission, 205, 206; Germany withdraws from, 297, 358

Dix, Dr, 548

Dobrudja, the, 25, 456

Dodecanese, 25, 88; Italian fortification of, 446–7; British occupy Samos, Cos, Leros, 503

Dodd, William E., 317

Dodd, —, American interrogator at Nuremberg, 546–7

Doenitz, Admiral Karl, 291, 550, 553, 564, 570

Doernberg, —, 530

Dollfuss, Engelbert, charges against Papen regarding assassination of, 101; negotiations with Herriot, 178; outlines Austria's difficulties to Papen, 178; bans Austrian Nazis, 299; attempt on life of, 299–300; murder of, 332, 339; installation of authoritarian régime by, 348; his independence policy, 364

Donovan, General, 271

Drang nach Osten, Churchill's warning against, 494

Dresden, 235, 303, 304, 443–4, 530

Dresden, German cruiser, 17

Dual Monarchy. *See* Austria-Hungary

Dubsky, Count, 357

Duesterberg, Colonel Theodor, 147, 148; leader of the Stahlhelm, 241; Nazi campaign against, 292

Dülmen, 59, 109, 536

Dumba, Count Constantin, 48, 49, 50, 51

Dunkirk, 461

Dupont Powder Company, the, 37

Düsseldorf, 7, 10, 11, 125, 226, 231

Earle, George H., Roosevelt's personal representative in Turkey, 499, 500, 503–4; and Papen's peace plan, 517, 522–3

Eastern Mediterranean, Turkey's military position in, 447; Papen's formula after the fall of France, 456; Turkey and Russian ambitions in, 527

East German Republic, 141

East Jordan, 77, 82

'Eastman Girl,' the. *See* Reiss, Mena

East Prussia, at mercy of Poles, 95; draft law for resettlement of, 167; Versailles and, 172, 221; military district, 240; Papen visits Hitler's headquarters in, 481

Ebert, Friedrich, 86, 96, 104, 107, 120, 122, 123, 165, 189

Eckenbrecher, —, 7

Eden, Anthony, 301, 359; arrives in Ankara, 472; meets Menemencioglu, 506; turns down suggestion to break off relations with Turkey, 516

Edward VIII, King of England, 386

Edwards. *See* Reiss, Mena

Egypt, 23; British Army builds railway line from Cairo, 70; Cicero seen in, 519

Eire. *See* Ireland

Eisenhower, General Dwight, 500, 523, 540, 543

Eisner, Kurt, 86, 95

El Alamein, Rommel at, 490; British counter-offensive, 493

Elbe, the, 27, 128, 165, 586

Electoral reform in Germany, 141, 193–4, 245

Elias. *See* Cicero

Eltz, Peter Paul von der, 219, 220, 240, 243, 260, 290, 291

Emperor, German. *See under* Wilhelm II

'Ems' Telegram, the, 429

Enabling Law (1933), 273–5, 324, 333–4, 336; passed by Reichstag, 274; helps towards Hitler's dictatorship, 274; Brüning on, 274–5

Engels, Friedrich, 324

England. *See* Great Britain

English Channel, the, 47, 201, 515

Entente Cordiale, 24

Entente Powers, 20, 35, 40, 87, 88

Enver Pasha, 23, 25, 69, 76, 81, 118

Eppinger, Dr, 502

Erbach, Prince Victor zu, 350, 381, 470, 565

Erden, General Ali Fuad, 72, 103, 488

Erfüllungspolitik, Brüning's, 136

Eskişehir, 471

Es Salt, 77, 78, 79, 80

Ettel, —, 480

Euphrates River, 69

Europe, Germany's rôle in defence of against Asia, 27; Germany as part of, 93; needs of, subordinated to Wilsonian principle, 94; Balkanization of,

95; ideological battle in, 129–30; re-organization of, 296–7; Holy Roman Empire decisive factor in, 343; Bismarck and, 343–4; political situation (1934–35), 357–65; situation as result of Italian invasion of Albania, 444; Papen urges Hitler to pay attention to reorganization of, 462
Europe, Council of, 128
European Union, 138
Evangelical Churches, 278, 281; suffer ill-treatment under Nazis, 282

Fahri Pasha, 77
Faisal I. See Feisal
Falkenhausen, General Alexander von, 76
Falkenhayn, General Erich von, 44, 60, 61, 62, 63, 64, 68, 71, 72, 74, 75, 77, 82, 523
Falmouth, 49, 53, 54, 57
Far East, Russia's defeat in, 28; Britain's lines of communication to, 447
Farmer's Association, the, 147, 232, 235; at Bad Harzburg conference, 143
Fatherland Front. See under Austria
Faupel, —, 96
Feisal I, King of Iraq, 77, 80
Feldherrnhalle, Munich, Hitler's march to, 104
Felmy, General, 477
Fevzi Pasha. See Çakmak, Marshal
Fey, Emil, 353; ousted from position as Austrian Chief of Police, 377; Schuschnigg breaks with Starhemberg and, 379
Fez, 24
Fierlinger, —, 351
Finland, Russia and, 467; Molotov demands withdrawal of German troops from, 469; Russia's attack on, 572
First World War, peace lost before end of, 86; Reichstag enquiry into responsibility for, 87
Fischboek, Dr, 414, 417, 418
Fischer, Keresztes, 508
Flanders, 65, 66, 81, 97
Flandin, Pierre Etienne, 359
Flossenbürg concentration camp, 539
Flynn, Father, 547
Foch, Marshal Ferdinand, 101
Foreign Press Association, 205
Fourteen Points, Wilson's, 94, 296, 405
France, Papen's desire for understanding with, 2, 9, 113; relations with Germany over Saar, 11; German plans for operations against, 12; expansionist policies in North Africa, 23; occupies Fez, 24; and Entente Cordiale, 24; tension with Germany over Morocco, 26; closer

link with St Petersburg, 26; policy directed towards regaining Alsace-Lorraine, 28; and partition of Turkish Empire, 88; treatment under Congress of Vienna, 89; occupation of Ruhr, 101, 119; encourages German separatism, 101; opposition to Hindenburg, 107; and Soviet Russia, 118, 119, 360; Papen seeks personal connections with, 124–5; her foreign policy after 1918, 127; contacts between Germany and, 127–8; and German reparations, 137, 139, 178–9; attitude to German crisis of 1931, 137–8; relations with Germany, 175–6, 204, 205, 345; differences of opinion with Britain, 177; objection to Austrian Customs Union with Germany, 178; closer to Britain after Lausanne, 186; bluntly rejects German approach on disarmament, 203; perturbed at events in Germany, 297; and Saar referendum, 301; attitude to union of Austria and Germany, 345, 400–1, 421, 424–5; multilateral pacts, 358; attitude to Anglo-German discussions, 359; press comments on July Agreement between Germany and Austria, 371; share in Austrian plebiscite idea, 425; Daladier's attitude to Munich Agreement, 442; military missions in Moscow, 444; negotiations for mutual aid pacts with Poland and Rumania, 444; gives guarantee to Poland, 445–6; treaty with Turkey and Great Britain, 456; German attack on, 460, 461; allowed by Hitler to keep fleet, 461; Papen's idea for winning over to co-operation with Germany, 462; Hitler's idea for military pact against Great Britain, 463; German Gauleiters' plans for, 463; Allied invasion through, 515, 518, 525, 533; Laval on relations with Germany, 526
Francis I, Kaiser, 343
Franco-British Entente, 186
Franco-British guarantee to Poland, 445
Franco-German Study Group, 128
François-Poncet, André, 140, 156, 201, 204, 244, 246
Frank, Hanns, 320, 544, 552
Frankfurt Congress, the, 168 and n
Frankfurter Zeitung, 310
Franqui, —, 177
Franz-Ferdinand, Archduke, 354, 393
Franz Joseph, Emperor, 357
Frederick the Great, King of Prussia, 272, 329
Frederick-William I, King of Prussia, Hitler's admiration for, 329
Free Corps, 96, 119, 122

Freiburg, 185
Freiheitsbund, 349
French Congo, slice conceded to Germany, 24*n*
French Military Government, in Germany, 575
French Revolution, 92, 291, 308
Frick, Dr Wilhelm, 164, 195, 208, 241, 276, 291, 427; Nuremberg trial, 553
Friede, —, 490
Friedrich, Prince, 329
Fritsch, General Werner von, 11, 240, 288–9, 318–9; Gestapo's accusations against, 365; disturbed at too rapid expansion of the Army, 388; invites Papen to manœuvres, 399; opposes, Hitler's plans, 405; the Fritsch affair, 409
Fritzsche, Hans, at Nuremberg, 554
Fuerth, labour camp hopital at, 578
Funk, Walter, 312
Funston, General Frederick, 19, 20
Furtwängler, Wilhelm, 498
Fyfe, Sir David Maxwell, 327, 556, 564, 567–8

Gaelic American, the, 35
Galen, Cardinal Clemens August von, 111, 126, 128, preaches against Nazi persecution of the Churches, 481
Galhau, Adolphe von, 9
Gallup poll, 246
Ganghofer, Ludwig, 553
Garmisch, 325, 404, 578
Gaunt, Admiral Sir Guy, 49, 50
Gayl, — von, 159, 165, 190, 195
Gaza, 70, 73, 74
Gegenwart, Die, 190
Geheime Front, Die, 440
Geldbronnen van het Nationaal-Socialisme, De, 229
Gemünden, near Coblenz, 446, 535, 537, 575
Geneva, 127, 139, 140, 186, 201, 202, 205; Jewish World Congress at, 285; declaration of December 1932, 297; disadvantages of Germany's absence from, 358; Schuschnigg's unsuccessful visit to, 368
Geneva Protocol, 178, 345–6
George VI, King of England, Coronation of, 386; and Papen's peace plan, 472; Horthy appeals to, 543
Georgia, Hitler's Gauleiter for, 503
Gerasium, 79
Gerede, Hüsrev, 482–3, 519
German Army, foreign misconceptions regarding, 5; virtues of, 10; adoption of training methods by Mexico, 16;

expeditionary force for Turkey, 69; Palestine campaign, 69, 70–9, 81, 82, 83; offensive of 1918, 81; territorial divisions on Maritza, 82–3; troops interned at Moda, 84, 85; demobilization decreed by Allies, 86; Papen leaves, 86; Free Corps formed, 96; rôle in 'twenties, 115; 'Black Reichswehr' formed, 119, 120, 121; tradition of neutrality in political affairs, 122–3, 220; inability to carry out duties against extremists in emergency, 220–2, 236; rumour of *Putsch* by, 243; traditions unsympathetic to Weimar system, 252; younger officers favourable to Nazis, 252; riddled with Nazi cells, 252–3; failure to maintain independent position under Blomberg, 258; Hindenburg's wish to strengthen independence, 288; Roehm presses for introduction of militia system in, 306, 319–20; Hitler's method of securing loyalty of, 307; Roehm's *Putsch* to control, 313–22; Blomberg opposes intervention during Roehm *Putsch*, 319; stronger after neutralization of Brownshirts, 319; new oath of loyalty to Hitler, 335–6; strengthening of, 359; over-rapid expansion of, 388; Fritsch on, 399; struggle for power and influence within, 404–5; crisis in, 406, 407, 410, 420; Hitler assumes rank of Commander-in-Chief, 407; dismissal of generals, 407; order for march into Austria cancelled, 429; march into Austria ordered, 430; Papen requested to serve again, 443; marches into Prague, 443, 445; mobilization of, 451; campaign in Poland, 456; enters Russia, 479; disaster before Moscow, 484; change in system of command, 497; retreats in Northern France, 533–4
German Asia Corps, 69, 71, 83
'German Club,' the, 354–5
German General Staff, 10, 106, 404–5; Papen accepted for duties on, 11; relations with Austria, 11; desire to maintain peace, 12, 13; sensitivity to shifts in balance of power, 21; instructions to military attaché in U.S., 30, 33; instructions to Papen to interrupt transport of troops in Canada, 34; name Irish nationalists for sabotage work, 35; authorize sabotage on American territory, 46; attempts to postpone offensive in West, 459; memorandum on methods of continuing war, 470
German High Command, 81, 83; unprepared for retreat in France, 533

Germania, 111, 112, 113, 134, 186, 311

German-Italian alliance, 448

German Nationalists, 211, 214; in Prussia, 191; in Election of November 1932, 212, 232, 233; oppose Schleicher, 234, 236; desire for dictatorial Cabinet under Papen, 238; offer conditional support to Hitler Cabinet, 239

German National Party, 169; boycotts Reichstag, 141; at Bad Harzburg conference, 143

German Navy, prevents Allied blockade of German harbours, 41; submarine warfare, 41–2, 60, 61–4, 523; accused at Nuremberg, 41–2; sinks *Lusitania*, 42; preponderant influence on foreign affairs, 61

German People's Party, 104–5, 166

German Red Cross, 39, 42, 45

German State (Democratic) Party, 104, 135, 212; supports Enabling Law, 274

German Workers' Front, 284

Germany, her rôle in last fifty years, 1, 3; thesis of exclusive war guilt of, 3, 22, 89, 585; relations with France, 2, 9, 11, 24; unification of, 4; traditions of, 6; declaration of war on Russia (1914), 20; ordinances of the occupying powers in, 22; influence in Europe loses ground, 23; relations with Russia, 23; no desire for preventive war against Russia, 23; alliance with Italy, 23; friendship for Turkey, 23, 25; and Agadir, 24; intervention in Morocco, 24; conceded slice of French Congo, 24; and British position in Near East, 25; seeks export markets, 25; co-operation with Britain during Balkan conflict, 26; difficulties with France over Moroccan affair, 26; conflict of interests with Britain over Baghdad railway, 26; seeks to prevent outbreak of war in 1914, 26; duty of defending Central Europe, 27; exclusion from historical rôle by Versailles Treaty, 27; errors in Wilhelmian era, 27–8; and violation of Belgium (1914), 28; regards war in 1914 as a defensive war, 28; misrepresentation of, by Allies, 29–30, 31–2; plan to defeat placing of Allied orders in U.S., 38–9; decides on submarine warfare, 41; prohibits areas to enemy and neutral shipping, 41–2; submarine warfare, 42, 43, 52, 60–1, 61–4; support for Indian and Irish independence movements, 35–6, 40; British propaganda campaign against, 53, 54; American companies' claims for damages against, 55; Black Tom Case decided in favour of, 57; agree-ment with Lehigh Valley Company, 58; Papen's statement of her interests to Falkenhayn, 60–1; her inept diplomacy, 61; not waging aggressive war, 61; no ambitions in conflict with U.S., 61; Tirpitz favours unrestricted submarine warfare by, 62, 64; Allied blockade of, 61–2; U.S. and submarine policy of, 61–4, 65; plan to enter alliance with Mexico, 65; news of defeat of, 84; Wilson's refusal to deal with Kaiser's régime in, 84; Red Flag planted in, 84; revolution in, 86; error of policy in not declaring war aims, 87; absence of political leadership in, 87; effects of Versailles Treaty on, 89; in defeat, 90; Republic in, 90, 91, 93; effect on people of disappearance of order, 93; decisive part in building up Western civilization, 93; democracy in, 94; Wilson's Fourteen Points greeted with relief in, 94; historic mission of, 94, 496; Allies' fear of, 94; peace treaties and, 95; threats to national existence after peace treaties, 95; civil war in, 95; characteristics of Weimar Constitution, 97–100; at its nadir, 100–1; inflation, 101, 102–3, 111; denied assistance against separatists, 102; destruction of currency in, 102–3; on brink of collapse, 102–4; radical parties in ascendant, 104; economic crisis of 1930, 109; unemployment, 109, 135, 139, 210; currents of political thought in 'twenties, 114–5; assists Soviet Russia to build up war industry, 118–9; desperate situation in 1925, 120–1; Concordat with Vatican, 127, 281, 350, 351, 357, 432; contacts with France, 128; André Siegfried's attitude to, 128; moral vacuum in, 129; burden of Young Plan, 131–2; reparations, 131, 136, 139, 141, 171–2, 173–4, 177, 182–4; worsening crisis in, 134, 136; Election of 1930, 135; plans for Customs Union with Austria, 136; grave economic situation in 1931, 136–7, 143; Communist threat to, 141; right wing parties' conference at Bad Harzburg, 143; Presidential Elections (1932), 146–8; uniformed organizations in, 148–9; negotiations leading to formation of 'Presidential Cabinet', 150–8; 'Presidential Cabinet' formed, 159–60; Papen as Chancellor, 159–214; new ban on uniformed formations, 163; *Osthilfe* scandal, 164–6; Lausanne Agreement, 185, 187, 188; Election of July 1932, 193–4; Roehm demands Chancellorship for Hitler, 195; Potempa incident, 199–200; attempts to negotiate with France, 201–2, 203, 204, 205; sharp British note to, 204; and Disarmament Conference, 201–6, 358; granted equality of rights, 206; Papen's Government defeated, 209; Papen's economic recovery programme, 209–10; national debt, 210; Election of November 1932, 211–2; Papen's negotiations with parties, 212–4; Papen resigns, 214, 223; Schleicher's policy, 225; Schleicher's Government, 226, 227, 232, 233, 234, 235, 236, 237; Schleicher resigns, 238; Hitler asks to form 'Presidential Cabinet', 239; Hindenburg decides to appoint Hitler Chancellor, 241; threat of Reichswehr *coup* under Schleicher, 242–3; Hitler Cabinet formed, 244; the eventful January of 1933, 251; Hitler's Enabling Law, 250, 252, 258, 262, 273–5; psychology of, under Weimar, 253–4, 255; bitter struggle of working class in, 254; disruption of bourgeois values in, 254; desperation in, 255; growth of Nazi domination in, 256–7; amorality of Nazis regarded by middle class as temporary manifestation, 257; party system in, 259; dissolution of parties, 259, 303–4; explanation of lack of resistance to Hitler, 262–3; Papen formulates coalition programme, 265; 'Black-Red-White' electoral bloc, 266–8; Reichstag Fire, 268–71; Election of March 1933, 271–2; Papen's efforts as Vice-Chancellor to counter Nazi influence, 276–7; labour legislation by Coalition Cabinet, 283–4; Nazi extremists' attack on Jews begins, 285–6; working of Hitler's Coalition Cabinet, 290–2; foreign policy of Hitler's Coalition Cabinet, 295–6; right to equal armaments recognized, 297; leaves League of Nations, 297–8, 358; deterioration in relations with Austria, 298–300; and the Saar, 300–2; flood of Nazi excesses, 304–5; Papen's Marburg speech, 307–12; the Roehm *Putsch*, 313–9; attempts to restore monarchy in, 329–30, 332; law combining offices of President and Chancellor, 333–4; death of Hindenburg, 334–5; Hitler assumes Presidency, 335; faced with breakdown in international relations, 339–40; relations with Austria, 342, 344–51, 354, 357, 409–28; Austrian Nazis in, 352, 397; no rearmament between 1932–34, 359; conscription reintroduced, 359; Naval Treaty with Britain, 360, 373; Saar plebiscite, 358,

360; Hitler's recognition of Austrian independence, 361–3; Papen's reports on relations with Austria, 365, 368; July agreement with Austria, 369–72, 376–7, 383, 387, 391, 395, 396, 397, 401, 403, 408, 409, 411, 415, 421; Lord Londonderry's visit, 399–400; Hitler dismisses Papen, 406; Ribbentrop appointed Foreign Minister, 407; Hitler cancels orders for troops to march into Austria, 429; Hitler orders march into Austria, 430; Munich Agreement, 441–2; marches into Prague, 443, 445; commercial agreement with Rumania, 444; Hitler revokes Naval Agreement with Britain and cancels non-aggression pact with Poland, 445; representations to Italy on Turkish fears, 448; signs Italian alliance, 448; non-aggression pact with Russia, 451–2; declaration of war by Great Britain on, 452–3; policy in Bulgaria, 455; invasion of Denmark and Norway, 460; attack on Belgium, Netherlands and France, 460; end of French campaign, 461; refusal to meet Italy's territorial demands, 461; allows France to keep fleet, 461; policy in France, 463; preparations for war against Russia, 469; resolution to invade Great Britain abandoned, 469; worsening relations with Russia, 473; Turkey her only source of chromium, 475; relations with Turkey, 478–9, 487–8, 507; declaration of war on United States, 484; Japanese suggestion for compromise with Russia, 491; fate sealed during 1943 campaign, 493; Turkish fear of complete defeat of, 495; reaction to Papen's Istanbul speech, 496; Allied intentions towards, 514–5, 517; Turkey suspends chromium deliveries to, 524; cities destroyed from the air, 534; monarchy swept away, 580; her responsibility for second world war, 583–4; her part in the future, 587

Gestapo, Papen on liquidation list of, 2; Ketteler's death at hands of, 276; formed, 294; Diels as chief, 294–5; granted judiciary powers at outbreak of war, 295; confiscates copies of Papen's speech, 311; arrests Edgar Jung, 312–3; suppresses Roehm *Putsch*, 315–6, 325; occupies and seals Vice-Chancellery, 315–6, 321, 322; refuses to investigate Roehm purge, 323–4; powerful position in Prussia, 324; visits Papen, 337; interference with Papen's work, 365–7; in Austria, 433, 434, 435, 436, 437; Hitler frees Papen

from supervision by, 445; its information services, 481; Canaris and, 481;
activities in Ankara, 487, 510; Moyzisch
representative of, 510; plan to kidnap
Papen, 520–1; Papen expects to be
arrested by, 529; watches Papen, 535;
and concentration camps, 539; Horthy's
treatment by, 541

Gienanth, General, 388

Gieseking, Walther, 521

Gisevius, Hans Berndt, Schacht's principal witness at Nuremberg, 554

Glaise von Horstenau, Edmund, 377,
414; becomes Minister of the Interior,
379; appointed by Schuschnigg as
Minister without Portfolio, ᵇ395;
demanded formally in the Keppler
Protocol, 416, 418; called as witness at
Nuremberg, 566

Godesberg talks, 441–2

Goebbels, Dr Paul, and *Germania*, 112–3;
anti-Semitic campaign, 113; influences
Hitler's attitude to Churches, 261;
demands Dr Wingen's dismissal, 276;
campaign against Catholics, 281;
becomes Propaganda Chief, 289; his
appearance, 289; his methods of argument, 291–2; bans Papen broadcast,
310; fails to win response at Hamburg,
311; complete control of press, 327;
death of, 554

Goerdeler, Dr, 159

Goering, Hermann, as *Reichstagspräsident*,
207, 208–9; Dresden speech (1932), 235;
Schleicher's approach to, 242; his police
squads, 255, 268, 316; at Reichstag
Fire, 269; swears no responsibility for
Reichstag Fire, 271; limits opposition's
electoral campaign in Prussia, 271;
imposes his ideas by weight of personality, 291; control of Prussian
police, 293; becomes Prussian Prime
Minister, 294; declines to delegate
authority to Papen, 315; heated discussion with Papen during Roehm
Putsch, 315–6; prevents Papen's liquidation, 317; apologies for Papen's continued arrest, 317–8; his story of
Roehm purge, 320; visits Rome, 387;
correspondence with Austrian Foreign
Minister, 401–2, 408, 438; meeting
with Austrian Nazi leader, 423; intervention in Austrian plebiscite on independence, 427; orders Seyss-Inquart
to resign and form new Cabinet, 428;
telephone conversations with Vienna,
429; accusations against Ketteler,
435–6; increased domination in international affairs, 438; in favour of ending war, 458; during his imprisonment,

543; suicide, 551, 576; outstanding personality at Nuremberg, 554–5; after
his sentence, 570

Goerlitzer, Arthur, 312

Gold Medal of the Nazi Party, Papen
awarded, 431, 434

Goleyevsky, Colonel, 20

Goltz, Count von der, 147

Goltz, Field-Marshal Colmar von der, 68

Goltz, Horst von der. *See* Bridgeman-
Taylor

Good Hope, H.M.S., 19

Gordon, Mrs., 56

Gotha, 539

Gottfried III, Count of Arnsberg, 4

Grandeurs et Misères d'une Victoire, Les, 101

Grandi, Count Dino, 175

Grand Mufti of Jerusalem, joins Rashid
Ali, 477; flight to Persia, 477

Great Britain, Papen's visits to, 8–9;
Papen's admiration for, 13; and U.S.-
Mexican crisis (1914), 18; and Germany (1914), 19; prevents passage of
Turkish troops through Egypt, 23;
alliance with France and Turkey (1939),
24; attitude to Agadir incident, 24; and
Entente Cordiale, 24; Italy more
closely associated with, 24; and
Baghdad railway, 25, 26; co-operation
with Germany during Balkan conflict,
26; naval blockade of Germany, 34, 35,
37, 40–1; declares U-boat warfare
illegal, 41; naval supremacy not
threatened by U-boats, 43; propaganda
campaign against Germany, 53, 54, 82;
promises to Arabs, 80; agreement with
Russia on Dardanelles, 88; agreement
with Japan, 88; and partition of
Turkish Empire, 88; differences with
Arab world, 88; deterioration in Germany's relations with, 94; intervention
in Communist Russia, 101–2; declares
Herrenklub a criminal organization,
114; successful coalition government
in, 141; differences of opinion with
Herriot Cabinet, 177; Franco-German
Pact unacceptable to, 177, 180; 'divide
and rule' policy, 181; brought closer to
France by Lausanne, 186; sharp note to
Germany, 204; and the Saar, 301; re-
armament, 358, 390, 442; discussions
with Germany, 359–60; White Paper
on breaking of Versailles Treaty, 360;
Naval Treaty with Germany, 360, 373;
questionnaire to Hitler on reoccupation
of Rhineland, 368; Papen suggested as
Ambassador to, 372; Ribbentrop as
Ambassador to, 375–6; Coronation of
King George VI, 386; attitude to
German proposals for Austria, 421;

Munich Agreement, 441–2; defence estimates increased, 444; negotiations for mutual aid pacts with Poland and Rumania, 444; military missions in Moscow, 444, 446; consideration of guarantees to Poland, Rumania, Greece and Turkey, 444; guarantee to Poland, 445–6; declaration of war on Germany, 452–3; negotiations for Rumanian military aid to Poland, 455; treaty with Turkey and France, 456; its parliamentary institutions, 459; losses at Dunkirk, 461; resists peace feelers, 461; military mission to Turkey, 461; reported readiness to recognize Balkans as Russian sphere of interest, 463; Hitler's idea for French military pact against, 463; Hitler's resolution to abandon invasion of, 469; intervention by expected in Greece, 470; relations with Turkey reach nadir, 480, 521; pressure on Turkey to enter war, 487; demands Turkey's rupture with Axis, 507; considers Turkey's demands excessive, 519; Vermehren deserts to, 520; fails to overcome Turkish opposition to joining war, 521. *See also* British Empire

Greater Berlin, 190

Greece, in anti-Turkish alliance, 25; receives Salonika and Crete, 25; Bulgarian attack on, 25; Britain considers guarantees to, 444; Italian attack on, 464; Italian offensive halted in, 470; and Balkan front with Yugoslavia and Turkey, 472; British intervention, 470, 471, 473; Bulgaria's demands on, 473–4; German campaign concluded in, 475, 476; German airborne corps in, 476; programme to relieve distress in, 481

Grey, Sir Edward, 24

Gritzbach, —, 293

Groeber, Archbishop, 280

Groener, General Wilhelm, 84, 87, 123, 124, 143, 144, 148; his resignation, 149, 150

Gros, Prof., 556

Guertner, Franz, 83, 159, 219, 220, 240, 260, 286, 290, 291, 324

Gueules Cassées, 127

Gustav, King of Sweden, 286, 442, 443; Papen's peace approach to, 472; Papen's appeal from captivity, 543

Habbaniya, 475

Habicht, Theo, Gauleiter for Austria, 299, 338, 339, 340–1, 371; death on the Russian Front, 460

Hacha, Emil, 443

Haeften, Hans von, 350, 530

Hagen, Walter, 440, 441

Hague Convention, 542, 572

Haifa, 88

Hainburg, 437

Haldane, Lord, 26

Halder, General Franz, 471

Haltern, 536

Hamburg, 221, 311

Hamburg-Amerika Line, 36, 64

Hames, Mr, 8

Hammerstein, General, 10, 118, 149, 150, 243, 288, 319

Haniel family, 7, 15, 125

Hanover, 8

Hapsburgs, the, 25–6, 95, 343, 344, 354, 378, 393

Harbou, —, 118

Harcourt-Barrington, Major J., 560

'Harzburger Front,' the, 144, 147, 236, 237, 241

Hashemite family, the, 80

Hasse, —, 118

Hassell, Ulrich von, 326, 331, 406

Hatzfeldt, Prince Hermann, 128

Haus Merfeld, 96

Haydarpasha, 71

Hebron, 72, 74

Hedjaz, the, 80

Heimannsberg, Colonel, 191

Heimwehr. See under Austria

Heinz, — von, 350

Heisig, —, 269

Held, Dr Heinrich, 214

Heldt, Mrs, 56

Helldorf, Count Wolf Heinrich von, discussion with Papen, 195; change in attitude to Hitler of, 498; Papen prepared to arrange for meeting of Earle with, 522; arrest of, 527

Henderson, Sir Nevile, 444

Herren, definition of, 113

Herrenklub, the, 113, 225, 247

Herriot, Edouard, at Lausanne Conference, 138, 172, 174–86, 201; attitude to Franco-German relations, 176–7; reaction to German withdrawal from Disarmament Commission, 203–5; attitude to Versailles Treaty, 256

Herwarth, — von, 15

Hess, Rudolf, 104*n*, 227, 339; at Nuremberg, 553–4

Heydrich, Reinhard, campaign against alleged immorality in Catholic monasteries, 281; takes over Gestapo, 295; increase of influence of, 304; determined to liquidate Papen, 316; Bose's files on excesses of, 322, 325; questioned by Papen on disappearance of Ketteler,

433–5; ordered by Hitler to drop investigation into Papen's files in Switzerland, 441; at reception for Molotov in Berlin, 467; relations with Canaris, 481

Heydebrandt, Ernst von, 6

Heydekamp, Colonel C. von, 293

Heye, 7

Heynen, Carlos, collaborates with Papen in Mexican deals, 40

Himmler, Heinrich, 394, 407, 441, 515, 533; at Hitler-Papen meeting in Cologne, 227; takes over Gestapo, 295; influence increases, 304; promises release of Jung, 313; and Roehm purge, 315, 316, 317, 318, 322; Bose's files on activities of, 322, 325; and Fritsch, 405; denies Gestapo responsibility for disappearance of Ketteler, 434, 436; plan to capture, 498; Abwehr placed under, 520; his suicide, 554

Hindenburg, Oscar von, 123, 124, 165–6, 235, 242, 332–3, 334

Hindenburg, Paul von, President of Germany, adopted as right wing candidate for Presidency, 107–8; elected President, 108; Herrenklub and, 114; his qualities, 116–7; and Schleicher, 123, 124; personal message to Hoover asking for help, 137; carries out duties in objective manner, 142; negotiations to extend his term as President, 146–7; in Presidential Election (1932), 146–8; differences with Brüning, 148, 150, 151, 157; calls on Papen to accept Chancellorship, 158; signs order lifting ban on S.A., 163; and Osthilfe scandal, 164–6, 167; agrees to forbid uniformed demonstrations, 188; refuses to appoint Hitler Chancellor, 197; Hitler's interview with on August 13, 1932, 197–8; determined not to abandon concept of 'Presidential Cabinet', 214; calls on Schleicher, 215; discussions with Papen and Schleicher, 215–8; prepared to accept unconstitutional solution, 218, 244; decides to offer Chancellorship to Schleicher, 223; letter of gratitude to Papen, 223; relations with Papen, 232; declines Schleicher's request for dissolution of Reichstag, 236, 237, 238; interviews with Papen after Schleicher's resignation, 238–9, 240–1, 242; decides to appoint Hitler Chancellor, 240–1; decides to appoint Blomberg as War Minister, 242; Schleicher's quarrel with, 247–8, 249; gradually ceases to impose personal authority, 258; Hitler's influence on, 262; agrees to Enabling Law, 262; surrenders to pressure on

Nazi flag issue, 287; and Blomberg, 288; Papen sees him for last time, 306; rejects Roehm's plan to incorporate S.A. in Army, 313; Papen's efforts to get in touch with during Roehm purge, 317, 322, 323; congratulates Hitler on suppression of Roehm Putsch, 326–7; favours return to monarchy, 330; his testament, 330–1, 332–3, 336; death of, 328, 333, 334; his faculties during last years, 328; funeral of, 332, 335; on his deathbed, 334; friendship for Papen, 334; his record, 334–5; his final words, 335

Hintze, Admiral von, 16

Hirtsiefer, —, 189, 190

Hitler, Adolf, corollary of Versailles Treaty, 3, 80; support from German electorate, 3; destroys Army's responsibility, 12; undoubted responsibility for second world war, 22; Putsch of 1923, 104, 120; industrialists and, 126; increases arbitrary demands, 144; negotiations with Brüning, 146, 147; refuses to support Hindenburg's candidature, 147; in 1932 Presidential Election, 148; promises tacit support to 'Presidential Cabinet', 153; Papen meets for first time, 162; interview with Papen after 1932 Election, 195–7; interview with Hindenburg, August 13, 1932, 197–8; and Potempa incident, 199; declines discussions with Papen, 213; refuses to form parliamentary Cabinet, 215–6; restores Party discipline, 227; refuses to join Schleicher Cabinet, 227, 235; Papen's meeting with at Cologne, 226, 227–8, 231, 232, 247, 248; final break with Strasser, 234; meeting with Hugenberg, 234; Papen meets at Ribbentrop's house, 235; Papen sees after Schleicher's resignation, 239; his demands to Papen, 239; Hindenburg decides to appoint as Chancellor, 240–1; his conditions of acceptance of Chancellorship, 241, 243; suggests new elections, 243; forms Cabinet, 244; brought to power by democratic processes, 244, 250; younger generation supports, 253–4; his social programme, 254; his appeal to patriotic feeling, 254–5; his 25-point programme, 256; insatiable lust for power, 257, 261; his personality, 259–62; rage at Brownshirt indiscipline, 260; backs up Papen's efforts to support Churches' rights, 261; influence on Hindenburg, 262; his coalition programme, 265; wishes to ban Communist Party, 270; transfers opening ceremony of Reichstag to

Potsdam, 272; insists on special powers, 273; Reichstag speech, March 21, 1933, 273; and Christianity, 273–4; compared with Mussolini, 279; accepts Vatican Concordat proposal, 280; his anti-Semitism, 285–6; replaces Weimar flag by Nazi flag, 287; his attitude to Cabinet majority decisions, 290; breaks with radical wing of Nazi Party, 307; Papen offers resignation to, 310–11, 318, 322, 323; and Roehm, 313, 314, 320; Papen sees after Roehm *Putsch*, 318; unpredictable mood after *Putsch*, 321; Papen's letters to following *Putsch*, 321–3; offers post of Ambassador to Papen, 323; and the monarchy, 329; admiration for Mussolini, 331; meetings with Mussolini, 332, 398–9; and Hindenburg's testament, 332–3; sees Hindenburg on his death bed, 334; takes over Presidency, 335; suppresses second part of Hindenburg's testament, 336; orders Papen to go as Minister to Vienna, 337–8; agrees to possible union between Austria and Germany, 342; documentary evidence of warlike intentions, 347; 1944 plot against, 350, 525, 527–8, 530, 531, 532; proclamation on reintroduction of conscription, 359; suggests naval pact with Britain, 360; Papen's appeal for recognition of Austrian independence, 361–2; attitude to July agreement with Austria, 370–2; suggests Papen as Ambassador to London, 372; receives leader of Austrian Nazis, 376–7; Austrian Foreign Minister visits, 379–80; Papen's and Schacht's plan for controlling ambitions of, 388; his ignorance of economics, 388; effect of Abyssinian adventure on foreign policy of, 389; meeting with Papen on flag incident, 392–3; honorary corporal in Fascist militia, 398–9; approves suggestions for co-operation with Austria, 401–2; concern over loyalty of Army, 405; dismisses Papen, 406; assumes rank of Commander-in-Chief, 407; meeting with Schuschnigg, 412–21; instability of, 420; meeting with Austrian Nazi leader, 423; cancels order for march into Austria, 429; orders march into Austria, 420; orders Papen to go to Vienna, 431; in Austria, 431–2; meeting with Cardinal Innitzer, 432–3; Papen's appeal to, on disappearance of Ketteler, 434; alleged plan by Ketteler to assassinate, 435; Munich Agreement with Chamberlain, 441–2; interviews President Hacha, 443; marches into Prague, 443, 445; attitude to Italian invasion of Albania, 445; agrees to Papen's request for freedom from Gestapo supervision, 445; tells Papen of non-aggression pact with Russia, 451; his Polish policy, 452; refusal to meet Italy's territorial demands, 461; allows France to keep fleet, 461; discussions with Papen on possible peace moves, 462; attitude to Italian attack on Greece, 464; discussions with Papen on Russia and Turkey, 466, 468; willing to share British Empire with Russia, 466; discussions with Molotov, 467; rejects Russian demands in Balkans, 469; orders preparations for war against Russia, 469; resolution to abandon invasion of Great Britain, 469; realistic about Turkey's position, 471; King Boris presents demands to, 473–4; Papen visits at Yugoslav headquarters, 473; Papen gives account of sinking morale to, 481–2; agrees to arm Turkey, 488; changes system of command in the Army, 497; his lack of military ability, 497; his technical flair, 497–8; hatred of Italian Royal Family, 502; his conduct of the war, 508; decline in Papen's relationships with, 517; not shown all 'Cicero' reports, 517; places Abwehr under Himmler, 520; overrules Ribbentrop on recall of Papen, 525; rejects Laval's complaints, 526; on Turkey's defection, 531; awards Papen Military Merit Order, 532

Hoadley, George, 38, 45
Hoegen, —, 54
Hoegner, —, 575
Hoesch, —, 372
Hoffinger, —, 397, 411
Hoffmann, Hitler's photographer, 458
Hohenberg, Prince, 393–4
Hohenstaufen, the, 343
Hohenzollern dynasty, 6, 329
Holland. *See* Netherlands
Holtzendorff, Admiral von, 62
Holy Places, the, 77, 81
Holy Roman Empire, 4, 27, 297, 343, 430
Hoover, Herbert, 137, 141, 177
Hoover moratorium, the, 138, 139, 141
Hopffgarten, Count Eric, 7
Horn, Werner, 34, 53
Hornbostel, Dr von, 397
Horthy, Admiral Miklos, 361, 378, 492, 508–9, 540–1, 542, 543, 546, 565
Hossbach Protocol, the, 347, 388, 405, 442, 569
Hötzendorf, General Conrad von, 11, 12
Huber, Frau, 394

Hudal, Dr Aloys, 382–3

Huecking, Dr, 59

Huerta, President, 18

Hugenberg, Alfred, lack of qualities as Conservative leader, 104, 135, 169; calls on Hindenburg to respect Constitution, 142; declines to co-operate in extension of Hindenburg's term of office, 146; attitude to reparations, 185–6; received by Hindenburg, 215; Nationalists suggest his inclusion in Cabinet, 232; discussion with Hindenburg, 233; discussion with Hitler, 234; defection of, 235; attitude to Hitler as Chancellor, 236–41; relations with Hitler, 291–2; resignation from Cabinet, 303

Humann, Hans, 153, 154, 324

Hummelsheim, —, 316

Hungary, 365, 433; alliance with Axis Powers, 468–9; conversations between Nazi Party emissaries and nationalists, 508–9; Nazi proposal to incorporate, 509; Russia's occupation of, 515; German relations with, 521; Horthy's appeal on behalf of, 543. See also Austria-Hungary

Hussein, King, 80

Hymans, Paul, 177

Ibn Saud, King, 80

Iburg, 296

Igel, — von, 53

In der Maur, —, 384, 410

India, independence movement supported by Germany, 35; German arms shipments to, 40

Indo-China, 586

Industrial Revolution, the, 91

Industrieklub, 252

Innitzer, Cardinal Theodor, 357, 432, 433, 561

Innsbruck, 425

Inönü, Ismet, 77, 444, 472–3; Papen's discussions with, 446–7; meeting with Papen on anniversary of founding of Turkish Republic, 465; Churchill's letter to, 471–2; willingness to act as mediator, 477–8, 531; impresses on Churchill need for bringing war to an end, 494–5; attends Cairo Conference (1943), 513–4; parts company with Çakmak, 520; Papen's final audience with, 527; informs Churchill of Papen's peace plans, 528; Hitler informed of his mediation offer, 531

Institut Catholique, 127

International Workers' Congress in Hamburg, 386

Iraq, 72; Arabian freedom movement in, 475, 476–7

Ireland, independence movement supported by Germany, 35

Ismet Pasha. See Inönü, Ismet

Ismit, Gulf of, 466

Istanbul, possible German reprisal raid on, 512, 516, 531; Cicero seen in, 519

Istanbul, Treaty of, 466

Istria, 88

Italy, conflict with Turkey over Libya, 12, 23–4; Abyssinian adventure, 23, 364, 368, 383, 387, 388; closer association with Great Britain, 24; state of confusion in, 83; treaties with Entente Powers, 88; Papen visits, 279, 280–1; divisions on Brenner Pass, 358, 387; influence in Austria, 360–1, 364, 378; relations with Germany, 368; British demand for sanctions against, 387; failure to apply sanctions to, 389; support of Hitler's proposals for Austria, 421; invasion of Albania, 443–4, 445, 446, 447, 448; alliance with Germany, 448; entry into war, 460; Hitler's refusal to meet territorial demands of, 461; attack on Greece, 464; German confidence in sinks to zero, 471; defeat of fleet, 476; capitulation of, 503

Izmir, 88, 466, 503, 514, 516

Jackson, Justice R. H., 556, 564

Jaffa, 71, 72

Jagow, Hans von, 64

Jannings, Emil, 329

Japan, 22, 23; British agreement with, 88; attack on Pearl Harbour, 484; relations with Germany during second world war, 491

Jenke, —, 509, 510, 512, 519, 528

Jerash, 79

Jericho, 78

Jerusalem, 73, 74, 75, 76, 77

Jerusalem, S.S., 85

Jewish Agency, 522

Jewish World Congress, the, 285

Jews, 88, 560; Nazi antipathy to, 256; S.A. excesses against, 260, 293; Papen helps, 276–7, 285; tragedy of, under Hitler's régime, 285; Nazi attacks on, 285–6, 290; in Austria, 356; refugees, 500, 521–2; persecution of, 521, 552

Jodl, General Alfred, 551, 570, 575

Johst, Hans, 295

Jordan, the, 77, 78, 520

Judiciary, Nazi campaign against, 305

July Agreement, between Germany and Austria, 369–72, 376–7, 383, 387, 391,

395, 396, 397, 401, 403, 408, 409, 411, 415, 421

Jung, Edgar, 312–3, 324; death of, 322, 324, 325, 340

Kaas, Dr, 134, 155, 156–7, 158–9, 209, 212, 234, 252; supports Enabling Law, 274; assists Cardinal Pacelli, 279, 280
Kallay, Miklos, 509, 521
Kaltenbrunner, Ernst, in charge of Vienna police, 437; and 'Operation Cicero', 511, 518; at Nuremberg, 552
Kaltschmidt, Albert, 34
Karachi, 40
Karapunar, 71, 83, 84, 94
Kareski, —, 285
Karinhall, Goering's shooting lodge, 400; Guido Schmidt visits, 401
Karl, Kaiser, 354
Katyn forest affair, 560
Keitel, Field-Marshal Wilhelm, 320, 413, 415, 417, 427; and the invasion of Austria, 429; Nuremberg trial of, 553, 555
Keppler, Wilhelm, 227, 228, 396, 412, 420, 423, 562
'Keppler Protocol,' the, 415–7
Kerkerinck zur Borg, — von, 97
Kerrl, Hans, 294
Ketteler, Wilhelm von, 317, 340; assistant to von Bose, 276, 277; assistant to Papen, 338; disappearance and murder of, 326, 367, 481, 433–7; Nazi campaign against, 365; and Papen's papers, 407, 424, 440
Keyserling, Count, 129
Kinsky, Prince Karl, 357
Kirdorf, Emil, 252
Kiruna, Horst Heinz, 19 and n
Kitzbühl, 424
Klagenfurt, 380
Klausner, —, 423
Kleist, Field-Marshal Paul Ludwig, 319
Klenze, —, 8
Klepper, —, 189, 190, 191
Kloeckner, Dr Florian, 111, 125
Kluge, Field-Marshal Gunther, 319, 388
Knatchbull-Hugessen, Sir Hughe, Papen's opinion of, 450–1, 454; visits King of Bulgaria, 456; informed of Papen's peace plan, 456; opinion of inadequacy of Turkish Army, 460; visits Inönü, 465; kept informed about Turco-German negotiations, 478; Adana Conference, 495; note to Turkish Government, 507; and 'Operation Cicero', 509–16; suggests breaking off relations between Britain and Turkey, 514

Knights of Malta, 126
Koenig, Paul, 36, 42
Koestler, Arthur, 548–9
Kolberg, 85
Korea, 573, 586
Kreditanstalt, 136
Kressenstein, General Kress von, 70, 71, 72, 73, 74
Kreuzeck, the, 404
Kreuznach, 457
Kroll, Dr, witness for Papen at Nuremberg, 565, 568
Krüger, Prof. Paul, 355
Kubuschok, Dr, 548
Kulturbund, the, 356
Kurihara, —, 491
Kut el Amara, 68

Laboulay, M. de, 176
Labour Day, 283
Labour Party, British, 104, 141, 168, 538
Lammers, Hans Heinrich, 323, 371–2, 406, 431, 481–2
Landsberg gaol, 104n
Landtag, Prussian, 6, 100, 116, 294
Langwasser, labour camp at, 578
Lansing, Robert, 43
Lardy, —, 454
Lateran Treaties, Mussolini's, 279
Laurent, Charles, 128
Lausanne, German Colony in, 177
Lausanne Conference, 172–4, 175–7, 181–5, 201, 204, 205, 212, 255
Lauzanne, —, 179
Laval, Pierre, 138, 139, 359, 360; prevents sanctions against Italy, 387; Papen's conversation with, 526
Lawrence, Lord Justice, President of the Court at Nuremberg Tribunal, 559, 563, 569–70
Lawrence, of Arabia, 68, 77, 80, 83
League of Nations, 94, 95, 186–7, 206; acknowledges Germany's right to equal armaments, 297; Germany leaves 297–8, 358; and independence of Austria, 344–5; Soviet Russia becomes member, 358; and sanctions against Italy, 387, 389
Léger, Alexis, 203
Lehigh Valley Railroad Company, 55, 56, 57, 58, 59
Leipart, —, 238
Leipzig, 252–3
Lenin, N. I., 94, 103, 324
Leo XIII, Pope, 93, 97, 254
Leopold, Captain, 381, 394, 395, 396, 408; leader of Austrian Nazis, 370; character and record of, 384; Hitler agrees to expel from Austria,

403-4; Nazi aim of a government under, 404; Schmidt approves the removal of, 410; Hitler decides he must live in Germany, 423

Leros, British occupation, 503

Lersner, — von, 15, 16, 67, 116, 332; peace negotiation mission in Rome, 489; contacts Mr Earle regarding possible peace negotiations, 499, 517, 522; Papen sends questionnaire from Nuremberg, 565

Leutze, Emanuel, 7

Leverkuehn, Dr, 499, 500

Levetzow, Admiral von, 293

Lex, Ritter von, 274

Ley, Robert, speech after July plot, 527; commits suicide at Nuremberg, 550

Libya, 478; Italo-Turkish conflict over, 23-4; Enver Bey organizes resistance in, 23

Liebet Eure Feinde, 229

Liebknecht, Karl, 86

Liegnitz, 27

Lippe-Detmold, elections in, 230, 232, 233-4

Little Entente, the, 351, 391

Lloyd-George, David, 24, 88

Locarno, Treaty of, 104, 105, 179, 187, 205, 255, 581

Loebe, Paul, 346

London, 13, 14, 58, 202, 205, 368, 400; first impact of, on Papen, 8-9; Brüning and Curtius visit, 137; Papen offered post of Ambassador to, 372; Coronation of George VI, 386; Nuremberg Statute drawn up in, 556

London, Treaty of (1912), 25

Londonderry, Lord, visits Germany, 399-400

London Economic Conference, 292

Loritz, —, 577, 578

Lorraine, 9, 28

Lossow, General von, 120

Los von Rom movement, 285n

Lubbe, Marinus van der, 269-70

Ludendorff, General Erich Friedrich Wilhelm, 65, 67, 68, 81, 104, 107, 116, 117, 123

Ludin, —, 253

Ludwig, Dr, 416

Lusitania, the, 42, 43, 60

Luther, Dr Hans, 209

Luxembourg, 9, 343; aerodrome, 543

Luxemburg, Rosa, 86

Lyautey, Pierre, 128

Lynar, Count, 49

MacArthur, General Douglas, 18-19

McCloy, John, 58

McCoy, Captain, 15

MacDonald, Ramsay, 171, 202, 205, 256; and German economic crisis, 137; and Lausanne Conference, 138, 174, 175, 176, 177, 178-80, 181, 182-3, 185, 186-7; at Stresa, 360

Macedonia, 25; Bulgarian interest in, 456, 473

Mackensen, Hans Georg von, 448

Madrid, 532, 534

Maglione, Cardinal, 489

Magyars, 95

Maier, —, 274

Malkasten, 7

Mannerheim, Baron Carl Gustav von, 102

Marburg, Papen's speech at, 298, 307-10, 311-2, 324-5, 326, 340, 442; speech referred to at Nuremberg, 560, 567

Maritza River, 82, 474

Market Harborough, 8

Marne, battle of, 36, 45

Marsal, François, 127

Marshall, General George, 538

Marshall Plan, the, 95, 586

Mars la Tours, 126

Marwitz, Admiral von der, 526

Marx, Karl, 324

Marx, Wilhelm, 107, 108

Marxism, 91, 92, 93, 253, 283, 284

Masaryk, Tomas, 345

Massigli, René, 127, 461, 463-4

Matapan, battle of, 476

Matin, 179, 194

Matthes, —, 7

Maveric, S.S., 40

Mayrisch, Emile, 128

Mecca, 77

Mecklenburg, 319, 399

Medina, 77, 80

Mediterranean, 468, 470, 476; British interests in, 24; Mussolini's threat to Britain in, 390; Hungarian aspirations in, 543

Megerle, Dr, 530

Meissner, Dr Otto, Hindenburg's chef de cabinet, 165, 235, 242, 243, 467; to blame for Hindenburg's isolation during Roehm Putsch, 317; and Hindenburg's telegram to Hitler, 320; on Hindenburg's faculties, 328

Melcher, —, 192

Mendelssohn, Franz von, 128

Menemencioglu, Numan, 460, 478, 524; Papen's appreciation of, 449; meets Ribbentrop, 450; relief at German attack on Russia, 479; takes over Foreign Ministry, 492; determination to keep Turkey out of war, 493, 507; opposes entry into war at eleventh hour, 506; Papen's interventions with, 511–2; assurance that Turkey will join war, 512–3; accompanies Inönü to Cairo; cool response to Western Allies' overtures to Turkey, 519; disquiet at bad relations with Britain and America, 521; démarche on Levantines living in France, 522; resigns, 526, 527

Menghin, Prof., 394, 395, 412

Merfeld, Westphalia, 125

Mersin, 516

Mesopotamia, Germany's interests in recognized, 26; Papen sent on active service to, 68; campaign in, 68–70, 71; Baghdad enterprise postponed, 71–2; thinly held Turkish front in, 77; awarded to Britain, 88

Messersmith, George, 351, 561, 565

Mettlach, 9, 92, 93

Metz, 525, 533, 545

Mexico, Papen's visit to, 16–20; civil war in, 16–7; U.S. intervention, 17–9, 391–2; war material sold to, by German agents in U.S., 39–40; German plan to enter into alliance with, 65

Mezöhegyes, 508, 540

Middle East, the, 68, 76, 585

Mierendorff, Karl, 193

Miklas, Wilhelm, President of Austria, 370, 421, 428; refuses to entrust Seyss-Inquart with formation of Cabinet, 429

Militia system, Roehm demands, 306–7

Minorities, Hitler's policy declaration on, 296; Iburg Festival of, 296

Mixed Claim Commission, 57, 59

Moda, 84, 85

Molotov, V. M., 452, 463, 465, 466, 515; visits Berlin, 467–8; replies to Ribbentrop's alliance proposals, 469

Moltke, Field-Marshal Helmuth von, 11

Moltke, General Helmuth von, 11, 13, 28, 37, 117

Monarchy, attempts to restore, 329–30, 332; Hitler favours restoration, 329; Hindenburg favours restoration, 330

Mondorf, 541, 543

Monroe Doctrine, the, 34

Montenegro, in anti-Turkish alliance, 25; attacks Turkey, 25

Montini, Monsignor, 489

Montreux, Treaty of, 455, 460, 465, 466

Morgan, J. Pierpont, 32

Morgenthau Plan, the, 579, 584

Morocco, Franco-German friction over, 24

Moscow, 95, 118, 103, 118–9, 207, 270, 293, 359, 451, 455, 460, 463, 484; Allied Foreign Ministers' Conference at, 506, 512–3

Moselle, 533, 534, 535

Mosse and Ullstein, 185

Mosul, 477

Moyzisch, L. C., and 'Operation Cicero', 509, 510–11, 512, 517, 518–9

Mudania, 70, 83

Muehlmann, Dr, 394, 413, 419

Muff, General, 427

Mulay Hafid, Sultan, 24

Müller, Hermann, 132, 133

Müller, Admiral Karl von, 62

Munich, 96, 126, 213, 229, 297, 398; revolution in, 85; Habicht's head-quarters, 299; Agreement (1938), 441–2, 443

Munk, Professor, 317

Münster, 97, 199, 246

Münster, Treaty of, 458

Mussala Peak, 502

Mussolini, Benito, 198; Mare Nostrum cry, 24, 444; Papen meets for first time, 279; contrasted with Hitler, 279; urges speed in signing Vatican Concordat, 280–1; expresses surprise at lack of resistance to Roehm purge, 326; disturbed at behaviour of Nazis in Austria, 331; agrees to State visit to Hitler, 331; agrees to persuade Hitler to restore monarchy, 332; meetings with Hitler, 332, 398–9; influence on Austrian Government, 360–1, 365, 378; Goering visits, 387; abandons objections to Anschluss, 407; warns Schuschnigg about plebiscite, 426; attitude to Munich Agreement, 442; remarks on the Turks, 448; freed from mountain prison, 503

Mustafa Kemal. See Atatürk

Napoleon, 4, 27, 343, 503

Napoleon III, Emperor, 344

Napoleonic Wars, the, 89

Nationalism, era of, 94; exacerbated by victors in 1919, 95; revival of, 296; European, 537

Nationalists. See German Nationalists

National Socialism, result of years of development, 131; Weimar Germany fertile ground for, 253; conception of worker-employer relationship in, 284

National Socialist Party, Austrian, Papen hated by, 2; German 'inspector', 299; banned by Dollfuss, 299; illegal activities of, 300; Mussolini's concern over, 331; German control, 338, 339; Papen's policy towards, 347; recognition of Hitler as head of, 348; underground activities, 352; activities against Heimwehr, 353; Papen's report to Hitler on, 364; legalization proposition, 369;

Hitler's meeting with Party leader, 376–7; attitude to July Agreement, 384; headquarters raided by police, 391; Leopold's orders to Party members, 394; Leopold and Papen, 396; Schuschnigg agrees to expulsion of Leopold, 403–4; informed of events leading to Anschluss, 412; leader's meeting with Hitler, 423; new campaign against Schuschnigg, 426; connection with German Nazi Party, 437–8

National Socialist Party, German (Nazis), anti-Communist attitude of, 27; growth of, 109; growing tension with Government, 115; and the monarchy, 121; young officers attracted to, 122; gains in 1930 Election, 135; boycotts Reichstag, 141; Bad Harzburg conference with other parties, 143; Hitler demands recognition of, 146; striking increase in strength in 1932, 148; increasing radicalism, 170; development based on exploitation of Versailles grievances, 172; in Prussia, 191; gains 230 seats in Reichstag, 193; reverse at November (1932) Election, 211, 223, 227, 246; refuses support to Zentrum, 215; unbridled behaviour of, 216; Schleicher's plan to split, 217, 236; Papen's Government in open conflict with, 220; Strasser breaks with, 226; no contributions to finances by Papen, 229, 230; stories about source of finances, 229–30; opposition to Schleicher, 236; attempts by Papen to limit prerogatives of, 239; funds placed at disposal of by industrialists, 252; chief support from younger generation, 254; gradual domination of Government, 256–7; middle class attitude to, 257; influx of Socialists and Communists into, 261; huge vote in Election of March 1933, 271; excesses of, 276; increasing control of press, 277; Blomberg's sympathies with, 291; Papen suggests dissolution of, 304; flood of excesses of, 304–5; Hitler breaks with radicals in, 307; Papen and radicalism in, 307–9; gains in Lippe-Detmold, 234; denial of complicity in Vienna Putsch, 338; Papen's condition on non-interference in Austrian affairs, 340; anti-clerical policy as barrier to Austrian union, 357; centralization tendencies, 364; interference with Papen's work, 365; assurance against interference in Austrian affairs, 369; Pope's attitude to, 382, 432; contacts with Austrian Nazis, 391, 437–8; Papen awarded Gold Medal of, 431, 434; meddles with

Papen's work in Ankara, 489–90; emissaries to Hungarian nationalists, 508–9; campaign against Jews, 521; born of despair, 581

Naval Treaty, Anglo-German, 373, 445, 567

Nazareth, 71, 76, 79, 82

Near East, 447; German High Command in, 69; German Asia Corps in, 69, 71; question of Central Powers command in, 72

Netherlands, the, 343; van der Lubbe's life in 269–70; Papen's plan for mediation on Poland and Czechoslovakia, 456–7; Queen's letter to Hitler offering mediation, 458; Germany attacks, 460; and co-operation with Germany, 462

Neubabelsberg, 153

Neudeck, 117, 165, 188, 194, 199, 306, 311, 317, 333, 343; Hindenburg wishes to be buried at, 335

Neue Zeitung, 44–5

Neurath, Konstantin von, 58, 175, 392, 427; becomes Foreign Minister, 159; at Lausanne Conference, 180; presses for equal rights for Germany, 201, 203, 206; in Hitler's Coalition Cabinet, 240, 243, 286, 290, 299, 300; and League of Nations, 297, 298; and Duce's visit to Hitler, 331–2; and the *Kulturbund*, 356; and Tschirschky, 366; and Austro-German agreement, 370; and Ribbentrop, 373, 375, 386; Schmidt visits, 379, 380; and the Hossbach protocol, 388; visits Vienna, 389–90; dismissed by Hitler, 406, 410; and Austrian request for intervention, 429; at Nuremberg, 550; trial of, 553, 555

Neustaedter-Stuermer, —, 379

Neven du Mont, August, 8

New Jersey Agricultural Company, the, 48

New York, 21, 31, 34, 40, 42, 55

New York World, the, 44

Nicholas II, Czar, announces Russia's support for Serbia, 26; orders partial mobilization (1914), 26

Niedermayer, German explorer, 80

Nikitchenko, General, 556, 559–60, 564

Nile Delta, 471, 477, 491

Nimitz, Admiral William, 41, 564

Nordam, S.S., 53, 64

North German Lloyd Company, 40

Norway, 39; invasion of, 460, 564

Noske, Gustav, 86, 104, 238, 251

Nothomb, Baron Jean Baptiste, 9

Nuber, —, 49

Nuremberg, party rally at, 543

Nuremberg gaol, 492

Nuremberg racial laws, 268, 356
Nuremberg Tribunal, 388, 415, 419, 442; Papen and, 19; indictment based on thesis of Germany's exclusive guilt, 22; accusation against German Navy, 41–2; prosecution's case at, 120; Papen's letter to Hitler described as 'undignified' at, 213; prosecution's case against Papen, 226, 321, 327, 335, 409, 445, 453; theory of joint criminal responsibility presented at, 253; suggestion that Reichstag Fire be investigated, 271; Papen's acquittal opposed, 367; prisoners' régime before, 549–51; the indictment, 548, 556–8, 560–6; story of the trial, 551–5, 559–60; Papen's examination, 566–69; verdict, 569–70; consideration of, 570

Oberndorff, Count, 128
O'Connor, Father Sixtus, 547, 552
Oder River, 27
Odessa, 83; fall of, 524
Oeder, —, 7
Old Comrades' Association. See Stahlhelm
Olden, Rudolf, 165
Oldenburg, 141
Oldenburg-Januschau, — von, 165, 317
Omurtak, General Salih, 520
'Operation Barbarossa,' 469, 478
'Operation Cicero,' 509–17
'Operation Overlord,' 515, 518, 526
Oranienburg concentration camp, 538
Orbay, General Kasim, 520
Orient Association, the, 489
Orient Bank, Ankara, 503
Ormesson, Vladimir d', 128
Osthilfe, the affair of, 164–6
Ott, Major, 220, 222, 227, 246, 253
Ottawa, 53, 182
Ottawa Conference, the, 184
Otto, Archduke, 354, 370, 378
Ouchy Peace Treaty (1912), 25
Oulman, Gaston, 574

Pacelli, Cardinal. See Pius XII
Pacific Ocean, 40, 88
Page, Walter Hines, 53
Palairet, Sir Arthur, 35
Palatinate, the, 120
Palestine, campaign in, 68, 69, 70; Papen visits, 71; Papen reorganizes defensive system in, 72–3, 448; Allenby's attack in, 74; German-Turkish reverse, 74; British advance, 75; Jerusalem evacuated by Germans, 76; stabilization of front in winter of 1917–18, 76; new British

attacks (1918), 77–9; situation in, reported to Ludendorff, 81; British offensive on whole front in, 81–2; Balfour Declaration and, 88; weak British forces in, 476
Pan-Slavism, 11
Panther, German gunboat, at Agadir, 24n
Papacy, its solution to problem of capital and labour, 254
Pape, Albert, 4
Papen, Friedrich Franz von, 317, 338, 492, 525, 539–40; joins German army march on Moscow, 482; friendship with Knatchbull-Hugessen family, 509; at Stockhausen, 536; assists father at Nuremberg trial, 548
Papen, Frau von, 9, 92, 232, 316, 317, 481, 485–6, 524, 530, 546, 577
Papen, Isabelle von, 475, 524, 535, 37, 546
Papen, Wilhelm von, 4
Papen, — von, 4–5
Paris, 32, 525; Brüning and Curtius visit, 137; Planck sent to, 246; Schuschnigg's visit, 368; Papen's visit to World Exhibition, 402
Paris Exhibition (1937), 386; German pavilion at, 387–8
Parker, John J., 559
Parliamentary democracy, 199
Pas de Calais, 32
Peace negotiations, Papen's efforts, 455–9, 462, 472, 534; Great Britain announces intention of resisting, 461; Papen discusses with Hitler, 462; Inönü ready to act as mediator, 478, 531; Ribbentrop denies any movement towards by Germany, 483–4; Lersner's approaches through Vatican, 489; Roosevelt and, 504–5, 522–3; Horthy's efforts towards, 509; German attempts at, 522–3;
Pearl Harbour, 484
Pechel, Dr, 164
Pelet-Narbonne, Colonel von, 11
People's Courts, the, 498, 546
Peppo, — de, 449
Pera, 519
Pergamon altar, the, 154 and n
Pershing, General John Joseph, 15
Persia, 22, 88, 470, 477; severs relations with Germany, 480
Persian Gulf, the, 22, 26, 476; vital to Britain, 447; Hitler considers offering to Russia, 466
Peter the Great, 466
Petrie, Sir Charles, 23
Peyerimhoff, — de, 128
Pfeffer, — von, 58
Philadelphia Enquirer, the, 523
Picot, Colonel, 127

Pieck, Walther, 270
Pietri, —, 402
Pilsudski, Marshal Jozef, 102, 445
Pinkafeld incident, 391–3
Pius XI, Pope, 127, 279, 382, 432
Pius XII, Pope, 126–7, 279, 280, 281, 282
Planck, —, 234, 246
Plettenberg, Countess, 520
Poensgen, family of, 7, 125, 128
Poincaré, Raymond, 119, 120
Poland, France and, 119, 127; threats from, 119, 120; Germany and, 296; British and French negotiations for mutual aid pacts, 444; Hitler cancels non-aggression pact with, 445; Franco-British guarantee to, 445–6; Hitler's policy, 451–2; German campaign in, 455–6; peace conditions regarding, 505; deportation of Jews to, 522
Popitz, Dr Johannes, 304
Posth, —, 503, 504
Potempa, incident at, 199, 200, 227, 246, 250
Potsdam, 11, 530, 538; Putsch, 248; Conference, 538
Prague, 359, 443, 445
Prinkipo, 84
Progrès et Union Committee, 25
Protestantism, in Prussia, 350
Prussia, 4, 5, 6; attempts to join with Russia, 27; State Parliament, 97; conservatism in, 97; and the Central Government under Weimar Constitution, 98–100; preponderance of, 99; a State within a State, 100; coalition in, 105–6; 1924 Election in, 106; 1932 Election, 109–10; Vatican Concordat with, 126; rôle of, 128; violence in, 132; Government stops Stahlhelm referendum project in, 142; Social Democrat-Zentrum collaboration, 169; anxiety about situation in, 188–9; threat of alliance between Social Democrats and Communists, 189, 192; Papen appointed Reich Commissioner for, 189; emergency measures to combat threatening situation, 189–91, 192–3; limits on electoral campaign by Goering, 271; relations with Vatican, 278; police taken over by Nazis, 293; situation after Papen's appointment as Reich Commissioner, 293–5; elections in 1933, 294; Goering elected Prime Minister, 294; concentration camps in, 294–5; Gestapo's power in, 324
Puaux, —, 350, 362, 425
Punktationen, the, 411, 420; Schmidt at Nuremberg proves that Papen had no knowledge of, 565
Pytchley pack, 8

Quadragesimo Anno, Papal Encyclical, 284
Queen's pack, 8
Quéretaro, 16
Quorn pack, 8

Rabenau, General Friedrich von, 121 and n
Racial laws, Nuremberg, 268
Radek, Karl, 118, 119
Raeder, Admiral Erich, 149, 553, 570
Rahn, Rudolf, 476, 477
Rainer, Dr, 394
Rainer, Gauleiter, 384, 412, 566
Rapallo, Treaty of, 118–9
Rashid Ali, el Gailani, 475, 476, 477
Ravensbrück concentration camp, 539
Refet Pasha, General, 73
Regensburg, labour camp at, 269, 578
'Reich Complaints Office,' 276
Reichenau, Field-Marshal Walter von, 288, 413, 415
Reichsbank, the, 136, 137, 388
Reichsbanner groups, 119, 149, 191
Reichslandbund, 232–3
Reichsrat, the, 97, 100
Reichstag, 6, 207, 420; Goering becomes President, enquiry into responsibility for war by, 87; Schleicher asks for powers to dissolve, 236, 237, 238; Fire, 268–71; opening ceremony transferred to Potsdam, 272; Hitler's speeches, 273, 421–2, 445, 462–3; passes Enabling Law, 274; reduces autonomy of German States, 329; amends Constitution regarding position on death of President, 333
Reichswehr. See German Army
Reinhardt, Severin, 230
Reiss, Mena, 56
Reisswitz, —, 34
Remagen, 535
Renner, Dr Karl, 345
Rennes, 525
Rentenmark, the, 103
Reparations, 101, 102, 103, 162, 171–2, 255
Rerum Novarum, Pope Leo XIII's Encyclical, 93, 254
Return of the Dark Invader, the, 58
Reuter's News Agency, 201
Révin, 540
Reynaud, Paul, 402
Rheims, 540
Rheinthaller, —, 394, 395, 412
Rhine, the, 221, 534, 535
Rhineland, the, 97, 101, 172, 350, 581; remilitarization of, 327; German re-occupation of, 368, 438, 560
Rhine Republic, 101, 120

Ribbentrop, Joachim von, French-German Committee set up by, 128; requests post of Permanent Secretary of Foreign Office, 373; as Ambassador to London, 376, 427; views on British Empire, 376, 386; his conclusions on abdication of King Edward VIII, 386; appointment as Foreign Minister, 407, 410; discussions with Papen and Austrian Foreign Minister, 414–5; action over Papen's address to Swedish-German Society (in Stockholm), 442–3; offers Papen post of Ambassador in Ankara, 443–4; informs Papen of Italian invasion of Albania, 443–4; his Polish Corridor policy, 445; anger over Papen's talk with Ciano, 448–9; discussion with Menemencioglu, 450; suggests Russian negotiations for Turkish neutrality, 455; forbids Foreign Office officials' discussions with Papen, 457–8; and peace plans, 457–8, 482–4; discussion with Papen on talks with Russia, 465; reception for Molotov, 467; urges that Turks denounce pact with Britain, 471; Papen visits in Berlin, 474–5; desire to ensure chromium supplies from Turkey, 475; his insistent demands on Papen regarding Turkey, 477; refuses agreement mentioning Turkey's obligations to Britain, 478; Papen's brush with on ciphers, 482; complains of Papen's indiscretions, 482–4; supports Papen's ban on party activities in Turkey, 489–90; orders Friede's reinstatement, 490; Papen declines his order to proceed to Berlin, 492; blames 'bourgeois clique' for Stalingrad defeat, 496; refuses suggestion of German meeting with Spellman, 500; and 'Operation Cicero', 511, 512, 515, 517, 518; approves Gestapo plan to kidnap Papen, 521; orders Papen to Berlin, 524; Papen meeting with, 524–5; orders Papen to return to Germany, 527; anger at the Turks, 530; condemns suggested negotiations, 534; arrested, 543; during Nuremberg trial, 552

Ribbentrop Bureau, the, 372–5, 414

Ribes, Champetier de, 127

Richelieu, Cardinal, his 'divide and rule' policy, 402

Riegele, Frau, 394

Rieth, Dr, 338

Rintelen, Captain von, 46, 47, 48, 58

Robertshaw, Captain, 540

Rock Creek Park, 16, 51

Roeber family, 7

Roehm, Ernst, close associate of Hitler,

195; *Putsch*, 244, 249, 260, 305, 306, 313–27, 338, 351, 365–6, 440–1, 546, 582–3

Rohde, General, 461

Rohr-Demin, — von, 165

Rolland, Louis, 127

Roman Catholic Church, democratic thesis opposed to, 91; German Socialists' lack of tolerance for, 92; in Prussia, 97; in Austria, 348, 349, 357, 382, 432

Rome, 127, 129, 229; Fascist march on, 198; Papen's visits, 278–81; German religious foundation 'Anima', 382; Goering pays State visit, 387

Rommel, Field-Marshal Erwin, 477, 490–1, 493

Roncalli, Monsignor, 524, 565

Roosevelt, Franklin D., 141, 553; Yalta Conference, 27, 570; speeches result of teamwork, 325; requests for guarantees against aggression, 445; at Casablanca Conference, 493–4; Papen appeals to, 495–6; Papen's approach to, 499, 508, 516–7, 522–3, 528; visitor to Papen from, 504–5; and peace negotiations, 504–5, 508; Cairo Conference, 513; Teheran Conference, 513, 514; confidence in Stalin, 515; death of, 537–8

Roosevelt, Theodore, 14, 32

Rose, Maria, 433, 436, 452–3, 512

Rosenberg, Alfred, 261, 357; influence on Hitler, 458; under arrest, 543–4; at Nuremberg, 552

Rote Bude, 11

Rotfront, the, 149, 242

Rotterdam, 54

Rotterdam, S.S., 49

Rousseau, Jean-Jacques, 90, 324

Rudenko, General R.A., 559–60, 569

Ruethen, 536

Ruhr, the, 32, 95, 96, 99, 101, 119, 194, 221, 293, 298, 399, 536, 581

Rumania, Dobrudja ceded to, 25; campaign in, 68; Great Britain considers guarantees to, 444; commercial agreement with Germany, 444; Hitler anxious to deflect Russian ambitions in, 466; German divisions sent to, 470; Black Sea ports, 473; forces cross Russian border, 479; Allied attacks on oil wells, 511

Rumbold, Sir Horace, 167, 194, 199, 201, 202, 205; his view of situation in Germany, 211

Rundstedt, Field-Marshal Karl von, 190, 191; in France, 525–6; Ardennes offensive, 535

Russia, von Hötzendorf's view of inevitability of war with, 11; deteriora-

tion in Germany's relations with, 12;
relations with Austria (1913), 13; German declaration of war on (1914), 20;
Anglo-Russian Convention disturbs
balance of power, 22; sphere of interest
in Persia, 22; security on Asian side,
22; agrees to maintain *status quo* in
China, 22; designs in West checked by
Bismarck, 22; weakened condition
after defeat by Japan, 23; designs in
south and west Europe, 24; threat of
war with Austria (1913), 25; sponsors
anti-Turkish alliance, 25; Czar announces support for Serbia, 26; comes
to Serbia's assistance, 26; threatens
European balance of power, 26; partial
mobilization against Austria, 26; total
mobilization against Germany ordered
by War Minister, 27; efforts to incorporate in European family, 27; an
Asiatic power, 27; policy in Europe,
28; and partition of Turkish Empire,
88; threat of, 94; Bismarck's view of,
344. *See also* Soviet Russia
Russian Front, the, 77, 488; death of
Habicht on, 460
Russo-German Pact, 451-2, 460, 572
Russo-Japanese war, 32
Rüstow, Prof., 503-4

S.A. *See* Brownshirts
Saar, Franco-German relations in, 11,
301; international control of, 95;
Papen's home in, 96; Papen Reich
Commissioner for Saar affairs, 301;
political parties in, 301; Nazis in, 301;
referendum (1935), 301, 302, 358, 360;
importance of a solution to problem
of, 587
Saarbruecken, 442, 525, 533
Saarlouis, 533
Sabath, Dr, 276, 325
Sachs, Dr, 577, 579
Sachsenhausen concentration camp, 538
Sadowa, 334
St Croix River, 34
Saint Germain, Treaty of, 95, 178, 344-5
Saint Jean de Maurienne, Treaty of, 88
Salata, ——, 370
Salis, Baron, 535, 536
Salonika, 25, 473-4, 516, 517, 521
Saltillo, 17
Salzburg, 413, 420, 436, 526; referendum
on the Anschluss, 345
Samos, British occupation, 503
Sanctions, against Italy, 387
Sanders, Marshal Liman von, 77, 78, 79,
81, 82, 83, 84, 85, 116
San Diego, 40

Saracoglu, Sükrü, 460, 477; Papen's regard
for, 449; suggests air attack on Baku,
463-4; agreeable to pact with Germany,
478; concern at Russia, 479-80, 494; be-
comes Prime Minister, 492; emphasizes
Turkey's intention to remain neutral,
492; devises new tax, 493
Sarajevo, 19, 26, 338, 354
Saseno, 88
Sauerbruch, Ferdinand, 295, 343, 356, 502
Savigny, —— von, 276, 316
Saxon kings, 343
Saxony, 95, 120, 123, 189
Saydam, Refik, his statement on
attempted Papen assassination, 486;
death of, 492
Scandinavian countries, Papen's idea for
winning over to co-operation with
Germany, 462
Schacht, Dr Hjalmar, 141, 143, 230, 292,
295; opens German pavilion at Paris
Exhibition, 387-8; at Nuremberg, 547,
548, 550, 554; his acquittal, 570, 575
Schadow, Wilhelm von, 7
Schaeffer, Dr, 239-40
Schaffgotsch, Count, 548
Scheele, Dr, 48
Scheidemann, Philipp, 119, 122
Schirach, Baldur von, 553
Schlange-Schoeningen, Dr Hans, 166 and
n, 167
Schleicher, General Kurt von, outstanding personality in Reichswehr, 115;
suggests Papen be given Chancellorship, 116; Seeckt's opinion of, 121-2; a
'political general', 123; his record,
123-4; his character, 124; intrigues
against Brüning, 140; duplicity of, 149-
50; calls Papen to Berlin, 150-1; suggests that Papen should lead Cabinet,
152-6; choses 'Presidential Cabinet',
159; perturbed at possibility of
Ministry of Interior falling into Nazi
hands, 189; insistent that authority not
be given to Hitler, 197, 198; plan to
form Government, 217; change of
attitude towards Papen, 218-9; declines
to support Hindenburg's directive,
220; plan to divide Nazi Party, 226,
236, 246; his Government, 226, 227,
232, 233, 234, 235, 236, 237; suspicions
of Papen, 231; his friendship with
Papen, 232; refuses post for Hugenberg, 233; forms Government, 223,
225; negotiations with Strasser, 232,
233, 234; German Nationalists oppose,
234, 236; lack of support for, 234-5;
Nazi opposition to, 236; asks for powers
to dissolve Reichstag, 236; threatens to
resign, 237; inspires article in *Tägliche*

Rundschau, 237, 238; his demand for full powers again refused, 238; resigns, 238; private approach to Goering, 242; offers to mobilize Potsdam garrison against Hindenburg, 242; rumour of Reichswehr *Putsch* by, 243; unable to answer for rôle of Army, 244; his account of Papen's 'intrigues', 244; his attitude to Papen, 245; Papen's view of 244–9; his rôle, 245–9; tragedy of his quarrel with Hindenburg, 249; his death, 249, 318, 320, 327; his wife's ambitions, 249

Schlieffen, Field-Marshal Count Alfred von, 11, 17

Schlumberger, Jean, 128

Schmidt, Dr Guido, 368, 370, 376–7, 379–80, 389, 395, 400–2, 409–14, 417–21, 422, 426, 565–6

Schmidt, Dr Paul, 387

Schmieden, — von, 530

Schoenebeck, General von, 502

Schönburg-Waldenburg-Hartenstein, Colonel-General Prince, 354

Schöneberg Town Hall, 270

Schönerer, Georg von, 285 and *n*

Schoup, J. G., 230

Schreiber, Dr, 128, 134

Schroeder, Baron, 225, 226, 227, 228–9, 248, 252, 396, 560

Schulenburg, Count Friedrich Werner von der, 530; German Ambassador in Moscow, 455; informs Germany of British offer to Russia, 463; and the impending Balkan-Axis alliance, 468; arrives in Ankara, 480; meeting with Papen in France, 525; death of, 525

Schulenberg, — von der, 330–1

Schuman, Robert, 119, 128

Schuman Plan, the, 95, 586

Schuschnigg, Dr Kurt von, bans political parties except Fatherland Front, 349; refuses to meet Papen, 357; declaration on Austria as German State, 361; moves for negotiations on Austro-German relations, 368–71, 376–7; relations with Heimwehr, 377–8; reshuffles Cabinet, 379; decision for arrangement with supporters of union with Germany, 391; forms Committee of Seven, 394; asks Seyss-Inquart to join administration, 395; his accusations against Nazi Party, 396; discussions with German delegation, 397; stops entry of new members into Fatherland Front, 403; and expulsion of Nazi leader to Germany, 403; Papen accused of enticing him to Berchtesgaden, 409; discussions with Papen, 409–11; meeting with Hitler at Berchtesgaden, 412–21; replies to Hitler's speech, 422; Papen's farewell visit, 423–4; announces plebiscite on independence question, 425; rejects Papen's suggestions for changes in wording of plebiscite, 426; refuses to postpone plebiscite, 427; resigns, 428; lack of understanding of Papen, 438–9

Schwerin, General Count, 540

Schwerin-Krosigk, Count Lutz von, 159, 174–5, 183, 240, 243, 290–1, 542

Scotland, 343

Sebastopol, 490

Second Front, Stalin's demand for, 489

Seeckt, General Hans von, 82, 120–2, 124, 143, 151; his outstanding personality, 116, 117; Chief of Staff in Turkey, 117; his opinions, 118; and the Soviet Government, 118

Seeger, Major, 540

Seipel, Dr Ignaz, 346

Sekuna, Ernst, 40

Selby, Sir Walford, 351

Seldte, Franz, 241, 290, 291, 292

Self-determination, national, 296; Wilson's insistence on, 89

Serbia, 95; in anti-Turkish alliance, 25; receives North Macedonia, 25: Bulgarian attack on, 25; conflict with Austria, 26

Severing, Carl, 132, 144, 189, 190, 194; released from prison, 274; votes for Hitler's foreign policy, 296

Seyss-Inquart, Dr Artur von, 412, 413; member of Committee of Seven, 394; joins administration, 395; discussions with Papen, 404; Germany proposes him as Minister of Interior, 414, 416, 417, 418, 419, 420; requested by Hitler to intervene for postponement of Austrian plebiscite, 426–7; ordered by Goering to form new Cabinet, 428; Miklas refuses to entrust with formation of Cabinet, 429; during Nuremberg trial, 551–2

Sicherheitsdienst, 325, 481, 510, 517, 518

Siegfried, André, 128

Siegfried Line, the, 440, 443

Silesia, 95, 97, 353

Simeon, Crown Prince of Bulgaria, 501

Simmern, 535

Simon, Sir John, 186, 202, 203, 205, 358, 359

Simpfendoerfer, —, 274

Skal, — von, 54

Skubl, Chief of Police, 418

Slavs, 61, 94, 501

Smyrna. *See* Izmir

Social Democrats. *See* Socialists

Socialists, British, 104

Socialists, French, 104

Socialists, German, 92, 95, 123; opposition to Liebknecht, 86; cling to list system, 99; in Prussia, 100, 110, 189; characteristics of, 104; loss of only leader of stature, 107; Brüning's dependence on, 109; eradication of Kaiser's Germany by, 114; opposition to Reichswehr, 120; and the monarchy, 121; indifference to moral decay in Germany, 129; withdraw support from Coalition, 132; and the Brüning Government, 133, 136; refuse concessions to right parties, 146; organize Reichsbanner, 149; and Papen, 155, 210; doctrinaire attitude of, 168, 169; their failure in the 'twenties, 169; negotiations with Communists in Prussia, 189; alliance of the Nazis and Communists, 208; opposition to Papen's economic programme, 210; in Election of November 1932, 212; refuse part in coalition, 215; Schleicher and, 234; meaning of refusal to postpone Reichstag meeting, 242; decision not to call strike against Hitler, 259; influx into Nazi Party of, 261, 280; in Election of March 1933, 271; oppose Enabling Law, 275; opposition to Church schools, 278; vote for Hitler's foreign policy, 296; recommend support for National Socialist reconstruction, 304

Socorro Island, 40

Sofia, 459, 474, 501–2, 511, 529

Somme, Battle of, 66, 67

Sonderegger, René, 230

Soviet Union, strategic conception behind submarine weapons, 43; negotiations with von Seeckt, 118; Germany assists in building up war industry, 118–9; and Versailles Treaty, 118, 119; France and, 127, 360, 444; membership of League of Nations, 358; British and French military missions to, 444; non-aggression pact with Germany, 451–2; and Turkey, 460; desire for revision of Montreux Convention, 460, 465, 466; Papen's discussion with Hitler on neutrality of, 462; Cripps' discussions in Moscow, 463; reported British readiness to recognize Balkans as sphere of interest of, 463; proposed guarantee to Bulgaria, 467, 468; Hitler orders preparations for war against, 469; worsening German relations with, 473; mission in Sofia, 474; Germany attacks, 479; Churchill pledges help to, 480; Turks blame for attempted assassination in Ankara, 487; Turkish fear of, 493; occupation of Bulgaria, Yugo-

slavia and Hungary, 515; Roosevelt disagrees with Earle's view of, 523

Soziale Arbeitsgemeinschaft, the, 349

Spa, 123

Spain, 39; civil war in, 387, 389, 415

Spartacists, the, 102, 122

'Special Courts,' 498

Spee, Count, 85

Speer, Albert, 322, 497–8, 547, 553

Spellman, Cardinal, 499–500

Sperrle, Field-Marshal Hugo, 413, 415

Spezia, 85

Spiecker, Dr, 191

Sportpalast, Berlin, 299

Springorum, —, 125

Spy and Counter-Spy, 49

SS., 264, 540; banned, 148; excesses of, 293; suppress Roehm Putsch, 315, 316; occupy Vice-Chancellery, 315–6; surround Papen's home, 316–7; relative weakness at time of Roehm Putsch, 320

Staatspartei, German. See German State Party

Staatsrat, Prussian, 98

Stadelheim prison, 320

Stadler, Madame de, 128

Staël, Madame de, 128

Stalevski, Baron, 20

Stahlhelm, 119, 264, 353; attempts to organize referendum in Prussia, 142; at Bad Harzburg Conference, 143; refuse to support Hindenburg's candidature, 147; leaders undertake to support Hitler Cabinet, 241; a stabilizing factor, 241–2; members vote for Nazis, 266; leader's conversion to Nazism, 292; crisis in, 292; joins Nazi Party en bloc, 292

Stalin, J. V., 446, 489, 514, 515, 537; Ribbentrop's meeting with, 452; Yalta Conference, 570

Stalingrad, the battle for, 493, 495, 496

Starhemberg, Prince Ernst Rüdiger von, 353–4, 377–9; and Mussolini's plan, 361; gains in influence, 364–5; character, 365; leaves Austrian Cabinet, 369

State, Marxist view of, 91; Socialist view of, 92; anonymity of administration by, 93; menace of its omnipotence, 130; masses drawn to overthrow of, 254; Papen's conception of its authority, 256–7

Steengracht, Baron Moyland von, 534, 542

Steeplechasing, 8

Stegerwald, Adam, 144, 156, 166–7

Stein, — von, 381, 403, 426, 427

Steinhardt, Laurence, 492

Stenay, 548

Stimson, H. L., 139, 202, 203, 204
Stockhausen, 536
Stockhausen, Max von, 540
Stockholm, 442
Stotzingen, Baroness von, 316, 434
Strasbourg, 11, 128
Strasser, Gregor, 217, 226, 232, 233, 234
Strasser-Leipart 'axis', the, 238
Streicher, Julius, 544, 547, 552
Strength Through Joy organization, 284
Stresa Conference, 360, 388
Stresa Powers, the, 368, 376, 383
Stresemann, Dr Gustav, 57, 58, 102, 104, 131, 132, 144, 187, 194
Strong, General, 540
Stülpnagel, Heinrich von, 526
Stuttgart, 300
Sudeten crisis, the, 441–2
Suez Canal, 70, 72, 477; vital to Britain, 447, 470
Svilengrad, 479, 529
Sweden, 30, 39, 107, 443; Kageneck escapes to, 441; Papen invited to speak in, 442
Swedish-German Society, Stockholm, 442–3
Switzerland, 177, 343; Papen sends papers to, 424, 435–6; 440–1; Red Cross, 500–1
Sykes-Picot Treaty, the, 88
Syria, 70, 72; French Protectorate, 88; German line of advance through, 470–1; German desire to establish line of communication through, 476; Free French reach, 477
Syrup, Dr, 159

Tägliche Rundschau, the, 237, 238, 242
Talleyrand, 341
Tampico, 17, 391
Tannenberg, 117, 332, 336
Tardieu, André, 127, 139
Tatra mountains, the, 69, 70, 71, 83, 84, 94, 471
Taurus mountains, 69, 70, 71, 83, 84, 94, 471
Tauscher, —, 40, 54
Tauschitz, —, 370
Tavs, Dr, 384, 404, 410
Teheran Conference, 514–15; Cicero's information re, 512; résumé of, sent to British Ambassador, 517–8; Papen discusses decisions with Hitler, 525
Teleki, Count Paul, 468
Tempelhof aerodrome, 338, 431
Terentiev, —, 460
Teutoburg Forest, 128
Thaelmann, Ernst, 148
Therapia, 480

Thiépval, 75
Thirty Years' War, the, 458
Thrace, 25; Turkish, 511
Thuringia, 120, 123, 141
Thyberg, —, 472
Thyssen, Fritz, 125, 230, 252
Tibet, 22
Tirpitz, Admiral Alfred von, 61, 62, 63, 64
Tobruk, 490
Tocqueville, Count de, 308
Todt, Fritz, 497
Tokyo, 491
Torgler, Ernst, 208, 270
Townsend, General, 68
Trentino, the, 88
Trier, 11, 533
Trieste, 88
Triple Entente, 23, 24
Tripoli, 12. See also Libya
Trotsky, Leon, 118
Trott zu Solz, Adam von, 504, 530
Truman, Harry S., 95, 538
Tschirschky, Baron Fritz-Günther von, 276, 300, 312, 314, 315, 316, 333, 365-7, 565
Tunisia, 500
Turkey, decline of Empire, 23; conflict with Italy over Libya, 12, 23–4; German friendship for, 23, 24, 25; deprived of Libya and Dodecanese (1912), 25; wins back Adrianople, 25; Government brought down by Enver Pasha, 25; urgent appeal for help to Germany, 68; reverses after von der Goltz's death, 68; lose Baghdad, 68; German reinforcements for, 69; Papen on service in, 69; reorganization of 7th Army near Aleppo, 69; signs armistice of Mudania, 70, 83; failure of offensive against Suez Canal, 70; Liman von Sanders' appointment and, 77; occupies Medina, 77; resists political concessions to Arabs, 81; and the Holy Places, 81; armies attacked by British, 82; no position to fight on, 83; final collapse of, 83; Allied decision to partition, 88; Seeckt as Chief of Staff in, 117; Ribbentrop offers Papen post of Ambassador, 443–4; agreements with Balkan States, 444; Great Britain considers guarantees to, 444; Papen's arrival, 446; Stalin's personal emissary in, 446; neutral diplomats' relations with Papen, 454–5; Russian negotiations for neutrality, 455; relations with Bulgaria, 456; inadequate Army equipment, 460–1; Allied efforts to induce Turkey to join in war, 461, 464, 487, 493, 512–3; British military missions,

461, 494, 495, 521; attitude to Italian attack on Greece, 464; anniversary of Republic ceremonies, 464–5; obligations under Balkan Pact, 470; Ribbentrop urges to denounce pact with Britain, 471; Papen urges Hitler to guarantee inviolability of, 471; possibility of including in Balkan front explored, 472; Papen reiterates arguments in favour of neutrality, 472; Germany's assurances, 472, 495; policy of neutrality, 473, 492, 503; and Bulgaria's demands on Greece, 473–4; relations with Bulgaria, 474; King Boris' attitude to, 474; German chromium supplies from, 475; allows transport of German petrol, 477; her interest in arranging a peace, 478; Papen works for neutrality and friendship of, 478; agreement with Germany, 478–9, 480; and German attack on Russia, 479–80; relations with Britain at nadir, 480; Gestapo and Abwehr activities in, 481; Hitler agrees to arm, 488; foreign political party work forbidden, 489; Papen orders Nazi Party activities to stop, 489–90; Friede's activities, 490; German nationals in, 490; Churchill warns against German *Drang nach Osten*, 494; tax on foreigners' income and property in, 493; concern about Russia, 494, 495; Moscow Conference decision regarding, 506; opposed to eleventh-hour entry into war, 506; prepared to declare war under Allied pressure, 507–8; Allied use of air and naval bases, 513, 514, 516; demand for materials, 516, 519; attitude to increasing Allied pressure, 517; divergent groups on question of breach with Germany, 519; refuses to abandon extra territorial rights, 521; German emigrés in, 521–2; suspends chromium deliveries to Germany, 524; grants permission for German ships to pass through Dardanelles, 526; severs relations with Germany, 527; Papen leaves, 528–9; Hitler on defection of, 531

Twentieth Century-Fox Film Company, 519

Tyrol, 345

U-boats, 36, 40, 41, 43, 52, 60–1, 62, 63–4, 65, 563–4

Uhlan Regiment, of Düsseldorf, 5; Westphalian Fifth, 7, 10; First Regiment of the Guard, 11; old friends, 15, 117; 39th Regiment, 117

Ukraine, independent State proposal, 505

Ulbricht, —, 141, 270

'Unconditional surrender,' Allies' policy of, 493–4, 499, 505, 514–5, 517, 522, 525, 540

Unemployment, 3, 109, 135, 160, 163, 170, 199, 210, 283

Union Club, 498, 533

Union of German Princes, the, 343

United Nations, 537, 573; intentions towards Germany, 514

United States, divorced from European alliances, 13; intervention in Mexico, 17–19; German intelligence and information service in, 20, 30–1, 32–3, 36, 37; Papen's activities in, 29–31, 32–6; 37–40, 42–3, 43–52, 55–7, 59, 82; Allied propaganda to bring active intervention of, 29, 32; Papen only military representative of Central Powers in, 30; isolation of Germans in, 31–2; effect of Wilson's advent on foreign policy of, 32; German propaganda in, 32–3; German immigrants demand neutrality of, 33; pro-Allied feeling in, 35, 60; productive capacity of, 37, 60; Allied purchasing agents in, 37, 38; German orders for war materials, 38–40, 50; Allied war effort in, 37, 38, 39; German cause suffers in, 40–1; declares German U-boat warfare illegal, 41; proclaims principle of freedom of seas, 41; arms shipments to Europe, 42; reaction to *Lusitania* sinking, 42, 60; stiffer attitude to Germany under Lansing's ægis, 43; attitude to U-boat warfare, 43; an inexhaustible arsenal for Allies, 43; British purchasing agents in, 44; German efforts to prevent shipments of war material from, 44–5, 48; British propaganda to bring into conflict, 45, 53; German counterpropaganda in, 45–6; sabotage by German sympathizers in, 45–6; sabotage is authorized by German General Staff, 46, 56–7; Rintelen's mission in, 46–8; the Dumba episode, 45–50; Ambassador Dumba declared *persona non grata*, 50; press campaign against Papen in, 50–1; Allied campaign against Papen in, 51; declares Papen *persona non grata*, 51; effect of U-boat campaign on opinion in, 52; Papen leaves, 52; explosions caused by German agents in, alleged, 55–9; Allied efforts to persuade to enter war, 60; Papen advises against sabotage in, 60; no German ambition in conflict with interests of, 61; likely effect of unrestricted submarine warfare, 61–5; Papen's account of situation in, 61–3; Kaiser's view of situation in,

63–4; brings about turning point in war, 81; and peace negotiations, 94; intervention in Communist Russia, 101–2; successful coalitions in, 141; opposed to cancellation of reparations, 179; German declaration of war on, 484; Army reaches Rhine, 535; Army arrests Papen, 536; European recovery under guidance of, 538; Horthy prisoner of, 541–3; leadership of world passes to, 586

Untertürkheim, Stuttgart, 300

Upper Austria, referendum on the Anschluss banned, 345

Upper Silesia, 99

Vabres, Prof. Donnedieu de, 559

Valona, 88

Vanceboro bridge affair, 35, 53

Vatan, 519

Vatican, Concordat with Prussia, 126; Concordat with Germany, 127, 278, 279–81, 350, 351, 357, 432; Concordats with German States, 278; Lersner visits with peace negotiations proposal, 489

Veesenmayer, —, 509

Venice, 332

Vera Cruz, 17, 18, 19, 40

Verdun, Battle of, 68, 72, 76

Vereinigte Stahlwerke, the, 125

Vermehren, Dr, 520

Versailles, Treaty of, compared with Congress of Vienna, 89; lack of vision in, 95; efforts to lift discriminatory clauses of, 105, 180, 201, 212; Soviet Russia and, 118, 119; 'Black Reichswehr' a breach of, 119; Hitler on errors of, 162; effect on Germany, 172; U.S. and, 203; Nazi Party feeds on discriminatory clauses, 212; effects of restrictions of, on internal order in Germany, 221–2; no lessening of restrictions imposed by, 255; ascribed to Jewish influence, 285; German obligation to maintain Austrian independence, 345; British White Paper on breaking by Germany, 359; Danzig Corridor question and, 444; Bulgarian attitude to, 459; seeds of another war in, 537

Vichy, General Dentz loyal to, 476

Vienna, 299, 344, 391; Papen as Ambassador in, 350–439, 546

Villa, Pancho, 17

Villa Wolkonski, 331

Villers, Count Lamoral, 9

Vimy Ridge, 66, 67, 70, 73

Vinogradov, —, 473; and bomb attempt on Papen, 486

Visser, Philips Christiaan, 455, 456, 459, 460, 472, 565

Voegeler, Albert, 125

Vogt, —, 270

Voguë, Count Félix de, 127

Völkische Beobachter, the, 188, 285, 452

Volkspolitisches Referat, the, 350

Vollgruber, —, 421, 424–5

Voska, Captain, 49

Wachendorf. *See* Bridgeman-Taylor

Wagner, Robert, 276

Wallerfangen, 9, 150, 337, 352, 408, 440, 530, 533, 535, 561

Wannsee, the, 154

War Academy, 10, 117

Warburg, Max, 128

Warburg, James P., 230

Warburg, Paul M., 229

'Warburg, Sidney', 229, 230

War criminals, 548

Warmbold, Prof., 159

Warr, Lord de la, 8

Warsaw, 359, 387

Washington, 7, 9, 13, 15, 16, 20, 43, 51

Weber, —, 370

Weberstedt, Major, 270

Wedell, —, 35, 54

Wedemeyer, Hans, 533

Weimar Constitution, political parties under, 3, 254, 255; characteristics of, 97–100; causes of failure, 168–9; failure of its conception of democracy, 253; position in event of President's death, 330, 333

Weisse Hirsch sanatorium, 443

Weizsäcker, Baron von, 397

Welland Canal, 34, 51, 53

Wels, 397–8

Werl, 4, 500, 536

Western Allies, propaganda against Nazi régime, 459–60; pressure on Turkey, 464, 512–4, 517, 527; prevent chromium supplies to Germany, 475; Lersner tries to start negotiations with, 489; Conference in Moscow, 503; Horthy puts out peace feelers to, 509; readiness to make concessions to Stalin, 516; intentions concerning Germany, 517; protest to Turkey, 526; offer protection to Papen, 528; fail to take advantage of German retreat, 534

Western Front, 34, 44, 64, 523; Papen's service on, 66–8; Allies threaten breakthrough on, 66–7; British and Canadian divisions supported by tanks on, 66; failure of British to exploit successes, 67; fantastic Allied losses, 67; new German defensive methods on, 67;

German High Command seeks final decision on, 77; Papen asks for transfer to, 79; position in August 1918, 81, 83; Papen's report to Hitler on, 457–8

Western Powers, Papen's appeal for understanding of Germany's rôle, 495–6

Westfalen Post, 101

Westphalen, Count, 9

Westphalia, 55, 96, 97, 98, 125, 312, 350, 437, 458, 575

Westphalia, Peace of, Hitler's obsession with, 460

Westphalian Farmers' Union, 97, 125; Papen's speech to, 199

West Wall, the, 533

Whyte-Melville, George, 8

Wied, Prince zu, 25

Wiesbaden, 443, 536, 538

Wilhelm I, Kaiser of Germany, Coronation at Versailles, 334

Wilhelm II, Kaiser of Germany, 12, 19, 77; Papen's audience with (1913), 14, 16, 37; action over Morocco, 24; declines to promise German help to Austria, 25; did not seek war, 28; supporter of Tirpitz' naval policy, 61; Papen's audience with on return from U.S.A., 63–4; view of situation in U.S., 63–4; social reforms under, 93

Wilhelmina, Queen of the Netherlands, 458

William, Crown Prince of Germany, 11, 21, 121, 245, 329, 580

Wilson, Woodrow, 6, 16, 32, 43, 47, 64, 84, 87, 89, 94, 95, 296, 537; rights of European self-determination laid down by, 344; declares war on Mexico, 392; Fourteen Points, 94, 296, 505

Windthorst, Ludwig, 97

Windischgrätz, Prince, 357

Wingen, Dr, 276

Winter Aid Collections, in Turkey, 489

Wirth, Dr Joseph, 118, 119, 141, 143

With Burning Anxiety, Papal Encyclical, 432

Witzleben, General von, 457

Wolff News Agency, 204

Wolff, Theodor, 211

Wolfsschanze, 496

Wood, General Leonard, 15–6, 5

Work Law (1934), 284

Wuerttemberg-Baden, 304

Yalta Conference, 27, 537, 538, 570–1

Young Plan, the, 131, 332, 141, 147, 173

Yugoslavia, 344, 345, 390, 455, 456, 524; possibility of Balkan front with Greece and Turkey, 472; German campaign in, 473; Bulgaria's part in war against, 474; Russia's occupation, 515

Zapata, Emiliano, 17

Zeit, Die, 518

Zentrum Party, 6, 101, 104, 105–6, 107, 155, 156–7, 159, 166, 214, 215, 351, 371; in Prussia, 97, 98, 110, 192; Papen's opposition to policy of, 106; and Hindenburg's candidature, 107–8; Papen and, 111, 115, 125, 245; organ of, 111–3; liquidation of, 112; and the Socialists, 125, 133; fight for religious freedom, 126; calls for National Socialist Government, 161; failure of, 169; and Lausanne Conference, 185; supports proposal to elect Goering as *Reichstagspräsident*, 207; joins with Communists and Nazis, 209; in Election of November 1932, 212; declines co-operation with Papen, 212; regards Hitler Cabinet as necessary, 212; Schleicher's Government and, 234; objections to coalition with Nazis, 237; opposition to Papen's Cabinet, 245; gains in Election of March 1933, 271–2; record between 1919 and 1932, 272; supports Enabling Law, 274; efforts to reach understanding with Rome, 278; places itself under Hitler's leadership, 304

Zernatto, ——, 411, 419, 565

Zetkin, Klara, 207, 209

Zimmermann, Werner, 229, 230

Zimmermann Telegram, 39, 65

Zurich, 230, 411

Zita, Empress, 354